Engaged Buddhism

Engaged Buddhism

Buddhist Liberation Movements in Asia

EDITED BY

Christopher S. Queen
and Sallie B. King

STATE UNIVERSITY OF NEW YORK PRESS

Published by
State University of New York Press, Albany

For information, address State University of New York
Press, State University Plaza, Albany, NY, 12246

Production by Diane Ganeles
Marketing by Nancy Farrell

Library of Congress Cataloging-in-Publication Data
Engaged Buddhism: Buddhist liberation movements in Asia / edited by
  Christopher S. Queen and Sallie B. King
    p. cm.
    Includes index.
    ISBN 0-7914-2843-5 (alk. paper).—ISBN 0-7914-2844-3 (pbk. :
  alk. paper)
    1. Buddhism—Social aspects—Asia. I. Queen, Christopher S.,
  1945– . II. King, Sallie B.
  BQ270.E54   1996
  294.3'378'095—dc20   95-17232
                                                                CIP

10 9 8 7 6 5 4 3

To non-violent Buddhist social activists everywhere—
To those in prison or house arrest and those who are free,
To those who have suffered torture, abuse, and threats,
To those who have given their lives and those who live—
We dedicate this book in the spirit of *Dhammapada* 1.5:

Hatred is never appeased by hatred.
Hatred is appeased by love.
This is the eternal law.

Contents

Preface

To most people in the West, the term "Buddhism" means a religion of introspective withdrawal. Yet the reality of contemporary Asian Buddhism is often something very different. "Buddhism" in contemporary Asia means energetic engagement with social and political issues and crises at least as much as it means monastic or meditative withdrawal. During the war in Vietnam, for example, Buddhists constructed a "Third Way" alternative to the "sides" represented by North and South Vietnam; their view represented the wishes of the majority of the people of South Vietnam; their power was sufficient to bring hordes of demonstrators into the streets and to bring down successive governments in South Vietnam. In Sri Lanka today, large numbers of Buddhist monks can be seen working to rejuvenate village life, laboring side by side with villagers to install roads, latrines, and schools. In India today, millions of Untouchables have converted to a form of Buddhism that actively works for social change and promises an end to the misery caused by the caste system. Throughout Asia, Buddhist nuns have organized themselves to bring institutional change to the Buddhist Sangha within which they have always been second-class citizens. On the international level, the contributions of Buddhists to the conceptualization and actualization of nonviolent action for social justice have been so great that two recent Nobel Peace prizes have gone to Buddhist leaders, the Dalai Lama of Tibet and Aung San Suu Kyi of Myanmar (Burma).

These are some of the contemporary manifestations of Asian Buddhism as a vehicle of social and political activism. Yet this aspect of contemporary Buddhism, significant as it is, remains largely unrecognized in the West. The editors of the present volume believe that this aspect of the contemporary face of Buddhist Asia needs to be brought to the attention of Westerners interested in Buddhism in order to correct a fundamental misapprehension of what Buddhism is today.

This volume began as a panel on "Buddhist Liberation Movements" organized by Christopher Queen at the 1990 national meeting of the American Academy of Religion. At that time, the editors realized that no scholarly study of Buddhist liberation movements existed in the West, despite the fact that these movements represent arguably the most important development in contemporary Asian Buddhism. Consequently, we conceived this volume as an introduction to this facet of contemporary Buddhism, which would be comprehensible to anyone familiar with the basic teachings and general history of Buddhism. Certainly, other stories could have been added to those collected in this volume; our account does not attempt to be exhaustive. (In particular, we were unable to include a chapter on Aung San Suu Kyi, given the delicacy of her situation and the unavailability of sufficient material on the Buddhist elements in her thought and action.) Nonetheless, we believe that the volume will amply demonstrate how widespread and significant socially and politically engaged Buddhism is.

Our subtitle, "Buddhist Liberation Movements in Asia," requires clarification. Individually, the terms, "liberation" and "movement" seem fitting enough for Buddhism: Gautama's order of mendicants in India and its successors throughout Asia were by all accounts dynamic movements devoted to spiritual liberation through ethical, meditational, and devotional practices. However, the phrase "liberation movement," may conjure up images of social protest and insurgency not usually associated with the spirit and reality of traditional Buddhism.

In the industrialized democracies of the post–World War II period, "liberation movement" has come to signify the collective, generally peaceful protest of various minority or politically underrepresented groups—the poor, African-Americans, Hispanics, Native Americans, women, gays, and lesbians. On the other hand, in the developing countries of Latin America and Africa, in the Middle East and South Asia, and in the ethnically complex regions of the former Soviet world, liberation movements have not been typified by peaceful or symbolic protests, but rather by open ethnic and class warfare, terrorism, and protracted armed struggle.

Our Buddhist liberation movements have little in common with the latter category of liberation movements but much in common with the former. These Buddhist movements are always nonviolent and, indeed, often contribute innovative ideas and actions to the global discourse on the theory and practice of nonviolence. Like Christian "Liberation Theology," these movements are characterized by a fundamental commitment to making Buddhism responsive to the suffering of ordinary Buddhists. They are concerned to mobilize the Buddhist laity to address their own economic, social, political, and spiritual needs; to contribute to the amelioration of conditions that produce suffering for all living beings; and, finally, to reform, in light of the demands of modernity, Buddhist doctrines and institutions. It is, finally, their focus upon the relief of concrete economic, social, political, and environmental ills that qualifies these movements as "liberation movements," and it is their commitment to pursue this end on the basis of Buddhist spirituality and heritage that makes them "Buddhist liberation movements."

In inviting our colleagues to contribute to this volume, the editors noted that in nearly every case the movements were founded, inspired, and directed by charismatic individuals, and that these persons' stories were often deeply revealing of the conditions and challenges faced by their followers. Consequently, the chapters devoted to each movement are developed in three dimensions: (a) *biographical,* dealing with the life and career of the leaders; (b) *ideological,* dealing with the ways in which traditional Buddhist teachings have been reinterpreted to address contemporary social realities; and (c) *institutional,* dealing with the shape and constituency of the movement. Paralleling the Three Refuges of Buddhist practice—the Buddha (exemplar), the Dharma (teaching), and the Sanga (Buddhist community)—this scheme offers opportunities to assess the ideals of personal transformation, spiritual/social visions, and community formation that make these movements authentically Buddhist.

Each chapter of the volume represents the story of an individual or group that has responded to the challenge of contemporary conditions, and often crises, from a Buddhist perspective. The chapters are arranged in simple geographic order, moving from India east to Japan, with the pan-Asian nuns' movement situated in the center. They are preceded by an introduction that surveys common features of the movements chronicled and places them in the context of Buddhist history. The central question examined in the introduction concerns whether the activist impulse of contemporary Asian Buddhism is historically new—a series of responses to uniquely modern conditions and historical forces—or whether there exist substantive precedents for such engagement with social and political concerns in Buddhist history. The volume closes with a concluding study of the themes and issues that recur throughout the independent narratives, constructing a more systematic picture of the nature and meaning of contemporary Buddhist social activism as such.

We hope that *Engaged Buddhism* will be useful both to the Buddhist Studies community and to the growing number of readers interested in religious practice and social change. To make the text more accessible to the general reader, the editors have transliterated most foreign terms for ease of pronunciation rather than using the diacritical marks of scholarly transliteration. *Bhikshu,* rather than *bhiksu,* is used for the Sanskrit for "Buddhist monk", for example, and *dhammachari* for *dhammacari* for "lay leader" in the Ambedkarite movement in India. Frequently used foreign terms may appear in italics until they are defined or identified in the text, after which they may appear in plain type.

The editors are grateful to the contributors for their willing involvement in the project and for their patience as the book took form. Sallie King would like to thank James Madison University for the time released in the summer of 1993, which allowed her the opportunity to write the conclusion and to complete her share of editing of this volume. Chris Queen thanks deans Michael Shinagel and Peter Buck for release time for Asian research, Masatoshi Nagatomi, Charles Hallisey, and Tara Doyle for valuable insights on contemporary Buddhism, and Diana Eck, Study of Religion chair, for supporting the teaching of Buddhism and social change at Harvard.

The editors gratefully acknowledge permission from the Center for Southeast Asian Studies to reprint as chapter 6 of this volume Donald K. Swearer's "Sulak Sivaraksa's Buddhist Visions for Renewing Society," which appeared in *Crossroads*, volume 6, number 2, in 1992. We are grateful as well to A. K. Narain and D. K. Publishers (Delhi) for permission to reprint as chapter 2 of this volume Christopher Queen's essay, "Ambedkar, Modernity and the Hermeneutics of Buddhist Liberation," which appeared in *Dr. Ambedkar, Buddhism and Social Change* (1994), edited by A. K. Narain and D. C. Ahir.

1

Introduction: The Shapes and Sources
of Engaged Buddhism

Christopher S. Queen

No recent event has revealed the social and political dimensions of
modern Buddhism as powerfully as the fiery death of Thich Quang Duc on
a Saigon street in 1963. Because the image of a meditating monk in flames
was broadcast by wire service and television, and because Quang Duc and
thirty-six other monks and a laywoman died voluntarily, their message of
anguish and protest over the Vietnam war was engraved on the heart of the
world. Yet the Buddhist meaning of these deaths was lost on most viewers
and commentators. Was it common for Buddhist monks to engage in political protest? Did these monks represent broad popular sentiment or were
they a radical fringe group? Was self-immolation a traditional practice or an
aberration?[1]

Thich Nhat Hanh, a young leader of the Buddhist movement that
contributed to the fall of the repressive Diem regime, later wrote to the Rev.
Dr. Martin Luther King, Jr.,

> The self-burning of Vietnamese Buddhist monks in 1963 is somehow diffi-
> cult for the Western Christian conscience to understand. The press spoke
> then of suicide, but in the essence, it is not. It is not even a protest. What
> the monks said in the letters they left before burning themselves aimed only
> at alarming, at moving the hearts of the oppressors, and at calling the
> attention of the world to the suffering endured then by the Vietnamese. [2]

Nhat Hanh explained that candidates for ordination in the Mahayana Buddhism of Vietnam traditionally burn small spots on their bodies while vowing
to observe the 250 precepts of the order. The idea is that words uttered
while experiencing intense pain "will express all the seriousness of one's

1

heart and mind, and carry much greater weight." Thus the immolation of a monk will carry the greatest weight of all.[3]

What Thich Nhat Hanh did not attempt to explain to Dr. King, to mention in his speaking tours to nineteen countries, or to record in his book on the struggle, *Vietnam: Lotus in a Sea of Fire,* was that self-immolation by fire reminds Mahayana Buddhists of dramatic episodes in the *Lotus Sutra,* one of their oldest and holiest scriptures. In the twenty-third chapter a bodhisattva, or enlightened being, burns his fingers, toes, arms, and finally his whole body in a living sacrifice to the Buddha. So the sacrifice of Thich Quang Duc and the others held meanings that only those raised in a Mahayana Buddhist culture could fully fathom.[4]

Despite the great distances of space and culture separating the Vietnamese and Americans, the message of peace of Quang Duc, Nhat Hanh, and other Vietnamese Buddhists has touched many in the West. Dr. King, the Nobel laureate and soon-to-be martyr for racial justice, nominated Thich Nhat Hanh for a Nobel prize. Thomas Merton, the Trappist author and mystic, described him as "a contemplative monk who has felt himself obliged to take an active part in his country's effort to escape destruction in a vicious power struggle between capitalism and communism. . . . [He] speaks for his people and for *a renewed and 'engaged' Buddhism* that has taken up the challenge of modern and Western civilization in its often disastrous impact upon the East."[5] And now, thirty years after the death of the Saigon monks, thousands of Americans—many of them new converts to Buddhism—follow the teachings of Thich Nhat Hanh, the Vietnamese Zen Master who coined the expression "engaged Buddhism" and introduced its implications to the West.[6]

Today many more Buddhist voices and movements have entered the world stage. Perhaps the best known are the recent Nobel Peace laureates Tenzin Gyatso, the fourteenth Dalai Lama of Tibet (1989), and Aung San Suu Kyi, the Burmese opposition leader (1991). The forced exile of hundreds of thousands of Tibetans and the systematic repression of their compatriots who remained (or were born) in Tibet since the Chinese crackdown in 1959, have made the Dalai Lama's tireless campaign for reconciliation and restoration a model of engaged Buddhism. Likewise, the resolute courage of Aung San Suu Kyi, a Buddhist laywoman and diplomat, elected national leader in democratic elections in 1989 and then held under house arrest in Rangoon by the ruling military junta, is another striking example of Buddhist nonviolent resistance.[7]

Less well-known movements and leaders have also helped to define the meaning of socially engaged Buddhism. The mass conversion to Buddhism of millions of India's "Untouchables" since 1956 is the legacy of Dr. B. R.

Ambedkar, India's fiery civil rights leader and statesman, and an ongoing experiment in urban economic development and grass roots religious revival.[8] In Sri Lanka, the participation of 8,000 villages and 300,000 volunteers in the Sarvodaya Shramadana movement ("All Awaken through Volunteer Service") represents the oldest and largest Buddhist-inspired rural development program in Asia. And the gathering momentum among Asian Buddhist women to restore full ordination for women and to rebuild the Buddhist Order of Nuns, or *bhikkhuni sangha,* connects engaged Buddhism to the global struggle for gender equality.[9]

Three of the studies presented here do not deal with "liberation movements," as that term is commonly understood. Two are devoted to individual figures—the Thai reformers, Buddhadasa Bhikkhu and Sulak Sivaraksa—whose followers are only loosely organized, while a third presents a movement that is highly organized, materially prosperous, and politically influential—the Soka Gakkai lay movement of Japan. Yet these three cases exemplify essential traits of contemporary engaged Buddhism and the liberation movements surveyed. The late Buddhadasa Bhikkhu was arguably the most prolific scholar-teacher in the history of Theravada Buddhism. Leaving more than fifty volumes of religious and social commentary and founding the temple-retreat-training-conference center of Suan Mokkh in Chaiya, Thailand, Buddhadasa may be regarded as the senior philosopher of engaged Buddhism. Thousands of pilgrims, students, ecumenical and community leaders, resident monks, and lay practitioners are likely to use Suan Mokkh ("Garden of Liberation") for generations to come. Similarly, the lay Thai activist and author, Sulak Sivaraksa, a longtime protégé of Buddhadasa, has become a kind of a one-man liberation movement, founding numerous grass-roots, volunteer organizations for peace, community development, and ecumenical dialogue, including the International Network of Engaged Buddhists (INEB, founded in 1989), and publishing a flood of pamphlets, articles, and books, including A *Socially Engaged Buddhism* (1988) and *Seeds of Peace* (1992). Although not representing a specific constituency (such as the Untouchables or Buddhist women), Buddhadasa Bhikkhu and Sulak Sivaraksa, like Nhat Hanh and the Dalai Lama, speak the universal language of human suffering, wisdom, compassion, and liberation we associate with traditional Buddhist teachings.

The inclusion of a chapter on the Japanese lay Buddhist movement, Soka Gakkai, has raised objections. In spite of its energetic engagement in the political, economic, educational, and cultural realms of Japanese society; its consistent espousal of material as well as spiritual well-being (both tenets shared by other engaged Buddhists); and its significant size for a movement founded less than fifty years ago (numbering 8 million in Japan and 1.26 million in 120 other countries), some Buddhist practitioners and scholars argue that Soka Gakkai is fundamentally unlike the liberation movements in South and Southeast Asia. Because of its considerable wealth, its appeal to the class aspirations of its members, and its affiliation with the Komeito, Japan's third-largest political party, critics question its "social location." Secondly, the Gakkai's intolerance of other Buddhist sects and practices (not to mention other religious traditions), its aggressive missionary outreach through one-to-one proselytizing, and, most recently, the breakup of its historical ties with the orthodox Nichiren Shoshu priesthood have raised questions about its status within the Nichiren tradition and its compatibility with the rising spirit of world Buddhism. Finally, the public activities of Soka Gakkai's energetic leader, Daisaku Ikeda, have perplexed and offended some observers, who question his motives and admit that they prefer a more retiring and "gentle" style of Buddhist leadership. It has been said that Ikeda's high-profile meetings with world leaders, frequent lecture and book promotion tours, and even the focus on global issues such as human rights and environmentalism are unfitting for a Buddhist public figure whose sect (if not he himself) stands to benefit materially from the attention.

For the purposes of this volume, such worries over Soka Gakkai's designation as a Buddhist liberation movement or as an exemplar of socially engaged Buddhism have underscored the need to analyze the similarities and differences of the movements and individuals surveyed, and to introduce the larger topic of the place of engaged Buddhism within the history of the Buddhist tradition as a whole.[10] The first task—the need for a phenomenology of Buddhist liberation movements—is addressed in the following section, while the historical question—engaged Buddhism's relation to traditional teachings—is addressed in the final sections of the Introduction.

Buddhist Liberation Movements: A Phenomenology

Beginning our discussion on the streets of Saigon in 1963, we enter a world of people's movements and liberation fronts surrounded by war, violence, and superpower intervention. In the developing nations and border states surrounding the great powers, the immediacy of death by bullet, car bomb, and poverty has spawned liberation theologies and religious revival movements for generations. Yet the presence of religion has been no guarantee of social harmony or diminished violence. Indeed religion, when embodied by true-believers and closed communities, often increases tensions, triggers new outbreaks of hostility, and prevents adversaries from resolving their differences.[11] Sadly, Buddhists cannot claim exemption from this pattern, as Stanley Tambiah has shown in his study of religion, politics, and violence in Sri Lanka.[12] Nor have Buddhists, compared to other religious people, played notable roles in the resolution of local and international tensions. Like the followers of other faiths, Buddhists have responded to local challenges in provisional ways, sometimes pursuing collective action, including institutional pronouncements, nonviolent intervention, and even the principled use of force. On the other hand, like the followers of other faiths, Buddhists have as often declined or failed to lead in shaping the flow of social change.

Despite these caveats, all of the engaged Buddhists in our collection—from Thich Nhat Hanh to Daisaku Ikeda—have been consistent advocates and activists for world peace. The unprecedented awarding of Nobel Peace prizes to two Buddhists in a three-year period, and the prevalence of the theme of "inner peace and world peace," suggesting the conjunction of spiritual and political practice, in the writings of Buddhadasa, Sulak Sivaraksa, Thich Nhat Hanh, and the Dalai Lama suggest this as a distinguishing mark of contemporary engaged Buddhism. The tone and style of Buddhist activism does not always match the stereotype of the mild and self-effacing monk; indeed, the tensed arms and clenched fist of a robed monk addressing a public gathering in Sri Lanka makes a striking cover for Tambiah's *Buddhism Betrayed?*, while Ambedkar's slogan "Educate! Agitate! Organize!" sounds unlikely as an update of the ancient Buddhist precepts.

In a comparative study of Third World liberation theologies, Deane William Ferm observes that Christian liberation theology has two salient features. First, "it stresses liberation from all forms of human oppression: social, economic, political, racial, sexual, environmental, religious"; and second, it insists that theology must be truly indigenous. "For this reason liberation theology coming out of Peru cannot be merely transported to Sri Lanka or South Korea"; each locality must devise its own moral and political response to the vicissitudes it faces.[13]

While the first of Ferm's observations—the worldly perspective of liberation theologies—is fully consistent with the Buddhist liberation movements surveyed, the second feature—the cultural particularism of liberation theologies—does not match (despite obvious local elements) the pervasive universalism of engaged Buddhism.[14] Thich Nhat Hanh's letter to America's best-known civil rights leader was motivated not by a desire to promote Vietnamese Mahayana Buddhism, self-immolation, or a particular political outcome to the war. It was rather, like the sacrifice of Quang Duc, "to call the attention of the world to the suffering" of the Vietnamese in a universal language—not unlike the ecumenical or nonsectarian expressions and gestures of many engaged Buddhists chronicled in this volume.[15]

As an expedient way of presenting several related aspects of engaged Buddhism in Asia, let us use the terms "Buddhist," "liberation," and "movement" to stand, respectively, for the personal, doctrinal, and institutional dimensions of the phenomenon. Like the traditional Three Refuges (*tisarana*) or vows of homage to the Buddha (personal exemplar, savior, or symbol of enlightenment), the Dharma (doctrine, truth, way), and the Sangha (practicing community, both ordained and lay), this threefold scheme will enable us to draw out important patterns of thought and action in the emerging Buddhism.

Interpretive Pattern for Comparing
Buddhist Liberation Movements

Buddhist	Liberation	Movements
personal	doctrinal	institutional
leader	teachings	actions
[Buddha	Dharma	Sangha]

A New Kind of Leader

Each of the movements surveyed here has coalesced around a popular leader or leaders whose identity and mission are understood by followers to be distinctively *Buddhist*. Perhaps the preeminent example in this respect is that of the Dalai Lama, who is venerated as an incarnation of the Bodhisattva Avalokiteshvara, the patron saint of Tibet and the epitome of divine compassion. Throughout the world, followers of the Tibetan tradition show respect for the Dalai Lama by displaying his photograph on altars or on the walls in their homes. Similarly, in the years since Dr. Ambedkar's death, a devotional cult has grown up among his followers, who display his image in their homes in the form of posters or small busts, or outdoors in the form of plaster, stone, or bronze monuments. What is significant in both instances, one old (Dalai Lamas have long been venerated as symbols of wisdom and compassion by Tibetan Buddhists) and one new (never before had an Indian Untouchable been venerated as a Buddhist leader), is that the image is often combined or juxtaposed with that of the Buddha, and the ensemble is found not only in a temple or shrine complex but in the home or on the street corner.

In a study of religious symbolism and political change in Ceylon, Gananath Obeyesekere noted the appearance of images and statues in the home and on street corners—Buddha statues that sprang up on nearly every major intersection in urban Sri Lanka, and private Buddha altars or *Budu ge* that became a common sight in middle-class Buddhist homes by the 1960s.[16] Obeyesekere called this importation of religious symbols into the secular realm "a spatial shift symbolizing the entry of Buddhism into the 'world,' " and went on to analyze its key elements:

1. the emergence of a leader who provides a charter for change, a model for emulation, and becomes a symbol of a new order;

2. role shifts, specifically a this-worldly asceticism directed to political and social goals; and

3. 'a rationalization of the religious life' involving the discrediting of folk religious elements (such as theistic devotionalism or ritualism) and an emphasis on mental and moral development through education and virtuous living.[17]

Many leaders of the Asian Buddhist liberation movements embody these elements. Most came from relatively privileged circumstances and benefited from intensive early education.[18] Indeed, when one considers the Dalai Lama's rarefied monastic education, Ambedkar's doctoral degrees from Columbia and London universities, and the origins of Soka Gakkai in the educational reform movement of Tsunesaburo Makiguchi, we can see the extraordinary role that formal education has played in the origins of engaged Buddhism.[19] On the other hand, none of the leaders chose the most traditional role for Buddhist leaders in the past, that of the forest or temple monk. Buddhadasa, Thich Nhat Hanh, and the Dalai Lama, three ordained movement leaders, have embarked on nontraditional careers involving travel, administrative responsibilities, contact with members of the opposite sex, and financial affairs. Most ordained women of Taiwan and female lay renunciants of Sri Lanka (*dasa sil mata*), Thailand (*mae ji*), Burma (*thila shin*), and Tibet (*ani*) eschew the traditional monastic rules of subordination to monks and emphasize community service. When one adds the institutional and temporal duties of head of state (Dalai Lama), cabinet minister, minority leader, constitutional lawyer (Ambedkar), and chief executive officer of nongovernmental organizations numbering thousands or millions of members (Ariyaratne, Ikeda), one recognizes the magnitude of the social, psychological, and ideological shifts that have occurred.

In spite of the fortunate backgrounds and extensive influence of the liberation movement leaders, each one has had to confront and overcome daunting obstacles. Ambedkar's childhood (and perhaps more painfully, his adulthood) as an Untouchable was the source of his moral authority and his attraction to Buddhism. The activist women, especially in South Asia, have confronted staunch resistance to change from lay and ordained sectors of

Buddhist society. Other leaders have had great personal sadness to bear: for the Dalai Lama, exile and the near extinction of his culture; for Thich Nhat Hanh, the protracted civil and superpower war in his country; for the first Soka Gakkai leaders, Makiguchi and Toda Josei, imprisonment and (for Makiguchi) death at the hands of the wartime Japanese government; for Sulak Sivaraksa, imprisonment and exile for denouncing the Thai throne; for leaders of the Ambedkarite movement in central India and the Sarvodaya Shramadana movement in Sri Lanka, the intractable poverty and backwardness of rural and urban slum populations; and for Buddhadasa, the deterioration and decadence of Sangha and society in rapidly industrializing Thailand. In the process of struggling through these hardships, the new Buddhist leaders exemplify Obeyesekere's role models for change, popular emulation, and a new symbolic order.

New Readings of Ancient Dharma

The *liberation* that these leaders envision and articulate in their addresses and writings is consistently based on their own distinctive readings of traditional Buddhist doctrines, particularly those of selflessness, interdependence, the five precepts, the four noble truths, nondualism, and emptiness. Virtually all of these leaders have written creatively and copiously on the contemporary application of traditional Buddhist teachings. Ambedkar's *The Buddha and His Dhamma* was conceived and written as a kind of Buddhist bible for the Untouchable converts to Buddhism, while the flood of addresses and essays from the other leaders has been directed at a full range of religious and social issues.

The anthropologist Clifford Geertz has identified "scripturalism" as a distinctive mark of religious change in classical cultures. By this he meant a heightened reliance on ancient teachings in rapidly changing times. Such attention to tradition might take the form of new popular reverence for scripture and for scriptural literacy, a belief in the inerrancy of the canonical tradition, or alternatively, the prodigious efforts of scholars and public figures to reinterpret ancient teachings in the light of modern problems. One thinks, for example, of the contrast between the Vietnamese association of a monk's death by fire with a well-known chapter in the Lotus Sutra, on the one hand, and the Soka Gakkai faith in the single-minded chanting of the title of the same scripture, on the other hand.

Given such a wide range of possible responses, Geertz offered the following caution:

> For scripturalism to become a living religious tradition rather than merely a collection of strained apologies, its adherents would have to undertake a serious theological rethinking of the scholastic tradition they can, apparently, neither live with nor live without.[20]

Buddhadasa Bhikkhu's historic rereading of the Theravada tradition is already regarded as a major contribution to Theravada commentarial literature, as the Dalai Lama's writings and pronouncements on Buddhist philosophy and ethics occupy a similar place in the Tibetan context. Sulak Sivaraksa and A. T. Ariyaratne have been notably resourceful in invoking traditional Pali scriptures, such as the *Kutadanta Sutta*, *Sigalovada Sutta*, *Jatakamala*, *Buddhacarita*, and others to formulate a viable lay ethic in a world of multinational corporations, mass media, political corruption, and mounting violence. Daisaku Ikeda's imaginative melding of doctrines from the T'ien T'ai and Nichiren traditions—especially those of *mappo*, "degenerate age," and *obutsu myogo*, "engaged religion"—with contemporary reflections on a wide range of planetary issues (and in dialogue with well-known political and academic figures) have been appearing at a rate of nearly a book per year, translated and distributed in English, German, French, Spanish, Italian, Portuguese, Romanian, Chinese, Korean, Thai, Indonesian, and Malay.

It has been said that the word "liberation" is like a chameleon, "changing its color with each new attachment: animal liberation, women's liberation, liberation theology, gay liberation, or the liberation of Kuwait."[21] In traditional Buddhism, liberation (Pali *vimutti*, Sanskrit *vimoksha*) has also meant many things, from the Theravada freedom from desires, passions, and delusion to the Mahayana freedom from conventional views of reality to the Vajrayana freedom from moral and ethical dualism. All of these meanings have been tied to the ultimate promise of a personal, spiritual liberation that transcends the material, psychological, and social confines of this world: *nirvana*, a state of peace, devoid of passions and attachments; *bodhi*, the condition of wisdom and compassion that is "gone far beyond" (*parasamgate*) mundane conditioning and comprehension; or *mahasukha*, the sublime happiness that results from advanced ritual practice.

Yet in the socially engaged Buddhism of modern Asia, the liberation sought has been called a "mundane awakening" (*laukodaya*), which includes individuals, villages, nations, and ultimately all people (*sarvodaya*), and which focuses on objectives that may be achieved and recognized in this lifetime, in this world. George Bond has summarized the comprehensive nature of the liberative vision that inspires volunteers in the Sarvodaya Shramadana movement, including moral, cultural, spiritual, social, political, and economic dimensions. Thus, in addition to being a society based on the Buddhist precepts and offering opportunities for obtaining wisdom, happiness, and peace, Ariyaratna and his colleagues have focused on the "ten basic human needs" that must be met for liberation to be possible: a clean and beautiful environment, an adequate and safe water supply, clothing, balanced diet, simple housing, basic health care, communication facilities, energy, education related to life and living, and free access to cultural and spiritual resources. The list is offered as a modern version of the Buddhist "middle way"—a balancing of the material and spiritual aspects of social change.[22]

We may conclude that a profound change in Buddhist soteriology—from a highly personal and other-worldly notion of liberation to a social, economic, this-worldly liberation—distinguishes the Buddhist movements in our study. The traditional conceptions of karma and rebirth, the veneration of the bhikkhu sangha, and the focus on ignorance and psychological attachment to account for suffering in the world (the second Noble Truth) have taken second place to the application of highly rationalized reflections on the institutional and political manifestations of greed, hatred, and delusion, and on new organizational strategies for addressing war and injustice, poverty and intolerance, and the prospects for "outer" as well as "inner" peace in the world.[23]

Skillful Means for Social Engagement

It is this new awareness of the social and institutional dimensions of suffering and the liberation from suffering that has contributed to the rise of contemporary Buddhist liberation *movements*. Let us stipulate that a modern liberation "movement" must be more than a collection of people who happen to live in a geographic area and participate in a cultural tradition—whether religious, ethnic, or political. Moreover, a liberation movement must be more than a voluntary association guided by exemplary leaders and a common vision—when that vision is related only to the personal or spiritual needs if its members. (Most intentional religious communities, including the order of monks that followed Shakyamuni Buddha, would fall within that definition.) Rather, let us propose that a modern liberation movement is a voluntary association guided by exemplary leaders and a common vision of a new society (or world) based on peace, justice, and freedom. Today's Buddhist liberation movements in Asia exemplify these features, appropriately expressed in language and styles of conduct that its members deem to be "Buddhist."

In framing our definition in this way, we avoid language that would restrict the membership of liberation movements to those persons who are objectively oppressed, disadvantaged, or marginalized—or who regard themselves as such. For if it is true that liberation movements have initially grown out of historical oppression—from the Hebrews of the Biblical exodus, to the industrial "proletariat" of the nineteenth century, to the Christian liberationists of Latin America—it is also true that the theologies and institutions that emerged from these roots were formulated and nurtured by leaders and groups who had escaped (or been "liberated") from oppressive circumstances.[24]

We have noted that the most distinctive shift of thinking in socially engaged Buddhism is from a transmundane (*lokuttara*) to a mundane (*lokiya*) definition of liberation. Accompanying this shift is a de-emphasis on the stages of transmundane liberation (for example, the Theravada stages of "stream-enterer," "once-returner," "non-returner," and "arahant," or the Mahayana stages of the Bodhisattva path), and a new focus on the causes, varieties, and remedies of worldly suffering and oppression. Thus contemporary Buddhist liberation movements are as likely to apply their interpretive and organizational efforts to the critique and reform of social and political conditions as they are to propose and practice new spiritual exercises. The evils of war and genocide, of ethnic hatred and caste violence, and of economic disparity and degradation figure prominently in engaged Buddhist writings. On the other hand, the democratization, if not the transformation, of spiritual practices—for example, meditation and ritual initiations as now appropriated by lay practitioners—has been seen as an integral concomitant to the shift to mundane awakening.[25]

To advance their vision of a new world, Buddhist liberation movements have harnessed modern methods of education, mass communication, political influence and activism, jurisprudence and litigation, and yes, even fund-raising and marketing. Many examples of these new "skillful means" may be cited.

If practical education is a basic human need, according to villagers in Sri Lanka, then the Buddhist liberation movements have concentrated major resources to this end. Among the first activities of the Buddhist women reformers in Sri Lanka at the turn of the century was the founding of primary schools for girls. Today the Trailokya Bauddha Mahasangha Sahayaka Gana (TBMSG), or Western Buddhist Order in India, is proud of its nursery schools, which permit parents to work full-time or to attend school themselves. The TBMSG also offers vocational training in tailoring and other trades for women, who would ordinarily not have the opportunity or the skills to work outside the home. Sarvodaya Shramadana has carried on the ancient tradition of founding and supporting Buddhist primary and secondary schools in cooperation with the Bhikkhu Sangha in Sri Lanka. To promote higher education, Ambedkar founded the People's Education Society and its member institutions, Siddharth and Milind colleges, and Thich Nhat Hanh and his associates were instrumental in founding Van Han University. The Soka Gakkai, in recognition of its founder's lifetime commitment to educational reform, has established the Soka schools from kindergarten through graduate school, with Soka University and its affiliated research institutes at the apex of the system. Buddhadasa Bhikkhu and the Dalai Lama have labored to preserve and improve monastic education but also to broaden access of the laity to spiritual and cultural training.

The printing press, the public address system, and the speaking tour
have been skillfully employed by Asian Buddhist liberation movements and
leaders, as we have seen; yet some of them have gone considerably farther.
By staging highly newsworthy media events and by associating—or "networking"—with celebrated personalities to reach a worldwide audience,
engaged Buddhists have sought to bring international pressure on governments and individuals perpetrating violence and suffering. Was this not,
after all, the effect of the Buddhist self-immolations in Saigon in 1963 and
of Thich Nhat Hanh's follow-up letter to Dr. Martin Luther King, Jr., two
years later? The letter explicitly places the matter in the context of mass
communication ("The press spoke then of suicide . . . ") and then goes on
to underscore the intention of Thich Quang Duc and his followers, "moving
the hearts of the oppressors, and calling the attention of the world to the
suffering endured then by the Vietnamese." If Mahatma Gandhi used street
theater, newsreel, and print media to communicate with his adversaries
during the Indian struggle for independence, now television, Fax, and
E-mail make it possible for engaged Buddhists to enter the offices and
homes of the rich and powerful: heads of government and multinational
corporations, and the middle class who rule by checkbook and ballot box.

The memoirs of Ambedkar's close associates offer a revealing glimpse
at the feverish planning that led up to the mass conversion of Untouchables
to Buddhism in Nagpur on October 14, 1956—and a prime example of the
role image making has played in twentieth-century engaged Buddhism. The
date had been set for years (Ambedkar had decided to convert at least five
years earlier): 1956 would mark the worldwide celebration of the 2,500th
birthday of Buddhism, and October 14 was the traditional date of the conversion of Asoka Maurya, Buddhism's greatest king. But the location and
the text of the ceremony were sources of contention among Ambedkar's
inner circle up to the final weeks. Some said Bombay, with its millions of
potential converts; others said Nagpur, with its central Indian location and
legendary associations (the Naga people played a key role in protecting and
preserving the Buddha's teachings). More controversial was the question of
the Three Refuges: Ambedkar reportedly refused until the final days to take
refuge in the Sangha, because of the wealth and apathy of monks he had
met in Sri Lanka and Burma ("an army of idlers"). At last, Ambedkar's aides
convinced him that the conversion would not be authentic unless the
universal custom of taking all three refuges was observed. India's oldest
Theravada monk was invited to preside.[26]

Can it be doubted that these negotiations, like the plans surrounding
the Saigon immolations, were intended to maximize the social and political, as well as spiritual, impact of the events? It is interesting to compare

the public relations skills of the Dalai Lama and Daisaku Ikeda, both of whom have met frequently with statesmen, scholars, and scientists to promote their movements; have cooperated with film and publishing interests to place their views before the largest audience; and have waged highly sophisticated campaigns for the understanding and support of followers at all strata of society, not least, the educated elite.[27] As the Dalai Lama has impressed the world with his sincerity and integrity, so Mr. Ikeda must be credited for his skillful leadership of the most rapidly growing and widely dispersed Buddhist sect on earth.

To sum up our phenomenology of Buddhist Liberation movements, it is instructive to return to the Soka Gakkai as a kind of test case. Clearly, Soka Gakkai shares essential elements of leadership, doctrine, and organization with the other groups. It fits the definition of a liberation movement we have proposed, and it is dedicated to the social and political ideals of engaged Buddhists elsewhere: a dual emphasis on *inner peace* (associated with spiritual practice—chanting for Gakkai members, meditation, devotional ritual, and study for most other groups) and w*orld peace* (the use of a wide range of educational, social, cultural, and political means to reduce violence, injustice, and environmental degradation). The sticking points for some critics remain the historical intolerance of Nichiren Buddhists for other sects, and Soka Gakkai's overt use of politics and propaganda to achieve public acceptance and influence.[28] Yet when these aspects of Nichirenism are compared with well-known and recurrent patterns of exclusivism and political power found elsewhere in Buddhist history—the strident sectarianism of the early Mahayana, as manifested in the Lotus Sutra, for example, or the proclamation of ideological and political hegemony through the mass media of the Indian Asoka Maurya's rock and pillar edicts or the Japanese Prince Shotoku's Ten Article Constitution—the critique loses much of its force.[29]

In 1970 Donald Swearer wrote in the introduction to his influential *Buddhism in Transition*, "The times in which we live demand that the historic religions find within themselves the strength of reorientation and the wisdom of genuine reformation. Certain aspects of Buddhism in Southeast Asia indicate there is some hope that such revitalization will take place."[30] Twenty-five years later, as Swearer's and other chapters in this volume confirm, Buddhist revitalization, in the forms we have come to call "engaged Buddhism" and "Buddhist liberation movements," is a fact—albeit still "in transition." With these reflections on the common characteristics of the movements surveyed in this volume, we turn now to the question of engaged Buddhism's origins, including the complex issue of its continuity or discontinuity with models of traditional Buddhist social teaching and action.

Buddhism and Social Service

"Buddhism is based on service to others," wrote Walpola Rahula, the eminent Sinhalese scholar-monk and activist, in 1946. The occasion was a heated debate over the social role of the Buddhist monk (*bhikkhu*) in Sinhalese society in the final months before independence. Responding to the disparaging remarks of the new prime minister, a rising chorus of letters and editorials in the press, and the official warnings of chief monks of the ancient monastic orders—all denouncing the involvement of monks in public affairs—Rahula delivered a major address in which he argued on historical grounds that political and social engagement was the "heritage of the bhikkhu" and the essence of Buddhism.[31]

Rahula was not alone in this view. One of the premier monastic colleges in Ceylon, the Vidyalankara Pirivena, had earlier issued a declaration on "Bhikkhus and Politics" that read, in part:

> We believe that politics today embraces all fields of human activity directed towards the public weal. No one will dispute that the work for the promotion of the religion is the duty of the bhikkhu. It is clear that the welfare of the religion depends on the welfare of the people who profess that religion. . . . We, therefore, declare that it is nothing but fitting for bhikkhus to identify themselves with activities conducing to the welfare of our people—whether these activities be labeled politics or not—as long as they do not constitute an impediment to the religious life of a bhikkhu.[32]

Within months the firebrand Rahula founded the United Bhikkhu Council to promote "a great awakening of the bhikkhus and laymen regarding current religious, social, economic, and political problems," organized mass meetings and strikes, and published *The Heritage of the Bhikkhu: A Short History of the Bhikkhu in Educational, Cultural, Social, and Political Life.*

In calling his essay a "short history," Rahula did not mean to imply that the involvement of Buddhist monks in politics was a recent phenomenon. His thesis was that Buddhist monks had traditionally "resolved to remain in *samsara* (the circle of existence and continuity) to serve the world," and moreover that monks, following the example and exhortation of the Buddha, have always vowed "to wander from village to village preaching to the people for their good and for their well-being."[33] Rahula's book, then, stands as a manifesto of socially engaged Buddhism, written by a movement leader who was shortly to land in jail for his public agitations, a monk who exemplified the new religious militancy, and a recognized scholar and university administrator. Like other Sinhalese Buddhist works of the period, *The Heritage of the Bhikkhu* was the work of a passionate participant-observer.[24]

Rahula's summary of the history of monastic engagement in the social and political life of Ceylon begins with a picture of the primitive sangha at the time of the Buddha. Here the founder and his followers are seen giving practical advice to villagers who were "poor, illiterate, not very clean, and not healthy . . . [who] needed simple moral ideas conducive to their material well-being and happiness rather than deep and sublime discourses on philosophy, metaphysics, or psychology as taught in the *Abhidhamma*."[35] Such ideas, taken from early Pali scriptures (*suttas*) Rahula was well-qualified to interpret, included the view that crime and immorality in society are rooted in poverty (*Cakkavatti-sihanada-sutta*), that employment opportunities must be provided to ensure the common weal (*Kutadanta-sutta*), that merchants should be diligent, savvy, and scrupulous in their dealings and that laypersons should seek economic security, freedom from debt, good health, and wholesome associations (*Sigala-sutta*; *Anguttara-nikaya*), and that political leaders should observe the Ten Duties of the King, including liberality, morality, self-sacrifice, integrity, nonviolence, and so on (*Dhammapadatthakatha*). In short, "the Buddha and the bhikkhus taught such important ideas pertaining to health, sanitation, earning wealth, mutual relationships, well-being of society, and righteous government—all for the good of the people."[36]

In the following chapters, Rahula traces the evolution of monks' roles and social teachings in Sinhala Buddhism, stressing the unique and intense symbiosis that developed between the sangha and the state in Ceylon between the third century B.C.E. and the nineteenth century C.E. Not only did the monastic establishment legitimate the throne by developing an ideology of Buddhist kingship, but monks ended up in key advisory and bureaucratic roles throughout the government. In addition to serving as king makers (in a kind of ancient electoral college), monks served as education ministers, physicians, judges, architects, and military advisers. We learn of the rise of state Buddhism and Buddhist holy war. During the reign of Sri Lanka's most illustrious king, Dutthagamani (101–77 B.C.E.), large numbers of bhikkhus accompanied the king on his military campaigns, some disrobing to join the army and others providing moral blessing by their presence. During this period "both bhikkhus and laymen considered that even killing people in order to liberate the religion and the country was not a heinous crime."[37]

In the course of time, according to Rahula, a profound evolution of monastic roles took place, from a sangha founded on the preeminence of religious practice (*patipatti*) to one founded on study (*pariyatti*), from the prestige of the ascetic monk (*pamsukulika*) to that of the learned monk (*dhammakathika*), and from the dominance of the forest-dweller (*aranyavasi*) to that of the village-dweller (*gramavasi*). And if the reader grants Rahula's thesis that scholarship is a form of service, and that the vocation of book-wielding scholar-monk (*gantha-dhura*) increasingly attracted more talented and service-oriented youth than the vocation of meditation-master (*vipassana-dhura*), then one is persuaded that, in Ceylon at least, the heritage of the bhikkhu lay in the public sphere and not in monastic retreat.

In the last chapters of *The Heritage of the Bhikkhu*, Rahula chronicles the forced reversal of Buddhist monastic engagement by successive waves of European colonialists and their Christian missionary allies. With the arrival of the Portuguese (1505), the Dutch (1602), and the British (1815), most of the traditional roles of the Buddhist sangha—especially their social and welfare activities—were usurped by the missionaries. Finally, all that was left to the bhikkhu was "the recitation of the *Suttas* (*Pirit* chanting), preaching a sermon, attendance at funeral rites and alms-giving in memory of the departed, and an idle, cloistered life in the temple."[38]

Rahula convincingly shows that the Buddhist revival that began in the nineteenth century with the new militancy of such monastic leaders as the Ven. Hikkaduve Sri Sumangala and the Ven. Migettuvatte Sri Gunananda was the heroic response of the sangha to three centuries of political and religious domination. Once again "political monks" could join in the tradi-tional tasks of nation-building and public service, protected both by a re-stored national government (independence came to Sri Lanka in 1948) and, not incidentally, by the historical legitimation of scholarship like Rahula's.

Buddhism: Spiritual or Political?

The reactions of historians to *The Heritage of the Bhikkhu* have been mixed. S. J. Tambiah found Rahula's treatment of the colonial period "innova-tive and compelling" and endorsed the epitome of the book's thesis offered in its introduction by Edmund F. Perry, that "colonial administrators dis-possessed the bhikkhus of their influence on the public life of their people, and actually succeeded in instituting a tradition of Buddhist recluses, to the near exclusion of other types of clergy."[39] Nevertheless, Tambiah shows how Rahula's career and writings, along with those of numerous other ordained and lay supporters of the political bhikkhu cause, contributed to the rise of religiously inspired violence in postindependent Sri Lanka.

Other reviewers have not been as favorable. The Ven. Sangharakshita, an English Buddhist monk whose own credentials as an engaged Buddhist are documented in Chapter 3 of this volume, denounced *The Heritage of the Bhikkhu* as suffering from "extreme confusion of thought," especially with respect to its central proposition that "Buddhism is based on service to others." Sangharakshita reminds the reader that the earliest bhikkhus were sent out to preach enlightenment and *brahmacarya*, the holy life, not primarily to give practical advice. Yet, in Rahula's account,

> the impression is created that 'a true Buddhist' is concerned with the promotion exclusively of the material well-being of humanity. In other words, having in effect dismissed Nirvana as a sort of anti-social selfishness, the Bodhisattva ideal [of postponing one's own liberation for others] is equated with the secular concept of social service. Could the degradation of a sublime spiritual ideal be carried further than this? Despite his extensive scholarship, the author seems totally unaware of the true significance either of the 'transcendental' state of Nirvana, the goal of the Theravada, or of the transcendental 'career' of the Bodhisattva, the ideal of the Mahayana schools.[40]

Sangharakshita defends his position with a detailed critique of Rahula's argument, noting, for example, that villagers in the Buddha's time were more likely to be prosperous and healthy than poor and dirty, judging from the large numbers of Buddhist monks supported by public philanthropy.[41]

Scholars have long questioned the ancient origins of engaged Buddhism. In an influential study, Max Weber depicted ancient Buddhism as an "anti-political status religion, more precisely, a religious 'technology' of wandering and of intellectually schooled mendicant monks . . . the most radical form of salvation-striving conceivable, [whose] salvation is a solely personal act of the single individual."[42] Today, after eighty years of new research, many specialists are inclined to agree with Weber that, in its essence, primitive Buddhism was not based on service to others, but on the quest for individual enlightenment. Bardwell L. Smith writes,

> The primary goal of Buddhism is not a stable order or a just society but the discovery of genuine freedom (or awakening) by each person. It has never been asserted that the conditions of society are unimportant or unrelated to this more important goal, but it is critical to stress the distinction between what is primary and what is not. For Buddhists to lose this distinction is to transform their tradition into something discontinuous with its original and historic essence. Even the vocation of the bodhisatta is not as social reformer but as the catalyst to personal transformation within society.[43]

Richard Gombrich adds that the Buddha should not be seen as a social reformer: "his concern was to reform individuals and help them to leave society forever, not to reform the world. . . . He never preached against social inequality, only declared its irrelevance to salvation. He neither tried to abolish the caste system nor to do away with slavery"—and ultimately the sangha came to own slaves and to be submerged in the caste system of greater India.[44]

Joseph M. Kitagawa's "Buddhism and Social Change: An Historical Perspective," (a chapter written, significantly, for the *Festschrift* honoring Walpola Rahula) extends the discussion to China and Japan.[45] In a survey of the evolution of Buddhist beliefs and institutions amidst historical change throughout Asia, the author concludes that, "while Buddhism had lofty universal principles (Dharma) as well as moral codes for individual life, it made little effort in developing what might be called 'middle principles' to mediate between universal principles and the empirical socio-political and economic situations in any given society."[46] Kitagawa joins others in pointing out that, "contrary to the popular notion that the Buddha was a crusading social reformer, fighting for the cause of common man against the establishment of his time, there is no evidence that he attempted, directly at any rate, to change society."[47]

Later stages of assimilation and symbiosis placed Buddhism under the patronage of kings in India, China, Japan, and neighboring states. According to Kitagawa, this left the sangha "detached from the everyday aspect of life—typically uninterested in customary law and political matters, marriage and family affairs, contracts, and business relationships." In China, for example, amidst the vast property holdings of the sangha, and its popularity among the genteel classes, the cosmic bodhisattvas Avalokiteshvara and Maitreya (known for their heroic intervention on behalf of suffering humanity) are transformed, respectively, into the gentle Kuan-yin and the pot-bellied Pu-tai, epitomizing "the long and tragic process of particularization and domestication of the 'universal' dimension of Buddhism throughout its history in China."[48] Similar transformations are cited in other culture areas, yielding the conclusion that

> rarely did [Buddhist] rulers, even the pious ones, tolerate a prophetic judgment, based on Buddhist principles, directed toward the norms and structures of the socio-political order.[49]

We may conclude that engaged Buddhism, as exemplified in the liberation movements in this volume, has not been a typical pattern in the social history of Asia. This is not to say that the role of Buddhist monks in the political life of premodern Ceylon is without parallel. The continuous and often intimate relations between sangha and state in the Theravada lands of Southeast Asia, in China, Tibet and the Himalayan region, and in imperial Japan from the time of Shotoku Taishi are well documented.[50] But the kind of Buddhism exemplified in the careers and writings of figures like Thich Nhat Hanh, Ambedkar, Ariyaratne, Sulak Sivaraksa, and Daisaku

Ikeda—and, incidentally, in the nonviolent activities of the political bhikkhus in Sri Lanka since the 1940s—is significantly different from the state-sponsored "service to others" in Rahula's account.

The model of engaged Buddhism presented in *The Heritage of the Bhikkhu*—that of monks legitimating and staffing the government in all of its functions, including warfare—does not resemble contemporary engaged Buddhism. The intimate relationship between sangha and state, which lies at the heart of Rahula's account, is antithetical to the independent, some-times adversarial, relationship between movements and power structures claimed by many Buddhist activists today. Even in the cases of the clerically directed Tibetan community-in-exile, and the lay-directed Soka Gakkai, where great authority is vested in the leader and where the community is actively involved in political affairs, these movements are neither state-controlled nor state-sponsored.[51]

A liberation movement, we proposed, is a voluntary association of people, guided by exemplary leaders and a common vision of a society based on peace, justice, and freedom. Such a movement is significantly different in character and function from a sovereign state, which exercises temporal power over its citizens in the name of a common purpose. Socially engaged Buddhists direct their energies toward social conditions over which the state has legal authority, if not control; but their objective is to influence the exercise of temporal power, not to wield it. Sulak Sivaraksa is fond of contrasting the "capital-B Buddhists" who cultivate privileged relations with state power brokers, with the "small-b Buddhists" who change society by manifesting qualities of wisdom, compassion, and peace:

> Buddhism, as practiced in most Asian countries today, serves mainly to legitimize dictatorial regimes and multinational corporations. If we Bud-dhists want to redirect our energies towards enlightenment and universal love, we should begin by spelling Buddhism with a small "b." Buddhism with a small "b" means concentrating on the message of the Buddha and paying less attention to myth, culture, and ceremony.[52]

This does not mean a strategic retreat from social activism, but rather the avoidance of excessive wealth and power.[53] Consequently, the status of non-governmental organization or "NGO" well describes Sulak's International Network of Engaged Buddhists, Sarvodaya Shramadana, Soka Gakkai Inter-national, TBMSG, and other Buddhist groups treated in this volume—groups working for social change with or without the alliance of the nation-state.

We may also conclude that the history of engaged Buddhism, as exem-plified in the liberation movements presented here, is a brief one. Once we have identified the common characteristics of contemporary Buddhist liberation movements (voluntary groups and nongovernmental organizations committed to realizing a just and peaceful society by Buddhist means), and once we have rejected two extremes of historical reconstruction (the extreme of a primitive Buddhist counterculture bent on social reform, and the extreme of a sangha directing social change from its position within the power elite), we recognize that the shape and style of contemporary engaged Buddhism does not appear in Buddhist history until about the year 1880. Here we may thank Rahula for providing the setting.

It is only in the late nineteenth-century revival of Buddhism in Sri Lanka —and particularly in its two principal figures, the American Theosophist, Col. Henry Steel Olcott (1832–1907) and his protégé, the Sinhalese Anagarika Dharmapala (1864–1933)—that we first recognize the spirit and substance of the religious activism we call "socially engaged Buddhism." And it is only in this context that we first meet the missing ingredient— in effect, the primary explanation for the appearance of socially engaged Buddhism in its contemporary form following the arrival of Colonel Olcott and Madame Blavatsky in Ceylon on May 17, 1880. This ingredient is the influence of European and American religious and political thought (and perhaps equally important, western methods of institutional development and public communication) on the evolution of modern Buddhism.

Imagine the scene, as the first Americans to embrace Buddhism as a personal faith arrived in the coastal town of Galle.

> The harbor was lined with brightly painted fishing boats, a thousand flags flew in the sun, and white cloth was spread out on the dock to lead them to their carriage. On May 25, [Blavatsky] and the Colonel knelt before a Buddhist priest at a temple in Galle and performed the ceremony of "taking *pansil*"—the five lay precepts of undertaking to refrain from killing, lying, stealing, intoxicants, and sexual misconduct. They repeated the vows in Pali, as well as the refuge in Buddha, Dharma, and Sangha, before a large crowd. "When we finished the last of the Silas," Olcott wrote in his diary, "and offered flowers in the customary way, there came a mighty shout to make one's nerves tingle."[54]

Engaged Buddhism as Cultural Interpenetration

In "Religious Symbolism and Political Change in Ceylon," Gananath Obeyesekere coined the term "Protestant Buddhism" to refer to the Buddhist revivals associated with Olcott's Buddhist Theosophical Society in Ceylon (1880) and Dharmapala's Maha Bodhi Society in India (1891). Not only were these societies and the attitudes, institutions, and literature they fostered deeply derivative of the Victorian Christianity which Olcott and Dharmapala encountered and imported from the West, but they were also, significantly, a *protest* against Victorian religion and the political dominance it represented in preindependence South Asia. Thus, according to Obeyesekere, we cannot consider the Buddhist revival in South Asia in purely Buddhist terms. We are forced to acknowledge and to trace the ways in which Buddhist and Christian—Asian, European, and American—traditions have become inextricably intertwined in the brief history of socially engaged Buddhism.[55]

A narrative history of the Buddhist revivals of Sri Lanka and elsewhere since the 1880s is not our purpose here. Rather, to give a sense of the profound cultural interpenetration that shaped the personalities of Olcott and Dharmapala and laid the groundwork for engaged Buddhism today, let us return to the three schematic "refuges"—the personal, the doctrinal, and the institutional—that structured our earlier analysis above. Here we may refer to the reformers, the scriptures, and the public symbols of Buddhist modernism. To illustrate the correspondence of the careers and contributions of Olcott and Dharmapala with those of our current survey, let us add Ambedkar to the account, as a leader who embodied the goals and methods of the later Buddhist liberationists.

Three Exemplars: Olcott, Dharmapala, Ambedkar

While 1880, the year of Olcott's arrival in Ceylon, may be taken as a focal date in the appearance of engaged Buddhism as we know it, 1891, the year of Ambedkar's birth in a British army barracks near Bhopal, offers a more useful introduction to our three *reformers*.[56] Ambedkar was the fourteenth child in an Untouchable family. His father, thanks to the British policy of recruiting and promoting Hindus of all castes in the colonial army, served as a military school headmaster and for years as young Bhimrao's academic tutor. These childhood years of a provincial outcaste were decisively to shape the future direction of engaged Buddhism.

It was also in 1891 that the Baptist Missionary Society in Ceylon reported resistance to its efforts to Christianize the population:

> The Buddhist opposition . . . is now an active and organized force which must be reckoned with. With a European at its head to direct, it is strenuously waging war against us. The head men are gathering around their European leader, and are using all their influence to overthrow our weekday and especially our Sunday-school. . . . In the Buddhist newspapers have appeared columns of print against us. Public subscriptions have been started for funds to oppose us. Buddhist emissaries have been sent out from

Kandy to stir up the people. Now, after twelve months' agitation, their
school is to be started in the very next compound to ours. We cannot but
lose ground.[57]

The "European" in question was, rather, the American Colonel Olcott,
age 59, who had been agitating against the British since he and Blavatsky
arrived. The son of New Jersey Presbyterians, Olcott had served in the Civil
War, investigated military procurement fraud for the War Department, and
worked as an attorney and journalist in New York City before returning to
his youthful interest in spiritualism.

In 1891, we also meet the twenty-seven-year-old Anagarika Dharmapala,
born Don David Hewavitarne to a wealthy furniture merchant in Colombo,
educated in Catholic and Episcopal missionary schools, and then "born
again" as a militant Buddhist under the influence of Blavatsky and Olcott.
Making his first pilgrimage to Bodh Gaya in northeast India, the traditional
site of the Buddha's enlightenment, Dharmapala was shocked at the condition of the shrine, which had been under the control of Hindu landlords for
generations. Nevertheless, in a passage reminiscent of the call of the Biblical prophet Isaiah, the young activist (who had memorized much of the
Christian Bible in missionary school) illustrates the cultural interpenetration of Christian and Buddhist sentiment that typified the Theosophy of
Blavatsky and Olcott:

> Jan. 22. How elevating: the sacred Vihara—the Lord sitting on his throne
> and the great solemnity which pervades all around makes the heart of the
> pious devotee weep. How delightful: as soon as I touched my forehead to
> the Vajrasana, a sudden impulse came to my mind. It prompted me to stop
> there and take care of the sacred spot.

A few weeks later, after a midnight return to the Maha Bodhi temple:

> February 17. This night at 12 for the first time in my life I experienced
> that peace which passeth all understanding. How peaceful it was. The life
> of our Lord is a lofty and elevating subject for meditation. The Four
> Truths and the Noble Eight-fold Path alone can make the devoted pupil of
> Nature happy.[58]

In the following months, Dharmapala wrote hundreds of letters to
Buddhist leaders in India, Burma, and Ceylon to raise funds to purchase the
Maha Bodhi temple and surroundings; he sailed to Rangoon and Colombo
to meet with leaders; he founded the Maha Bodhi Society in Calcutta; he
installed four monks at the Burmese Rest House in Bodh Gaya with representatives from Ceylon, China, Japan, and Bengal; and he made prepara-

tions for the publication of the *Maha Bodhi Journal,* which, with the society, was to wage a successful public relations and legal campaign for the renovation of the ancient Buddhist shrine.[59]

These highlights of the events of the year 1891 illustrate some of the common features of the careers of Olcott, Dharmapala, and Ambedkar— features we may list as characteristics of contemporary engaged Buddhism, and evidence of its multicultural parentage

First, *the engaged Buddhists were high-profile personalities whose careers straddled and sometimes blended East and West.* All three were trained in English-speaking or Christian schools and universities. Olcott was the "White Buddhist" with flowing beard, a military title, and the anomaly of adult conversion to a religion that was practically unheard of back home. Ambedkar renounced Hinduism for a religion that was now of greater interest to the British than to most Indians. He is revered as "Dr. Babasaheb Ambedkar," a mixture of Eastern and Western honorifics, whose followers have been known to chant his academic degrees like a mantra: "M.A., Ph.D., D.Sc., LL.D., D.Litt., Bar.-at-Law." He is usually pictured in horn-rimmed glasses and Western suit and tie in the ubiquitous wall calendars and memorial statuary. Hewavitarne, more the survivor of a foreign religion than a convert to one, invented for himself the liminal persona "Anagarika Dharmapala," "homeless protector of the doctrine," betwixt and between layman and monk, Asian and European. He wore white robes, the traditional garb of Buddhist laity, and practiced celibacy, the universal mark of the monk; he wore his flowing hair long, in the manner both of the Indian sadhu and the Victorian artist, yet spent decades in the Indian courts seeking legal control of the Bodh Gaya shrine. With his biblical diction and his gift for oratory, Dharmapala made an unforgettable impression on the Christians, Buddhists, and Hindus of Asia, and with Swami Vivekananda, he was a star attraction at the 1893 World's Parliament of Religions in Chicago.

Second, *the engaged Buddhists were dauntless activists for cultural renewal, social change, and an ecumenical World Buddhism.* Olcott, Dharmapala, and Ambedkar were spellbinding orators and prolific writers who used the print media and the mass rally to further the causes they espoused. All three traveled widely in Asia and the West to publicize their campaigns, win concessions, or raise money. All three founded journals and newspapers to promote their aims; all three used the courts and lawmaking bodies to achieve their objectives; and all three faced physical dangers and threats at various points in their careers.

Olcott's and Dharmapala's trip to Japan in 1889, and their shuttle diplomacy between Rangoon and Colombo were taken up in the spirit of a dawning unity among Theravadins, Mahayanists, and Vajrayanists. Sixty years later, Ambedkar was to give addresses at the first three meetings of the World Federation of Buddhists, held in Colombo, Rangoon, and Kathmandu. Of course, for Ambedkar and Olcott, the oddness of being a Buddhist and then serving as a missionary took some getting used to. Recalling his recitation of Buddhist vows in Pali before a Jodo Shinshu altar in Kyoto, Olcott later wrote,

> I could not help smiling to myself when thinking of the horror that would have been felt by any of my Puritan ancestors of the seventeenth century could they have looked forward to this calamitous day! I am sure that if I had been born among them at Boston or Hartford, I should have been hanged for heresy on the tallest tree.[60]

Third, *the engaged Buddhists are honored by their followers as saints and bodhisattvas*. On Olcott Day, an annual school holiday in Sri Lanka, brass lamps and incense are lit to commemorate the death of the American Buddhist saint. Saffron-robed monks bow before the Colonel's photograph as children offer gifts and pray, "May the merit we have gained by these good deeds pass on to Colonel Olcott, and may he gain happiness and Peace."[61] Dharmapala Day is similarly celebrated in Sri Lanka to commemorate the native son who took higher ordination as a monk in the last weeks of his life and was buried amid the ruins of Sarnath, the traditional site of the Buddha's first sermon. Today, followers of Dr. Ambedkar reverently call him Babasaheb or simply Baba ("father"), but they have also been known to refer to him as a Bodhisattva or enlightened being, and as the Second Manu, linking the ancient Hindu law giver with the architect of the modern Indian Constitution.

In the opening scene of his book on the rising sectarian militancy in India in the 1980s, V. S. Naipaul described his taxi ride from the Bombay airport one April day:

> Bombay is a crowd. But I began to feel, when I was some way into the city from the airport that morning, that the crowd on the pavement and the road was very great, and that something unusual might be happening. . . . Many of them seemed freshly bathed, with fresh puja marks on their foreheads; many of them seemed to be in their best clothes: Bombay people celebrating an important new day, perhaps.[62]

Unable to question his Marathi-speaking driver about the festive crowd, now five deep and extending more than a mile along the road, the author finally learned the answer from a cleaning woman: April 14 is the birthday of Dr. Babasaheb Ambedkar, savior of the Untouchables. In spite of Ambedkar's untimely death only weeks after his conversion to Buddhism, "he had remained their leader, the man they honoured above all others; he was almost their deity." And despite the chaos and pathos of the "million mutinies" described in the course of Naipaul's 500-page journey, the atmosphere of the Ambedkarites' witness—a quiet gaiety, a new confidence—stands out as an unexpected glimpse of liberation Buddhism.

Catechism, Discipline, and Bible for Engaged Buddhists

A new reliance on the authority of *scripture*—indeed a propensity to create new scriptures, that is, authoritative and prescriptive texts—in the Buddhist liberation movements is exemplified in radical forms by the early engaged Buddhists. Not content with the mere veneration or reinterpretation of the ancient canon, the new Buddhists contributed quasi-canonical works of their own. Olcott's *Buddhist Catechism* (1881), Dharmapala's *Gihi Vinaya* or "Lay Discipline" (1898), and Ambedkar's *The Buddha and His Dhamma* (1957) aimed at re-presenting the essence of the ancient Dharma for modern practitioners.

Olcott wrote his *Buddhist Catechism* within a year of his arrival in Sri Lanka, frankly hoping to counter the effects of "similar elementary handbooks so effectively used among Western Christian sects."[63] Prefaced by a "Certificate" from "H. Sumangala, High Priest of the Sripada and Galle, Principal of the Widyodaya Parivena," authenticating the faithfulness of the work to the teachings of the southern (Theravada) Buddhists and recommending it to Buddhist school teachers and beginners waiting to learn "the essential features of our Religion." Here is a sample of its style and contents:

127. Q. *Are charms, incantations, the observance of lucky hours, and devil-dancing a part of Buddhism?*

A. They are positively repugnant to its fundamental principles; they are the surviving relics of fetishism and pantheistic and other foreign religions. In the Brahmajala Sutta, Buddha has categorically described these and other superstitions as pagan, mean, and spurious.

137. Q. *Are there any dogmas in Buddhism which we are required to accept on faith?*

A. No; we are earnestly enjoined to accept nothing whatever on faith, whether it be written in books, handed down from our ancestors, or taught by the sages. Our Lord Buddha has said that we must not believe a thing said merely because it is said. . . .[64]

The *Buddhist Catechism* eventually went through forty editions and appeared in more than twenty languages. It is still used in Buddhist parochial schools today.[65]

The nineteenth edition of Anagarika Dharmapala's *Gihi Vinaya*, appearing in 1958, sold more than 49,000 copies. As a code of lay ethics, the pamphlet imitated Christian missionary etiquette manuals, offering a total of two hundred rules under twenty-two categories: table manners (twenty-five rules), how to chew betel nuts (six rules), how to use the toilet (four rules), how females should behave (thirty rules), how children should behave (eighteen rules), and so on. The manual also covered festivals and domestic ceremonies associated with Buddhist lay practice. Gombrich and Obeyesekere comment on the "Protestant" elements in this manual:

> In India Victorianism found a happy home in Brahmanic values; in Middle Eastern nations like Egypt and Turkey it was harmonized with Islam and in Sri Lanka with Buddhism. The Sri Lankan case is especially striking since the new value system was articulated into a powerful ethic of this-worldly asceticism. We have labeled this value system Protestant Buddhism, not only because of its incorporation of Protestant values but also because of *its radical protest against traditional Buddhism*, which in Sri Lanka was essentially geared to a peasant society and economy and a peasant moral code. [66]

Thus modern engaged Buddhists hone their critique not only of the colonial powers but of traditional Buddhism, which, as we have seen, was also deeply invested in the legitimation of state power.

Dr. Ambedkar's magnum opus, *The Buddha and His Dhamma*, was written in English and based on the author's extensive library of Western scholarship (at thirty thousand volumes, said to be the largest personal library in India). Each sentence is versified, and the style imitates that of the English orientalist T. W. Rhys Davids, whose renderings of the Pali scriptures were featured in Max Muller's *Sacred Books of the East* and the Pali Text Society's complete *Tripitaka*. The original working title of the book was "The Gospel of the Buddha." Like Olcott and Dharmapala, Ambedkar presents a highly rationalized and moralistic Buddhism: Book V, Part V, for example, is titled "Vinaya for the Laity" and contains sections for the wealthy, the householder, children, pupils, spouses, masters, servants, and girls. For his prologue, Ambedkar chose a paragraph from James Hastings's *Encyclopedia of Religion and Ethics* (1908), in which the modern revival of interest in religion "as a subject of critical and scientific inquiry" is explained by the rise of scientific knowledge, the inherent intellectual interest of religion, worldwide tendencies to "reform and reconstruct religion along more rational and scientific, and less superstitious, lines; and finally because of *social, political, and international events which have impinged upon religious communities*."[67] One hears echoes of the liberal Protestant theologians Schleiermacher, Bushnell, and Rauschenbusch and of the American pragmatists James and Dewey—all of whom exercised great influence at Columbia University and Union Theological Seminary during Ambedkar's years as a graduate student on Morningside Heights in New York City.

Flags, Monuments, and Colleges

Finally, we turn to the public symbols and institutions that manifested engaged Buddhism at the turn of the century and down to the present. The most famous item is probably Olcott's Buddhist flag, which was designed and paraded on ceremonial occasions to promote the ecumenical spirit of World Buddhism. More significant for the fabric of Sinhalese Buddhism were the hundreds of secondary schools and voluntary Buddhist organizations—most notably the Buddhist Theosophical Society, Young Men's Buddhist Association, and the All-Ceylon Buddhist Congress—that mobilized the urban elite to collective action and ultimately prepared the way for independence.

Dharmapala's chief contribution was his protracted and passionate campaign to recover and restore the ancient Buddhist monuments and pilgrimage sites in India. As public symbols of Indian Buddhism, the run-down condition of the stupas and monastic ruins at Sanchi and Sarnath, and the Hindu worship activities now carried on at the Mahabodhi Temple at Bodh Gaya told of the sorry fate of the Dharma in the land of its origin.[68] Some have speculated that Dharmapala's dogged campaign for control of Bodh Gaya was a harbinger of the violent communal struggles over religious sites in India today, such as the Hindu destruction of the old Muslim mosque at Ayodhya in 1991. On the other hand, Dharmapala's proprietary interest in Buddhist ruins, like his missionary travels to North America, East Asia, and Europe, signaled both a revival of ancient devotional patterns (pilgrimage and relic worship) and the emergence of a muscular new Buddhism. Suddenly South Asian Buddhists, along with Japanese Zen Buddhists like Soen Shaku and D. T. Suzuki, felt a connection to Buddhists everywhere. The unexpected mass appeal of Dharmapala, Soen Shaku, and Swami Vivekananda at the World's Parliament of Religions in Chicago in 1893 stands as an early high-water mark in the confluence of East and West.

Ambedkar, as a member of Nehru's first cabinet, proposed the use of the Buddhist *dharmachakra* or "wheel of the law" on the new flag of India and the Ashokan lion-capital on the national currency. The national constitution, with its combination of Western due process and separation of powers, and derivative legislation reserving scholarships and government jobs for the Scheduled Castes and Tribes, illustrates one of Ambedkar's favorite distinctions: that between a "salvation-giver" (*moksha-data*), who robs the devotee of initiative and effort—an allusion to savior religions such as devotional Hinduism or Christianity and to the total welfare state—and the "path-giver" (*marga-data*), who offers the practitioner access to a program of self-improvement through hard work—an allusion to the inner-worldly asceticism of Theravada Buddhism and the progressive government policies of equal opportunity and access. Another expression of Ambedkar's affinity for Buddhist symbols was his naming of the colleges he founded under the People's Education Society. With their provision of government-subsidized educational opportunities for the lower classes, Siddharth College in Bombay (named for the Buddha) and Milind College in Aurangabad (named for Buddhism's first Western convert) reflect as much the pragmatism and progressivism of the Americans Dewey and Rauschenbusch as they do the celebrated role of the Buddha as teacher (*sattha*).

Unlike the symbiotic relations between Buddhist leaders and state officials we encounter in Rahula's account of the heritage of the bhikkhu, we see Olcott, Dharmapala, and Ambedkar as independent actors who used or opposed the state to achieve their goals for society. And while their mastery of the media of law and diplomacy, mass communication, and world travel is not unprecedented in the annals of Buddhism, we must ask whether the message of these leaders falls within the broad heritage of Buddhist teaching or whether their unmistakable focus on the conditions and institutions of worldly life represents a new kind of Buddhist "heresy."[69]

Engaged Buddhism: Heritage or Heresy?

Despite the freshness and utility of Gananath Obeyesekere's concept of Protestant Buddhism, he has reserved harsh criticism for the reality behind the term. In his 1972 article, Obeyesekere suggested that the monumental Buddha statues in and around Colombo are a kind of "reaction-formation or overcompensation" for the deep sense of inferiority that the Sinhalese continue to feel after centuries of colonial domination. Even today, monks who become involved in political and social service activities are perceived as unvirtuous (*dussila*) and are subject to open contempt and "salacious gossip" by the laity; yet, in the wake of Dharmapala's unorthodox career, monks who pursue the traditional paths of spiritual practice and teaching feel equally unvirtuous for their dependency on public charity and their impotence to affect the social and political crises of the day.

In 1991 Obeyesekere wrote again on Buddhist modernism, alleging the disastrous affects of Protestant Buddhism on the cultural life of Sri Lanka. Calling Olcott's thought the "Western intellectualist view of Buddhism," he concluded that "like many contemporary intellectuals, [Olcott] seemed to accept implicitly the missionary critique of [popular] Buddhism," namely as a mass of incantations, lucky charms, and devil dancing that Gotama had ruled out 2,500 years ago. Following Olcott, Dharmapala ignored the "religion of the heart," which Buddhists have followed from the time of the founder. Such a faith is rooted in a semi-divine founder, miraculously conceived, who possessed supernormal powers and was worshipped by his followers. Robbed of this rich mythology and cosmology—especially the high drama of moral pilgrimage over many lifetimes contained in the Jataka tales of the Buddha's former births—the new Buddhism fails to communicate vital social values to the masses, especially to children.[70]

As a result of the transformation of Buddhism from a religion of the heart to one of the head, Obeyesekere argues, the Sinhalese have lost their moral compass. The social consequences have been disastrous. "I do not think one can fully grasp the terrible violence in contemporary Buddhist Sri Lanka without an understanding of the processes that led to this dismantling of the Buddhist conscience."[71] In Obeyesekere's final assessment, the rationalist and moralist reading of the dharma we associate with Olcott, Dharmapala, and by extension, the social engagement of modern Buddhist liberation movements in Asia, is called "the dark underside of Buddhism."[72]

Obeyesekere's conclusions, and those of his compatriot and fellow anthropologist, S. J. Tambiah, point to a Buddhism "transformed" and "betrayed," and to a religious heritage gone wrong. Both scholars follow Walpola Rahula in painting a tragic picture of the long descent of Sinhala Buddhism first into passivity and finally into sectarian, ethnic, and political violence. In 1956, following a national election in which between 3,000 and 4,000 monks—about a fourth of the national total—participated as campaign workers, the newly elected prime minister, S. W. R. D. Bandaranaike, was assassinated by a monk associated with one of the island's leading temples. Two years later the first postindependence wave of violence against the Tamil Hindus in the northern part of the island was unleashed.[73]

But the connection between Buddhist modernism and ethnic warfare in Sri Lanka is not an obvious one. Just as the history of Sinhala monks in government service is insufficient to account for the appearance of socially engaged Buddhists in late nineteenth-century Ceylon, so the recent history of civil war in Sri Lanka is not obviously related to the story of the rise of Buddhist liberation movements in Asia—even of Sarvodaya Shramadana, the movement that has had to coexist with the rising violence. The long-term depredations of Western colonialism, the restive presence of the Tamil minority, acute population pressure, deteriorating economic and environmental conditions, the uneasy ethos of a multicultural island society, and the rise of revolutionary socialism—all these would seem to offer more compelling answers to the puzzle of Sri Lankan instability than would the evolution of clerical roles in Theravada Buddhism.

We have seen evidence of the constructive role that engaged Buddhism has played as a result of Olcott's and Dharmapala's activism. There seems little ground for terming their activities a "religion of the head and not the heart," given their intense (perhaps un-Buddhist) passion for Buddhism and its revival, and their deep empathy for people they perceived to be suffering cultural marginalization. Both reformers—like Ambedkar, Ariyaratne, and the Buddhist liberationists who followed throughout Asia— were energetic exemplars of the late-Victorian crusader ethic, motivated by a vision of a restored Buddhism and a just and peaceful world. Their brand of religion appealed to millions of followers from all segments of society, both urban elite and rural peasant. The social engagement of Buddhist liberationists may indeed be seen as a rejection of the other-worldly asceticism of the traditional monk and the routinized devotionalism and merit-making of the lay masses, but this cannot credibly be blamed for the rising tide of political violence in the Buddhist countries of the Third World.[74]

In *The American Encounter with Buddhism: 1844–1912,* Thomas Tweed paints a detailed picture of the intellectual and spiritual currents that attracted and mingled Buddhists, Protestants, free-thinkers, agnostics, and social reformers in the late-Victorian age. From Thoreau's Hindu musings on Walden Pond to the runaway success of Edwin Arnold's heroic life of the Buddha, *The Light of Asia,* the appeal of Indian philosophy and religion was palpable in the English-speaking world. The Buddhism that attracted Americans was not one of pessimism, resignation, and retreat, but a vigorous religion of optimism and activism. Tweed shows that these two attributes were ultimately more dear to American religionists than were theism and personalism, the hallmarks of Western religion.

> With few exceptions, Buddhist apologists stood united with American critics, travelers, and scholars in implicitly or explicitly affirming the role of religion in stimulating effective economic, political, and social activity. Almost all participants in Victorian culture and contributors to the public discourse about Buddhism agreed: whatever else true religion was, it was optimistic and activistic. In many ways, then, nineteenth-century Euro-American Buddhist sympathizers had more in common with their mainline Protestant contemporaries than with nineteen-century Asian-American or twentieth-century Caucasian Buddhists.[75]

While nineteenth-century Asian-Americans (Chinese and Japanese immigrants) were occupied in the ritual observance of their imported faiths and twentieth-century Caucasian readers of D. T. Suzuki, Alan Watts, and the Beats were increasingly attracted to the aesthetic and psychological ethos of Zen Buddhism, it has been the mainstream Protestant Buddhist sympathizers and adherents who forged the conception of an activist, socially engaged Buddhism.

And it was this amalgam of Eastern and Western elements—nontheistic, ethical, contemplative, reformist, communitarian, utopian—that was transmitted back to Asia by figures such as Olcott. This "pizza effect," as the anthropologist Agehananda Bharati has called the process by which a cultural export is transformed and reimported to the land of its origin (e.g., the alleged popularity of American-style pizza in Italy), has been interpreted in terms of modern linguistic theory by Stephen Prothero. Henry Steel Olcott's religion was a "creolization" of liberal Protestantism (progressive, rational, and worldly), metropolitan gentility (fostering voluntary associations for social, economic, political, and spiritual uplift), academic orientalism (seeking cultural origins and essences in Asian history), and Theravada Buddhism. "Just as a creole language can be analyzed as a combination of grammatical and lexical elements," Prothero writes, "so Olcott's creole faith can be described as a combination of a deep structure and a more superficial lexical idiom. While the lexicon of Olcott's faith was Buddhist, its grammar was liberal Protestant, genteel, and orientalist."[76]

Yet to stress the discontinuity of engaged Buddhism with its classical and medieval predecessors, and to suggest its significant debt to styles of thought and action we associate with non-Buddhist cultures—those of the Hebrew prophets, the framers of the American constitution, or late-Victorian social reformers, for example—is not to discredit its authority. A tradition may be transformed without being betrayed, and heresies may enrich and broaden a cultural heritage while leaving behind those elements—beliefs, practices, institutional forms, public roles—that no longer meet the needs of living communities in a changed world. The question becomes, rather, one of terminology: if the "deep structure" of Olcott's Buddhism is Protestant, according to one interpreter, must not the faith be called Christianity, not Buddhism? Can such a designation be made in the face of informants' claims to be Buddhist? Or do sufficient touchstones of sentiment and conduct remain to justify the continued use of old categories?

Problems of identity, continuity, and semantics are hardly new in the history of Buddhism. In a new study of the ritual and soteriological roles of women in the emerging Tantric Buddhism of ancient India, Miranda Shaw illustrates the powerful contradictions of thought and practice separating the erotic spirituality, or "passionate enlightenment" of the new Buddhists from "the religion of the elders" (Theravada). Her observations on the extent of the transformation are highly suggestive for our context.

The Tantric movement represented a radical revision of the reigning values, practices, and symbols of Buddhism. As a new religious paradigm, Tantric Buddhism stimulated vigorous literary and artistic creativity. Tantric adherents introduced a new body of scriptures called *tantras*, for which they claimed the status of divine revelation. Tapping into the same wellspring as Hindu Tantric and Sakta (goddess-worshipping) movements, the Buddhist *tantras* arose from a dynamic inter-change among diverse elements of society that revitalized Buddhism with fresh infusions of cultural energy. These works introduced a dramatic and colorful array of rituals, initiations, magic, mantras, yoga, sacramental feasting, and ecstatic practices.[77]

Shaw demonstrates that few of the touchstones of Theravada Buddhism—the primacy of the male monk, of individual spirituality, of ethical orthopraxy, and of otherworldliness—remain in the sensuous ritualism of the lay Tantric societies. *Yet the new practitioners were still Buddhists.* How is this possible?

In this introduction we have used the traditional rubric of the "Three Refuges" (Pali *tisarana*) or "Three Jewels" (Skt. *triratna*) as a heuristic device for collecting and analyzing themes and styles of action common to the movements under review. Now it is time to suggest that the refuge formula, expressing homage to Buddha, Dharma, and Sangha, offers a standard for regarding a thinker or movement as "Buddhist," regardless of the presence of non-Buddhist cultural elements, and regardless of the absence of other traditional teachings. This was the position of the Ambedkarites on the eve of their mass conversion to Buddhism in 1956. In spite of Ambedkar's deep misgivings about the third refuge, his advisers persuaded him that to take anything less than three refuges would be to fail to embrace Buddhism. At the same time Ambedkar was putting final touches on *The Buddha and His Dhamma*, which questioned the intelligibility, if not the authenticity, of many central teachings: the Buddha's renunciation of family life, the Four Noble Truths, the insubstantial self, and karma and rebirth. Yet the decisive willingness to take the three refuges—in essence, to have faith in and to swear by the power of Buddha, Dharma, and Sangha, and to orient all of one's thoughts and actions to these hoary categories of Buddhist understanding—this was the act that made the followers of Ambedkar, like those of the Dalai Lama, Thich Nhat Hanh, and the nuns of Taiwan, Buddhists.

In the accounts of Buddhist liberation movements and leaders in this book, we shall witness countless patterns of continuity and discontinuity. We will see, for example, that a movement may be "scripturalist" in its simple veneration of a text (Soka Gakkai), as well as in a systematic re-reading of the canon (Buddhadasa), and in the creative application of traditional teachings to new circumstances (Ariyaratne, Thich Nhat Hanh, Sulak Sivaraksa). Whether we are justified in speaking of a localized Buddhist "heresy," of an emerging "heterodoxy" encompassing several cultural areas, or of a "new Buddhism" of truly global significance, it becomes apparent that a complex interpenetration of spiritual, intellectual, and behavioral habits—"habits of the heart" as Robert Bellah has called them, echoing Alexis de Tocqueville—from Buddhist and Christian societies has evolved. Like the radical transformations of faith and practice that occurred in India after Asoka and followed the transmission of the dharma south to ancient Ceylon, north to China and Tibet, east to Korea and Japan and to the cultures of Southeast Asia—in each case assimilating and being assimilated to local cultural forms—so the great transmission of Buddhism to the West has entailed a profound mutual assimilation.

In his introduction to the writings of contemporary engaged Buddhists, Kenneth Kraft has noted their agreement that "the principles and even some of the techniques of an engaged Buddhism have been latent in the tradition since the time of its founder. Qualities that were inhibited in pre-modern Asian settings . . . can now be actualized through Buddhism's exposure to the West, where ethical sensitivity, social activism, and egalitarianism are emphasized."[78] When these principles and techniques, regardless of their provenance, are proclaimed and practiced in the name of the the Awakened One, in accord with the teachings of wisdom and compassion, and in the spirit of the unbroken community of those seeking human liberation—that is, in harmony with the ancient refuges of Buddha, Dharma, and Sangha—then we may regard the catechism of the transplanted Civil War colonel, the Biblical cadences of Anagarika Dharmapala, the educational projects of Soka Gakkai International, and the sacrifice of the Ven. Thich Quang Duc as authentically Buddhist.

Notes

1. Malcolm E. Browne, the Associated Press photographer who recorded the event recalls, "The expression of agony on the old monk's face and the smell of his scorched flesh would have overwhelmed me if I had had to watch without busying myself with something. As it was, I knew I must work, just as Thich Quang Duc was working at his act of protest. His suicide (and my photographs of it) played some role in bringing down the Saigon government, but all that mattered to me was to close out the horror by working." The *New York Times Magazine*, October 3, 1993, p. 102.

2. Thich Nhat Hanh, *Vietnam: Lotus in a Sea of Fire* (New York: Hill and Wang, 1967), p. 106.

3. Ibid.

4. See *The Lotus Sutra*, trans. Burton Watson (New York: Columbia University Press, 1993), pp. 280–285. Watson comments, "One chapter of the Lotus does in

fact describe a bodhisattva who burned his own body as a form of sacrifice, but the passage is clearly meant to be taken metaphorically. Despite this fact, some believers of later times, in their eagerness to emulate the bodhisattva's example, have interpreted it with tragic literalness" (p. xxi). Paul Williams observes, "The Vietnamese immolations were by way of political protest rather than a direct attempt to offer devotion to the Buddhas. Nevertheless, the form of suicide, burning, was undoubtedly indicated by the age-old precedent of the *Lotus Sutra.*" In *Mahayana Buddhism: The Doctrinal Foundation* (New York and London: Routledge, 1989), p. 155.

5. Thomas Merton, Foreword to *Vietnam: Lotus in a Sea of Fire*, p. vii (emphasis added).

6. The term "engaged Buddhism" is attributed to Thich Nhat Hanh, who published a book by that title in 1963, according to Kenneth Kraft, *Inner Peace, World Peace: Essays on Buddhism and Nonviolence* (Albany: State University of New York Press, 1992), p. 18. While I have seen no other reference to the work, it seems likely that the French term "engagé", meaning politically outspoken or involved, was common among activist intellectuals in French Indochina long before the 1960s. The term "socially engaged Buddhism" appeared in two titles in 1988: *A Socially Engaged Buddhism* by Sulak Sivaraksa (Bangkok: Thai Inter-Religious Commission for Development), and *The Path of Compassion: Writings on Socially Engaged Buddhism,* edited by Fred Eppsteiner (Berkeley, Calif.: Parallax Press). The term has achieved currency within the Buddhist Peace Fellowship, founded in 1978, and the International Network of Engaged Buddhists, founded in 1989. A reliable summary of the rise of the movement, both in the United States and internationally, is Kenneth Kraft's "Prospects of a Socially Engaged Buddhism," in Kraft, op. cit., pp. 11–30. A more personal interpretation is offered by Ken Jones, *The Social Face of Buddhism: An Approach to Political and Social Activism* (London and Boston: Wisdom, 1989).

7. See Aung San Suu Kyi, *Freedom from Fear,* edited by Michael Aris (London and New York: Penguin Books, 1991).

8. The practice of untouchability—hereditary and ritual restrictions placed on the lowest members of Hindu society—was officially outlawed by the Indian Constitution, ratified in 1949. Yet the continued use of euphemisms (Harijan and Scheduled Caste) attests to the continuity of the practice in many parts of India. The terms "ex-Untouchable," *Dalit* ("oppressed," a name some untouchables prefer to use), and "Buddhist" are all used today to refer to Ambedkar's followers.

9. Bibliographies for these movements are provided following each chapter.

10. Many of the issues treated in this introduction are independently addressed by the contributors. In this and the concluding chapter, the editors do not speak for the contributors, although consensus in many areas will be noted.

11. See Mark Juergensmeyer, *The New Cold War? Religious Nationalism Confronts the Secular State* (Berkeley, University of California Press, 1993). The author makes frequent reference to the violence spawned by militant Buddhism national-

ism in Sri Lanka, as well as to the more familiar Islamic, Jewish, Sikh, and Catholic/ Protestant examples.

12. Stanley Jeyaraja Tambiah, *Buddhism Betrayed? Religion, Politics, and Violence in Sri Lanka* (Chicago and London: The University of Chicago Press, 1992). See also Trevor Ling, *Buddhism, Imperialism, and War: Burma and Thailand in Modern History* (London: George Allen and Unwin: 1979), and Paul Demiéville, "Le bouddhisme et la guerre," in *Melange* (Paris, 1957), vol. 1, pp. 375–385.

13. Deane William Ferm, *Third World Liberation Theologies: An Introductory Survey* (Maryknoll, N.Y.: Orbis Books, 1992), pp. 1–2.

14. By "universalism" I mean the belief that the central teachings of the Buddhist tradition are applicable to all people in all times and places, and not that Buddhists are tolerant of other people's religions, including other Buddhist's versions of the central teachings. Indeed universalism often entails exclusivism and intolerance, as in the case of fundamentalist Christians, Islamic nationalists, and Nichiren Buddhists. On the other hand, most of the engaged Buddhists surveyed here stress tolerance and openness to divergent religions and world views—as a distinctive tenet of Buddhism.

15. One may argue that the travels of the Dalai Lama, Thich Nhat Hanh, Sulak Siveraksa, and before them Anagarika Dharmapala, Ambedkar, D. T. Suzuki, and Sangharakshita (founder of the Western Buddhist Order in Britain) rival those of many heads of state and international business leaders. Ferm is correct in suggesting that Christian liberationists are not nearly as interested in proselytizing or publicizing their witness at the global level.

16. Gananath Obeyesekere, "Religious Symbolism and Political Change in Ceylon," in *The Two Wheels of Dhamma: Essays on the Theravada Tradition in India and Ceylon,* Bardwell L. Smith, editor, American Academy of Religion Studies in Religion, no. 3 (Chambersberg, Penn.: American Academy of Religion, 1972), pp. 63–65.

17. Ibid., p. 78 (emphasis added).

18. Even in Ambedkar's case, his father's unlikely position as a schoolmaster on a British army base enabled young Bhimrao to begin his education under the ambitious and watchful eye of an Untouchable who had escaped the dead-end faced by most Indian outcastes.

19. While notable, the formal academic training of modern engaged Buddhists does not distinguish them from Buddhist leaders of the past, who typically benefited from advanced monastic training in the academic as well as the spiritual arts. Nor would this factor distinguish Buddhist leaders from those of other scripturally based traditions in which high degrees of literacy are often combined with broad general education in the arts and technologies of the day.

20. Clifford Geertz, *Islam Observed: Religious Development in Morocco and Indonesia* (Chicago: University of Chicago Press, 1968), p. 115.

21. Stuart Smithers, "Freedom's Just Another Word," *Tricycle: The Buddhist Review,* vol. 2, no. 1 (Fall 1992), p. 34.

22. This list, garnered from an opinion survey of 660 Sri Lankan villagers, did not include employment and income because these were considered means rather than ends. George Bond, *The Buddhist Revival in Sri Lanka: Religious Tradition, Reinterpretation and Response,* (Columbia, SC: University of South Carolina Press, 1988), pp. 266–267.

23. This new outlook may not be ascribed to all of the millions of followers and practitioners of contemporary Buddhism, but it is certainly characteristic of leaders of the new Buddhism—those who are actively promoting social change.

24. It is interesting to note, for example, that many Ambedkarite Buddhists chose until recent years to call themselves *Dalits,* or "the oppressed." This term is not longer favored by many, whether because they prefer to invoke their new positive identity as "Buddhists," or, perhaps more significantly, because they have moved up the social ladder as a result of their new assertiveness and the legal protections of Ambedkar's Indian Constitution.

25. Engaged Buddhists have often combined the spiritual and political in innovative new exercises, such as Thich Nhat Hanh's meditation on "my true names" (I am both oppressor and oppressed). Similarly, in answer to a question on the mental attitude of the Buddhist activist, Sulak Sivaraksa described his own meditative approach to writing protest letters to political figures and the press—remaining mindful of the suffering of all sentient beings, including the perpetrators of social evil, and extending loving-kindness (*metta*) to all parties involved. The writing of such letters was described as tantamount to a regular spiritual practice—not unlike those of sitting and walking meditation for the monk (public address, Boston, April 21, 1992). The accounts of Sarvodaya and TBMSG offer examples of group spiritual exercises in a political context.

26. Dhanajay Keer, *Dr. Ambedkar: Life and Mission* (Bombay: Popular Prakashan, 1971), p. 495; and Shankaranand Shastri, *My Memories and Experiences of Babasaheb Dr. B. R. Ambedkar* (Ghaziabad, India: Smt. Sumithra Shastri, 1989), p. 125–126.

27. The Dalai Lama, Thich Nhat Hanh, Daisaku Ikeda, and Sulak Sivaraksa have included Harvard and numerous other campuses on their frequent intineraries in the United States.

28. In *Freedom and Influence: The Role of Religion in American Society* (Santa Monica, Calif.: World Tribune Press, 1985), former head of North American operations for Soka Gakkai, George M. Williams, compares the arrival and growth of Nichiren Buddhism in America with the flourishing and adaptation of other faiths in the New World since colonial times. The argument stresses the rapid growth in numbers, public visibility, and acceptance of the missionary faith.

29. See *A Time to Chant: The Soka Gakkai Buddhists in Britain* by Bryan Wilson and Karel Dobbelaere (Oxford: Clarendon Press, 1994) for a thorough, criti-

cal study of the personal, ideological, and social dimensions of the movement in the United Kingdom. The authors note that "politics" occupies a relatively low rung on the value ratings of these Western Buddhists, following, in order, family, religion, work, friends, and leisure time (pp. 125ff). It is thus primarily in its Japanese manifestations that Soka Gakkai conforms to our profile of engaged Buddhism, and not thus far in its Western transplants. It may be noted that Nichiren Buddhism in the United States has been more attractive to African Americans than other sects, although, like their British counterparts, the American Nichiren Buddhists have been politically conservative, if not unengaged.

30. Donald Swearer, *Buddhism in Transition* (Philadelphia: The Westminister Press, 1970), p. 16.

31. Walpola Rahula, *The Heritage of the Bhikkhu: A Short History of the Bhikkhu in Educational, Cultural, Social and Political Life,* (New York: Grove Press, 1974), p. 3. Originally published as *Bhiksuvage Urumaya* (Colombo, Sri Lanka: Svastika Press, 1946).

32. Ibid., p. 132. "Bhikkhus and Politics, Declaration of the Vidyalankara Pirivena, Passed Unanimously on February 13, 1946," is Appendix II in Rahula, pp. 131–133.

33. Ibid., p. 3. Rahula later published a detailed exposition of the role of monks in the history of Sinhalese Buddhism, an expansion of his doctoral dissertation, under the title *History of Buddhism in Ceylon* (Ceylon: Gunasena, 1956).

34. Other defining documents of the time were *Dharma-Vijaya, or the Revol in the Temple* by the wealthy layman, D. C. Vijayawardhana (Colombo, Sri Lanka Sinha Publications, 1953); and *The Betrayal of Buddhism,* the report of the Bud dhist Committee of Inquiry, made up of distinguished scholar-monks and lay educators (Colombo, 1956). All are discussed at length by Tambiah, op. cit.

35. Rahula, op. cit., pp. 3–7. The Abhidhamma is the third and formally speculative division of the Pali canon, after the Sutta, or didactic, and Vinaya, or regulatory, divisions.

36. Ibid.

37. Ibid., p. 21.

38. Ibid., p. 91

39. Tambiah, op. cit., p. 29, citing Rahula, p. xii.

40. Sangharakshita, "Religio-Nationalism in Sri Lanka," in *Alternative Tra tions* (Glasgow: Windhorse, 1986). pp. 70–71

41. "As for [the villagers] being illiterate, *of course they were.* With the p sible exception of a few traders, who may have used writing for purposes of busir correspondence, everybody in that society was 'illiterate'—including the Bud and His disciples." Ibid., p. 71.

42. Max Weber, *The Religion of India: The Sociology of Hinduism and Buddhism* (New York: The Free Press, 1958), p. 206. Weber continues, "A sense of 'social' responsibility resting on a social ethic which operates with the idea of the 'infinite' value of the individual human soul, must be as remote as possible from a salvation doctrine which, in any value emphasis upon the 'soul,' could discern only the grand and pernicious basic illusion. Also the specific form of Buddhistic 'altruism,' universal compassion, is merely one of the stages in the wheel of life, a sign of progressive intellectual enlightenment, not, however, an expression of active brotherliness. In the rules for contemplation, compassion is expressly defined as being replaced, in the final state of mind, by the cool stoic equanimity of the knowing man." Ibid., p. 213.

43. Bardwell L. Smith, "Sinhalese Buddhism and the Dilemmas of Reinterpretation," in Smith, et al., eds., *The Two Wheels of Dhamma: Essays on the Theravada Tradition in India and Ceylon* (Chambersberg, Penn.: American Academy of Religion, 1972), p. 106.

44. Richard Gombrich, *Theravada Buddhism: A Social History from Ancient Benares to Modern Colombo* (London and New York: Routledge & Kegan Paul, 1988), p. 30.

45. Joseph M. Kitagawa, "Buddhism and Social Change: An Historical Perspective," in *Buddhist Studies in Honour of Walpola Rahula,* Somaratna Balasooriya, et. al., eds. (London: Gordon Fraser, 1980).

46. Ibid., p. 100.

47. Ibid., p. 87.

48. Ibid., p. 98. Commenting elsewhere on the "domestication" of the messianic Maitreya, Kitagawa writes, "any attempt to criticize the ills of the empirical social and political order was abandoned. Only in the modern periods has the [Maitreyan] ideal become associated with anticolonial revolutionary movements. . . . In retrospect, it is evident that the potentialities of Maitreya as the symbol of eschatological vision as well as the religious and ethical critique of empirical sociopolitical order have rarely been actualized in the history of Buddhism." "The Many Faces of Maitreya: A Historian of Religions' Reflections," in *Maitreya, the Future Buddha,* Alan Sponberg and Helen Hardacre, eds. (Cambridge: Cambridge University Press, 1988), pp. 17–18.

49. Ibid., p. 100.

50. See, for example, Bardwell L. Smith, editor, *Religion and Legitimation of Power in Sri Lanka* (Chambersberg, Pa.: ANIMA Books, 1978) and *Religion and Legitimation of Power in Thailand, Laos, and Burma* (Chambersberg, Pa.: ANIMA Books, 1978) for treatment of the Southeast Asian material. Robert A F. Thurman, *The Politics of Enlightenment,* in press, deals with Buddhist government in the Tibetan cultural area, and is prefigured in "The Politics of Enlightenment," *Tricycle: The Buddhist Review,* vol. 2, no. 1 (Fall 1992), pp. 28–33. For a vivid account of

Buddhist collaboration with imperial power in China, see Arthur F. Wright's account of the career of the early missionary, Fo-t'u-teng (fourth century C.E.), who used his magical powers to influence the weather, warfare, medicine, and politics in the service of his royal patron (*Studies in Chinese Buddhism*, New Haven, Conn.: Yale University Press, 1990). Regarding Buddhism and politics in ancient Japan, Robert N. Bellah writes, "the early history of Buddhism, too, is bound up very closely with political considerations. The earliest introduction of Buddhism was associated with the jockeying for power of the powerful families around the throne. Once the position of Buddhism was secure at court, it was rather closely integrated with the political aspiration of the ruling family. Here was a new and powerful influence which could aid in bolstering the position of the monarchy." From *Tokugawa Religion: The Cultural Roots of Modern Japan* (New York: Free Press, 1957), p. 87.

51. Many regard the Dalai Lama as a head-of-state in exile, while the Soka Gakkai-affiliated Komeito party is currently a constituent of the ruling coalition in Japan. Yet in neither case do the respective leaders or groups posses the temporal power—legal authority to levee taxes and direct armed forces—which defines the sovereign state. On the other hand, Ambedkar's cabinet-level position as law minister under Nehru afforded him the opportunity of drafting the new constitution, but it became clear with the failure of his campaign to reform Hindu religious law from within the government (through his controversial Hindu Code Bill) that his influence, as a token minority appointee, was severely limited.

52. Sulak Sivaraska, *Seeds of Peace: A Buddhist Vision for Renewing Society* (Berkeley, Calif.: Parallax Press, 1993), p. 68.

53. "It is easy, particularly as we get older, to want softer lives and more recognition, and to be on equal terms with those in power. But this is dangerous." Ibid., pp. 71–72.

54. Rick Fields, *How the Swans Came to the Lake: A Narrative History of Buddhism in America* (Boulder, Colo.: Shambhala, 1981), p. 97.

55. Gananath Obeyesekere, op. cit., pp. 62ff. For more extended treatment of the concept and features of "Protestant Buddhism," see Richard Gombrich, op. cit., pp. 172–197; Richard Gombrich and Gananath Obeyesekere, *Buddhism Transformed: Religious Change in Sri Lanka* (Princeton, N.J.: Priceton University Press, 1988), pp. 202–240; and George Bond, op. cit., pp. 45–74. For a valuable critique of the term, see John C. Holt, "Protestant Buddhism?" In *Religious Studies Review*, 17:4 (October 1991), pp. 307–311.

56. Although Olcott was a central player in the Buddhist revival in Asia and a forerunner of the engaged Buddhism of today, it would be too much to anoint him the "founder" of engaged Buddhism, which independently emerged in diverse Asian settings over the century that followed.

57. "The Annual Report of the Baptist Missionary Society" (London: Alexander & Shepheard, 1891), pp. 41, 45, cited by Stephen R. Prothero, *Henry Steel Olcott*

(1832–1907) and the Construction of "Protestant Buddhism," Ph.D. dissertation, Harvard University (Ann Arbor, Mich.: UMI Dissertation Services, 1991), p. 249.

58. Maha Sthavira Sangharakshita, *Flame in Darkness: The Life and Sayings of Anagarika Dharmapala,* (Pune, India: Triratna Grantha Mala, 1980), pp. 64f. Note the Christian "peace which passeth understanding." The reference to Buddha as "our Lord" is not alien to Buddhism, as Shakyamuni was addressed as *bhagavan,* "Lord," from earliest times. But for Dharmapala, the expression undoubtedly had the paradoxically "Protestant" overtones Obeyesekere has identified: as both an echo and an alternative to the Christianity that pervaded young Hewavitarne's education.

59. See Ananda Guruge, ed., *Return to Righteousness: A Collection of Speeches, Essays, and Letters of Anagarika Dharmapala* (Colombo, Sri Lanka: The Government Press, 1965); and Alan Trevithick, *A Jerusalem of the Buddhists in British India: 1874–1949.* Ph. D. Dissertation, Harvard University (Ann Arbor, Mich.: UMI Dissertation Services, 1992), for primary and secondary accounts of Dharmapala's career.

60. Prothero, op. cit., p. 10.

61. Ibid., p. 1.

62. V. S. Naipaul, *India: A Million Mutinies Now* (New York: Viking, 1990), p. 1.

63. Prothero, op. cit., p. 164.

64. Henry S. Olcott, *Buddhist Catechism, According to the Canon of the Southern Church,* First American Edition (Boston: Estes and Lauriat, 1885), pp. 60–64. At the time of this first American edition, only four years after its first appearance in Ceylon, 17,000 copies in Sinhalese had been distributed in schools and homes on the island, a Burmese edition of 15,000 in Burmese and English versions were in press, and German and French editions were in production and distribution, respectively.

65. Ibid., p. ii.

66. Gombrich and Obeyesekere, op. cit., pp. 212–215.

67. B. R. Ambedkar, *The Buddha and His Dhamma,* 3rd ed. (Bombay: People's Education Society, 1984), p. xliii, citing James Hastings, ed., *Encyclopedia of Religion and Ethics* (New York: Scribner's Sons, 1908), vol. 10, p. 669 (emphasis added).

68. It is interesting to contrast this view with the remark of Thich Nhat Hanh that a Buddhist would prefer peace in Vietnam at the expense of all the Pagodas and physical manifestations of Buddhism, if such a choice were possible. Eppsteiner, op. cit., p. 16.

69. It is worth recalling here the extraordinary travels of the Indian Buddhist missionaries (e.g., Mahinda, Padmasambhava), and Chinese pilgrims (e.g., Fa-hein, Hsuan-tsang), the innovative proselytizing of the Pure Land Masters (e.g., the Chinese T'an-luan, the Japanese Kuya), the economic and political independence of the Chinese Ch'an communities and the Japanese Samurai, and the incandescent mavericks who lit up a dreary political landscape (e.g., the Chinese Fo-t'u-teng, the

Japanese Nichiren). The fact that these figures are less well-known today, except by historians and secretarian devotees, underscores the negative assessment of Buddhism's contribution to social and political thought we associate with Weber, Kitagawa, Bardwell Smith, and others; indeed, few contemporary scholars have successfully challenged the conventional wisdom that, until recent times, Buddhism focused on personal liberation, not on social transformation.

70. Gananath Obeyesekere, "Buddhism and Conscience: An Exploratory Essay," in *Daedalus* 120:3 (Summer 1991).

71. Ibid., p. 237.

72. Ibid., p. 238.

73. See Tambiah, op. cit., pp. 42–57 for a full account of the political events of 1956.

74. Mark Jeurgensmeyer, op. cit., includes Buddhist examples of violent "religious nationalism" alongside the more familiar (and numerous) ones from Islamic, Jewish, and Christian societies. His thesis is that the confrontation between traditional conceptions of social and religious order and those of secular modernity represents a new, global "cold war" that transcends the core ideologies and institutions of the religions. Thus the conflict of local cultural interests may be played out in personal and religious terms (e.g., in the careers and writings of liberationists like Olcott and Dharmapala), but the scale of the struggle is better understood in transpersonal and transnational terms.

75. Thomas A. Tweed, *The American Encounter with Buddhism: 1844–1912* (Bloomington: Indiana University Press, 1992), p. 155.

76. Stephen Prothero, op. cit., pp. 293f.

77. Miranda Shaw, *Passionate Enlightenment: Women in Tantric Buddhism,* (Princeton, N.J.: Princeton University Press, 1994), pp. 21–22.

78. Kraft, introduction to Eppsteiner, op. cit., p. xiii.

References

Ambedkar, B. R. *The Buddha and His Dhamma*. Bombay: People's Education Society, 1984.

Bellah, Robert N. *Tokugawa Religion: The Cultural Roots of Modern Japan*. New York: Free Press, 1957.

Bond, George. *The Buddhist Revival in Sri Lanka: Religious Tradition, Reinterpretation, and Response*. Columbia: University of South Carolina Press, 1988.

Eppsteiner, Fred, ed. *The Path of Compassion: Writings on Socially Engaged Buddhism*. Berkeley, Calif.: Parallax Press, 1988.

Ferm, Deane William. *Third World Liberation Theologies: An Introductory Survey*. Maryknoll, N.Y.: Orbis Books, 1992.

Geertz, Clifford. *Islam Observed: Religious Development in Morocco and Indonesia*. Chicago: University of Chicago Press, 1968.

Gombrich, Richard. *Theravada Buddhism: A Social History from Ancient Benares to Modern Colombo*. London and New York: Routledge & Kegan Paul, 1988.

Guruge, Ananda, ed. *Return to Righteousness: A Collection of Speeches, Essays, and Letters of Anagarika Dharmapala*. Colombo, Ceylan: The Government Press, 1865.

Holt, John C. "Protestant Buddhism?" *Religious Studies Review* 17:4 (October 1991).

Jones, Ken. *The Social Face of Buddhism: An Approach to Political and Social Activism*. London and Boston: Wisdom, 1992.

Juergensmeyer, Mark. *The New Cold War? Religious Nationalism Confronts the Secular State*. Berkeley: University of California Press, 1993.

Keer, Khananjay. *Dr. Ambedkar: Life and Mission*. Bombay: Popular Prakashan, 1971.

Kitagawa, Joseph M. "Buddhism and Social Change: An Historical Perspective," in *Buddhist Studies in Honour of Walpola Rahula*. Somaratna Balasooriya, et al., eds. London: Gordon Fraser, 1980.

Kraft, Kenneth. *Inner Peace, World Peace: Essays on Buddhism and Nonviolence*. Albany: State University of New York Press, 1992.

Ling, Trevor. *Buddhism, Imperialism, and War: Burma and Thailand in Modern History*. London: George Allen and Unwin, 1979.

Naipaul, V. S. *India: A Million Mutinies Now*. New York: Viking, 1990.

Nhat Hanh, Ven. Thich. *Vietnam: Lotus in a Sea of Fire*. New York: Hill and Wang, 1967.

Obeyesekere, Gananath. "Religious Symbolism and Political Change in Ceylon," in Bardwell L. Smith, ed., *The Two Wheels of Dhamma: Essays on the Theravada Tradition in India and Ceylon*. Chambersberg, Penn.: American Academy of Religion, 1972.

———, and Richard Gombrich *Buddhism Transformed: Religious Change in Sri Lanka*. Princeton, N.J.: Princeton University Press, 1988.

———. "Buddhism and Conscience: An Exploratory Essay," in *Daedalus* 120:3 (Summer 1991).

Olcott, Henry S. *Buddhist Catechism, According to the Canon of the Southern Church*. Boston: Estes and Lauriat, 1885.

Prothero, Stephen R. *Henry Steel Olcott (1832-1907) and the Construction of "Protestant Buddhism."* Ph.D. dissertation, Harvard University. Ann Arbor, Mich.: UMI Dissertation Services, 1991.

Rahula, Walpola. *The Heritage of the Bhikkhu: A Short History of the Bhikkhu in Educational, Cultural, Social and Political Life.* [First published in 1946.] New York: Grove Press, 1974.

Sangharakshita. *Alternative Traditions.* Glasgow: Windhorse, 1986.

———. *Flame in Darkness: The Life and Sayings of Anagarika Dharmapala.* Pune, India: Triratna Grantha Mala, 1980.

Shastri, Shankaranand. *My Memories and Experiences of Babasaheb Dr. B. R. Ambedkar.* Ghaziabad, India: Smt. Sumithra Shastri, 1989.

Shaw, Miranda. *Passionate Enlightenment: Women in Tantric Buddhism.* Princeton, N.J.: Princeton University Press, 1994.

Sivaraksa, Sulak. *A Socially Engaged Buddhism.* Bangkok: Thai Inter-Religious Commission of Development, 1988.

———. *Seeds of Peace: A Buddhist Vision of Renewing Society.* Berkeley, Calif.: Parallax Press, 1993.

Smith, Bardwell L., ed. *The Two Wheels of Dhamma: Essays on the Theravada Tradition in India and Ceylon.* Chambersberg, Penn.: American Academy of Religion, 1972.

———. *Religion and Legitimation of Power in Sri Lanka.* Chambersberg, Penn.: ANIMA Books, 1978.

———. *Religion and Legitimation of Power in Thailand, Laos, and Burma.* Chambersberg, Penn.: ANIMA Books, 1978.

Smithers, Stuart. "Freedom's Just Another Word," in *Tricycle: The Buddhist Review,* vol. 2, no. 1 (Fall, 1992).

Sponberg, Alan, and Helen Hardacre, eds. *Maitreya, the Future Buddha.* Cambridge: Cambridge University Press, 1988.

Suu Kyi, Aung San. *Freedom From Fear.* Edited by Michael Aris. London and New York: Penguin Books, 1991.

Swearer, Donald K. *Buddhism in Transition.* Philadelphia: Westminster Press, 1970.

Tambiah, Stanley J. *Buddhism Betrayed? Religion, Politics, and Violence in Sri Lanka.* Chicago and London: University of Chicago Press, 1992.

Thurman, Robert A. F. "The Politics of Enlightenment," in *Tricycle: The Buddhist Review,* vol. 2, no. 1 (Fall 1992).

Trevithick, Alan. *A Jerusalem of the Buddhists in British India (1874–1949).* Ph.D. dissertation, Harvard University. Ann Arbor, MI: UMI Dissertation Services, 1992.

Tweed, Thomas A. *The American Encounter with Buddhism 1844–1912: Victorian Culture and the Limits of Dissent.* Bloomington: Indiana University Press, 1992.

Vijayawardhana, D. C. *Dharma-Vijaya, or The Revolt in the Temple*. Colombo, Ceylon: Sinha Publications, 1953.

Watson, Burton, trans. *The Lotus Sutra*. New York: Columbia University Press, 1993.

Weber, Max. *Religions of India: The Sociology of Hinduism and Buddhism*. New York: Free Press, 1958.

Williams, George M. *Freedom and Influence: The Role of Religion in American Society*. Santa Monica, Calif.: World Tribune Press, 1985.

Williams, Paul. *Mahayana Buddhism: The Doctrinal Foundations*. New York and London: Routledge, 1989.

Wright, Arthur F. *Studies in Chinese Buddhism*. New Haven, Conn.: Yale University Press, 1990.

2

Dr. Ambedkar and the Hermeneutics
of Buddhist Liberation

Christopher S. Queen

In *The Heretical Imperative: Contemporary Possibilities of Religious Affirmation* (1979), the sociologist Peter Berger characterized modernity as the "universalization of heresy," deriving "heresy" from its ancient Greek root, meaning the exercise of personal choice. Berger cited the explosion of options in modern life, from consumer preferences to reproductive choice, and argued that all these point in turn to a master choice—the choice that marks both our liberation and our alienation from the certainties of the past—the choice of religious belief.

> In premodern situations there is a world of religious certainty, occasionally ruptured by heretical deviations. By contrast, the modern situation is a world of religious uncertainty, occasionally staved off by more or less precarious constructions of religious affirmation. . . . For premodern man, heresy is a possibility—usually a rather remote one; for modern man, heresy typically becomes a necessity. . . . [M]odernity creates a new situation in which picking and choosing becomes an imperative.[1]

This is the context in which I believe we should consider the life and thought of Bhimrao Ramji Ambedkar (1891–1956). The leader of India's Untouchables in the decades leading up to Indian independence, the architect of the Indian Constitution, and the celebrated convert to Buddhism, Ambedkar began life as a premodern man. As a member of the lowly Mahar community, required by Hindu law to perform menial work and avoid polluting contact with the upper classes, young Bhimrao inhabited a world of certainties dating back two thousand, perhaps three thousand, years. But over his long career Ambedkar evolved into Berger's modern man, one who rejected the sacred canopy of Hinduism, systematically studied the religious options available in India, and finally adopted Buddhism as the faith that met the complex requirements of reason and morality he stipulated along the way. Ambedkar, the apostate Hindu, the agnostic seeker, the heretic Buddhist: this was a pilgrimage few outside of India's Untouchable community could comprehend.

In his final years, having announced his leaning to Buddhism and begun his magnum opus, *The Buddha and His Dhamma*, Ambedkar went beyond Berger's typology to become a *postmodern man*, I would suggest—one driven not only to choose a religious tradition, but to dismantle and reassemble it with elements of faith and practice appropriated in his wide-ranging studies and travels in Asia and the West. This was a hermeneutic task, a critical assessment of ancient and modern meanings, their interplay, and their applicability to the exigencies of the age. Unlike the deconstructive postmodernisms that negate the unity of past and present, however, Ambedkar's was a constructive, revisionary postmodernism that sought "a new unity of scientific, ethical, aesthetic, and religious intuitions."[2]

Ambedkar's preoccupation with the religious meaning of social oppression suggests parallels to the rise of twentieth-century liberation theology in the West. Like the social gospel of the Christian liberationists, Ambedkar's version of the Buddhist *dhamma* (Pali; Sanskrit *dharma*: "teaching," "truth") is directed to the dispossessed and wrapped in sacred injunction. Like the writings of the Third World theologians, Ambedkar's voluminous output addresses the economic, political, social, and spiritual vicissitudes of historical communities, with scant reference to a life to come.

To countless new Buddhists from the Mahar and other Scheduled Caste (lowborn) communities today—young professionals, workers, children, and particularly the elderly who lived through the turbulent transition to Indian independence—Ambedkar is "Dr. Babasaheb Ambedkar," the most highly educated man in India, the father of his people, lawyer and legislator, author, orator, labor leader, cabinet minister, and educator. He was "the Second Manu" (replacing the oppressive laws of the ancient Hindu lawgiver), and the beloved "Bodhisattva" (a Buddhist who vows to save all afflicted beings) whose memory inspires the daily greeting "Jai Bhim," "Victory to Ambedkar!"

To traditional Buddhists and scholars of Buddhism, however, Ambedkar's life and thought pose difficulties. It is clear that his conversion to Buddhism in 1956 triggered a mass movement, as the number of Buddhists reported by the Indian census increased over a thousand percent in a decade, from 181,000 in 1951 to 3,250,000 in 1961.[3] It is also clear that, after his systematic study of alternatives to Hinduism, Ambedkar concluded that Buddhism was the only viable religion, not only for the Untouchables of India, but for the modern world at large.

But Ambedkar's Buddhism is different from any Buddhism of the past. Missing is the emphasis on monastic life, meditation and enlightenment, karma and rebirth, and the miraculous trappings of the old scriptures—the divine intervention of buddhas and bodhisattvas, the practice of magic and ritual, and the cosmic realms of time and space. Missing are the philosophical and psychological speculations of the Abhidhammikas, Madhyamikas, and Yogacharins, and missing most notably are the Four Noble Truths, which Ambedkar regarded as the misguided interpolation of monastic editors of the Buddha's sermons. Human suffering (the first noble truth in traditional accounts) is not chiefly caused by the sufferer's ignorance and cravings (the second truth), he held, but by social exploitation and material poverty—the cruelty of others.

Ambedkar came to believe that the Buddhist dhamma is a superior religion aimed at human freedom and liberation. Writing in the journal of the Maha Bodhi Society in 1950, he proposed four criteria for a satisfactory religion. Such a faith must foster morality; accord with scientific reason; offer liberty, equality, and fraternity; and not sanctify or ennoble poverty. "So far as I know," he concluded, "the only religion which satisfies these tests is Buddhism." In addition to *ahimsa*, the principle of nonviolence, the Buddha taught

> social freedom, intellectual freedom, economic freedom, and political freedom. He taught equality, equality not between man and man only but between man and woman. It would be difficult to find a religious teacher to compare with Buddha, whose teachings embrace so many aspects of the social life of a people, whose doctrines are so modern, and whose main concern was to give salvation to man in his life on earth, and not to promise it to him in heaven after he is dead.[4]

Ambedkar's redefinition of Buddhist liberation—as the amelioration of material conditions and social relationships in this life—did not find ready acceptance among Buddhist intellectuals in India. Following the posthumous publication of *The Buddha and His Dhamma*, a reviewer in *The Maha Bodhi* found the book "enough to shock a real Buddhist," particularly in its denial of the Buddha's infallibility, its rejection of karma and enlightenment, its omission of the Four Noble Truths, and its reduction of the First Sermon to "a merely social system."[5] Meanwhile, the reviewer for *The Light of Dhamma*, another Buddhist journal, attacked Ambedkar for failing to cite his sources and for allegedly fabricating scriptural support for his own secularist viewpoints.[6]

In two unpublished studies analyzing Ambedkar's use of the Pali scriptures in *The Buddha and His Dhamma*, Adele M. Fiske documents

Ambedkar's repeated use of omission, interpolation, paraphrase, shift of emphasis, and rationalization in passages that are presented as, in Ambedkar's words, "simple and clear statement[s] of the fundamental Buddhist thoughts." Perhaps the most notable example is his treatment of the future Buddha's motivation for retiring from the world. According to Fiske, the canonical *Buddhacarita's* depiction of the Buddha's

> longing for peace, for passionless meditation, for the homeless mendicant life for "the sake of liberation" is replaced by [his] political initiation into a "sangha" remarkably like a parliament, in which there is party conflict, debate and voting. Gautama is the Opposition, the minority leader; he yields to the best interests of the commonweal; he upholds an anti-militaristic *ahimsa* position. All poetic and fantastic elements in the tale of his departure—the gods causing the harem girls to look repulsive in sleep, the gods opening the doors as he escapes by night—are replaced by a sober account of a daytime leaving of his family.[7]

In this and many other cases, Ambedkar's alteration of the particulars of sacred narrative and doctrine in the Buddhist tradition raises a familiar question in the history of religion. How far may a reformer deviate from the core teachings of a tradition and still be a reformer—and not a schismatic, the founder of a new tradition?

The answer to this question involves the intellectual and spiritual dynamics of the tradition in question, and the conventions of interpretation that the tradition has evolved to meet the challenges of history. These are the hermeneutics of the religious tradition, and they are tacitly at work whenever new utterance is given to the teachings.

The life and thought of B. R. Ambedkar cannot be considered, thus, without attention to the related problems of *modernity,* the imperative to choose values and patterns of life, and *hermeneutics,* the dynamics of in-terpretation and innovation that mark the evolution of a religious tradition. In the following section I examine some of the experiences and influences that contributed to Ambedkar's heresy from Hinduism. Then I approach the question of Ambedkar's standing as a heretic or a bona fide reformer in the context of Buddhist hermeneutics. Finally I turn to Ambedkar's historical significance as a postmodern man of faith.

From Untouchable to Buddhist

As an Untouchable boy in village India at the turn of the century, Bhimrao Ambedkar faced continuous abuse. In grade school, he and his brother were made to sit silently on a piece of burlap in the back of the classroom; their notebooks could not be handled by the teacher, and drinking water was poured into their mouths from above to avoid physical contact. Beatings followed the inadvertent trespassing on private property, and the local barber refused to cut their hair.[8]

Nevertheless, Bhimrao was fortunate in having devoted parents who were ambitious for his future. Both sides of the family were active in the devotional cult of the poet-saint Kabir (1440–1518), known for his rejection of caste and his vision of universal brotherhood. Bhim's father, a career officer and military school headmaster in the British army, drilled his children in Marathi and English translation, arithmetic, and long passages from the Hindu epics. An activist for Untouchable rights in his later years, Ambedkar's father was a friend and admirer of Mahatma Jotiba Phule (1827–1890), the Maharashtrian social reformer and founder of the first Indian School for Untouchables.[9]

Years later, Ambedkar claimed that the greatest influences on his thought were the lives of Kabir, Mahatma Phule, and the Buddha. Upon his graduation from high school in 1907—he was only the second Untouchable to reach this level—Bhimrao was given the *Life of Gautama Buddha* (in Marathi) by K. A. Keluskar, a well-known local author and social reformer. Inspired by the social teachings of the great reformers and by the intense ambition of his father, Ambedkar entered college in Bombay, where his tuition was paid by the liberal Hindu Maharaja of neighboring Baroda state, Sayajirao Gaekwad.

With the continued financial support of the Gaekwad, Ambedkar became one of the most highly educated men in India, receiving M.A. and Ph.D. degrees from Columbia University in New York, and the M.Sc. and D.Sc. degrees from the University of London between 1913 and 1923. He was also admitted to the bar in London and pursued postdoctoral studies at the University of Bonn.

In spite of these historic achievements and his entry into professional life in the following years—as a government worker, newspaper editor, college professor, law school dean, and elected official—Ambedkar was repeatedly victimized by caste violence, including eviction from housing, beatings, and death threats. These experiences convinced him that neither the well-wishes of liberal Hindus, the random support of the British, nor the efforts of isolated Untouchables like himself could make a lasting difference in India; only a social revolution with broad support of the masses could lessen the violence and prejudice.

In an early speech, Ambedkar revealed the moral intensity that became his trademark, whether addressing hostile caste Hindus or the masses of low-born Indians. Here, he addresses one of the many political gatherings of the Untouchables:

> My heart breaks to see the pitiable sight of your faces and to hear your sad voices. . . . Why do you worsen and sadden the picture of the sorrows, poverty, slavery and burdens of the world with your deplorable, despicable, and detestable miserable life? . . . If you believe in living a respectable life, [then you must] believe in self-help, which is the best help![10]

The hortatory yet compassionate tone of the address reflects Ambedkar's typical impatience but also, one suspects, his shock after ten years abroad, studying the causes and remedies of historical oppression—only to return to an India sinking deeper in economic and spiritual decay.[11]

The challenge of self-help and independence (*svaraj* in Hindi) was indeed the guiding theme in India during the 1920s, 1930s, and 1940s. For Mahatma Gandhi and the Congress Party, this meant the epic struggle against the British Raj by means of *satyagraha*, nonviolent protest, along with endless rounds of political negotiation, both at home and in London. In his own right as the fiery spokesman for the depressed classes, Dr. Ambedkar was a major player in this period, yet his analysis of India's crisis was diametrically opposed to Gandhi's. It was the caste system that crippled India, he declared at every opportunity, not the British. And while Ambedkar fully supported the movement toward national independence, he took strong exception to the reformist liberalism of Gandhi and the Congress leaders, who believed that caste—purged of untouchability—must remain the social backbone of India.

For twelve years, Ambedkar led sit-ins and demonstrations for equal access to temples and public facilities, negotiating with Hindu leaders and pressing the case of Untouchable rights in the courts. This was a period of deep ambivalence regarding his religious identity and, by extension, the identity of all Untouchables. In 1927, on the failure of a massive demonstration for access to the water supply at Chowdar (which the caste Hindus claimed to have to "re-purify" with sacred cow dung and urine after its use by Untouchables), Ambedkar declared that Hinduism itself had become the fighting issue. Some weeks later, before a gathering of fifteen thousand, he burned a copy of the *Manusmriti*, the ancient Book of Manu, which includes among its penalties the pouring of molten lead into the ears of lowborn Hindus who hear the recitation of the Vedas.

In 1935 Ambedkar made the most daring speech of his career, announcing that, because of the intransigence of the Hindus and the failure of a decade of nonviolent protests, he had resolved to abandon Hinduism and to seek another faith. He urged the ten thousand Depressed Class leaders at the conference at Yeola to consider their religious identity as a *choice,* not as a fact of destiny. In a voice rising with emotion, he enumerated the benefits of heresy:

If you want to gain self-respect, change your religion.
If you want to create a cooperating society, change your religion.
If you want power, change your religion.
If you want equality, change your religion.
If you want independence, change your religion.
If your want to make the world in which you live happy, change your religion.[12]

Ambedkar's declaration at Yeola sparked years of intense debate in the Untouchable communities and throughout India, not only on the suitability of Hinduism vis-à-vis other faiths—Islam, Christianity, Sikhism, and Buddhism—but also on the very claim that one may choose a religious identity. Upon hearing of Ambedkar's speech, Gandhi remarked that "religion is not like a house or a cloak, which can be changed at will. It is a more integral part of one's self than one's own body."[13]

For his part, Ambedkar approached the task of choosing a religious identity as if it were a massive research project. Letters and cables poured in from the contending religions. The former Nizam of Hyderabad offered 50 million rupees—about a rupee a head—for the wholesale delivery of Untouchables to Islam. The Methodist Episcopal Bishop of Bombay observed that true conversion requires an individual change of heart, but the Christians would surely welcome the Untouchables *en masse* on the approval of their leader. The vice president of the Golden Temple wired that only the Sikh faith met the Untouchables' requirement of equality under God, and the secretary of the Buddhist Maha Bodhi Society (a Brahmin) cabled:

> Shocked very much to read your decision to renounce Hindu religion. Very sorry. . . . Please reconsider. . . . But if you still persist in embracing another religion, you with your community are most cordially welcome to embrace Buddhism which is professed by the greater part of Asia. Among Buddhists there are no religious or social disabilities. We grant equal status to all converts. There are no caste distinctions amongst us. We are willing to send workers.[14]

The Untouchable leader devoted increasing energy to the question of conversion. He sent delegations of his followers to attend and report back on religious conferences, he corresponded with religious thinkers and clerics, and he traveled to religious gatherings abroad. A voracious reader and book collector since his student days, he amassed a personal library of thousands of volumes in philosophy, history, the social sciences, and comparative religion, including critical editions and translations of the sacred literatures.

In the end, Buddhism won out. But the process and criteria of evaluation were as significant as the result, especially in light of the transformation that Buddhism underwent along the way. Ambedkar's consideration and ultimate rejection of the competing traditions was rationalized to a remarkable degree and reported in his writings and speeches of the period. On the eve of Indian independence, political issues of national identity and security were weighed along with the moral and ethical criteria that Ambedkar stressed.

A revealing glimpse of the process is afforded by Ambedkar's provisional statement of preference for Sikhism, reported in the *Times of India* for July 24, 1936:

> ... Looking at these alternative faiths purely from the standpoint of Hindus, which is the best—Islam, Christianity, or Sikhism? Obviously, Sikhism is the best. If the Depressed Classes join Islam or Christianity, they not only go out of the Hindu religion, but they also go out of the Hindu culture. On the other hand, if they become Sikhs they remain within Hindu culture. This is by no means a small advantage to the Hindus. What the consequences of conversion will be to the country as a whole, is well worth bearing in mind.
>
> Conversion to Islam or Christianity will denationalize the Depressed Classes. If they go over to Islam, the numbers of Muslims will be doubled; and the danger of Muslim domination also becomes real. If they go on to Christianity, the numerical strength of the Christians becomes five to six crores [fifty to sixty millions]. It will help to strengthen the hold of Britain on the country. ... Thus it is in the interest of the country that the Depressed Classes, if they are to change their faith, should go on to Sikhism.[15]

In the following years Ambedkar released similar progress reports as he wrestled publicly with his decision. Increasingly, moral and ethical considerations predominated. In his 1945 book on the issue of the partition of Pakistan, he compared Islam's record of social justice in India to that of Hinduism. Among Islam's failings were its acquiescence in the abuses of caste and untouchability, in spite of the egalitarian spirit of the Qur'an; its oppression of women by its sanction of Purdah, polygamy, and concubinage; and, in Ambedkar's words, its "spirit of intolerance which is unknown anywhere outside the Muslim world for its severity and its violence, which is directed towards the suppression of all rational thinking which is in conflict with the teachings of Islam."[16]

Like Gandhi, Ambedkar was a great admirer of the Christian Gospels. He was aware of the prophetic cry for justice and mercy for the disinherited and of the influence of Christian social teachings in Western societies. In the late 1930s he developed a close friendship with Dr. J. W. Pickett, the Methodist Episcopal Bishop in Bombay. Over a period of eight years the two men dined together monthly in the bishop's residence and discussed religion. Ambedkar came to believe that St. Paul's stirring message of liberation was "the perfect antidote to the poison Hinduism has injected into our souls" and, according to Dr. Pickett, he twice inquired whether the bishop would be "willing to baptize him secretly on the understanding that within a few years he would make confession of his faith."

But finally, according to Pickett, Ambedkar rejected this option, concluding that the Indian Christians, especially converts from the Depressed Classes, did not live up to the Gospel:

> [The Christian converts] don't care a snap of their finger what becomes of their former caste associates so long as they and their families, or they and the little group who have become Christians, get ahead. Indeed their chief concern with reference to their old caste associates is to hide the fact that they were in the same community. I don't want to add to the number of such Christians.[17]

Gradually the alternatives to Buddhism were eliminated one by one. Untouchable converts to Christianity, acting on their own after the Yeola speech, were ignored. A delegation of followers sent to Amritsar to study Sikhism returned instead as converts, and were disavowed. Jainism was ruled out because its adherence to *ahimsa*, nonviolence, was too extreme. On the other hand, hints of Ambedkar's preference for Buddhism appeared with increasing frequency. In 1940 he proposed the theory that Untouchability was Brahminism's punishment of those who clung to Buddhism in ancient times (a theory he developed in his book, *The Untouchables*, in 1948). In a 1944 speech before the Madras Rationalist Society he contrasted the empiricist (and by implication, modern scientific) epistemology of Buddhism with the scriptural fundamentalism of the Brahmins. The following year he named the new college founded under the auspices of the People's Education Society—which he also founded—Siddharth College, after the Buddha.[18]

With Indian independence in 1947 came Ambedkar's appointment as first law minister in Nehru's cabinet, and then as chairman of the drafting committee for a new constitution. In spite of these new duties, he continued his religious quest. In the preface to his 1948 reissue of P. Lakshmi Narasu's classic, *The Essence of Buddhism*, Ambedkar managed to associate Indian patriotism with Buddhist faith and to advertise many of his own commitments in his tribute to the author.

Prof. Narasu was the stalwart of the 19th century who had fought European arrogance with patriotic fervour, orthodox Hinduism with iconoclastic zeal, heterodox Brahmins with nationalistic vision and aggressive Christianity with a rationalistic outlook—all under the inspiring banner of his unflagging faith in the teachings of the Great Buddha.[19]

In the same preface, Ambedkar revealed that he was working on his own life of the Buddha in order "to deal with some of the criticisms which have been levelled against the teachings of the Buddha by his adversaries." This volume undoubtedly became *The Buddha and His Dhamma*, which appeared posthumously.

In 1950 Dr. Ambedkar wrote in *The Maha Bodhi* that only Buddhism is compatible with the ethical and rational demands of contemporary life. At the same time he and his wife traveled to Ceylon to attend the first meeting of the World Fellowship of Buddhists. Arriving at Colombo airport, he announced that there were those who believed the time might be auspicious for a revival of Buddhism in India, and that he was in Ceylon to assess the vitality of Buddhism in a traditionally Buddhist country. In view of the eremitic life of most bhikkhus in Ceylon—who, in spite of the activist wing of the sangha dating back to the middle of the last century, did not appear to contribute to the welfare of the people—Ambedkar questioned the conference's focus on "fellowship," asking whether it should not rather be upon outreach and sacrifice.[20]

Upon his return to India, Ambedkar announced that he would devote the rest of his life to the revival and spread of Buddhism. Following his retirement from public office in 1951, he labored tirelessly on this project, writing articles, giving speeches, twice traveling to Burma to attend Buddhist conferences, establishing the Indian Buddhist Society, and working all the while on his book.

Finally, in 1955, speaking to a throng of Untouchables who gathered to dedicate an image of the Buddha he had brought back from Rangoon, Ambedkar confirmed that, upon the completion of his book the following year, during the world celebration of the 2,500th anniversary of the Buddha's Nirvana, he would become a Buddhist.

The conversion ceremony, or *diksha*, took place on October 14, 1956, a date associated with Emperor Ashoka's conversion to Buddhism, in the central Indian city of Nagpur, also associated with Buddhist folklore and history. Approximately 380,000 Untouchables took part in the outdoor ceremony, as Dr. Ambedkar and his wife took refuge in the Three Jewels, pledged to observe the Five Precepts, and, in a litany of twenty-two vows composed by Ambedkar, pledged to avoid the beliefs and practices of the Hindu religion. The vows were first administered to the Ambedkars by

Chandramani Maha Thera, the oldest Buddhist monk in India, and then, the following day, by Ambedkar to his jubilant followers. In a thirty-six-hour period, following the arrival of latecomers, nearly a half million people embraced the Buddhist faith.

Six weeks later, Ambedkar passed away, having fulfilled his pledge, made twenty-one years earlier, not to die a Hindu.

The Hermeneutics of Liberation

In Peter Berger's terms, Ambedkar epitomized the modern spirit in an epic way. By deliberately choosing a religious faith from among the competing traditions in a richly pluralistic society, Ambedkar set off perhaps the largest mass religious conversion in the twentieth century. The method and style of Ambedkar's heretical quest—that of publicly announcing and then painstakingly investigating the problem of religious choice—also illustrate Berger's model of modern consciousness.

But the Buddhism of Ambedkar's mature writings has posed a stumbling block to traditional Buddhists and academic critics. What is the historian to make of his theory that India's Untouchables are the descendents of the ancient Buddhists, who were, in turn, the descendents of the pre-Aryan aboriginals of India? How can Buddhists and scholars of Buddhism accept his retelling of the legend of the Great Going Forth or his rejection of the Four Noble Truths, of karma and rebirth, and of the contemplative mission of the Bhikkhu?

Is the Buddhism presented in Ambedkar's major work, *The Buddha and His Dhamma*, Buddhism at all, or should it perhaps better be termed "Ambedkarism," as some proposed at the time? And, since this volume is the equivalent of the Bible for the millions of new Buddhists who have followed Babasaheb to Buddhism, can they be considered true Buddhists?

Some commentators, claiming a radical shift in spirit and emphasis in Ambedkar's Buddhism, have attempted to put a good face on it. Joanna Macy writes that "the converts' background, as Untouchables in a caste society, colors their views of the faith they espouse—casting into bold relief the social teachings of the Dhamma and those interpretations of the Buddhist past that speak to their need for self-respect."[21] Richard W. Taylor compares Ambedkar's compilation of *The Buddha and His Dhamma* to his work on the Indian Constitution, with its borrowings from American, British, and Indian law. In the book, Ambedkar

> has taken what seemed to him the most relevant parts of several Buddhist traditions, edited them, sometimes drastically, added material of his own,

and arranged them in an order. Like the Constitution, this too has become much more than another document. Just as the Constitution is at the heart of the nation's political life, this canon is at the heart of the religious life of the new Buddhists.[22]

Perhaps more significantly, Bhadant Anand Kausalyayan, the respected scholar who translated *The Buddha and His Dhamma* from the original English to Hindi and checked all Pali references in the process, concluded that Ambedkar's presentation is a "new orientation, but not a distortion" of Buddhism, and that all the central doctrines of the tradition are present.[23]

While it is not feasible here to verify Kausalyayan's assertion in detail, we may test it with respect to Ambedkar's treatment of the Four Noble Truths, by all accounts a cardinal teaching of the Pali scriptures. In the introduction to his book, Ambedkar declares that the formula "cuts at the root of Buddhism," constitutes "a great stumbling block in the way of non-Buddhists accepting the gospel of Buddhism," denies hope to man, and thus represents a later addition by the monks who formulated and collected the Buddha's teaching.

In the chapters of the book titled "The Buddha's First Sermon," Ambedkar's paraphrase of the opening section of the *Dhammachakkappavattana Sutta*, involving the middle path, follows the original. But when the five wanderers demand to know the essence of the Buddha's teaching, the familiar presentation of the Four Noble Truths is missing; instead,

> He began by saying that his path which is his Dhamma (religion) had nothing to do with God and Soul. His Dhamma had nothing to do with life after death. Nor has his Dhamma any concern with rituals and ceremonies. The center of his Dhamma is man and the relation of man to man in his life on earth. This he said was his first postulate. His second postulate was that men are living in sorrow, in misery and poverty. The world is full of suffering and that how to remove this suffering from the world is the only purpose of Dhamma. . . .
>
> The Parivrajakas then asked him, "If the foundation of your Dhamma is the recognition of the existence of suffering and the removal of suffering, tell us how does your Dhamma remove suffering!" The Buddha then told them that according to his Dhamma if every person followed (1) the Path of Purity; (2) the Path of Righteousness; and (3) the Path of Virtue, it would bring about the end of all suffering.[24]

In the following sections, the Path of Purity is identified as the traditional Five Precepts, the Path of Righteousness is identified as the Eightfold Path (equivalent to the fourth Noble Truth), and the Path of Virtue is the ten traditional *paramis*, "perfections," including the four *brahmaviharas* or "blessed abodes." In addition to these interpolations, the treatment of several items is unexpected. The eighth step on the Eightfold Path, *samma samadhi*, "right concentration," is defined as the "habit of mind to think of good . . . [and] the necessary motive power to do good"—rather than "mere concentration [which] leads to Dhyanic states which are self-induced, holding the five hindrances in suspense."

The Eightfold Path is interpreted not as a means to *nirvana* ("the traditional Theravada Buddhist goal)" but as the way "to remove injustice and inhumanity that man does to man." *Dana* and *karuna* ("generosity" and "compassion") are directed to the "suffering of the needy and the poor," *maitri* ("loving-kindness") "means fellowship not merely with human beings but with all living beings," and *prajna* ("wisdom") is identified as the "understanding and intelligence" that motivates and rationalizes all acts of virtue.[25]

Thus, of the Four Noble Truths, the first and fourth—Suffering and Path—appear in recognizable formulations as elements in the first sermon, but the second and third—suffering's Arising (from mental craving) and Cessation (in Nirvana)—are unmistakably reinterpreted as social teachings. One is forced to look elsewhere in *The Buddha and His Dhamma* to find additional commentary on these teachings. On the arising of suffering, Gautama, in Ambedkar's version, upon hearing of the resolution of a violent dispute between neighboring clans, the Sakyas and Koliyas, reflects,

> The conflict between nations is occasional. But the conflict between classes is constant and perpetual. It is this which is the root of all sorrow and suffering in the world.[26]

In another place, the Buddha speaks of craving—the traditional cause of suffering—but quickly relates it to the violence of class struggle: "blows and wounds, strife, contradiction and retorts; quarrelling, slander and lies."[27]

As for Nirvana, the Buddhist goal of liberation, Ambedkar writes of a "kingdom of righteousness on earth" and describes the Buddha's enlightenment not as the ripening of an individual's cosmic potential but as a simple realization of the plight of others:

> On the night of the last day of the fourth week, light dawned upon him. He realized that there were two problems. The first problem was that there was suffering in the world and the second was how to remove this suffering and make mankind happy.[28]

This dramatically understated reading of the central epiphany of Buddhism has alarmed even sympathetic critics. Macy finds that "the jolt to a traditional Buddhist of reading such a description of the enlightenment, with its absence of a sense of radical transformation or transcending insight into the nature of reality, epitomizes the problems inherent in Ambedkar's 'Turning of the Law.'"[29] Taylor concludes that "suffering is still central to the insight of the enlightenment, but it is a much paler insight, and indeed a paler suffering, than that usually communicated by the four Truths, even to those who themselves have no real understanding of their trans-empirical dimensions." The omission of the second and third truths is "little short of an emasculation" of the Buddha Dharma.[30]

We noted that Ambedkar presents both the traditional truths of *samudaya* (arising [of suffering]) and *nirodha* (cessation [of suffering])—as well as accounts of Nirvana (Pali *nibbana*) and Parinirvana (the Buddha's final rest)—elsewhere in the *The Buddha and His Dhamma*.

> What makes man unhappy [he has the Buddha say] is his falling prey to his passions. These passions are called fetters which prevent a man from reaching the state of Nibbana. The moment he is free from the sway of his passions, i.e., he learns to achieve Nibbana, man's way to happiness is open to him.

And again,

> As the Udana says, 'Parinibbana occurs when the body becomes disintegrated, all perceptions become stopped, all sensations die away, the activities cease and consciousness goes away. Thus Parinibbana means complete extinction.' Nibbana can never have this meaning. Nibbana means enough control over passion so as to enable one to walk on the path of righteousness.[31]

But here again the emphasis is redirected to ethical life in society; cessation of passions is seen as a precondition for righteousness, as if the third truth of the traditional formula (cessation) leads causally and temporally to the practice of the fourth truth (the path), a clear reversal of the traditional order.

Why has Ambedkar denied the authenticity of the Four Noble Truths in their canonical presentation, leading scholars and traditional Buddhists to conclude that he has abandoned or distorted the Dhamma?

The answer to this question—and the key to understanding Ambedkar's redefinition of Buddhist liberation—hinges on the hermeneutical principles that undergird *The Buddha and His Dhamma* and Ambedkar's other writings on Buddhism. And perhaps more critically, the answer hinges on an appreciation of the centrality of hermeneutic transformations in the history of Buddhism itself.

Most commentators on *The Buddha and His Dhamma* cite the pivotal section near the middle of the book that treats the problem of the transmission of the Dhamma and its frequent misunderstanding. The burden of the argument is that because of oral transmission and the vast scope of the Buddha's teachings, inadvertent misreporting of the *Buddha-vacana* or authentic Buddha-sayings took place, as acknowledged in five suttas. Thus it becomes necessary today to apply certain tests of authenticity to the scriptures. These are three in number:

> If there is anything which could be said with confidence it is: [the Buddha] was nothing if not rational, if not logical. Anything therefore which is rational and logical, other things being equal, may be taken to be the word of the Buddha.

> The second thing is that the Buddha never cared to enter into a discussion which was not profitable for man's welfare. Therefore anything attributed to the Buddha which did not relate to man's welfare cannot be accepted to be the word of the Buddha.

> There is a third test. It is that the Buddha divided all matters into two classes. Those about which he was certain and those about which he was not certain. On matters which fell into class I, he has stated his views definitely and conclusively. On matters which fell into class II, he has expressed his views, but they are only tentative views.[32]

These three criteria—rationality, social benefit, and certainty—are applied to the traditional and supplementary material that Ambedkar reworks. And they may be seen as the proximate answer to critical questions of inclusion and arrangement.

But these criteria must be transparent to the life needs and sensibilities of the community from which Ambedkar and his Buddhism arose—narrowly, the Mahars of Maharashtra, more broadly, the Untouchables of India, and ultimately, the oppressed of every age. This means that the rationality, social benefit, and certainty of the Buddha Dhamma must be intelligible and relevant to *these* people first and foremost. This is the final answer to questions of inclusion and arrangement and constitutes the master hermeneutic principle of Ambedkar's Dhamma.

Ambedkar knew that the traditional presentation of the Four Truths—which blame the victims for their own suffering—would be offensive and unacceptable to people whose sufferings were caused by others' cruelty and a heartless social system. He recognized that the metaphysics of karma and rebirth intensified self-blame by alleging the sufferers' misconduct in former lives. Furthermore, he knew that the voluntary poverty and contemplative pursuits of the traditional bhikkhu could not offer a viable ideal for people locked in structural poverty. And he responded to the need for an uplifting historical construction to explain the origins of the Untouchables, the rise and fall of ancient Buddhism, and the present supremacy of caste Hinduism.

"What are the teachings of the Buddha?" Ambedkar asked. No two followers of the Buddha or students of Buddhism agree, he replied. Some say *samadhi*, some *vipassana*, others, metaphysics, mysticism, or abstraction from the world. But the key question for the Untouchables was, "Did the Buddha have a Social Message?" Did he teach justice, love, liberty, equality, fraternity? Could the Buddha answer Karl Marx? "These questions are hardly ever raised in discussing the Buddha's Dhamma," Ambedkar observed. "My answer is that the Buddha has a Social Message. He answers all these questions. But they have been buried by modern authors."[33]

In 1978 Robert Thurman published an influential essay on Buddhist hermeneutics. Defining hermeneutics as "a philosophical discipline of rational interpretation of a traditional canon of Sacred Scriptures," Thurman argued that the salience of hermeneutics in Buddhism may be understood in light of Shakyamuni's resourcefulness as a teacher "who sought to encourage the individual disciple's ability to think for himself," and his "affirmation of empiricism, a rational acknowledgement of the fact that reality, even ordinary reality, is never, in the final analysis, reducible to what we may say about it."[34] In his survey of Buddhist hermeneutic strategies from the time of the founder to that of the Tibetan commentator, Tsong-khapa (14th–15th centuries), Thurman illustrates the internal developments, innovations, and shifts of emphasis that Buddhist thinkers have wrought over the centuries.

More recently, Ronald Davidson has argued that standards of scriptural authenticity in the Buddhist tradition were progressively reformulated from the outset to accommodate the changing circumstances of the sangha. "From the beginning," he writes, "there were formal factors in the transmission of the Buddhist dispensation which virtually assured that the early Samgha would modify the literal content of the sayings of the Buddha"[35] These included the use of varying dialects in preaching; the Buddha's authorization of missionaries to speak in his name; the doctrine that "the dharma went beyond the speech of the Buddha" and could be learned from inspired disciples (*sravakas*); the idea that the dharma "has one taste, the taste of final release"; the expectation that the individual must verify, textually or experientially, the truth of the dharma; the traditional emphasis on orthopraxy, not orthodoxy; and "the role of non-Buddhist literature in the formation of new genres of scripture, the classification systems of the scriptures, the lack of centralized authority, and the proliferation of various sects."[36]

Ambedkar's hermeneutics of Buddhist liberation may be seen as a striking contemporary example of these patterns. Like Nagarjuna, Aryadeva,

Asanga, Chih I, Candrakirti, Fa Tsang, and the Ch'an Master Pai Chang—who, Thurman shows, reframed and reinvented central elements of Buddhist teaching—Ambedkar offered a fresh reading of the Dhamma for his time. Ambedkar's use of English idioms and thoughtforms in his writing on Buddhism, his assumption of license in interpreting the Buddha-word, his emphasis on moral practice (orthopraxy) over tenets of doctrine (orthodoxy) like karma and rebirth, his reliance on Western critical scholarship (non-Buddhist literature) in his reconstruction of Buddhist history and thought, his original approach to classifying and presenting Pali source materials, and his independence from sectarian authority and influence all reflect the dynamics of canonical evolution in Davidson's detailed treatment of the Indian Buddhist tradition.

Great shifts in Buddhist thought have typically entailed assertions that appeared at first to negate or compromise the original teaching. For example, a famous utterance of the ideological and practical shifts we know as Mahayana Buddhism is found in the verses of the *Heart Sutra* that conclude, "There is no suffering, no origin, no cessation, no path, no exalted wisdom, no attainment, and also no non-attainment." At the literal (or "conventional") level, a more radical repudiation of the Four Noble Truths ("suffering, origin, cessation, path") and the totality of Buddhist faith and practice ("wisdom and attainment") can scarcely be imagined. At the figurative (or "ultimate") level, the sutra's blunt presentation of the Mahayana's central teaching, the "emptiness" (metaphysical groundlessness) of conceptual forms, reflects an equally drastic departure from the moderate tone and practical message of the Buddha's first sermon.

By comparison, Ambedkar's assertion that man's suffering is caused by class struggle, which is caused in turn by human passions, can be considered a new reading of, but hardly a radical break from, the canonical Buddha-word. The author marshalls familiar social teachings and paradigmatic actions of the Buddha in support of his interpretation. The tradition's early commitment to the inclusion of outcastes and women in the sangha, for example—widely recognized by historians as a revolution in the ancient world—is presented at length in *The Buddha and His Dhamma*. Based on the Pali sources, separate sections are devoted to the Buddha's conversion of various social groups: *parivrajakas* (mendicants); the low and lowly, including Upali the barber and Sunita the sweeper (both outcaste occupations in Ambedkar's day); Sopaka and Suppiya the Untouchables (brought up by a cemetery guard); and Suprabuddha the leper; women, including Mahaprajapati and Yashodhara, Gautama's aunt and wife, and Prakrti, the Untouchable (Chandalika) girl—all members of the first women's religious order in recorded history; and the fallen and criminals, including Angulimala ("Garland of Fingers") the serial killer.

In short, the Buddhism of Ambedkar's late writings recasts the central tenets of ancient Buddhism: the reality of human suffering, the availability of relief through self-cultivation and compassionate action, and the potential for a liberated society based of equality and opportunity. As one who shared the pain and sorrow of the disinherited in his time, Ambedkar affirmed Gautama's stress on the noble truths of pain and the liberation from pain. But he translated the ancient stress on spiritual wisdom, meditation, and mindfulness into the modern emphasis on critical reason sharpened through education and science, and the ancient values of generosity, moral striving, and skillful means into the struggle for social justice.

It may be said that to turn the wheel—the ancient Buddhist metaphor for preaching the Dharma—is to change the wheel; each rotation suggests a new "angle" on the truth. Over many centuries, Buddhist teachings have been worn, mended, and changed like ancient cartwheels; today some have been traded in for the rubber tires of the automobile. Yet the function remains: to convey passengers to their destination. By assembling Ambedkar's best-known teachings under the rubrics of the traditional Four Noble Truths, one may discern the spokes and axles of a distinctive new vehicle. (The term *Navayana* or "new vehicle" has been proposed for Ambedkar's new Buddhism since its first appearance.) For Ambedkar, the *first noble truth* for the present age was the widespread suffering of injustice and poverty; the *second truth* was social, political, and cultural institutions of oppression—the collective expressions of greed, hatred, and delusion; the *third truth* was expressed by the European ideals of "liberty, equality, and fraternity"; and the *fourth truth* was the threefold path of Ambedkar's famous slogan, "Educate! Agitate! Organize!"

By seeking to account for both the personal and the collective dimensions of Buddhist liberation, Ambedkar attempted to move beyond the narrow focus on psychology and moral striving he encountered in early Buddhism. On the other hand, he was anxious that his position not be misinterpreted as a one-sided call for social and political activism at the expense of the individual or as a strident demand for improved material conditions without concomitant advances in self-respect and confidence in the future. In an address before seventy thousand activists of the All-India Depressed Classes Conference in 1942—years before his public turn to Buddhism—Ambedkar attempted to counter the charge that his movement was merely warmed-over socialism:

> My final word of advice to you is educate, agitate, and organize, have faith in yourself. With justice on our side, I do not see how we can lose our battle. The battle to me is a matter of joy. The battle is in the fullest sense spiritual. There is nothing material or social in it. For ours is a battle not

for wealth or for power. It is a battle for freedom. It is a battle for the
reclamation of human personality.[37]

In the end, Ambedkar's "battle for freedom"—sometimes "a matter of
joy," but more often a matter of bitter struggle—encompassed every level
of human experience: the personal (emotional and intellectual), the communal (particularly the caste-based and religious communities in India),
and the national (the fight for *swaraj* and constitutional democracy).
Ambedkar was a holistic thinker with advanced training in the arts and
social sciences of his time. Only by invoking all of these in his redefinition
of Buddhism could he conclude his twenty-one-year quest for a spiritual
home.

Ambedkar's Legacy

The more one learns about the Untouchable leader who earned advanced academic degrees in the West; launched a civil rights movement,
newspapers, service organizations, colleges, and political parties for the
outcastes; drafted India's constitution; and led millions to a revitalized
Buddhism, the more one is struck by the silence of most histories of the
period, including histories of contemporary Buddhism, regarding this important figure. In modern histories of India, Mahatma Gandhi reigns, not
only as "the great soul" of the independence struggle but also as the father
and protector of the Untouchables (or *harijans,* "children of God," as he
called them). Few in the West are aware of Gandhi's opposition to the
abolition of caste—or of the Untouchable leader who demanded it. Few
scholars write of the encounter of the two figures at Pune in 1932, when
Gandhi threatened suicide by fasting if Ambedkar insisted that the Untouchables be allowed to vote as a block (as the Muslims did) in the latest
blueprint for independence. Fewer have heard of Gandhi's rejection of the
modernist premise that one may choose one's religion or of Ambedkar's
growing conviction of its necessity.[38]

To assess the place of B. R. Ambedkar in the history of social movements, political thought, and world religions, therefore, it becomes necessary to seek interpretive frameworks outside as well as inside the Indian
context—sources of Ambedkar's thought and practice, historic figures who
parallel Ambedkar's career, and categories of understanding drawn from
social and religious thought. Among the few writers who have addressed
Ambedkar's legacy—the historian, Eleanor Zelliot, the English monk,
Sangharakshita, and a handful of writers in India and the United States—
none has considered Ambedkar in the contexts of Buddhist hermeneutics,

liberation theology, and the cultural categories of modernity and postmodernity. To this end let us conclude by considering Ambedkar's American experience, parallels with American civil rights leaders, the rise of liberation theology, and the notion of postmodernity as a new age of faith.

Ambedkar's graduate school years in New York City, 1913–1916, had a profound impact on the young Indian scholar. Columbia University was in its heyday, and Ambedkar availed himself of its greatest professors, not the least of whom was the philosopher, social thinker, and educational reformer, John Dewey. Like Dewey, Ambedkar later based his campaigns for social justice on the European Enlightenment principles of reason and experience and the quest for universal education. He founded the People's Education Society and its affiliated colleges, Siddharth College in Bombay and Milind College in Aurangabad, to provide educational opportunities for Untouchable youths. In *Annihilation of Caste* (1936), Ambedkar supported his scathing critique of Hindu society by quoting Dewey ("to whom I owe so much"): "Every society gets encumbered with what is trivial, with dead wood from the past, and with what is positively perverse. . . . As a society becomes more enlightened, it realizes that it is responsible *not* to conserve and transmit the whole of its existing achievements, but only such as make for a better society."[39] Years later, in his first published essay on the superiority of Buddhism, "The Buddha and the Future of His Religion" (1950), Ambedkar echoed Dewey's language and pragmatism in his tribute to the Buddha,

who claimed no infallibility for what he taught . . . He wished his religion not to be encumbered with the dead wood of the past. He wanted that it should remain evergreen and serviceable at all times. This is why he gave liberty to this followers to chip and chop as the necessities of the case required. No other religious leader has shown such courage.[40]

In a more general way, Ambedkar cannot have missed the progressivist and modernist *zeitgeist* that permeated Morningside Heights, including Columbia University Graduate School, Columbia Teacher's College, and Union Theological Seminary, all within a few blocks of Ambedkar's apartment. This was the height of the Social Gospel movement in liberal Protestantism, characterized by the belief that religion is a key element in shaping social change; that religion may itself be adapted to the changing needs of society; that the divine or sacred is immanent in the cultural developments of the day; that God's kingdom may be implemented on earth through the good works of his people; and that religion may be experienced and practiced in a great variety of ways.[41] This was the era of the liberal theologian Walter Rauschenbusch's *Christianity and the Social Crisis* (1907) and *The-*

ology for the Social Gospel (1917). "It is not a matter of saving human atoms," Rauschenbusch wrote, "but of saving the social organism. It is not a matter of getting individuals to heaven, but of transforming the life on earth into the harmony of heaven."[42]

All of these elements of religious modernism may be found in Ambedkar's philosophy of religion and his views concerning religious and social praxis. His use of an extended passage from James Hastings's *Encyclopedia of Religion and Ethics* (1909) as the prologue to *The Buddha and His Dhamma* touches on all the themes of the era: religion and science, religion and social reform, and religion "as the source of ethical and moral values and deep-stirring experiences."[43]

Throughout his career Ambedkar led the ranks of social activists in India who saw that freedom cannot be bought at the expense of justice. Here the American civil rights movement and the rise of liberation theology offer valuable parallels to the struggle for Untouchable rights in India. Martin Luther King, Jr., and Malcolm X, the dominant figures in the African-American struggle in the decade following Ambedkar's time, curiously recall aspects of Ambedkar's brooding personality: the Ph.D. with a booming voice and the grudging respect of politicians and pundits (King) and the strident iconoclast who embraced an exotic religion which offered world brotherhood to the underclass (Malcolm). Like Ambedkar, Dr. King and Malcolm X blended politics with spirituality.

Liberation theology appeared in America shortly after the violent deaths of these two African-American leaders. The year 1970 saw the appearance of James H. Cone's *A Black Theology of Liberation*, which begins, like Ambedkar's Buddhism, with the fact of social oppression. "There can be no Black Theology," wrote Cone, "which does not take seriously the black experience—a life of humiliation and suffering."[44] A year later, Gustavo Gutierrez brought out *A Theology of Liberation*, with its analysis of Roman Catholic and Marxist teachings against a backdrop of social injustice and oppression.[45] Both books, and the flood of liberation theologies that appeared throughout the Americas and in other parts of the Christian Third World in the 1970s and 1980s revive the optimism and activism that animated the Social Gospel writers at the turn of the century and parallel the engaged Buddhism of Ambedkar and his followers today.

Finally, we return to consider Ambedkar as a "postmodern" figure. Modernity, as we have seen, involves alienation from the past, the contest of dying traditions in the present, and the necessity of picking and choosing a future from the scraps of possibility at hand. I have shown the extent to which Ambedkar exemplified Berger's modern man in his deliberate exercise of the heretical imperative: he selected and modified a religious tradition to meet the needs of his community. Indeed, in the application of the hermeneutic criteria of rationality, social benefit, and certainty, Ambedkar appears more an heir of Kant and other Western Enlightenment thinkers—the ancesters of modernity—than of Buddha and the East.

Why, then, a postmodern man? In an essay on "Postmodernity and Faith," Alan M. Olson argues that modernity—characterized by Kant's Enlightenment values of critical understanding and universal ethics—ran aground in the repressive absolutisms of the late nineteenth century and the "man-made mass death" of the twentieth. One reason for the demise of rationalist modernity is that "moral and religious conversion do not necessarily follow intellectual conversion." In postmodernity all "metadiscourse"—the explicit appeal to some "grand narrative" for the legitimation of action—is rejected ("deconstructed"). Thus deprived of the authority of reason and tradition, the only alternative to the "psychological and moral limbo which some have sensed in the so-called blank postmodern generation"—is *faith,* which Olson locates in the "freedom principle" of the Pauline-Lutheran tradition of Protestant Christianity.[46]

I believe that somewhere along the way to conversion, Ambedkar came to feel that, in their classical formulations, none of the religions, philosophies, and political traditions of India or the West—the metadiscourses and grand narratives of world culture—could meet all the spiritual and social needs of the Untouchables or, of *any* group in society. Babasaheb's twenty-one years of hesitation from the Yeola speech to the Nagpur conversion were years of political struggle but also years of deep personal turmoil. One of his close associates reports that Ambedkar was frequently overcome with tears in his last months as he reflected on the continued vulnerability of the Scheduled Castes in independent India, the precariousness of the Buddhist revival, and his own failing health.[47] Yet his training as a scholar, his practice of the law, and most of all, his lifelong experience as a social pariah in the eyes of most Hindus (the civil protections of the new Constitution notwithstanding) reinforced his awareness that religious beliefs, like worldviews and legal systems, grow out of personal and social struggles and cannot be handed down from the past.

In compiling *The Buddha and His Dhamma*, Ambedkar could not have been unaware of the shock effect his version of the tradition would have on conservative Buddhists and scholars. Yet he never faltered in his belief that Buddhism was finally compatible with Indian demands for social justice and democratic institutions. He believed that a religious symbol system cannot be justified solely by its faithfulness to the past, but it must also resonate with and satisfy the requirements of the present. Of course, his "freedom principle" was not that of St. Paul and Martin Luther (except, perhaps during that interlude of lunches with a hopeful Methodist bishop), but that of "my Master, the Buddha," as he confessed in a radio address for the B.B.C. in 1954.

Ambedkar's construction of a socially engaged Buddhism was not, in the end, the discovery or the creation of a religious faith but an act of religious faith. His was the faith that religious symbols and values are indispensible for lasting social change and that self-respect and personal dignity (the Marathi word *manuski* was used in the rhythmic cadences of his Yeola declaration) could only come with religious identity and commitment. But his was not merely a faith in religion in general. Ambedkar's deep attraction to the Buddha and his teachings began at an early age and intensified throughout his life. The blossoming of this Buddhist faith in his final years provided rich resources for a new hermeneutics of liberation, a new sense of identity and hope for millions of his low-caste followers in India, and a new conception of social activism for engaged Buddhists of the coming generation.

Acknowledgment

I wish to thank Eleanor Zelliot, Carleton College historian and the dean of Ambedkar research in America, for her friendship and guidance; Vasant Moon, editor of Ambedkar's writings and speeches, for his good counsel and hospitality in Bombay and Nagpur; S. S. Rege and Srikanth Talwatkar for their assistance in the Ambedkar archives at Siddharth College, Bombay; Yogesh Varhade, for his generosity as a guide to Ambedkarite family and friends in India; and the American Philosophical Society for travel support.

Notes

1. Peter Berger, *The Heretical Imperative: Contemporary Possibilities of Religious Affirmation* (Garden City, N.Y.: Anchor Press Doubleday, 1979), p. 28.

2. For the distinction between deconstructive/eliminative and constructive/visionary postmodernisms, see David Ray Griffin, in *Varieties of Postmodern Theology* by David Ray Griffin, William A. Beardslee, and Joe Holland (Albany: State University of New York Press, 1989), pp. xi–xiv.

3. D. C. Ahir, *Buddhism in Modern India* (Nagpur: Bikkhu Niwas Prakashan, 1972), p. 3.

4. D. C. Ahir, *Dr. Ambedkar on Buddhism* (Bombay: Siddharth Publications, 1982), pp. 27–28.

5. *The Maha Bodhi* (1959), pp. 352–353.

6. *The Light of Dhamma* 6 (1959), pp. 68–70.

7. Adele M. Fiske, "The Use of Buddhist Scriptures in Dr. B. R. Ambedkar's *The Buddha and His Dhamma*" (New York: Columbia University, unpublished thesis, n.d. 2), pp. 59–69. The episode recalls Ambedkar's own thankless years as opposition leader under the Congress Party, and his resignation, retirement, and retreat from Nehru's cabinet following the bitter defeat of his Hindu Code Bill in Parliament in 1951. Like the Buddha, although much later in life, Ambedkar devoted his remaining years to the formulation and spread of spiritual teachings. See also Adele M. Fiske, "B. R. Ambedkar's Interpretation of Some Passages of the *Mahavagga (Vinaya Pitaka)* in his book, *The Buddha and His Dhamma*" (Purchase, N.Y., Manhattanville College, unpublished thesis, n.d. 1).

8. Dhananjay Keer, *Dr. Ambedkar: Life and Mission,* Third Edition (Bombay: Popular Prakashan, 1971), pp. 12–15.

9. Ibid., pp. 8–12.

10. Ibid., p. 60.

11. One is reminded of the early sermons of the Buddha, who had also just returned from years of self-imposed exile and solitary reflection on the ills of life and their remedy: the penetrating analysis of the first two Noble Truths and the Fire Sermon, followed by the clarion call to liberation through self-help.

12. Ibid., p. 255.

13. Sangharakshita, *Ambedkar and Buddhism* (Glasgow: Windhorse Publications), p. 62.

14. B. A. M. Paradkar, "The Religious Quest of Ambedkar," in T. S. Wilkinson and M. M. Thomas, *Ambedkar and the Neo-Buddhist Movement* (Madras: Christian Literature Society, 1972), p. 56–57.

15. Keer, op. cit., pp. 279–280.

16. Paradkar, p. 55.

17. Ibid., p. 60.

18. Sangharakshita, p. 69.

19. P. Lakshmi Narasu, *The Essence of Buddhism* (Delhi: Bharatiya Publishing House, 1948). p. viii.

20. Joanna Rogers Macy and Eleanor Zelliot, "Tradition and Innovation in Contemporary Indian Buddhism," in A. K. Narain, ed., *Studies in the History of Buddhism* (Delhi: B. R. Publishing Corp., 1980), p. 134.

21. Macy and Zelliot, p. 134.

22. Richard Taylor, "The Ambedkarite Buddhists," in Wilkinson and Thomas, op. cit., p. 146.

23. Macy and Zelliot, pp. 134–135.

24. B. R. Ambedkar, *The Buddha and His Dhamma*, Third Edition (Bombay: Siddharth Publications, 1984), p. 83 (Section II.II.3).

25. Ibid., pp. 88–90 (Section II.II.5).

26. Ibid., p. 45 (Section I.II.6).

27. Ibid., pp. 168–169 (Section III.III.4).

28. Ibid., p. 55 (Section I.IV.2.9).

29. Macy and Zelliot, p. 142.

30. Taylor, pp. 159–160.

31. Ibid., pp. 166–167 (Section II.III.49).

32. Ibid., pp. 254–255 (Section IV.I.13–15).

33. Ibid., pp. 158–159 (Section III.II.1).

34. Robert A. F. Thurman, "Buddhist Hermeneutics," in *The Journal of the American Academy of Religion,* vol. 46, no. 1 (1978), p. 19.

35. Ronald M. Davidson, "An Introduction to the Standards of Scriptural Authenticity in Indian Buddhism," in Robert E. Buswell, Jr., ed. *Chinese Buddhist Apocrypha* (Honolulu: University of Hawaii Press, 1990), p. 292. I should like to thank David Eckel for this reference.

36. Ibid., pp. 292–294, 316f., passim.

37. Keer, p. 351.

38. See Eleanor Zelliot, "Gandhi and Ambedkar: A Study in Leadership," in Zelliot, *From Untouchable to Dalit: Essays on Ambedkar Movement* (New Delhi: Manohar, 1992), pp. 150–178.

39. B. R. Ambedkar, "Annihilation of Caste," in *Dr. Babasaheb Ambedkar Writings and Speeches,* vol. 1, Vasant Moon, ed. (Bombay, Education Department, Government of Maharashtra, 1989), p. 79. Ambedkar does not identify the source of the quote.

40. B. R. Ambedkar, "The Buddha and the Future of His Religion," in *The Maha Bodhi,* vol. 58, April-May, 1950; cited in D. C. Ahir, *Dr. Ambedkar on Buddhism* (Bombay: People's Education Society, 1982), pp. 24–25. Eleanor Zelliot reports that Ambedkar's widow, Mrs. Savita Ambedkar, recalls her husband affectionately imitating Dewey's classroom mannerism decades after their studies together. See Zelliot, "The American Experience of Dr. B. R. Ambedkar," in her *From Untouchable to Dalit: Essays on the Ambedkar Movement* (New Delhi: Manohar, 1992), p. 84.

41. See William R. Hutchinson, *The Modernist Impulse in American Protestantism* (Durham and London: Duke University Press, 1992), pp. 2–4.

42. Walter Rauschenbusch, *Christianity and the Social Crisis* (New York: Harper and Row, 1964; originally published 1907), p. 65.

43. Ambedkar, *The Buddha and His Dhamma,* p. xlii, quoting from James Hastings' *Encyclopedia of Religion and Ethics,* volume 10, p. 669.

44. James H. Cone, *A Black Theology of Liberation* (Philadelphia and New York: J. B. Lipincott Company, 1970), p. 54.

45. Gustavo Gutierrez, *A Theology of Liberation* (Maryknoll, N.Y.: Orbis Books, 1973).

46. Alan M. Olson, "Postmodernity and Faith," in *The Journal of the American Academy of Religion,* vol. 63, no. 1 (1990), p. 47.

47. N. C. Ratthu, personal communication, New Delhi, March 26, 1991.

References

Ahir, D. C. *Buddhism in Modern India.* Nagpur: Bikkhu Niwas Prakashan, 1972.

———. *Dr. Ambedkar on Buddhism.* Bombay: Siddharth Publications, 1982.

Ambedkar, B. R. *The Buddha and His Dhamma.* Third edition. Bombay: Siddharth Publications, 1984.

———. Dr. Babasaheb Ambedkar Writings and Speeches. Vasant Moon, ed. Volumes 1–14. Bombay: Education Department, State Government of Maharashtra, 1982–

Berger, Peter. *The Heretical Imperative: Contemporary Possibilities of Religious Affirmation.* Garden City, N.Y.: Anchor Press Doubleday, 1979.

Cone, James H. *A Black Theology of Liberation.* Philadelphia and New York: J. B. Lippincott Company, 1970.

Davidson, Ronald M. "An Introduction to the Standards of Sciptural Authenticity in Indian Buddhism," in Robert D. Buswell, Jr., ed., *Chinese Buddhist Apocrypha.* Honolulu: University of Hawaii Press, 1990.

Fiske, Adele M. "B. R. Ambedkar's Interpretation of Some Passages of the *Mahavagga (Vinaya Pitaka)* in His Book *The Buddha and His Dhamma.*" Purchase, N.Y., Manhattanville College, unpublished thesis, n.d. 1.

———. "The Use of Buddhist Scriptures in Dr. B. R. Ambedkar's *The Buddha and His Dhamma.*" New York: Columbia University, unpublished thesis, n.d. 2.

Griffin, David Ray; William A. Beardslee; and Joe Holland. *Varieties of Postmodern Theology.* Albany: State University of New York Press, 1989.

Gutierrez, Gustavo. *A Theology of Liberation*. Maryknoll, N.Y.: Orbis Books, 1973.

Hutchinson, William R. *The Modernist Impulse in American Protestantism*. Durham and London: Duke University Press, 1992.

Keer, Dhananjay. *Dr. Ambedkar: Life and Mission*. Third edition. Bombay: Popular Prakashan, 1971.

Lakshmi Narasu, P. *The Essence of Buddhism*. Delhi: Bharatiya Publishing House, 1948.

Macy, Joanna Rogers, and Eleanor Zelliot. "Tradition and Innovation in Contemporary Indian Buddhism," in A. K. Narain, ed., *Studies in the History of Buddhism*. Delhi: B. R. Publishing Corp., 1980.

Narain, A. K., ed. *Studies in the History of Buddhism*. Delhi: B. R. Publishing Corp., 1980.

Olson, Alan M. "Postmodernity and Faith," in *The Journal of the American Academy of Religion*. Vol. 63, No. 1 (1990).

Paradkar, B. A. M. "The Religious quest of Ambedkar," in T. S. Wilkinson and M. M. Thomas, *Ambedkar and the Neo-Buddhist Movement*. Madras: The Christian Literature Society, 1972.

Rauschenbusch, Walter. *Christianity and the Social Crisis*. New York: Harper and Row, 1964.

Sangharakshita. *Ambedkar and Buddhism*. Glasgow: Windhorse Publications.

Taylor, Richard. "The Ambedkarite Buddhists," in T. S. Wilkinson and M. M. Thomas, *Ambedkar and the Neo-Buddhist Movement*. Madras: The Christian Literature Society, 1972.

Thurman, Robert A. F. "Buddhist Hermeneutics," in *The Journal of the American Academy of Religion,* Vol. 46, No. 1 (1978).

Wilkinson, T. S., and M. M. Thomas. *Ambedkar and the Neo-Buddhist Movement*. Madras: The Christian Literature Society, 1972.

Zelliot, Eleanor. *From Untouchable to Dalit: Essays on the Ambedkar Movement*. New Delhi: Manohar, 1992.

3

TBMSG: A Dhamma Revolution in Contemporary India

Alan Sponberg

After originating in India and leaving an indelible mark on practically every aspect of South Asian culture, Buddhism had virtually ceased to exist in its homeland a thousand years ago, even as it thrived as an export religion across much of the rest of Asia. The last century has seen a revival of Indian interest in this ancient tradition, however, a revival rife with both anomaly and irony. One is struck first of all by the curious fact that this Buddhist rebirth has manifested itself at opposite ends of the country's complex social spectrum. Since the mid-nineteenth century, Buddhism has become quite fashionable among a small but influential segment of the Brahmin intelligentsia, typically members of a Western-oriented and often Western-educated elite seeking to find in Buddhism a venerable and indigenous synthesis of traditional spirituality and modern rationalism. At the opposite end of the social spectrum, one finds also, arising from a quite disparate set of social circumstances, a major Buddhist mass-conversion movement among the "Untouchables," those outcastes who are among the most destitute factions of India's traditionally caste-structured society. These two expressions of India's fledgling "Buddhist Renaissance" are historically related to be sure. Yet each has arisen in response to very different social needs, and each has found its advocates among quite different and not infrequently antagonistic elements within Indian society.

The first of these two forms of Buddhist revivalism has received relatively more attention in the scholarly literature to date. Several studies have traced the emerging interest in Buddhist philosophy among certain segments of the Brahmin intelligentsia since the mid-nineteenth century,

TBMSG Activities Across India

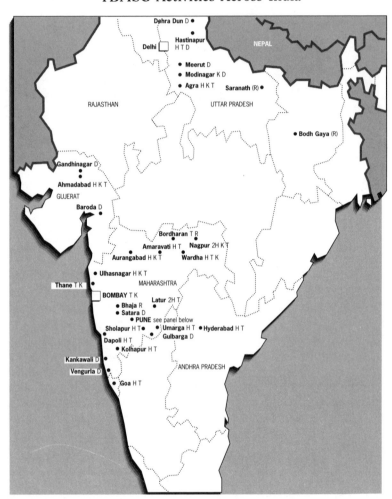

Dehra Dun D

Hastinapur
Delhi H T D

NEPAL

Meerut D
Modinagar K D
Agra H K T   Saranath (R)

RAJASTHAN

UTTAR PRADESH

Bodh Gaya (R)

Gandhinagar D

Ahmadabad H K T

GUJERAT

Baroda D

Bordharan T R
Amaravati H T   Nagpur 2H K T
Aurangabad H K T   Wardha H T K

Ulhasnagar H K T

Thane T K   MAHARASHTRA

BOMBAY T K
Bhaja R   Latur 2H T
Satara D
PUNE see panel below

Sholapur H T   Umarga H T   Hyderabad H T
Dapoli H T   Gulbarga D
Kolhapur H T

Kankawali D

Vengurla D

Goa H T

ANDHRA PRADESH

Key

H	Hostels for Schoolchildren
K	Kindergarten
I	IBMSG Center
R	IBMSG Retreat Center
(R)	Proposed IBMSG Retreat Center
D	Regular Dharma Class

Pune

1 Boys and 1 Girls hostel, 21 Kindergartens
Homework classes, Girls and womens literacy classes
Sewing classes
Mother and child community health programme, Health Clinic
Mobile library, Sports and cultural activities
Creche
Achvagosha performing arts project

Bahujan Hitay Funding 1994
19 hostels: 799 Children, 47 Kindergartens
Other organizations supported
Indo Tibetan Buddhist Cultural Institute, Kahmpong
Mahabodhr International Meditation Centre, Ladakh, Girls hostel

an interest stimulated by British scholarship on the Pali Canon and inspired by English and American Theosophists who sought the origins of their own eclectic faith in a Buddhism the Victorian world was wont to perceive as the most rational and ethical of the major world religions. In this case we surely have a classic example of what some sociologists call the *pizza effect,* the process whereby an export product takes on new significance in the country of its origin after meeting with success (and transformation) abroad. If the Buddhist revival at the top end of the social spectrum thus reveals a highly complex sociological process, what we find at the other end of the scale, although less well documented as yet, represents an even more complicated and intricate web of spiritual inspiration, cross-cultural fertilization, and modernization.

The Trailokya Bauddha Mahasangha Sahayaka Gana, or TBMSG, the subject of this chapter, illustrates this interwoven complexity especially well.[1] One finds here a Buddhist liberation movement that was initially inspired by one of India's foremost modern statesmen, B. R. Ambedkar, yet one that was actually founded by a prominent Western Buddhist, Ven. Sangharakshita. The first of these two key figures, an Indian-born Untouchable, was a social reformer whose primary intellectual influences derive from Anglo-American liberalism and philosophy of law, sources he mastered while studying in Europe and the United States. The second, an English-born Buddhist convert, is a scholar-monk who studied and practiced Buddhism in Asia for twenty years before returning to England to found the Friends of the Western Buddhist Order (FWBO), an international Buddhist organization that would eventually make its way back to India. From those singular and seemingly incongruous roots has grown a highly implausible yet surprisingly successful movement in contemporary Maharashtra—a social as well as religious liberation movement, one in which we find sons and daughters of the British Raj working side by side with some of the most oppressed of India's indigenous peoples in a common effort to reestablish Buddhist practice and culture in the land of its birth. In this self-proclaimed "Dhamma Revolution" we see surely one of the most peculiar and intriguing historical ironies of the latter half of this internationalist century.[2]

By the end of 1992 the TBMSG Dhamma Revolution was working out of some twenty urban centers and two rural retreat centers to administer a diverse array of activities, including day-care centers, kindergartens and residential hostels for school-age children, health-care programs for mothers and children, as well as adult literacy classes and vocational training courses.[3] Additional ongoing activities and facilities include a number of adult residential communities, two regularly published and widely read magazines, several "right livelihood" business ventures[4] and, of course, the full program of Dhamma study classes and retreats that lie at the heart of the movement's effort to establish the Buddha-dhamma on a more solid footing in the ex-Untouchable communities.[5] Because of the disparate nature of these activities, it is difficult to specify the total number of people involved. Those receiving direct services on a regular and ongoing basis would probably easily number ten thousand, whereas the number would be in the tens, indeed hundreds, of thousands if one were to count everyone who attends TBMSG dhamma lectures or cultural events on a more irregular basis. While TBMSG is most active in the major urban areas of the central Indian state of Maharashtra, there are centers, hostels, and other permanent facilities in neighboring Gujarat and Andhra Pradesh as well as Uttar Pradesh, and irregularly scheduled activities in several other states as well. The potential for this movement to grow is considerable. While the current numbers are certainly impressive for an Indian-managed organization not yet fifteen years old, we must also remember that they represent contact with only a fraction of India's ex-Untouchable Buddhist population, a potential constituency currently estimated to be anywhere from 9 to 20 million depending on what criteria one uses to determine Buddhist affiliation.[6]

To appreciate the uniqueness of this Dhamma revolution we must first understand something about the personality and teaching of its two disparate founders, each with his own distinctive bicultural background, each with his own experience and understanding of Buddhism. We can then move on to chart the current state of the movement and to assess the significance and success of its various activities. Although typically referred to loosely as the Trailokya Bauddha Mahasangha Sahayaka Gana (lit: "the Association of Friends of the Buddhist Order of the Three Realms") or TBMSG, we shall see that technically this movement comprises three interrelated organizations or institutions: a modern Buddhist order of both lay and monastic members known as the Trailokya Bauddha Mahasangha (TBM), a legally constituted religious organization that is the TBMSG proper, and finally the social work branch of TBMSG that secures its own separate financial support under the name Bahujan Hitay. Clarifying this tripartite structure in India is complicated, moreover, by the fact that TBMSG developed historically and institutionally as the Indian branch of the Western Buddhist Order (WBO) and the Friends of the Western Buddhist Order (FWBO) founded by Sangharakshita in the late 1960s. Although the roots of TBMSG were laid during the decade that Sangharakshita worked with the Ambedkarite Buddhists before his return to the West, the present institutional structure of TBMSG was inaugurated only in 1979, well after FWBO was established in the West. Confusing things still further is the fact that the literal meaning of TBMSG is more inclusive or universal than the "Western" orientation of the FWBO, and hence Indian members of the movement are as likely to refer to FWBO as "the western branch of TBMSG." Actually the later understanding is not inappropriate since the Indian and Western organizations are in fact ideally meant to be two branches of the same worldwide movement, even though each has its own distinctive historical roots and development, with Ambedkar playing a far less prominent role in the Western branch of the movement than that of Sangharakshita in the Indian branch. The close link between TBMSG and FWBO is all the more evident moreover in the fact that the Indian movement relies substantially on the financial support it receives through the Karuna Trust, a registered charity in Britain founded and run by members of the Western Buddhist Order. And while this funding is critical to the success of TBMSG in India, we shall also see that the relationship between the Indian movement and the Western Buddhist movement is one that goes well beyond financial support alone.

Considered as a whole, the TBMSG movement is still quite young and, by Indian standards, still relatively small. Nonetheless, the historically significant nature of its hybrid pedigree, the substance of its social welfare and Dhamma education programs, and the remarkable growth it has experienced thus far together suggest the possibility that the new Buddhists among India's 100 million "ex-Untouchables" may have found in TBMSG a singularly effective vehicle to fulfill both the social and the spiritual aspirations articulated so eloquently by the late Dr. B. R. Ambedkar and his English associate, the Ven. Sangharakshita.[7]

Imagine this scene: amidst the squalor of a Bombay slum one comes upon a small hut with a corrugated tin roof. Inside, seated on the floor in front of old-fashioned, portable sewing machines, are a group of women. While their children attend a nearby TBMSG *balwadi* or day-care center for several hours, these ex-Untouchable women are learning a skill that will add a significant new source to their families' income. At one end of the room is a simple shrine with a plaster image of the Buddha flanked by two candle holders and a vase holding a single flower. The expected congeries of popular Hindu divinities is conspicuously absent, the only additional items on the altar being two modestly framed photographs. One depicts a stern but portly, dark-skinned Indian dressed in a double-breasted Western-style suit and holding a legal tome in one hand. From the other smiles a bespectacled, middle-aged Englishman, looking very much the Edwardian country vicar except for his flowing Buddhist monastic robes. Later that day several of the women seated before this modest shrine will board a train to nearby Bhaja to attend a weekend meditation retreat, for one of them the first time she will ever have been on a train or away from her family by herself. Deceptive in its simplicity, this scene depicts a major change in the lives of these and other ex-Untouchable Indians, people who have converted to Buddhism in an effort to free themselves from the debilitating legacy of generations of social discrimination and self-deprecation. To analyze the hidden complexity of this scene we must first begin with the two key figures portrayed in the photographs on the shrine, B. R. Ambedkar on the left and Sangharakshita on the right.

Sangharakshita and the Origins of TBMSG

The prominence of the Ambedkar photograph on a TBMSG shrine may at first seem puzzling, especially since the movement was not even founded until 1979, more than twenty years after the death of the ex-Untouchable political leader. And indeed it may seem all the more puzzling since the Ambedkarite political movement had become during those same two decades increasingly ineffectual with the increasing factionalization and decline of Ambedkar's Republican Party. Nonetheless Ambedkar's posthumous role in the inception of TBMSG cannot be underestimated. Without the inspiration and example of this man, whom many new Indian Buddhists consider a modern-day bodhisattva, TBMSG quite literally could never have come into existence. TBMSG was founded, in the words of its principal organizer, as "a response to the needs, spiritual and social, of the new ex-Untouchable Buddhists in India."[8] And it was Ambedkar who conceived and initiated the mass conversion movement that created these new Buddhists, converts whose zeal to practice their new religion was often matched only by their lack of the knowledge and instruction necessary to do so. Without Ambedkar there would have been no Buddhist movement among the ex-Untouchables and hence no need or place for TBMSG, literally no audience for it to address.

Even with the powerful impetus and model provided by their revered leader, however, a growing number of Ambedkarite Buddhists had begun to feel by the 1970s that much of the promise of his vision remained unfulfilled by the political orientation that prevailed within the broad and disjointed movement. Some began to question whether any exclusively political approach could ever be effective in achieving Ambedkar's vision.[9] It was among this group of Ambedkarites that TBMSG quickly grew, among those seeking a broader and more explicitly spiritual expression of Ambedkar's socially engaged Buddhism. Ambedkar and his conception of the role Buddhism must play in the social and spiritual emancipation of the Untouchables have been treated in chapter 2 of this volume. In this chapter I explore how Sangharakshita and his followers, both Indian and Western, have sought to develop their version of the Ambedkarite vision, one that in spite of its early success has been criticized by some Ambedkarites precisely because it attempts to ground the socially radical aspects of Ambedkarite Buddhism in a broader framework of traditional Buddhist practice and doctrine.

Turning then to the second photograph on the ex-Untouchable shrine in Bombay, we must now take up the role played in the creation of TBMSG by the Ven. Sangharakshita, the Western monk born Dennis Lingwood in the Stockwell district of London in 1925.[10] In marked contrast to the challenges of Ambedkar's youth, the young Lingwood enjoyed a seemingly conventional working-class childhood in prewar England as the elder child of an antique restorer and his English-Hungarian wife. The most notable features of Lingwood's earlier years were the precocious interest he demonstrated in the arts and the two years from age 8 to 10 that he spent confined to a bed because of a misdiagnosed heart condition. Rather than being stifled by that period of enforced confinement, the young boy became a voracious reader, laying the foundation for a largely self-acquired education that went well beyond the standard fare of an English grammar school education. By the age of 15 when he was evacuated from London at the beginning of the Blitz, he had read his way through the English poets, been profoundly moved by Milton's *Paradise Lost,* and was beginning to develop a lifelong interest in philosophy as well.

On completing his schooling at the age of 15, Lingwood was already an avid poet and soon completed a novel inspired by D. H. Lawrence. He was reading widely on his own by then, having worked his way through Kant, Hegel, and Schopenhauer with explorations into Gnosticism, Rosicrucianism, and the Neo-Platonists as well. He was also developing a passionate interest in music, especially Bach and Beethoven, which he reported often left him in a state of mystical absorption.[11] Finally in 1943, as Europe sank ever deeper into the cataclysm of the Second World War, the young Lingwood was wrenched rather abruptly from his budding philosophical and artistic pursuits by two events that propelled him quite literally into a very different world, one fraught with both uncertainty and suffering. First he was conscripted to serve in the British army, and shortly thereafter his family home was totally destroyed by a V-1 rocket. The grim destruction and random chaos that characterized life during the London Blitz served, no doubt, to encourage what was already becoming the central thread in the young poet's life. As early as 1941, after reading the *Diamond Sutra,* Lingwood came to feel that he "had always been [a Buddhist],"[12] and on his return to London in 1942 he became an increasingly frequent participant at the meetings of Christmas Humphreys' Buddhist Society. At the Society's Wesak Celebration in 1944, several months after his induction into the British Army, Signalman Lingwood took the Refuges and Precepts from U Thittila, a respected, if unconventional, Burmese bhikkhu who became well-known for his unstinting humanitarian efforts as a stretcher-bearer during the Blitz.

By 1944 Lingwood was thus already definite in his commitment to Buddhism, and quite by chance the Signal Corps unit to which he was assigned was transferred to India. He served out the remainder of the war in Asia, with temporary postings in Sri Lanka and Singapore as well as India. Continuing throughout his Army days to pursue his studies in Buddhism, he gradually reached a resolution to take up the spiritual life on a full-time basis at the first possible opportunity. Although somewhat discouraged by the institutionalization of Sri Lankan Buddhism, the young English Buddhist found himself strongly drawn to the traditional Indian ideal of the wandering mendicant. When his unit was being demobilized at the end of the war he simply walked away, going AWOL in his determination to remain in India to pursue the life of a Buddhist monk. From 1946 through early 1950 the ex-signalman turned *sadhu* wandered across India seeking out both Buddhist teachers and Hindu sages, eventually receiving ordination as a novice monk in 1949 from U Chandramani, the most senior Burmese Theravadin monk in India, and subsequently the full *bhikkhu* or monk's ordination in 1950. As the newly ordained monk Sangharakshita, he undertook study with the Ven. Jagdish Kashyap, a Bihari Kayastha convert to Buddhism, who held the chair of Pali and Buddhist Studies at Banaras Hindu University. One of the most respected Buddhist monks in India, Kashyap was also one of India's foremost scholars of Buddhism. He strongly encouraged both the spiritual and scholarly aspirations of the young English monk, eventually directing him "to work for the good of Buddhism" among the Buddhist Newars of Kalimpong, the hill station on the Tibet border where Sangharakshita was to spend the next fourteen years.[13]

At the age of 25, soon after taking up residence at the local Newari Buddhist temple in Kalimpong, Sangharakshita began a variety of activities that provided the basis for the understanding of Buddhist thought and practice he was gradually to develop over the next forty years. He had already developed a strong meditation practice based in the mindfulness tradition of the *Satipatthana Sutta* and refined by his study of Buddhagosha's *Visuddhimagga* under Jagdish Kashyap. In addition to these contemplative pursuits, he also undertook a number of more outwardly directed activities, from founding a local Young men's Buddhist Association to coordinating the Kalimpong Buddha Jayanti Celebration. The years between 1950 and 1964 saw a period of considerable literary activity as well. Besides editing the *Maha Bodhi Society Journal* and his own Buddhist literary magazine

Stepping Stones, Sangharakshita wrote several books, including *The Three Jewels* and the first edition of his *Survey of Buddhism* as well as a collection of poetry. Because of Kalimpong's proximity to Tibet, moreover, the English monk also had the opportunity to befriend and work with a number of visiting European Buddhists and Buddhologists, including among others Marco Pallis, David Snellgrove, Rene de Nebesky-Wojkowitz, John Driver, Herbert Guenther, Lama Govinda, Prince Peter of Greece, and Dr. George Roerich.

The most significant aspect of Sangharakshita's fourteen-year residence in Kalimpong, however, was his encounter with Tibetan Vajrayana Buddhism, a tradition well represented in that border hill station filled with Tibetan refugees. Although ordained a Theravadin, the English bhikkhu had long felt an affinity with the spiritual heights of the Mahayana, an interest encouraged by his first teacher, the Ven. Kashyap. After several years of contact with the Vajrayana in Kalimpong, Sangharakshita received his first Vajrayana initiation in 1956 from Chetul Sangye Dorje,[14] and later received further teachings and initiations from other prominent Vajrayana masters, including Khachu Rimpoche, abbot of Pemayangse Gompa, the royal monastery of Sikkim; Dilgo Khyentse; Dudjom Rimpoche; and also his "root-guru" Jamyang Khyentse.[15] Of all his Tibetan teachers, however, his strongest bond was with Geshe Dhardo Rimpoche, a Geluktrained Nyingmapa who was abbot of the Ladakhi monastery at Bodhgaya and later of the famous Yi Ga Chöling Monastery at Ghoom not far from Kalimpong.[16] It was from Dhardo that Sangarakshita received Bodhisattva Ordination, and the connection between the two eventually became one of deep friendship as well as discipleship. When deciding to return to the West for good in order to found his new Western Buddhist Order, it was Dhardo Rinpoche's advice and blessing that Sangharakshita was most anxious to secure.

Under the guidance of these Tibetan teachers Sangharakshita's practice of the Mahayana and the Vajrayana matured in Kalimpong, but the same period of his life saw the beginnings of another significant influence, one that would link him very closely to quite a different Buddhist community, the ex-Untouchable Buddhists of Maharashtra. It was this latter connection, through the figure of Dr. B. R. Ambedkar, that was eventually to come to fruition in the "Dhamma revolution" of TBMSG.

Ambedkar and Sangharakshita

Ambedkar and Sangharakshita met in person on only three occasions, yet the influence they exerted upon each other through these meetings and through their correspondence was substantial. It was to Sangharakshita that Ambedkar first turned when he sought a Buddhist monk to confer upon him the refuges and precepts ceremony that would mark his conversion to Buddhism.[17] And it was Ambedkar that Sangharakshita credits with demonstrating for him the full substance of the social dimension of the Buddha-Dharma, an influence that is manifestly evident in the Western Buddhist Order that Sangharakshita subsequently founded, as well as in the TBMSG movement.[18] What Ambedkar saw in the newly ordained English monk Sangharakshita was an example of the "new bhikkhu" that he felt was so crucial, crucial not just to the revival of Buddhism in India but to the very survival of this ancient tradition in the modern world. Much of the contemporary bhikkhu-sangha had lost, in Ambedkar's view, the Buddha's original commitment to serve and to educate all. He argued frequently and vehemently that only monks who were willing to come out of their monasteries to teach and who recognized the Buddha's teachings on social justice in general as well as his critique of the caste system in particular were to be considered true bhikkhus. And Sangharakshita was one of the few such monks Ambedkar had encountered. According to some of his closest lieutenants, Ambedkar often expressed his high regard for the English monk, saying on various occasions that there were only two bhikkhus his followers should trust, Sangharakshita and an Indian bhikkhu who was known for his consistent denunciation of caste prejudice.[19] The respect the often fiery leader ex-Untouchables extended to Sangharakshita was initially not so easily won, however.

It was Sangharakshita who first initiated indirect contact between the two when he wrote Ambedkar in 1950, responding favorably to a number of points the latter had raised in his article on "The Buddha and the Future of his Religion" that had just been published in the journal of the Maha Bodhi Society.[20] It was not until 1952 that their paths crossed. Sangharakshita had just finished writing a monograph on Anagarika Dharmapala, commissioned by the Maha Bodhi Society, and had been invited to Bombay to act as adviser for a Buddhist film project.[21] He made an appointment to visit the ex-Untouchable leader at his home, looking forward to their first meeting in person after corresponding for more than two years. Sangharakshita reports of the meeting that, on being ushered into Ambedkar's study, he was taken by surprise when Ambedkar immediately demanded with some belligerence, "Why does your Maha Bodhi Society have a Bengali Brahmin for a president?"[22] Sangharakshita explained that he did not actually work for the Maha Bodhi Society, that he in fact had specifically decided not to join the venerable Buddhist organization precisely because he shared the concern of Ambedkar and many other Indian Buddhists that the leadership of the society was dominated by caste Hindus who were not particularly sympathetic to the plight of the ex-Untouchables.[23] Only once that common ground had been established was the relationship between Ambedkar and Sangharakshita to develop.

The second meeting took place three years later in Bombay, just at the time when Ambedkar was beginning to make plans for his public conversion to Buddhism. After explaining to Sangharakshita at some length his vision for a revival of Buddhism in India among the ex-Untouchables, he questioned the young monk quite closely about the technical details involved in becoming a Buddhist. Sangharakshita reports that he explained that formal conversion to Buddhism involved "going for refuge" to the Three Jewels—the Buddha, the Dharma, and the Sangha—and also undertaking the five basic principles or precepts of ethical behavior.[24] Later, following further discussion, Ambedkar informed the English monk that after many years of reflection he had decided to proceed with his own formal conversion to Buddhism, a step that had been long anticipated by many of his followers. He then asked if Sangharakshita would be willing to administer the refuges and precepts to him and to his fellow ex-Untouchables.[25] Sangharakshita expressed his willingness to do so but pointed out that the conversion ceremony would carry more weight in the broader Buddhist world if it were performed by the oldest and most senior monk in India who, at that time, was U Chandramani, the Burmese monk from whom Sangharakshita had received his *sramanera* ordination in 1949.[26] Apparently impressed with the English monk's advice, Ambedkar asked him for a more complete written account of his views and invited him to address an upcoming rally of 3,000 of Ambedkar's followers, an event that marked Sangharakshita's first formal involvement with the ex-Untouchable Buddhist movement.

Ambedkar and Sangharakshita remained in contact over the following year, but they were unable to meet again until a few weeks after Ambedkar's public conversion ceremony on October 14, 1956, an event Sangharakshita was unable to attend because of a prior commitment to lecture in Gangtok, Sikkim. This meeting, which took place at Ambedkar's home in Delhi, was to be their last, and Sangharakshita reports that both he and Ambedkar were very aware of the latter's failing health. Not surprisingly, the conversation on that occasion focused on Ambedkar's concerns for the future of the conversion movement he had inaugurated, and it was an encounter that left a lasting impression on the English bhikkhu, who found himself increasingly drawn to the plight of the new Ambedkarite Buddhists. Less than a month later Ambedkar was dead, though by that time some 750,000 ex-Untouchables had already accepted his call to adopt Buddhism formally through the simple but highly significant conversion ceremony of receiving the refuges and precepts along with the twenty-two special vows Ambedkar added specifically to counteract the negative effects of caste conditioning still operative among many of the new Buddhists. Millions more were to follow in the months to come.

Quite by chance Sangharakshita was visiting the ex-Untouchable Buddhist community in Nagpur when Ambedkar died. Nagpur was the center of Mahar Buddhist activity in Maharashtra and also the city Ambedkar had chosen as the site for his conversion ceremony, which had been attended by some 380,000 followers just seven weeks before. The news of Babasaheb's death thus fell especially heavy in that community, and Sangharakshita was immediately drafted to preside over a hastily convened memorial service. He addressed at least 100,000 mourners who had converged on Kasturchand Park by that evening and as many again over the next four days in a series of more than forty talks he subsequently gave in the outlying Buddhist localities of Nagpur. The message was the same in each talk: while the new Buddhists had indeed suffered a great loss, Babasaheb would live on in them—he would live on in them "to the extent to which they were faithful to the ideals for which he stood and for which he had, quite literally, sacrificed himself."[27]

The events of that week forged an even stronger link between the English bhikkhu and Ambedkar's now leaderless followers. Sangharakshita remained based in Kalimpong following the direction of his Tibetan Vajrayana teachers until his return to England in 1964, but during the seven years following Ambedkar's death he scheduled regular teaching tours in Maharashtra, often spending as much as six months of the year working with the Ambedkarite Buddhists. While it appeared that his decision in the mid-1960s to found a new Western Buddhist movement based in London might bring to an end his close relationship with the ex-Untouchable Buddhists of India, the actual outcome proved to be even more surprising, for in 1978 Dh. Lokamitra, one of the senior members of Sangharakshita's ten-year-old Western Buddhist Order, decided that he would take up the work Sangharakshita had left behind in India, a decision that soon led to the creation of TBMSG. Before tracing that next phase of the story, however, we should look more closely at Sangharakshita's distinctive understanding of the Buddhist tradition, at the teaching that he brought from India to shape his fledgling Western Buddhist Order and that those order members subsequently reintroduced into India as TBMSG, the Trailokya Bauddha Mahasangha Sahayaka Gana.

Sangharakshita's Neo-traditional Buddhism

Both Sangharakshita and Ambedkar were keen scholars of early Buddhism, each using his historical research to help shape and justify his respective visions of what Buddhism in the modern world might become.

It is evident from the preceding discussion of their interaction that their relationship was significant for both, each having had a formative influence on the other's subsequent conception of the Dhamma Revolution. We must thus be all the more careful to recognize the distinctive features of Sangharakshita's understanding of Buddhism. The structures and ideals of TBMSG reflect much that is specific to Sangharakshita's vision of Buddhism, even as the movement seeks also to identify itself as part of the broader Ambedkarite legacy. As converts to Buddhism, both Ambedkar and Sangharakshita felt the need for a new formulation of the Buddhist tradition, one that would address specifically modern needs. Yet each of these two "new Buddhist" leaders sought to ground his respective vision in a historical reconstruction of early Buddhism. This "neo-traditionalist" approach is especially rich and variegated in the Buddhism of Sangharakshita, who has spent the decades since Ambedkar's death elaborating a Buddhist vision that intentionally draws on all the various historical and cultural expressions of Buddhism, while tying itself to no single Buddhist school or tradition exclusively.[28]

Although ordained in the Theravada tradition, Sangharakshita is quick to acknowledge that he has been most profoundly influenced by his Tibetan teachers, Dhardo Rimpoche in particular. But it would be misleading nonetheless to present him simply as a Theravadin with Mahayana and Vajrayana sympathies. While attracting some notoriety because of his criticisms of the institutional indolence and intolerance of the Theravada establishment, Sangharakshita is also quite prepared to criticize the *triyana* inclusivism of Vajrayana because of its often explicit assertion that each subsequent historical and doctrinal phase of Buddhism superseded the previous—with Mahayana thus being both richer and more "complete" than Hinayana, and Vajrayana in turn surpassing the Mahayana. Respecting the value of each of these phases of Buddhism, Sangharakshita prefers to advocate, like Ambedkar, a new or contemporary expression of Buddhism, seeing Hinayana, Mahayana (including its East Asian forms) and Vajrayana as complete and valid expressions of Buddhism, each addressing the particular needs and problems of its respective time and culture. Central to his vision is the notion of an essential or universal Buddhist teaching, a core of principal doctrines underlying all the varied expressions of Buddhism. The job of the modern Buddhist, in Sangharakshita's view, is thus to find a distinctly contemporary expression of these core teachings, and undertaking that requires a deep respect for, though not subservience to, the various cultural traditions that survive in Buddhist Asia. Lest this depiction of his views begin to sound too "Protestant" however, we must also recognize the emphasis this English monastic places on the place of ritual and spiritual hierarchy, as well as his strong advocacy of the traditional Buddhist ideal of celibate *brahmacharya* as the culmination of the spiritual life. While a Weberian would undoubtedly see much of the "prophetic" leader in Sangharakshita, the distinctive mix of neo-traditionalist elements in his encyclopedic conception of Buddhism has more the spirit of an Aquinas than a Luther—or, to put it in a more appropriate historical context, more the spirit of a Chih-i or a Tsong-khapa than of a Nichiren or even a Shinran.[29]

Central to Sangharakshita's formulation of Buddhism and to the TBMSG program to fulfill Ambedkar's vision is the notion of a Buddhist Order that is, strictly speaking, neither lay nor monastic. It is important to stress this is *not* a critique of monasticism per se but only of the notion that the central Buddhist act is the taking of monastic vows. Without reference to the complete picture of Sangharakshita's vision of the Buddhist path, it is easy to misunderstand his effort to distinguish ordination from the taking of monastic vows as an expression of Western Protestantism in Buddhist guise. In fact, however, Sangharakshita remains quite traditional in his view that cenobitic monasticism is the most ideal and effective mode of spiritual life. Indeed, after giving up his own robes for a more worldly lifestyle during the 1970s, he subsequently returned to monastic life, even reaffirming his vow of celibacy and encouraging the more spiritually mature of his followers to do likewise. What Sangharakshita does seek to criticize is the tendency in many contemporary Asian Buddhist traditions to see monastic ordination as the act by which one becomes a truly committed Buddhist, as the watershed that separates the serious Buddhist practitioner from the simple lay supporter. In his view what constitutes the Buddhist's fundamental commitment to the tradition is the act of going for refuge to the Three Jewels—the Buddha, the Dharma, and the Sangha—and it is this act, when it becomes *effectively* expressed, that is marked by ordination into the Western Buddhist Order or its more recently founded Indian counterpart, the TBM.[30] Whether or not the order member then (or subsequently) decides to adopt also a more monastic lifestyle, including vows of celibacy or any of the other rules of the traditional Pratimoksa monastic code is a secondary consideration, one to be considered in the light of individual circumstances, including existing family responsibilities, and so on. One's basic commitment to the Buddhist path of growth and development—evidenced by effectively, not just formally, "going for refuge"—is thus seen to be the Buddhist act of primary importance, whereas the particular lifestyle in which one chooses to express that commitment remains a secondary consideration. Secondary though it is, however, this is not to mean that lifestyle is unimportant or insignificant, for ultimately the ideal spiritual life (or "lifestyle") is still seen to be one free of the cares and responsibilities of the householder's life.

The point is thus not to do away with monasticism, but to locate the focus of ordination within the ordinand's commitment to the spiritual life rather than in his or her compliance with a particular set of monastic strictures. But a simple formal recitation of the Three Refuges does not itself constitute commitment in Sangharakshita's view; rather "effective going for refuge" occurs only when the aspiring Buddhist has reoriented every aspect of his life to reflect and express, both inwardly and outwardly, that commitment to the spiritual life, in particular, the cultivation of morality, meditation, and wisdom, to use the traditional *trishiksha* formula. Thus it is quite possible to be "effectively going for refuge" and to be ordained into the WBO or TBM while still living in a family situation, for example. Just as it is, in Sangharakshita's view, quite possible to be living as a monk or a nun without yet have having reached the point of *effective* going for refuge. Indeed, it typically takes from five to ten years to become a member of the Western Buddhist Order, whereas one can become a monk in many Buddhist traditions in a year or even less, in some cases without any preliminary training or subsequent supervision.

This central focus on "going for refuge" and of a Buddhist Order that is neither lay nor monastic is indeed a radical departure from the primacy of the lay-monastic distinction so characteristic of modern Asian Buddhism. Yet it is a departure that Sangharakshita sees as "radical" in the literal sense of the word, asserting that this view of ordination is much closer to the spirit of the earliest community of followers that grew up around the Buddha. Hence his choice of the ancient, but nontechnical Buddhist term *dharmachari* (fem.: *dharmacharini*)—lit.: "dharma-farer"—to designate the members of his order, a choice that seeks to avoid the dichotomy implicit in the more conventional designations of *upasaka* (lay-Buddhist) versus *bhikshu* (monk).[31]

The other salient features of Sangharakshita's Buddhism follow for the most part from this central theme of effectively "going for refuge." For all members of the movement, whether ordained or not, great importance is placed on exploring within one's immediate life effective applications of ethical conduct, of meditative practice, and of dharma study. Within that framework, meditative practice draws initially on the *samatha* techniques of mindfulness of breathing and the cultivation of loving kindness and subsequently on various *vipassana* techniques and Vajrayana visualization practices. Communal devotional ritual (*puja*) also plays an especially prominent role in FWBO/TBMSG Buddhism, with the primary ritual form being the sevenfold puja derived from the Shantideva's *Bodhicharyavatara,* a typical liturgical format common to many traditional Mahayana and Vajrayana *sadhanas.* This emphasis in Sangharakshita's teaching on communal as well as individual practice highlights another distinctive point of emphasis: the importance he places on the traditional Buddhist doctrine of spiritual friendship (*kalyana-mitrata*). One sees this in the ritualized respect and appreciation expressed to the lineage of teachers reaching back to the Buddha and also in the importance given to the cultivation of peer friendship as well—not just ordinary, mundane friendship but friendship based on mutual exploration of the shared commitment to the Three Jewels. Undertaking friendship of this sort as a significant part of one's practice is, in fact, deemed an indispensable part of the path within the FWBO/TBMSG.

Ethical conduct or morality is seen not only as a personal or individual endeavor but also, by extension, as a call to move toward community-based "right livelihood ventures," small businesses and co-ops that will provide a spiritually conducive daily environment as well as an ethically appropriate means of material support. Dharma study too is seen both as a crucial part of one's individual path as well as a valuable opportunity for enhancing communal ties. FWBO/TBMSG study courses and retreats draw on the Buddhist classics of the Pali Canon as well as later Mahayana and Vajrayana works, again always with the attempt to recognize the basic Buddhist principles that underlie the doctrinal and cultural variations of the different traditions.

Creation of the TBMSG—A New Buddhist Movement

While Sangharakshita's understanding of Buddhism as well as his commitment to help the ex-Untouchable Ambedkarite Buddhists played a crucial role in the creation of TBMSG, he himself was only indirectly involved in its initial inception. In fact, TBMSG was inaugurated only in 1979, some fifteen years after Sangharakshita had left India to return to Britain, initially to serve temporarily as the spiritual director of the Hampstead Buddhist Vihara and eventually to found his own Buddhist organization, the FWBO. The seed engendered through the contact between Ambedkar and Sangharakshita thus did not germinate until many years after the former's death and the latter's departure from India. For it to sprout and to thrive the nurturing efforts of a skilled gardener were needed, and this third key figure in our story, Dharmachari Lokamitra, arrived on the scene in Maharashtra in 1977. The son of a prominent English anthropologist, Lokamitra was born Jeremy Goody in 1947. After a student trip to India in the late 1960s. Goody had become a follower of Sangharakshita in 1972 and an ordained member of the Western Buddhist Order in 1974.[32] Having given up his career as a secondary school teacher in 1973, he went to work full-time for Sangharakshita's budding FWBO movement. In 1977, having taken additional monastic vows subsequent to his WBO ordination and donning the saffron robes of a bhikkhu, he took a leave of absence from his work within the Order to attend an Iyengar Yoga course in Pune, India.

Traveling across India, he arrived in Nagpur, quite by chance, on the day of the twenty–first anniversary of Ambedkar's conversion. Immediately drafted by some of Sangharakshita's ex-Untouchable friends to join the speakers at a memorial service, he soon found himself addressing a half-million new Buddhists who had converged at the *diksha-bhumi* site. That experience and the enthusiasm for Buddhism that Lokamitra experienced among the ex-Untouchables over the next few days had a profound effect, he reports, leading rapidly to his decision to commit his life to Dharma work among the Ambedkarites.[33] Within a matter of months after arriving back in England he had settled his affairs there, and he soon returned to India to begin working with the ex-Untouchable Buddhists. TBMSG was officially inaugurated a few months later by Sangharakshita on a visit to India that also included the ordination of several of his earlier Indian followers into the Trailokya Bauddha Mahasangha (TBM), the new Indian wing of the WBO. Although Lokamitra began his work as a saffron-robed *anagarika,* after his first several years as a TBMSG organizer he found the monastic persona increasingly limiting, both socially and administratively. This led him to give up his monastic vows and eventually to marry into the ex-Untouchable community, a change of status he found personally as well as culturally more appropriate since most of the new Indian order members were also married householders.

Throughout the 1980s other Western-born members also played vital roles in the early growth of TBMSG, especially the physician-nurse team of Dh. Virabhadra (Dr. William Stones) and Dh. Padmashuri (Hilary Blakiston), who established the first Bahujan Hitay public health project in Pune.[34] Visa and immigration restrictions have severely limited the activity of Western-born order members in India, especially in recent years, and the only on-going English presence in the organization over the years has been Lokamitra's substantial contribution. As the Indian wing of the Order has grown, however, the need for outside help has decreased to the point that the administration of both TBMSG and Bahujan Hitay is now almost entirely in the hands of ex-Untouchable order members, with Lokamitra serving in an advisory capacity as president of TBMSG and as the field representative of Karuna Trust, the United Kingdom's registered charity that provides much of TBMSG's outside funding. Given the esteem with which he is held by TBMSG Buddhists, Lokamitra's influence, even in his current, technically limited capacity, is not to be underestimated, of course. Still, his very success in developing strong indigenous leadership within TBMSG will likely turn out to be an even greater achievement than his initial efforts in organizing the movement.

In introducing the three key figures who have played a role in shaping this Dhamma Revolution in modern India—B. R. Ambedkar, Ven. Sangharakshita, and Dh. Lokamitra—I have indicated in the following table that it now encompasses a complex movement comprising several interrelated parts: TBMSG (Trailokya Bauddha Mahasangha Sahayaka Gana), denoting the Indian organization proper; Bahujan Hitay, its social work branch; TBM (Trailokya Bauddha Mahasangha), the Indian wing of Sangharakshita's new Buddhist order; and Karuna Trust, the Oxford-based foundation funding much of the work. As one can see, the movement in India has a two-level structure mirroring that of the WBO and FWBO that Sangharakshita founded in the West. While this link between TBMSG and FWBO is quite significant, as we shall see, there is also a widely expressed concern that the Indian wing of the movement should be organizationally as independent and self-sufficient as possible. To consider how these complex interrelations work in practice we must turn now to consider each facet of the Indian movement in more detail.

The Trailokya Bauddha Mahasangha—A New Order of New Buddhists

The leadership of TBMSG's Dhamma Revolution is based in the new Buddhist order founded by Sangharakshita. Known in India as the Trailokya Bauddha Mahasangha (TBM), the order itself is, however, not formally or legally an organization. A key feature of Sangharakshita's understanding of Buddhism is that the spiritual community of ordained individuals, as an entity, be kept quite distinct from organizations in which those individual order members pursue their Dharma work. Looking to the radically decentralized character of the original community of ordained followers of the Buddha, the TBM sees itself as a voluntary fellowship of individuals sharing the same spiritual commitment without need of a formal ecclesiastical structure. And, following Sangharakshita's principle discussed earlier of linking ordination to effective "going for refuge," TBM is not a monastic order. Like their Western counterparts in the WBO, some Indian order members of TBM are householders while others are not. What they share is a full-time commitment to work on behalf of the Dhamma Revolution as effectively as their circumstances allow.

Both Ambedkar and Sangharakshita are well known for their frequent criticism of the current state of Buddhist monasticism in Asia, Ambedkar noting the bhikkhu-sangha's frequent lack of concern for the social and material needs of the lay community, and Sangharakshita focusing more on the traditional tendency to exclude lay Buddhists from any serious pursuit of Buddhist practice beyond merit-making through their support of the monks. However, neither Ambedkar nor Sangharakshita ever advocated an abolition of monastic Buddhism. Sangharakshita, living himself as a celibate monk, is adamant in fact that Buddhism cannot survive either in the

Organizations Founded by Ambedkar and Sangharakshita

Dr. B. R. Ambedkar (1891–1956), affectionately known as Babasaheb

- **Bahishkrit Hitakarini Sabha** (Organization for the Welfare of the Excluded), 1924
- **Independent Labour Party**, 1936 → **Scheduled Caste Federation**, 1942 → **Republican Party**, 1957
- **People's Education Society**, 1945: Siddharth College in Bombay, 1946, Milind College in Aurangabad, 1950
- **Bharatiya Bauddha Mahasabha** (Buddhist Society of India), 1955

Trailokya Bauddha Mahasangha (TBM)
Indian Wing of the Buddhist order founded by Sangharakshita

- **Trailokya Bauddha Mahasangha Sahayaka Gana** (TBMSG):
  Dharma Work Branch of Indian Wing; 1979
- **Bahujan Hitay** ("For the Welfare of the Many"):
  Social Work Branch of Indian Wing; 1979

Ven. Sangharakshita (1926–   ), born Dennis Lingwood in London

Western Buddhist Order (WBO)
Western Wing the Buddhist order founded by Sangharakshita

- **Friends of the Western Buddhist Order** (FWBO):
  Dharma Work Branch of Western Wing, 1968
- **Aid for India**, 1980 & **Karuna Trust**, 1987 (AFI & KT)
  Charitable Trust and Foundation to support Social Work and Dharma Work projects in India & the West

East or the West without a strong monastic branch. Both have argued, nonetheless, that the traditional emphasis on monastic ordination is fraught with dangers, having obscured and distorted the Buddha's historical ministry to lay Buddhists, many of whom in the Buddha's day were active practitioners as well as donors, a number even gaining the fruit of liberation (*arhattva*) as householders, according to the canonical discourses. Both Ambedkar and Sangharakshita felt that modern Buddhism must reassert the centrality of commitment to going for refuge to the Three Jewels. It was this commitment that must be primary they agreed, and in their view it is thus a commitment to be made by all Buddhists, whatever their subsequent choice of a lay or monastic lifestyle. For all his criticism of monastic indifference and arrogance with regard to the plight of ex-Untouchable Buddhists, Ambedkar nonetheless recognized the role that committed, full-time Buddhists could play, proclaiming eloquently in 1950 the need for a "new kind of bhikkhu."[35]

For Ambedkar, the single most important Buddhist act for an ex-Untouchable was conversion (*diksha*), the act of formally renouncing one's outcast status within Hinduism by going for refuge to the Buddha, Dhamma, and Sangha and by undertaking the five moral precepts of the traditional five *pansil* along with Ambedkar's own list of twenty-two additional vows. As we have already seen, Sangharakshita too saw the active decision to go for refuge as the central Buddhist act, but he went a step further to distinguish between what he calls "provisional" and "effective" going for refuge. Any sincere affirmation of the Refuges and Precepts, as in the Ambedkarite conversion ceremony, marks the first or "provisional" stage of going for refuge, of truly being a Buddhist. But the conversion, in Sangharakshita's view, is only the beginning, only a preliminary commitment, still to be made "effective" through one's actual actions in transforming both one's self and one's society. For Sangharakshita ordination then—whether in the WBO or TBM—signifies an individual's transition from provisional to effective going for refuge, the development of a commitment evidenced in one's spiritual practice as well as one's social activism. Whether the WBO/TBM order member chooses to express his or her "effective going for refuge" as a lay person or as an *anagarika* (lit.: "homeless one") in robes then becomes a secondary decision, one that takes into account the practical advantages of monastic freedom from mundane responsibilities, but also the fact that many new Buddhists may not be inclined immediately to give up existing familial responsibilities. The crucial point here is that the monastic lifestyle is neither a prerequisite for or even a guarantee of, "effective" going for refuge, although its spiritual value is readily recognized. As we saw previously, this notion of a Buddhist order that is thus neither lay nor monastic is a distinctive characteristic of Sangharakshita's understanding of the Dhamma. While the terminology and distinctions are unique to his teaching, they present a conception of Buddhist ordination that many new Buddhists have found to be very much in the spirit of Ambedkar's own teaching, a notion that many feel comes the closest yet to Babasaheb's call for a "new kind of bhikkhu."

The TBM is currently made up of over 150 order members, virtually all former ex-Untouchables who were active in other Ambedkarite groups before coming in contact with TBMSG.[36] For most TBM order members ordination has meant remaining within their extended families and maintaining some "householder" responsibilities, though many have arranged their lives to work full-time for the movement—a number having given up more lucrative and secure secular positions as teachers, engineers, or government bureaucrats. A small but significantly growing number have taken the additional step of adopting a formally monastic lifestyle donning the robes of a celibate *anagarika* who has gone forth from conventional worldly life. The anagarikas are not recognized as full monastics by the Buddhist establishment outside of TBMSG, not having been duly ordained as bhikkhus by a forum of other bhikkhus, but within TBM this is seen more as an asset than a limitation. Indeed, most TBM order members are quite happy to remain "robe-less" altogether and thus freer to interact in a less formal way with their fellow ex-Untouchable Buddhists. It is ironic, actually, that although not technically enjoying the full status of the bhikkhus within the broader international Buddhist community, the TBM Dhammacharis and Dhammacharinis are generally recognized within the ex-Untouchable community to be both better trained and more committed than many of their monastic counterparts in bhikkhu robes, a fact hardly surprising given that it takes significantly more time and effort, more actual study and practice of the Dhamma, to become an TBM order member than it does to become a bhikkhu. But how is the aspiring order member to gain that training and experience, especially if, as most, he or she comes from the poorest and most downtrodden segments of Indian society? And, once commitment to the Dhamma Revolution has been made and eventually ordination received, what is it that the TBM order members actually do to express their new Buddhist identity? To answer those questions we must consider two other aspects of the movement, TBMSG and Bahujan Hitay.

Dhamma Work: The Spiritual Dimension

The Trailokya Bauddha Mahasangha Sahayaka Gana, or TBMSG proper, is the organization that supports the Dhamma work of the movement. It is the administrative entity that constitutes the movement legally, holding title to the various facilities. Its membership comprises members of the Order (TBM), Dhammamitras (lit. "Dhamma-friends") and Dhammasahayaks (lit. "Dhamma, helpers"). Actually there is no formal membership requirements for TBMSG—one simply takes part in TBMSG activities as much or as little as one chooses. To become a Dhammamitra one undertakes to become more seriously involved with the movement, but one is quite free to remain a Dhammasahayak with no formal responsibilities or obligations for as long as one wishes. TBMSG seeks primarily to address the needs of ex-Untouchables who have already become Buddhists, and in that sense its mission is not so much to convert ex-Untouchables to Buddhism, but rather more to assist those who are seeking some way to fulfill their already expressed aspiration to follow Babasaheb Ambedkar into Buddhism. When requested, TBMSG will and often does organize conversion ceremonies, but at present it sees a greater need in assisting those who have already converted to Buddhism. Although quite sincere in their aspiration to follow Ambedkar's example, most of the ex-Untouchable Buddhists have found few opportunities for serious Buddhist education or practice. How are these new Buddhists to be helped then? One TBMSG publication from the late 1980s states that the movement seeks to enable ex-Untouchable Buddhists to learn "how, through the practice of the Dhamma, they can transform themselves and can work with others to transform society.[37] This dual transformative focus lies at the heart of TBMSG's conception of the Dhamma Revolution.

Transformation of the self and of society requires education in the Dhamma, the teachings of the Buddha, and also the opportunities and facilities necessary to put those teachings into practice. TBMSG, as an organization, seeks to do this in three primary ways: through Dhamma courses and lectures, through retreats offering an opportunity for periods of more intensive Buddhist practice, and through the creation of residential communities where order members and friends may together pursue their mutual commitment to realizing the Buddhist ideal of a Dhammic life. These three spheres of activity are, of course, closely interrelated yet they have led to the establishment of three different types of specialized facilities within the movement: public centers, retreat centers, and residential community houses. Other types of facilities have also been created to address the social welfare mission of the movement, but they will be presented later in the discussion of Bahujan Hitay.

The first and most immediately visible of the various TBMSG facilities are the public centers.[38] While they also serve as the local administrative offices of TBMSG, the primary function of these centers is to offer Dhamma instruction in the form of regular lectures and classes. With the exception of the recently completed Mahavihara in Dapodi most of these centers are quite modest in scale, little more than a one- or two-room hut, yet often the only local focus for Buddhist activities and hence likely to be in continual use throughout the day and evening. Several of these buildings have been donated to TBMSG by the local Buddhist community, often having previously served as the local *vihar* or Buddhist temple without any program of activities because of lack of staffing. TBMSG centers are typically run by teams of order members working and often living together in residential communities, although in some cases there may be only one order member resident in the community on a full-time basis.

Newcomers to TBMSG's activities will typically first encounter the movement at a lecture organized by one of the centers. Public lectures on any topic are a highly popular form of outdoor evening entertainment in India, with such publicly advertised lectures on Buddhism easily drawing an audience of hundreds or even thousands in any area with a large ex-Untouchable community. Popular veneration, indeed devotion for Babasaheb Ambedkar still runs very high in these communities, even thirty-five years after his death, and dhamma talks among the new Buddhists thus always begin with an evocation of his legacy. A TBMSG speaker will typically remind the audience how important Ambedkar considered Buddhist practice to be in his program for the moral and social liberation of the Untouchables. They will be reminded that he insisted that his followers be Buddhists not just in name alone, that they be "100 percent Buddhists," in a very frequently cited phrase. This, the audience is told, means that it is not enough simply to have taken the Diksha ceremony of conversion, that they must now strive actually to live as Buddhists by following the precepts, studying the Dhamma, and undertaking a regular practice of meditation. At the conclusion of these talks those interested in following the injunctions of the speaker will be invited to join the classes offered at the nearest TBMSG center.

TBMSG centers offer intensive classes in the principles of the Dhamma as interpreted by both Ambedkar and Sangharakshita, as well as in the practice of meditation. The demand for these classes often exceeds the capacity of the center's facilities, overflowing into various outdoor venues. Because there have been so few Bhikkhus with either the training or the motivation to work within the ex-Untouchable communities, TBMSG classes are often the first opportunity many new Buddhists have had to explore seriously the tradition they may have originally adopted a quarter of a century ago or more. Dhamma study in TBMSG focuses on the application of the teachings in the daily life of those participating, often seeking to find ways in the Dhamma to deal with specific social issues such as domestic violence and alcohol abuse, as well as the broader problems of poverty, lack of self-esteem and confidence, and the difficulties encountered in taking advantage of educational and employment opportunities now guaranteed by law.

Meditation, though typically not considered a lay practice by many contemporary Asian Buddhists, is an important part of the TBMSG program. In the first classes they attend, all newcomers to the movement are introduced to two basic and traditional Buddhist meditation techniques: mindfulness of breathing (*anapana-sati*) and the cultivation of loving kindness (*metta-bhavana*) All "Friends" of the movement are encouraged to establish a regular daily meditation practice, even though this can be extremely difficult given the very crowded conditions typical of ex-Untouchable life in the urban hutments. To help counteract these difficulties, the various TBMSG centers offer regularly scheduled meditation retreats, often held beneath a rented canopy in a temporarily donated field with the participants sleeping out under whatever blankets they manage to bring along. The need for more consistent opportunities for longer-term meditation practice has led to the creation of the second major type of TBMSG facility, the rural meditation retreat centers. Two such facilities have already been built by TBMSG, the first between Bombay and Poona and another in eastern Maharashtra. Opened in 1983, the Saddharma Pradeep Retreat Center is situated on the forested slopes of a lovely valley just below the ancient Buddhist cave-monastery site at Bhaja. Although still limited in scale, it runs a continual program of one- to fourteen-day retreats with accommodations for 150 people that are sometimes stretched to include as many as 450 through the use of *pandal* tents. Much-needed additional retreat space recently became available at the Hsüan-tsang Retreat Center at Bor Dharan, twenty-five miles from Wardha. Newly opened in 1992 and funded largely with contributions from Taiwanese Buddhist supporters of TBMSG, this facility will house 350 retreatants when the final phase of construction is complete.

Costs for attending these retreats are kept to a bare minimum—only a couple of rupees a day—but even so, many of the poorest new Buddhists can attend only with financial support, many never before having even been able to travel any distance from their homes. It is especially significant that women in large numbers take part in these retreats, a circumstance only possible because of special provisions, including the exclusion of men, that are made to reassure anxious relatives and to minimize the breach of conventional social expectations a married woman commits in leaving her family even for as little as a single day. Terry Pilchick reports that some women attend TBMSG retreats knowing that on their return home they will be berated and even beaten by their husbands or in-laws.[39]

Finally there is a third type of TBMSG facility, the residential communities, which are more numerous but less visible than the public centers and retreat centers. The communities vary considerably both in size and in function, though all serve primarily as a residence for order members as well as interested Dhammamitras and Dhammasahayaks.[40] The function of these communities is not simply practical, however, since they also are meant to be workshops for the development of spiritual friendship and community, one of the central features of Sangharakshita's understanding of Buddhism. The Sangha of committed Buddhists is, in his view, to be an actual community of individuals striving through their various forms of practice to live more harmoniously together. Order members also feel that by living and working together they are responding to a problem Ambedkar saw in contemporary Buddhism, the need for a sangha that would truly lead and serve the people, a sangha that "would live up to the Buddhist ideal embodied in the principles of Buddhism and serve as a model to the laymen."[41] The residential communities are thus a vital part of the institutional structure of TBMSG, and it is in these communities that many prospective TBM order members receive a crucial part of their training and socialization into the order. Several of the communities, especially those most important in training prospective order members, are also directly associated with one of the boys' or girls' hostels run by the social work wing of the movement to which we now turn.

Bahujan Hitay: The Social Dimension

Ambedkar was adamant that Buddhist liberation was emancipation from material as well as spiritual suffering, that the latter could be truly pursued only after the former was sufficiently secure. Although Ambedkar was influenced by key aspects of his Western education—Anglo-American liberalism, in particular—we should not overlook the many traditional Buddhist sources for this view, well-known Buddhist stories exemplifying the social concerns of Shakyamuni Buddha as well as historically prominent later Buddhists like the Emperor Ashoka and the great philosopher Nagarjuna.[42] Although concern for the welfare of others is typically presented as a special concern of the Mahayana, the earlier Buddhist texts contain numerous references to the practical nature of the Buddha's compassion. In one well-known story associated with the popular *Dhammapada*, for example, the Buddha was about to deliver a Dhamma talk at the village of *Alavi* when a poor laborer arrived late. Sensing that the man had not eaten all day in order to attend the meeting, the Buddha insisted that he be fed before the Dhamma talk proceeded. When the monks later complained about the Buddha's unseemly concern for food, the Buddha used the occasion to point out that no one suffering from hunger could comprehend the Dhamma he taught, adding that "hunger is the greatest of afflictions."[43]

Given the prominence of its Ambedkarite roots it is not surprising to find this concern for the social dimension of the Dhamma well developed in TBMSG. Within a year of its inception TBMSG had begun the Pune Project, an ambitious four-stage plan to develop a community resource center, a full-time medical team, a school hostel, and eventually a local school in the ex-Untouchable slum community in the Dapodi suburb of Pune. This plan, with its emphasis on the long-term benefits of preventative medicine and increased educational opportunities has provided a model for the movement's subsequent social welfare activities in other communities. As the work expanded, a separate registered trust, Bahujan Hitay, was established to take advantage of the charity provisions of the Indian Tax Law. An allusion to the Buddha's frequent exhortation to his monks to work "for the welfare of the many," Bahujan Hitay was thus an appropriate appellation for this aspect of the movement's work. Although TBMSG sees social welfare work as essential to and ultimately inseparable from its Dhamma education activities, care has been taken to ensure that the social programs are open to all community residents, whether they be Buddhist, Hindu, Moslem, or Christian. Although the distinction between social and religious work becomes somewhat arbitrary at times, it has also allowed donors, both in Asia and the West, to specify a preference if they choose to support one set of programs over the other. Western supporters have tended to favor the social programs, while Asian donors typically favor the Dhamma programs.

At the end of 1992 Bahujan Hitay's main projects included forty-two *balwadis* (kindergartens) serving more than 1,200 children, and fifteen residential school hostels serving some 600 primary and secondary pupils, with a number of new, often purpose-built facilities due to open in the coming year. Those basic educational programs are supplemented by non-residential study classes serving 280 students, women's literacy classes serving 190 adults, vocational classes serving 125 adults, and by a health-care outreach program serving a community of 7,000 slum dwellers with local health-workers and a centralized outpatient clinic. Additional, less formally structured programs include a mobile library as well as variety of sports and cultural programs in various localities.

Recently inaugurated projects also have begun to expand beyond the basic focus on health and education, adding more adult-oriented programs as well as a number of right livelihood cooperative ventures. The Nagpur Stationery and Book Store, a joint TBMSG-Oxfam funded project, opened in July 1990 with a long-term plan to develop a book-binding business to provide low-cost recycled college textbooks for poor students. The Wardha Women's Cooperative runs several small-scale business enterprises in that city, including a shop selling basic staples that is located in the local Bahujan Hitay hostel. These vocational programs, especially those moving toward greater economic independence, have been slow to develop. The ex-Untouchables were traditionally unskilled agricultural laborers, and those who have moved to the urban slums more recently are typically employed as unskilled construction or factory workers at very low wages. After generations of social and economic oppression, it will take a substantial effort to develop the skills and the confidence necessary to run a business. One especially promising step in that direction is a joint venture between Windhorse Trading, a very successful FWBO wholesale import business in the United Kingdom, and the Ajanta Handicrafts Co-op. Windhorse, which retails to over 1,000 gift shops across Britain, has recently undertaken to provide Ajanta Handicrafts with the administrative training necessary for the women co-op members to successfully market their products abroad. While still at a relatively experimental stage, this project will be a proving ground for exploring new routes to economic independence. It is also a remarkable example of direct cooperative interaction between Western and Indian Buddhists, economic cooperation that is seen by both sides as an integral aspect of their practice of the Dhamma.

These efforts toward developing new sources of livelihood and self-reliance within the ex-Untouchable community are extremely significant. In 1972, J. Michael Mahar concluded a volume of articles on the ex-Untouchables with the observation that the Ambedkarite Buddhist conversion movement might turn out to be a self-limiting interim measure rather than an ultimate solution to the plight of the Untouchables, due, he argued, to "the separateness fostered by the new identity and the regional basis" of the movement. In his view, the characteristic focus of the Ambedkarite Buddhist movement on education—on the creation of schools and hostels—may ultimately fail to address the underlying problem of economic improvement, an especially pressing concern for the landless agricultural laborers who are most vulnerable to the pressures of population growth. Describing the pre-TBMSG Ambedkarite movement he points out that, "[w]hile adult education classes and community libraries have also been established as part of the Buddhist movement, there is little evidence that this organizational base has been used to create credit cooperatives, labor unions, or similar organizations for the fostering of Untouchable economic interests."[44]

Mahar makes two crucial points here, both with some bearing on the more recent developments within the TBMSG movement. First, he rightly notes the inherent limitations of a policy too narrowly focused on education and not on the creation of new economic opportunities; and second, he underscores the fact that it is much more difficult to bring the benefits of Ambedkar's revolution to Untouchables still living as landless laborers in the villages. And it is still in the villages that the vast majority of the Untouchables live. To date the Dharma work of TBMSG and the social work of Bahujan Hitay have been primarily, although not exclusively, focused on the urban slums, which offer a much greater concentration of ex-Untouchables than the dispersed villages, most of which will typically have only two or three ex-Untouchable families banished to the least desirable outskirts. TBMSG, in particular, does have regular outreach programs providing Dharma talks to many village areas in Maharashtra, and it hopes to do more in the future. Meeting that objective, however, will first require many, many more TBM order members than the 150 or so who have been ordained to date.

Some critics of the TBMSG and Bahujan Hitay have suggested that the Dhamma Revolution should focus its efforts more exclusively at the village level, on the assumption that it would be better to actively encourage the ex-Untouchables to remain rooted in their ancestral villages rather than migrating to the already over-populated slums of the cities. The model sometimes suggested is that of Thich Nhat Hanh's work in the villages of Vietnam, but the analogy is seriously flawed in that it overlooks a significant difference between the rural ex-Untouchables in India and village Buddhists in Southeast Asia. The latter are undoubtedly better off staying within the supportive context of their traditional culture. But the opposite is often true for the ex-Untouchables of India, who are striving to escape a discrimination and oppression that has its strongest roots precisely in the traditional village culture. For outcastes religiously prohibited from owning their own land village life offers little more than indentured bondage. That the worst hutments of Bombay, with even their minimal opportunities for paid labor and for education, nonetheless look relatively attractive to many of the new Buddhists gives some measure of just how bad village life for ex-Untouchables can be. Far from glamorizing life in the urban slums, the programs of Bahujan Hitay and of TBMSG simply recognize that for most ex-Untouchables the first step out of caste subjugation must be a step away from the traditional locus of the oppression—in other words, a step away from traditional village life.

Financing the Dhamma Revolution

When Dh. Lokamitra first began planning how to develop TBMSG two things were very clear. For the movement to grow effectively, project funding would have to be found outside the economically destitute ex-Untouchable community, whereas staffing, on the other hand, would need to come from among the indigenous new Buddhists themselves, both because they needed the confidence that would come from administering their own projects and because the number of Westerners and other Asian Buddhists willing to make a long-term commitment to living in the poverty-stricken hutments would be quite limited in any case. Significant progress has been made on both fronts. We have seen already that although a number of Western Buddhists did provide substantial assistance in the early days of TBMSG, the administration of all TBMSG activities is now in the hands of Indian order members. We shall now turn to consider how the movement has been financed, yet another aspect of our story that illustrates the crucial link between TBMSG and Sangharakshita's Friends of the Western Buddhist Order (FWBO) movement in Britain, Europe, the Antipodes, and the United States.

While a number of Lokamitra's Buddhist friends in England were ready to provide him with personal support when he decided to return and work full-time in India, the scale of Dhamma and social welfare work he envisioned would require much more substantial sources of funding. Within a year FWBO supporters in the United Kingdom had established "Aid for India" (AFI), a registered charitable trust that quickly developed an innovative program for soliciting funds from the general public as well as from other Western Buddhist organizations. A crucial decision was made early on to focus the fund-raising efforts on covenanted contributions, a strategy that provided special benefits under British tax law. Under that system the government will provide a registered charity with matching funds equivalent to the tax paid on that portion of the donor's income if—and this was the crucial feature of the law—the donation was in the form of a seven-year covenant pledging an annual contribution.

To secure these ongoing covenants is a very contact-intensive form of fund-raising, one based on educating the potential donor about the nature of the project and establishing a long-term relationship rather than asking for a simple one-time donation. Recognizing that this contact-intensive aspect of covenanted fund-raising could eventually be an asset rather than a hindrance, AFI developed over the 1980s a distinctive style of team-based door-to-door appeals, a fund-raising technique that has subsequently been copied by other charities in Britain, especially some of the environmental groups. Andrew Goodman (Dh. Mahamati), secretary and director of AFI, points out that this style of fund-raising also provides an opportunity for Western Buddhist AFI-workers to become more seriously involved in the project and in their own Buddhist practice, in that they typically will take off from their normal responsibilities to work full-time on an appeal team for one to two months, time the team spends living and doing their Buddhist practice together as well as working as a fund-raising team.[45]

The financial benefits of the covenant system were evident already in the figures published in AFI's first annual report published at the end of 1981. Total receipts for the first thirteen months of fund-raising amounted to £33,091. More significant, however, was the fact that over half that amount was convenanted pledges that would eventually bring in over £300,000 as the seven-year commitments ran their course. Although founded in the middle of a major economic recession, the fund-raising progressed well with steady gains in total receipts over the succeeding years, as indicated in the table below.

Supporting the work of TBMSG and Bahujan Hitay remains the main priority for the charity, although in 1987 AFI was expanded to become the Karuna Trust with a charter to fund Buddhist humanitarian projects throughout the world.[46] Patrons (official sponsors) of the new charitable trust or foundation include Sir Edmund Hillary, Dame Judi Dench, and Dr. David Morley, Professor of Tropical Child Health at the University of London. While Karuna Trust's team-based door-to-door fund-raising appeals continue to provide most of the funding for capital projects, new sources of funding have been developed as well. Grants from the Overseas Development Administration of the British government have become an important source of project-specific funds—totaling £20,826 in 1989 and £35,960 in 1990. And plans are underway to explore additional sources of grant funding including other foundations and the newly created European Community grant programs.[47] Within India, grants have been obtained under a government program to support school hostels, and Lokamitra has been increasingly successful in fund-raising among the Buddhist communities of other Asian countries, especially in Taiwan.

The ultimate goal of TBMSG and Bahujan Hitay is economic self-sufficiency, at least with regard to ongoing expenses if not new capital projects. That will take some time, however, and the need for externally funded capital development will remain in any case. Besides, the fund-raising activities initiated by Karuna Trust and by Lokamitra in his Asian travels have proved to have a double benefit. The funding itself is directly useful, and the contact it establishes abroad has begun to bring the plight of India's ex-Untouchable Buddhists to the attention of much more of the

Funds Raised by AFI & Karuna Trust

1982	£82,640
1983	180,914
1984	228,049
1985	260,378
1986	295,592
1987	308,284
1988	337,408
1989	351,240
1990	413,345

world. While most of Karuna Trust's funding is coming from non-Buddhists in Britain, significant support from other Buddhist groups across the world is increasing.

An Assessment: Prospects and Problems for the Future

TBMSG's Dhamma Revolution is still too young for anything beyond the most provisional assessment in this study. As we approach the close of the twentieth century, it is, however, clear that this hybrid movement combining the "new Buddhism" of an Indian statesman with that of an English monk has found a warm reception among many of the ex-Untouchables of Maharashtra and increasingly in other Indian states as well. What accounts for this success? Three crucial factors emerge from the data we have explored in this chapter. The first of these lies in the fact that TBMSG's Dhamma Revolution is closely tied to the bodhisattvic figure of Babasaheb Ambedkar and his vision of liberation for the former Untouchables. While unquestionably a necessary condition, this single factor is not by itself sufficient to account for the success of TBMSG, however, as demonstrated by the history of the many ineffectual and ephemeral Ambedkarite groups that have come and gone during the thirty-five years since his death. Although Ambedkar stressed the central role of Buddhism within his program for social and spiritual emancipation, his premature death left no opportunity for him to work out a comprehensive model for applying the Dhammic principles and practices to the particular needs of the new Buddhists of India. He exhorted his followers to take up Buddhism, pointing out certain aspects of Asian Buddhist practice that he felt warranted criticism. Yet at the time of his death he had only barely begun the more demanding task of presenting a concrete model of *how* Buddhist thought and practice could address the special needs and circumstances of this new Buddhist community. The bulk of his magnum opus, *The Buddha and his Dhamma*, remained little more than a visionary outline.

We can see the second aspect of TBMSG's strength then in Sangharakshita's ability to provide the critical piece that remained lacking in Ambedkar's vision, the reformulation of traditional Buddhist thought and practices into a practical model that would address the particular needs of new Buddhists living within the constraints of contemporary society. Ambedkar saw in Buddhism the spiritual basis for his program, but he also realized that the currently existing Asian forms of tradition would not adequately address the needs of his ex-Untouchable followers. Hence the need he saw for a radical, yet thoroughly modern critique of the available Buddhist institutions as well as a "new Buddhism," a *navayana* formulated with the special needs of "new Buddhists" in mind. Providing this comprehensive reformulation of the Buddhadhamma was Sangharakshita's key contribution to TBMSG's current success. But even this second component would itself have remained insufficient, without the addition of yet one further crucial piece of the puzzle.

Sangharakshita's blueprint for a "modern Buddhism" drew heavily on his many years of experience within the prevailing forms of Asian Buddhism, the Theravada of Southeast Asia and Tibetan Vajrayana in particular. Yet it was not until he had returned to the West that the fruition of his long apprenticeship began to emerge in the form of the Western Buddhist Order, a "new Buddhism" to be sure, yet one formulated more specifically to meet the needs of Western Buddhists. The third factor still needed was the master builder who could adapt Sangharakshita's blueprint to the particular materials back in India. This was Dh. Lokamitra's role, and Sangharakshita has reportedly said that he himself could not have done as good a job constructing the Dhamma Revolution that has emerged, stone by stone, over the last decade in India without Lokamitra's guidance.[48] The vision and the blueprint were both essential, but their successful implementation in India has required the creation of an effective institutional structure built ultimately on the commitment of a highly dedicated and well-trained indigenous cadre of both social workers and Dhamma teachers. Without Lokamitra's organizational genius and his ability to build and to empower a dedicated core of Indian order members TBMSG could never have flourished, however grand the vision, however comprehensive the plan.

If TBMSG's current success demonstrates the potential of this tripartite formula, the future of the movement, will lie in its ability to integrate further and more effectively all three of these critical components—Ambedkar's visionary inspiration, Sangharakshita's Dhammic blueprint, and Lokamitra's organizational structure. The prospects seem quite bright, but the movement's very success will itself inevitably reveal new obstacles in the future. What are the problems TBMSG will face as it moves from its expansive adolescence to a more established maturity? To conclude this preliminary survey of the TBMSG's Dhamma Revolution, I shall briefly identify three areas that will require sustained and creative response if this movement is to fulfill its early promise. First, TBMSG must convincingly demonstrate the sense in which it offers a legitimate development of the Ambedkarite vision. Second, TBMSG must secure and even intensify its Buddhist critique of the social conditioning obstructing the individual and social transformation advocated by both Ambedkar and Sangharakshita. And finally, the Dhamma Revolution must sustain the full spiritual as well as social scope of the Ambedkarite Buddhist vision among the ex-Untouchables even as they become, through the very success of Ambedkar's legal reforms, increasingly more integrated into the bourgeois materialism of middle-class professional life in contemporary India. These three challenges are obviously interrelated, but it will help to consider each of them separately.

The Challenge of Legitimacy

The second chapter of this volume has already addressed the problems that some Buddhists have had with the legitimacy of Ambedkar's "new Buddhism." The problem for traditionally minded Buddhists lies not so much in his message of social revolution, which has its place even within the tradition. Rather what they see as problematic is Ambedkar's critique of several central features of the tradition: especially monasticism and the doctrine of karma and rebirth. Christopher Queen has suggested how Ambedkar's efforts to formulate a *navayana,* a "new Buddhism," can be understood as a legitimate response with historical precedent, and this is a crucial point for those evaluating Ambedkar from the outside, whether as historians of religion or as Buddhists of other traditions. But this is not the question of legitimacy that most concerns the Ambedkarite Buddhists them- selves. They are far more concerned with whether new Buddhist develop- ments within India remain true to the vision of Babasaheb Ambedkar, who himself provides for them the necessary standard of "orthodoxy." This double- headed concern for legitimacy puts TBMSG in the unique position of hav- ing to assert the "orthodoxy" of Ambedkar's conception of the Dhamma in the broader context of world Buddhism, while also needing to convince the ex-Untouchable Buddhists that the more broadly based Buddhist teaching of Sangharakshita and Lokamitra in fact remains true to its Ambedkarite legacy. We have already seen how Sangharakshita's more comprehensive model of Buddhist thought and practice is one of the crucial elements accounting for TBMSG's current success. The full promise offered by this synthesis will be fulfilled, however, only to the extent that TBMSG is able to establish itself within Ambedkarite circles as a legitimate development of Babasaheb's vision. TBMSG is unique among the various Ambedkarite groups in the central place it gives to Dhamma work and in the importance it places on addressing social problems within the context of a broader spiri- tual program of individual as well as social transformation. This has troubled some of the more politically oriented Ambedkarites. Sangharakshita's em- phasis on the actual practice of Buddhism—both meditation and devotion (*puja*)—has in fact led to charges that TBMSG is overly "spiritualizing" the original social and material thrust of Ambedkar's teaching, a claim some feel substantiated by the movement's efforts to work outside of the political arena (as much as this is possible in India).[49]

This is a charge that must be assessed quite carefully: if there indeed were a fundamental divergence between Sangharakshita and Ambedkar, the future of TBMSG would be quite limited. If, on the other hand, Sangharakshita and his followers have succeeded in effectively expressing a spiritual dimension that was in fact central to Ambedkar's thought, then their Dhamma Revolution may be the fulfillment rather than the betrayal of his vision. Is there then any significant conflict between Ambedkar's Buddhist vision and Sangharakshita's program for putting that vision into practice? Is TBMSG in fact "spiritualizing" Ambedkar's vision in a way that will vitiate its original intent? Lokamitra and the Indian order members of TBM do indeed feel that any effort to improve the material welfare of the ex-Untouchables will succeed only to the extent that effort is securely grounded in Dhammic principles and practice, including both study and meditation on an ongoing daily basis. And a critic might well argue that the large amount of energy devoted, both organizationally and personally, to these Dhamma activities limits the time available for less "spiritual" pursuits. What this critique overlooks, however, is Ambedkar's own recognition and insistence that social transformation, a point born out, it would seem, by the TBMSG's very success in the social sphere, a record arguably unmatched by any of the other less "spiritually" and more politically oriented Ambedkarite organizations.[50]

Dh. Lokamitra has argued the fundamental compatibility of Ambedkar's vision and Sangharakshita's model on several occasions, most recently in a retrospective survey of articles published in *Golden Drum,* the house organ of the FWBO. In his discussion of "the basic concord" between the Buddhism of Ambedkar and that of Sangharakshita, Lokamitra points out that both share a nonsectarian perspective, drawing on the full historical breadth of the tradition rather than affiliating themselves with one school or cultural tradition. Both are concerned, Lokamitra continues, to provide a cultural critique of the theistic assumptions of their respective native cultures, stressing the Buddhist focus on morality as an alternative. Both, moreover, are concerned to articulate the social dimension of the Dhamma, and both saw the need for a new type of Buddhist order, one more actively dedicated to "the welfare of the many."[51] While this preliminary statement of Lokamitra's does much to lay the groundwork for resolving the challenge to legitimacy, much more will need to be done in the years to come since it is likely that the controversy has only begun to assert itself. As TBMSG becomes increasingly more successful its claim to Ambedkar's mantle will only be contested all the more. Some Ambedkarites feel that any devotional practice (other than the veneration of Ambedkar) is incompatible with his teaching, especially if that practice shares any features of Hindu devotion, including even the designation *puja.*[52] Yet devotional *puja* based on traditional Buddhist sources does, as we have seen, play a central role in TBMSG practice—as does meditation, another traditional Buddhist practice about which even Ambedkar himself appears to have expressed some ambivalence.[53]

These are issues that TBMSG will have to address more directly in the future, as is the problem with the central Buddhist doctrines of karma and rebirth. As pointed out in the previous chapter, Ambedkar was inclined to minimize or even deny the place of rebirth in the Buddha's thought, seeing only the way it is used within Hinduism to rationalize the inequities of the caste system.[54] But the traditional Buddhist doctrine of rebirth saw this karmic process in quite different terms: as moral law that ensured the opportunity of the human individual to change and grow even within this lifetime, not as a fatalistic doctrine holding that one's lot in this life was inextricably fixed or predetermined by one's actions in a previous life. The doctrine of karma in Buddhism has never been used to delimit human potential, nor to legitimize suffering in a fatalistic manner. Karma and rebirth, in this traditional Buddhist sense, do play a central role in the Buddhism of Sangharakshita, but this is something quite different from the Hindu sense of karma, reincarnation, and caste of which Ambedkar was rightly so wary.

This discussion suggests that much remains to be done in working out the ultimate compatibility between the Buddhisms of Ambedkar and Sangharakshita, but it should also suffice to show that the two are not as incompatible as TBMSG's critics might seek to charge. Sangharakshita's design for a "new society" and its concrete implementation in the institutions of TBMSG do indeed go well beyond what Ambedkar was able to outline at the end of his life. Nonetheless, the radical social concerns so dear to the Indian reformer certainly are represented in the Buddhism of Sangharakshita, and the latter's efforts to expand in more positive terms Ambedkar's primarily critical stance toward traditional Buddhism may, moreover, provide the key that will help integrate the Ambedkarite Buddhists into the broader world of contemporary Asian (and Western) Buddhism. It may thus provide the necessary bridge to those who have been inclined to question the Buddhist "orthodoxy" of Ambedkar.[55] In expanding the Buddhist dimension of Ambedkar's vision while also muting some of its seemingly discordant themes, Sangharakshita's more doctrinally conservative formulation of Buddhism thus offers the prospect of resolving both aspects of the challenge of legitimacy.

The Challenge of Persistent Cultural Conditioning

While the task of establishing TBMSG as a legitimate heir to the Ambedkarite legacy may prove to be quite manageable, success on this front may also turn out to be little more than a pseudo-victory, for the challenge of legitimacy is likely to be eclipsed by still greater problems. The second challenge I wish to identify comprises a cluster of issues all related to the general theme of cultural conditioning. While the new Buddhists of India are profoundly sincere in their aspiration to leave their position as Untouchables behind, there is much residual conditioning that must be consciously addressed and overcome. We have already considered the psychological problems arising from generations of oppression, the difficulty in mustering the self-confidence necessary to effect any significant transformation. Another instance can be seen in the problem of caste identity itself. While many of the Ambedkarite Buddhists of Maharashtra have firmly renounced their Untouchable identity, most still think of themselves first of all as Mahars, the ethnic subgroup (*jat*) into which they were born. Indeed the designation "Buddhist" has become, in Maharashtra at least, virtually synonymous with "Mahar." For Ambedkar's vision to succeed, however, this tendency to turn Buddhism into simply another caste (or outcaste) identity must be firmly resisted, both among the ex-Untouchables as well as among the caste-Hindus. The future of TBMSG's Dhamma Revolution will be significantly restricted if its Buddhism remains linked exclusively with the Mahars (Ambedkar's own *jat*), a problem that is just beginning to arise as the movement expands beyond its Maharashtran roots. While some non-Mahar ex-Untouchables have enthusiastically embraced Ambedkar's call to Buddhism—most notably the Jatavs of Agra—other groups, especially in the south, have been much more reluctant to ally themselves with the Mahars. The persistence of caste conditioning and its ability to reemerge in new forms is not to be underestimated in India. Some communities of Indian converts to Christianity, for example, officially repudiate the notion of caste, yet nonetheless maintain separate facilities, both churches and cemeteries, to keep former Untouchable congregants separate from those who come from a caste-Hindu background.

Another instance of persistent cultural conditioning that is already a problem for TBMSG has to do with traditional restrictions on the role of women. Although the movement is thoroughly committed to social and personal emancipation of all, extending the opportunities of Ambedkar's vision to women has proved a far greater challenge than addressing the needs of men. The problem here is evident in the fact that among the 150 Indian members of the Order at the end of 1992, there were only two active Dhammacarinis.[56] TBMSG's struggle to secure funding and facilities for girls' as well as boys' hostels, as well as the effort to create socially acceptable single-sex retreat opportunities, demonstrates a significant recognition of the special needs of women. Indeed Eleanor Zelliot credits TBMSG as the only sustained Buddhist effort ministering to women in Maharashtra.[57] Yet in spite of substantial accomplishments a significant lag remains in developing the women's wing of the TBM Order in India. The reasons for this are complex, involving several mutually reinforcing circumstances. First there is reluctance on the part of many ex-Untouchables, both men and women, to see any change in the traditional roles of women. This restriction is further compounded by the fact that the special needs of aspiring women ordinands are not best met by male order members, leaving the movement in the paradoxical quandary of not being able to ordain more women order members until there are more women order members. One solution is to bring in more women order members from the West to work with the Indian women seeking ordination, although so far this has proved difficult to do, both because of visa restrictions and a shortage of Western dharmacharinis able to make the substantial commitment to work in India on a long-term basis.

Interestingly this is another instance in which the aspirations of TBMSG echo those of Babasaheb himself. The issue of spiritual and social empowerment for women was one that Ambedkar had seen as especially important for his new Buddhists to address, going so far as to suggest that the oppression of women, even caste-Hindu women in traditional India was not unrelated to the oppression of the Untouchables. In 1950 he wrote an impassioned article titled, "The Rise and Fall of the Hindu Woman. Who was responsible for it?"[58] Citing at some length Buddhist scriptural sources and the traditional Hindu legal code attributed to Manu, Ambedkar argued that Buddhism had offered women far greater opportunities, including access to all aspects of the spiritual, whereas the *Manu-smriti* has decreed that even caste-Hindu women were not to recite the sacred Vedic texts and hence had little more spiritual empowerment than the Untouchables. He goes on to note that the Buddha, in contrast, "kept his way open to all classes of women, married, unmarried, widows and even to prostitutes. All could acquire merit, freedom, dignity and equality along with men."[59]

I have outlined only a few of the specific forms of social conditioning the Dhamma Revolution will have to address even more vigorously in the future. While this second challenge is likely to be more vexing and persistent than the first, we must not overlook the substantial resources available within the Buddhist tradition. From the days of the Buddha himself the Dhamma has been a teaching that has sought to challenge the conditioning of prevailing social norms, whether the Brahmanic ritualism and caste system of ancient India or the secular morality of Chinese Confucianism. Both Ambedkar and Sangharakshita were acutely aware of the socially critical dimension of the tradition when formulating their respective visions of a "new Buddhism." If TBMSG remains true to their understanding of Dhamma, confronting these problems of residual social conditioning should

Alan Sponberg

prove to be a central focus in the years to come. One might even say that precisely this is the task that TBMSG has set for itself. Transformation, both individual and social, will be possible only to the extent that conditioning of oppression is overthrown—within the minds of the oppressed as well as the oppressors.

The Challenge of Secular Assimilation

The last challenge to the continued success of TBMSG's Dhamma Revolution might well be another instance of the problem of cultural conditioning discussed in the previous section. The distinctive nature of this particular problem warrants special consideration, however, for unlike the previous instances of cultural conditioning this one is a problem borne of the very success of Ambedkar's visionary program. With better opportunities for education and a substantial affirmative action program in both the state and federal civil service, increasing numbers of ex-Untouchables have begun their ascent up the economic and social ladder of the urban middle classes. Having managed to leave much of the stigma of their outcaste status behind, there is now strong incentive to leave behind their Ambedkarite Buddhism as well. Indeed for the most successfully urbanized and secularized ex-Untouchables the only remnant of their previous outcaste status may be precisely their Buddhist identity. Ironically, their veneration of Ambedkar and the Buddha thus becomes the only thing that might enable their new colleagues and coworkers to recognize their Untouchable origins.

At present only a tiny fraction of the Ambedkarite Buddhists have achieved this degree of social success and assimilation, most having only traded the poverty and exclusion of their ancestral villages for the less discriminatory but equally impoverished slums and hutments of the cities. Nonetheless the potential problem here is clear: Why would an industrious and talented young ex-Untouchable choose to remain associated with Buddhism, once he or she has secured the government job that assures financial security not just for oneself but generally for one's entire extended family as well?"[60] J. Michael Mahar, one of the first Western Scholars to research the Ambedkarite movement in India, has recently gone so far as to suggest that, given the trend toward secularization among the emerging urban professional classes, the very success of Ambedkar's legal and social reforms makes the Buddhist dimension of his vision superfluous.[61] To the extent that this is true, however, many Ambedkarites including those in TBMSG would argue that the original vision has been lost, because, they assert, Ambedkar sought not just a materialistic improvement for his people but an ethical and even spiritual transformation as well. Some of this idealism seems to have survived even the co-opting influence of modern secularism among the Ambedkarites in TBMSG. Several of the new Indian order members have given up relatively lucrative jobs to work full-time for the movement, a decision that we must remember affects not just the one individual, but his extended family as well. But will these notable examples prove to be only eccentric exceptions to an already well-established social trend among educated ex-Untouchables? Or will TBMSG succeed in further channeling the energy of emancipation back into remaining segments of the profoundly impoverished ex-Untouchable community?

To sustain the degree of social idealism necessary for successful ex-Untouchables to return to aid their communities will surely require some motivation that goes beyond the aspirations of secular materialism. Hence Ambedkar's insistence that the Dhammic aspect of his emancipation program was as essential as the legal and educational components. TBMSG's response to this challenge is to stress the importance of developing a substantial core of educated and socially active order members whose idealistic motivation will arise as a part of their shared commitment to the ideals of both individual and social transformation. But many more bright, young ex-Untouchables, both men and women, will have to follow the lead of the early Indian order members for TBMSG's ambitious plans for the future to be realized. This means developing more extensive programs for effectively educating and socializing potential postulants into the values and ideals of the order. It also will require the development of opportunities for economic security and growth that will remain wholly within the Buddhist culture of the community. As we have seen, TBMSG has begun to make significant though still tentative steps in this direction with its residential communities and its "right livelihood" business ventures. Still more will need to be done on both these fronts, however, before the Dhamma Revolution will fulfill the full promise of Ambedkar's vision.

Notes

1. I must express my appreciation to all the members the Trailokya Bauddha Mahasangha and the Western Buddhist Order who have assisted my research for this chapter. Special thanks go to the Ven. Sangharakshita who sat for over ten hours of recorded interviews with me in December 1991; also to TBMSG's principal organizer, Dh. Lokamitra, with whom I spent a delightful and informative week in the fall of 1988; and to Dh. Mahamati, who generously offered me much of his time and many helpful archive documents when I visited the Oxford home office of Karuna Trust for four days in late 1991. Further thanks also to the many other Order members and friends of the movement I interviewed over the last three years: especially Virabhadra and Padmashuri, the medical team that organized the

movement's first public health project in 1983; Subhuti and Suvajra, the team of preceptors responsible for ordaining many of the TBM Order members; Vajraketu, one of the first English order members to work with Lokamitra in India and currently codirector of Windhorse Trading, the movement's most financially successful right livelihood business enterprise; also Dh. Manjuvajra and Ginny Keegan, U.S. representatives of Karuna Trust—and dozens of others whom I shall regrettably have to leave unnamed for lack of space. Financial support for this research was provided by a faculty research grant from the University of Montana, supplemented by additional travel funds from the Office of the Dean of Arts and Sciences.

In the fall of 1994, I had the opportunity to update some of the research presented here during a two-month visit to TBMSG centers in Poona, Bhaja, Aurungabad, Amravati, Bor Dharan, and Nagpur. In addition to reconnecting with both Lokamitra and Mahamati, I was especially appreciative of the time I was able to spend with Dhammacharis Vimalakirti, Ratnasagar, and Amoghasiddhi. TBMSG has continued to grow quite rapidly since this chapter was written in 1992. There are many new developments that go beyond the basic structure of the movement outlined here, but adequate documentation of these will have to await a more substantial monograph-length study.

2. See page 91 for a schematic overview of the various organizations discussed in this chapter. "Dharma" and "Dhamma" are linguistically equivalent terms, the first the Sanskrit form and the second the Pali form of the same word. In spite of this philological equivalency, Ambedkarite Buddhists consistently adopt the Pali form "Dhamma" to distinguish the Buddhist meaning of the term from the Hindu notion of "caste duty" often associated in India with the Sanskrit "dharma." In its Buddhist context dharma/dhamma refers to Truth or the ultimate reality of existence, and more specifically to the Buddha's formulation of that Truth, that is, to his teachings or doctrines. What we would refer to as "Buddhism," Asian Buddhists would thus designate as the Buddha-dharma or, in this case, the Buddha-dhamma. (Other Sanskrit/Pali equivalencies, such as *bhikshu/bhikkhu,* monk, will appear later; the Sanskrit is generally used by the FWBO, while the Pali forms are preferred by the TBMSG.)

3. While the TBMSG movement is too new to have attracted much scholarly attention as yet, there are two excellent journalistic accounts documenting many aspects of the movement: Terry Pilchick's (Dh. Nagabodhi) *Jai Bhim!—Dispatches from a Peaceful Revolution* (Glasgow: Windhorse Publications; and Berkeley, Calif.: Parallax Press, 1988) and *But Little Dust—Life amongst the ex-Untouchables of Maharashtra* (Cambridge, England: Allborough Press, 1990) by Hilary Blakiston (Dh. Padmashuri). My research for this study has also benefited greatly from interviews on several occasions with each of these authors.

4. Right livelihood is one aspect of the Buddha's doctrine of the eightfold path leading to the elimination of suffering. Within the context of FWBO/TBMSG a "right livelihood business" is one that is established and operated to support its employees' spiritual as well as material needs while providing an ethically acceptable product or service.

5. A note on nomenclature: the term "Untouchable" is a rather nonspecific blanket term that was traditionally used to refer to all of those subcastes considered to fall outside the four primary castes or estates of the Hindu *varna* system, that is, those whose touch was considered to be ritually defiling. Legally referred to as the "scheduled castes," these groups became officially "*ex*-Untouchables" when the first Indian constitution (drafted by Ambedkar) outlawed caste discrimination in 1949. More recently some ex-Untouchables have adopted the term "Dalit" (lit. the oppressed, downtrodden) to refer to themselves, especially since the founding of the Dalit Panther political party. While TBMSG has enjoyed a good working relationship with several prominent Dalit Panther leaders, most TBMSG followers still prefer to call themselves ex-Untouchables (if not simply Buddhists) because of the often more narrowly political connotations of the term "Dalit." "Harijan" (lit. children of [the Hindu god] Hari) was a designation for the Untouchables adopted by Gandhi and still popular among liberal caste-Hindus. Although Gandhi generally is portrayed as a champion of these helpless "children of God," the ex-Untouchables themselves rejected Gandhi's paternalistic concern because of his advocacy of the caste system, and they resent the name "harijan," which is also used to refer to the fatherless children of temple prostitutes.

Ambedkarite Buddhists are often referred to as neo-Buddhists, a term that Ambedkar himself used on occasion when speaking in English of the need for a *navayana*, a new, reformed dispensation of Buddhism. Many of his followers, including most of those associated with TBMSG, have come to prefer calling themselves simply "new Buddhists," however, feeling that "neo-Buddhist" has pejorative overtones suggesting questionable orthodoxy or legitimacy. They point out that Indian converts to other religions are only rarely called neo-Christians or neo-Muslims, for example.

6. On the occasion of Ambedkar's own formal conversion to Buddhism on October 14, 1956, he, in turn, administered the refuges and precepts to a crowd of followers in Nagpur variously estimated to have numbered from 300,000 to 600,000. By the time of the 1961 census the number of those identifying themselves to government officials as Buddhists had risen to 3,250,277 an increase from the previous census figures of 1,671 percent. Current estimates of new Buddhists run between 6 and 7 million, these figures are likely to be underreported since many Ambedkarites have been reluctant to officially identify themselves as Buddhists out of fear of losing the affirmative action benefits they legally enjoy as ex-Untouchable Hindus.

For further analysis of the social and political implications of the 1961 census figures, see Eleanor Zelliot's "Buddhism and Politics in Maharashtra," in *South Asian Politics and Religion,* edited by Donald E. Smith, (Princeton, N.J.: Princeton University Press, 1966), esp., pp. 191–193.

7. Ambedkar's career has received surprisingly little attention outside of the ex-Untouchable community in India. The best monograph-length studies of his life and work are Sangharakshita's *Ambedkar and Buddhism* (Glasgow: Windhorse, 1986)

and Dhananjay Keer's *Dr. Ambedkar: Life and Mission,* 2nd rev. ed. (Bombay: Popular Prakashan, 1962). Also very helpful in understanding the relative disregard among both Indian and Western intellectuals of Ambedkar's role in the founding of modern India is Eleanor Zelliot's "Ambedkar and Ghandi—A Study in Leadership" in *The Untouchables in Contemporary India,* ed. by J. Michael Mahar, (Tucson: University of Arizona Press, 1972)

8. Interview with Dh. Lokamitra, November 1988.

9. On the problems of factionalization and disorganization among the many Ambedkarite groups that arose (and often declined) in the first decade after their leader's death, see Adele Fiske's "Scheduled Caste Buddhist Organizations" in *The Untouchables in Contemporary India,* pp. 113–142, and especially pp. 140–141.

10. Insight into the spiritual development of Sangharakshita can be gleaned from the three volumes of memoirs he has published over the last two decades: *The Thousand-Petalled Lotus* (London: William Heinemann, Ltd., 1976) is a lively and literary account of the years he spent wandering in India leading up to his ordination; *Learning to Walk* (Glasgow, Windhorse, 1990) tells of his childhood, focusing on his early education and initial attraction to Buddhism, and *Facing Mount Kanchenjunga* (Glasgow: Windhorse, 1992) recounts in some detail the trials and aspirations of the young monk living in Kalimpong in the 1950s. The account of Sangharakshita's life included in this chapter also incorporates material from a series of interviews I conducted with him in London in December 1991 and also from a draft of the forthcoming biography, A New Voice: *The Life of Sangharakshita,* which was generously made available to me by the author Alex (Subhuti) Kennedy.

11. *Learning to Walk,* pp. 102–103.

12. Ibid, p. 118.

13. *Facing Mount Kanchenjunga,* p. 1.

14. On the substantial influence this same elusive recluse (also spelled Chatral Sangye Dorje) was later to have on another prominent Western monk, see *The Asian Journal of Thomas Merton* (New York: Norton New Directions, 1973), pp. 142–145; Harold Talbott provides further background on the relationship between Merton and Chetul in "The Jesus Lama—Thomas Merton in the Himalayas," *Tricycle* (New York), I.4 (Summer, 1992), pp. 14–24.

15. Sogyal Rinpoche offers a good introduction to all three of these leading Nyingma masters in his *Tibetan Book of Living and Dying,* (San Francisco: Harper Collins, 1992).

16. For more on this influential monk, see Suvajra (Morgan Findlay), *The Wheel and the Diamond—the Life of Dhardo Tulku* (Glasgow: Windhorse, 1991).

17. *Buddhism and Ambedkar,* p. 20.

18. Interview with author, London, December 10, 1991.

19. Alex (Subhuti) Kennedy, *A New Voice,* chap. 4 (p. 53 in the as yet unpublished datafile version provided to me by the author).

20. *The Maha Bodhi* (Calcutta), April–May 1950.

21. The Dharmapala biography is currently available as *Anagarika Dharmapala, A Biographical Sketch,* Wheel Publication Series no. 70–72, Kandy, Sri Lanka: Buddhist Publication Society, 1964.

22. *Ambedkar and Buddhism,* p. 18.

23. The Bengali Brahmin president of the society at the time was, in fact, Shyama Prasad Mookerjee—former president of the Hindu Mahasabha, a very conservative Caste Hindu organization. In that role Mookerjee had helped lead the opposition to Nehru's and Ambedkar's failed Hindu Code Bill, which had sought to reform many of the more egregiously discriminatory aspects of traditional Hindu religious and social practice. That a staunch Hindu traditionalist could also turn up as the president of the country's most influential Buddhist organization is an intriguing detail that helps reveal the complexity of India's current Buddhist revival.

24. Commonly referred to as *pansil* (Skt. *pancha sila*), the traditional five precepts are: (1) to refrain from harming, (2) to refrain from taking what is not given, (3) to refrain from sexual misconduct, (4) to refrain from untruthful speech, and (5) to refrain from intoxicants that cloud the mind.

25. Christopher Queen reports that he was able to confirm this fact in a meeting he had with Mrs. Ambedkar in 1992 (personal communication).

26. *Ambedkar and Buddhism,* p. 20.

27. *Ambedkar and Buddhism,* p. 26–27.

28. On Sangharakshita's distinctive notion of "Western Buddhism" see his *New Currents in Western Buddhism* (Glasgow: Windhorse, 1990) and also "Buddhism in the West," an address he gave at the European Buddhist Union Congress held in Berlin during September, 1992 (published under the same title by Windhorse, 1992).

29. Sangharakshita has recently published a long essay exploring some of these issues under the title *The FWBO and 'Protestant Buddhism'—An Affirmation and a Protest,* (Glasgow, Windhorse, 1992).

30. A good exposition of Sangharakshita's views on what it means to be a Buddhist and to be an WBO/TBM order member and also of his notion of different "levels" of going for refuge is found in his *History of My Going for Refuge* (Glasgow: 1988).

31. The WBO has anglicized this term as Dharmachari (fem.: Dharmacharini; abv. Dh.), while Indians in the TBMSG prefer the Pali forms Dhammachari and Dhammacharini for reasons discussed in endnote 2.

32. The best source currently available on Lokamitra's early involvement with Buddhism, FWBO and TBMSG is a partially autobiographical chapter he has recently written for *Dr. Ambedkar, Buddhism, and Social Change*, A. K. Narain and D. C. Ahir, editors (Delhi: D. K. Publishers, 1994). See also Pilchick, *Jai Bhim,* pp. 33–36, 150–151.

33. Personal conversation with the author, November 15, 1988.

34. This work was based on the needs established by an extensive public health survey undertaken in 1983–1984 and subsequently published as the *Bahujan Hitay Pune Project: A Report on Slum Localities in Dapodi* by R. W. Stones, (Pune: Bahujan Hitay, 1984; reprint 1987)

35. "The Buddha and the Future of His Religion," in *Maha Bodhi,* 58 (April–May 1950).

36. The original TBM order members were ordained personally by Sangharakshita during his visits to India in 1979, 1983, and 1988. Because of constraints on his ability to travel to India, he subsequently delegated this responsibility to teams of ordination preceptors among both the men's and women's wing of the WBO that now perform the ceremony for TBM in India and WBO in the West. As yet there is not a separate all-Indian TBM ordination team, but this is anticipated in the foreseeable future as the order there matures.

37. "Buddhist Revival in India" (Pune, n.d.), p. 6.

38. By the end of 1991 TBMSG Centers had been established in a number of Maharashtra cities and communities including Bombay, Ulhansnagar, Aurangabad, Nagpur, Kolhapur, and Wardha, with five separate facilities in the Pune area: Pimpri, Dapodi, Camp, Yerawada South, and Yerawada North. Elsewhere in India, major centers included Ahmedabad in Gujarat along with Hastinapur and Agra in Uttar Pradesh, with invitations to open centers in Delhi, Hyderabad (Andhra Pradesh), and Bangalore (Karnataka) under consideration.

39. *Jai Bhim,* p. 96.

40. At the end of 1991 the principal residential communities included those in Dapodi, Bombay, Aurangabad, Nagpur, Wardha, Ahmedabad, and Hastinapur.

41. This is a theme recurring in Ambedkar's frequent critiques of the bhikkhu-sangha as he encountered it in India and Sri Lanka, "a huge army of idlers" in whom "there is neither learning nor service"; see, for example, his article in the May 1950 issue of the *Maha Bodhi,* (excerpted in D. C. Ahir's *Dr. Ambedkar on Buddhism,* pp. 52–53).

42. The current discussions of "socially engaged" Buddhism often overlook traditional Buddhist concerns for "the welfare of the many," suggesting even that Buddhism has become "socially engaged" only recently under the influence of Western or even specifically Christian models. While contact with the West has undoubtedly inspired (or even provoked) a renaissance of socially active Buddhism, we must

be careful not to overlook the traditional sources for this perspective, sources well surveyed in Robert Thurman's two articles on the "Edicts of Asoka" and "Nagarjuna's Guideline for Buddhist Social Action" in *The Path of Compassion,* ed. by Fred Eppsteiner, (Berkeley, Calif.: Parallax Press, 1985).

43. *Dhammapadatthakatha,* N iii. 261–264; trans. by E. Burlingame in *Buddhist Legends,* (Cambridge, Mass.: Harvard University Press, 1921), vol. 3, pp. 74–76. This story is part of the commentary to verses 203–204 of the Dhammapada, which assert that hunger is the greatest of afflictions and health the greatest of possessions.

44. J. M. Mahar (ed.), *The Untouchables in Contemporary India,* (Tucson: University of Arizona Press, 1972), p. 423. This observation certainly holds true for the majority group of new Buddhists, the Mahars in Maharashtra—though perhaps somewhat less so for the Jatavs in Agra, who were studied by Owen Lynch, *The Politics of Untouchability: Social Mobility and Social Change in a City of India,* (New York: Columbia University Press, 1969). The Jatavs differ from most of the other ex-Untouchable subcastes in that for generations they have had a strong urban artisan tradition as leather workers, experience that left them much better equipped in terms of both skills and confidence. They responded very enthusiastically to Ambedkar's Buddhist vision beginning in the early 1950s, successfully organizing themselves into the guilds and cooperatives that have made Agra famous as a center for leather work.

45. Interview with the author at the Karuna Trust headquarters in Oxford, December 7, 1991.

46. In addition to its support for TBMSG, Aid for India (and now the Karuna Trust) has been the primary funding source for the operation and expansion of the Indo-Tibetan Buddhist Cultural Institute in Kalimpong, a boarding school for Tibetan refugee children founded by Sangharakshita's teacher and friend Dhardo Rimpoche.

47. Besides its ongoing support for the ITBCI school for Tibetan refugee children mentioned in the previous note, Karuna Trust also has extended grants to the People's Education Society, to the Centre for Development Studies and Activities, to the Centre for Learning Resources in Pune, and to the Progressive Education Society in Phaltan, Maharashtra, to fund its educational work serving 372 children.

48. Personal conversation with Dh. Subhuti, December 29, 1992; see also Pilchick, *Jai Bhim,* p. 150.

49. See, for example, Gopal Guru's "Hinduisation of Ambedkar in Maharashtra" (*Economic and Political Weekly,* February 16, 1991), which was followed by Dh. Lokamitra's response and Guru's subsequent follow-up (*Economic and Political Weekly,* May 18 and July 6, 1991). Guru's charge is that in "spiritualizing" Ambedkar's social message TBMSG is insidiously reasserting "Hindu" values and practices among the ex-Untouchables. He is particularly wary of the "other-worldly" and socially deleterious effects of meditation and devotion (*puja*).

50. Ambedkar articulated the relationship between the political and spiritual dimensions of his program quite clearly in a broadcast for the All India Radio series, "My Personal Philosophy": "Positively, my social philosophy may be said to be enshrined in three words" liberty, equality and fraternity. Let no one, however, say that I have borrowed my philosophy from the French Revolution. I have not. My philosophy has roots in religion and not in political science. I have derived them from the teachings of my Master, the Buddha" (October 3, 1954); transcribed in D. C. Ahir's *Dr. Ambedkar on Buddhism*, p. 15.

51. "A Basic Concord," *Golden Drum* (Glasgow), no. 25 (May–July, 1992), pp. 4–7; see also Dh. Lokamitra's reply to the Gopal Guru critique cited in note 48.

52. On the tendency among Marathi-speaking Ambedkarites to favor *vandana* (devotion) and *vihar* (temple) in place of *puja* and *mandir* because of their Hindu associations, see "Tradition and Innovation in Contemporary Indian Buddhism" by Joanna Macy and Eleanor Zelliot in *Studies in History of Buddhism*, ed. by A. K. Narain (Delhi: B. R. Publishing, 1980), p. 146. TBMSG recognizes the importance of asserting a clear difference between Buddhist and Hindu forms of spiritual practice, yet it retains the use of both the terms, pointing out their prominent place within long-established Buddhist tradition.

53. It is sometimes charged that Ambedkar was critical of the practice of meditation, but this seems less than clear. There are passages where Ambedkar was critical of the practice of meditation, but those of which I am aware are actually a criticism of monks who use their meditation practice as an excuse for neglecting the Buddha's injunction "to work for the welfare of the many" (*bahujan hitay*). This criticism is a recurrent theme in Ambedkar's discussion of what he felt to be the much needed "new Bhikkhu" in his article on "The Buddha and the Future of His Religion," in *Maha Bodhi*, 58 (April–May, 1950), for example.

54. Eleanor Zelliot reports one Ambedkarite list of nine Buddhist tenets that states flatly, "There is no rebirth"; p. 98 in "Buddhist Women of the Contemporary Maharashtrian Conversion Movement," in José Cabezón, ed., *Buddhism, Sexuality and Gender* (Albany: State University of New York Press, 1992).

55. The recent efforts on the part of Taiwanese Buddhists to finance a TBMSG retreat center reported earlier is one example of both the possibility and the significance of this development. We must not forget that significant (and supportive) contact among the culturally different Buddhist traditions of Asia is a quite modern phenomena, and it may be one upon which the future vitality of Asian Buddhism in fact depends.

56. Two more women were ordained early in 1993, and ten more in early 1994.

57. "Buddhist Women . . . ," p. 100.

58. *Maha Bodhi*, 58 (March, 1950), reprint in Ahir, *Dr. Ambedkar on Buddhism*, 75–96. Along with an earlier piece in the same journal by Lama Govinda,

Ambedkar's article was written specifically to refute an article published in *Eve's Weekly* earlier the same year arguing that it was Buddhism that was historically responsible for the subjugation of women in Hindu society.

59. Ambedkar, ibid., p. 89, in Ahir, Dr. *Ambedkar on Buddhism.*

60. The emerging tension between educated, socially assimilated ex-Untouchables and those still impoverished was already documented two decades ago by Harold R. Isaacs in "The Ex-Untouchables," (esp. pp. 396–403) in *The Untouchables in Contemporary India*, ed. by J. Michael Mahar, op. cit.

61. Michael Mahar, in a response to my paper, "*Dhamma* and Human Rights: the Ambedkarite Legacy in Contemporary India," at the Association of Asian Studies, Western Division, Western Conference, October 4–5, 1991.

Bibliography

Ahir, D. C. *Dr. Ambedkar on Buddhism.* (Collected excerpts from writings and speeches.) Bombay: Siddharth Publications, 1982.

———. *Buddhism in Modern India.* Nagpur: Bhikku Niwas Prakashan, 1972.

Blakiston, Hilary. *But Little Dust—Life amongst the Ex-Untouchables of Maharashtra.* Cambridge, England: Allborough Press, 1990.

Joshi, Barbara R. (ed.). *Untouchable!: Voices of the Dalit Liberation Movement.* London: Minority Rights Group and Atlantic Highlands, N.J.: Zed Books, 1986.

Kennedy, Alex (Subhuti). *Sangharakshita: A New Voice for Traditional Buddhism,* Glasgow: Windhorse Publications, 1994.

Keer, Dhananjay. *Dr. Ambedkar: Life and Mission,* 3rd ed. Bombay: Popular Prakashan, 1971 (rpt. 1990) [1st ed. 1954].

Ling, Trevor. *Buddhist Revival in India.* New York: St. Martin's Press, Inc., 1980.

Lokhande, G. S. *Bimrao Ramji Ambedkar: A Study in Social Democracy.* New Delhi: Intellectual Publishing House, 1977; 2nd rev. ed., 1982.

Macy, Joanna Rogers and Eleanor Zelliot. "Tradition and Innovation in Contemporary Indian Buddhism," in *Studies in History of Buddhism,* edited by A. K. Narain. Delhi: B. R. Publishing Co., 1980.

Pilchick, Terry. *Jai Bhim! Dispatches from a Peaceful Revolution.* Glasgow, Scotland: Windhorse, 1986.

Sangharakshita. *Facing Mount Kanchenjunga.* Glasgow, Scotland: Windhorse Publications, 1991.

———. *The History of My Going for Refuge.* Glasgow, Scotland: Windhorse Publications, 1988.

————. *Learning to Walk*. Glasgow, Scotland: Windhorse, 1990.

————. *New Currents in Western Buddhism*. Glasgow, Scotland: Windhorse, 1990.

————. *The Thousand-Petalled Lotus—the Indian Journey of an English Buddhist*. London: William Heinemann, Ltd., 1976; rpt. Gloucester: Alan Sutton Publishing, 1988.

Wilkinson, T. S., ed. *Ambedkar and the Neo-Buddhist Movement*. Bangalore: Christian Institute for the Study of Religion and Society, 1972.

Zelliot, Eleanor. "The Psychological Dimension of the Buddhist Movement in India" in G. A. Oddie, ed., *Religion in South Asia: Studies in Conversion and Revival Movements in Medieval and Modern Times*. Delhi: Manohar, 1977.

————. "Buddhism and Politics in Maharashtra" in *South Asian Politics and Religion*, edited by Donald E. Smith. Princeton, N.J.: Princeton University Press, 1966.

4

A. T. Ariyaratne and the
Sarvodaya Shramadana Movement in Sri Lanka

George D. Bond

The Sarvodaya Shramadana Movement in Sri Lanka represents one of the oldest and most celebrated Buddhist social liberation movements. Founded by a Buddhist layman, Dr. A. T. Ariyaratne, Sarvodaya arose in Sri Lanka in 1958 as one manifestation of the Buddhist revival that began in the late nineteenth century and continued into the twentieth century and the post-colonial period. This revival occurred in almost all of the countries where Theravada Buddhism was present. In Sri Lanka it can be said to have had two interconnected aims: it represented a quest by the Buddhists, first, to rediscover their Buddhist heritage and identity and, second, to respond rationally to the modern social, political, and economic context. To some extent this process of reinterpreting Buddhism was nothing new because religious traditions such as Buddhism are not static or monolithic but represent cumulative historical movements whose identities are continually being reinterpreted and reconstituted. What was significant about the Buddhist revival was the extent to which the Theravadins had to reconstruct their viewpoint because of the erosion caused by over four centuries of colonial rule. S. J. Tambiah has described the Buddhist revival in Sri Lanka as a process of resuscitating a tradition that had virtually died out.[1]

One of the central themes of the Buddhist revival was universalism, expressed as a newly discovered confidence in the spiritual potential of the laity. The reformers had a definite optimism about what Mary Douglas has called "the human potential for sustaining great spiritual achievement."[2] The revival in Theravada countries, carried out in large part by the new laity, emphasized the lay person's spiritual potential by teaching in various ways that the laity has both the opportunity and responsibility for their own liberation. A standard theme in reformist movements, this universalism

121

also implies an opposition to hierarchicalism and clericalism. In contrast to the traditional and neotraditional Buddhist idea that great sanctity is exceptional and that if it exists at all it is the province of the ordained clergy, the reformers have held that lay persons have at least as good, or perhaps better, chances to attain the goal in this life. Richard Gombrich and Gananath Obeyesekere have identified this feature as one of the hallmarks of "Protestant Buddhism," "the view that the layman . . . can and should try to reach *nirvana*."[3]

The Sarvodaya movement began as a lay Buddhist movement that has at its center a belief in the human potential for spiritual achievement.[4] Sarvodaya, however, went farther than other groups in the revival in arguing that Buddhist liberation involves not only individuals but also society. The Dhamma entails a dual liberation; there is a necessary and dependent relation between the freedom of the individual and the freedom of society. Neither the classical Theravada monastic interpreters nor the other reformers had stressed as clearly as Sarvodaya the implications of the Dhamma for social change. Sarvodaya affirmed the world by arguing that the path to individual liberation ran through social liberation.

Influences on Sarvodaya

In developing its interpretation, the Sarvodaya movement was influenced by two historical figures from this period: Mahatma Gandhi and Anagarika Dharmapala. Mahatma Gandhi coined the term "Sarvodaya" or "the wellbeing of all," as the title of his Gujarati translation of John Ruskin's work, *Unto this Last*. Ariyaratne studied Gandhi's ideas and worked with Gandhi's successor in India, Vinoba Bhave. Ariyaratne has often said that he did not borrow or import the Indian Sarvodaya ideas when he was beginning his Sri Lankan movement, and to a large extent this is true because the distinctive culture and problems of Sri Lanka required distinctive approaches. Nevertheless, there can be no doubt that the Gandhian movement inspired and influenced Sarvodaya in Sri Lanka. A close associate of Ariyaratne has described the early days of the Sri Lankan movement when "In public meetings the pictures and sayings of Gandhi and Vinoba were given prominence and in study classes it was their thought that provided the much needed inspiration for the young Sarvodayans."[5]

The Indian Sarvodaya movement influenced the fundamental orientation and outlook of Sarvodaya in Sri Lanka in at least three important ways. First, the Gandhian example of selfless service for humanity as the highest form of religious practice lies at the heart of the Sarvodaya movement. When

Gandhi formulated this idea, India was attempting to revive Hinduism and liberate India; in this process it was facing some of the same problems as the Buddhists in Sri Lanka. Gandhi's view presupposed a belief in the unity of humanity and the need for religion to address human need. Gandhi said, "God demands nothing less than self-surrender as the price for the only real freedom that is worth having. And when a man thus loses himself, he immediately finds himself in the service of God's creation."[6] Second, Gandhi and his movement used the term *Sarvodaya* to refer to a new, nonviolent, socioeconomic order. Working for this new social order was the highest form of religious vocation. "The spiritual law," Gandhi said, "expresses itself only through the ordinary activities of life. It thus affects the economic, the social and the political."[7] Gandhi's immediate successor, Vinoba Bhave, with whom Ariyaratne worked, spoke of trying to bring about a threefold revolution. "Firstly, I want to change people's hearts. Secondly, I want to create a change in their lives. Thirdly, I want to change the social structure."[8]

The third kind of influence that shaped Sarvodaya in Sri Lanka was the Gandhian movement's focus on the village as the heart of this new social-economic-religious order. Gandhi opposed industrialization, materialism and the drive for wealth. In his campaign for *khadi,* or homespun cloth, Gandhi was one of the pioneers of appropriate technology. The peaceful life of the village with its basic Hindu values rather than the industrialization of the city became the ideal for Gandhi. Gandhi said that the spinning wheels that he encouraged people to use in order to become self-sufficient, stood for "simple living and high thinking." All of these ideas permeated and shaped the Sri Lankan Sarvodaya movement's orientation and programs.

Supplementing these ideas of Gandhian Sarvodaya as influences on the Sri Lankan Sarvodaya movement were the ideas of Anagarika Dharmapala, the patriarch of the Buddhist revival and the charismatic advocate of Sinhalese Buddhist independence. Dharmapala, who worked for the revival of Buddhism in Sri Lanka and India during the late nineteenth and early twentieth centuries, was a living sermon on this-worldly asceticism. In order to reform Buddhism, he took on the role of an "anagarika," or homeless one. Since an "anagarika" was neither a monk nor a layman, this status enabled Dharmapala to pursue the religious life and be active in the world without having the restrictions of the monastic life. Although few Buddhists after Dharmapala took up the role of an "anagarika," Dharmapala's life and preaching established for all later Buddhist reformers the importance of worldly activity. He described Buddhism as a "Gospel of Activity" preached by the Buddha who "was engaged in doing good in the world of gods and men for twenty-two hours each day." Dharmapala proclaimed that "Greater than the bliss of sweet Nirvana is the life of moral activity."[9]

In advocating a Buddhism of activity and service, Dharmapala was undoubtedly responding to the Western and Christian criticism of Buddhism as too other-worldly. The British officials and Christian missionaries had promoted this idea from the outset of colonial rule in Sri Lanka and had used it as an argument for promoting Christianity and Christian schools. Since Christianity was identified with Western culture and knowledge, the British praised it as progressive and condemned Buddhism as backward. Buddhism came to be regarded by the Westerners and by many Sinhalese also as a religion that lacked a social ethic. To counter this argument, Dharmapala wrote extensively of the emphasis that early Buddhism placed on a social ethic. "To build a rest house for the public good, to build a bridge, . . . to help the poor, to take care of parents and holy men, . . . to establish free hospitals . . . all these are productive of good karma."[10] He criticized the Buddhism of his day, saying that "The bhikkhus are indolent, they have lost the spirit of heroism and altruism of their ancient examples."[11] In words that were to be echoed by Sarvodaya, Dharmapala wrote, "The ideal of the Buddhist faith consists in realizing through spiritual experience and moral acts, the continuity of life in man and nature and the fellowship of all beings."[12]

Dharmapala's central message, which profoundly influenced later Buddhist reformers including Ariyaratne, was that the Sinhalese should return to the *Dhamma* in order to solve the dual dilemma of discovering their identity and responding to the modern context. Reestablishing Buddhism and Buddhist values would enable the Sinhalese to reestablish the glorious civilization of Buddhist antiquity, where "free from foreign influences, . . . with the word of Buddha as their guiding light" the Sinhalese people enjoyed happiness and prosperity.[13]

In response to Dharmapala's preaching and to the missionaries' criticism that Buddhism lacked a social ethic and social concern, some Buddhist organizations began social service agencies. The All Ceylon Buddhist Congress and the Young Men's Buddhist Association, for example, established orphanages, hospitals, and homes for the elderly. It was not until the Sarvodaya movement emerged, however, that social service was given a distinctively Buddhist rationale and organized to achieve Buddhist objectives.

Building upon these influences, the leaders of Sarvodaya reinterpreted both the path and the goal of Buddhism to develop the blueprint for the Sarvodaya Shramadana Movement. The path became a path of selfless service in the world, and the goal became the development of a new social structure that embodied the Buddhist ideals and facilitated a dual liberation process.

Sarvodaya's Reinterpretation of the Dhamma for Social Action

Sarvodaya affirms the Gandhian and rationalist view that selfless service in the world represents the true path to the goal of the religion. Thus,

Ariyaratne is critical of any forms of Buddhism that lack a social and this-worldly focus or that have primarily other-worldly goals. He rejects all interpretations of the monastic life that expect the monks to live aloof from worldly matters. He also placed little value on the traditional Theravada path for lay Buddhists that interprets Buddhism as a system of rituals and rules for the acquisition of merit for rebirth. The monks, Ariyaratne explains, should do more than merely "look after the souls of people after death." Because that is all many temples do, he writes, "We are not getting full use out of them."[14] Explaining the difference between the Gandhian Sarvodaya based on Hindu ideas and the Sri Lankan Buddhist Sarvodaya, Kantowski observed that, "Gandhi tried to realize his true Self through dedication to the Service of All; Sarvodaya workers in Sri Lanka express their Non-Self by Sharing with All. Starting from different assumptions both concepts lead Sarvodaya in India and Sri Lanka into society and not out of it."[15]

Sarvodaya finds a charter for this path of selfless service to the world in the *Tipitaka,* the ancient Pali Canon of Buddhist scriptures. Sarvodaya's publications cite *suttas,* the discourses attributed to the Buddha, that support its interpretation of Buddhism as a religion that has as much to say about how to exist in the world as it does about how to transcend the world. Sarvodaya's apologists claim that this interpretation of the scriptures "represents not so much a departure from tradition as a return to the early teachings of its founder and a reclamation of their original meaning."[16] To support its call for social and economic change and the relevance of such changes to individual awakening, Sarvodaya holds up *suttas* dealing with social and economic teachings. Ariyaratne points out, for example, that the Buddha set out guidelines for economic activity in *suttas* such as the *Kutadanta Sutta.*[17] In other *suttas* the Buddha gave social-ethical teachings for Buddhists to follow. Sarvodaya publications remind their followers of the importance of the social philosophy contained in the *Sigalovada Sutta* with its teachings about one's duties toward others, in the *Mahamangala Sutta* with its thirty-eight keys to living happily in the world, and in the *Parabhara Sutta* that explains those actions that lead to one's defeat or downfall. Sarvodaya also regards other texts such as the *Jataka Tales,* the life story of the Buddha and the stories of the arahants as scriptures that "emphasize nothing but the value of serving others as the surest means of eventually attaining the ultimate goal."[18]

Sarvodaya's reinterpretation is, however, not limited to these *suttas* that explicitly contain Buddhist social teachings. Rather, citing these *suttas* as an indication of the intentionality of early Buddhism, Sarvodaya goes beyond them to reinterpret the central principles of the Dhamma by showing that they constitute a path for action in the world. For traditional Theravada Buddhism, the basic nature of the path was summarized in the formula of the Eightfold Path. Traditional texts, such as the *Visuddhimagga* ("The Path of Purification"), taught that the path was lengthy and gradual, requiring many lifetimes to fulfill. Progress on this path presupposed renunciation of the world and dedication to meditation and the monastic life. Sarvodaya reinterprets the Eightfold Path, however, by saying that everyone who works for the goals that Sarvodaya seeks can and should follow the Eightfold Path in daily life in the world. When I asked Ariyaratne whether renunciation is necessary to reach the goal of enlightenment, he replied that it depends on the person. Some are inclined to renunciation, others to activity. Each person should decide how he or she can make the greatest contribution. Clearly, however, Sarvodaya's whole program presupposes that renunciation does not represent the only path—or even the most suitable path—for the majority of people. Ariyaratne says, "According to the extent of each person's mental development and determination this spiritual path can be followed while living in society."[19]

Ariyaratne justifies his reinterpretation of the path by pointing out that the Buddhist tradition and its texts include many elements, some spiritual and moral, some social, economic, and political. All of these elements have to be taken together; they exist in balance. An interpretation should not limit Buddhism to spiritual teachings only: "otherwise," Ariyaratne said, "we end up confining Buddha's teachings only to the other world."[20] That idea represents a serious misinterpretation, in his view, because if that had been the Buddha's intention he would not have given so many teachings about social responsibilities and social philosophy.

The extent of Sarvodaya's reinterpretation of the *Dhamma* for social engagement is evident in its explanation of the Four Divine Abidings *(Brahma Viharas)* as central factors in the this-worldly path. The Four Divine Abidings comprise loving-kindness *(metta)*, compassion *(karuna)*, sympathetic joy *(mudita)*, and equanimity *(upekkha)*. Classical Theravada taught that these four represented enstatic states of mental tranquility reached by withdrawing from the world and practicing the meditation of calmness, *samadhi*. The texts of Theravada describe the process whereby a meditator employing these Divine Abidings in *samadhi* meditation could attain the *jhanas* or trance states. These four states of tranquility were cultivated traditionally by withdrawing from the world, not by acting in the world. As subjects of meditation these topics produced calm mental states, not an ethic for social involvement. The meditator who perfected the mental states of loving-kindness or compassion infused these qualities into the world not by social work but by a process that Winston King has described as "individualized radiation of virtue and health out into society by holy persons."[21] To be sure, some or many Arahants are said to have lived lives of compassionate service, but there was no requirement that meditation leads to service.

The Divine Abidings represented exercises in mental purification, intended to calm the mind and produce both equanimity and the world-recessive trance states. Sarvodaya, however, teaches that the Four Divine Abidings serve primarily as guidelines for social action. Although the tradition may have seen them as meditation subjects or thoughts, Ariyaratne says that is not sufficient. "Loving-kindness towards all is the thought that an awakening personality should have. But this thought is not enough; it is only the motivation which should lead us to compassionate action."[22] Clearly Sarvodaya has shifted the focus in its understanding of the Divine Abidings; however, even in classical Theravada these ideas have ethical implications on the mundane or this-worldly plane and seem logically to imply a social philosophy.

Ariyaratne maintains that in Sri Lankan culture traditionally the awakening of the personality was based on these four principles.[23] Therefore Sarvodaya promotes them as central elements of its plan for employing the Dhamma to assist and uplift the rural poor. Sarvodaya takes the first principle, *metta* or loving-kindness, to mean "respect for all life," cultivating love for all beings. This principle leads to the second, *karuna,* or compassion, which Sarvodaya understands as "compassionate action."

Mudita, or sympathetic joy, results from acting on the first two principles because one sees how one's efforts have helped others. This joy represents an important factor in Sarvodaya's mundane awakening, for to be awake and liberated is to be joyful. Sarvodaya does not downplay the element of joy derived from losing oneself in the service of society. The fourth principle, *upekkha,* or equanimity, becomes important for developing a personality structure unshaken by praise or blame, by gain or loss.

Sarvodaya's distinctive method for cultivating these ideals and implementing a this-worldly path is *shramadana,* the work camp. Sarvodaya has regarded shramadana as a reinterpretation of the Buddhist virtue of generosity, *dana.* Shramadana is understood to mean "the gift or sharing of one's time and labor." Sarvodaya volunteers assist villagers to organize shramadana camps to solve problems such as the need for a well or the building of a road. To carry out the project the villagers join with Sarvodaya volunteers and neighbors to work for a week or more in an atmosphere in which Buddhist values are explicitly cultivated and discussed. Each day of the camp begins and ends with a "family gathering" in which ideas such as the Divine Abidings are considered and the day's work is planned. During the period of the camp, all participants follow the four *sangaha vatthuni,* grounds of kindness, as the social application of the Buddhist ethical ideals. These four principles of group behavior include *dana,* generosity, *peyyavajja,* kindly speech, *atthacariya,* useful work, and *samanattata,* equality. Ariyaratne regards these principles as the foundation of traditional village communal life and the antithesis of modern, materialist social life. Following them leads to a life governed by sharing and nonaggression rather than by individuality and competition. Ariyaratne described the value of these principles for traditional village society when he says, "This social philosophy and practice at the rural level laid a strong infrastructure for the stability and strength of the nation."[24] So, in a *shramadana* or work camp, the participants relate to each other on the basis of these principles and thereby establish a psychological and social infrastructure for authentic development and awakening.

Through living out the Divine Abidings in the concrete action of *shramadana*, Sarvodayans implement the path of this-worldly asceticism that leads to the goal of dual liberation. Ariyaratne said that "To change society we must purify ourselves, and the purification process we need is brought about by working in society."[25] The Buddhist path, including the factors of the Eightfold Path and the Four Divine Abidings, constitutes the crucial link between the individual and society in Sarvodaya's whole scheme of awakening and development, for it provides a means to awaken both self and society together. At times Ariyaratne compares Sarvodaya's conception of the path to that of the Bodhisattva, the being who postpones his own enlightenment in order to remain in the world to work for the enlightenment of all.[26] The *Bhagavad Gita*'s ideal of the *karma yogi,* the one who sees doing service and work as the highest form of religion, especially as updated by Gandhi, also functions as a central paradigm for Sarvodaya's path.

Sarvodaya has been criticized for this reinterpretation of the Buddhist path as this-worldly asceticism by many Buddhists and scholars of Buddhism who have understood the tradition as world-denying and the path as one that required detachment from the world. Almost since the inception of Buddhist studies in the West, scholarly opinion has held that Theravada represents a world denying or world renouncing tradition. As one Western scholar wrote, "Buddhism was (and largely is) ahistorical in viewpoint. It deals not with man in society or among his fellows but with the individual man facing his eternal destiny. And it turns man supremely toward seeking a Good (*Nibbana*) above all time and space. To tell the truth the Buddha had little . . . concern for society as such or firm conviction of its possible improvability."[27]

Does Sarvodaya's interpretation of the Buddhist teachings sacrifice continuity with the Theravada tradition for the sake of relevance to present problems? This is the question that Sarvodaya's view of the path raises for many people. An example of the criticism of Sarvodaya on this point was stated by Obeyesekere: "The Buddha had a realistic view of human life in society: the achievement of the ultimate Buddhist goals cannot be realized

in the world; it requires the arduous path of the homeless monk and systematic meditation. . . . By contrast Sarvodaya attempts to achieve the great
goals of Buddhism by living in the world and participating in this-worldly
activity."[28] The answer to this question of whether Sarvodaya has sacrificed
continuity lies in understanding Sarvodaya's interpretation of the goal of its
this-worldly path.

Sarvodaya's Goal of Dual Liberation

The goal of the path for Sarvodaya is signified by its name, which it
translates to mean "the awakening of all" or "the uplift of all." It represents
a dual liberation because it is the awakening of both the individual and the
society. These two forms of liberation are integrally related as a dual process in which the liberation of the individual depends upon the liberation
of society and vice versa. An individual living in a society that is poor
materially as well as spiritually will have great difficulty awakening to the
reality of his or her own greed, hatred, and delusion. But unless some
individuals awaken to these problems, social change and alleviation of poverty
will never be sought. Ariyaratne explains this dual process saying, "I cannot
awaken myself unless I help awaken others. Others cannot awaken unless
I do."[29] Ariyaratne contends that both of these forms of liberation have
continuity with the original goals of the Buddha's path.

Awakening the Individual

Sarvodaya calls the awakening of the individual "personality awakening" or "personality development." In the spirit of the Buddhist revival,
Ariyaratne has written that "every human being has the potential to attain
supreme enlightenment."[30] Because of the present condition of both individuals and society, however, the kind of "personality awakening" that the
average person can achieve in this life is far below the level of supreme
enlightenment but nevertheless represents a start on the gradual path toward the "ultimate goal of Buddhism." Therefore, Sarvodaya teaches that
before people can awaken to the supreme, supramundane dimension of
truth, they must awaken to the mundane dimensions of truth that surround them in society. Before people can see the supramundane meaning
of the traditional Four Noble Truths, for example, they must see the mundane meaning of these truths. To illustrate this idea, Sarvodaya has given
these truths social interpretations.

The first truth, *dukkha,* suffering or unsatisfactoriness, is translated as
"There is a decadent village." This concrete form of suffering becomes the

focus of mundane awakening. Villagers should recognize the problems in their environment, such as poverty, disease, oppression and disunity. The second truth, *samudaya,* the origin of suffering, now signifies that the decadent condition of the village has one or more causes. Sarvodaya teaches that the causes lie in factors such as egoism, competition, greed, and hatred.

The third, *nirodha,* cessation, understood in traditional Buddhism as an indicator of *Nibbana,* becomes hope that the villagers' suffering can cease. The means to solving the problem lies in the fourth truth, the Eight-fold Path. Joanna Macy offers an excellent example of the mundane expli-cation of the stages of the Eightfold Path when she cites a Sarvodaya teacher's explanation of Right Mindfulness or Awareness, *sati.* "Right Mindfulness—that means stay open and alert to the needs of the village. . . . Look to see what is needed—latrines, water, road. . . ."[31]

If persons can awaken to the mundane truths about the conditions around them, then realizing the need for change they can work in society in the spirit of the Divine Abidings. As society is changed, the individual is changed. One who addresses mundane problems with compassion, finds the mundane world becoming more compassionate. And in a more compas-sionate world it is easier to develop wisdom. Ariyaratne explains the interconnectedness of this process of dual liberation when he says that "The struggle for external liberation is a struggle for inner liberation from greed, hatred and ignorance at the same time."[32]

Awakening Society

Sarvodaya spells out the interdependent nature of this process of awak-ening and development by specifying six levels of human awakening: per-sonality awakening, family awakening, village/community awakening, urban awakening, national awakening, and global awakening. Sarvodaya's view of the awakening of society on these levels—the other side of the dual libera-tion process—constitutes a radical reinterpretation of the nature of social and economic development. For Sarvodaya, development is an integrated process involving six elements that reinforce each other to bring about the best society: in this process the reform of the social, political, and economic elements of a society should take place in conjunction with the reassertion of its moral, cultural, and spiritual elements. Integrated development of these six elements leads to a society based on spiritual and traditional values where people can live together in harmony and where individuals will have an opportunity to awaken their personalities to the fullest.

Sarvodaya's ideal of an integrated development supported by spiritual values critiques the materialistic, capitalistic model of development domi-

nant in Sri Lanka since the colonial period. Opposing the kind of materialistic development schemes that the government and international
agencies have brought about in Sri Lanka, Ariyaratne says, "In production-
centered societies the total perspective of human personality and sustain-
able relationships between man and nature is lost sight of. . . . The higher
ideals of human personality and social values are disregarded."[33] Produc-
tion-centered societies define wealth in quantitative terms and create desires for the objects that they produce; Sarvodaya declares that spiritual
values represent the true wealth. Sarvodaya's model of development is
"people-centered" and has as its primary aim "human fulfillment" rather
than the creation of material wealth. Ariyaratne argues that the "advancement of people in a quantitative sense is meaningless and even unachievable"
unless the spiritual and qualitative factors are included also.[34] The economic ideal of the social order Sarvodaya seeks is described as one of "no
poverty and no affluence."

In addition to basing these ideas on Buddhist texts, Ariyaratne grounds
Sarvodaya's alternative ideal of development on the village culture of ancient Sri Lanka. These "old societies" were human-centered and established
on Buddhist values. With this ancient village culture in mind, Ariyaratne
speaks of a "spiritual and cultural inheritance coming not from artificial
and affluent societies" of today but from "no-poverty societies of days
gone by."[35] Ariyaratne has a romantic image of this ancient village culture
where equality, justice, and Buddhist spiritual values governed all aspects
of life. He says, for example, that in precolonial village culture "The king,
the monks, the physician, the agents of the state, the black-smith, the
washerman, the aged and the widowed, all received their share (of the
harvest) . . . everyone's worth and dignity was well recognized."[36] In this
"old society" in Sri Lanka, people lived meaningful lives and had harmonious relations that enabled them to produce the great works of art and
architecture found in Anuradhapura and other ancient sites. In modern
society, by contrast, "machine and machine-like men" have exterminated
all of the traditional arts and crafts.[37] On this point Ariyaratne cites William
Blake, a poet whom John Ruskin also admired for his vision of the evils of
the industrial age.

> When nations grow old,
> the arts grow cold,
> And commerce settles on every tree.[38]

Ariyaratne contends that this traditional culture still exists in the rural
villages of Sri Lanka and that this rural, village culture constitutes one of
the main sources from which Sarvodaya has gleaned its ideas about the

values that should govern development. Sarvodaya maintains that its aim is not to institute a new plan of development, but "to revive the indigenous, age-old perception of reality that the people still possess and assist them to organize themselves on the basis of their own resources."[39] Among the values that these vestigial "old societies" continue to embrace Ariyaratne lists "nonviolence, sharing, smallness, decentralization, relevant technologies, production by the masses and unity."[40] In these village societies the "concept of the well-being of all, the awakening of all, or what we call Sarvodaya is well understood."[41] Ariyaratne argues that most of the problems in Sri Lanka came about because Western powers imposed foreign values along with a foreign economic system on the country during the colonial period. Violence, nonequality, lying, and unpleasant speech came to replace the traditional Buddhist or "old society" values. Nevertheless, the traditional values can still be found in the rural villages where Sarvodaya works.

This idealizing of the village recalls the similar emphasis by Gandhi on the Indian village as the hope for society and the place where traditional values survived during the colonial period. For Sarvodaya it serves to give their program of development an indigenous legitimation over against the materialism that stems from foreign sources. Ariyaratne asks whether the U.S.A., the U.S.S.R., Japan or Singapore should be the models that the people of Sri Lanka should emulate, or whether the Sri Lankans should follow their own tradition that enabled people to build the great civilizations of the past.

Sarvodaya's political model for a new, or renewed, social order is also drawn from this romantic notion of the ideal village: its government should operate without political parties. The new society, Ariyaratne says, "should be free from the stranglehold of party politics and based on the people's own power . . . "[42] This ideal, which has also been discussed extensively in contemporary Sri Lankan political circles, Ariyaratne derived from the "pure culture of the ancient village." In that context "The king was no different from the common man" because the king had to uphold the traditional morality that stressed equality. According to Ariyaratne, the king and the ordinary villager worked together "knee-deep in the mud of the paddy field."[43] The ideal here is a political system in which the leaders do not manipulate and divide the people for the leaders' own enrichment.

Ariyaratne's advocacy of the superior "spiritual and cultural inheritance from the old society" of the village represents a reprise of a theme from the early Buddhist revival. Nineteenth-century British historians, such as William Knighton and James Tennent, wrote histories of Sri Lanka that emphasized its glorious ancient civilization.[44] They described its greatness in Victorian terms by alluding to a cultural and national superiority of the

Sinhalese that had gone into decline. As John Rogers has noted, these historians "pictured Sinhala Buddhists as possessing an inherent identity separate from both the Veddas . . . and the Malabars."45

In the early Buddhist revival, Dharmapala, taking up the ideas of historians such as Tennent and Knighton, argued for the evolution and superiority of Sinhala Buddhist culture. He said, "No nation in the world has had a more brilliant history than ourselves."46 Dharmapala proclaimed that when the ancestors of the British "were running naked in the forests of Britain with their bodies painted," the ancient Sinhalese had already developed a "glorious and peaceful civilization based on Buddhist spiritual values."47

Ariyaratne and his Sarvodaya colleagues, in advocating the superiority of the "old structure," continue this view of the cultural superiority of Sri Lanka. They have changed the argument somewhat, however, by cleansing it of racial claims for the superiority of the Sinhalese. Sarvodaya speaks of Sri Lankan culture, not Sinhalese culture, a distinction that is not only more correct politically but probably is also more accurate historically. Nevertheless, Sarvodaya's claims about the village culture reflect the nineteenth-century views of culture in general and of Sri Lankan culture in particular. Along with Dharmapala, Ariyaratne extols the preeminence of the "old culture" based on Buddhist values and calls upon the people to put off Western values and to restore this more viable and valuable culture.

Although Sarvodaya's identification with village society serves to support its advocacy of grass roots development, its glorification of the village raises significant questions. It seems highly unlikely that the ideal village, as Ariyaratne describes it, ever existed. Ariyaratne, however, responds to those who criticize the veracity of his picture of village life by saying that he has tried to emphasize "all that is good or positive" about the "old society" of the village rather than to dwell on the negative aspects. Sarvodaya's view of the ideal village of the past represents what Milton Singer has called an "archaization."

To conclude this discussion of Sarvodaya's philosophy, we can return to the question raised earlier as to whether Sarvodaya's social activist interpretation of the dharma sacrifices continuity with classical Theravada's view of the goal of Buddhism. It seems accurate to say that Sarvodaya has maintained continuity while introducing a social interpretation of the gradual path. Mundane awakening to the realities of the social context represents a new stage of the path correlative to the new path of social activism. But mundane awakening and social reform never become the supreme goals for Sarvodaya; the supreme goal remains the spiritual enlightenment of Nirvana. In Sarvodaya's view, what it has done is simply to explicate some important steps in the long gradual path to Nirvana. Mundane awakening represents a basic step on the spiritual path, and those who awaken now to the Four Noble Truths or the Divine Abidings in a mundane sense can progress later in this life or in their next incarnation to higher understandings of these ideas. Ariyaratne recognizes this distinction between the mundane and supramundane goals and writes, "In other words, Sarvodaya as applied to the individual is the emergence of the best in him at any time culminating in the accomplished (awakened) personality... who is then capable of progressing on his own towards still higher goals of perfection such as purely spiritual pursuits."[48] Clearly though, Sarvodaya's concept of mundane awakening represents an innovative reinterpretation of what the gradual path of Buddhism involves in today's society. The concept of mundane awakening reforms both Buddhist spirituality and materialist development.

The exact nature of the interrelationship of the spiritual and social goals in Sarvodaya's vision of development is illustrated by a saying used by the movement to described shramadana camps: "We build the road and the road builds us." This saying catches the point that material development work done on behalf of society also serves spiritual purposes. As Ariyaratne explains, Sarvodaya actually cannot fail; the road may fail by being washed out, but the awakening that occurred in the building of it will endure. This saying demonstrates that although the social and spiritual factors in development depend on each other, for Sarvodaya the spiritual retains priority.

History of the Sarvodaya Movement

The Sarvodaya movement is completing its fourth decade of engaged Buddhism. Over this time, both the vision and the movement itself have evolved as Sarvodaya has sought to implement its programs in Sri Lanka. The growth and evolution of the Sarvodaya movement can be traced by noting a few of its landmark events. For a movement that was ultimately to reach out from its headquarters near Colombo to thousands of villages in Sri Lanka, Sarvodaya had somewhat modest origins as what Ariyaratne himself has called an educational experiment. It had its genesis in 1958 in a series of work camps conducted by Nalanda College in Colombo for its students. Ariyaratne, then a faculty member at the school, helped to organize the work camps to enable the students, who came from urban, middle-class backgrounds, to have some experience serving others in a poor village. For this experience, the students traveled to the village of Kanatoluwa, a poor, low-caste village in the North Central Province, about 80 kilometers north of Colombo. They worked there for eleven days, painting buildings, digging latrines, planting gardens, and teaching the villagers about subjects such as health care. From this first work camp, the movement began as Ariyaratne and his friends went on to organize more work camps in other depressed villages around the island. The movement soon grew beyond the bounds of Nalanda College, and the work camps came to involve youth and adults from various parts of the country. The camps came to be called *shramadanas,* or the donation of labor. Between 1958 and 1966 hundreds of these shramadanas were held, involving more than 300,000 volunteers.

In 1961 the young movement held a shramadana camp at Anuradhapura as part of a nationwide efforts to restore the ancient city.[49] During this camp the participants approved the name Sarvodaya for the movement and in a meeting held beneath the sacred Bo-tree adopted a resolution pledging to further "the cause of the movement in the service of the spiritual and economic regeneration of Sri Lanka according to Buddhist Values and principles."[50] In 1967, Sarvodaya declared its "Hundred Villages Development Scheme," which was a plan to carry out *gramodaya,* or village awakening, in one hundred selected villages. This scheme was so successful that by 1971 the movement was conducting shramadanas and village awakening in four hundred villages, and by the end of the decade it was working in some two thousand villages.

In 1972 Ariyaratne resigned from the faculty of Nalanda College to devote his full time to directing the Sarvodaya movement. By then the movement had begun to receive funding from foreign donor organizations, such as the German organization, Friedrich Naumann Stiftung (FNS), and the Dutch organization, NOVIB. As Sarvodaya grew and came to the attention of groups beyond Sri Lanka, Ariyaratne received international recognition for his work, and this recognition contributed to the movement's success at home. Among Ariyaratne's awards—at this time and later—were the Ramon Magsaysay Award for Community Leadership (Philippines, 1969), the King Baudouin Award for International Development (Belgium, 1982), the Feinstein World Hunger Award (United States, 1986), and the Niwano Peace Prize (Japan, 1991).

As Sarvodaya grew, it evolved from a student work camp movement into a nongovernmental organization (NGO) dedicated to facilitating alternative development. Many young people were attracted to the ideals of this movement/organization that sought to assist disadvantaged rural villages. These young people became Sarvodaya volunteers, who worked without salary and lived among the villagers whom they were assisting. Through the help of international donor organizations Sarvodaya built a large development education complex at Moratuwa, near Colombo, with a training center, a library, a media center, a conference hall, and administrative offices. A sign on the front of this headquarters complex declared:

> This abode of young men and women trainees who strive to establish a
> Sarvodaya social order in Sri Lanka and the world in keeping with the
> noble eightfold path of the Buddhist philosophy is named the "Damsak
> Mandira" and it is built in the shape of the Dhamma Chakka (Wheel of
> Doctrine).

By the late 1970s, as Sarvodaya entered its third decade, it had become a huge movement that blanketed the country with development
services. Much of its expansion was made possible by the rapid growth of
donor funding during this period. In the early 1970s there had been only
a few outside donors supporting the movement, but by the 1980s there
were over twenty foundations providing support. The major supporters
were European foundations such as NOVIB (Netherlands), FNS (West
Germany), NORAD (Norway), and Helvetas (Switzerland). With the support of these donors, Sarvodaya established vocational training schools,
community farms, preschools, shramadana camps and other programs
that had an impact on the lives of thousands of people. Sarvodaya became
a powerful national entity that at times rivaled the government in terms
of both the effectiveness of its programs in assisting the people and its
popularity in all parts of the island. By 1985 the number of villages in
which Sarvodaya was active was said to be 8,000, which represented one
third of the island's villages.[51]

The most severe test of Sarvodaya's effectiveness and even of its survival came about because of the ethnic conflict that has ravaged Sri Lanka
since the late 1970s. This intractable conflict thrust Sarvodaya into a major
role as a peace broker. Since Sarvodaya has been active in all parts of the
island, including the Tamil areas, from an early period of its history, it can
claim with accuracy to have been attempting to overcome ethnic differences even before the conflict erupted in violence. Recognition of the
multicultural nature of Sri Lankan society led Sarvodaya to attempt to
translate its Buddhist ideology into a nonsectarian ideology stressing "traditional values." Tamils have held prominent positions of leadership in
Sarvodaya and Sarvodaya has organized Shramadana camps and training
programs of various kinds for Tamil youths. Tamils who worked with
Sarvodaya have not regarded it as a Sinhala-Buddhist organization but as
a Sri Lankan organization. By all accounts, Sarvodaya was very successful
in its development programs in the northern part of the island before the
terrible riots of July 1983 and the emergence of the militant Tamil separat-
ist movements.

After the riots erupted in July 1983, Sarvodaya began arranging peace
conferences and peace marches involving the various ethnic groups in the
country. In the immediate wake of the violence in 1983, Sarvodaya, along

with other groups organized refugee camps for some of the victims and held a national conference. This conference issued Sarvodaya's "People's Declaration for National Peace And Harmony" calling for nonviolence and national integration. Part of that declaration stated that one aim of the conference was "to create a spiritual, mental, social and intellectual environment" for peace in the nation. Toward that end, Ariyaratne planned a Gandhian-style peace march or "peace walk" from the southern tip of the island to Nagadeepa in the north. The march was set to begin on December 6, 1983, and as the date approached, thousands of people began assembling at Kiri Vehera near Kataragama to take part. The march by representatives from all ethnic groups was to cover a thousand miles in one hundred days and to pass through some of the most troubled areas of the country. The plans for this dramatic march put Sarvodaya in the national and international spotlight. Ultimately, however, the march was not to be. Led by Ariyaratne, the marchers had gone only a few miles when the President of Sri Lanka, J. R. Jayawardene, requested them to stop. Jayawardene's stated reason for stopping the march was that he feared it would disrupt the work of the government's negotiations at the impending All Party Conference. Jayawardene also said that the government had information that terrorists were plotting to assassinate Ariyaratne during the march in order to cause further rioting by the Sinhalese. The march was therefore stopped so as to prevent further violence.

Sarvodaya did not, however, abandon the peace march as a strategy. It continued to organize other major and minor peace marches, including one from Kandy to Sri Pada in March 1990. These peace marches had great symbolic value at a time when most people in the country longed for peace but felt helpless in the face of the increasing violence. Through the peace marches, Ariyaratne and his supporters stood up to the terrorists in protest. During one march Ariyaratne said, "Let it be known to those who bear arms that there are about two million members in Sarvodaya who are prepared to brave death anywhere and anytime."[52] Understandably, these marches drew significant attention to Ariyaratne and Sarvodaya. A Sarvodaya publication of the time drew an analogy that many Sri Lankans thought was not inappropriate when it noted in a story about the Sarvodaya "peace walk" that, "History records that the Buddha undertook a series of walks in his forty-five years of existence for the well-being of humanity."[53] Through the marches and other means, Sarvodaya has continued to work for peace in the country. In 1994, Ariyaratne made a widely publicized trip to Jaffna to meet with the leaders of the Tamil insurgent group, LTTE, in an attempt to find a solution to the long conflict. That Ariyaratne was able to arrange these negotiations testifies to the national status that he and his movement have achieved.

The most recent chapter of Sarvodaya's history—its evolution during its fourth decade—has been marked both by Sarvodaya's great successes, such as its role in the quest for peace, and by serious problems. Somewhat paradoxically, the problems have been caused to some extent by the successes. These problems can be summarized under two headings: problems with the government of Sri Lanka and problems with Sarvodaya's foreign donors.

Sarvodaya and the Sri Lankan Government

Sarvodaya's relations with the government have been complex from the outset. Although Sarvodaya has sought to be politically neutral, it has found that principle difficult to follow in a small country such as Sri Lanka. After 1977, Ariyaratne and Sarvodaya became very closely associated with the UNP governments of Jayawardene and Premadasa. It is no secret that Premadasa's very successful *Gam Udawa* program borrowed many of its ideas as well as its name from Sarvodaya's *gramodaya,* or "village reawakening program." For several years, Ariyaratne supported the government and encouraged Premadasa's efforts at grass-roots development, seeing these government programs as supplementary to Sarvodaya's programs. The ethnic conflict in general and the repressive measures used by the government against the JVP in particular, however, drove a wedge between Sarvodaya and the government. Disillusioned, Ariyaratne began to speak out in criticism of the government

When R. Premadasa became President of Sri Lanka in 1989, the government launched a comprehensive attack on Sarvodaya and Dr. Ariyaratne. As part of its campaign the government set up, in 1990, a Presidential Commission to investigate nongovernmental organizations, of which Sarvodaya was the largest and most prominent in the country. The state-run television and radio stations ceased almost all coverage of Sarvodaya events and all mention of Ariyaratne. Indicating the extent to which the government viewed Ariyaratne as a threat, the government-controlled newspapers began a vigorous campaign of negative news stories about Sarvodaya. Articles in these newspapers questioned Sarvodaya's use of the foreign funding that constitutes its major source of support. Carrying this theme even further, the papers charged in 1991 that Sarvodaya had raised funds by selling Sri Lankan children to foreign adoption agencies. A story on this subject in the *Sunday Observer* carried the heading, "Exposing Sarvodaya." Indicating the intent of the campaign, the story said, "the readers will be able to judge the character of the leaders of the Sarvodaya Movement who allowed themselves to be part of such a sordid deal." Ariyaratne wrote an immediate reply to the papers stating that in all the years that Sarvodaya had cared for children in its homes, it had never given any children for foreign adoption. The papers, however, did not print his letter. Although the stories resembled the worst tabloid journalism and were patently false, they, nevertheless, constituted a powerful campaign of negative publicity about Ariyaratne and the Sarvodaya movement.

The government's motives for this campaign of attacks were doubtless complex. It seems clear, however, that a major factor behind them was the success and power of Sarvodaya and Dr. Ariyaratne. President Premadasa was threatened by Ariyaratne's popularity among the rural masses. Premadasa also resented the way that these Buddhists held Ariyaratne in high regard as a spokesman for Buddhist values and ideals—possibly higher than they held the President himself, who longed to be seen as the champion of Buddhism. That the government was threatened by the size and power of Sarvodaya was revealed in an editorial in the government press during the height of the attacks on the movement. The article asked whether an NGO that had received foreign funds intended to assist the country, should be allowed "to use against a people's elected government the nearly 100 million (Rupees) worth of property, buildings and vehicles that they have country-wide?"[54]

The campaign against Sarvodaya ended in 1993 when the new government of President Wijetunge, who took over after President Premadasa was assassinated, disbanded the NGO commission and issued presidential orders stopping all of the attacks by government agencies against Sarvodaya. The Sri Lankan courts have recently ruled that the government press was guilty of libel against Sarvodaya for some of the malicious stories that it published, including the stories about the orphans. The ultimate effect on Sarvodaya of the four years of attacks and negative publicity remains to be seen, however. Can time and truth erase the cloud of doubt that the government created with its campaign against Sarvodaya?

Sarvodaya and Its Foreign Donors

The period of the government's attacks coincided with a time when Sarvodaya's donors began to insist that they should have more control over Sarvodaya. Although the donor organizations officially sided with Sarvodaya in its battle with the government, the attacks by the government seemed to erode some of the donors' confidence in Sarvodaya and its leaders. From the beginning, Sarvodaya had defined its development objectives in qualitative terms; however, the donors now brought pressure on Sarvodaya to adopt a quantitative approach and to accept quantitative measures of developmental success. In earlier times when Sarvodaya had been strongly supported by the government and the public, the donors would not have been able to make such demands. It is also the case that the original representatives of the foundations who began supporting Sarvodaya had been much more in sympathy with Sarvodaya's goals and philosophy of development. In the last few years, however, the current representatives of the donors have attempted to push Sarvodaya to make changes that are inconsistent with the aims and identity of the movement.

The donors have tried to impose on Sarvodaya what have been called "World Bank-type financial and administrative systems," and to force it to comply with the foundations' expectations about the meaning of development. In one meeting with the donors, when Sarvodaya leaders pointed out that these demands ran counter to Sarvodaya's philosophy and ideals, the project director from NOVIB replied, "We are not interested in philosophy. For NOVIB, development is a business. There is nothing idealistic about it."[55] The donors have insisted, for example, that Sarvodaya centralize its administration and adopt a highly centralized system of financial management—changes that run counter to Sarvodaya's philosophy of grass-roots organization and leadership. The donors have sought also to have more frequent assessments of Sarvodaya's development projects. Previously, Sarvodaya had always refused to accept the notion that the kind of development that it sought could be assessed in quantitative terms. The donors, however, wanted Sarvodaya to be able to say when development in a particular village or area is complete and when the donors could stop supporting that development. Although philosophically Sarvodaya believed that this question was unanswerable because the development of a village like development of a person could never be considered finished, Ariyaratne and the other leaders had to accede to the donors demands for more quantitative assessments of progress.

Relations between Sarvodaya and the donors reached a crisis in 1993 when NOVIB announced that it would reduce its funding to Sarvodaya by 42 percent. This reduction was made despite a long-term commitment that NOVIB and other donors had previously entered into with Sarvodaya. NOVIB cited various reasons for the cutbacks including the Dutch government's dissatisfaction with Sarvodaya's audit reports. These reductions were devastating to Sarvodaya, coming as they did hardly three months after President Premadasa had died and things had begun to return to normal for Sarvodaya. As a result of this reduction in its funding, Sarvodaya had to lay off over one thousand staff members. This number included two thirds of the district-level staff and large numbers of the village workers. These cutbacks brought many of Sarvodaya's programs to a complete standstill. Sarvodaya district centers throughout the country, that had once been busy with activities to assist the people, now stood empty.

Conclusion

Sarvodaya grew and succeeded in Sri Lanka because it discovered that development required spiritual rather than material goals as a basis. Sarvodaya enabled Buddhists to address the difficult questions of social change and liberation from a Buddhist perspective. This was the secret of Sarvodaya's popularity as well as its success. Ariyaratne and his followers regarded Sarvodaya as more than an NGO or a development organization; it was a crusade. The Buddhists of Sri Lanka, having recently (1947) attained their freedom from colonialism, felt that the wheel of Dhamma was turning again and could provide the solutions to their modern problems. Ariyaratne was a charismatic preacher of this kind of Buddhist optimism about a future of freedom and quality. He proclaimed that Buddhism alone provided the force to temper the power of science and "channel it along the path of general progress and well-being for all in society."[56] Ariyaratne's speeches and writings issued a challenge to the youth to join not a development organization but a "People's Movement for a Sarvodaya Social Order." He wrote that, "Calling a halt to exploitation or violence in all fields, economic, political, administrative, or social—by nonviolent direct action—is the duty of all who believe in total freedom. The movement provides the youth a humble opportunity to do that duty."[57] Large numbers of Sinhalese young people responded to this challenge and enlisted in Sarvodaya as volunteers because they wanted to work for this social revolution based on a Buddhist credo for the modern age. Kantowski has observed that "Sarvodaya is not an extension agency that hopes to improve the so-called 'quality of life' in certain rural areas through technical advice and capital aid. . . . It is not the extension of appropriate techniques which is the main mission of the movement, but the propagation of the message."[58]

The attacks of the government and the cutbacks by the donors have now raised serious questions about the future of this revolution. Sarvodaya faces several challenges to its survival. These include the challenge of establishing a new base of financial support and the challenge of rediscovering its identity and charting a new course for the future. There is no question, however, about Ariyaratne's determination to meet these challenges. When the donors first threatened to withdraw their support, Ariyaratne's first reaction was to say that Sarvodaya would simply do without donor support and "restart the movement." He said, "We cannot abandon our vision just to please the donors."[59]

Fortunately for Sarvodaya, the present time seems to be auspicious for a rediscovery of its values and its identity and for doing exactly what Ariyaratne says—"restarting the movement." At one time, Sarvodaya's approach represented an alternative that was foreign to the views of most development planners. Today, however, some development thinking—although unfortunately not that of Sarvodaya's recent donor consortium—seems to be moving in the direction of endorsing Sarvodaya's original objectives of a human-centered development. *The Human Development Report* for 1994 from the United Nations Development Program (UNDP), for example, calls for a "new development paradigm . . . [that] puts people at the center of development, regards economic growth as a means and not an end . . . and respects the natural systems on which all life depends."[60] If this report of the UNDP signals real changes in the development community, Sarvodaya may be able to solve its funding crisis.

If Sarvodaya can simultaneously resolve the questions about its identity and direction that the challenges by the government and the donors raised, then it can continue to be a force both in Sri Lanka and the world. Dr. Ariyaratne is prepared to extend Sarvodaya's engaged Buddhist path and goals to the world. In receiving the Niwano Peace Prize in 1992, he said, "Now the time has come when science and technology on the one hand and spiritual wisdom on the other have to be synthesized on a global scale to build a nobler, more just and more peaceful global community."[61]

Notes

1. S. J. Tambiah, *World Conqueror and World Renouncer* (New York: Cambridge University Press, 1976), p. 217.

2. Mary Douglas, "The Effects of Modernization on Religious Change," *Daedalus*, vol. 3, no. 1, p. 4.

3. Richard Gombrich and G. Obeyesekere, *Buddhism Transformed: Religious Change In Sri Lanka* (Princeton, N.J.: Princeton University Press, 1988), p. 216.

4. Although Sarvodaya affirmed the potential of lay persons, it did not take an anticlerical stance. It has tried throughout its history to enlist the monks in its programs for social liberation.

5. N. Ratnapala, *Sarvodaya in Sri Lanka* (Moratuwa, Sri Lanka: Sarvodaya Publications, 1978), p. 6.

6. Gandhi, M. K., *Young India*, December 20, 1928, p. 420.

7. Gandhi, M. K., *Young India*. September 3, 1925. p. 304.

8. Cited in Hans Wismeijer, *Diversity in Harmony*. Privately published dissertation from the Department of Cultural Anthropology, Heidelberglann, Utrecht, Netherlands, p. 33.

9. A. Guruge, *Return to Righteousness* (Colombo, Ceylon: Government Press, 1965), p. 737.

10. Ibid., p. 337.

11. Ibid., p. 748.

12. Ibid., p. 339.

13. Ibid., p. 489.

14. *Collected Works,* vol. 1, p. 124.

15. Kantowski, p. 75.

16. Joanna Macy, *Dharma and Development: Religion as Resource in the Sarvodaya Self-Help Movement* (West Hartford, Conn.: Kumarian Press, 1983), p. 76.

17. *Kutadanta Sutta* in *Digha Nikaya,* vol. 1, ed. Rhys Davids and Carpenter (London: Pali Text Society, 1967), pp. 127–148.

18. L. G. Hewage, *Relevance of Cultural Heritage in Development Education.* A published paper presented to the Conference on Sarvodaya and Development, 1976, p. 31.

19. *In Search of Development,* p. 14.

20. Interview with Ariyaratne, 1984.

21. Winston King, *In the Hope of Nibbana* (LaSalle, Ill.: Open Court Press, 1964), p. 183.

22. *Collected Works,* vol. 2, p. 49.

23. *Collected Works,* vol. 1, p. 119.

24. *Sarvodaya Shramadana: Growth of a People's Movement,* (Sarvodaya, 1973), p. 17.

25. This comment was made during one of our interviews.

26. Collected Works, vol. 2, p. 84.

27. King, p. 177. Ariyaratne responds to this kind of criticism of Sarvodaya's interpretation by charging that it is this interpretation of Buddhism as a world-denying system that is in error. He contends that this viewpoint began during the colonial period when the Western powers wanted to subvert the indigenous culture and marginalize the monks.

28. *Buddhism Transformed,* p. 246.

29. *A People's Agenda for Global Awakening,* Ninth Niwano Peace Prize Ceremony, 1992. p. 3.

30. *Collected Works,* vol. 1, p. 133.

31. Ibid.

32. *In Search of Development,* p. 16.

33. *Dana,* vol. 14, no. 9 (September 1989), p. 13.

34. "Political Institutions and Traditional Morality," *Dana,* vol. 14, no. 9, (September 1989), p. 13.

35. "Dwellings for Humanity with a View to Total Human Fulfillment," (Address to conference on Dwellings for Humanity, Japan, 1984), *Dana,* vol. II, no. 3, p. 6.

36. *Collected Works,* vol. 1, p. 52–153.

37. Ibid.

38. Ibid., p. 9.

39. "Political Institutions and Traditional Morality," *Dana,* vol. 14, no. 9 (September 1989), p. 16.

40. *Dana,* vol. II, no. 3, p. 4.

41. Ibid.

42. "Sarvodaya: Non-Partisan But Committed," *Dana,* vol. 13, nos. 9–12 (September–December 1988), p. 2.

43. Ariyaratne, *Collected Works,* vol 1, p. 53.

44. William Knighton, *The History of Ceylon from the Earliest Period to the Present Time* (London, 1845); James Tennent, *Ceylon: An Account of the Island; Physical, Historical, Topographical,* 2 vols. (London, 1859).

45. John D. Rogers, "Historical Images in the British Period," p. 92.

46. Dharmapala, Return to Righteousness, p. 506.

47. Ibid., p. 502.

48. Ibid., p. 99.

49. Detlef Kantowski, *Sarvodaya the Other Development* (New Delhi: Vikas Publishing House, 1980), p. 44.

50. Ibid.

51. *Sarvodaya Annual Service Report,* April 1983–March 1984, p. 34. and Dana, vol. II, no. 9, (1986), p. 5.

52. Speech delivered on 9/26/86 at the "Peace Walk Ceremony in Vavuniya on behalf of Mr. K. Kadiramalai," *Dana,* vol. II, nos. 10–11, p. 16.

53. "Editorial," *Dana,* vol II, no. 6 (May 1986), p. 1.

54. "It is damaging for Non-Governmental Organizations to get involved in politics," Sri Lanka *Daily News,* April 6, 1992.

55. *The Future Directions of Sarvodaya,* (Moratuwa; Sri Lanka: Sarvodaya Press, 1994), p. 10.

56. A. Ariyaratne, *Collected Works,* vol. I (Moratuwa, Sri Lanka: Sarvodaya Publication, n.d.), p. 57.

57. Ibid., p. 73.

58. Kantowski, *Sarvodaya, the Other Development,* p. 68.

59. Comment made by A. T. Ariyaratne to the Donor Liaison Officer in 1994.

60. United Nations Development Program, *Human Development Report,* 1994, p. 4.

61. "A People's Agenda for Global Awakening" Niwano Peace Prize acceptance speech. Published by the Niwano Peace Foundation, 1992.

Bibliography

Ariyaratne, A. T. *Collected Works.* Volumes I–V. Moratuwa, Sri Lanka, Sarvodaya Research Institute, 1978–1991.

———. *In Search of Development: The Sarvodaya Movement's Effort to Harmonize Tradition with Change.* Moratuwa, Sri Lanka: Sarvodaya Press, 1982.

Bond, George D. *The Buddhist Revival in Sri Lanka.* Columbia, S. C.: University of South Carolina Press, 1988.

Dasgupta, Sugata. *Sarvodaya in Sri Lanka.* Calcutta: Jayaprakash Institute of Social Change, 1982.

Gombrich, Richard and Obeyesekere, Gananath. *Buddhism Transformed: Religious Change in Sri Lanka.* Princeton University Press, 1988..

Goulet, Denis. *Survival with Integrity: Sarvodaya at the Crossroads.* Colombo: Marga Institute, 1981.

Kantowski, Detlef. *Sarvodaya, The Other Development.* New Delhi: Vikas Publishing House. 1980.

King, Winston. *In the Hope of Nibbana: An Essay on Theravada Buddhist Ethics.* LaSalle, Ill.: Open Court, 1964.

Macy, Joanna. *Dharma and Development: Religion as Resource in the Sarvodaya Self-Help Movement.* West Hartford, Conn.: Kumarian Press, 1983.

Perera, Jehan; Marasinghe, Charika; and Jayasekera, Leela. *A People's Movement Under Siege.* Moratuwa: Sarvodaya Publishing Services, 1992.

Wismeijer, Hans. *Diversity In Harmony: A Study of the Leaders of the Sarvodaya Shramadana Movement in Sri Lanka.* Privately published dissertation from the Department of Cultural Anthropology, University of Utrecht, Netherlands, 1981.

5

Buddhadasa Bhikkhu: Life and Society through the Natural Eyes of Voidness

Santikaro Bhikkhu

I offer this life and body to the Lord Buddha.
I am the slave of the Buddha, the Buddha is my master.
For this reason, I am called "Buddhadasa."*

Buddhadasa Bhikkhu is a Thai Buddhist monk whose dedication in service to the Lord Buddha has produced the largest and most innovative body of work of any bhikkhu in recent Thai history. He has been a pioneer in the application of Buddha-Dhamma to the realities of the modern world during the recent decades of rampant modernization and economic growth and has forthrightly criticized the immorality and selfishness of many modern social structures. Further, he has been Thailand's most vocal proponent of open-mindedness toward other religions.

Buddhadasa means "Servant of the Buddha"[1] and *bhikkhu* refers to a monk, a person who has left home in order to fully undertake Buddhist spiritual training, *dhamma-vinaya*. While *buddhadasa* itself is a generic term, a certain young Thai bhikkhu took it as his name when he began a unique experiment within Thai Buddhism called *Suan Mokkh* (The Garden of Liberation). In the more than sixty years since, he has initiated and inspired many innovations in the teaching and application of Buddha-Dhamma. Primarily, as he sees it, his life's work has been to restore the Buddha's teaching to its pristine state. Over the centuries many cultural

---

* The quotation is from *Tam Roi Phra Arahant* (In the Footsteps of the Arahant), Sukhapap Jai, Bangkok, 1986.

practices and superstitions inevitably have obscured the essential Dhamma. Buddhadasa Bhikkhu has dedicated his life to distinguishing one from the other—that which leads to absolute liberation from self and its suffering, and that which does not—without limiting himself to the traditionally narrow religious concerns of the orthodox Theravada. His truly radical reform has been to go back to the original source of all Buddhism, that which is even more original than the scriptures or the Buddha himself, something he has come to call "the natural religion of non-selfishness."

Buddhadasa Bhikkhu has interpreted the Pali *Tipitaka* of Theravada Buddhism in light of its primary principles—noble truths *(ariya-sacca),* not-self *(anatta)* or voidness *(sunnata),* and dependent origination *(paticca-samuppada)*—so that all of the core teachings fit together and are more deeply understood through each other. In doing so, he moved away from some cherished, albeit secondary, dogmas of orthodox Theravada belief. The consequences of this reappraisal have been many, including an emphasis on the here–and–now rediscovery of the spiritual dimension of everyday life, a bridging of the lay-monastic fracture, greater compatibility with science, greater intellectual rigor, and the reintegration of political and social issues within a Dhammic worldview. The last achievement is the focus of this chapter.

Buddhadasa Bhikkhu and Suan Mokkh[2]

Childhood

Six hundred kilometers south of Bangkok, where the Malay peninsula suddenly widens, are ruins belonging to the Sri Vijaya Empire, which dominated the sea-lanes of Southeast Asia between India and China 1,200 to 1,500 years ago. Although Siam has been a Theravada Buddhist country for centuries, the archaeological evidence shows that Mahayana Buddhism came to what is now southern Thailand first.[3] Among the Sri Vijaya ruins, numerous beautiful images of Mahayana Bodhisattvas have been found. Thus, the Buddhist roots of the Chaiya area are ancient and diverse.

At the turn of the twentieth century,[4] the rubber economy and electricity had not yet come to Chaiya. Life followed the old traditions, which were centered in Buddhism, the effects of which were pervasive and profound. The customs and values of the people still showed the Buddhist roots of their culture. Life was simple and family–oriented. Sharing was common and crime rare. The seasons and cycles of rice planting passed on along with the festivals of the people. This was the climate in which Ngeuam

Panich (later Buddhadasa Bhikkhu), his brother Yikey (later Dhammadasa), and their sister Kimsoi were born and raised.

In 1906, Ngeuam Panich was born at Pum Riang, then the provincial seat of Chaiya Province,[5] into a small merchant family. Ngeuam's father was second-generation Chinese (Hokkien) and his mother a native Thai. Their relatives were spread up and down the local seaboard. Many of his relatives were and had been bhikkhus and even abbots. The family kept a small store in the Pum Riang market.

In speaking of his childhood, Buddhadasa Bhikkhu emphasizes three primary influences: his mother, the Wat ("temple"), and Nature. His mother was Buddhadasa's first spiritual guide. She taught the morality and values that have underpinned all of his later insights and accomplishments. Her home was firmly based in the five ethical precepts (*sila*) and there was a daily contact with Buddhism through offering food to the monks on their daily alms round and other activities. The family was thrifty and hardworking. Even at a young age, Ngeuam and his brother learned to shred coconut meat more carefully so that more coconut milk, a staple in traditional Thai cooking, could be extracted. In a recent Mothers' Day talk, Buddhadasa Bhikkhu said that his mother's influence was crucial in the formation of his character. "Whatever abilities, knowledge, and such I have now, where do they come from? Let me say that they come from my mother most of all."[6]

At the age of 10, Ngeuam was taken by his parents to stay at Wat Pum Riang, where he was a temple boy for the next three years. This is where he learned to read and write, had his introduction to Buddhist ceremonies, heard many traditional stories, and made frequent forays into the forest to collect medicinal herbs for the abbot. Ajarn[7] Buddhadasa speaks fondly of his experiences among the temple boys, with whom he learned discipline, hard work, cooperation, punctuality, responsibility, humor, cleverness, and, most importantly, unselfishness. In "A Single Solution for All the World's Problems" he suggests this temple boy education as a way of overcoming the immorality and selfishness that is destroying the world.[8]

The influence of Nature was experienced while taking his father's cows into the field to forage and in collecting herbs from the forest for his abbot. The sea was always nearby, along with the mangrove forests that then covered much of the shore. The forest then was still primal, full of trees more than a meter wide. Rural life followed the natural cycles of the seasons and animal birth and death. Ajarn Buddhadasa also tells of an early passion for Siamese fighting fish, which much later developed into a hobby of raising exotic fish at Suan Mokkh. His study of the fish and other animals, as well as plants, especially orchids, provided many insights into Nature, an important source of material in his teaching.

Ngeuam left the Wat in 1911 to enter Wat Potharam School where he completed the four-year primary school curriculum. In 1921, his father opened a second store in Chaiya, near the new railroad station. Ngeuam went to stay with him there and began secondary school. The following year his father died, compelling Ngeuam to leave school in order to help his mother run the family stores. He was now the head of the family at the age of 16.

Besides the obvious effects of running a store for four years, there were other important influences on Ngeuam during his late teens. First, he had access to a large number of new books, including many concerning Dhamma, which were sold in the store. This was a period when writers and thinkers like Krom Phraya Vajirananavarorasa and Luang Wichit Wattakarn were challenging many traditional Thai beliefs and beginning to demythologize Thai Buddhism. Ngeuam also had daily opportunities to discuss and debate Dhamma and other issues with local officials, the educated elite of rural Siam. By the time he was ordained as a monk, Ngeuam had read and discussed all the basic Dhamma books, and much more, that a young monk would be expected to learn. These contacts and responsibilities gave him some understanding of the wider world.

Early Days in the Sangha

At the age of 20, in line with Thai custom, Ngeuam undertook *upasampada* (the higher training) as a bhikkhu for the annual Rains Retreat *(Pansa)*.[9] He was given the Pali name Indapanno, which he later used on official documents. At first, his motivation was simply to express gratitude to his parents and ancestors; he had no intention to remain a monk longer than the customary three months of the Rains Retreat. Phra Ngeuam took to the bhikkhu life, however, and had an easy time of his studies.[10] He also became a popular preacher from the very start. Taking what he learned in his daily Dhamma classes, he gave nightly sermons that explained the Buddha's teachings in simple, straightforward terms.

Enjoying the bhikkhu life, Phra Ngeuam decided not to disrobe after the initial Rains Retreat was over. This made it necessary for his brother to leave the university in Bangkok and come home to run the family business. Phra Ngeuam continued his Dhamma studies and began to teach newly robed bhikkhus. He had a natural facility for teaching and greatly enjoyed the responsibilities. Eventually, older bhikkhus and relatives noticed his intellectual abilities and sent him to Bangkok to further his studies and career.

At that time, the only way to advance within the institutional Sangha was to study Pali in Bangkok. Such studies were the opportunity to prove oneself to senior monks and obtain patrons and positions within the ecclesiastical hierarchy. An uncle, who had been a bhikkhu at an influential Bangkok temple (Wat Pathum Kongkha) for many years, arranged for him to live and study there, but Phra Ngeuam found Bangkok to be noisy and dirty. Worse, the lifestyle and behavior of many monks made a bad impression on him. After only two months he returned home dismayed, intending to disrobe. At the last minute, he decided to stick out a third Rains Retreat (1928) and passed the third and final level of Dhamma studies. Afterward, he forgot his plan to disrobe. The following year he taught at the Dhamma School of the royally sponsored Wat Boromathat Chaiya.

In 1930, Phra Ngeuam's relatives and friends convinced him to try Bangkok again. There he was more interested in visiting Wats, attending lectures, and experimenting with photography, than the rote learning of Pali. Still, he passed the first Pali examination (*Parien 3*, Third Level). He also made his first attempt at writing, in which he showed a modern perspective and expressed the conviction that the highest levels of Buddhist realization are still possible today.

Nonetheless, Bangkok did not suit Phra Ngeuam. He was increasingly put off by the noise, crowding, busyness, and pollution, and his health suffered. He missed the calm and simplicity of his hometown. As he continued his studies, he began to do more outside reading. The Pali curriculum itself did not include readings from the *Tipitaka,* but Phra Ngeuam began to read it anyway. The contradiction between the lifestyles, behavior, and practices of the monks around him in Bangkok and the lifestyle and practices of the original Sangha gradually became obvious to him. He began to think that Bangkok was not the path and doubted that peace could be found there.

> We have decided that Bangkok certainly is not the place to find purity. Our stumbling into the academic Dhamma studies *(pariyattidhamma)* has had the good result of making us aware that it was a mis-step. If we didn't realize this in time, we would take many more steps until it would be hard to extricate ourselves, as has happened with some people. From just this awareness of going astray has come a hint of how we are to take the right step.[11]

Dissatisfied and suspicious of the rote translations expected in the Pali schools, he deliberately failed the next year's examination by giving answers he believed in but that were not what the examiners wanted. For now, he had something better to do than climbing the ecclesiastical ladder.

> We have walked according to the world from the moment of birth up until the moment of this insight. From now on, we won't follow the world

anymore and will give up the world to search for that which is pure as the Noble Ones did until finding it.[12]

Founding of Suan Mokkh[13]

Phra Ngeuam left Bangkok and returned to Pum Riang with the intention of living in a natural setting conducive to the practice of Dhamma as taught by the Buddha. This move had already been prepared through letters to his brother, who also was keenly interested in the problem of adapting the timeless Buddha-Dhamma to modern realities and who now called himself "Dhammadasa." A group of his friends called the "Dhammadana Group" helped. Phra Ngeuam returned home on May 12, 1932, and moved into Wat Trapang Jik, an abandoned temple about a kilometer from the Pum Riang market. Here, just one month before Thailand switched to "democracy" in the form of a constitutional monarchy, Phra Ngeuam began his experiment, *Suan Mokkhabalarama,* "The Garden of the Power of Liberation" (for short, *Suan Mokkh,* "The Garden of Liberation"), the institutional expression of his emerging resolve to reform Thai Buddhism. In so doing, he went beyond the official and politically controlled religious institutions of his time without resort to harsh words, judgments, or condemnations.

Alone in an abandoned Wat, where he had to confront socially conditioned fears of spirits, Phra Ngeuam set about his intention to dedicate his life to the practice of Dhamma. He already knew, however, that his understanding of exactly what and how to practice was insufficient. Thus, for the sake of practicing Dhamma, he went back to the Pali texts for guidance. Unlike the forest Wats built around famous teachers, Suan Mokkh turned directly to the Dhamma and Vinaya (discipline) of the Buddha as the teacher.[14] During that first Rains Retreat of Suan Mokkh, Buddhadasa Bhikkhu began to compile the Dhamma principles that would guide him. At first he thought this would only take five or six months, after which he would live a wandering life, perhaps in India. Circumstances turned out otherwise, and he never left Suan Mokkh.

As Buddhadasa Bhikkhu pursued these studies, he also experimented with their application in life. Along with his Dhamma studies and practice, he was kept busy speaking at other Wats and functions set up by the Dhammadana Group. From the start, we see the three central components of life at Suan Mokkh: study, practice, and Dhamma teaching.

In the second year of Suan Mokkh, the two brothers began to publish the quarterly journal *Buddha-Sadana,* which was then the only Buddhist magazine in Thailand published outside of Bangkok and since then the longest running Buddhist periodical in the country. It soon developed a reputation for new ideas, readability, and insight. In the third Rains Retreat of Suan Mokkh (1934), Buddhadasa Bhikkhu spent the entire three months in silence[15] and recorded his experiences in the form of a Dhamma Log Book. He treated his life as a kind of Dhammic laboratory experiment: for example, investigating the effect of different foods on his body and mind, as well as keeping careful track of mental states. He kept a meticulous record of these experiences and wrote many short essays based on observations of Nature and insights into the workings of the human mind.[16]

In his writings, Buddhadasa Bhikkhu began to explore the connection between study and practice, arguing for their complementariness rather than their dichotomy. It should be noted that young Buddhadasa Bhikkhu's approach was unique in Thailand. For at least a millennium, going way back to the Sri Lankan commentators, there had been a strict separation between city monks *(gamavasin)*, who studied and performed ceremonies, and forest monks *(arannavasin)*, who lived a simple meditative life. Buddhadasa Bhikkhu integrated both strands of monastic life, something that had not been seen in Siam for centuries, if ever. Here was a forest monk who kept many of the traditional ascetic practices *(dhutanga)*[17], ate one meal a day, lived alone, yet was a diligent scholar and a prolific writer and speaker. Rather than emphasizing one or two elements of traditional Buddhism, such as the moral precepts or meditation practices, as has been done with more recent reform groups, he tried to integrate everything genuine into a balanced middle way.

The Growth of Suan Mokkh

Buddhadasa Bhikkhu lived alone for most of the first four years, but the quality and innovation of the writing and ideas in *Buddha-Sasana* inevitably attracted increasing attention. After five years some monks came to stay with him. Visitors included high-ranking monks, such as the Somdet of Wat Thepsirinda, who was then administering the Thai Sangha on behalf of the Supreme Patriarch, and influential civil servants, who were to provide important support and recognition. Later, they were also to provide protection against those threatened by Buddhadasa Bhikkhu's ideas.

Beginning in 1940, Buddhadasa Bhikkhu gave a series of lectures at the Buddha-Dhamma Association in Bangkok. Until this point, he had been teaching on the fringes of Thai intellectual society and lacked the podiums supplied by rich Bangkok Wats and royal patronage. In his first Bangkok lecture, he spoke for over two hours concerning the way to realize Buddha-Dhamma. In this and subsequent lectures we can see the primary features of Buddhadasa Bhikkhu's mature teaching style. His presentations were in plain language, rational, clear, and unencumbered by literary profuseness and old-fashioned monkish phrases. He left out accounts of miracles and divine beings and focused directly on the Dhamma, trying to show that anyone of average intelligence could study, understand, practice, and realize its truth for themselves. In this first lecture, he even dared to suggest meditation to the Bangkok intellectuals.

In subsequent years, he gave lectures titled "Peace as Being the Fruits of Realizing Buddha-Dhamma" (1942), "Buddha-Dhamma and Peace" (1946), and "Buddha-Dhamma and The Spirit of Democracy" (1947). The series concluded with his first major controversy in June 1948 after speaking about "The Mountains of the Buddha-Dhamma Way," in which he asserted that the Buddha, Dhamma, and Sangha of most Buddhists were obstacles obstructing their way to liberation, *nibbana*. Because of their egoistic attachments they did not have the true Buddha, Dhamma, and Sangha that alone can liberate us from suffering, *dukkha*. The idea that all aspects of Buddhism must be cleansed of attachment to "I" and "mine" was hard for many to swallow. Through these lectures and *Buddha-Sasana*, Buddhadasa Bhikkhu was firmly established as an innovative free-thinker who was unafraid to express views that were not acceptable to the majority, when he thought the old way of understanding hindered people's spiritual insight and growth.

By the early 1940s, the original site of Suan Mokkh had become crowded, and so a large tract of land was purchased around long-abandoned Wat Tarn Nam Lai ("Temple of the Flowing Water") through which ran a beautiful stream. In the center of this Wat was Golden Buddha Hill on which were scattered remnants of an ancient temple or stupa. In 1944, Buddhadasa Bhikkhu moved there permanently and others followed.

At this point Suan Mokkh and Buddhadasa Bhikkhu had become well-known to educated Buddhists throughout the country. It is time we considered the Dhamma teaching that led to this recognition; however, a final comment is necessary as we conclude this biographical sketch. Buddhadasa Bhikkhu always felt that the person and its biographical details were not very important. Personal stories too easily distract us from the Dhamma and strengthen the illusion of self. "The person doesn't really exist. Who are you talking about?" he would ask. So may the foregoing be forgiven and taken with a grain of salt as we turn our attention to the Dhamma, which Buddhadasa served for the sake of liberating humanity from dukkha and making world peace possible.

The Social Teachings of Buddhadasa

In line with the overall purpose of this book, this chapter focuses primarily on the "social teachings" of Buddhadasa Bhikkhu. However, we must consider a few qualifications. First, for Buddhadasa Bhikkhu there was no ultimate separation between the social and spiritual. They are two inter-penetrating aspects of the one reality (Dhamma) according to the Law of Nature (Dhamma), that is, interdependency. "Don't separate them, otherwise world peace is not possible."[18] Further, because Ajarn Buddhadasa looked at everything from certain basic perspectives—those he considered the heart of Buddhism—we must examine those perspectives at least briefly. And the more deeply we wish to explore the social teachings, the more we must be rooted in the spiritual teachings in which they are based.

Ajarn Buddhadasa used the word "spiritual" in a way that includes the material, physical, and social. Previously, Theravada had spoken only of body *(kaya* or *rupa)* and mind or heart *(citta).* For Ajarn Buddhadasa, a problem arises when we overemphasize the distinction between body and mind—any duality for that matter—because one cannot be understood without the other. To avoid polarizing this pair, he used "spiritual" to en-compass and transcend them both.

> Buddhism is neither materialism or mentalism, but is the correctness between the two or is both of them in the right proportions. The religion which can be taken as the best social science must not be a slave of materialism nor crazy about mental things.[19]

The spiritual does not reject the body, society, economics, politics, or any other area of life but understands all the dimensions of life in a fundamental way, that is, in the context of Dhamma. Essentially, the spiritual is concerned with the central issue of life—the illusion of self and the voidness of self—that permeates all aspects of human life.

Truth is One

When exploring the teachings of Buddhadasa Bhikkhu it is dangerous to focus much on any one principle as central or primary, as some writers have done. The noble truths, impermanence, not-self *(anatta)* or voidness *(sunnata),* conditionality *(idappaccayata),* dependent cooorigination *(paticca-samuppada),* and thusness *(tathata)* have all been called "the heart of Bud-dhism". We cannot have one without the other; to overemphasize any one principle would distort their understanding, for these natural principles clarify and illuminate each other and the fundamental reality of the uni-verse. Ajarn Buddhadasa utilized the full range of the Pali Canon, plus other religious traditions, modern science, and the phenomena of Nature to explore the Dhamma, which is a whole *(kevala).* As he often said, citing the Buddha, "Truth is one, there is no second."[20]

Now let us consider some of Buddhadasa Bhikkhu's main themes, aware that there is not enough room in a chapter of this length to do them justice. We must be content with merely sketching the general picture.

The Power of Understanding

Ajarn Buddhadasa liked to stress that the noble eightfold path—that is, our spiritual life—begins with right understanding *(sammaditthi)*. Whatever the problem to be solved, he emphasized the need for changing the way we understand and think about things, which means educating or training ourselves correctly. To live happily, we require a worldview that fosters and makes such happiness possible. Personally we must study, reflect upon, and investigate the Dhamma; socially we must educate our children and each other in unselfishness.

Ajarn Buddhadasa believed world peace is the goal of the Buddha and his servants. What then is the means appropriate to the end? Bhikkhus have given up worldly power and cannot force people to do or believe things. Instead, they seek to persuade by example and teaching, especially so that people can experience the truth for themselves. In working for peace, Ajarn Buddhadasa chose to clarify the meaning of Buddha-Dhamma and its relevance to modern society through "Dhamma Proclamation" *(Dhammaghosana)*.[21] He took this to be the most pressing matter and concern. Thus, his work was in the area of ideas, meanings, values, and perspectives using a variety of media, including lectures, books, a journal, poetry, audiovisuals, and Suan Mokkh and its facilities. He did not involve himself in direct political work or even Buddhist institution-building. Even within Suan Mokkh he avoided organizational trappings.

Other writers have discussed Buddhadasa Bhikkhu's hermeneutical tools, especially the principle of "people language and Dhamma language," so we can skip the details of them here.[22] The key point is the importance of meaning and interpretation when we work with Dhamma and its understanding. Throughout our lives as human beings we accumulate, make, and remake meanings. How we do so individually and collectively determines the degree of peace, happiness, and freedom in our lives. Ajarn Buddhadasa daily met people with endless hurts and read about social problems in the newspaper or heard about them on the radio. He saw that something was missing or incorrect in their lives and understanding of life. People lack the means to interpret life and make meanings that liberate them from *dukkha*. This is why Ajarn Buddhadasa chose to focus on *ditthi* (understanding, views).

Dukkha and Its Quenching

Right understanding begins with the experience, awareness, and understanding of suffering, *dukkha*. The Buddha himself declares the purpose and scope of his teaching: "In the past, Bhikkhus, as well as now, I teach only *dukkha* and the utter quenching of *dukkha*."[23]

Buddhadasa Bhikkhu referred to these words repeatedly, and they provide the proper context of his own life and work, for anyone who calls himself "The Servant of the Buddha" must faithfully carry on the Buddha's work and objective. *Dukkha* and its quenching is a summary of the Four Noble Truths, the framework of Buddhism. Here we have the entire scope and range of the Buddha's teachings, although its heights and depths may not be immediately apparent. None of Ajarn Buddhadasa's words can be understood properly, except in this context. In particular, his social commentaries require this context in that the reason why we must discuss politics and economics is that they are the sources of so much *dukkha* in individuals and conflicts in society.

Much more than "suffering," dukkha includes stress, conflict, ugliness, dissatisfaction, meaninglessness, and imperfection. According to the Buddha, "The five aggregates [constituents of personality] are the essence of *dukkha*." Thus, *dukkha*—whether we translate it as pain, misery, or dissatisfaction—boils down to egoistic life, which as the Buddha repeatedly points out, arises from ignorance, desire, attachment, and egoism. This, then, is where Buddhadasa Bhikkhu attacked social problems.

The final quenching of *dukkha*, Ajarn Buddhadasa stressed, comes about only through the relinquishment or "tossing back" of all egoism and clinging. When we have no feelings or thoughts of "me" or "mine" toward anything in the universe, including our own consciousness, then there can be no more *dukkha*, no more birth and no more death. Peace in our societies also depends on letting go of egoism and selfishness. As we shall see later, this idea formed the basis of Buddhadasa Bhikkhu's social teaching.

Having understood what the Buddha had discovered, Buddhadasa Bhikkhu pursued the same course and objective; all that matters to him is *dukkha* and liberation from *dukkha*. For Buddhadasa Bhikkhu, something is Buddhist solely because it quenches *dukkha*. When asked if something is "good" or "correct," Ajarn Buddhadasa asked in return, "Does it quench *dukkha?*" *Dukkha* provides the existential test to all ideas and experiences. Is there *dukkha?* Then, something is not yet right *(samma)*. If no *dukkha* can be found, then things are correct, at least for a while. In this way, spirituality is based in tangible experience rather than beliefs, theories, and concepts. Further, since we need not conceptualize it, *dukkha* and its quenching is a standard that escapes the confusion of dualities such as "good and bad." This standard is central to everything discussed here.

When we decide that the life without dukkha is the life for us, then we must find out how that life is lived. Ajarn Buddhadasa pointed to the heart of this way of living by recalling the Buddha's one-sentence summary of his entire teaching: "All things ought not to be attached to (as 'I' or 'mine')."[24] There is no thing in this universe—no concept, belief, experience, possession, heaven, God or Truth—worth regarding as "I" or "mine." Here we have a second central principle, inseparable from the first and the rest, in Buddhadasa Bhikkhu's teaching. *Dukkha* can only be understood in light of attachment or clinging *(upadana)* and Buddhadasa Bhikkhu insisted that all attachment boils down to regarding something as being "I" or "mine." Conversely, the quenching of *dukkha* only occurs when attachment is quenched. Thus the path is one of nonattachment, of letting go. If you don't want to suffer, don't attach yourself to anything.[25]

Is nonattachment just an idea, just a theory? Not for Ajarn Buddhadasa. If we approach it as such, it may not help us very much or may even make us suffer more. But if we see that nonattachment is a natural consequence of the way things are (the Law of Nature), then there will be more to it than just an idea. Here we must come to terms with and personally experience the fact of selflessness *(anatta)* or voidness *(sunnata).*[26] Why is it *dukkha* to attach to things as "I" or "mine"? Because they are void of any independent substance, core, or "thingness" that can correctly be regarded as a "self." To cling to an illusion, something that is not really there, grounds the mind in falsehood and conflict. This insight follows from the realizations that all created things are impermanent, are characterized by *dukkha*-ness, and depend on causes and conditions. Therefore, to overcome our deeply ingrained habits of attachment, we must realize that everything is void of self.[27]

For Ajarn Buddhadasa, voidness has two applications. First, it is an inherent characteristic of all things, similar to *anatta* (not-self). Not only are "things" *(dhammas,* natures) not "me" and not "mine," they are void of selfhood and any independent entities that can be rightly taken as being selves. This characteristic is a primary object of insight. The second application refers to the "void mind" *(cit-wang).* Void of what? Void of I-making *(ahamkara)* and my-making *(mamamkara),* void of the clinging to "I" and "mine," void of selfishness, void of *dukkha.* This is an experience to be developed. Here Ajarn Buddhadasa used a common Thai word, *"wang,"* which is used in expressions like "the chair is *empty*" and "*free* time." An immensely profound insight is thus expressed in a very simple term. Other teachers picked up on "voidness" and "letting go," until they became well-known terms among Buddhist practitioners in Thailand.

Ajarn Buddhadasa pointed out that the void mind happens in different ways. The first way is accidental or coincidental. In ordinary life, even for the most spiritually indifferent people, circumstance can arise such that the concept of self does not get stirred up. This is more or less "forgetting oneself," for example, when we act spontaneously in an emergency or when we are so awed by the power and beauty of Nature that the mind becomes momentarily silent. The second way is the suppression of the self-concept and selfish feelings through strong concentration *(samadhi)*. The third way happens when Dhamma practice is well established and contact with sense experiences occurs with sufficient mindfulness and wisdom. Then, ignorance is not given an opportunity to concoct desire, attachment, ego, and *dukkha*. Ultimately, through full realization of the fact of the inherent voidness of things so that all tendencies to perceive and conceive things in terms of self are eliminated, "supreme unsurpassable voidness" is realized. In this way, Ajarn Buddhadasa showed that voidness is accessible to all human beings. It is not just some absolute metaphysical truth; it is a way of practice leading to the ultimate voidness—*nibbana*. In fact, the mind can only be void because its nature is voidness and we can only realize that void nature when the mind is void. In practice, the two meanings are inseparable; Ajarn Buddhadasa switched frequently between the two to make the point. Following the Buddha, he also described the realization of progressively deeper *"nibbanas."*[28]

Here it would be good to remember that the Dhamma we are discussing is not primarily the Buddha's "teachings," although the word "Dhamma" is commonly understood in this limited way. Rather, Dhamma is the Truth, Reality, Law, or that to which the teachings point. Or, as Ajarn Buddhadasa liked to remind us, Dhamma is Nature.

Everything is Nature

For Ajarn Buddhadasa everything is Dhamma and

> Dhamma means Nature, which can be distinguished in four aspects: Nature itself *(sabhavadhamma)*, the Law of Nature *(saccadhamma)*, the Duty of living things according to Natural Law *(patipattidhamma)*, and the results that follow from performing duty according to Natural Law *(pativedhadhamma)*. All four are known by the single word "Dhamma."[29]

The Thai word for Nature is *dhammajati* and like the Latin root of the English word "nature," *jati* means "birth." Thus, *dhammajati* is "that which is born out of the natural order," which means that all things are "natures" and that everything is Dhamma, is Nature. For Ajarn Buddhadasa, this was the fundamental reference of Buddhism. By contemplating this most basic meaning of Dhamma, we come to the other primary "dimensions of Dhamma," according to Buddhadasa Bhikkhu: the law of Nature that governs all natures *(dhammas)*; the duty required of every *dhamma*, especially human beings, each moment by natural law; and the natural fruits of that duty correctly or incorrectly done.[30]

Natural Law Similarity / Contrast?

Nature is the sum total of reality; there is no thing that is not Nature, not even the Absolute or Ultimate Reality, whatever we call "it." Everything is produced out of Nature by the law of Nature. Nature and humanity are not separate; human beings and all their creations are as much a part of Nature as are insects, trees, rivers, and stars. Thus, in Ajarn Buddhadasa's understanding, we are not set against or above Nature but are only a part of Nature that must find and fulfill its natural role or duty (Dhamma). This insight is important for overcoming both personal egoism and collective or structural egoism, such as the materialism and consumerism of modern societies.

Another way that Buddhadasa Bhikkhu used the theme of Nature is his advice to live in intimate contact with Nature (in the more limited sense of trees, insects, rocks, and weather), especially the natures not yet altered by human greed, anger, and delusion. By living close to Nature, we are closer to Dhamma and it is easier for us to understand Dhamma. "The trees can speak, the rocks can speak, the pebbles and sand, the ants and insects, everything is able to speak!"[31] When we listen, we can hear them say: "You crazy people, learn to stop, to cool down, to give in, just a little bit!"[32] "You stupid people. . . . Don't fight and kill so much!"[33] There is no better teacher or classroom than Nature itself. "A dry leaf is a symbol of the mind that has no 'I' and ' mine.' "[34] For this reason, Ajarn Buddhadasa stressed that all Buddhas are born outdoors, awakened outdoors, and enter *parinibbana* outdoors.[35] Or, as he put it, "No Buddha was ever enlightened in a university."[36]

Ajarn Buddhadasa never insisted that Nature be left untouched, but that we live in mindful and respectful harmony with it. If we listen to and learn from Nature, we will not be selfish towards it, nor abuse it. But now most of our environments are no longer natural because human artifice, fired by selfishness, has interfered almost everywhere.

> They nurture each other. Material progress nurtures selfishness and selfishness nurtures material progress, until the whole world is filled with selfishness.[37]

This is one of the tragedies of the modern world. Our selfishness out of control, everything we see, hear, smell, taste, and touch becomes a manifestation of selfishness. These further stimulate confused, stressful, selfish states of mind. By cutting down the forests, we cut ourselves off from Dhamma.

When our interactions with Nature are solely for the sake of survival, selfishness does not ruin and destroy.[38] When we maintain our "inner Nature," the outer Nature will be taken care of.

Only the genuine Buddhists (those who have Dhamma and know the
Buddha) can conserve Nature, while those who are Buddhists in name
alone cannot do it. True Buddhists are able to conserve the deeper Nature,
that is, the mental Nature. Non-genuine Buddhists can't conserve Nature,
even the material kind. When the mental Nature is well conserved, the
outer material Nature will be able to conserve itself.[39]

Then we can live close to and learn from Nature. We see, hear, and are
touched by things that express peacefulness and interdependency. This influences our minds in ways conducive to spiritual insight and nurtures a much
healthier perspective on life. We learn to look on and act toward the world
unselfishly. Then, we can perform our duties toward life, family, and
society—in addition to the spiritual duty—without creating more problems.

The Law of Nature

Nature is not meaningless or pointless; there is something that governs it all. Our investigation of Nature leads to the discovery of a principle
that comes closest to being Ajarn Buddhadasa's fundamental teaching,
namely, the law of Nature, *idappaccayata*.[40] *Idappaccayata* means "the
state (or fact) of having this as condition," that is, conditionality or interdependency.[41] The formula the Buddha used most often to explain
idappaccayata is:

This being, that exists; because this arises, that arises.
This not being, that does not exist; because this ceases, that ceases.[42]

For Ajarn Buddhadasa, this was the universal law of Nature that governs all
of Nature. He liked to call it "the Buddhist God," emphasizing that it is an
impersonal God rather than a personal God. It is the creator, preserver, and
destroyer all rolled into one. It is omnipotent, omniscient, omnipresent,
eternal, and absolute, thus having all the necessary qualities of the "Supreme Thing."

Everything is conditional *(idappaccayata)* and the principle of everything
is conditionality; according to this principle all actions are conditional and
dependent. Thus, if we would like to have a God like they do, we must take
idappaccayata (conditionality) as God. It will be a more powerful God
than any other; at best, the others are equal to it. If we take *idappaccayata*
as our God, we'll have a God which no other surpasses. . . . God the

Creator is nothing more than conditionality, God the Destroyer is nothing more than conditionality, God the Preserver is nothing more than conditionality, Omnipresent God is nothing more than conditionality, God which is everything is nothing more than conditionality. If Buddhism has a God, it is in *idappaccayata* (conditionality).[43]

Not a supreme being, or non-being, it is the Supreme Truth, Law, and Reality—one that is void of self.

A specific case of *idappaccayata* is dependent origination *(paticca-samuppada)*, which examines our fundamental problem of *dukkha* according to the law of conditionality. The key elements in the dependent origination of *dukkha* are ignorance, sense consciousness and experience, feeling, desire, attachment, and ego-birth. When we live without mindfulness and wisdom, these elements continually flow out of sensory experience and bring us into *dukkha*. When we are mindful of Dhamma, ignorance cannot set off the process of blind conditioning into *dukkha*. Such mindfulness is to know and see the law of Nature in everything we experience and do. Knowing it, we live according to it, which is our natural duty. Then, there is no *dukkha*.

Buddhists aim to penetrate deeply to the inner Nature, the spiritual Nature, the Nature which is the Law of Nature, which is the source of everything. We try to study so that we realize the Nature within which is called "Dhamma-element" *(dhammadhatu)*, namely, the law of dependent coorigration or conditionality. If we realize this Nature, we have no way that selfishness can happen.[44] Understanding of dependent co-origination *(paticcasamuppada)*, when it develops correctly and completely, leads to clearly seeing that there is no real self. The thought one has a self doesn't arise. So we must study dependent co-origination. We will have no self when we fully understand dependent co-origination, which can be called the "heart" or "essence" of Buddhism.[45]

These observations about Nature and natural law are central to Ajarn Buddhadasa's approach both to spiritual questions and to moral and social questions. In fact, the natural principle of conditionality allows us to set aside distinctions between self and other, between personal and social. In Nature there is one reality, there is no second.

This has been a brief overview of Ajarn Buddhadasa's favorite Dhamma teachings. Because he reexamined and reworked almost all the standard terms and categories of Theravada Buddhism, much has had to be left out. As we look into the social dimensions of Dhamma, please keep these perspectives in mind and remember that they are only some of the key elements in a thorough-going and consistent reinterpretation of the Pali texts.

Dhamma and Society

When words and teachings are mined for their deepest spiritual potential, when interdependency and voidness are the central teaching, when Nature is the primary reference, and when the goal is the end of all *dukkha*, does one have anything meaningful to say about society and all the suffering found and caused therein? Buddhadasa Bhikkhu has addressed this pressing question since the beginning of Suan Mokkh.

> There tend to be people who wrongly understand that Buddhism doesn't have much to do with society or that the connections are only on a lower level. Some people misunderstand so far as to say that those who strictly train themselves according to Buddhist principles find it difficult to do anything tangibly beneficial for society. I feel that such understanding is not yet in line with the truth. However, there is a way for us to develop the kind of understanding through which our socially beneficial actions become the highest spiritual benefit for ourselves, also. So I've tried to distinguish and make obvious social benefits. . . . In addition I try to point out that the social goods and acting for the benefit of society are prerequisites of traveling beyond to *nibbana*.[46]

The Buddhist goal of quenching or ending *dukkha* is not to be falsely spiritualized into an other-worldly end, for the genuinely spiritual does not denigrate or reject the body. *Nibbana* can only be found right here in the middle of *samsara,* the whirlpool of birth and death. So when we talk about ending *dukkha*, we mean both personal and social problems.[47]

As early as the 1940s, in the series of lectures at the influential Buddha-Dhamma Association through which Buddhadasa Bhikkhu made his first big impact on the national scene, he discussed issues such as "Buddha-Dhamma and Peace" and "Buddha-Dhamma and the Spirit of Democracy."[48] In "Buddha-Dhamma and Peace" (March 1946) he pointed out that there was more to peace than getting rid of the Japanese occupation forces. He argued that without a proper understanding of Buddha-Dhamma, human desires expand endlessly and lead to violence and oppression. The Buddha pointed out an unconditioned peace "above the world," which can only be reached when we act correctly according to the law of nature. Social and spiritual peace appears when, through the realization of Buddha-Dhamma, we can abandon our desires. "This world lacks peace because it is unable to grasp the thing which is close at hand, so close it is actually in hand, that is, within everything."[49] The only hope for genuine peace is when everyone realizes Dhamma. At that time, Ajarn Buddhadasa seemed to emphasize the personal realization of *nibbana* as the meaning he gave to "peace," but there were also hints that the more individuals realized the unconditioned peace, the more social peace could be achieved. In the years since, while always giving primacy to the absolute peace of *nibbana,* he increasingly spoke of achieving world peace, such that he came to say, "the Buddha's purpose is world peace."[50]

"Buddha-Dhamma and the Spirit of Democracy" (1947) explored the importance of democratic values—freedom, equality, and brotherhood—in the Buddha's teaching and in the original Sangha. At the same time, he explored the spiritual meaning of these three values: freedom from the law of karma and from defilements; equality of opportunity in realizing *nibbana;* and fraternity among those who live the homeless spiritual life together. The subtitle of the talk was "Moral and Wisdom Perspectives Have Nothing To Do With Politics." He explained that they "have nothing to do with politics" because there is no need to make democracy into something political, which is a complicated and troublesome business. But here, whoever hears the word 'democracy' thinks it is about politics."[51] To some extent, he was being careful to stay within the boundaries expected of monks; more importantly, however, he wanted to give deeper meaning to the word "democracy" than was common.

Buddhadasa Bhikkhu specified that democracy has a "natural spirit" and to "understand this democracy clearly we must rely on the Buddha's words."[52] After giving examples of how the Lord Buddha exemplified freedom, equality, and fraternity in his life, teaching, and the organization of the Sangha, Buddhadasa Bhikkhu related these democratic virtues to Nature and Dhamma.

> These three conditions *(bhava)* are determined by Nature. If we are to love one another, live together in harmony, and survive in this world peacefully, Nature merely determines that there must be these three conditions. All people will be happy when they can think as pleases them, are equal, and have fraternity.[53]
>
> These are examples to demonstrate that freedom, equality, and fraternity—in terms of *siladhamma*—exist fully in Buddhism and in the Lord Buddha's behavior. Buddhism already had the character of democracy as understood morally. There is no need to fear that we misunderstand this thing, that is, that we will turn Buddhism into politics.[54]

Buddhadasa Bhikkhu used the *Aggañña-sutta*[55] to illustrate how differences developed among human beings. At first, all beings were equal. Later, variations in physical appearance developed due to differences in behavior, that is, morality. As morality deteriorated—causing laziness, theft, sexual wantonness—social problems grew. To deal with crime, "the democratic system appeared in the world for the first time," a king *(raja)* was chosen, and the people "stipulated that he must punish those deserving punishment, must capture those requiring capture, and must banish those deserving banishment."[56]

Thus, Buddhadasa Bhikkhu insisted that democracy is a moral rather than political issue. Our value as individuals and societies is determined by moral decency, not by aristocratic birth, education, or wealth. "Dhamma alone makes the difference. . . . Whatever we will be, whether democratic or not democratic, is because of the power of Dhamma."[57] He always insisted on this point, as we will see later, with the twist that politics is also a moral issue when properly understood. Only selfish people treat politics as a matter of power. The limited democracy of morality is difficult but possible, while absolute democracy—synonymous with *nibbana*—is in the world but not of it. Absolute freedom, equality, and brotherhood cannot be found in the world, in things under the power of time; they can only be found in the realization of Buddha-Dhamma.

Later, in the 1970s, Ajarn Buddhadasa began giving talks such as "A Socialist Type of Democracy," "Socialism According to Religious Principles," and "The Type of Socialism which Can Help the World," all of which were published and discussed in Bangkok.[58] This was a direct response to the Thai sociopolitical situation. At that time, the Vietnam war was still going on and the United Stated had official and secret (although not to the local people) air bases in Thailand. Many GIs came to Bangkok for "R & R," which contributed to a rapid expansion of the sex and tourism industry. Thais were fighting with the United States against the Vietnamese and the Thai military continued to be the dominant force in Thai politics. At the same time, the student and labor movements were growing strong and demanding the removal of the United States bases.[59] In such a climate, the polemics flew fast and the easiest way to get somebody thrown in jail or killed was to accuse him of being a communist. To many of the power elite, socialism was the same as communism, that is, the enemy. Further, Thai monks were expected to stay clear of politics, which means that most of the senior monks in Bangkok tacitly supported the ruling elites. At such a time, Ajarn Buddhadasa chose to speak out on socialism and gradually develop what has come to be called "Dhammic Socialism."

Why must we speak about socialism? Is it crazy or is it just chasing after current fashions? There are many angles with which to consider this question. We need not chase the socialist fad anywhere because Buddhism already has an excellent and special socialist system. Further, the present world is having problems concerning socialism and there are some forms of socialism which are like malignant germs which will cause infections and disease for human beings in the world.[60]

Ajarn Buddhadasa was attempting to bring a moral and spiritual perspective to the situation, in hopes of avoiding violence. Many intellectuals were interested in socialism but only from political and economic points of view. For Ajarn Buddhadasa, that was too shallow; he felt it could never really succeed. Therefore, he began to articulate a view of socialism that was in harmony with, in fact, grew organically out from, Buddhist principles and insights. With the necessary moral underpinnings and the guidance of Buddhist wisdom, he felt, a genuine socialism could emerge that would bring peace.

At first, it was necessary to make clear that the socialism he advocated was not the kind motivated by revenge. Thai society does not tolerate monks who advocate or support violence for the sake of changing the political and economic status quo. (Nonetheless, monks who have supported the use of state violence in order to maintain the status quo have been well rewarded.) More important, he himself believed that monks should stay free of partisan politics and should not support the use of force. On the other hand, he consistently made clear the inherent immorality of capitalism and never spoke of "Dhammic Capitalism." While the socialism he read about in books and newspapers was still caught up with selfishness, he felt that socialism, when properly understood, could be a vehicle for unselfish social relationships and, thereby, peace.

Dhammic Socialism

Let us begin with basic definitions. "Socialism" (Thai *samgama-niyama,* literally, "preference for society") as understood by Ajarn Buddhadasa is foremost the point of view and attitude that the common good comes first, that society is more fundamental than the individual, that the interests and needs of society as a whole come before those of the individual.

> Here, Dhammic Socialism according to Buddhist principles holds that Nature created beings which must live in groups. Both plants and animals live together in groups or communities. This system we will call 'socialism': the correctness necessary for living together in groups which Nature has dictated. In short, it is living for the benefit of society, not for the individual benefit of each person.[61]

Out of this understanding, political, economic, and social structures can emerge that are peaceful, moral, and just. Here, society is the collective of all the individuals grouped together on a certain level for mutual benefit and support. In this respect, socialism can be contrasted with individualism and liberal democracy, both of which, as Ajarn Buddhadasa saw them, share the common root of selfishness.

Dhammic means to be composed of, based in, governed by, and in line with Nature and the Law of Nature. It means to see and fulfill one's natural duty (Dhamma) in all situations. It is to be "correct for the sake of survival, every step and stage of human evolution, both for oneself and for others."[62] "To be Dhammic, besides being honest and virtuous, also requires knowledge. If one's knowing is incorrect, no matter how honest and virtuous one may be, one will not be able to make it Dhammic. They might make laws which go against Nature or that create suffering and danger."[63] Thus, "Dhammic Socialism" is a preference for society as a whole in a way that is in line with Nature and the Law of Nature. Ajarn Buddhadasa stressed that our socialism must be Dhammic because the modern understanding of the term "socialism" is overwhelmingly materialistic, centering only on economic and political factors more or less devoid of moral considerations.

> We can see that there are many kinds of socialism. For example, the socialism of Karl Marx is just the revenge of the worker. There's nothing to it other than revenge by the workers or laborers. Such socialism of revenge is angry and acts through its anger. The socialism of Buddhists, however, must include the word 'Dhammic,' which means consisting of or having Dhamma, that is, correctness: acting and practicing correctly in line with Dhamma principles, not acting out of anger or revenge. 'Dhammic' means connected with and going according to Dhamma.[64]

Ajarn Buddhadasa insisted that moral concerns and higher spiritual insights must be primary. For him, capitalism and communism—especially in their recent historical forms—were the same in that they are fundamentally selfish. In both, classes are opposed to each other and one is dominant. He felt that this violates a deeper social reality and our duty toward it.

> Everyone is indebted to society and is bound by the social contract from the moment one was born from one's mother's womb, or even from the time one was in the womb.[65]

In short, "Dhammic Socialism" is the principle that society should be governed for the sake of genuine peace. Over and over again Ajarn Buddhadasa stressed that peace is the purpose of Buddhism, both personal inner peace *(santisukha)* and world peace *(santipap)*. Such peace can only be achieved when nonselfishness informs all aspects and levels of society.

There are many implications to and consequences of this insistence that socialism—in fact any political, economic, and social system or government—be grounded in and governed by natural truth (Dhamma). I will draw out some of the more important ones here.

First, this socialism can only exist within Nature since everything is Nature. All social realities—economics, politics, culture, language, art, crime, religion—are part of Nature and must be understood and responded to accordingly. Thus, Dhammic Socialism cannot be separated from Nature, and, therefore, is under the Law of Nature, that is, the law of interdependence.

Second, the interdependence of Nature makes Nature inherently socialistic. We should observe that from birth through our entire lives we are dependent on parent, relatives, friends, the government, and even enemies. Our lives, well-being, and meaningfulness depend on those of others, which makes us social creatures. The animals and plants are socialistic through their mutual dependencies. As we also depend on them, human socialism depends on the larger socialism of all living things. Socialism, as Ajarn Buddhadasa understood it, is a natural consequence of the natural order and of human beings gathering together in mutually beneficial and supportive groups.

> So we aren't surprised by all the different ideological, dogmatic, biased (*saccabhinivesa*) socialist systems when humanity is unable to achieve the genuine socialist system of Nature. When we don't realize the natural truth of this matter, we get stuck in views and opinions, that is, many varied forms of dogmas and biases about this word.[66]

Third, there is a social contract arising from the place of human beings within Nature. Because society gives us everything, we ought to be grateful and recognize the duty (Dhamma) to act for the benefit of society.

> As for practicing benefits for society, the meaning is that Buddhists still respect and accept the social contract, that is, the fact that everyone in the world has rights, duties, and obligations inseparably and unconsciously linked, which ought to cause everyone to consider that he has the duty to bring benefits in gratitude to each other, which is important for humanity or the honor of humanity. We can say that the one who violates the social contract does not deserve the name "human." Therefore, Buddhists, whether those who are not yet liberated or those who are liberated must recognize the social contract and practice correctly in situations concerning it, namely, having the duty to benefit society.[67]

Fourth, this is not merely a social duty, it is our religious duty. Those who do not see this duty have failed to understand their religion, especially if they are Buddhists.

That there are bhikkhus, samaneras, upasakas, and upasikas [ordained and lay Buddhists] who are careless in this matter derives from their not knowing this aspect of the Buddha's purpose, or from their knowing but wrongly understanding that it is a trivial matter. In fact, this matter is important enough to cause significant harm for that individual and for the religion collectively. That it is harmful for that person doesn't mean that he will lose the benefits he ought to get from society, but means that such behavior shows that his capacity for sympathy and kindness *(nam jai)*, or his subconscious personality, is hard and crude. Or he is soaking in a character which grows more crude with each day. When a person's capacity for sympathy and kindness has become habitually hard like this, how ever can his mind be gentle, subtle, pliant, and ready for understanding or for higher practices of body, speech, and mind such as *sila, samadhi, and panna?* It amounts to the closing of the gate of realizing the path, its fruits, and *nibbana.*[68]

When we look deeply enough, we see that the social duty of working for the common good, that is, the maintenance of peace, justice, and morality in society, supports our spiritual duty, that is, the abandonment of ignorance and egoism in order to realize *nibbana.* For Ajarn Buddhadasa, there was no conflict between the interests of the individual and the interests of society as a whole when we consider genuine needs and benefits. That which is truly beneficial for society is beneficial for its members. Of course, there must be short-term disadvantages for some individuals sometimes, but when the welfare to its members is not served in the long run, no society will survive.

Fifth, socialism is nothing new, especially for Buddhists. It is not a Western property to be imported into Asia. As Ajarn Buddhadasa understood it, socialism has been around since at least the Buddha's time.

> We already have the ideal of socialism without being aware of it. Whether in the administrative system of the Sangha from the Buddha's time until now, or within the Dhamma system of Buddhism, or in the Buddha's way of behaving toward other beings in the world, we can see that it is the highest socialism.[69]

A tangible example of "Buddhist Socialism" was King Asoka of India, the traditional exemplar of Buddhist rulers. Ajarn Buddhadasa also felt that Ramkhamhaeng of Sukothai (the ancient Thai kingdom) demonstrated socialism. Further, because of its long association with Buddhism Thai culture has socialistic roots. "Our ancestors taught us to act so that all lives can live together correctly in kindness and friendliness, in line with the standard of Nature."[70]

To be Buddhist is to be socialist, and Thais can find their own form of socialism in their cultural roots.

> If one believes in Buddhism, the spirit of socialism will be in one's flesh and blood. One sees fellow human beings as comrades in *dukkha,* friends in birth, aging, illness, and death. We are comrades in suffering such that we can't sit and watch.[71]

What of indiv enlightened ethic?

It is time Buddhists knew the socialism of Buddhism and unsheathed it as a weapon in withstanding the blood-crazy socialism of dogmatism (ideology) which does wrong by itself then puts the blame on others.[72]

Ajarn Buddhadasa seemed to try to accomplish two things here. First, he legitimized socialism as an issue and an approach appropriate to Buddhism, Thai culture, and the current situation. Socialism is not something to be shunned as Western or foreign, for it can be found in Thailand's cultural and religious heritage. In fact, it is more appropriate for Thailand than the Western forms (capitalism, consumerism, technocracy, etc.) currently being mimicked. Socialism, as he understood it, would allow Thai society, as well as Asian culture as a whole, to preserve and further develop those elements of their heritage that are superior to what is being imported from the West.

Finally, he argued for a more religious understanding of socialism, one based in Dhamma principles. He tried to raise or enlighten the level of discourse on these matters beyond the usual elements of power and materialism. The human being is much more than a mere "economic animal" or "political animal"; therefore, theories that disregard our cultural, psychological, and spiritual aspects will fail to satisfy all of our needs. The spiritual dimension, being the aspect of our lives that provides ultimate meaning and happiness, requires special attention. Only by so doing can correct socialism be found.

Politics is Morality

While Buddhadasa Bhikkhu took pains in earlier talks, such as "Buddha-Dhamma and The Spirit of Democracy," to specify that Buddha-Dhamma has nothing to do with politics,[73] he eventually dropped the distinction. In fact, he said that the Lord Buddha is "the supreme politician." Still, he insisted on the distinction between the politics that is based in morality and the politics that is about power, exploitation, and self-interest. Only the former is acceptable to Buddhists.

Ajarn Buddhadasa insisted that socialism—like politics, economics, education, and other social concerns—is a moral issue, despite frequent criticism from those Buddhists who feel a dirty word like "politics" should never be mentioned in the same breath as Buddhism, and from politicians who do not want morality to interfere with their activities. Recognizing socialism's relationship to morality is crucial to understanding and using it for the common good.

> Western thinkers from ancient times have said that everyone once born is inescapably a social being, an economic being, a political being. But here we must say that this isn't enough, isn't sufficiently correct. It lacks an adequate foundation, So we ask to add another point: we must also be moral beings.[74]

Morality *(siladhamma),* for Ajarn Buddhadasa, was more profound than merely following rules or precepts, as *siladhamma* is often understood. It must always be rooted in Natural Law if it is to be wise, peaceful, and successful.

Ajarn Buddhadasa defined *siladhamma* (or simply *sila,* morality) as "1. the condition of being normal, 2. the Dhamma that causes normality, and 3. the thing that is normality (itself)."[75] The key term here is normality *(pakati),* which the Pali Text Society dictionary defines as "original or natural form, natural state of condition" and in its instrumental form means "by Nature, ordinarily, as usual."[76] In Thai usage, these meanings are retained but with an emphasis on ordinariness, normality, and naturalness. The true normality of *"pakati"* must be natural, that is, derived from the law of Nature rather than thought. "*Sila* means *'pakati.'* If anything leads to *pakati* and not to disorder, it is called *'sila.'* The Dhamma that brings this state about is called *'sila-dhamma.'* "[77] Without sacrificing the popular meaning of morality, Ajarn Buddhadasa informs it with more profound roots. Let us examine this further.

When we consider *sila-dhamma* as it is usually understood, that is, applied to our actions, speech, and means of sustaining life (corresponding to the third, fourth, and fifth factors of the noble eightfold path), "normality" concerns our relationships with other people, other living things, and the rest of Nature. As these relationships are naturally those of interdependency *(idappaccayata),* they are *pakati* (normal and natural) when they are free of conflict, for only then are they mutually beneficial. Freedom from conflict is absence of violence, injustice, exploitation, and abuse. In short, our relationships and the actions that compose them are moral or "normal" when they harm neither us nor others. "The word *pakati* means not to collide with anyone and not to collide with oneself, that is, not to cause distress for oneself or for others."[78] All of society should be organized on this principle. "Setting up a system which makes society *pakati* or happy is called 'socialism.' If something causes disorder, it is a kind of immorality in society."[79]

Moral, normal, natural relationships that are both beneficial to all involved and free of harm require unselfishness. When the mind functions under the influence of ignorance—when it lacks wisdom—desire, attachment, and egoism take over.[80] Unless carefully restrained, egoism turns into selfishness and selfish behavior is always harmful, tends toward conflict, and often becomes violent. Ideally, by replacing ignorance with wisdom there is a selflessness that automatically creates the conditions for peaceful, harmless actions and relationships. "With mindfulness controlling the flow of *paticcasamuppada,* self doesn't arise and selfishness doesn't happen. Then we are able to have Dhammic Socialism."[81]

But there is still more to this natural normalcy. *Pakati,* and thereby *sila-dhamma,* is not limited merely to the realm of speech and actions, as morality is commonly understood in Theravada Buddhism. Normalcy must refer also to our inner state, to the *citta* (heart-mind). When the mind-heart is *pakati,* it is free of attachment and defilement, that is, it is in its natural or original state, which in Pali is called the *"pabhassara-citta"* (luminous mind). Mind is "abnormal" when it is clouded by selfishness and defilement; mind is "normal" when it is free of "I" and "mine."

Further, there is the spiritual level of *pakati* that consists of direct knowledge and experience of truth, namely, impermanence, unsat—isfactoriness, not-self, and interdependency. Lastly, the ultimate *pakati* corresponds to the absolute, that is, *nibbana.* The unchanging, timeless, unconditioned, Supreme Reality is the ultimate level and standard of *pakati.* When we examine *sila-dhamma* fully, we see that it cannot be taken as just one level of human life, separated from the entirety of experience. Rather, it connects with all levels of human experience and reality from the deeply personal to the familial and communal to the universal and back. Thus, Ajarn Buddhadasa's understanding of *sila-dhamma,* whether we translate it as "morality" or "normalcy," and with it Dhammic Socialism, is clearly holistic *(kevala).* Rather than setting up a dichotomy between the social and the individual, or between the moral and the spiritual, which would force them into conflict and confuse us, he saw them as being naturally integrated.

In short, Ajarn Buddhadasa emphasized that Dhammic Socialism must be governed by wisdom, that is, it must be based in profound understanding of Nature, its law, and our corresponding duty. Morality and wisdom depend on each other. By extension, wisdom and Dhammic Socialism depend on each other, also. Why did Ajarn Buddhadasa bother to emphasize this? Once again, because of his concern for *dukkha.* He observed that anyone stuck with the traditional idea of *sila-dhamma* will only be avoiding evil and doing good because of a limited conception of right and wrong. If our avoidance of evil and doing of good lacks the illumination of higher understanding, we cannot avoid identifying with the not doing of evil—"I'm not bad," "I don't do anything wrong"—and the doing of good—"I only do good," "I'm a good person." This attachment to our actions—the "doer"— no matter how good, traps us in dualistic concepts of right and wrong and makes the morality egoistic and caught up with *dukkha*. Such a morality is profoundly unsatisfying. Not only does it fail to liberate us from *dukkha*, it can even be a source of further *dukkha*.

The situation is much different when the *sila-dhamma* is grounded in *paramatha-dhamma* (ultimate reality, transcendent truth). Then, the understanding of voidness and dependent origination prevents attachment. Those in whom such understanding is not sufficiently developed to avoid all attachment can reflect on not-self and interdependency so as to understand better the Nature of clinging and mitigate its painful consequences. From this understanding, avoidance of evil is natural and done automatically. "Good deeds" are done, without regarding them as "good," not for the sake of "goodness," but because they are required by the Law of Nature. Everything is done simply as a wise and compassionate response to the way things are.

Ajarn Buddhadasa taught Dhammic Socialism because he thought we needed it to get out of the terrible trap of egoism and *dukkha*, both personal and collective. Needless to say, a society based on standards of nonselfishness would not face the environmental, crime, drug, violence, and moral crises that confront Thailand, the United States, and the rest of the world. These very crises prove, to Ajarn Buddhadasa at least, that selfishness will be our ruin. So long as political, social, ecological, educational, and religious institutions and systems do not serve the cause of human liberation, and even heap more *dukkha* upon us, for that long we will be in danger of destroying ourselves. Ajarn Buddhadasa proposed Dhammic Socialism as the basic solution, the necessary response to the reality of many layered, pervasive, intertwined *dukkha*. Ajarn Buddhadasa tried to clarify the main principles; many details remain to be worked out concerning appropriate political, economic, and other social systems.

Dictatorial Dhammic Socialism

Due to the ambiguity of democracy—the Thai version of liberal democracy in particular—Ajarn Buddhadasa challenged us with "dictatorial dhammic socialism." He asked what will happen with a government of, for, and by the people if the people are selfish. This question and his advocacy of "dictatorship" has raised some hackles.[82] Some people accused Ajarn

Buddhadasa of justifying dictators—perhaps unintentionally, perhaps not—and creating openings for the likes of Stalin and Hitler. Others feel frustrated when a generally progressive religious leader contradicted some of their cherished beliefs. There would be less confusion if critics paid more attention to what Ajarn Buddhadasa meant by "dictator."

> Now almost everyone in Thailand fails to understand the word "dictator." They're afraid of dictators the same as they're afraid of ghosts; it's stuck in their hearts. Tyrants have brought disaster to the world. That's what they call "dictatorship," meaning tyranny with evil leaders who dictate according to their own interests.[83]

For English speakers, the use of the translation "dictator" loses some of the connotations of the original Thai word. The Thai term is *"phadetkarn,"* a noun meaning "the use of absolute governing power,"[84] derived from *phadet, a* verb meaning "to cut, eradicate, break"[85] and also "to expedite, to dispose of quickly, to dictate."[86] In using this term, Ajarn Buddhadasa emphasized the qualities of absoluteness, firmness, and decisiveness needed to solve many intractable social problems.

> 'Dictatorial' means to do something absolutely and decisively (resolutely, unequivocally). This 'absolute' must be correct. If there is Dhamma, it dictates absolutely and correctly. Dictatorship is merely a tool, the means of decisiveness. Thus, dictatorship is neither evil nor good in itself, but depends on the people who use it. If used evilly, it's evil; if used well, it's good. . . . Now we are speaking of the dictatorship which is used in a good way and has Dhamma as the dictator. Would everyone please give justice to the word 'dictator.'[87]

If people would behave unselfishly on their own, "dictatorship" would not be needed. But when they choose to chase after their own selfish desires, strong qualities are needed to clean up the mess.

Ajarn Buddhadasa's critics tend to interpret dictatorship as being human dictators, that is, they recognize only the conventional meaning of "dictator" as a person or self. In Dhamma terms, however, "dictator" is the absolute power of the world, which is the law of Nature or Dhamma rather than a person or self. In other words, the dictator is voidness. Ajarn Buddhadasa's primary reason for using the word "dictator" was to emphasize that absolute decisiveness is needed to overcome the self and its selfishness. On the other hand, he used the term "dictator" fully conscious of the connotations it has for modern people. He knew it would stir up interest and discussion, and he did not mind if these were critical.

For the authority of Dhamma to function in society, it must act through social institutions, in particular, the rulers. Although secondary, an individual or group that dictates on behalf of Dhamma may be needed. Ajarn Buddhadasa insisted that such a ruler must have Dhamma, in particular, the Ten Virtues of Rulers *(rajadhamma).*[86]

> If a good person dictates, that is even better. If a bad person, it is hopeless. When the socialist system is well, it must have a tool to dictate. A ruler who fulfills the *rajadhammas* is the best kind of dictator. There probably aren't any political science books from the West to teach us this, maybe because they never had this kind of ruler or King.[89]

The real power is the Law of Nature or Dhamma. By carrying out the ten *rajadhammas,* a ruler (individual or collective) conforms to Dhamma. In Dhammic Socialism, a human dictator—whether an individual or group— is only legitimate when carrying out the dictates of natural law for the sake of peace. Should any person or group usurp or abuse power—that is, use it selfishly and oppressively—the people are justified in deposing them. In fact, this in inherent in the original meaning of the word *"raja,"* according to the *Aganna Sutta.*[90] Here, in an origin story of sorts, the Buddha is reported to have said that the man chosen to protect the fields and property of the people is given three titles: *Maha-Sammati* meaning "Authorized by the People," *Khattiya* meaning "Lord of the Fields," and *Raja* meaning "He Who Satisfies Others."[91] Thus, the *Raja* must rule for the sake of the people and with their consent. To satisfy the people, a ruler must have Dhamma; without Dhamma, he is merely a usurper or tyrant. The Dhammic dictator, by definition, cannot oppress the people or use violence against them.

Critics complain that such a teaching justifies dictatorships in a part of the world where democracy is not very strong and where many governments tend to be corrupt and abusive of human rights. Ajarn Buddhadasa responded that liberal democracy does not have a better record when we look at it without bias.[92] He believed that dictatorship—as he defined it— is better able to get things done. He cited events from Thai and local history to illustrate his point. Those of us who have been raised to hate fascism may not agree with him, but we should recognize that he is not talking about fascism or totalitarianism. Further, perhaps we should consider whether he had a valid point when he asked, Which is more important, clinging to our democratic ideology or solving society's problems? If democracy does not solve the problems, is it really better? If it does solve the problems, there will be no need for a human dictator, only the dictatorship of Dhamma.

Dhamma as Democracy

Ajarn Buddhadasa felt that "democracy," especially as it is being touted by Western governments, businesses, and missionaries—that is, capitalistic liberal democracy—is vague and ambiguous. Here, he was not speaking as a political scientist or ideologist but as a person practically concerned with the well-being of society. Therefore, he spoke of "democracy" as it is popularly understood in Thailand; this is the "democracy" he criticized. He also gave the word his own twist, as he had done with "socialism." Whether democracy is beneficial or harmful depends on the kind of democracy being discussed.

> "Democracy" is a word we hear every day, but it is a word which is ambiguous and most deceitful. This is because each person uses his personal defilements to give his own meaning to "democracy." One kind [of democracy] is a tool for taking advantage of or harming others; another kind is a tool for building peace.[93]

The democracy that is primarily concerned with the good of the individual and the rights of the individual is wide open to exploitation by individual defilements. While there can be a kind of democracy that genuinely champions the common good, the democracy idealogues do not speak of it nor does U.S. foreign policy support it. Further, this defiled and selfish "liberal democracy" creates divisions and violence in society.

> It creates simultaneously both capitalists and laborers, which are usually seen as opposites or opponents. Because democracy is blurred, there are capitalists. Because democracy is blurred, there occurs the right to seize from the capitalists, that is, the rights of laborers. Because democracy is blurred to the point at which nobody really knows where it is, everything is left to the desires of each person in each case.[94]

The great danger, then, is that the freedom of democracy will be used selfishly, that is, according to the defilements *(kilesa)*. As Ajarn Buddhadasa sees it, the vast social problems of our era—increasing poverty, crime, militarization, environmental destruction, suicide, drug abuse, to name only a few—demonstrate that democracy is in fact being used selfishly, incredibly so.

> Liberal democracy is totally free and doesn't define clearly what freedom it means. This allows the defilements in people to take advantage of the situation to be free according to the power of defilement. Although the ideal is set out in a philosophically beautiful way, in practice it doesn't

work. Philosophy doesn't have the strength to stop the defilements. Thus, we must be very careful about liberal democracy for it can be terribly dangerous. Anyone can claim freedom, both fools and sages. If they don't get what they want, they will say there is no freedom.[95]

Freedom, like democracy and socialism, is another concept or value that must be qualified. Is it wise or blind? Is it just or selfish? Is it freedom from *dukkha* or merely from responsibility? For Ajarn Buddhadasa, the only safe freedom is the kind which fits with Dhamma. Let me stress that Ajarn Buddhadasa was not necessarily against all forms of democracy, only the forms that encourage or give too much freedom to selfishness.

As one might expect, Ajarn Buddhadasa had his own definition of "democracy." He felt that "Buddhism has the spirit of democracy" because it recognizes the equality of sharing the common experiences of "birth, aging, illness, and death equally." In short, because all human beings suffer, they are equal and therefore naturally have "the spirit of democracy." Further, he reasoned, "the Buddhist Sangha lives together in a democratic system" and because it can be taken as the Buddhist ideal of communal living its democratic characteristics mean that Buddhism is democratic.[96] In short, "democracy is Dhamma or is *siladhamma*."[97]

Notice that he here used "democracy" in the same way as he used "socialism." Both terms were described from the same perspective and as being important for the same reasons. It seems that Ajarn Buddhadasa turned them into synonyms, at least when understood in his way. On the other hand, he clearly stated that democracy, as he understood it, is not synonymous with capitalism. In fact, capitalism is undemocratic.

> If there is democracy, there is no way for there to be capitalists. If there are capitalists, there cannot be democracy. There is no equality or freedom in that kind of democracy, not to mention brotherhood. . . . Nobody can obstruct the interests of the capitalists.[98]

This point has not always been made as forcefully or directly as it could be, perhaps because of the military dictatorships that have run Thailand throughout most of Ajarn Buddhadasa's teaching career. Direct criticism of the government and political system was not tolerated until recently. Censorship of the press and self-censorship by the monks have been the rule. Nonetheless, Ajarn Buddhadasa made it clear that he considered capitalism to be selfish and immoral, a cause of violence and an obstacle to peace.

On the other hand, Ajarn Buddhadasa was suspicious of Marxist revolutionary movements, primarily because of their emphasis on class struggle, which seemed to him to be motivated by revenge, and because of their use of force. Nonetheless, he still believed that true socialism is ideal, as is true democracy. For him, "Dictatorial Dhammic Socialism" is a middle way between the contending ideologies of liberal democracy and vengeful communism.

> If small countries like ours have a dictatorial Dhammic Socialist system of government it will be like burning the area around our house to clear away the grass so that forest fires won't endanger our house. The forest fire is blood-crazy socialism which is epidemic in the world at this time. Even the capitalist system should be considered as a forest fire. If we must face these forest fires we must clear around our homes. If we have dictatorial Dhammic Socialism we can face both capitalism and the blood-crazy revenge of some workers because pure socialism doesn't create capitalists or laborers. It creates only *sappurisa* or human beings who are correct, who are neutral and without bias.[99]

In the end, the primary issue is not a debate between democracy and absolutism, but whether the political system of a particular society is in line with Dhamma or not; that is, whether it is selfish and immoral or leads to genuine peace. "Suan Mokkh believes in the democracy which has Dhamma as dictator, or, to put it another way, has love as dictator. Kindness and compassion are a dictator like parents who love and care for their children but sometimes must punish them"[100]

It should be clear that Ajarn Buddhadasa's main objective all along was to overcome selfishness. He played with political terms because they stir up people's interest, not because he was a politician or political scientist. People had already "invested much thought" in issues like peace, democracy, and socialism; he attempted to attract this interest and "apply it to a better understanding of Buddha-Dhamma."[101] The more people understand Dhamma, the less selfishness there will be in society.

Some critics feel that Ajarn Buddhadasa's ideal is unrealistic, that a moral, unselfish society will never happen. His patient response was that no other principles could bring about peace. If it is difficult to accomplish, put blame on one's own selfishness, not Dhammic Socialism. For now, the task is to call attention to the issues that have been discussed here, so that a proper debate may take place. For the most part, our social, political, and economic discussions are too narrow and flat. We must give them moral and spiritual life, which is the proper contribution of Buddha-Dhamma. Then, together, we can work out the appropriate forms needed in each cultural, historical situation. If the end result is peaceful, nonselfish, and rooted in natural law, Ajarn Buddhadasa's objectives will have been achieved. Thus, his Dhammic Socialism can be democratic or dictatorial or both, for he defines these words in ways that do not put them in conflict. The key is that the principles work, that is, lead to world peace. "Any political system, if permeated with Dhamma, can solve the problems."[102]

And lest we forget, working for the common good and for world peace cannot be separated from our spiritual practice. "This helping others is a matter of helping to destroy selfishness."[103] For individuals, there is a spiritual side to our responsibility. When it is practiced by society, it can be called "Dhammic Socialism." That Nature forces us to do so in order to survive makes it "dictatorial Dhammic Socialism." This is Ajarn Buddhadasa's vision of world peace in which social and spiritual practice are made one through the destruction of selfishness.

Ajarn Buddhadasa's Influence

The teachings discussed in this essay aim to end *dukkha* and bring about peace. Have they indeed brought such results? What influence have these teachings had in Thailand? The direct result of Ajarn Buddhadasa's work is difficult to measure, for its fruits are found in the understanding and attitude of those who study and practice accordingly. These cannot be quantified. A further complication is that there are many who claim to be Ajarn Buddhadasa's disciples (and their numbers have escalated since his death). It is not easy to determine who is genuinely putting the principles he taught into practice. We must rely on what people tell us about themselves, as well as observe their actions, work, and lifestyle. Roughly, the people influenced by Ajarn Buddhadasa fit into four groups: Buddhist groups and organizaitons, social elites, progressives, and other religions. Here, we can mention only some prominent examples.

Buddhist Groups

Through his life, writings, talks, and Suan Mokkh, Ajarn Buddhadasa has influenced many individuals who have in turn gone on to their own work, groups, and Wats. Of these, monks and novices are foremost, as Suan Mokkh was originally intended to train them and they made up the majority of residents until recently. Many monks, after a few years of study at Suan Mokkh, went on to start their own Wats or to take up responsible positions, primarily teaching, in established Wats. Well-known examples are Phra Payom of Wat Suan Kaew in Nontaburi, who is very popular with youth and working-class people, and numerous monks at Wat Cholapratan Rangsarit, including the Abbot, Luang Paw Panna (Phra Depvisuddhimedhi), who is probably the best known Buddhist teacher among Thais. Some monks, such as Luang Paw Panyat of Wat Pah Dhammada (Ordinary Forest Temple), have been involved in grass-roots development work. A number of well-known nuns and women Dhamma teachers have also been deeply influenced by Ajarn Buddhadasa, for example, Upasika Ki Nanayon (known as Ajarn Kor Khao-suan-luang in her later years) and, more recently, Upasika Runjuan Indarakamhaeng, a former university lecturer.

In addition to these individuals and institutions, many lay Buddhist organizations were inspired by Buddhadasa Bhikkhu, including the Teachers of Morality Club of Thailand, which works in schools; the Sublime Life Mission, which publishes books; and the Buddhadasa Foundation. In the 1960s and 1970s, Ajarn Buddhadasa was the first to have university students ordain as monks during the summer break and come to the monastery for religious instruction and meditation teaching. In doing so, he helped to apply the ancient Thai custom of temporary ordination for young men to the modern situation.

A brief mention should also be made of foreign Buddhists from Nepal, India, Japan, and the West who have met with and become friends of Ajarn Buddhadasa. The Dalai Lama and he met in Bangkok during 1967. When His Holiness was able to return to Siam in 1972, Ajarn Buddhadasa hosted him at Suan Mokkh. Their main topic of conversation was meditation, specifically, the systematic practice of *anapanasati* (mindfulness of breathing).

Social Elites

Among the elites of Thai society, the groups that have been most influenced by Ajarn Buddhadasa are judges (Ministry of Justice), teachers and educators (Ministry of Education), and doctors (Ministry of Public Health), all of whom work in the civil service, have higher education and social status, and are somewhat conservative. The ones who have been most drawn to Ajarn Buddhadasa are those who share his concern for morality, for Thai culture and society, and some degree of religious understanding and growth. Although they represent the status quo to some degree, his influence helps them to look further and deeper

In 1938, Suan Mokkh was visited by three well-respected jurors and lawyers, who became lifelong supporters of Buddhadasa Bhikkhu. One of them, Dr. Sanna Dhammasakdi was Thailand's only civilian prime minister (1973–1976) and is now chairman of the king's privy council, as well as honorary president of the World Fellowship of Buddhists. Another, Phraya Ladpli Dhammapragalbha, then director of the appellate courts, arranged for Ajarn Buddhadasa to give Dhamma training to prospective judges. This training, consisting of ten lectures given over a three-week period, began in 1956 and lasted for fourteen years, after which Ajarn Buddhadasa handed the responsibility over to Pannananda Bhikkhu (Phra Depvisuddhimedhi), his close friend and coworker for many years, who continues training the judges up to the present. Many of these lecture series were published as books (and many are still in print), including the well-known *Handbook For Mankind*. Regularly, judges came to pay respect to Ajarn Buddhadasa and express their gratitude for his teaching. If he has helped 10 percent of them to be more wise, compassionate, and just in their work, then Thai society is the better for it.

Ajarn Buddhadasa considered education to be very important and spoke on the subject a great deal. Dhammic Socialism can only come about if youth are educated appropriately. In 1936, the Dhammadana Group opened its Buddhanigama School in Chaiya, the first tangible manifestation of the Suan Mokkh—Dhammadana Group's interest in education. This school became well known due to the high number of its students who went on to high government positions and yet retained a moral foundation. Graduates include former cabinet ministers, Supreme Court judges, and the current commander-in-chief of the army.

Ajarn Buddhadasa's ideas on education were taken seriously, and still are, among teachers, professors, and education administrators. In 1955, he lectured on "Ideals of Teachers from the Buddhist Perspective" to teachers from around the country. A few years later he began to appear increasingly at the major universities and spoke to large audiences, as many as three thousand at a time. He also gave many talks at the Teachers' Congress *(Guru Sabha)*. While the education system has not yet been overhauled to reflect his ideas and still mimics the West, some of his students have implemented policies and projects that have tried to mitigate the competitive and selfish aspects of the current system.

In 1985, officials responsible for the ethics component of the new primary school curriculum met and worked at Suan Mokkh. Ajarn Buddhadasa guided their work with daily talks on ethics, education, social responsibility, and nonselfishness. Runjuan Indarakamhaeng, who formerly worked for the Ministry of Education and then became a well-known lecturer at a Ramkamhaeng University (Bangkok), now a resident of Suan Mokkh and one of Siam's most respected woman Dhamma and meditation teachers, was directly involved in the work. Although there have been many problems in implementing this ethics curriculum, such as entrenched bureaucratic interests, the input of Suan Mokkh provided a deeper vision and strengthened the small steps that were made.

Again, there has been little effect on the medical system as a whole, which continues to follow the Western capitalist model wholeheartedly. Nevertheless, individual doctors, including administrators and teachers in the main teaching hospitals, have changed the way they practice so as to better live up to Buddhist principles. These doctors are less interested in money and more committed to service and social well-being. This group of doctors often invited Buddhadasa to lecture to the Buddhist clubs at their hospitals.

Even prime ministers have taken an interest in Ajarn Buddhadasa. H. E. Pridi Panomyong, leader of the 1932 Revolution and Thailand's senior statesman at that time, attended the "Buddha-Dhamma and the Spirit of Democracy" lecture in 1947 and invited Buddhadasa Bhikkhu, who was only forty–one years old then, for private consultations. Usually, Thailand's political leaders have only sought advice from elder and high-ranking monks. It seems Buddhadasa Bhikkhu had a knack for relating the highest teachings of Buddha-Dhamma with the key issues of the day in a way that intelligent people could understand and benefit from. Pridi even attempted to build a Buddhist center modeled after Suan Mokkh in Ayuddhaya, his home province. The attempt failed when Pridi was driven into exile by rightist politicians and generals.

Progressive Groups

In addition to Buddhist circles, Ajarn Buddhadasa has also had some influence among progressive social groups. One reason for this influence is that he has articulately, directly, and forcefully criticized the current state of affairs in Thai Buddhism, Thai society, and the world. His critiques may not come from the same perspectives as the progressives, but there has been room for common cause. In fact, just the fact that someone of his stature is critical is important when most of the monastic hierarchy is conservative, passive, silent, and often co-opted. The progressives had little access to the government-controlled mass media in the 1960s and 1970s and welcomed anything that seemed to support their cause. While he said some things that made the progressives uncomfortable—his idea of dictatorial Dhammic Socialism for example—for many years he was the only prominent monk to teach in ways supportive of their efforts. Many in the student movement of the 1970s, the main force for social change then, found inspiration and guidance in Ajarn Buddhadasa's teaching and example. Even now, important Buddhist social workers—such as Sulak Sivaraksa and Pracha Hutanuvatra, founders of the International Network of Engaged Buddhists—are profoundly affected by the life and work of Buddhadasa Bhikkhu.

On the other hand, Ajarn Buddhadasa did not exactly take the side of the progressives. He felt strongly that taking sides is not correct, is selfish, and goes against Dhammic Socialism.

> Now the time has come that there is a socialism which conflicts with natural truth. Some individuals and groups behave as rebels against Nature and separate into two sides. One side has the power of money and the other side has the power of labor. Separating humanity into groups, then setting them against each other as enemies, is not the wish of Nature, nor is it the wish of any religion.[104]

While it is probably true that the progressives are not the main cause of such separations and conflicts, they often help maintain the divisions.

One prominent social activist, unfortunately little known in the West, who has been deeply influenced by Buddhadasa Bhikkhu is Dr. Prawet Wasi. A tropical hematologist on the faculty of Siriraj Hospital of Mahidol University, Dr. Prawet was a leading researcher for many years. He also has become a leading figure in the network of Thai nongovernment organizations (NGOs). He heads the Foundation for Children, one of the country's best known NGOs, and has been influential in the herbal medicine movement, which has regained a significant role in rural health care. Partly because of the prestige of being a Magsaysay Award winner,[105] but also because of his nonoffensive style, Dr. Prawes also commands attention in government circles. Because he is listened to by groups as diverse as the National Security Council and democracy activists, he fulfills the important function of bridging opinions that tend to be opposed and in conflict. Creating a middle ground for constructive dialogue is one way he tries to apply Ajarn Buddhadasa's teachings. Since his retirement from the university, he lectures widely in Thailand and abroad, serves on the boards of most of Thailand's universities, and advises a number of NGOs. He is interested in developing a Buddhist-based alternative education and for this reason visits Suan Mokkh regularly to support the new project for training foreign monks at Suan Atammayatarama.

We should also mention artists, such as the poet Naowarat Pongpaiboon and the painter-poet Angkarn Kalayanapong, who have woven Buddhist themes and perspectives into their work, including poems about Suan Mokkh and Ajarn Buddhadasa.

Dialogue with Christianity

In 1939, Buddhadasa Bhikkhu wrote a long article titled "Answering the Questions of the Priest," in which he strongly criticized the idea of a personal God, that is, a God that is conceived in personal or anthropomorphic terms. This was a response to a visit by an Italian missionary priest who had been living in Thailand for many years. At that time, Buddhadasa Bhikkhu was not impressed by the teachings of the Christian missionaries, especially what he heard on the radio broadcasts. He found what he heard rather simplistic and superstitious, exactly what he was trying to overcome in Thai Buddhism. Further, like many educated Buddhists, he was suspicious of motives of Christian missionaries, the tactics they used, their wealth, and their support from the Western powers.

Ajarn Buddhadasa had been reading the Bible himself and began to study it more deeply. On his own, more or less as he had done with the Buddhist *Tipitaka,* he found there was more to the Christian tradition than he heard on the radio. Eventually, he concluded that there was no point in criticizing the superstitious interpretations of some Christians. There was much more to be gained by working with open-minded Christians. For Ajarn Buddhadasa, all religions are the same in one central respect—eliminating selfishness. Thus, all religions share the same enemy—materialism. Should not they work together then, each in its own way, for the welfare of all humanity? He has espoused this theme for many years, expressed in his "Three Resolutions" *(panidhana):*

1. To help everyone realize the heart of their own religion;

2. To help bring about mutual good understanding among religions;

3. To work together to drag the world out from under the power of materialism.[106]

Beginning with the Thompson Memorial Lectures in Chiang Mai (1957), which he was the first non-Christian to give, Ajarn Buddhadasa repeatedly called for mutual understanding and cooperation among religions. He was the most important voice for Inter-Religious Exchange in Siam, and was often criticized by other Buddhists for it. Two of his books on Christianity have been translated into Western languages. *Christianity and Buddhism*[107] is a Buddhist understanding of the Bible, with particular emphasis on the recorded teachings of Jesus, directed mainly at Christians. *Christianity as Far as Buddhists Ought to Know*[108] is for Buddhists, explaining how they can learn from the Christian teachings as the Christians themselves present them, focusing mainly on the theme of Love. To this day, Suan Mokkh is the Wat where Christians feel most at home. A number of Thai and foreign Christians, both lay and religious, looked to him as a teacher.[109] There is even a small Catholic reform movement in the Philippines partly inspired by his life and work.

Final Remarks

In his mid-eighties, in poor health, Ajarn Buddhadasa continued to work and innovate. He initiated a few last projects that expanded the work of Suan

Mokkh. Over the last five years, Ajarn Buddhadasa directed the development of the International Dhamma Hermitage. It has been built by Ajarn Poh Buddhadhammo, the current abbot of Suan Mokkh, on seventy acres of former coconut groves beside two limestone hills across the highway from Suan Mokkh. Also known as Suan Mokkh International, the Hermitage is a retreat center at which monthly meditation courses are given in English and almost monthly in Thai. Usually the courses are attended by over a hundred people. The Hermitage is also used for meetings and workshops, especially those for interreligious exchange and understanding.

Another facility—tentatively named Suan Atammayatarama—is newly completed. Near the International Dhamma Hermitage, thirty acres of land have been set aside as a training center for foreign monks (Western and Asian). Ajarn Buddhadasa conceived of it as a school for "Dhamma Missionaries" where men who wish to dedicate their lives to world peace can live a simple life close to Nature, study Dhamma thoroughly, establish a profound meditation practice, develop teaching skills, and learn to apply the principles of Dhamma to the many problems afflicting the world. A curriculum is being developed, and there are plans for periodic seminars exploring the relationships between Dhamma and social issues, for example, education, AIDS, and feminism. The facilities for this school were completed in 1993.

A similar project is being considered for women. Acknowledging that bhikkhus are not always able to help women and that women have an important contribution to make in solving society's problems, Ajarn Buddhadasa wanted to establish a center for women who wish to become Dhamma Mothers *(dhamma-mata),* "those who give birth through Dhamma." He felt that the status of women had been dropping steadily since his youth and that this decline should be reversed. Because it is not yet possible to reestablish the Bhikkhuni Order in Thailand and since the white–robed *mae chi* have important limitations, he felt a new approach was needed. Although he was not in a position to give the Dhamma Mothers the same social status as bhikkhus receive, he believed that material support can be provided so that women are also able to live the homeless life and have spiritual opportunities equal to those of the bhikkhus. He envisioned that the Dhamma Mothers would live a simple life focussed on meditation, with some supporting study. They would not travel much, perhaps would be flexibly cloistered. Then, he hoped, as the Dhamma Mothers live up to their name, through example and teaching, society will give them the respect they deserve.

In his last two years, despite poor health following a heart attack and strokes, Buddhadasa Bhikkhu continued to work on various projects. When he died, many were left unfinished. The disciples who are cataloging his notes will publish some manuscripts that were sufficiently complete, such as his *Dhamma Will and Testament,* which he playfully warned might get him defrocked. A large number of his lectures, including many designed as part of the *Dhamma Proclamation Series,* remain to be published. Various groups, especially the Dhammadana Foundation, which is still headed by his brother Dhammadasa, intend to continue bringing them into print. As Buddhadasa said repeatedly in his later years, "Buddhadasa does not die. I will be present wherever the Dhamma is being discussed and practiced."

Postscript

The final section of this chapter was originally written in the present tense, since Ajarn Buddhadasa was still active despite a heart attack, minor strokes, and other serious physical ailments endured over the last couple of years. Then, on May 25, 1993, two days before his eighty-seventh birthday and the sixty-first anniversary of Suan Mokkh, he had a serious stroke that soon deteriorated into a coma. After six seeks of hospitalization, he returned to Suan Mokkh and died on July 8, 1993.

Although he was unconscious for the final six weeks, he inadvertently provided another opportunity for Thailand to question its values and morals. Previously, he had refused to be taken to the hospital and put limitations on the treatment he would accept, for example, no blood transfusions and no surgery, including the most minor. Nonetheless, the medical establishment and popular opinion forced the monastery to allow him to be "kidnapped" to Bangkok's leading teaching hospital. Although it was obvious to many that there was no chance for recovery, the medical team insisted on "fighting" to the very last moment. His body was finally released from the hospital just in time to return to Suan Mokkh for its last breaths. These events have prompted an important discussion and evaluation of Thailand's health-care system and its ethics. Thus Ajarn Buddhadasa's teachings on Nature, nonattachment, and the middle way are being applied in yet another area of modern life.[110]

Notes

1. *Dasa* can also be translated "slave."

2. Primary resources for this section are *Lao Wai Meua Wai Sondhaya: Atajivaprawat kong Tan Puttatat (As Told in the Twilight Years: The Memoirs of Venerable Buddhadasa),* interviewed and edited by Phra Pracha Pasannadhammo (Bangkok: Komol Kimtong Foundation, 1986); *Phap Jivit 80 pi Puttatat Phikkhu (Pictorial Life of Buddhadasa Bhikkhu's 80 Years),* ed. Phra Pracha Pasanna-dhammo

and Santisuk Sophonsiri (Bangkok, Komol Kimtong Foundation, 1986); and the author's personal conversations with Buddhadasa Bhikkhu. In this chapter, works for which no translator are given have not yet been published in English and translations are this writer's own.

3. There is a traditional belief that two of Emperor Asoka's missionaries—the monks Sona and Uttara—came to *Suvarnabhumi,* the capital of which is now Nakorn Pathom, in the third century (B.E.).

4. Christian Era. 1900 C.E. corresponds to 2443 Buddhist Era (Thai reckoning) and 2500 B.E. corresponds to 1957 C.E. Thais count 1 B.E. as the year following the Lord Buddha's *parinibbana,* whereas the Singhalese and Burmese count 1 B.E. as the year of the *parinibbana.*

5. In 1909, the provincial seat moved to Ban Don, at the mouth of the Tapee River, and was renamed Surat Thani, "City of Good people." Pum Riang remained the district seat until 1921, when it moved to the Chaiya market.

6. *Phra Khun kong Mae keu Santipap kong Lok* (The Virtue of Motherhood is Peace for the World), (Bangkok: Atammmayo, n.d., original talk given on Mother's Day, August 12, 1989).

7. *Ajarn* is the Thai form of the Pali *acariya,* teacher or master.

8. "A Single Solution to the World's Problems" (*Nam Prik Tuay Diow*) in *Messages of Truth from Suan Mokkh, (Saccasara jak Suan Mokkh)* published in Thai and English (Bangkok: The Dhamma Study and Practice Group, 1990), translators unknown.

9. The *Pansa* (Pali, *Vassa*) literally means "rain" and refers to the three-month period when bhikkhus temporarily cease their wanderings. It is also the traditional way of counting years and seniority within the bhikkhu Sangha.

10. *Phra* is the common Thai term for monks. It is derived from the Pali *vara* (excellent, splendid, noble).

11. *Pictorial Life of Buddhadasa Bhikkhu's 80 Years,* p. 55.

12. Ibid.

13. Two valuable books concerning the early years of Suan Mokkh are *The First Ten Years of Suan Mokkh* (Sip Pi Nai Suan Mokkh), tr. Mongkol Dejnakarintra (Bangkok: Dhamma Study and Practice Group, 1990) and *The Style of Practice at Suan Mokkh (Naew Patipat Thamm Nai Suan Mokkh)* tr. Santikaro Bhikkhu (not yet published).

14. Cf. *Mahaparinibbana Sutta, Digha-nikaya* (D.ii.100, 154).

15. Children in the neighboring Muslim village liked to make fun of him, "Crazy Monk, Crazy Monk."

16. *Anutin Patibat Tham: Suksa Jivit Yang Pen Witayasat (Dhamma Practice Diary: Scientific Study of Life),* (Bangkok, Pacarayasarn, 1986).

17. Not to be confused with the more extreme forms of asceticism and mortification found in other religions.

18. From personal conversation with the author (February 28, 1993) concerning the fifth conference of the International Network of Engaged Buddhists.

19. "Dhammic Socialism According to Religious Principles" (*Dhammika Sanghaniyama tam Lak Sasana*) in *Dhammic Socialism* (*Dhammika Sanghaniyama*), ed. Donald K. Swearer (Bangkok: Komol Kimtong, 1986), p. 52. All citations from this book are this writer's own translation from the Thai portion of the book, although the translations of Swearer, et al., have been consulted.

20. Reference uncertain. The Words of the Buddha cited in this paper are all passages from the *Tipitaka* frequently mentioned by Ajarn Buddhadasa.

21. *Ghosana,* in a modified Sanskrit form, is currently used in Thai for "advertising" and "propaganda."

22. "People language" is more literally and conceptually accurate than the "everyday language" used by some translators. Some of Ajarn Buddhadasa's own writings in this area can be found in "People Language and Dhamma Language" in *Keys to Natural Truth,* ed. Santikaro Bhikkhu (Bangkok: Dhamma Study and Practice Group, 1988) and "Help, Kalama Sutta" in *Evolution/Liberation* #5, ed. Santikaro Bhikkhu. Donald Swearer, Louis Gabaude, and Peter Jackson have all emphasized Buddhadasa Bhikkhu's hermeneutics, although there are some problems in Peter Jackson's version.

23. *Majjhima-nikaya, Mulapannasaka, Alagaddupama-sutta* #22, (M.i.140).

24. *Majjhima-nikaya, Mualpannasaka, Culatanhasamkhaya-sutta* #37 (M.i.251) and elsewhere.

25. Here and elsewhere we run into difficulties with language. In English, "attachment" is given various connotations by various thinkers and disciplines. Often it is understood only in a positive sense, e.g., being attached to a spouse, or love. *Upadana,* however, can be negative as well. Further, the thing one is attached to doesn't matter nearly as much as the activity of attachment itself: the feeling of "I" or "mine" concocted by ignorance.

26. For the purposes of this essay, voidness and not-self *(anatta)* can be treated as more or less the same thing. "Because it is not self, it is void of any meaning of self, of selfhood."

27. Here it is worth noting, in passing, that Ajarn Buddhadasa's insistence that voidness is essential for all Buddhists has been controversial in Thailand. Senior monks even used to ask him to stop teaching it to lay people.

28. Ajarn Buddhadasa gave Pali names to these different ways or levels of voidness and *nibbana,* distinctions the Lord Buddha had applied to *viraga,* a synonym of voidness.

29. *Dharmaghosana Atthanukrom (Dhamma Propagation Book of Meanings)*, Bangkok: Alliance for the Propagation of Buddhism, 1990), p. 67.

30. These "Four Dimensions of Dhamma" roughly correspond to the four noble truths.

31. *Siang Takon jak Dhammajati (The Shouting from Nature)*, p. 5 (Wuddhidhamma Fund, Bangkok: 1991). When the title of a source is given in Thai, it has been published only in Thai and this writer provided the translation.

32. Ibid., p. 9.

33. Ibid., p. 13.

34. Ibid., p. 10.

35. He believed this to be true for all the prophets of all religions.

36. *Asitisamvaccharayusamanusarana jak Puttatat Phikkhu (The Eighty Years of Age Memorial from Buddhadasa Bhikkhu)*, Buddhadasa Bhikkhu (Thailand: Chaiya, Suan Mokkh, 1986), p. 142.

37. *Buddhasasanik kap Kananurak Dhammajati (Buddhists and the Conservation of Nature)*, (Bangkok: Komol Kimtong, 1990), p. 13. (This writer hopes to publish an English translation soon.)

38. For Ajarn Buddhadasa, "survival" was not merely physical or genetic, and must include spiritual salvation.

39. Ibid., p. 3.

40. A common synonym and special application of *idappaccayata* is called *paticcasamuppada* (dependent co-origination).

41. *Ida,* this; paccaya, condition; *-ta,* state of being.

42. This formula appears throughout the *Tipitaka,* e.g., M.iii.63 and S.ii.28, 95.

43. *Idappaccayata* (Conditionality), (Chaiya: Dhammadana Foundation, 1989), p. 27.

44. *Buddhists and The Conservation of Nature,* p. 12.

45. *Buddhadasana kap Udomgati Dhammika Sangkhom-niyom (Buddhism and the Ideal of Dhammic Socialism)*, (Bangkok: Vudhidamma Fund, date uncertain, probably 1991), p. 19.

46. From the Introduction to *Buddhadasana kap Sangkhom (Buddhism and Society)* in *Desana lae Ovada (Sermons and Talks)* (Suhkapapjai, Bangkok: 1989), p. 167. Original talk given September 22, 1952.

47. *Kam Sawn Puu Buat (Teaching for Those Gone Forth)*, (Bangkok: Sublime Life Mission, date unknown), p. 6.

48. *Chumnum Pathakatha Chut Buddha-Dhamma* (*Collection of Buddha-Dhamma Lectures*), (Chaiya: Dhammadana Foundation, 1987).

49. Ibid., p. 234.

50. Numerous public talks, as well as conversations with this writer.

51. *Collection of Buddha-Dhamma Lectures*, p. 242.

52. Ibid., p. 251.

53. Ibid., p. 245f.

54. Ibid., p. 253.

55. Digha-nikaya #27, (D.iii.80).

56. Ibid., p. 271.

57. "The Spirit of Democracy," p. 276.

58. One talk on "Socialism"—to judges' assistants—was actually requested by the Ministry of Justice (September 15, 1974 at Suan Mokkh).

59. Similar developments occurred in other Southeast Asian countries, especially the Philippines under Ferdinand Marcos, another U.S. client-dictator.

60. "The Kind of Socialism Which Can Help the World" from *Dhammic Socialism*, p. 94.

61. *Buddhism and the Ideal of Dhammic Socialism*, p. 4f.

62. *The Eighty Years of Age Memorial from Buddhadasa Bhikkhu*, p. 119.

63. *Dhamma kap Karn Meuang* (*Dhamma and Politics*), p. 267.

64. *Buddhism and the Ideal of Dhammic Socialism*, p. 4.

65. Buddhism and Society, p. 177.

66. "The Kind of Socialism Which Can Help the World," p. 96f.

67. "Buddhism and Society," p. 175f.

68. Ibid., p. 174.

69. "The Kind of Socialism Which Can Help the World," p. 96.

70. Ibid, p. 102.

71. Ibid., p. 97.

72. Ibid., p. 98.

73. *Collection of Buddha-Dhamma Lectures*.

74. *Fa Sang Rawang 50 Pi Ti Mi Suan Mokkh* (*Dawning During the 50 Years of Suan Mokkh*), Part I, (Bangkok: Suan Usom Foundation, 1986), p. 44f.

75. *Book of Meanings,* p. 216.

76. Rhys-Davids and Steede, ed., *The Pali Text Society's Pali-English Dictionary* (London: The Pali Text Society, 1979), p. 379.

77. "The Value and Necessity of Having Morality" from *Dhammic Socialism,* p. 134.

78. Ibid., p. 136.

79. "Socialism According to Religious Principles," p. 46.

80. This is the essence of the Buddha's *paticcasamuppada* (dependent coorigination), as Ajarn Buddhadasa understands it.

81. Ibid., p. 27.

82. One American journalist could barely keep from shouting while interviewing Ajarn Buddhadasa, then later exploded on this writer and others, insisting that "politics is about power, not morality."

83. *Dawning During the 50 Years of Suan Mokkh,* Part I, p. 32.

84. *Bacananukrom Ohabab Pajapanditayasathan 2525* (*Royal Academy Dictionary 1982*), (Bangkok: Aksornjaroentat, 2525), p. 554.

85. Ibid.

86. So Sethaputra, *New Model Thai-English Dictionary,* (Bangkok: Thai Watana Panich, 1965), p. 627.

87. *Dawning During the 50 Years of Suan Mokkh, Part I,* p. 33.

88. The Ten *Rajadhammas* are generosity, morality, self-sacrifice, integrity, gentleness, self-control, nonanger, nonviolence, patient endurance, and conformity to Dhamma (*Khuddaka-nikaya, Jataka Book* 5, 378).

89. "Socialism According to Religious Principles," p. 83.

90. Digha-nikaya #27 (D.iii.93).

91. Ibid. and "Buddha-Dhamma and the Spirit of Democracy," p. 271.

92. In the area around Suan Mokkh, the destruction of the environment and the increase in crime with consumer capitalism give evidence to his point.

93. "Socialism According to Religious Principles," p. 55.

94. Ibid., p. 56.

95. Ibid.

96. Ibid., p. 30 for all quotes in this paragraph.

97. p. 38.

98. *Dhamma and Politics,* p. 322.

99. "Socialism According to Religious Principles," p. 90.

100. *Dawning During the 50 Years of Suan Mokkh,* Part I, p. 36.

101. *Collection of Buddha-Dhamma Lectures,* p. 242.

102. *Dhamma and Politics,* p. 289.

103. *Gay Dhammaputra* (*Children of Dhamma Camp*) (Bangkok: Karn Pim Phra Nakorn, 1975), p. 133.

104. "The Kind of Socialism which Can Help the World," p. 110.

105. Named after the late Ramon Magsaysay of the Philippines, and sometimes called "The Asian Nobel Prizes," these awards are given yearly to Asians who have made significant contributions to their countries and the region.

106. The exact wording varied over the years and according to the audience. See, in particular, the talks he gave on his eightieth birthday, which were broadcast nationwide, *Panidhana Sam Prakarn kong Buddhadasa Bhikkhu* (The Three Resolutions of Buddhadasa Bhikkhu), (Bangkok: Sublime Life Mission, 1986).

107. Various translators, (Bangkok: Sublime Life Mission, 1967). A New English translation will be published soon.

108. *The Essence of Christianity as far as Buddhists Ought to Know.* This series of twelve lectures was published as *Putth-Khrit Nai Tasana Tan Buddhadasa* (*Buddhism and Christianity as seen by Venerable Buddhadasa*), (Bangkok: Tianwaan Press, 1984).

109. He has many friends from other religions, especially Muslims, who are numerous in southern Thailand.

110. This writer was at the center of the crisis as one of the monks who attended upon Ajarn Buddhadasa's body in the I.C.U. of Siriraj Hospital. In response to requests, I hope to write a Dhamma reflection on the events and issues raised, which may be completed in 1997.

Bibliography of Buddhadasa's Work in English translations

Dhammic Socialism, ed. Donald Swearer (Bangkok: Komol Kimtong Foundation, 1986).

Evolution/Liberation (periodical), tr. & ed. Santikaro Bhikkhu (Chaiya: Suan Mokkh, 1988–).

The First Ten Years of Suan Mokkh, tr. Mongkol Dejnakarintra (Bangkok: Dhamma Study and Practice Group, Bangkok: 1990).

Handbook for Mankind, tr. Roderick Bucknell, (Bangkok: Dhamma Study and Practice Group, 1989).

Heartwood of the Bodhi Tree: The Buddha's Teaching on Voidness, ed. Santikaro Bhikkhu, tr. Dhammavicayo (Boston: Wisdom Publications, 1994).

Keys to Natural Truth, tr. Santikaro Bhikkhu & Roderick Bucknell (Bangkok: Dhamma Study and Practice Group, 1988).

Me and Mine: Selected Essays of Bhikkhu Buddhadasa, ed. and with an introduction by Donald K. Swearer (Albany: State University of New York Press, 1989).

Mindfulness with Breathing: Unveiling the Secrets of Life, tr. Santikaro Bhikkhu, (Bangkok: Dhamma Study and Practice Group, 1988).

No Religion, tr. Bhikkhu Punno & Santikaro Bhikkhu (Hinsdale, Ill.: Buddha-Dhamma Meditation Center, 1993).

Practical Dependent Origination, tr. Steven Schmidt (Bangkok: Dhamma Study and Practice Group, 1992).

Radical Conservatism, ed. S. Sivaraksa, et al. (Bangkok: Sathirakoses-Nagapradipa Foundation, 1990).

Toward the Truth, ed. Donald K. Swearer (Philadelphia: Westminster Press, 1971).

6

Sulak Sivaraksa's Buddhist Vision for Renewing Society

Donald K. Swearer

Since the end of the nineteenth century Theravada Buddhism in Southeast Asia has experienced several kinds of transformation in response to challenges from the modern West. Buddhism has informed the development of the modern nation-states of Sri Lanka, Burma (Myanmar), Thailand, and to a lesser extent, Laos and Cambodia. At the same time the modernization represented by these new political and economic structures also served to challenge the traditional Buddhist worldview and the forms of religious life associated with it. Since World War II in particular, political, economic, and social change has greatly accelerated with dramatic consequences in Cambodia and Laos and with substantial impact on Buddhism in Thailand, Sri Lanka, and Burma.

Under the guidance of an enlightened monarchy and an educated aristocracy, Thai Buddhism developed an institutional structure, a well-organized educational program, and a modernized worldview that served the country reasonably well until the end of the absolute monarchy in 1932.[1] Since that time, however, competing secular institutions, the dramatic social and cultural changes accompanying the building of an increasingly industrialized market economy, and the rapid erosion of a village-based subsistence way of life have undermined the integrity and future viability of the Thai Buddhist tradition.[2]

Several kinds of development have taken place within this milieu, shared, in part, by the Buddhisms of other Theravada cultures. Specific institutional trends include the increasing laicization of a monastic-based tradition, a widespread lay interest in meditation, and the participation of women in religious roles formerly filled largely by males. These trends are particularly evident in urban areas, the context for the most rapid changes taking place in Southeast Asia. In Theravada countries there have also been various efforts to modernize the Buddhist worldview, especially to interpret the tradition in a socially, economically, and politically relevant manner. These changes, as might be expected, have included a critique of mainstream Buddhism for succumbing to the onslaught of modernization, westernization, and secularization.[3]

Among the general trends two seemingly opposed developments have emerged. One might be labeled fundamentalism or fundamentalist-like movements; the other may be characterized as liberal and reformist. Both trends lament the loss of a Buddhistically defined moral community but differ in their approach, analysis, and solution. The fundamentalist solution often seems doctrinally simplistic and moralistic, advocating a return to an idealized personal piety that either ignores or misunderstands the nature of systemic economic, social, and cultural problems and tensions. The reformist solution, on the other hand, engages head-on the tensions, dislocations and "evils" of the contemporary age, applying creative interpretations of traditional beliefs and practices as part of their solution. In contemporary Thailand Santi Asoka and Dhammakaya can be seen at different ends of the fundamentalist spectrum.[4] Buddhadasa Bhikkhu, one of Thailand's most famous and controversial interpreters of Buddhadhamma; Phra Dhammapitaka (Prayudh Payutto), the *sangha*'s most noted scholar-monk; Dr. Prawet Wasi, former vice-rector of Mahidol University and chair of the Local Development Foundation; and Sulak Sivaraksa, the country's best known lay Buddhist intellectual and social critic, all stand out as liberal advocates of doctrinal and institutional reform. In recent years the work of Buddhadasa, in particular, has received considerable attention.[5] Although Sulak is relatively well-known in the West, little has been written about him outside of Thailand.[6] With this chapter I hope to provide an introduction to Sulak's Buddhist vision for the renewal of society, a title taken from one of several volumes of his English-language essays.

Sulak Sivaraksa—A Controversial Siamese

Sulak's fame as a social critic, intellectual gadfly, and activist has made him a controversial figure, especially in Thailand. For twenty years he has carried on *ad hominem* attacks against M. R. Kukrit Pramoj—essayist, novelist, newspaper editor, actor, university lecturer, banker, former member of parliament, prime minister, and an Oxford-educated Thai aristocrat.[7] More dramatically, in 1984 Sulak was arrested, imprisoned, and finally released after four months on charges of *lèse majesté* for defaming the

King of Thailand in one of his publications.[8] Sulak's most recent notoriety resulted from a lecture he gave at Thammasat University on August 22, 1991.[9] In some respects the talk was reminiscent of Kukrit Pramoj's 1968 column in the *Siam Rath* newspaper attacking the American presence in Thailand. Kukrit concluded his editorial with the phrase, "American dogs get back to your holes." While Sulak has been equally critical of American influence in Thailand, at his Thammasat University lecture he attacked the National Peace Keeping Council (NPKC) headed by General Suchinda Kraprayoon, the commander-in-chief of the Royal Thai Army, and General Sunthorn Khongsomphong, the former Armed Forces supreme commander, which had overthrown the elected government of Prime Minister Chatichai Choonhavan, on February 23, 1991, in a bloodless coup d'état. In the course of his remarks Sulak traced what he considers to be the continuous threat to democracy in Thailand by the military. Arguing that the military's rationalization for taking control of the government in 1991 was virtually the same as that used to justify the first military coup in 1947, he challenged the NPKC in his typically acerbic, rhetorical manner: "In the past forty-four years, the military has not had one new idea; they are all outrageous. It is a pity that the civilians are not more clever. The present council of senators are kowtowing and obsequious servants of the military."[10]

Sulak's lecture, although critical of the NPKC, was basically a constructive plea for democracy in Thailand, for a constitution that protected the civil rights of the Thai people, for more just and humane economic development, and for the place of the royal family as the "center of unity in the country . . . above manipulation by politicians, businessmen, and multinational corporations."[11] Increasingly under attack by academics, nongovernmental organizations (NGOs), and activist Buddhist monks concerned about the manipulation of villagers by powerful economic, political, and military interests, the NPKC decided to silence their most outspoken critic.

On September 13, 1991, the NPKC issued a warrant for Sulak's arrest on the charges of *lèse majesté* and defaming General Suchinda Kraprayoon. Sulak, who was in northern Thailand at the time, was given political asylum in a Western embassy sympathetic to his critical stance on the Thai government's collusion with Burma's repressive, autocratic, military regime. On October 1, with the help of friends who assisted his departure from Thailand, Sulak began a ten-week tour of Sweden, Denmark, England, and Germany, lecturing and attending meetings of Western Buddhists. He arrived at the University of Hawaii on December 12 for a similar itinerary throughout the United States. A lecture and seminar program was organized for him at over two dozen American colleges and universities, as well as meetings with international peace and human rights groups in the country. He continued to teach and lecture in the United States, Europe, and Japan until his return to Thailand a year later.

Sulak's courageous stand was subsequently vindicated by political events in Thailand. When General Suchinda appointed himself to the position of prime minister after the May, 1992 elections, tens of thousands of demonstrators took to the streets in Bangkok and other metropolitan areas. The armed forces, fearful of losing power, responded with brutal, repressive force killing over seven hundred demonstrators. In the face of an increasingly aroused public and with the mediation of the king and other officials, General Suchinda stepped aside and an interim prime minister was appointed. On April 26, 1995, the Criminal Court dismissed the case of *lèse majesté* and defamation filed by General Suchinda Kraprayoon against Sulak. The hearing was attended by over 500 of Sulak's supporters including representatives of the Assembly of Small-scale Farmers of the Northeast and the Student Federation of Thailand as well as noted social and political activists.[12]

Sulak has earned the respect and support of numerous organizations and individuals throughout the world. In January, 1994, he was nominated for the Nobel Peace Prize by the American Friends Service Committee. The AFSC letter of nomination read, "Sulak Sivaraksa has throughout his life been a courageous and articulate voice for peace, human rights, and social justice. Rooted deeply in his Buddhist faith and the traditions and indigenous culture of Siam, Professor Sulak has created organizations and publications which have helped to form and nurture a community of persons dedicated to non-violence in a region particularly torn by violence and war."

In this brief survey of Sulak's life and work I would like to suggest that his controversial and often contentious nature stems from his paradoxical or "betwixt-and-between" personal and social status. Sulak is of Chinese ancestry yet is so Thai that he insists on calling Thailand by its traditional name, Siam, and on wearing traditional Siamese clothing either of the peasant or aristocratic variety depending on the occasion; he is a populist who prizes democratic, egalitarian values but is known as a royalist and strong supporter of the king; he is an urbanite who elevates the values of village life. Sulak began his formal education in a temple school in Thailand but ended it at St. Davids College, Lampeter, Wales, and at the Middle Temple, London; he is an admirer of the early twentieth-century scholars of Thai culture, Princes Damrong, Naris and Dhani Nivat, and the elevated commoner, Phya Anuman; but he is also a student of modern Western philosophy and social science. He is one of Thailand's most articulate lay Buddhist apologists, yet he studied in Christian schools and admires the spirituality of the Trappist monk Thomas Merton and the Quakers of Philadelphia. Sulak prizes peace and solitude but has probably founded more periodicals, written more books, given more lectures, traveled to more conferences, and established more nongovernmental organizations than anyone in modern Thai history.

Above all, Sulak is a practical man whose practicality is rooted not in utilitarian values but in a personally and socially transformative religious commitment. I would argue that Sulak's controversial image derives from all these contradictions but most of all from a religiously based idealism that places him "in the world but not of it"—or, in Buddhist terms, at the intersection of *lokīya* (the mundane) and *lokuttara* (the transmundane). Our examination of Sulak's vision for renewing society will focus on the theme of Sulak's controversial nature, or, more appropriately, his paradoxical nature born of his religiously based idealism. First, however, we shall explore Sulak's life and work.

Early Years and Emerging Career

Sulak was born in Bangkok in 1933, the son of a chief clerk in a Western import-export firm. After receiving his primary and secondary education in Thailand he took his university and law degrees in Wales and England respectively. In 1961 at age 28 Sulak returned to Thailand to begin the first of an ongoing series of periodicals. He became the founding editor of the *Social Science Review (Sangkhomsat Parithat)*, considered by many to have been the leading Thai intellectual journal of its time. The journal not only brought to fame such currently noted artists as Ankarn Kalyanapong, but by 1968 it had become the intellectual voice of the nation: "Much of the revitalized spirit of intellectual curiosity and skepticism during the 1963–1968 period may be attributed to the energetic work and contributions of Sulak and his journal. He succeeded in arousing intellectual concern over the social, economic, and political problems facing Thai society."[13] The government tolerated the strong antigovernment and antimilitary views often expressed in the journal in part because the military leaders felt their position to be largely impervious to the criticisms of a small group of Western-educated intellectuals without a power base. The royal support of Prince Wan Waithayakorn, the president of the Social Science Association that sponsored the journal, also protected Sulak's literary endeavor. *Sangkhomsat Parithat* was eventually closed down by the government in 1976 during the period of government repression after the country's three-year "experiment with democracy" (October 1973–October 1976). By that time Sulak had stepped down as editor.

Shortly after his return from England Sulak opened what was to become the best international bookstore in Thailand. He was also in constant demand as a visiting lecturer in philosophy at Chulalongkorn, Thammasat, and Silapakorn universities in Bangkok. From 1963 to 1968 he was instrumental in helping to establish informal discussion groups on university campuses, including one known as *Sapha Kafe* (Coffee House Council).[14] Sulak continued this tradition with monthly meetings held in a second-floor "council" room above his coffee shop, located adjacent to his Suksit Siam Bookstore. Several of the leaders of the October 14, 1973, student uprising were active members of those early discussion groups.

Sulak and his young family—Sulak married in 1964 in a ceremony presided over by H. H. Prince Dhani Niwat—resided in a modest wooden family home on a small lane in a busy, crowded section of the city. Sulak's material lifestyle has remained essentially the same over the past thirty years. The shaded compound, graced by a traditional pile-raised house and verdant vegetation, stands as a quiet oasis in the midst of the roar of Bangkok's current out-of-bounds development.

In the late 1960s and 1970s Sulak laid the foundations of a career pattern that has continued to the present—a life as writer and publisher, lecturer, perapatetic international conferee, peace and human rights activist, founder of NGOs, Buddhist social critic, and intellectual moralist. For thirteen years he was the honorary editor of *Visakha Puja,* the annual publication of the Buddhist Association of Thailand. He was the first chair of the South East Asian Study Group on Cultural Relations for the Future and a member of the Pacific Ashrama, headed by Dr. Soedjatmoko, the first rector of the United Nations University in Tokyo.

In 1971 Sulak was invited by Professor Sanya Dhammasakti, president of the Buddhist Association of Thailand (and later prime minister), and Dr. Puey Ungphakorn, governor of the Bank of Thailand, founder of the Thailand Rural Reconstruction Movement and rector of Thammasat University, to found the Komol Keemthong Foundation. Komol, a brilliant, idealistic student at Thailand's prestigious Chulalongkorn University in the late 1960s, had turned down a university lectureship to become a schoolteacher in the southern province of Surat Thani. There he sought to awaken the hearts of his students to a new sense of Siamese identity, one defined neither by the policies of a development-oriented national government nor the radical politics of Thailand's active southern communist movement. In 1971 Komol was shot to death by communist agents. Komol's friends, determined that his example of idealistic service not be lost, established a foundation in his name.

Sulak's characterization of the purposes of the Komol Keemthong Foundation provide insight into the basic principles behind his own dedication to the founding of voluntary NGOs as a counterbalance or counter option to the status quo: "[T]his was probably the very first social action project to take place . . . outside of government to do something for the people. Our main objective was to promote idealism among the young so that they would dedicate themselves to work for the people. We tried to revive Buddhist values. . . . We [also] felt that the monkhood could play a role again through education and public health. . . .[15]

The list of nongovernmental organizations Sulak has founded or helped direct does more than bear testimony to his frenetic activism; it sheds light on his deepest commitments and concerns. A participant in the Asian Cultural Forum on Development (ACFOD) since its first Asian Regional Workshop in 1977, Sulak was appointed its coordinator and the publisher of its newsletter, *Asian Action,* two years later. ACFOD is a regional nongovernment organization that has consultative status with the Economic and Social Council of the United Nations, liaison status with the Food and Agriculture Organization of the United Nations (FAO), and is a partner to the World Council of Churches commission on the Churches' Participation in Development. ACFOD's international and interreligious networks illustrate Sulak's own propensity to build networks of people within Thailand, between Thailand and other countries, and among different religious traditions and organizations.

ACFOD is committed to working for the uplift of the rural and urban poor, consistently one of Sulak's major areas of endeavor. The organization seeks to provide linkages and solidarity for individuals and organizations "who are working for integral human development . . . who believe that such development should be founded on religio-cultural values of people in community . . . [and] who, whether members of or uncommitted to institutional religions, possess a deep concern for the moral and humanist aspects of development."[16] In its 1983 council meeting ACFOD formulated the idealistic vision for its mission (summarized in tabular form on the following page).[17]

In 1976, seven months before the Thai government's brutal repression of the student demonstrations on the Thammasat University campus that marked the end of the 1973–1976 period of democratization, Sulak promoted the founding of the Coordinating Group for Religion and Society (CGRS). The CGRS is an ecumenical Buddhist and Christian human rights organization that publishes the quarterly, *Human Rights in Thailand Report* (HRTR).[18] At the time of the *coup d'état* that led to violent reprisals at Thammasat, the CGRS was there as Sulak put it, "asking people to meditate, asking people to pray and fast . . . ", in short to practice their religion in the midst of a violent situation.[19] CGRS members visited their friends in prison even though they risked arrest by doing so. Because of their commitment to the principles of nonviolence and reconciliation, they also visited injured soldiers in the hospital.

Asian Cultural Forum on Development (ACFOD)
Mission Statement (1983)

Dominant Existing System	*ACFOD Vision*
1. Emphasis on economic growth and material needs	1. Human-centered development of persons and their potential
2. Serves dominant interests (industrialists, local and foreign vested interests, landlords, bureaucracy, and military)	2. Serves peoples interest (in particular the poor and disadvantaged)
3. Increasing dependence on foreign capital, aid, technology, and power	3. National self-reliance
4. Export-oriented production	4. Production for use to meet basic needs
5. Inequality—control over resources by a few	5. People's control over resources: equal access to goods
6. Depoliticization/domestication/ condition people to preserve status quo	6. Awareness build-up; conscientization/politicization of the people for change
7. Fragmentation of people	7. Organization of people and forging linkages/coalititions among peoples/groups
8. Urban bias	8. Elimination of the urban/ rural contradiction
9. Neglect/discrimination/ oppression of women	9. Integration of women
10. Dominant culture	10. People's culture and traditions
11. Authoritarian/centralization/ militarization	11. Harmony with the environment/ conservation of resources
12. Pollution and destruction of the environment/wasteful resource use	12. Harmony with the environment/ conservation of resources
13. Suppression of minority rights and culture	13. Respect for minority rights and culture
14. Power (domination)	14. Counter-power (liberation)

The tragedy of October 1976 deepened Sulak's commitment as a peace activist, a commitment earlier inspired by a meeting with the Vietnamese Zen monk, Thich Nhat Hanh of Van Hanh University, Saigon.[20] More recently Sulak has been promoting nonviolence training in Theravada Buddhist countries torn by strife, violence, and repression, notably Sri Lanka and Burma. Sulak's commitment to peace and nonviolence is expressed by his leadership in various international peace organizations including the international advisory panel of the Buddhist Peace Fellowship (Berkeley, California), the Peace Brigade International (Philadelphia, Pennsylvania), and the Gandhi Peace Foundation (New Delhi, India). Closer to home, in 1983 Sulak proposed the establishment of the Pridi Banomyong Foundation and the Pridi Banomyong Institute named after one of Sulak's mentors who had played a prominent role in the 1932 revolution. Pridi had been a leader of the Free-Thai Movement during the Japanese occupation of the country during World War II. He was also prime minister briefly after the war, and he was forced into exile in 1947 by a military *coup d'état*. The purpose of the institute is to promote programs and research projects that will contribute to the search for peace and social justice in Thai society as well as globally.

Sulak himself was not on the Thammasat campus in October of 1976. He had left Thailand in September for the United States as one of only two representatives from Southeast Asia to speak at the Smithsonian Institution conference, "The United States and the World," as part of America's bicentennial celebration. Flying to Thailand via England after the meetings, he was advised there by Thai friends that his life might be in danger if he returned. Thus began eighteen months of exile spent largely in America and Canada as a visiting professor at the University of California, Berkeley; Cornell University; and the University of Toronto.

Sulak's ecumenical networking, involvement in peace-making activities, and efforts on behalf of the rural poor prompted him to help establish an interreligious organization, the Thai Inter-Religious Commission for Development (TICD) after his return to Thailand.[21] It has sought to encourage Buddhist student associations at Thammasat and Chulalongkorn universities to participate in social service and social change programs, to act as a bridge between rural and urban groups, and to cooperate with various organizations in short-term educational and recreational projects for children in slum areas. Through various Buddhist monasteries the TICD has also served impoverished farmers by establishing rice banks. As with most of the organizations Sulak has been instrumental in starting, the TICD publishes a periodical, *Seeds of Peace*. The journal has become a respected English-language forum, advocating issues of pressing social moment that include peace and justice, nonviolence training, Buddhist economics, women and religion, and ecology. The TICD also publishes a second periodical in Thai, *Withi* (A Way), which recently changed its name to *Sekhiyadhamma* (Training in the Dhamma). The journal focuses on issues of religion, especially Buddhism, and development.[22]

By 1982 Sulak recognized the need for establishing a coordinating body to bring together small NGOs to tackle common problems and support one another. As a consequence he helped found the Thai Development Support Committee (TDSC) with an initial group of seventeen member organizations. TDSC covers a wide range of activities that include rural and urban community development work, child-welfare activities, community health work, human rights activities, training of community workers, development publications, support for workers' rights, and appropriate technology services. Sulak himself fostered over half of the initial member groups. The TDSC's quarterly publication, the *Thai Development Newsletter*, contains information about the various member organizations and features articles on housing, malnutrition, human rights abuses, and other social problems.

These organizations and publications, founded, organized, or encouraged by Sulak, all address issues of justice, peace, violence, and civil and human rights. They often work with marginal peoples—the rural poor, slum dwellers, disadvantaged women, children, the war ravaged. Yet, Sulak has also been responsible for founding other types of organizations to support cultural, educational, and artistic interests and to promote international Buddhist and interreligious organizations. The most prominent of these is the Sathirakoses-Nagapradipa Foundation, which publishes the *Pacharayasara* journal, the intellectual successor to *Sangkhomsat Prithat*. The Foundation is named after the pen name of Phya Anuman Rajadhon (Sathirakoses) and that of his coauthor and cotranslator, Phra Sarapresert (Nagapradipa). Phya Anuman was a commoner with little formal education who became one of Thailand's most distinguished students of traditional culture, customs, and history as well as the director general of the Department of Fine Arts and the president of the Royal Institute and the Siam Society.[23] Phya Anuman's place as a role model for Sulak is illustrated by the following affectionate remarks:

> Phya Anuman Rajadhon['s] . . . pen name, Sathirakoses, symbolized the mentality that curiously probed into the depth and breadth of knowledge with the humility of an amateur but the enthusiasm of an expert. He attentively discussed etymological matters with his maid and people in the streets, while corresponding with princes and members of the nobility on historical and literary subjects. His writings ranged from an Introduction

to Graeco-Roman civilizations to an early pioneering survey of ancient states in mainland Southeast Asia, from a series of studies on Thai spiritual beliefs to a monumental work on *Our Asian Friends' Faiths*, . . . It is thus not surprising that this commoner whose formal education barely surpassed our present graduates from Secondary school would later be called a walking encyclopedia.[24]

For Sulak, Phya Anuman represents a true person of letters, someone who loves learning for its own sake, whose lack of pretension frees him to learn from everything and everyone, even the maid.[25] In Sulak's view Phya Anuman respected Thai culture in all its aspects, ranging from humble animistic beliefs and rituals to majestic royal ceremonies and the sublime heights of Buddhist philosophy. Phya Anuman, in short, understood what it meant to be a Siamese in the fullest sense of the word; he embodied the best of the Siamese traditions. Consequently, at a time when the Thai people are passing through a profound identity crisis, Sulak finds Phya Anuman to be a guiding representative of Thai culture. For this reason, almost single-handledly Sulak convinced the Ministry of Education to enlist the support of UNESCO to make the one hundredth anniversary of Phya Anuman's birth, December 14, 1988, a national and international event. Many of Phya Anuman's books in Thai and English were reprinted. Sulak also organized a photographic exhibit that he took to Japan, America, the Soviet Union, and several Asian countries. Furthermore, various artistic and literary events sponsored by the Sathirakoses-Nagapradipa Foundation were held in Bangkok.

Sulak's most ambitious project, however, is the establishment of the Phya Anuman Rajadhon Memorial Building and Park with two different but related purposes, a center of Thai studies and a place for spiritual development. In Sulak's view, both social activism and learning should be based in spiritual development, an awareness that politics, economics, and education are not independent ends in themselves but are interdependent parts of a total human being and human community.

Herbert Phillips employs a patron/client analysis to contrast Sulak's relationship to Phya Anuman and Angkarn Kalayanaphong, considered by many to be the country's most original traditional artist and greatest poet. Phya Anuman was Sulak's patron-mentor and teacher of literary criticism and social analysis, a relationship formalized in a ritual "in which Sulak literally prostrated himself before his teacher, swearing fealty and dutifulness."[26] By contrast, Sulak began as the reclusive Angkarn's patron, providing him with a national reputation by publishing his art, poetry, and essays in the *Sangkhomsat Parithat*. As Angkarn gained international fame Sulak's relationship shifted from patron to agent, and to a certain extent, to client.[27]

Sulak's relationships with Phya Anuman and Angkarn illuminate more than the dynamics of patron/client, intellectual mentor/student disciple, however. The diversity of Sulak's intellectual interests resonates with the broad, humanistic scope of his mentor, Phya Anuman, even though the latter's scholarly, empathetic, descriptive style contrasts with Sulak's intellectual–gadfly posture and social-critical agenda. Sulak's support of Angkarn, furthermore, reflects the nature of Sulak's primary network of friends and associates—intellectuals, academics, artists, writers, social critics, religious and cultural exemplars. I would also suggest that, at least in part, Sulak admires Angkarn and Phya Anuman because their success, like Sulak's, derives not from social class and economic privilege but from being "bright, imaginative, hard-working, up-by-the-bootstraps member[s] of the middle class...."[28]

I would contend, moreover, that Sulak's respect for classical scholars, poets, and artists reflects his Buddhist conviction that all things are interdependent. It may seem paradoxical that an outspoken, acerbic, social activist should buy the paintings of contemporary Thai artists or make the opening remarks at art exhibits and dramatic productions; or that one of Thailand's best known Buddhist laypersons should be a valued participant in World Council of Churches' symposia; or that the founder of the International Network of Engaged Buddhists (INEB) should invite a Christian to give the keynote address at INEB's 1989 annual conference. Sulak's actions are certainly unconventional; however, his ecumenicity and catholicity do not stem simply from a liberal broadmindedness or from a studied eccentricity but from his Buddhist understanding that all beings are mutually interdependent be they rich or poor, powerful or weak, urban or rural, sophisticated or humble, Buddhist or Christian.

Sulak's most recent activities can be seen, at least in part, from this perspective. On the international level there is the International Network of Engaged Buddhists, which convened its first meeting in February 1989 to discuss various activist issues: peace and nonviolence, human rights, the environment, alternative economics, family solidarity, women's issues. Its structure was to be nonhierarchical and nonauthoritarian as symbolized by the Buddhist Wheel of Dhamma. One of its stated purposes is to "encourage all involved groups to understand linkages between their own concerns and those of other groups, and help them to avoid narrow single-issue stances in favor of a holistic understanding...."[29]

Currently the most visible of Sulak's NGOs is the Santi Pracha Dhamma Institute (SPDI; Peace, Democratic Participation, Justice or Righteousness Institute). As I write this essay I have several SPDI project proposals before me that illustrate the breadth of the organization's concerns but that also express Sulak's conviction of the mutual interdependence of them all. The proposals are as follows: training programs of the Santi Pracha Dhamma Institute for new and prospective NGO workers from various organizations; the Thai Forum Programme to provide information to the mass media on matters of alternative ideas, approaches, and models for peace and social justice; a project to place a community development team in particular villages for a three-year period known as Community Organized Research into Development Alternatives (CORDA); Phya Anuman Rajadhon exhibitions in eleven Asian countries and an intercultural seminar in Thailand; a project to promote instruction in neighboring languages (e.g., Burmese, Lao), called Knowing Our Neighbours' Languages; an alternative development radio project to help publicize the innovative work being done in the areas of traditional medicine and self-cure, integrated farming methods, rural development, ecological preservation, and folk arts and crafts; and, the Thai-Indochinese dialogue project to facilitate dialogue between and among Thai, Lao, Cambodian, and Vietnamese peoples.

Why, we might ask, has Sulak expended so much time and effort founding NGOs, foundations, and journals, especially when so many of their aims and activities are overlapping? Does his frenetic pace not inevitably lead to overextension and superficiality, attempting too many projects with too little time to give to them? These questions are not easily answered. A more psychologically oriented researcher might argue that Sulak's style has something to do with his Sino-Thainess or that he suffers from a compulsive ego syndrome. It is certainly true that Sulak is a Sino-Thai and that by his own admission he has a sizeable ego. Yet, even those who accuse Sulak of unabashed egoism are quick to point out that he can be as brutally honest with himself as he is critical of others. A political scientist might contend that to be effective Sulak must build a power base of some kind, and since he is not one of the military, economic, or aristocratic elites he has to appeal to diverse groups on the margins of the mainstream power structures. The economically bent sociologist could take a more practical view, namely, that with virtually no government support Sulak has to create foundations and found journals in order to raise money. While various psychological, sociological, and political theories may illuminate Sulak's motivations, they ignore his specifically religious/Buddhist commitments to interaction, interdependence, and intercommunication and to affecting or realizing these fundamental human characteristics within communities (sanghas) of people. In short, I would argue that an interpretation of Sulak's activist style must take into account his unique Buddhistic understanding of the nature of things.

Sulak's career highlights the interactive, community-building dimensions of his work. Through his involvement in dozens of Thai and international organizations, he has touched the lives of hundreds of men and women. Through his publications he has influenced thousands more. It may be that Sulak has fashioned a diverse and informal power base and he has certainly had to raise significant sums of money; but, above all, he has built communities of people whose lives have achieved a sense of purpose and meaning in a chaotic and confusing world.

The staffs of such NGOs as the Santi Pracha Dhamma Institute tend to be young, college-educated men and women who share Sulak's "radical conservatism" or his Dhammic socialistic utopian vision. For example, Pracha Hutanuvatra, the assistant director of the Santi Pracha Dhamma Institute and one of the organizers within the International Network of Engaged Buddhists was one of the leaders in the Thai student movement who, after the government crackdown in October 1976, ordained as a monk at Wat Suan Mokkh under Buddhadasa Bhikkhu. He was thought by many to be Buddhadasa's heir apparent with an intellectual profundity matched by seriousness of practice. After he decided to leave the monkhood, he became associated with Sulak's *phuak,* or circle.

Herbert Phillips uses the term *phuak* in describing groups associated with certain key literary figures, including Sulak. He defines *phuak* as "the various colleagues, teachers, friends, and disciples with whom most writers surround themselves and who serve variously as critics, guides, and general sources of intellectual, emotional, and sometimes financial sources of support."[30] Appearance to the contrary, Sulak asserts that his main purpose in founding NGOs and other informal groups, such as the Siam Suksa Institute, is not to create a *phuak* around him as a "big man" *(phu yai)* would, but to give young men and women a purpose in life, to inspire them to contribute to a more equitable and just Thai society. I have heard Sulak make this same plea to Thai students studying in North America, namely, that they should return to Thailand to use their education to help others, especially those marginalized by an urban-centered, capital intensive system. Sulak's peer associates and collaborators (e.g., Dr. Prawet Wasi, Professor Chaiwat Sattha-Anand, Professor and Senator Chai-Anan Samudavanija, Professor Chatsumarn Kabilsingh, and Witoon Permpongsacharoen) are similarly involved in a wide range of political, humanitarian, and environmental causes.

Sulak's Critique of Contemporary Thai Society

Religious or utopian visions of a new and different social order often stem from dissatisfaction and disappointment with the status quo. By contrast, religion may also serve to legitimate or reinforce the present situation for those who are basically satisfied with their lives. These two opposing tendencies may overlap but often exist in tension with one another. Sulak exemplifies the first direction, enunciating a strong critique of the present age. Before analyzing Sulak's vision for a different kind of Thai social, political, and economic order, I shall explore his critique of Thailand's contemporary situation. I have chosen to focus on Sulak's criticisms of his own country since, despite his internationalism and his attacks on Western (particularly American) influence in Thailand, he is first and foremost a Siamese Buddhist.[31]

While Sulak analyzes Thailand's current problems from various perspectives, he frequently bases his critique on an interpretation of Thai history. In Sulak's view Thailand is in the midst of an identity crisis that began during the reign of Rama VI (King Vajiravudh) and accelerated in stages until the end of the absolute monarchy in 1932, continuing with Pibul Songkhram's accession to power in 1939 and Sarit Thanarat's coup in 1957. Within the past half century and more, Sulak sees two complementary challenges to Siamese identity: an erosion of traditional cultural, religious, and social values and a wholesale appropriation of a Western lifestyle. His analysis of modern Thai history documents these trends.[32]

Sulak shares most Thai intellectuals' appropriation of the modernizing instincts of King Mongkut/Rama IV (1851–1868) and his son, King Chulalongkorn/Rama V (1868–1910) who brought Thailand into the modern period and astutely balanced traditional Thai values with Western ones. As Sulak put it, "For Mongkut, Siamese identity meant bending along with the Western demand [in order] to preserve our independence politically, culturally and spiritually."[33] In Sulak's view some of the changes that did take place, especially in the judicial area, not only made Thailand's legal system more compatible with the West, but also were consistent with basic Thai Buddhist principles of righteous (dhammic) rule.

In Sulak's appreciation of Mongkut and Chulalongkorn we see one of the keys to his own position: "Mongkut's strength was not only his understanding of the West . . . but going back to the root of Siameseness which he claimed to be in accordance with the original teaching of the Buddha."[34] Sulak argues that Mongkut appropriated those aspects of the Sukhodayan monarchical tradition that were not only compatible with the West but that were inherently and universally just, namely the principles of independence, equality, fraternity, and liberty.[35] In short, in Sulak's opinion, Mongkut altered Siamese "outer identity," that is, learning English and Western technology, but preserved the essential core that was rooted in Buddhism. On the critical side, however, he contends that the failure of both Mongkut and Chulalongkorn to appropriate the democratic principles inherent in Buddhism contributed to the end of the absolute monarchy in 1932.

Sulak sees Rama VI (Vajiravudh) tampering with the core of Siameseness rather than merely the outer covering that his grandfather, King Mongkut, had appropriated. While Mongkut had coined the name, Siam, and had created a guardian spirit for the country (Phra Sayama Devadhiraja), Vajiravudh transformed the classical Sukhodayan three-world cosmology into the British trinity of God, King, and country. In the Thai case it became *Chat, Sasana, Phra Mahakasat*—the nation, the Buddhist religion, and the monarchy. As Sulak puts it, Rama VI "pursued his grandfather's concept of Siamese state to the extreme ideology of nationalism, patriotism and ethnicity. . . ," and he did so at the expense of non-Thais, especially the Chinese.[36] Chauvinistic nationalism and the development of a Thai civil religion accelerate after the 1932 coup, especially during the authoritarian rule of Phibul Songkhram before and after World War II.

Sulak characterizes the architects of the 1932 coup as a Western-educated elite with little if any appreciation of Siameseness and utter disdain for indigenous neighboring cultures—the Lao, Khmer, Malay, and Burmese. With the exception of Pridi Banomyong, the promoters of the coup seemed blindly to admire the West for all the wrong reasons, namely, for material progress and advanced technology. The revolution set in motion the beginnings of a consumer culture that Sulak sees as the principal culprit in undermining Siamese values and way of life:

> The great department stores or shopping complexes have now replaced our Wats which used to be our schools, museums, art galleries, recreation centres and cultural centres as well as our hospitals and spiritual theaters. The rich have become immensely rich, while the poor remain poor or even become much poorer. . . . Not only our traditional culture, but our natural environment, too, is in crisis.[37]

Although Sulak sees the Siamese identity crisis beginning with Rama VI and accelerating thereafter, he acknowledges positive contributions by both the sixth reign and the institution of the constitutional monarchy. His opinion of Phibul Songkhram, prime minister from 1938–1944 and again from 1948–1957 is unreservedly critical, however. Phibul turned Rama VI's nationalism and suspicion of the Chinese into a grand scheme for the Thai race and Thai empire in imitation of Hitler and Mussolini, whose writings he had translated into Thai. He changed the name of the country to Thailand; commissioned a new patriotic/racist national anthem; ordered that the national flag be saluted and the national anthem sung daily at 8 a.m. and 6 p.m.; fostered a policy of irredentism that resulted in a war against the French to seize territories lost to Laos and Cambodia; and even ordered the burning of ancient vernacular literature written in regional scripts.[38]

Phibul defined as his enemies the Chinese, the princes and old nobility, and all the foreign powers outside the Axis camp. He also forced or encouraged the appropriation of more and more Western habits and customs: "We were ordered to dress in western style. . . . The chewing of betel nut was prohibited. . . . Men . . . were strongly recommended to kiss their wives before going to work. . . . Any names or surnames which denoted Chinese origin . . . [had to be] changed. . . . Those who wished to join a naval or military academy . . . [had to] prove that their grandfathers were pure Thai. . . . Certain trades . . . [were] reserved for Thai."[39] Furthermore, it was Phibul, in Sulak's view, who laid the foundations for the country's anti-Communist stance that became obsessive under the Sarit Thanarat regime (1959–1963) largely due to America's support. American influence greatly enhanced the power of the military, speeded up the dissolution of Siamese culture in the face of an expanding culture of materialism, and involved Thailand in an immoral war: "At present the Siamese elite seem to care only for power and money, as well as other material aspects of life," Sulak wrote. "Most of them only pay lip service to social justice. . . . Those who think they are in control of the country whether they be in the army, the government, the civil service or in business, only work from day to day, solving one crisis after another in order to maintain the status quo."[40]

As we shall see in the following section, Sulak's analysis of Thai history sees more than villains who have undermined Siamese religious and cultural identity, whether those villains be Thais, Americans, or Japanese. There are also many heroes, both classical and contemporary. The observer of Thailand today, however, cannot help but agree with Sulak's views regarding the crisis of Siamese identity. The social, economic, and cultural changes in Thailand over the past twenty years have been spectacular. Rapid change always challenges traditional worldviews and cultural norms. Sulak is one of several prophetic voices challenging the direction that Thailand's military-economic ruling elite has fashioned for the country. In Sulak's view it has been devastating to both the human and natural environments.

Sulak's Buddhist Vision for Renewing Society

Sulak's vision, both the terms of his critique of modern society and his proposal for a more humane and livable world, derives from many sources. His religious commitment, however, constitutes a major ingredient in this vision. Although Sulak has studied other religions, especially Christianity, and has been influenced by their teachers and admires a variety of religious exemplars, including Mahatma Gandhi, Thomas Merton, Martin Luther King Jr., and Thich Nhat Hanh, he identifies himself incontestably as a Buddhist.

Within the Thai context Sulak may be characterized as the most prominent advocate of a liberal reformist Buddhist perspective. Included in this group would be Dr. Prawet Wasi, former vice-rector of Mahidol University, who has joined with Sulak on the board of directors of such organizations as the Thai Interreligious Commission for Development; Buddhadasa Bhikkhu, whose concept of Dhammic socialism has provided the underpinnings of a reformist Thai Buddhist political philosophy; and Phra Dhammapitaka, whose impeccable scholarship has made a major contribution to both Buddhist doctrine and Buddhist social philosophy.[41] In the following we analyze some of the major elements of Sulak's Buddhist vision, in particular, his adaptation and reinterpretation of traditional Buddhism and classical Buddhist teachings. Our interpretation relies primarily on Sulak's English-language books and articles in the hope that a Western audience unfamiliar with his writings will be encouraged to study them.[42]

It should be emphasized that while Sulak has published extensively in both Thai and English, he is principally an activist. Consequently, his published work is usually in the form of speeches, lectures, and contextual reflections rather than finely honed and critically polished books.[43] Sulak also speaks and writes from a committed perspective, one that prizes personal and social transformation, rather than meticulous, rationalistic argumentation. Indeed, Sulak has been an outspoken critic of self-serving intellectual pursuits that seem to lack any relevance to the development of a more humane existence.[44] The reader, therefore, should approach Sulak as an advocate rather than a scholar; as a prophet rather than a philosopher.

As we might expect, Sulak's stance gives his work a practical rather than a theoretical bent. He is concerned to see the classical Buddhist teachings of the Four Noble Truths, Nibbana, Interdependent Co-arising, Not-self, and others not as theories but as guidelines for personal and social transformation. As he put it in "A Working Paper on a Buddhist Perception of a Desirable Society in the Near Future," "people need to know how to apply the Four Noble Truths and the Noble Eightfold Path today, and how these methods can inspire people in the creation of a desirable society in the near future."[45] Consistent with various other Theravada Buddhist reformers of this century Sulak gives an ethical cast to his interpretation of Buddhist doctrine.[46] This does not mean that he ignores issues of "spirituality;" but, as Evelyn Underhill phrased it in her study of Western mysticism some years ago, it is a "practical spirituality." In agreement with his colleagues in the International Network of Engaged Buddhists, of which he is one the principal founders, spiritual development and dedication to the pursuit of a more humane world necessarily go hand in hand.[47]

The Living Past

For many people today the confusions of the present seem to promote a nostalgia for the past. In some cases the nostalgia is an escape back to a romanticized, secure, comfortable, and less threatening time. In Freudian terms, it is a retreat to the womb. For others the past provides a critical perspective from which to inform the present and guide the future. The latter use of the past typifies Sulak's view of the Buddhist tradition. It is a "living past" with the power to challenge and transform, to inspire people to be more generous and compassionate and for societies to be more just and nonviolent. This leads Sulak to a selective reading of Buddhist and Thai history, one that serves his prophetic role rather than scholarly purposes as such.[48]

As a Buddhist, Sulak uses the Buddha and the early Buddhist monastic order as exemplary models of personal virtue and social organization. The Buddha exemplifies the Middle Way of moral and mental cultivation between the extremes of sensory indulgence on the one hand and the ascetical rejection of ordinary social intercourse on the other. The Buddhist *sangha* embodies the ideals of personal community, economic simplicity, and spiritual cultivation. Both represent the values of wisdom, nonattachment and equanimity. Sulak also looks to the classic conceptions of Buddhist kingship, especially Asoka, as a model of political virtue and concern for every member of the social order. To be sure, Sulak's interpretation of the Buddha, the early *sangha,* and the classical conception of Buddhist kingship is not unique. It shares much in common with the views of other contemporary Theravada Buddhist reformers such as A. T. Ariyaratne, the founder of the Sarvodaya Shramadana movement in Sri Lanka. Of special interest to us is the way in which Sulak interprets Thai history from the thirteenth century to the present, from King Ramkhamhaeng to Buddhadasa Bhikkhu. In his reconstruction of Thai Buddhist intellectual history the seminal junctures are King Ramkhamhaeng's model of benevolent, righteous kingship; King Lu'thai's synthesis of Buddhist cosmology, politics, and ethics; King Mongkut's neo-orthodox Buddhist revivalism; and Buddhadasa Bhikkhu's reformist Buddhism, especially his utopian ideology of Dhammic socialism.

Sulak interprets King Ramkhamhaeng of Sukhothai (?1279–1298) as the exemplary "righteous ruler and father to his people" *(dhammaraja)* in contrast to the authoritarian model of the ruler appropriated later from Brahmanistic Cambodia by the rulers of Ayudhya. Sulak depicts this ideal Buddhist ruler as a great supporter of Buddhism as well as a moral example to his people. He sees Ramkhamhaeng's grandson, Phya Lu'thai, as continuing this *dhammaraja* tradition in a sermon attributed to him, "The

Three Worlds According to Phra Ruang" *(Traibhumi Phraruang)*, composed around 1345.[49] Although the text may well be the earliest elaborated Theravada cosmology, Sulak emphasizes its ethical aspects, namely, that kingship is a consequence of virtuous previous lives, the negative effects of human sinfulness, and the positive result of meritorious activities. Furthermore, Sulak argues, the mythological nature of the text is really the backdrop for the king's teachings about impermanence, rebirth, the Noble Eightfold Path, and the final release of Nibbana.[50] As an ethical treatise the text continued to be influential into the early Bangkok period.

As we have seen, Sulak is particularly appreciative of King Mongkut who was a monk for twenty-six years before he ascended to the throne in 1851. Mongkut not only revived the Thai monkhood, he refurbished the Sukhothai conception of the righteous monarch, regarding Ramkhamhaeng's famed 1292 inscription as a "Magna Carta of the Thai nation."[51] Part of Mongkut's legacy to the nation were his sons, Chulalongkorn and Prince Patriarch Vajirañavarorasa (1892–1921), who continued to revitalize and strengthen the Buddhist monkhood. One aspect of this revitalization was the development of a strong meditation, forest monastery tradition of which Phra Acariya Mun (1871–1949) and his disciples Phra Maha Boowa and Phra Acariya Cha are particularly exemplary.[52]

For Sulak, the essence of the Siamese Buddhist tradition lives on in a variety of exemplars, monastic and lay, royal and common, past and present. Previously we referred to Sulak's indebtedness to Pridi Banoymong and Puey Ungphakorn and his deep respect for Phya Anuman Rajadhorn. He has written about poets, artists, and princesses. He admires royal administrators who loved Thai history, literature, and culture and sought to ensure it was not swept away by the eroding power of Westernization. Sulak has a particular affection for two sons of King Mongkut, Prince Damrong and Prince Naris, who in different ways sought to sustain Thai identity during the early decades of the twentieth century. Damrong was founder of the Royal Council dedicated to the conservation of traditional arts, archaeological sites, and national treasures and to the shaping of national language and literature.[53] Sulak contends that for Damrong, Siamese identity had three aspects: "love of freedom and independence, a dislike of violence, and an ability to compromise and assimilate,"[54] qualities Sulak sees as necessary to maintain and refashion Siamese identity today. Prince Naris, assuming various ministerial portfolios under Chulalongkorn, was the artist responsible for the reconstruction of the Temple of the Emerald Buddha and for planning the beautiful Marble Temple (Wat Benjamabopitr). Sulak praises his artistic feats in and of themselves, but admires Naris even more because he was a modest, unassuming person despite his royalty: "While his contemporaries were building mansions in the city after the European fashion,

Naris bought a Siamese homestead and lived among farmers whom he regarded as friends."[55]

I stated earlier that Sulak appeals to the Buddhist *sangha* as an example of a minimalist, nonacquisitive, noncompetitive lifestyle that he believes is required for our survival in this day and age.[56] But Sulak has been especially encouraging to monks who have devoted their lives to serving the welfare of their communities in extraordinary ways. Particularly influential for Sulak have been Buddhadasa Bhikkhu and Phra Dhammapitaka.[57] Sulak's own reformist interpretation of Buddhism reflects Buddhadasa's demythologized, rationalized Dhamma. Furthermore, his political philosophy, which rejects both Western capitalism and Western Marxism, also resounds to Buddhadasa's notion of Dhammic socialism.[58]

Sulak tends to read the past in personalistic terms. There are villains the likes of Phibul and Sarit, but there are also many heroes who function as positive examples not of the past but for the present. In particular, there are exceptional individuals—often monks like Buddhadasa and Dhammapitaka—who not only embody life-enhancing cultural values but who also point to a timeless truth and meaning that Sulak as a Buddhist might refer to as Nirvana or *lokuttara* (trans-mundane). The paradox of this past is that it is ever-present.

Small "b" Buddhism

In February 1986 Sulak was interviewed by James Forest of the Catholic Peace Fellowship, biographer of Dorothy Day and friend of Thich Nhat Hanh. The interview was first published in *Reconciliation International* under the title, "Small 'b' Buddhism."[59] Sulak's small "b" Buddhism has three basic dimensions that we shall characterize as essentialist, universalist, and existentialist. In this context essentialist does not carry its usual metaphysical signification but refers to the essential core of Buddhism or Buddhist doctrine, a Buddhism stripped of what its author takes to be unessential. Capital "B" Buddhism, by way of contrast, is acculturated Buddhism, conventional ritualistic Buddhism, the *pro forma* Buddhism of civil religion, a Buddhism identified with Thai chauvinism and militaristic, aggressive values.[60] The existential dimension of small "b" Buddhism refers to its personal and socially transformative relevance. It has the practical applicability to solve contemporary problems as well as the power to fill one's life with meaning in a chaotic and threatening world.

While Sulak as a Buddhist interprets the essential core of small "b" Buddhism in Buddhist terms, he understands it to be the essential core of all the great world religions. In agreement with Buddhadasa Bhikkhu he interprets this universal core as the teaching of selflessness:

> You don't have to profess . . . [a particular] faith, you don't have to worship the Buddha, you don't have to join in any ceremonies. What is important is that you grow in mindfulness and awareness. You try to restructure your consciousness to become more selfless, to be able to relate to other people more meaningfully in order that friendship will be possible and exploitation impossible. To me the essence of Buddhism is this.[61]

For Sulak the moral equivalent of selflessness is "nonexploitation," one of the major themes of his talks in Europe and the United States during his most recent period of exile.[62] It provides an overarching perspective from which he interprets *dana* (charity, generosity) as "training in nonexploitation," *sila* (morality) as "understanding the consequences of exploitative action," and *bhavana* (meditation), as the critical self-awareness by which we can know if we are being exploitative.[63] To be selfless is to act empathetically and nonexploitatively toward ourselves, others, our community, and our world. Sulak applies a similar analysis to a discussion of nonviolence: Through the cultivation of mindfulness and the development of *metta,* or loving-kindness, one dissolves hatred, acquires the virtue of patience, and attains the state of neutral awareness essential to acting nonviolently.[64]

In this section of our study I shall focus on the essentialist and universalist dimensions of his small "b" Buddhism on the assumption that its existentialist character has been amply demonstrated by the prior discussion of Sulak's life and work. I shall analyze the essentialist dimension in terms of Sulak's reinterpretation of several fundamental Theravada Buddhist concepts: the Four Noble Truths, the Five Training Rules or Moralities *(pañca sila),* the Four Divine Abodes *(brahma vihara),* the Spiritual Friend *(kalayana-mitta),* interdependency *(idappaccayata),* and liberation or Nibbana.[65] We shall look very briefly at the universalist dimension using his ecumenical writings, especially regarding the relationship between Buddhism and Christianity.

The two foundational doctrinal formulae in Theravada Buddhism are the Four Noble Truths that include the Noble Eightfold Path and the Five Moralities, Precepts, or Training Rules. The Four Noble Truths are exposited in what is referred to as the Buddha's first discourse or sermon, "Setting the Wheel of the Law in Motion" *(Dhammacakkappavattana Suttanta).* The Five Precepts are an essential ingredient of every Buddhist sabbath meeting that begins with monks and laity pledging themselves to avoid killing, intoxicants, lying, stealing, and adultery.

In very brief terms the Four Noble Truths state that mundane existence is not ultimately fulfilling (i.e., life is suffering), that suffering *(dukkha)* arises because of the insatiable nature of worldly desires or grasping, that suffering will cease when these desires are overcome, and that the path to this goal involves moral and mental discipline leading to the inner realization that nothing exists independently and permanently. In Sulak's view this realization is the right view *(sammaditthi)* of small "b" Buddhism. It is basic to all other aspects of the fourth of the Four Noble Truths, that is, the Noble Eightfold Path (right view, right thought, right effort, right speech, right action, right livelihood, right mindfulness, right concentration). Although Buddhists have developed a variety of methods for developing right view, Sulak argues that its achievement entails three fundamental elements: overcoming selfishness, becoming detached from worldly gains, and realizing one's interdependence with others.[66]

Each of the Four Noble Truths relates to the nature, cause, and cessation of suffering. The story of Prince Siddhattha's renunciation sets out the classical Buddhist story about confronting and overcoming suffering. Sulak's treatment of the episode characterizes his hermeneutical approach to the interpretation of text and doctrine:

> When Prince Siddhattha saw an old man, a sick man, a dead man, and a wandering monk, he was moved to seek salvation, and eventually he became the Buddha, the Awakened One. The suffering of the present day, such as that brought about at Bhopal and Chernobyl, should move many of us to think together and act together to overcome such death and destruction, to bring about the awakening of humankind.[67]

Sulak interprets suffering in this example and countless others as dehumanizing social, economic, and political forces that sacrifice the long-term common human good for vested self-interest and short-term economic and political gain. The solution to this kind of suffering must come from broad-based, nonviolent, grass-roots movements that challenge narrow self-interest and dehumanizing power.

Sulak interprets the Five Precepts in a similar contemporaneous manner.[68] Not to take life does not simply mean the literal act of not killing another person or of not going to war; by extension it also entails a renunciation of the production and use of weapons, especially weapons of mass destruction.[69] Depriving people of the means to an adequate livelihood is also a kind of killing. The use of chemical fertilizers and insecticides that depletes the soil of rich microorganisms is also a form of taking life as is the destruction of forests, which has contributed to the loss of many animal species. Nuclear waste dumping and chemical contamination is a clear violation of the first precept for they threaten to destroy the human race. Sulak even applies the first precept to personal lifestyles. Living in luxury and consuming wastefully while others are dying of starvation contravenes the precept in Sulak's rather totalistic interpretation of the first precept. Vegetarianism, from this perspective, upholds the first precept because it avoids the taking of animal life but also since discouraging the consumption of meat is "doubly compassionate, not only towards animals but also toward the humans who need the grains set aside for livestock.[70] In short, for Sulak, the first precept grounds all Buddhist action: "that one should actively practice loving kindness towards all."[71]

Sulak contends that the notion of theft versus legal means of livelihood needs to be reconsidered. What are appropriate and inappropriate development models, right and wrong consumption? How are we to judge unequal and unjust marketing that leads to the degradation of natural resources and human exploitation? In Sulak's view much that passes as legal business, both nationally and internationally, often seems more insidious than traditional forms of petty theft. In short, the prohibition against theft becomes a basic principle of economic justice, of taking responsibility for the exploitation and violence of the economic system in which one lives. Typically, Sulak applies this principle both to one's personal life and to society: "To live a life of voluntary simplicity, out of compassion for all beings, is a meaningful way to set oneself against the unethical tendencies built into the status quo," but one may also need to "overturn the structures that compel others to live in poverty involuntarily."[72]

Sulak also greatly enlarges the purview of the traditional precept against adultery and sexual misconduct. It entails a broad range of issues including the rights of women; the widespread exploitation of women in the Third World, especially as prostitutes; attitudes toward abortion; and population control. Using traditional doctrinal terminology Sulak speaks of a collective "karma" of male dominance that limits both men's and women's potential to achieve their fullest self-realization beyond gender. Sulak contends that the fourth precept regarding truth and falsehood needs to be applied to advertising, the media, and education:

> We need a workable Buddhist education that is not limited to the classroom. We need to expand the [notion of] right view through the mass media so that truth will triumph over falsehood. The dignity of human beings should take precedence over a consumer culture wherein people have more than they really need.[73]

Finally, the fifth precept regarding intoxicants should be expanded to encompass a variety of dimensions of alcohol and drug abuse, including government support of alcohol, drug, and tobacco industries. He observes that military wars on drugs fail to address the problems of drug abuse and drug-related crime at their sources—unemployment, unequal distribution of wealth, and alienation from work: "If government leaders do not recognize their own addictive behavior involving alcohol or prescription drugs, if they do not work to alleviate the despair that makes drugs attractive, and if they continue to support regimes that profit from large-scale drug traffic, how can they expect symbolic measures such as a 'war on drugs' to succeed?"[74]

If Sulak's interpretation of the range and extent of the meaning of the Five Precepts can be said to represent an application of traditional Buddhist ethical principles and rules to contemporary situations, his treatment of the Four Divine Abodes, the Spiritual Friend, and the Four Dhammas exemplify his commitment to the truth of the mutually interconnected nature of all things *(idappaccayata)*. *Metta,* or love, the first of the four *brahma viharas* means sharing one's happiness with others. This is the first step in the development of right view followed by compassion *(karuna),* which means sharing in the suffering of others. Sulak contends that the increasing gap between the rich and the poor, the powerful and powerless must be addressed not only through government policies and economic programs but by developing oneself spiritually, "otherwise one would never be able to share suffering with others meaningfully."[75] *Mudita* or sympathetic joy, the third step in human development, transforms envy and enmity into friendship. Identifying one's own joys and sorrows with the joys and sorrows of others leads to the fourth and last of the Divine Abodes, equanimity *(upekkha)*. One becomes indifferent to success or failure, prosperity or adversity for oneself or for others. In such a state of neutrality all boundaries between myself and others fall away.

In Sulak's interpretation such a state of spiritual development must be cultivated through self-criticism and mental awareness *(yonisomanasakara)*. "Good friends" *(kalayanamitta)* play an especially crucial role in our spiritual development for they guide our way, protecting us from self-deception, spiritual pride, and religious escapism: "a Good Friend would be one's 'other voice' of conscience, to put one in the proper path of development, so that one would not escape from society, nor would one want to improve society in order to claim [it as] one's [own] achievement."[76] In short, the good friend is one who can lead others to the ideal balance between the inner journey of spiritual perfection and the outer path of social justice and harmony.

Individual spiritual perfection and social justice are inherently linked in Sulak's vision, another example of the truth of mutual interdependence. In a lecture on human rights delivered during his United States lecture tour in the spring of 1992, Sulak referred to the Burmese opposition leader, Aung San Suu Kyi's compassion as an example of her sense of interrelatedness with her captors: "She maintains a compassionate feeling for those who put her in jail, who killed her people, and for those who destroyed her political party. . . . If you take up arms against oppressors, you will end up destroying each other."[77] On a more mundane, practical level Sulak admonishes his Korean and Japanese friends to recycle their chopsticks and urges all of us to recycle paper: "We are all interrelated. I believe it was Thich Nhat Hanh who said that when we look at a piece of paper we must think of the trees. Without the trees, there would be no paper. . . . In my own country, a Buddhist monk who wanted to protect the forest was arrested by the military. Human rights . . . [is related] to a piece of paper."[78]

Sulak's exegesis of such traditional Buddhist moral teachings as the Five Precepts, the Four Divine Abodes, and the Four Dhammas—sharing *(dana)*, pleasant speech *(piyavaca)*, constructive actions *(atthacariya)*, and equality *(samanattata)*—functions to critique the contemporary moral order, to map constructive guidelines for personal and social moral transformation, and to demonstrate the unequivocally interdependent nature of things. Within this mutually interconnected world those in positions of power have a special responsibility. Traditionally, of course, this meant kings or rulers. Here, as elsewhere, Sulak often appeals to the Pali scriptures for support:

> When kings are righteous, the ministers of kings are righteous, When ministers are righteous, brahmans and householders also are righteous. The townsfolk and villagers are righteous. This being so, moon and sun go right in their course. This being so, constellations and stars do likewise; days and nights, months and fortnights, seasons and years go on their courses regularly; winds blow regularly and in due season. . . . Rains falling seasonably, the crops ripen in due season. . . . When crops ripen in due season, men who live on these crops are long-lived, well-favored, strong, and free from sickness.[79]

Those in positions of political and economic power have a special responsibility toward their human and natural environments, but each individual has a contribution to make. The first and foremost step is training in *self-awareness.* Our contribution to a more just world will arise naturally from knowing our inner condition:

> [W]e should adjust our inner condition, which should be calm and mindful, to be aware of the unjust external world. It is wrong to try to adjust the external world without training one's mind to be neutral and selfless. It is also wrong to be calm and detached without a proper concern to bring about better social conditions for all who share our planet as well as those who live in the same universe.[80]

Traditionally in Theravada Buddhism mindfulness and loving-kindness, or *metta,* accompany one another. Echoing the words of his friend, Thich Nhat Hanh, Sulak puts the interrelationship in concrete and specific terms: "In a family when there is one person who practices meditation the entire family will benefit from this loving kindness.... When in one village, a villager practices *metta,* the entire village will be influenced, thanks to the constant reminder given by the example of that one person."[81]

At its core, argues Sulak, Buddhism teaches selflessness. Its ethics of nonkilling and nonviolence flow from this teaching, as do such methods of spiritual cultivation as mental awareness and loving-kindness. Selflessness is at the heart of Sulak's universalism or ecumenical vision, especially his dialogue with Christianity. While Christianity and Buddhism differ in many respects, they share this common core of the ultimate value of selflessness. As a Buddhist, Sulak puts the affinity between Buddhism and Christianity in this way:

> A Buddhist ... [can] only reflect on Christianity from a Buddhist perspective; he ... [can] do no more. If a Buddhist understands that the Christian love of God makes him love his neighbors, his submission to God makes him selfless and compassionate to all beings—human or otherwise.... In his encounters with Christianity, he sees the cross as a sign that will strengthen him to share suffering—not only with his Christian friends but also with all god's creatures.[82]

Sulak has had numerous contacts with Christians on individual and institutional levels. He has worked with Quakers in international peace organizations and Mennonites serving in Laos and Cambodia. He has attended numerous conferences sponsored by the World Council of Churches and is on the editorial board of the journal, *Buddhist-Christian Studies.* Sulak is a great admirer of the Trappist monk, Thomas Merton, not primarily because Merton had a keen interest in Buddhism but because Merton's spirituality was much like his own—a paradoxical combination of contemplation and social action. In 1974 his review of Merton's *Asian Journal* for the *Journal of the Siam Society* demonstrated more than a passing knowledge of Merton and his writings. He concluded with the wry comment that *farangs* (foreigners) like Merton can help Thai Buddhists take their religion more seriously, especially the contemplative part of Thai Buddhist culture.

Buddhism and Christianity also share a common concern for liberation, a liberation from those dehumanizing powers that prevent the human spirit from its highest realization, whether that state be called Nibbana or the Kingdom of God. Utilizing the work of Phra Dhammapitaka *(Freedom—Individual and Social),* Sulak outlines four levels of freedom that are indispensable for the realization of peace and happiness: physical freedom, social freedom, emotional freedom, and intellectual freedom.[83] The first relates to the material world or physical environment and covers freedom from the shortage of the basic needs of life. Social freedom represents the freedom from oppression, persecution, exploitation, discrimination, violence, and terrorism as well as the positive promotion of benevolence and tolerance. Emotional freedom or freedom of the heart refers to freedom from mental defilements and suffering, a purified, sorrow-free, "Nibbaned" mind, full of the beneficial mental qualities of loving-kindness and compassion. Intellectual freedom is that gained through knowledge and wisdom, a freedom from distortion and bias, self-interest, or selfishness. It is the culminating state of selflessness shared by both Buddhism and Christianity.

Sulak's concern for social as well as individual or personal liberation promotes the emphasis on praxis of the Latin American liberation theologians (e.g., Leonardo Boff, Jon Sobrino). Sulak argues that grounding interreligious dialogue in praxis not only protects "against the persistent danger of the decay of doctrine into ideology" but it also provides a mutual starting point for "how Christians and others can struggle, together, against those things that threaten their common humanity, e.g. consumerism (greed), militarism (hatred), and the destruction of the environment (delusion)."[84] In his lecture at the Fourth International Buddhist-Christian Dialogue Conference held at the Boston University School of Theology in the summer of 1992, Sulak proposed that a liberation Christology provides a ground for Christians to be open to the possibility of encountering other "religious figures whose vision offers a liberating praxis and a kingdom equal to that of Jesus" without jeopardizing "the universal relevance of Jesus' vision."[85] Sulak's proposal reflects not only his own liberationist or transformationist religious vision but also his deeply held Buddhist conviction that to waste time debating ultimate reality claims "tends not to edification."

Sulak understands Nibbana to be that state of personal realization when one has extinguished worldly attachments and reaches "immediately in this life the deliverance of mind, the deliverance through wisdom, which is free from cankers *(asavas),* and which he/she himself/herself was understood and realized."[86] Ordinary language cannot encapsulate either the true nature or the full meaning of Nibbana. Typical of other modern Theravada Buddhist apologists, Sulak understands Nibbana to be not a metaphysical reality but a state of being, not a theory but an experience beyond the limits of the mundane. Thus, the *Udana* reference to Nibbana as "Unborn, Unoriginated, Uncreated, Unformed" is ultimately no more or less adequate a description than contemporary noncanonical characterizations such as "inner freedom, equilibrium, peace, void of angst and a sense of being entirely "at home" and unthreatened in the universe, which expresses itself both in a positive, affective state and in compassion for all forms of life."[87] That is to say, human language can only convey a likeness of the transmundane. For Sulak, Buddhist *upaya* or skillful means locates the core of religion in personal and social transformation governed by the principles of selflessness and nonexploitative compassionate love, rather than in conceptualizations of those outer reaches of human experience that both focus and expand our lives. Thus, while the cosmic significance of Nibbana can be conceptualized in a variety of ways, none constitutes the one and only correct way.[88] Such a position, Sulak believes, applies to all religious truth claims.

Conclusion

In concluding this essay I would like to suggest three different analytical perspectives of relevance to my interpretation of Sulak's Buddhist vision for renewing society: Reinhold Niebuhr's love and justice polarity; Robert Bellah's concept of "reformist"; and Gananath Obeyesekere's characterization of various twentieth-century developments in Sri Lankan Buddhism as "protestant Buddhism."

One of the most enduring issues in the study of religious ethics is the relationship between the highest religious ideals and goals (e.g. Nibbana, Kingdom of God) and moral norms (e.g. justice, fairness). Within the discourse of Christian ethics the debate over the nature of this relationship has focused on the polarity between an absolute and universal ethic of love (*agape*) and a prudentialist ethic of justice and fairness. This debate was initiated by Reinhold Niebuhr's *An Interpretation of Christian Ethics* (1956) and *Moral Man and Immoral Society* (1932). Although Niebuhr put love and justice in a dialectical relationship, he argued that the proximate norms of hardheaded justice should govern our collective behavior. Agapic love was a religious ideal that might be actualized in individual relationships but in the world of proximate justice love tended to become a sentimentalized, ineffectual, and fuzzy-headed pie-in-the-sky-by-and-by.

It might be argued that in the Buddhist case a rough parallel to the love/justice distinction is the differentiation between Nibbanic ideals and kammic justice/ethics. Scholars such as Max Weber, Melford Spiro, Winston King, and others have argued a Buddhist version of Neibuhr's distinction between love and justice, namely, that kamma and Nibbana define distinct realms (morality vs. religion) of human endeavor. Just as Niebuhr's distinction has been challenged by various ethicists, so the kammic/Nibbanic distinction has been challenged by both scholars and proponents. I would suggest that the reformist voices of Sulak and Buddhadasa frame a vision of the world in which the religious and the moral are essentially integrated. This integration not only gives Sulak's version of Dhammic socialism a utopian cast; it is at the heart of his paradoxical nature. Once again referring to Buddhist terms, Sulak stands at the intersection of mundane *(lokiya)* and transmundane *(lokkuttara)* values. That is, Sulak's project is to actualize what he understands to be the highest religious ideals of his Buddhist tradition in real life social, economic, and political situations.

This claim brings us to Robert Bellah's category, reformism, and Gananath Obeyesekere's notion of protestant Buddhism. In an earlier essay on religion and modernization in Asia, Robert Bellah suggests that in the confrontation between religion and modernization there have been four types of response: conversion to Christianity, traditionalism, reformism, and neotraditionalism.[89] The two main alternatives for reinterpreting and rationalizing religions have been what he terms reformism and neotraditionalism. Reformism is the more radical of the two. It represents the rationalization or deparochialization of both the means and ends of traditional religion. Neotraditionalism is more conservative, rationalizing only the means and not the ends. Reformism necessitates a thorough reinterpretation of the tradition. In doing so it appeals to early teachers and texts, rejects much of the intervening tradition, and proposes an interpretation that advocates social reform and national regeneration.[90] In my view Sulak can be interpreted as a representative of Bellah's category of "reformism." Within the Thai context I would ague that Sulak can be seen as the principal lay popularizer of the reinterpretation of the Buddhist religiomoral worldview proposed in a more sophisticated and creative way by Buddhadasa.[91] On the monastic side the nationally noted Thai monk, Pannananda, would be Sulak's counterpart.[92]

The rationalized Buddhist worldview defined by Buddhadasa and espoused by Sulak can be criticized from various perspectives. Monks like Phra Dhammapitaka, for example, while acknowledging Buddhadasa's creative genius, are also troubled by his original and sometimes idiosyncratic interpretations of the Theravada canon and its commentaries. Sulak's reformulation of the Buddhist religio-moral worldview rationalized even further to serve his prophetic and utopian goals, can be similarly critiqued for reifying the rich, multitextured, and diverse nature of the tradition. Sulak's utopian vision tends to interpret the cultural appropriation of Buddhist ideals as an inevitable diminution of their transformative power. This tendency seems to give his vision a reified, ahistorical cast. Yet, as we have seen, Sulak's vision lends itself to a selective reconstruction of the Theravada historical tradition based on his interpretation of the essential, universal principles of the Buddha's Dhamma. This observation brings us to Gananath

Obeyesekere's critique of a contemporary lay Buddhist reformer in Sri Lanka, A. T. Ariyaratne, founder of the Sarvodaya Shramadana movement, and the early twentieth century Sinhalese Buddhist apologist, Anagarika Dharmapala.[93]

Obeyesekere characterizes Dharmapala and Ariyaratne as "protestant Buddhists." He means by this term that they have been very much influenced by a modern, urban, Western, protestantized view that tends to define religion in terms of a core set of doctrinal beliefs. Such a view devalues much of the popular tradition—its myths and legends, its animistic accretions—and presents a neutered, excessively rationalized and urbanized form of Buddhism that sanitizes both the reality of village life and the moral ambiguity of its royal and religious history. Such a protestantized Buddhism can become neotraditional or fundamentalistic, as in the case of a Dharmapala in Sri Lanka or a Santi Asoka movement in Thailand, or it can become reformist as in the case of Ariyaratne and Sulak.

Sulak's vision for renewing society may be reformist but it is indisputably Buddhist. It is a vision fundamentally indebted to Buddhadasa Bhikkhu and one that finds resonant notes in the engaged Zen Buddhism of Thich Nhat Hanh, the liberation theology of Latin America, and the spiritual activism of Thomas Merton. Merton once referred to himself as being in the "belly of a paradox," an apt characterization of Sulak as a prophet caught in the intersection of the mundane and transmundane, the paradoxical posture of the idealistic hope-against-hope that the world may not simply improve but become a closer approximation of the vision of such religious founders as Sakyamuni the Buddha or Jesus the Christ.

Acknowledgment

I wish to express my appreciation to Swarthmore College, Mr. Eugene M. Lang, and the Council for the International Exchange of Scholars for sabbatical leave support during the academic year 1989–90 spent in Chiangmai, Thailand. I am especially grateful to Sulak Sivaraksa for numerous conversations during the year at meetings and conferences and for his critical reading of earlier versions of this chapter.

Notes

1. The development of modern Thai Buddhism has been discussed by many Western scholars. For a brief, neo-Weberian assessment of the development of a

"rationalized" Thai Buddhist worldview, see Charles F. Keyes, "Buddhist Politics and their Revolutionary Origins in Thailand," in *International Political Science Review* (1989), vol. 10, no. 2, pp. 121–142.

2. For a recent general assessment of the decline of Thai Buddhism, see Sirma Sornsuwan, "Buddha's Tears: The Decline of Buddhism in Thailand," in *Generation* (vol. 1, no. 1), Oct. 1989/B.E. 2532, pp. 39–55.

3. There have been various studies of contemporary movements in Thai Buddhism. One of the most recent is Peter A. Jackson, *Buddhism, Legitimation, and Conflict* (Singapore: Institute of Southeast Asian Studies, 1989). Gender issues in Thai Buddhism have been discussed by Charles F. Keyes, Thomas Kirsch, Chatsumarn Kabilsingh, Penny Van Esterik, and John Van Esterik; see Thomas A. Kirsch, "Text and Context: Buddhist Sex Roles/Culture of Gender Revisted," *American Anthropologist,* 12 (May 1985), pp. 301–320.

4. See Donald K. Swearer, "Fundamentalistic Movements in Theravada Buddhism," in *Fundamentalisms Observed,* eds. Martin Marty and Scott Appleby (Chicago: University of Chicago Press, 1991); Sulak Sivaraksa, *Panha Lae Thang Ook Karani Santi Asoka* [The Problem and the Solution to the Santi Asoka Case] (Bangkok: Thai Inter-Religious Commission, 1988). Peter A. Jackson also discusses Dhammakaya and Santi Asoka in *Buddhism, Legitimation and Conflict;* see chapters 7 and 8.

5. For example, see Louis Gabaude, *Une Herméneutique Bouddhique Contemporaine de Thailande: Buddhadasa Bhikkhu* (Paris: École Française D'Extrême-Orient, 1988); Peter A. Jackson, *Buddhadasa: A Buddhist Thinker for the Modern World* (Bangkok: The Siam Society, 1988); *Me and Mine: Selected Essays of Bhikkhu Buddhadasa,* ed. Donald K. Swearer (Albany: State University of New York Press, 1989).

6. For references to Sulak in recent anthropological, literary, and political studies, see Herbert P. Phillips, "The Culture of Siamese Intellectuals," in *Change and Persistence in Thai Society, Essays in Honor of Lauriston Sharp,* eds. G. William Skinner and A. Thomas Kirsch (Ithaca & London: Cornell University Press, 1975), pp. 324–358 (esp. pp. 349–351); Herbert P. Phillips, et al. *Modern Thai Literature, With an Ethnographic Interpretation* (Honolulu: University of Hawaii Press, 1987), esp. pp. 45–48, 257–273; David Morell and Chaianan Samudavanija, *Political Conflict in Thailand: Reform, Reaction, Revolution* (Cambridge, Mass.: Oelgeschlager, Gunn and Hain, 1981). See also Benedict R. Anderson and Ruchira Mendiones, *In the Mirror: Literature and Politics in Siam in the American Era* (Bangkok: Duang Kamol, 1985); the introduction contains a useful discussion of the kind of articles published in *Sangkhomsat Parithat.*

7. See Herbert Phillips, *Modern Thai Literature,* pp. 104–110, for an introduction to Kukrit, and pp. 46–47 for his explanation of three possible factors in Sulak's ongoing published attacks: in a seemingly paradoxical way Sulak exploits the omnipresent patron-client relationship pattern by using the older and better

known Kukrit to bring attention and importance to himself; Sulak's attacks represent a kind of karmic justice in which Kukrit is getting back the kind of treatment he's dealt out to others; and, finally, Sulak is attempting to inject the spirit of British literary rivalry and one-upsmanship into the Thai situation. Phillips sees Sulak's appeal within the contemporary Thai social context stemming in part from the role of the presumptuous outsider: "the perennial youth who has dared to criticize someone older and more important—something that in an ideal Thai world is not supposed to happen but when it does—is felt to be refreshing and emancipating...." (p. 47). For an English version of Sulak's article originally published in *Sangkhomsat Parithat,* see "M. R. Kukrit Pramoj Whom I know," in *Siam in Crisis,* 2nd rev. ed. (Bangkok: Thai Inter-Religious Commission for Development, 2533 B.E./1990 C.E.), pp. 36–46.

8. This charge was brought by the Bangkok Village Scouts Club in a letter to the prime minister. The letter charged that in an interview included in a book, *Lok Khrab Sangkhom Thai* (Unmaking Thai Society), Sulak made derogatory statements that affronted the monarchy. For thorough documentation in English, including a precise chronology of events, see Sulak Sivaraksa, *Siamese Resurgence: A Thai Buddhist Voice on Asia and a World of Change* (Bangkok: Asian Cultural Forum on Development, 1985), Appendix I, pp. 337–452. Included in the documents is an article Sulak wrote for the liberal newspaper, *Matichon,* published August 8, 1984. In the article Sulak draws a parallel between himself and Socrates for whom he has a great deal of admiration: "About the time of the Buddha, Socrates was prosecuted for degrading the basic virtue of young people. He was sentenced to capital punishment by drinking hemlock. If he was to be in Siam now, he might be charged with *lèse majesté* as I was, because, he had warned the people not to believe blindly in superstitions and the supernatural, but to use reason and intellect critically" (p. 356). For documentation in Thai see, *Khon Phon Khuk [Released from Prison]* (Bangkok: Yuwawithaya, 2928 B.E./1986 C.E.).

9. Sulak's lecture was titled, "Six Months of the National Peace-Keeping Council: A Tragedy in Thai Society," and is available in English translation through the International Network of Engaged Buddhists. References to Sulak's lecture will be based on this text.

10. Ibid., p. 7.

11. Ibid., p. 10

12. The details of Sulak's case to mid-1993 are traced in *When Loyalty Demands Dissent: Sulak Sivaraksa and the Charge of Lèse Majesté in Siam, 1991–1993* (Bangkok: Santi Pracha Dhamma Institute, Ashram Wongsanit, Sathirakoses-Nagapradipa Foundation, 1993).

13. David Morell and Chai-anan Samudavanija, *Political Conflict in Thailand, Reform, Reaction, Revolution* (Cambridge, Mass.: Oelgeschlager, Gunn and Hain, 1981), p. 140.

14. Ibid.

15. Sulak Sivaraksa, *Siamese Resurgence* . . . p. 316.

16. From the pamphlet, "ACFOD. Asian Cultural Forum on Development," 1981–1983.

17. Taken from Robert Bobilin, *Revolution from Below, Buddhist and Christian Movements for Justice in Asia* (Lanham, N.Y.: University Press of America, 1988), pp. 114–115. ACFOD's "vision" can be characterized as Sulak's version of Dhammic socialism, which, in my opinion, potentially has significant political implications. Herbert Phillips refers to Sulak's reformist activism as "apolitical." Although Sulak walks a narrow line in his criticism of the Thai government and military, his NGOs espouse a politically potent idealistic ideology.

18. The HRTR is the most significant human rights activist journal in the country. The journal not only reports on human rights violations in Thailand but includes articles on nonviolence training programs, women's issues, legal aid to the poor, and human rights situations in other Asian countries.

19. Sulak, *Siamese Resurgence*, p. 319.

20. Since the end of the Vietnam war Thich Nhat Hanh has continued his work as a peace activist dividing his time between residency at the Plum Village meditation ashram in France, peace activism, and meditation retreats. Sulak first published his widely reprinted meditation manual, *The Miracle of Mindfulness*, with the subtitle, "A Meditation Manual for Young Activists."

21. For a description of the activities of the TICD, see Bobilin, *Revolution from Below* . . . , chapter 6.

22. Sulak has done a remarkable job of straddling his national and international interests or the particularism of his commitment to Thailand (Siam) and the universalism of his concern for issues of peace and justice, the plight of the poor, and of nonviolent social change. This balance is reflected in the range of his publications in both English and Thai.

23. Three volumes of Phya Anuman Rajadhon's work in English were recently published as part of his 100th anniversary commemoration: *Some Traditions of the Thai: Essays on Thai Folklore, Popular Buddhism in Siam and Other Essays on Thailand Studies;* they are available through Sulak's bookstore, Suksit Siam, 117 Fuang Nakorn Road, Bangkok 10200.

24. From the announcement, "Phya Anuman Rajadhon's Centennary," p. 1.

25. See "Phya Anuman Rajadhon: A Common Man Or A Genius," in Sulak Sivaraksa, *Siam in Crisis* 2nd rev. ed. (Bangkok: Thai Inter-Religious Commission for Development, 1990), pp. 23–35.

26. Phillips, *Modern Thai Literature*, p. 48.

27. Ibid., p. 46. For a translation of a selection of Angkarn Kalyanapong's poetry into English see, *Angkarn Kalyanapong. A Contemporary Siamese Poet*, ed. Michael Wright (Bangkok: Santhirakoses-Nagapradipa Foundation, 1987).

28. Phillips, p. 47.

29. From the draft statement of the Progressive Buddhists Conference. (February 24–27, 1989), p. 1.

30. Phillips, p. 16.

31. "Siamese" is the key term in this statement. As a Sino-Thai, Sulak is very critical of the kind of modern chauvinistic nationalism represented by the term, "Thailand." For him, "Siam" denotes the best in classical Thai cultural and religious roots. Vira Somboon contends that while early Thai intellectuals, such as Prince Damrong Rajanuphab, addressed the question of "Thai–ness" in terms of ways of living, habits, inclinations, ways of doing politics, art and architecture, Sulak is the first Thai to explore the nature of "Thai–ness" (Siamese) in a generic sense. (Review of *Kansangsan Satipanya Yang Thai* [The Making of Thai Intellectual Tradition] in the *Journal of the Siam Society*, vol. 75, 1978, p. 287. Also see *Thasana Thang Kansu'ksa Phu'a Khwam Pen Thai*. [Views on Liberated Thai Education] (Bangkok: Yuwawithaya, 1990). Vira suggests that Sulak overemphasizes the Theravada Buddhist dimension of Thai identity.

32. I have chosen to base my analysis on Sulak's important essay, "Crisis of Siamese Identity," occasional paper, Santi Pracha Dhamma Institute (Bangkok, 1989), delivered as the keynote address at a symposium on Thai identity at the Centre of Southeast Asian Studies, Monash University, Australia, September 8–9, 1989.

33. Ibid., pp. 1–2.

34. Ibid., p. 2.

35. Sulak refers here to King Ramkhamhaeng's famous 1291 stone inscription that describes an Asokan-like conception of Buddhist kingship. Dr. Piriya Krairiksh has theorized that the inscription was an 1850's forgery by King Mongkut. See John Hoslin, "Dr. Piriya Krairiksh. Breaking Down the Ivory Towers," *Sawasdee*, vol. 19 (February 1990), pp. 24–31. See also various articles in *The Ramkhamhaeng Controversy: Collected Papers*, ed. James R. Chamberlain (Bangkok: The Siam Society, 1991).

36. Sulak, "Crisis of Siamese Identity," p. 3. Sulak couples modern Thai nationalism with a chauvinistic Thai ethnic exclusiveness. As a Sino-Thai, Sulak is particularly sensitive to this point, because the Chinese in Thailand were seen as the principal outsiders.

37. Ibid., p. 5.

38. For a more detailed history of the Phibun era, see David K. Wyatt, *Thailand: A Short History* (New Haven, Conn.: Yale University Press, 1984), chapter 9. Although Wyatt gives a more balanced account of Phibun, he agrees with Sulak's position that with Phibun's reign the military became the ascendant power in the country.

39. Sulak, "Crisis of Siamese Identity," p. 7.

40. Ibid., p. 12. See also Sulak's essay, "The Religion of Consumerism," in *Siam in Crisis* (1990), pp. 175–187.

41. Phra Dhammapitaka (former titles, Debvedi, Rajavaramuni) has written one of the most noteworthy interpretations of Buddhist social ethics available in English. See his, "Foundations of Buddhist Social Ethics," in *Ethics, Wealth, and Salvation,* eds. Russell F. Sizemore and Donald K. Swearer, (Columbia: University of South Carolina Press, 1990), chapter 1. His magnum opus, *Buddhadhamma* (Bangkok: Chulalongkorn Mahawithayalai, 1982) is regarded as the finest textually grounded contemporary interpretation of Theravada doctrine in Thailand. An earlier edition of this volume has been translated by Grant A. Olson (State University of New York Press, 1995). Olson's 1989 Ph.D. dissertation at Cornell University was a study of Dhammapitaka ("A Person-centered Ethnography of Thai Buddhism: The Life of Phra Rajavaramuni"). Dhammapitaka has also written essays on Buddhist doctrine and numerous issues in contemporary Buddhist social ethics. Dhamma-pitaka's published work is more scholarly than either Sulak's or such popular contemporary monks as Pannananda.

42. Sulak's books and occasional papers are available through the Santi Pracha Dhamma Institute and the Thai Inter-Religious Commission for Development, both of which are under the Santirakoses-Nagapadipa Foundation (4753/5 Soi Wat Thongnopbhakun, Somdejchaophya Road, Bangkok 10600, Thailand, GPO 1960). The following is a partial list of Sulak's English-language writings on which this analysis was based:

Siam in Crisis, 2nd rev. ed. Bangkok: Thai Inter-Religious Commission for Development, 1990.
Siamese Resurgence. A Thai Voice on Asia and a World of Change. Bangkok Asian Cultural Forum on Development, 1985.
A Buddhist Vision for Renewing Society, Collected Articles By a Concerned Thai Intellectual. Bangkok: Tenway Publishing House, 1986.
Religion and Development. Bangkok: Thai Inter-Religious Commission for De-velopment, 1986.
A Social Engaged Buddhism. By A Controversial Siamese. Bangkok: Thai Inter-Religious Commission for Development, 1988.

Occasional Papers in the Santi Pracha Dhamma Institute Series:
"Buddhism and the Socio-Political Setting for the Future Benefit of Mankind," 1987.
"Buddhism and Social Value: Liberation, Religion and Culture," 1988.
"Buddhism in a World of Change," 1988.
"Building Trust Through Economic and Social Development: A Buddhist Perspective," 1988.
"Crisis of Siamese Identity" 1989.
"Development for Peace," 1987.
"Buddhist Understanding of Justice and Peace: Challenges and Responses to Asian Realities," 1988.

"Reconciliation and Religion: A Buddhist Reflection on Religion's Claims and Reality," 1989.

"The Religion of Consumerism," 1988.

"The Religious and Cultural Data Center for Education and Development. The Thai Inter-Religious Commission for Development" 1989.

"Siamese Literature and Social Liberation," 1988.

"Science, Technology and Spiritual Values. A Southeast Asian Approach to Modernization," 1987.

"Buddhism in a World of Change," in *The Path of Compassion, Writings on Socially Engaged Buddhism,* ed. Fred Eppsteiner. Berkeley, Calif.: Parallax Press, 1988.

Eleven of Sulak's essays have been edited by Tom Ginsburg and published under the title, *Seeds of Peace* (Berkeley, Calif.: Parallax Press, 1992). The volume also includes Sulak's lecture at Thammasat University in August 1991, which occasioned the ensuing warrant for Sulak's arrest.

Sulak's writings in Thai are much more extensive than his English publications.

43. In reviewing Sulak's *Kansangsan Satipanya Yang Thai* [The Making of the Thai Intellectual Tradition], Vira Somboon comments that this book, like most of Sulak's writings, is designed to be a provocative argument for further studies and discussions rather than a definitive exposé of a subject; *Journal of the Siam Society,* vol. 75 (1987), p. 286.

44. Sulak has spoken and written extensively on this theme, for example, *Thit Thang Mai Samrap Mahawithayalai Phu'a Puang Chon* [New Directions for University Education for the People] (Bangkok: Suksit Siam, 1988).

45. *A Socially Engaged Buddhism* (Bangkok: Thai Inter-Religious Commission for Development, 1989), p. 50. Italics mine.

46. For Burmese Buddhist reformism see Winston L. King, *In the Hope of Nibbana* (La Salle; Ill.: Open Court Press, 1962), and *A Thousand Lives Away* (Cambridge, Mass.: Harvard University Press, 1964), chapters 2 and 4. For Sri Lanka see Heinz Bechert, *Buddhismus, Staat und Gesellschaft in den Landen des Theravada-Buddhismus,* vol. I (Weisbaden: Otto Harrassowitz, 1967), pt. 2.

47. Sulak's view of the symbiotic relationship between spiritual cultivation (especially meditation) and social activism is partially indebted to the noted Vietnamese Zen monk, Thich Nhat Hanh, whose widely read book, *The Miracle of Mindfulness* was first published by Sulak in Bangkok during the Vietnam War years. It was given the subtitle, "A Handbook for Young Activists." Sulak also has a deep appreciation for the manner in which Thomas Merton, the noted Trappist monk, insisted on the necessary relationship between spiritual discipline and social activism.

48. For example, Vira Somboon points out that Sulak chooses to ignore important elements in the Thai intellectual tradition, such as Ayudhya and Chiangmai, in his reconstruction of an idealized past. *Journal of the Siam Society,* vol. 75 (1987), p. 290.

49. *Three Worlds According to King Ruang: A Buddhist Cosmology,* translated by and with an introduction and notes by Frank E. Reynolds and Mani B. Reynolds (Berkeley, Calif.: Asian Humanities Press, 1982).

50. Sulak Sivaraksa, "Thai Spirituality," in *A Socially Engaged Buddhism* (Bangkok: Thai Inter-Religious Commission for Development, 1988), p. 28.

51. Ibid., p. 30.

52. See Stanley J. Tambiah, *The Buddhist Saints of the Forest and the Cult of Amulets* (Cambridge: Cambridge University Press, 1984) for an extended discussion of the forest monk tradition with a particular emphasis on the Phra Acharn Mun tradition.

53. For a lengthy paper on Prince Damrong, see "The Life and Work of Prince Damrong Rajanubhab (1862–1943)," in Sulak Sivaraksa, *Siam in Crisis,* 2nd revised edition (1990), pp. 47–70.

54. "Crisis of Siamese Identity," p. 3.

55. "H.R.H. Prince Naris," in Sulak, *Siam in Crisis,* 2nd revised edition, (1990), p. 18.

56. "The presence of Buddhist sages . . . means the presence of wisdom, love and peace. . . . In Buddhism we believe that such a presence is very important. . . . [It] has an influence on society." "Buddhism and Non-Violence," in *A Buddhist Vision for Renewing Society* (Bangkok: Tienwan Publishing House, 1986), p. 110.

57. Sulak refers to Phra Dhammapitaka in several of his writings and has been influenced by many of Dhammapitaka's recent themes, for example, the "good friend" *(kalayanamitta)* and essential interrelationship between the pursuit of spiritual perfection and social action. Sulak has actively supported Buddhadasa for years. See *Siam in Crisis,* pp. 224–248.

58. See Buddhadasa Bhikkhu, *Dhammic Socialism,* ed. Donald K. Swearer (Bangkok: Thai Inter-Religious commission for Development, 1986).

59. My essay was completed before the publication of Sulak's most recent collections of essays, *Seeds of Peace* (Berkeley, Calif.: Parallax Press, 1992), appeared. A revised version of "Small 'b' Buddhism" appears in that volume.

60. Sulak's reconstruction of the Theravada Buddhist historical tradition might be interpreted as either selective or inconsistent (see this essay's concluding analysis). At times Sulak seems to attack unequivocally the cultural institutionalization of the Sangha. Yet, not unlike the traditional Theravada chroniclers, Sulak praises and often idealizes a wide variety of Dhammic heroes at particular times and places from the Buddha to King Asoka and from King Mongkut to Buddhadasa. Sulak is certainly restructuring the Buddhist tradition in the light of his own vision, but when is a history of a tradition not a history of interpretation?

61. *Reconciliation International,* (February 1986), p. 5. Also found in *A Socially Engaged Buddhism* (Bangkok: Thai Inter-Religious Commission for Development, 1988), pp. 181–185.

62. A lecture Sulak delivered on several occasions during his tour across the United States from January through April was titled, "Not To Exploit Ourselves or Others: The Essence of Buddhism." He ended his remarks with the following comment, "Working toward peace and social justice, not to exploit ourselves or others, to me, is the essence of Buddhism. We can revive this essential element of Buddhism by working together. . . . Even the dictators will eventually have to work with us. We all must become more humble."

63. Lecture at Swarthmore College, April 2, 1992.

64. Sulak, "Buddhism and Nonviolence," in *Seeds of Peace* (Berkeley, Calif.: Parallax Press, 1992), esp. pp. 85 ff.

65. In his English-language writings one of Sulak's most straightforward and unadorened exposition of the doctrinal core of Theravada Buddhism is found in "Buddhism and a World of Change," in *Siamese Resurgence* (Bangkok: Asian Cultural Form for Development, 1985), pp. 3–16.

66. Sulak, "Buddhism and Development—A Thai Perspective," in *TICD Newsletter,* (January–June, 1982), p. 32.

67. Sulak, "Buddhism in a World of Change: Politics Must be Related to Religion," in *The Path of Compassion: Writings on Socially Engaged Buddhism,* ed. Fred Eppsteiner, rev. ed. (Berkeley, Calif.: Parallax Press, 1988), p. 9.

68. The following exposition is adapted from Sulak, "A Working Paper on a Buddhist Perception of a Desirable Society in the Near Future," in *A Socially Engaged Buddhism,* pp. 49–83, and his introduction to *Buddhist Perceptions for Desirable Societies* (Bangkok: Thai Interreligious Commission for Development, 1993).

69. "Buddhism and Contemporary International Trends," In *Inner Peace, World Peace, Essays on Buddhism and Nonviolence,* ed. Kenneth Kraft, (Albany: State University of New York Press, 1992), p. 127.

70. Ibid., p. 130.

71. Sulak, "Buddhism and Nonviolence," in *Seeds of Peace,* p. 83.

72. "Buddhism and Contemporary International Trends," p. 131.

73. Sulak, *A Socially Engaged Buddhism,* p. 67.

74. Sulak, "Buddhism and Contemporary International Trends," p. 133.

75. Sulak, "Buddhism and Development—A Thai Perspective," p. 73.

76. Ibid., p. 34.

77. Sulak, "Buddhism and Human Rights." Unpublished manuscript, p. 10.

78. Ibid.

79. Ibid., p. 39.

80. *A Socially Engaged Buddhism,* pp. 75–76.

81. *A Buddhist Vision for Renewing Society,* p. 108.

82. "Christianity in the Reflection of Buddhism" in *A Socially Engaged Buddhism,* p. 141.

83. "Siamese Literature and Social Liberation" in *A Socially Engaged Buddhism,* p. 141.

84. "A Theravada Response to Christian Upaya." Unpublished paper read at the Fourth International Buddhist-Christian Dialogue Conference, Boston, Massachusetts (July 30–August 3, 1992), p. 13.

85. Ibid., p. 14.

86. Quoted by Sulak in "A Theravada Response . . . ", p. 6.

87. Ibid.

88. Ibid., p. 9.

89. Robert N., Bellah, *Religion and Progress in Modern Asia* (New York: Free Press, 1965), p. 78.

90. Ibid., p. 210.

91. In this connection it should be recalled that Sulak cites Buddhadasa as the fourth major turning point in Thai Buddhist intellectual history.

92. A contemporary of Buddhadasa, Pannananda, the abbot of Wat Cholaphrathan outside of Bangkok, has been allied with Buddhadasa for decades. His published books are interpreted by many Thais as a popularization of Buddhadasa's teachings.

93. See Richard Gombrich and Gananath Obeyesekere, *Buddhism Transformed, Religious Change in Sri Lanka* (Princeton, N.J.: Princeton University Press, 1988), chapters 6 and 7.

Bibliography

Sulak Sivaraksa, *A Buddhist Vision for Renewing Society.* Bangkok: Thai Interreligious Commission for Development, 1994.

When Loyalty Demands Dissent: Sulak Sivaraksa and the Charge of lèse majesté in Siam. Bangkok: Santi Pracha Dhamma Institute, 1993 (no editor is listed).

Sulak Sivaraksa, *Seeds of Peace*. Berkeley: Parallax Press, 1992.

———. *Siam in Crisis*, 2nd ed., Bangkok: Thai Interreligious Commission for Development, 1990.

———. *A Socially Engaged Buddhism*. Bangkok: Thai Interreligious Commission for Development, 1988.

———. "Buddhism in a World of Change," in *The Path of Compassion*, ed. Fred Eppsteiner. Berkeley: Parallax Press, 1988.

———. *Religion and Development*. Bangkok: Thai Interreligious Commission for Development, 1987.

———. *Siamese Resurgence. A Thai Buddhist Voice on Asia and a World of Change*. Bangkok: Asian Cultural Forum on Development, 1985.

Sulak Sivaraksa et al., eds., *Buddhist Perceptions for Desirable Societies*. Bangkok: Thai Interreligious Commission for Development, 1993.

Books and occasional papers by Sulak Sivaraksa can be ordered from:
Suksit Siam
113–115 Fuangnakhon Rd., Opp. Wat Rajabopit
Bangkok 10200
Thailand

Engaged Buddhist Leaders

Fig. 1. Dr. B. R. Ambedkar in London, ca. 1920, studying for the bar and his second doctorate. Courtesy: Eleanor Zelliot.

Fig. 2. Dr. A. T. Ariyaratne. Photo by George Bond.

Fig. 3. Buddhadasa Bhikkhu. Courtesy: Santikaro Bhikkhu.

Fig. 4. Sulak Sivaraksa. Courtesy: Donald Swearer.

Fig. 5. His Holiness the Fourteenth Dalai Lama of Tibet, Tenzing Gyatso, receiving an honorary Doctor of Humane Letters degree at Columbia University, April 1994. Credit: Sonam Zoksang.

Fig. 6. Venerable Bhiksuni Ta Tao (Voramai Kabilsingh) in her temple, Wat Songdharmakalyani, Nakhonpathom, Thailand. The Venerable Bhiksni Ta Tao was the first Thai woman to become a fully ordained Buddhist nun. She is now 87 years old (August 1994). Credit: Chatsumarn Kabilsingh.

Fig. 7. Thich Nhat Hanh in the mid-1960s. Courtesy: Parallax Press.

Fig. 8. Soka Gakkai International President Daisaku Ikeda with Nelson Mandela, Tokyo, 1990. Courtesy: SGI.

Buddhist Liberation Movement Activities

Fig. 1. Dr. B. R. Ambedkar and Mrs. Savita Ambedkar on the occasion of their conversion to Buddhism, October 14, 1956. Nearly 400,000 ex-Untouchables took refuge in Buddhism at this time. Courtesy: Eleanor Zelliot.

Fig. 2. Self-immolation of Thich Quang Duc, June 11, 1963. Saigon. Credit: AP/Wide World Photos.

Fig. 3. TBMSG Women's Literacy class. Pune. Credit: Karuna Trust Archives.

Fig. 4. A TBMSG gathering, under handmade tapistries depicting B. R. Ambedkar, the Buddha, and Sangharakshita. Credit: Karuna Trust Archives.

Fig. 5. The Mahavihar, Headquarters of TBMSG in Pune. Credit: Karuna Trust Archives.

Fig. 6. Visrantwadi, the Girl's Hostel in Pune, a TBMSG institution. Credit: Karuna Trust Archives.

Fig. 7. An ex-Untouchable factory worker and union leader is ordained as a Buddhist lay leader, or Dhammachari, in the TBMSG organization, as the English monk Sangharakshita looks on. Yeotmal, India, ca. 1984. Courtesy: Eleanor Zelliot.

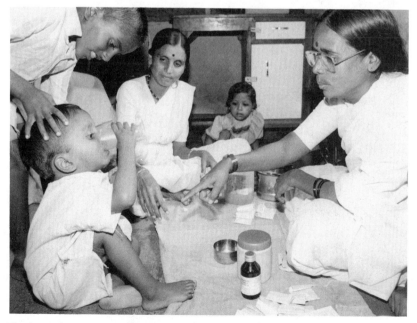

Fig. 8. A Bahujan Hitay Medical Clinic, TBMSG Program. Credit: Karuna Trust Archives.

Fig. 9. A. T. Ariyaratne addressing villagers and volunteers in the Sarvodaya Shramadana Movement, ca. 1993, Sri Lanka.Courtesy: George Bond.

Fig. 10. Buddhadasa Bhikkhu at Suan Mokkh, Chaiya, Thailand. Courtesy: Santikaro Bhikkhu.

Fig. 11. Sulak Sivaraksa leading discussions on engaged Buddhism, on one of his frequent lecture tours in the West. London, ca. 1984. Courtesy: Donald Swearer.

Fig. 12. Some of the 60,000 Buddhists who participated in the Kalachakra ceremony led by His Holiness the Dalai Lama in January 1995 in Mundgod, South India. The entrance gate inscription offers "Hearty Welcome to His Holiness the Dalai Lama, Nobel Peace Laureate." Credit: Sonam Zoksang.

Fig. 13. Tibetan refugees selling souvenirs at the 1995 Kalachakra ceremony in Mondgod, South India. Among the most popular items are photographs of H. H. The Dalai Lama and Dr. Babasaheb Ambedkar, whose ex-Untouchable followers have converted to Buddhism. Credit: Sonam Zoksang.

Fig. 14. *Mae ji* selling flowers and candles on *wanpra*, the Buddhist Sabbath, in Bangkok. The white-robed Thai *mae ji* are regarded merely as pious laywomen by monks and by other Thais. They are accorded no special status within the Buddhist community, although they devote their lives exclusively to religious practices. Credit: Chatsumarn Kabilsingh.

Fig. 15. Soka Gakkai International youth division members collect used radios to send to Cambodia. Tokyo, 1992. Credit: SGI.

7

Buddhist Women and the Nuns' Order in Asia

Nancy J. Barnes

Soon after Gautama the Buddha attained enlightenment under the Bodhi tree at Bodh Gaya in India, he established an order of male mendicants *(bhikshu sangha)*—men who were ready to renounce lay life so they could follow the Buddha's path of discipline and meditation and reach enlightenment and liberation from unhappiness. Somewhat later he founded an order of female mendicants *(bhikshuni sangha)* as well.[1] *Bhikshu* and *bhikshuni* were religious specialists, devoting full time to their personal spiritual development and the teaching of Buddhist doctrine *(dharma)* to lay people. For their food, clothing, and shelter they depended exclusively on the donations of the laity.

The order of *bhikshu* flourished in India for several hundred years after its foundation in the sixth century B.C.E., until Hindu revival and Muslim conquest drove Buddhism from India sometime after the twelfth century. Meanwhile, Buddhist missionaries had been carrying their religion to many other countries in Asia from about the third century B.C.E. on, and the *bhikshu sangha* was firmly established throughout Asia. It continues to flourish today in South and East Asia.

The *bhikshuni sangha* also flourished in India until the demise of Buddhism, and it, too, was transmitted to other countries in Asia—to Sri Lanka, China, and Burma. From China it was transmitted to Vietnam, Korea, and Japan. It eventually disappeared from both Sri Lanka and Burma, but it survives intact in China (the People's Republic, Taiwan, and Hong Kong) and in Korea and Vietnam. Today, there are several other Asian countries where Buddhism is a major religion, but where the *bhikshuni sangha* does not exist.[2]

In the twentieth century, some Buddhists in various countries have thought of trying to establish or reestablish the order of female mendicants.

Within the last ten years, efforts to fully establish the *bhikshuni sangha* throughout the world have become especially intense. Leading the effort are Asian women in Thailand and Sri Lanka, and some Western women who have converted to Buddhism. The leaders have as allies some of the most prominent members of the *bhikshu sangha,* most notably His Holiness the Dalai Lama of Tibet. But there are also many who oppose this movement.

Why should the *bhikshuni sangha* be established worldwide? Why do so many Buddhists oppose its establishment in their own countries? What are the issues involved in this controversy, and what is the outcome likely to be? These are the questions I take up in this chapter. The controversy cannot be adequately understood without knowing the history of the founding of the *bhikshuni sangha* in India in the sixth century B.C.E. as it is recounted in Buddhist canonical literature, so that is where I shall begin. Then, in order to clarify the important issues in the controversy, I will discuss the particular situations of Buddhist women in Sri Lanka, Thailand, and Tibet—the three traditions in which the question of the *bhikshuni sangha* is being most hotly debated at present. Buddhist women's lives in Burma (Myanmar) will be described as well, even though the *sangha* there is less involved in the debate over bhikshuni ordination. The Chinese *bhikshuni* tradition must also be examined, for it is from that tradition that the women's order would probably have to be propagated. Moreover, the Chinese women's *sangha* in Taiwan seems to be thriving brilliantly, and might serve as model and inspiration for Buddhist women elsewhere.

The Founding of the *Bhikshuni Sangha*

In the *Vinaya* (Books of Discipline for *Bhikshu* and *Bhikshuni*)[3] the founding of the order for women is described. It happened a few years after the men's order had been founded, according to the texts. Mahaprajapati, the aunt and foster mother of the Buddha, who had raised him after his mother's death, came to him and requested ordination as a female mendicant. She asked three times, but he refused her request each time. She departed, weeping.

Mahaprajapati returned home, cut off her hair as the *bhikshu* did, and donned saffron robes like those worn by the male mendicants. Several of her female relatives did the same, and together they walked many miles to where the Buddha was then staying. They arrived exhausted and covered with dust. Mahaprajapati stood outside the gate and wept. The young *bhikshu,* Ananda, who was a relative of both the Buddha and Mahaprajapati, saw her there, weeping, covered with dust, and with feet swollen from walking so far. He asked why she was crying, and she told him it was because the

Buddha would not allow women to leave home life and join his religious order. Ananda volunteered to intervene with the Buddha on behalf of the women, but the Buddha refused his requests, too. Ananda decided to try another tack. He asked the Buddha whether women were capable of attaining enlightenment, as men were, and the Buddha affirmed that women were fully capable of the highest spiritual accomplishments. Ananda then reminded the Buddha of all that Mahaprajapati had done for him, nurturing him after his mother had died. Finally he repeated his request that she and other women should be allowed to join the Buddha's religious order. The Buddha agreed, provided Mahaprajapati would accept these eight important rules, the eight *gurudharma:*

1. A *bhikshuni* who has been ordained even as long as a hundred years might rise, salute, and venerate every *bhikshu,* even one who had just been ordained that very day.

2. A *bhikshuni* must not reside for the rainy season in a place where there is no *bhikshu.*

3. Every half month the *bhikshuni* must ask the *bhikshu sangha* when a monk will be sent to give them the exhortation to keep the eight rules and when the *Uposatha* ceremony should be performed.

4. At the end of the rainy season retreat, *bhikshuni* should report any misdeeds committed before both the *bhikshu* and *bhikshuni sanghas.*

5. A *bhikshuni* who has transgressed an important rule must submit to formal discipline before both the *bhikshu* and *bhikshuni sanghas.*

6. After a female novice has trained for two years, she should seek ordination from both orders.

7. A *bhikshuni* must not abuse or revile a *bhikshu* in any way.

8. A *bhikshu* may admonish a *bhikshuni,* but no *bhikshuni* may admonish a *bhikshu.*

Mahaprajapati immediately agreed to observe the eight important rules and that constituted her ordination as a *bhikshuni.* Thus, the *bhikshuni sangha* was established.

Mahaprajapati's ordination was unique, since she was the first woman to be admitted into the Buddha's *sangha,* according to tradition. But for all women who have joined the *sangha* since her day, not only must they accept the eight important rules but they must be formally ordained by a quorum of both the *bhikshu* and *bhikshuni sanghas* in a ceremony known as *upasampada. Bhikshu,* too, are ordained in the same kind of ceremony, but their *upasampada* is carried out only in the presence of the *bhikshu sangha*. Men are not required to train in monastic discipline for a full two years as probationary students before admission to the order, as women are required to do. All the details of the ordination rituals for both men and women are recorded in the *Vinaya*.[4]

A novice *bhikshuni* requests two fully ordained *bhikshuni* to act as her instructors during the period of her training and to prepare her for her own ordination. (A male novice has two *bhikshu* instructors who prepare him for ordination.) On the day chosen for her ordination, the novice goes with her two instructors to present herself before the chapter of *bhikshuni*. There must be a quorum of at least ten *bhikshuni* present to confer ordination. The novice is asked a series of questions about her fitness for ordination. Then she is presented with robes and almsbowl, which are the basic equipment and the visible symbols of her religious vocation. She vows to wear only the fivefold robes of the *bhikshuni,* to live by begging her food with her almsbowl, and to use only the medications prescribed in the *Vinaya* in case of illness. Then, if she is deemed acceptable by the assembled chapter of *bhikshuni,* her ordination as the newest member of the order is proclaimed, and she is instructed as to all the rules she must observe as a *bhikshuni,* the *Pratimoksha* rules of the *Vinaya* that will regulate her life thenceforth. The number of these rules varies, from 290 to 380, depending on which school's *Vinaya* is used. Monks have somewhat shorter lists of rules to follow, but the rules are similar, often identical, for both men and women.

After she has been ordained by the *bhikshuni sangha,* she must then present herself before a quorum (at least ten members) of the local chapter of *bhikshu* and go through the entire ceremony again, after which she is recognized as a *bhikshuni* who has received the double ordination from both *sanghas.*

The historicity of this account of the founding of the *bhikshuni sangha,* that establishes a hierarchical relationship between the *bhikshu* and *bhikshuni sanghas,* with the women permanently subordinated to the men, has been questioned recently by several scholars. But, although the story told in the *Vinaya* and in other texts of the Buddhist canon of scriptures probably was created by monks some time after the Buddha's death, it does represent a very ancient tradition about how the women's order began, and it is accepted by most members of the Buddhist *sangha*. The eight important rules remain part of the heritage of the modern *bhikshuni.*

Buddhist Women in Sri Lanka: the *Dasa Sil Matavo*

In the third century B.C.E., both the *bhikshu* and *bhikshuni sanghas* were established in Sri Lanka by ordained men and women from India.

They established the Theravada school of Buddhism (School of the Elders) on the island.[5] It was the queen of Sri Lanka who requested that the *bhikshuni* ordination be instituted in her country and who became the first Sinhala *bhikshuni*. A residence for nuns was built for the former queen and the other Sinhala women who were ordained with her, and *bhikshuni* were an important part of Buddhism in the island kingdom for hundreds of years. Inscriptions from Sri Lanka show that the *bhikshuni sangha* was thriving until the eleventh century.[6]

But in the eleventh century Buddhism was nearly eradicated from Sri Lanka as a result of a long period of war and political instability that ended with the conquest of the land by the Chola king of southern India. So few *bhikshu* remained that a quorum could not be summoned to ordain new members of the *sangha*. Apparently the *bhikshuni sangha* was equally devastated. Both the *bhikshu* and *bhikshuni sangha* had been established by Sri Lankan Theravadin clerics in Burma by this time, however.[7] The king of Sri Lanka was able, therefore, to import monks of the Theravada ordination lineage from Burma to reinstate the *bhikshu* ordination in his country in the late eleventh century. It seems there was no effort to do the same for the *bhikshuni sangha*. There are no surviving records, in fact, of the fate of the *bhikshuni,* for the Buddhist chronicles of the period do not mention them at all. The women's order simply disappeared from Sinhala history.

Not until the end of the nineteenth century was the institution of female renunciants seen again in Sri Lanka.[8] It happened as Sri Lanka was emerging from a long period of colonization by European powers (Portuguese, Dutch, and British) that had demoralized Sinhala Buddhists and undermined their institutions. Buddhists began to resist domination by Western Christians in the nineteenth century and set out to restore and to reinvigorate their religion.[9] An important part of this Buddhist revival was women's efforts to make a place for themselves in the religion.

It was laywomen and laymen who led the Buddhist revival in Sri Lanka, and they realized that neither women's spiritual aspirations nor their educational needs were being addressed by existing Buddhist monastic institutions. Some laywomen took upon themselves the ten precepts that the most pious Buddhist devotees had traditionally taken up since the time of the Buddha.[10] But, in addition, they shaved their heads like the ancient *bhikshuni,* they put on saffron and white robes, and they lived together in religious communities *(aramaya)*. The color symbolism they chose for their dress—the saffron of the fully ordained monastic combined with the white of the pious layperson—was intended to show that they had chosen a new status for themselves that was neither that of the ordinary layperson nor that of a fully ordained *bhikshuni*. These first "ten-precept women," or *dasa sil matavo,* opened schools in their religious communities, to educate young girls—something that ancient *bhikshuni* are not known to have done. Sudharmacari (Catherine de Alwis)[11] founded one of the most important communities of *dasa sil matavo* in 1907 in Kandy, the Sudharmacari Upasikaramaya, with the support of many Buddhist laypeople.[12] The community and its school for young girls remains active today, and Sudharmacari and her community have been models for other Sinhala women desiring to go forth from home life into a spiritual path. The spiritual path followed by the *dasa sil matavo* is, however, distinct from that of the ancient *bhikshuni,* and it is so by design. A *dasa sil mata* is still a laywoman in her own eyes and in the eyes of the *sangha* and of the state. Because of this, the *dasa sil matavo* communities are not subject to the supervision of state or *sangha.*

At present there are more than two thousand *dasa sil matavo* in Sri Lanka. Many now live alone, scattered about over the island.[13] But many others live together in small communities. They teach children, counsel laypersons who request their help, sometimes minister to the sick, chant Buddhist scriptures for the laity, and assist in Buddhist religious ceremonies.[14] Most of their energies are directed toward religious observances and service to the lay community, but many of them also spend a certain amount of time each day meditating to develop themselves spiritually and to perfect their understanding so that they can ultimately attain enlightenment and liberation as the Buddha did. There is a certain tension between the responsibilities to the laity that the *dasa sil matavo* have accepted, which take a good deal of their time, and the powerful desire of some to follow the true renunciant's vocation and devote all their time to meditation. Those who aspire most strongly to the renunciant's vocation may take up residence in one of the secluded forest retreats on the island, where life is quite austere but where they can meditate without being distracted by other obligations.[15]

The cleric who cultivates purity by devoting his life to meditation is the religious ideal that the Buddhist laity of Sri Lanka look up to and respect most. Modern *dasa sil matavo* who live a pure life, even though they are not fully ordained members of the Buddhist *sangha,* have been greatly respected by laypeople, and they have been supported by donations of food, clothing, shelter, and medications, just as the *bhikshu* have been. But laypeople do not make gifts to *bhikshu* merely out of a spirit of generosity. Gifts given to members of the Buddhist *sangha* are believed to earn merit for the donor, merit that will lead to better rebirths in the future and eventually to liberation from unhappiness and from the cycle of rebirth *(nirvana).* Buddhist scriptures make it clear that gifts to a *bhikshu* or a *bhikshuni* earn such merit for the donor. But the scriptures do not promise such great merit to those who give gifts to pious laypeople. The *dasa sil matavo* are not *bhikshuni* and do not pretend to be. Their status is "in-

between," higher than that of ordinary lay Buddhists but not institutionalized like that of the *bhikshu.* When the *dasa sil matavo* first appeared in
the late nineteenth and early twentieth centuries, they were in the van-
guard of the Buddhist revival in Sri Lanka and were enthusiastically supported by the well-educated, affluent, urban laity of the cities of Colombo
and Kandy. As a group, they were highly respected, and some individual
dasa sil matavo, like Sudharmacari of the Kandy *aramaya* were extraordinary women who were deeply venerated. Most of the *dasa sil matavo* came
from an urban elite background themselves, up to the time of Sri Lankan
independence from British rule in 1948.[16]

Since independence, the majority of women who become *dasa sil
matavo* come from less affluent rural families. As a group they are not as
well educated as their predecessors in the first half of the twentieth century.
Their families do not always support their decision to renounce marriage
and to lead autonomous lives. Today's *dasa sil matavo* are neither as well
respected as their predecessors nor are they as well supported economically.[17] Monks are far better supported, and this is true both because the
laity regard them with greater respect, and also because the *bhikshu's*
position in Sinhala society is institutionalized. The *bhikshu sangha* enjoys
government recognition and support and its members have recognized legal
status. In every respect, by contrast, the *dasa sil mata*'s position is irregular
and indeterminate. If the *dasa sil matavo* were to be fully ordained, and
converted into an order of *bhikshuni,* thus restoring the *bhikshuni sangha*
to the country from which it disappeared eight hundred years ago, these
Buddhist women could achieve the social, economic, and educational security that the *bhikshu sangha* now enjoys. The restoration of the *bhikshuni
sangha* has been heatedly debated during the last thirty years, in government circles, in the *bhikshu sangha,* and among the *dasa sil matavo* themselves. Who is it who would like to see the saffron-clad *bhikshuni* once
again treading the roads and paths of Sri Lanka?

The government has sponsored a feasibility report on the restoration
of the *bhikshuni sangha* and has attempted to register the *dasa sil matavo*
and unite them in government-supported residences.[18] Further education
in Buddhist doctrine and scriptures has been made available to them, and
those who wish may sit for examinations along with the monks. Some
prominent Buddhist lay people have also lent their support to the effort to
restore the *bhikshuni sangha* to Sri Lanka. So have a few leaders of the
bhikshu sangha.

But most of the *dasa sil matavo* themselves do not want full ordination as *bhikshuni,* because it would mean institutionalized subordination to
the *bhikshu sangha* and supervision by the government. The *bhikshuni*
would have to accept the eight important rules, and would have to adhere

to the 311 regulations of the Theravada *Vinaya* for *bhikshuni*. At present, the *dasa sil matavo* have autonomy, they live without the interference of monks in their affairs, and they are able to follow a religious life that conforms to their own ideals. Their position in Sinhala society may be less secure than the monks' and they may be less honored than the *dasa sil matavo* of the earlier twentieth century, but laypeople still respect them as religious practitioners and functionaries, and they are honored above ordinary lay people. For the sake of their independence, then, most *dasa sil matavo* prefer to retain their present status, as a new kind of Buddhist woman renunciant.[19]

Some *dasa sil matavo* do favor the restoration of the *bhikshuni sangha*. Among the female renunciants of Sri Lanka there are a handful of Western women who have taken the ten precepts. They, and a few of the Sinhala *dasa sil matavo*, are in the forefront of the prorestoration effort. Most of the Western women have renounced worldly life in order to follow the path of meditation—in contrast to the majority of Sinhala *dasa sil matavo*, who follow the path of devotion and service.[20] Most articulate of this group of Western renunciants has been the Venerable Ayya Khema, the German-born *dasa sil mata* who founded Parappaduwa Nuns' Island in Sri Lanka.[21] She believes that the absence of the women's *sangha* denies Theravada women the opportunity to fully realize their religious aspirations, and she suggests that women could contribute much more to Sinhala society as *bhikshuni* than they can in their present capacity. Since it was not possible to receive *bhikshuni* ordination in Sri Lanka, Ayya Khema made the decision to take ordination in the Chinese lineage. In 1988, she was among the two hundred women ordained at the Hsi Lai Temple in Los Angeles. Five Sinhala *dasa sil matavo* were also ordained in this ceremony, having been invited by Sinhala sponsors to do so. But when the five returned as *bhikshuni* to Sri Lanka they returned to their original residences rather than forming a new *bhikshuni aramaya* as their sponsors had hoped they would. They have not changed their life-style, and at least two of them continue to wear the yellow and white robes of the *dasa sil mata* rather than the saffron of the *bhikshuni*. None of them wants to draw special attention to herself. They say that some monks vehemently oppose their ordination and write letters to the newspapers about it.[22] Venerable Bhikshuni Ayya Khema, too, was criticized in Sri Lanka for having taken ordination. She now resides primarily in Australia and Germany and spends little time in Sri Lanka.[23]

Opinions about the restoration of the *bhikshuni sangha* vary within the *bhikshu sangha*. Somewhat surprisingly, a great many monks, especially the younger ones, think favorably of the *dasa sil matavo* as Buddhist practitioners and would agree to their ordination as *bhikshuni*.[24] On the other hand, some of the best-known, most influential monks in Sri Lanka vehemently oppose the reestablishment of the *bhikshuni sangha,* which died a natural death so long ago. They assert that since there are no *bhikshuni* of the Theravada ordination lineage anywhere in the world, who could join with a quorum of Theravada *bhikshu* to ordain new *bhikshuni,* it is impossible to resuscitate the women's *sangha.* It will have to wait until Maitreya, the next Buddha, is born in this world.[25]

Thai Women in Buddhism: the *Mae Ji*

There never were any *bhikshuni* in Thailand. Buddhism penetrated most of Southeast Asia during the first centuries C.E., but there is no evidence that any *bhikshuni* were ordained in that early period. It was probably in the eleventh century C.E. that Theravada Buddhism reached Burma from Sri Lanka, and the *bhikshu* and *bhikshuni* ordination lineages were established there. Inscriptions indicate that there were still *bhikshuni* in Burma in the year 1279. It was apparently from Burma that the Theravada *bhikshu sangha* was introduced into Thailand in the thirteenth century, but the *bhikshuni sangha* seems never to have been transmitted.

As long ago as the seventeenth century, however, European travelers to Thailand were mentioning shaven-headed women in white robes who lived within the compounds of some Buddhist temples. These were the *mae ji,* women—often elderly—who had taken on themselves five or eight of the ten vows of the pious lay devotee and who shaved their heads and donned special white robes to mark themselves off from the rest of the population. As many as ten thousand are to be found in Thailand today. They are very different from the *dasa sil matavo* of Sri Lanka.[26]

An "order" of ten-precept women was deliberately founded and organized in Sri Lanka to answer the needs of aspiring and progressive Buddhist women for a religious vocation. The founders and patrons of *dasa sil matavo* communities were educated people with sound knowledge of their religion, their country's history, and also of Western civilization. Significantly, the patrons were quite generous in their financial support of the new Buddhist women's communities.

Thai *mae ji* have never been organized, and have received very little financial or moral support from anyone. *Mae ji* are women who have felt, individually, the desire to break their ties to worldly life and devote themselves to pious activities. They are scattered throughout the country, and they vary greatly in their practices and in their religious commitment. Many live in temple compounds with the permission of the abbot and receive minimal maintenance in exchange for cooking and cleaning for the monks. Some receive some support from relatives, and some must beg to subsist. Many are elderly without any families to help them. *Mae ji* do not receive many donations since they are not considered "fields of merit" as monks are—that is, gifts given to *mae ji* are not believed to accumulate much merit for the donor. Because *mae ji* are not ordained they have no religious status and no special status in society accruing from their religious activities. Many monks consider them a nuisance, and they are kept out of some temples. The most fortunate live in "nunneries" where they can organize their lives and their economic resources more effectively. *Mae ji* come mostly from poor farming families, and some 60 percent of them have had less than seven years of schooling. Most Thai monks come from a similar background, but they receive an education in their temples, the temples are the beneficiaries of laypeople's donations, and every monk has a respectable legal and social status because of his membership in the *sangha. Mae ji* can claim none of these benefits. Instead they live lives of hardship and poverty.[27]

The *mae ji* are a group with serious problems. However ambiguous the position of Sri Lanka's *dasa sil matavo,* they are a productive, socially beneficial group, and that makes them very different from the *mae ji.* The *mae ji* are not yet in a position to serve society religiously or socially. Because of their social backgrounds and lack of education, few *mae ji* have even thought of trying to improve their situation. The Thai government, which acts as protector of the religion, and religious reformers see the *mae ji* as a social group that needs assistance, and they are trying to make some fundamental changes in their lives. An Institute of Thai Mae Ji was formed by a group of senior monks in 1969 under the patronage of the Queen of Thailand, with the goals of uniting and organizing all *mae ji,* improving their status, providing religious instruction, and contributing to their social well-being. More than 4,000 *mae ji* have been registered so far, and religious education has been offered to them at the Institute in Bangkok. The *mae ji* themselves agree that education is the foundation on which their future development depends. But they also feel that the Thai government must fully recognize them now as women who have received the precepts from a *bhikshu* and are thus ordained. This would give them the dignity of a formal religious status, which would raise public awareness and support of them. That, they say, would be the essential first step in improving the situation of the *mae ji.*[28]

The *mae ji* have not aspired to ordination as *bhikshuni.* They are women who made individual decisions to lead a life of religious devotion, without ambition for a higher status. But in modern Thailand the *mae ji's* life is the only religious vocation available to women, and it is not attractive to better-educated women from the cities. Some of these women would like to see the *bhikshuni sangha* introduced into Thailand, so that a religious vocation with dignity and legitimacy would be available to Thai women.

The most vocal proponents of *bhikshuni* ordination in Thailand today are the mother-daughter team of Venerable Voramai Kabilsingh (Bhikshuni Ta Tao), founder of the first temple in Thailand for Buddhist women in Nakhonpathom province, and Dr. Chatsumarn Kabilsingh, a professor at Thammasat University in Bangkok. Voramai Kabilsingh, who had been a schoolteacher as a young woman, married and had a daughter. As she grew older her interest in religion deepened, as did her awareness of social problems in her country. When she was in her forties, she shaved her head and asked for the eight precepts from a respected *bhikshu* in Bangkok. Instead of putting on the white robe of a *mae ji,* however, she adopted a light yellow robe, to distinguished herself both from the *mae ji* and from the *bhikshu.* A year later, in 1957, she purchased property in Nakhonpathom province, near Bangkok, and established Watra Songdharma Kalyani there, a residence for Buddhist women. She also opened a school and orphanage for children and a press for publishing a monthly magazine. For the last thirty-six years the Venerable Voramai has carried out many projects to help laypeople in need. She also holds regular religious services at her temple on weekends for her many disciples. In 1971, Voramai learned that it would be possible to receive ordination as a *bhikshuni* from the Chinese *sangha,* and she was ordained Bhikshuni Ta Tao in Taiwan that year.[29]

The Venerable Vorami's daughter, Chatsumarn Kabilsingh, shares her mother's deep commitment to women's Buddhism. Chatsumarn studied Buddhism at universities in India and Canada, as well as at home in Thailand. She has become one of the best-known advocates for the *mae ji,* for the establishment of the *bhikshuni sangha* in Theravada Buddhist countries, and for women's leadership in Buddhism. In addition to her teaching at Thammasat University and her publication of several articles and books, she has organized international conferences on women in Buddhism. In 1984 she began to publish the *Newsletter on International Buddhist Women's Activities.* It now has subscribers in thirty-eight countries.

Chatsumarn Kabilsingh has remained a laywoman, but she actively promotes the establishment of the *bhikshuni sangha* in Thailand. Like Ayya Khema in Sri Lanka, she believes that Buddhist women should have the opportunity to fulfill their spiritual aspirations completely, and that is only possible if they can be ordained as *bhikshuni.* For it is the institution of the *sangha* that would provide women with real security and the opportunity to win the respect of the Thai laity. Dr. Kabilsingh does not foresee a *sangha* of *bhikshuni* who would devote their time exclusively to meditation, however, or to religious observances. *Bhikshuni* would be able to work to solve some of the country's and the world's horrendous social problems, with the force of the venerable *sangha* behind them. Thai monasteries offer many services to men and boys: they provide religious and practical education, and they are places where men can go for periods of retreat. Thai women have no such places to turn to. *Bhikshuni*, in their own "nunneries," could educate girls and women (as Venerable Voramai Kabilsingh does at Watra Songdharma Kalyani) and help and counsel women with family or personal problems. Chatsumarn Kabilsingh, like her mother the Venerable Voramai and like the Venerable Ayya Khema in Sri Lanka, believes that *bhikshuni* should engage in social services and that they will want to.[30]

The majority of Thai monks oppose the establishment of the *bhikshuni sangha* in their country. Most Thai monks come from rural areas and are not well educated.[31] They often hold and pass on traditional negative views of women. They are satisfied with the absence of any *sangha* of Buddhist women. When Voramai Kabilsingh put on pale yellow robes and opened her Watra Songdharma Kalyani for Buddhist women, she was challenged by *sangha* and civil authorities for usurping privileges reserved for the *bhikshu sangha*. An investigation by the council of Elders, the highest governing body of the Thai *sangha*, exonerated her, and she had no further difficulties with the government. But when Voramai was ordained as a *bhikshuni* in the Chinese lineage, the Thai *sangha* refused to verify her ordination. In her own country, therefore, she remains a Chinese, not a Theravada, *bhikshuni*.[32]

Some of the younger, educated Thai monks are changing the old negative attitudes toward women and toward the *bhikshuni sangha*, however. In the future these men will be the leaders of the *sangha*. The Thai *sangha* is hierarchically organized and centrally administered under the supervision of the government (unlike the *sangha* in Sri Lanka). Decisions of the Council of Elders determine what the entire *sangha* does. Thus, when younger monks who are favorably disposed toward the *bhikshuni* issue sit on the Council, the time may be ripe for the establishment of the Buddhist order for women.[33]

It will be necessary for the laity in Theravada countries to accept the *bhikshuni sangha*, too, for without their respect and their economic support the *sangha* cannot survive. The laypeople of Theravadin Southeast Asia have no experience with fully ordained Buddhist women. The idea that an order of ordained women could be introduced is unacceptable to many, especially to those who live in the villages of rural Thailand. Proponents of the *bhikshuni sangha* argue that the best way to win over the laity to the idea of *bhikshuni* is for Thai women to be ordained in the Chinese lineage, and then to gain the respect of the people by the purity of their practice.[34]

Bhikshuni ordination is something that a few, educated Thai women may aspire to. It is not something that *mae ji* have imagined for themselves. The problem of the *mae ji*'s situation is a different matter from the question of the establishment of the *bhikshuni sangha* in Thailand. At some future time *mae ji* may wish to be ordained. But they have other needs that must be met now. Above all they need to receive a basic education and they need adequate religious instruction and training in the precepts and other disciplinary rules they are to follow. After a number of them have been well trained, they will be ready to teach and lead others. And then they may wish to seek full ordination as *bhikshuni*.[35]

A few *mae ji* have already aspired to *bhikshuni* ordination. In 1988 and 1989, two *mae ji* and one Thai laywoman were ordained as novices by a Theravada *bhikshu* in the United States. Novice ordination is the first step in the ordination process for women and for men. It can be followed after two years (for women) by full *bhikshuni* ordination. Although these women were ordained as novices in the Theravada tradition, when they seek *bhikshuni* ordination, they will have to be ordained by Chinese, Korean, or Vietnamese *bhikshuni,* just as the Venerable Voramai Kabilsingh, the Venerable Ayya Khema, and the five *dasa sil matavo* from Sri Lanka were. That is because there is no quorum of Theravada nuns who could ordain them. Once again the *bhikshu sangha* will have to decide whether to recognize them as Theravada *bhikshuni.* What will they decide?

Bhikshuni and *Thila–shin* in Burma

Burma (now called Myanmar) was the only country in Southeast Asia to which the *bhikshuni* ordination lineage was transmitted, as far as is known. *Bhikshuni* and *bhikshu* brought the Theravada lineage from Sri Lanka to Burma in the eleventh century c.e., probably, as mentioned earlier. It is known from inscriptional evidence that *bhikshuni* were still active in Burma late in the thirteenth century. They are not found, however, in modern Burma; sometime after the thirteenth century the order disappeared. They were the last Theravadin *bhikshuni* in the world.

In modern Burma there are large numbers of eight- or ten-precept women called *thila–shin,* however. *Thila-shin* means those who keep the precepts, or those who observe the Buddhist code of moral discipline. In 1961 it was estimated that there were more than eight thousand *thila-shin* in Burma. The precepts they observe are the same ones kept by the ten-precept *dasa sil matavo* of Sri Lanka and the eight-precept *mae ji* of Thailand.[36] *Thila-shin* have doubtless been around for a long time.

The Burmese clergy have probably been the most honored and respected clergy in the world. The *thila-shin,* too, even though they are not fully ordained *bhikshuni,* enjoy a level of respect and support exceeding that given to Thai *mae ji* and even to the *dasa sil matavo* of Sri Lanka. In the nineteenth century King Mindon invited two famous *thila-shin* to his court to teach religion to his queens. At the present time there are a number of renowned teachers and scholars among the *thila-shin* of Sagaing, Mingun, and Rangoon.[37]

Thila-shin study religion in the "nunneries" *(gyaung)* where they live together. Some have excelled at their studies and have gained great renown. Most live more retiring lives in the *gyaung* and follow a strict routine of devotions, meditation, study, and collecting alms. They also spend much of their time preparing and serving food and performing menial tasks for any monks who live nearby. These are meritorious acts, and *thila-shin*'s lives center on making merit. For, although they themselves are regarded as fields of merit by the laity, and they are usually adequately supported by gifts of food, they consider themselves less pure than the monks and there-fore ceaselessly try to improve themselves by making merit.[38] Monks, as the "purer vessels," receive far more lavish donations from the laity than *thila-shin* do. Like the laity, *thila-shin* serve the *bhikshu*. (*Mae ji* do the same in Thailand, for the same reason, to make merit for themselves.)

The legal status of the *thila-shin* is that of laywomen. They can own property and handle money, for example, unlike monks. But with regard to civil status, they are considered religious persons and like the monks they are not allowed to vote in elections.[39] They are fields of merit, but they are not nearly so well supported or respected as the monks are. They are "in-between" clergy and laity, they do not have a secure religious status. Would they like to trade their present position for a status equivalent to the *bhikshu*'s, that of a fully ordained *bhikshuni*?

Other problems preoccupy Burmese monks and *thila-shin* at the moment because of the political situation in their country. As far as I know, *thila-shin* have not spoken out on the issue of restoration of the *bhikshuni sangha* to their country, as some women in Thailand and Sri Lanka have. A few Western women have become *thila-shin* and have expressed some dissatisfaction with the difference in status between religious women and men in Burma.[40] But at a 1992 conference on engaged Buddhism in Thai-land, when the possibility of ordaining Theravada women as *bhikshuni* was raised, a Burmese *bhikshu* asserted that women should not be ordained because the Buddha had predicted that the women's order would not endure.[41]

Tibetan Religious Women: the *Ani*

There is some disagreement over whether *bhikshuni* ordination ever existed in Tibet, but if it ever did the lineage was broken long ago. There were no fully ordained *bhikshuni* in any of the Tibetan Buddhist schools until the 1980s when eight Tibetan women took ordination in Hong Kong with the permission of their Tibetan spiritual teachers *(lamas)*.[42] Several Western women who have been trained in the Tibetan tradition have also taken ordination in the Chinese or Korean lineages. Now many Tibetan women express interest in being ordained as *bhikshuni,* and many of the most prominent Tibetan *lamas* are encouraging them to do it, led by His Holiness the Dalai Lama. The possibilities for women of the Tibetan tradition are much different, therefore, from those available to women from Theravada Buddhist countries.

All the schools of Tibetan Buddhism belong to the Mahayana tradition. Mahayana Buddhism—the name means the "Great Vehicle" that everyone can ride to enlightenment and liberation—was a movement that appeared in India around the beginning of the Common Era. It was soon carried by missionaries to China and thence to the other countries of East Asia— Korea, Japan, and Vietnam. Missionaries also took it to Tibet in the seventh and eighth centuries.[43] At the present time the world's Buddhists belong either to the Mahayana (in North and East Asia) or to the Theravada (in South and Southeast Asia). There has been antagonism between the two kinds of Buddhism. Today, most Theravada Buddhists believe that Mahayana has completely corrupted the Buddha's original teachings. That is one of the major reasons for unwillingness of Theravada monks in Thailand, Burma, and Sri Lanka to recognize as legitimate the ordination of Theravada women in the Chinese lineage: it belongs to the Mahayana. No such problem exists for Tibetans, for they, like the Chinese, are Mahayana Buddhists.

Although there was no *bhikshuni sangha* in Tibet, for centuries there have been women who have abandoned ordinary lay life and have taken the precepts. Most Tibetan renunciant women have taken not just five or eight or ten precepts, however, but thirty-six, and they are regarded as novice nuns. Since higher ordination was not possible in Tibet, these women remained novices permanently. In Tibet before 1959 it is estimated that there were over twelve thousand female novices. At present, they probably number more than two thousand.[44] They are called *ani,* which means "aunt," or *tsunma* or *chola,* which are more respectful terms.[45]

Ani have long been a familiar presence in Tibetan society. But they have never had a status comparable to the monks and *lamas.* Attitudes toward *ani* have been ambivalent, in fact, for, although many Tibetans believe that all women have keener minds than men, they also think that women's higher intelligence gets them into trouble and they are easily distracted from religious practice. Women who do become *ani* are often thought to have chosen that life because they were failures as daughters or wives. *Ani* themselves say they chose the religious life because they felt a strong vocation for it.[46]

In Tibet, and now in exile communities in India and Nepal, *ani* often lived together in nunneries. In the nunneries they were taught to read the

What about ... women in trouble

scriptures, but higher education, such as the monks enjoyed in the great monasteries, was available to very few of them. In Tibetan Buddhism, erudition and mastery of philosophy and logic are enormously respected. Without higher education *ani* could never attain positions of leadership in the religious hierarchy. The nunneries were even headed by male abbots, who were more learned than the women.[47]

Inevitably, nunneries were and are poor places compared to the residences for male religious. Pious laypeople preferred to endow the monasteries richly, for they were full of knowledgeable and accomplished *lamas*. Male religious were also the ones called upon by the laity to perform rituals, for which they received donations. Individual *ani,* like monks, were normally supported by their relatives, but monks also enjoyed additional donations from laypeople who sought their services and thus the monasteries became wealthy. Because the women's communities were poor they could not afford to pay *lamas* to come to them to teach them philosophy and logic; because they were not learned they could not improve themselves or their religious status.[48] Thus, much like the precept-keeping women of Southeast Asia, they were stuck on a low rung on the religious ladder in their country, even though they were recognized as ordained women.

During the past ten years, in the Tibetan communities in exile, the *ani*'s opportunities have improved, because many of the high *lamas* have realized that women's religious aspirations and their talents were not being adequately attended to. His Holiness the Dalai Lama and some other high *lamas* have ordained more women as *ani,* have trained them, and have encouraged their disciples to seek ordination as *bhikshuni.* There is now widespread interest, especially among the younger *ani,* in the higher ordination. Their interest has been stimulated also by the presence of many Western *ani* and *bhikshuni* in their midst. Western converts to the Tibetan traditions have often been outspoken in their championing of equality of opportunities in religion for women. Tibetan women have now begun to speak out as well.[49]

His Holiness the Dalai Lama stated publicly in 1985 that Tibetan *ani* could take *bhikshuni* ordination from the Chinese lineage. Later he said he was also investigating the Vietnamese tradition, which may be closer to the Tibetan. The Dalai Lama's government of Tibet in exile will give its recognition to a *bhikshuni* ordination lineage eventually, but, for the sake of credibility and in the hope of the future agreement of Theravada leaders, careful preparations for this step are being undertaken. Several issues must be investigated and resolved before a decision is made: Has the transmission of *bhikshuni* ordination remained unbroken? Has the ordination ever been performed only by *bhikshu,* with no senior *bhikshuni* present, and if so could such ordination be valid? Is it acceptable for modern ordinations to be held presided over by *bhikshu* and *bhikshuni* from several different traditions?[50]

The momentum for the institution of the *bhikshuni sangha* in the Tibetan tradition is much stronger than in the Theravada tradition. Obviously that is because the foremost Tibetan religious leaders are in the forefront of the effort.

Taiwan and the Chinese *Bhikshuni* Tradition

In 433 or 434 C.E. the first double ordination of *bhikshuni* was performed in China. Although many Chinese women had wanted to become *bhikshuni* before that date, it had not been possible to conduct the double ordination—an ordination with the requisite quorum of ordained *bhikshuni* and *bhikshu* present—because there were no *bhikshuni* in China. Women were, nonetheless, ordained by convocations of monks only, which is allowed by the *Vinaya* rules in places where the women's order does not yet exist. Toward the end of the fourth century C.E., the king of Sri Lanka sent an envoy to China, which was followed by further missions and trading expeditions in the fifth century. In 429 a small group of Sinhala *bhikshuni* arrived on a merchant's ship, and in 433 or 434 a second group arrived. A quorum of ten *bhikshuni* was finally at hand and a full double ordination, with Sinhala nuns and Chinese and foreign monks presiding, could at last be carried out. The Chinese *bhikshuni* ordination lineage was thus established under the auspices of nuns from Sri Lanka.[51] The Chinese sources do not mention the Buddhist school to which the Sinhala women belonged, and Sinhala records do not mention the incident at all. Theravada Buddhism has always dominated Sri Lanka, although some other Buddhist sects were also active in Sri Lanka in the fifth century.[52] It is probable that the Sinhala *bhikshuni* did belong to the Theravada, but it cannot be proven.

The Theravada *Vinaya* books never reached China, however, nor did that Buddhist school ever have any influence there. Which school's precepts were transmitted to the first Chinese *bhikshuni* at their ordination is not known. But for many centuries the *Vinaya* of the Dharmaguptaka school has been used in China. The Dharmaguptaka was a close relative of the Theravada, and the *Vinaya* of the two schools are very similar.[53] The Dharmaguptaka school itself has been defunct for centuries, as have all the other ancient Buddhist schools except the Theravada. But the Dharmaguptaka *Vinaya* is still very much alive and in use in Taiwan.

Even in the fifth century, when the first Chinese *bhikshuni* were properly ordained, Chinese Buddhists had taken the Mahayana scriptures to their hearts. But although Mahayana Buddhists produced volumes of scriptures that impart their own interpretations of the Buddha's teachings, they never bothered to create a *Vinaya* of their own. It was not necessary. Mahayana Buddhists have always observed the *Vinaya* rules for *bhikshu* and *bhikshuni* as they appear in the texts of the old schools. That includes the rules for the ordination of male and female religious. Buddhist clerics, throughout the world, follow nearly the same monastic discipline no matter what their school affiliation might be.

Since the fifth century there have always been significant numbers of *bhikshuni* in China. In a country where women were subordinated to men in most aspects of their lives, Chinese nuns had a great deal of autonomy in governing the affairs of their own religious communities. The *Vinaya* affords *bhikshuni* a great degree of control over their lives. In China, women were also employed, as the monks were, to perform rituals on behalf of the laypeople. The *Vinaya* makes no distinction between male and female religious in their ability to serve the spiritual needs of the laity.[54] In China in the past, as elsewhere in Buddhist Asia, the most famous and rich monastic institutions were men's, but the nuns were often also well endowed by lay patrons.

Monks and nuns were not always well respected in China, however, especially in recent centuries when Buddhism was in a state of decline. Monasteries and convents were often the only place of refuge for the poorest men and women, and the monastic institution came to be looked down upon by the rest of society. In China the family and kinship system has always been the most important social institution. To abandon one's family for a religious life was a drastic step, and it would take a person with a powerful sense of vocation to do it. Thus people who were members of a strong family usually preferred to remain in the family. If they were Buddhists, they practiced as laypeople. This has been true in Taiwan, too.[55]

Since 1949, however, when the government of the Republic of China and large numbers of mainland Chinese settled in Taiwan after losing the civil war to Mao Zedong's Chinese Communist Party, a real Buddhist revival has been occurring on the island. Some of the most senior Buddhist clergy moved to Taiwan from China in 1949. Since then, several outstanding new Buddhist leaders, both women and men, have appeared. Thirty to 45 percent of the people now identify themselves as Buddhists, and the numbers of women and men joining the *sangha*, especially from educated families, has been growing. There are now more than two thousand Buddhist temples and organizations in Taiwan.[56]

It is estimated that over ten thousand new clerics were ordained between 1952 and 1987, and 60 to 70 percent of these are *bhikshuni*. This is evidently because a remarkable number of young women perceive the life of a *bhikshuni* to be fulfilling. (Half of all the *bhikshuni* in Taiwan are less than forty years old.) Men in affluent Taiwan, on the other hand, are more inclined to go into business or the professions than to renounce worldly life. Ordained women and men have many opportunities available to them within the *sangha*, however, among which are the chance to continue their education and the chance to teach and engage in a variety of social services. *Bhikshu* and *bhikshuni* have the same opportunities and responsibilities. *Bhikshuni* are becoming quite influential to Taiwanese society as their numbers increase and as they expand their activities in society. Among the best known and most revered clerics in contemporary Taiwan are nuns such as Venerable Bhikshuni Cheng-yen who founded the Buddhist welfare society Tzu-chi, the largest charitable organization in Taiwan, and Venerable Bhikshuni Hiu Wan who is a respected scholar, teacher, artist, and Chan Buddhist master.[57]

The reasons for the current growth of Buddhism and *sangha* in Taiwan can be illuminated by examining the operation of Fo Kuang Shan, the largest temple on the island. Fo Kuang Shan was founded in 1967 by Venerable Master Hsing Yun who left the mainland for Taiwan as a young monk in 1949. He is a charismatic leader who has attracted over a million followers and has built a network of subsidiary temples in Taiwan and elsewhere in the world. Hsi Lai Temple in Los Angeles, where two hundred women received *bhikshuni* ordination in 1988, is a daughter temple of Fo Kuang Shan, the first in North America. A whole generation of young leaders, women and men, have been trained at Fo Kuang Shan, and their youth, energy, and abilities appeal to large numbers of new followers. Venerable Master Hsing Yun and the younger teachers at Fo Kuang Shan emphasize Buddhism in service to the living, which means programs that answer people's religious and practical needs here and now. They operate a free medical clinic with mobile units that serve remote villages, a program to distribute clothing and food to the needy in winter, a children's home, a home for the elderly, and wildlife conservation areas (reflecting the Buddhist attitude of compassion toward all living beings). There is also an extensive educational program that includes four Buddhist colleges, a high school, nursery schools, kindergartens, and Sunday schools and summer camps for children. The Fo Kuang Publishing House produces Buddhist books, magazines, and cassettes. Fo Kuang Shan teachers visit prisons and factories to lecture on the *dharma*, and they present Buddhist programs on radio and television; Venerable Master Hsing Yun himself was the first *bhikshu* in Taiwan to propagate Buddhism on radio and television.[58]

Clearly, Fo Kuang Shan monks and nuns are active everywhere in Taiwanese society, and people's response to them has been very positive. The young, well-educated clergy, and the army of well-organized, well-educated lay disciples who work with them, minister effectively to the people.

They act with a clear sense of responsibility and with real dignity, and consequently they have won the respect of much of the population.[59] They administer the organization efficiently and Fo Kuang Shan has received abundant financial support from donors. Women, both ordained and lay, are increasingly prominent in the Fo Kuang Shan structure. Fo Kuang Shan *bhikshuni* and other *bhikshuni* in Taiwan have emerged as leaders in modern Buddhism. Can they serve as a model for Buddhist women in the rest of Asia who aspire to ordination and to meaningful roles for themselves in the modern world?

Restoration of the *Bhikshuni Sangha:* Critical Issues

The possibility of establishing the *bhikshuni sangha* for Buddhist women everywhere has been discussed many times in the last hundred years by Buddhists in various Asian countries. In the last decade the discussion has attracted international notice because of the publication of numerous articles and books dealing with the subject and because of international conferences on Buddhist women that focused attention on the issue. In 1987 Buddhist women and Buddhist leaders from all over the world gathered in Bodh Gaya, India (the site of the Buddha's enlightenment), for the International Conference on Buddhist Nuns.[60] This first major conference on Buddhist women's issues was followed in 1991 by The First International Conference on Buddhist Women, in Bangkok, Thailand.[61] The conferences were organized by leading spokeswomen for the cause of the *bhikshuni sangha*—Dr. Chatsumarn Kabilsingh of Thammasat University, Bangkok; Venerable Bhikshuni Karma Lekshe Tsomo, an American woman trained in the Tibetan Buddhist tradition and ordained in the Korean *bhikshuni* lineage; and Venerable Bhikshuni Ayya Khema, founder of Parappaduwa Nuns' Island in Sri Lanka. The conferences provided a forum for various points of view concerning the *bhikshuni sangha*. The discussions also made it very clear that, although the question of finding an appropriate channel for Buddhist women to realize their spiritual aspirations is very important, it is only part of a bigger and more fundamental problem that must be addressed first: the situation of all women in the Buddhist societies of Asia.

There cannot be a *bhikshuni sangha* in Asia unless women who want to lead a spiritual life have the means to do it: an education in the *dharma,* economic support, and acceptance by monks, laity, and government. Education is the key to the rest, for as long as the *mae ji* of Thailand and the *ani* of Tibetan communities remain poorly educated, they will not be respected by monks and will not be economically supported by the laity. Sri Lanka's *dasa sil matavo* and Burma's *thila shin,* most of whom have received a basic general and religious education, are called upon to serve the laity's religious needs because they are perceived to be knowledgeable and capable. Their services are repaid with donations. Economically they are better off than the *mae ji*. The fully ordained *bhikshuni* of Taiwan are the best examples of how important education is for the advancement of women within the *sangha*. Taiwanese *bhikshuni* not only minister to the religious needs of the laity on an equal level with the *bhikshu,* many of them have become real leaders in Taiwanese society. Recognizing that education is the foundation on which the betterment of the situation of *mae ji* and *ani* depends, Chatsumarn Kabilsingh, His Holiness the Dalai Lama, and other religious and governmental leaders are now working to motivate these women to take advantage of the educational opportunities that are finally being offered to them. The result, for Tibetan women, is that some have already been able to take ordination as *bhikshuni.*

Many laypeople have advocated the restoration of the *bhikshuni sangha* in their own countries, but their visions of what the ordained women's life should be do not necessarily agree with the desires of the *dasa sil matavo, mae ji,* and *thila shin* themselves. The lay leaders of the Buddhist revival in Sri Lanka and Chatsumarn Kabilsingh and some of her associates in Thailand have envisioned an order of educated women who would dedicate themselves to helping other women with their personal and family problems and to alleviating the social problems of poverty, illiteracy, and ill health. Western women and men interested in restoring the Buddhist women's order imagine it as an order of meditators and religious teachers. But most *mae ji* and *dasa sil matavo* have chosen their paths for the sake of personal spiritual growth, to be accomplished by piously carrying out devotions to the Buddha. Neither social service nor meditation meet their ideals of what their own spiritual lives should be. *Thila shin* and *ani,* too, spend most of their time in devotions and in accumulating merit for the future.

There is an incongruity between what the better-educated Asians and the Westerners who are leading the effort to restore the *bhikshuni sangha* want and the more modest aspirations of the majority of Buddhist women who have already taken up the religious life. Most of the Buddhists of South and Southeast Asia come from a rural background, and most are not well educated. If a restored *bhikshuni sangha* is really to meet the spiritual needs of ordinary women, as well as the ideals of more sophisticated individuals, it cannot be an elitist institution with a narrow view of what the religious life should be. Current efforts to educate and broaden the outlook of *mae ji* and the other lay nuns, and dialogue between the women religious and the lay promoters of the *bhikshuni sangha* are helping to bridge the gap between their viewpoints. Here, too, the *bhikshuni* of Taiwan can provide a useful role model, for although education is greatly stressed within their *sangha* and younger women with an intellectual bent are attracted to it, there seems to be scope for a variety of spiritual vocations.

Without an order of fully ordained women in Thailand and the other Buddhist countries, opportunities for Buddhist women to be leaders within their religion are very limited. This is one of the main reasons for the attempt to restore the *bhikshuni sangha*. Taiwanese and Korean *bhikshuni* have been just as able to become leaders as have their male counterparts. East Asian *bhikshuni* have very creatively developed their own ways to fulfill their spiritual aspirations, whether as teachers, meditation masters, or healers of the sick. There are laywomen meditation teachers, scholars, and social activists in Asia who prefer to remain laywomen. But there are also many Asian women who deeply desire to be able to do such things with a degree of commitment they do not feel is possible while remaining in lay life. The Venerable Bhikshuni Voramai Kabilsingh is a woman who felt this way, and she therefore took the step of seeking ordination outside the Theravada tradition. She and women like her want it to be possible for Theravada women to do what Taiwanese *bhikshuni* can already do, but within a Theravada *bhikshuni sangha*.

Most of the *dasa sil matavo* of Sri Lanka would prefer to remain as they are, independent of control by the *bhikshu sangha,* lay reformers, and the government. For the restoration of the *bhikshuni sangha* would mean that the women would have to observe all the *Vinaya* rules that establish a hierarchical relationship between monks and nuns and that regulate all their interactions. By canon law, *bhikshuni* are subordinated to all *bhikshu.* Now the ten-precept women regulate their own daily lives. Many of them consider themselves purer in conduct than most monks are, as well. They do not feel that their opportunities in religion are limited by the absence of a *bhikshuni sangha*. They have a good sense of their own dignity. They appear ready to persevere as a new kind of women's institution that is distinct from the *bhikshuni sangha* but is every bit as fulfilling. The success of *dasa sil matavo* was due to the particular historical circumstances in Sri Lanka that led to the formation of groups of precept-taking women. But the *dasa sil matavo* have been in a period of decline since the 1950s. If they can successfully reverse that decline, as they have been trying to do by admitting only the best-quality recruits to the order and then training them well, the *dasa sil matavo* of Sri Lanka may present to the world the spectacle of a most unusual phenomenon in the history of Buddhist institutions: a new and viable religious order outside the *Vinaya*.[62]

But it remains to be seen whether such an institution can really endure. The ability of the *dasa sil matavo* to permanently attract the loyalty and support of the lay public will be crucial. A mutually respectful relationship between the ten-precept women and the *bhikshu* of Sri Lanka would have to be established as well. If the *dasa sil matavo* communities can thrive, it will be extremely interesting to see if other groups in other countries take them as models for new Buddhist institutions that can meet the spiritual needs of modern Buddhists. In short, is it possible to go against tradition and establish an enduring religious order outside the *Vinaya,* if *Vinaya* and *sangha* cannot be made flexible enough to fulfill the religious needs of modern people?

The *Vinaya* has been the touchstone of practice for members of the *sangha* for more than two thousand years, and the *sangha* is the central organization of the Buddhist religion. The *bhikshu* and *bhikshuni sanghas* are regulated by the rules of the *Vinaya.* It is precisely the observation of the *Vinaya* rules that distinguishes the ordained monk or nun from the layperson. Therefore the *Vinaya* rules are central to the identity of the cleric.

The *Vinaya* books of six of the ancient Buddhist schools survive, but only one of the ancient schools, the Theravada, remains active today. Each school's *Vinaya* contains a catalogue of basic rules, called the *Pratimoksha,* that govern the daily lives of *bhikshu* and *bhikshuni.* The rules cover the major ethical concerns, such as taking a life, theft, and sexual misconduct, and they also cover minute details of daily interactions between individuals, such as controlling one's temper, proper conduct when taking a meal, disposing of bodily wastes, and other matters of personal and social decorum. The rules are very similar in the six extant *Vinaya* books, but there are slight variations. A *bhikshu* must observe between 218 and 263 rules, according to the various *Vinaya;* a Theravada *bhikshu* observes 227. A *bhikshuni*'s life is somewhat more carefully regulated: she must observe 290 to 380 rules. The Theravada *Vinaya* contains 311, and the Dharmaguptaka *Vinaya* used by Chinese nuns has 348. Most of the rules are the same for both men and women.

The *Vinaya* rules are assumed by Buddhists to have been formulated by the Buddha, and to be, therefore, irrevocable. In fact, it is impossible to determine whether all or part or none of the rules actually originated with the Buddha, although regulation of the monks' and nuns' activities must certainly have begun soon after the two *sanghas* were formed.[63] But so far as monastic tradition is concerned, the rules were established by the Buddha and they cannot be changed. The *Vinaya* rules have not necessarily met all the changing needs of the *sanghas* through the centuries, however, and additional rules have been formulated as need has arisen. These additional rules exist outside the *Vinaya,* and each *sangha* in each country has its own set.[64] Thus, there have, in fact, been changes in the monastic regulations, but the changes have been made in such a way as not to compromise the *Vinaya,* which remains sacrosanct.

Modern monks and especially modern nuns have sometimes criticized the inflexible attitude of their fellow monastics toward the *Vinaya.* Some have even suggested reevaluation of the traditional rigid adherence to rules formulated centuries ago in response to problems of a specific time and place. Is there perhaps a more appropriate way to understand Buddhist moral discipline? Some have argued that the ten precepts that the novice monk and nun, as well as the most pious lay devotees, have always taken are the essence of Buddhist morality, and all other regulations are merely elaborations on the ten. Thus, to keep the ten precepts faithfully is truly to follow the path of moral discipline envisioned by the Buddha. The additional *Vinaya* rules are unnecessary.

Such a radical reevaluation of the importance of the *Vinaya* has been suggested by some of the *dasa sil matavo.* It reinforces their claim that their conduct is purer than that of the monks, and that there is no need for them to join the *sangha* in order to live the perfect Buddhist life. The majority of *sangha* members throughout Asia certainly do not share this view. There is a fundamental conflict here between tradition and change, the desire to preserve what has always been versus the willingness to innovate in order to create Buddhist religious orders that are entirely relevant to modern life. If the *bhikshuni sangha* is to be reestablished, or if new religious vocations are to be accommodated, the problem of traditionalism will have to be dealt with. The monks' *sangha* has in fact changed much during the last two millenia, but always under the guise of purification of the *sangha,* the notion that impure practices that had crept in were being purged and the original pure practices reaffirmed. It remains to be seen how much change the modern *sangha* is willing to accept.

Of all the rules that apply to *bhikshuni,* none have been so criticized by modern Buddhists and scholars as the eight important rules, the *gurudharma,* that the Buddha is said to have enjoined upon the first woman ordained a nun, the Buddha's aunt and foster mother, Mahaprajapati. The eight important rules clearly establish a hierarchical relationship between the *bhikshu* and *bhikshuni sanghas,* subordinating the women to the men. The eight appear in all the extant *Vinaya* books and in other scriptural texts as well. They are not literally the same in all texts, and the order of the eight varies from school to school, but all recensions are similar enough so that we can say they belong to an ancient, common heritage shared by all the ancient Buddhist schools. Moreover, the eight rules are the first and most basic rules imparted to the *bhikshuni,* according to tradition. They are more fundamental to the nuns' order than the 300 or so rules of the *Vinaya Pratimoksha.*[65] They are also extremely offensive to many modern women, both Asian and Western. Yet those progressive Asian and Western women who have taken the *bhikshuni* ordination in recent years have formally accepted the eight rules. But do they live by them?

Many modern women and men reject the eight rules outright, either because they seem inconsistent with the rest of the Buddha's teachings, or because they are inappropriate for modern Buddhists, or both. No doubt they do reflect the social situation of two thousand or so years ago. But in fact the eight rules relate to the formal interactions between the women's and men's *sanghas,* and in the formal business of the *sanghas* men simply take precedence over women. As Karma Lekshe Tsomo, the American *bhikshuni,* says, for the harmonious working of the *sanghas* there must be order, and somebody has to come first, somebody must be second.[66] The rules need not be personally humiliating. It depends on how a *bhikshuni* chooses to take them.

In fact, *bhikshuni* take them quite differently. Many *bhikshuni* make personal decisions not to observe the eight rules: the Venerable Bhikshuni Voramai Kabilsingh, for example, does not bow down before monks.[67] Others, like the Korean nun Il Jin Sunim, accept them as a form of beneficial personal discipline that she puts in service of her own spiritual development. When she was first ordained, she angrily rejected the eight rules, as did most of her sister nuns; but now she observes them not for the sake of the monks, but for her own sake. That, she believes, was what the Buddha intended.[68] Tibetan *ani* habitually venerate all monks to an extraordinary degree. It is their custom. To older nuns, it is not onerous to honor the *lamas* and to be humble in their presence. Yet younger *ani* think it is wrong for women to subordinate themselves to men, and are questioning the efficacy of the eight rules in this modern age.[69]

Bhikshuni in Taiwan do not keep the eight rules, nor do *bhikshu* expect them to.[70] The traditional sharply drawn hierarchical relationship between male and female monastics is not observed, according to the Venerable I Fa, a *bhikshuni* of Fo Kuang Shan temple. The eight rules are there, in the *Vinaya* that is transmitted to each *bhikshuni* when she is ordained, but though known, they are not acted upon. Should the Taiwanese *sangha* be a model for all other *sanghas* with respect to the eight important rules, too? Modern Buddhist women and men will have to decide what to do about the eight rules, and about *Vinaya* rules as a whole, but precipitous rejection of them would no doubt further antagonize those Theravada monks who are already resisting the idea of restoring the *bhikshuni sangha.* A more politic solution would be preferable.

The eight important rules do not, of course, apply to the *dasa sil matavo, thila shin,* or *mae ji* since they are not fully ordained religious. *Thila shin* and *mae ji* nonetheless treat monks with great deference and serve them. *Dasa sil matavo* maintain their distance from monks, and that is one of the freedoms they would have to give up if they should elect to form a true *bhikshuni sangha* in Sri Lanka.

Traditionalists in the *sangha* have questioned the validity of the Chinese ordination lineage, the lineage in which Tibetan *ani* and Theravada precept women have begun to take ordination in the absence of ordination lineages in their own traditions. Tibetan monastic leaders want to examine the Chinese lineage as carefully as possible so that they can make the wisest decision about how to establish a Tibetan lineage. Theravada leaders, and the rank and file of the *sangha,* have rejected the Chinese lineage outright because it is not Theravadin. Scholarship seems to promise a solution to this impasse, since it is not difficult to demonstrate that the Dharmaguptaka *Vinaya* and ordination ceremony are extremely similar to the Theravadin, and that the Mahayana doctrinal position of Chinese Buddhists has no bearing on the ordination practices they observe. But the real issue here, too, comes back to the conflict between tradition and change. Will the Theravada, the School of the Elders, the most conservative of the ancient Buddhist schools, be able to accept an ordination tradition that, though similar to their own, has nonetheless been separate for hundreds of years? And can old prejudices against the Mahayana finally be overcome in favor of a new spirit of cooperation from both sides?

It is not only monks who cling to tradition. The Buddhist laity does the same. In part this is true because they are instructed by the monks, who have been, in many parts of Buddhist Asia, the educators of the rural population. But it is also because Theravada laypeople (whether in Thailand, Sri Lanka, Burma, or the rest of Southeast Asia) have a practical interest in having the traditional monastic order continue as it always has. To the layperson, a monk is a field of merit, which means that a gift made to a monk will create merit for the layperson's future well-being and ultimate liberation from unhappiness in the cycle of rebirth. But a *bhikshu* is a valid field of merit for a layperson only as long as he scrupulously observes the *Vinaya* rules, which ensure that he is living a pure life. The *Vinaya* rules for daily behavior are very precise so that the ordinary conduct of monks will remain distinct from that of the laity. If monks become lax in their observance of the monastic rules and begin to act like laymen, the lines between monk and layman are blurred and the monk's efficacy as field of merit is destroyed. Thus the laity is generally unwilling to accept changes in the *sangha*'s long-established, traditional way of being. The laity reinforces the conservatism of Theravada monks.[71]

The laity of Thailand and the rest of Southeast Asia is, moreover, unaccustomed to the presence of an order of respectable, fully ordained women, who should also be looked upon as fields of merit. Introducing to the laity this new concept of the religious role of women in their lives will not be an easy matter, yet it must be done if there is to be a viable *bhikshuni sangha* in Theravada countries. The *bhikshuni* could not possibly survive without laypeople's acceptance and support. Traditionally in Thailand and Sri Lanka, women are valued as nurturers—wives and mothers, sustainers of the family—and not as religious specialists. Thus, to win the laity's acceptance of the *bhikshuni sangha* requires inducing them to change their attitudes about women as well as their assumptions about monastic purity and who can be a field of merit. In Sri Lanka and Burma, this problem has already been partly overcome, for *dasa sil matavo* and *thila shin* are respected and supported because of the purity of their religious lives. It is possible, therefore, for Theravadin laypeople to accept women as religious, and they can even regard women whose status between the lay and monastic worlds is ambiguous as legitimate fields of merit. But so that the situation for religious women in Asia can continue to be improved, it is essential that the sensibilities of the laity and the monks not be wounded by too hasty action. Some monks have already vented their outrage at what seems to them the intrusion of Western feminist notions into a very Asian matter. It is necessary to proceed with utmost care.

Conclusions

Can it happen? Can a universal *bhikshuni sangha* be established in our time? The creation of a *sangha* that embraces all national traditions has already begun in the West. In part, this is because Western women belonging to the Tibetan and Theravada traditions have found existing patterns for women in Buddhism unsatisfying and have taken the initiative to seek permission from their teachers to take *bhikshuni* ordination. Buddhist teachers working in the West are aware that Buddhism must be flexible enough to accommodate the spiritual aspirations of Western converts. Many of the Theravada monks in the West have decided to lead the way in establishing a *bhikshuni* ordination lineage for Theravada women. Consequently they have participated in *bhikshuni* ordinations at Hsi Lai Temple in Los Angeles and have ordained novices on their own.

In Asia, however, the introduction of a new religious structure will have to be accomplished slowly and carefully if it is to be done. It will undoubtedly be easiest for the Tibetan tradition to accept an order of fully ordained women. The fact that the foremost leaders of the Tibetan *sangha* favor the restoration of the *bhikshuni sangha* is of critical importance. The Tibetan community in exile is blessed with a group of outstanding leaders whose outlook is progressive. It seems likely to me that the uprooting of the traditional culture of Tibet since 1959 has enabled His Holiness the Dalai Lama and the other high *lamas* to implement change more quickly than might have been done if the Chinese had left Tibet in peace. Traditions have already been broken. It seems to be the opinion of the Dalai Lama that this is a time for change and growth. Because he is so enormously respected by his people, the decisions of the Dalai Lama and his advisers about the *bhikshuni sangha* will no doubt be readily accepted by Tibetan monks and laity.

The Thai *sangha* is hierarchically structured, like the Tibetan, but the Thai Sangharaja does not enjoy the authority or influence over the Thai people that the Dalai Lama has over Tibetans. Nonetheless, if the Sangharaja and the council of Elders should recommend to the government that the *bhikshuni sangha* be established, it could be accomplished. This seems to be what Chatsumarn Kabilsingh hopes for. The task of reconciling the rank-and-file monks and the laity, especially in rural areas, would remain, but with the authority of the *sangha* fully behind it, the *bhikshuni sangha* would probably have a reasonable chance of success. It is when problems like this one arise in the *sangha* that the practical advantages of a centralized structure become apparent, in contrast to the more democratic arrangement the Buddha himself favored. There will be no reason for the *sangha* hierarchy to do anything about women's Buddhism, however, unless there is a real demand that a *bhikshuni sangha* be established. There does not yet seem to be widespread interest in the issue among Thai women.

In Sri Lanka the office of Sangharaja ceased to exist during the colonial period, and the government ceased to function as purifier of the *sangha*. It was the devout and nationalistic Buddhist laity who took on the function of purifier of the religion in the nineteenth and early twentieth centuries. In the midst of the Buddhist revival they led, a new and innovative kind of religious order for women was born, rather than the restoration of a defunct body. This order, the *dasa sil matavo,* may be able to put down permanent roots and survive as a distinctive spiritual path for women that is self-directed and independent of both monastic and lay supervision. Their success, too, will depend on the commitment of a significant number of women to this calling. Interest in the restoration of the *bhikshuni sangha* itself in Sri Lanka does not seem to be widespread, even though it was in Sri Lanka that the ancient order of women religious once thrived.

If the *bhikshuni sangha* is actually established throughout Asia, then it will have to meet the greatest challenge of all: how to survive in the modern world. In most countries, the *bhikshu sangha* is shrinking, and interest in institutionalized religions is declining as Asian countries modernize and more and more of their populations move to urban centers. Will many educated, city-bred women choose a religious vocation? Will the rural laity, the traditional breeding ground of the Buddhist clergy, offer its daughters to the *sangha,* or will they turn away from a religion that they think has turned its back on them?

Once again, the Taiwanese *sangha* may be the place to look for revealing patterns. Taiwan is an affluent, industrialized, extremely literate and sophisticated modern society, which is experiencing a Buddhist revival. Buddhism is not the religion of the majority (Buddhists make up about a third of the population), but it does appear to be meeting the religious needs of a large proportion of the people. A *bhikshuni* of Fo Kuang Shan temple told me that "Buddhism is an important religion now because in a highly developed country it is [necessary] to have spiritual food."[72] It does seem that especially now, when Taiwan's economic growth and social change are so rapid, intelligent young women with a strong sense of social responsibility are feeling attracted to Buddhism. Many remain laywomen and may marry and raise families. But many choose the life of the ordained woman, the full-time religious specialist who can devote herself entirely to her calling. They seem to choose this life because it affords them the best opportunity for personal development through service to others. In Taiwan the *bhikshuni sangha* is alive and well and finding a creative place for itself in the modern world. This is a possible scenario for what could happen elsewhere in Asia, too, if the *bhikshuni sangha* were to be established.

Whether or not the effort to restore the order is successful, the effort itself is important as an issue around which Buddhist women can rally. In the past, Buddhist women have lingered quietly in the background, invisible and ignored by the *bhikshu sangha* and by scholars. But now Asian and Western women have taken the lead in a well-publicized international effort to bring about a fundamental change in Buddhist institutions. The effort is empowering. Buddhist women will lead more and more and will create new places for themselves under the umbrella of their religion. They have already wrought profound changes in the ancient religion and in the possibilities available to women in Buddhist Asia.

Notes

1. The Sanskrit terms *bhikshu* and *bhikshuni* mean male and female mendicant, respectively, one who begs alms and renounces conventional worldly ways of living. In this paper, the English words "monk" and "nun" will sometimes be used to refer to Buddhist religious, but this is done only for convenience. Christian monks, nuns, and priests live quite differently from their Buddhist counterparts.

2. There are still ordained women and men in Japan, but they do not follow the ordination procedures for *bhikshuni and bhikshu* preserved in the *Vinaya* or

Books of the Discipline for Monks and Nuns. Technically, therefore, they are not *bhikshu* and *bhikshuni*. Karma Lekshe Tsomo, ed., *Sakyadhita: Daughters of the Buddha* (Ithaca, N.Y.: Snow Lion Publications, 1988), pp. 53–54, 104–107, 124–130.

3. The books of regulations to be observed by *bhikshu* and *bhikshuni* in their daily lives are called *Vinaya*. Six *Vinaya* books are extant today, belonging to six of the ancient Buddhist schools. The narrative of the founding of the religious order for women, which follows in this chapter, was taken from the *Vinaya* of the Theravada School (School of the Elders), which is now followed in South and Southeast Asia. See I. B. Horner, *The Book of the Discipline (Vinaya-Pitaka),* volume V (*Cullavagga*) (London: Luzac and Company Ltd., 1963), pp. 352–358.

4. I have followed the description of the ordination ceremony as recorded in the Mahasanghika *Vinaya,* because the account in the Theravada *Vinaya* is quite abbreviated. I have used Akira Hirakawa, *Monastic Discipline for the Buddhist Nuns, An English Translation of the Chinese Text of the Mahasamghika-Bhikshuni-Vinaya* (Patna: K. P. Jayaswal Research Institute, 1982), pp. 50–68. The Theravada ordination ceremony for women is described in I. B. Horner, *Women Under Primitive Buddhism* (Delhi: Motilal Banarsidass Publishers, 1975), pp. 138–158.

5. Theravada is one of several ancient Buddhist schools and the only one to survive to the present. The schools differed somewhat from one another in their interpretations of the Buddha's teachings, but the *Vinaya* rules to which nuns and monks must adhere, and the ordination ceremonies, were very similar in all the schools.

6. Tessa Bartholomeusz, "Women Under the Bo Tree," Ph.D. dissertation, University of Virginia, Department of Religious Studies, 1991, pp. 66–71, 78.

7. The Theravada *sangha* was probably established in Burma in the second half of the eleventh century. Richard F. Gombrich, *Theravada Buddhism* (London: Routledge and Kegan Paul, 1988), p. 168; R. A. L. H. Gunawardana, *Robe and Plough: Monasticism and Economic Interest in Early Medieval Sri Lanka* (Tucson: University of Arizona Press, 1979), pp. 272–276.

8. Bartholomeusz, op. cit., p. 104 ff.

9. George D. Bond, *The Buddhist Revival in Sri Lanka: Religious Tradition, Reinterpretation and Response* (Columbia: University of South Carolina Press, 1988); Richard F. Gombrich and Gananath Obeyesekere, *Buddhism Transformed: Religious Change in Sri Lanka* (Princeton, N.J.: Princeton University Press, 1988).

10. The ten precepts are: to abstain from killing, stealing, sexual relations, lying, using intoxicants, eating after midday, dancing, self-adornment, using comfortable beds and chairs, touching gold and silver. See Etienne Lamotte, *Histoire du Bouddhisme Indien, des Origines a l'ere Saka* (Louvain: Publications Universitaires, Institut Orientaliste, 1958), p. 59. These precepts are considered the fundamental code of ethical conduct for Buddhists. From the Buddha's time until now, particularly devout lay disciples have frequently taken on themselves five or eight or occasionally all ten of the precepts, for a limited period of time or permanently. Pious lay

disciples who kept precepts were called *upasika* (female disciples) or *upasaka* (male disciples). Although *upasika* and *upasaka* were very pious, they did not abandon lay life and did not put on the saffron monastic robes or shave their heads. Normally they retained their property and served the religion by making gifts to the *sangha*. The same precepts are accepted by novices when they enter the monastic order. Novice monks and nuns, however, shave their heads and dress distinctively to symbolize their renunciation of conventional lay life.

11. Catherine de Alwis came from a prominent Christian Sinhala family, converted to Buddhism after her parents' death, went to Burma to study Buddhism, and took the precepts from a Burmese woman teacher who gave her the religious name, Sudharmacari. When she returned to Sri Lanka, she quickly became one of the central figures in the Buddhist revival movement. See Bartholomeusz, op. cit., pp. 281–282. See also Lowell E. Bloss, "The Female Renunciants of Sri Lanka: the *Dasasilamattawa*," *Journal of the International Association of Buddhist Studies*, vol. 10, no. 1 (1987), pp. 9–11.

12. The Sudharmacari Upasikaramaya was not the first women's religious community established in Sri Lanka at this period. The flamboyant American convert to Buddhism, Countless Miranda de Souza Canavarro, became a precept taker in the 1890s and established the Sanghamitta Sisterhood in Colombo. It did not last. Other women's communities were also established in these years, but Sudharmacari's was one of the most important and influential. One of Sudharmacari's more important lay patrons was Lady Edith Blake, wife of the British governor of Sri Lanka at the time. Consequently, Sudharmacari's community came to be popularly known as Lady Blake's *Aramaya*. See Bartholomeusz, op. cit., pp. 152 ff.

13. Karma Lekshe Tsomo, *Sakyadhita*, pp. 142–143.

14. Bartholomeusz, op. cit., p. 319.

15. Bloss, op. cit., pp. 8–17; Gombrich and Obeyesekere, op. cit., pp. 286–291.

16. Bartholomeusz, op. cit., pp. 378 ff.

17. Bartholomeusz, op. cit., pp. 367 ff, 385 ff.

18. *Newsletter on International Buddhist Women's Activities* (NIBWA), no. 5 (1985), 19; no. 34 (1993), 13–14.

19. Bartholomeusz, op. cit., pp. 389 ff, 398 ff.

20. Bartholomeusz, op. cit., p. 464 ff.

21. NIBWA, no. 20 (1989), pp. 16 ff; no. 27 (1991), p. 23.

22. Bartholomeusz, op. cit., pp. 496–497; NIBWA, no. 19 (1989), 21–23; no. 31 (1992), 3–4.

23. Nuns' Island continues to operate, however, under the direction of Ayya Khema's disciple, Ayya Kheminda. NIBWA, no. 20 (1989), pp. 16 ff; no. 27 (1991), pp. 23–24.

24. Bartholomeusz, op. cit., p. 459.

25. Bartholomeusz, op. cit., p. 452, note 39; pp. 460–464.

26. Chatsumarn Kabilsingh, *Thai Women in Buddhism* (Berkeley, Calif.: Parallax Press, 1991), 36–38. The origin and precise meaning of the term *mae ji* is uncertain. Most *mae ji* take the first five of the ten precepts listed previously.

27. Kabilsingh, op. cit., pp. 39, 41. See also Chatsumarn Kabilsingh, "The Future of the Bhikkhuni Sangha in Thailand," in *Speaking of Faith,* ed. Diana L. Eck and Devaki Jain (Philadelphia: New Society Publishers, 1987), pp. 152–153.

28. Kabilsingh, *Thai Women in Buddhism,* p. 39; NIBWA, no. 5 (1985), pp. 12–14; no. 20 (1989), p. 32; nos. 29–30 (1991–92), pp. 23–24.

29. Kabilsingh, op. cit., pp. 46–52.

30. Kabilsingh, op. cit., pp. 42–43.

31. Yoneo Ishii, *Sangha, State, and Society: Thai Buddhism in History* (Honolulu: University of Hawaii Press, 1986), pp. 86 ff.

32. Kabilsingh, "The Future of the Bhikkhuni Sangha in Thailand," pp. 152–156; *Thai Women in Buddhism,* p. 51; Ishii, op. cit., pp. 69–70.

33. Kabilsingh, "The Future of the Bhikkhuni Sangha in Thailand," p. 157.

34. NIBWA, no. 12 (1987), pp. 5–9.

35. Kabilsingh, *Thai Women In Buddhism,* 42–43; NIBWA, no. 35 (1993), pp. 15–17.

36. Mi Mi Khaing, *The World of Burmese Women* (London: Zed Books, 1984), pp. 80, 82; Hiroko Kawanami, "The Religious Standing of Burmese Buddhist Nuns (thila-shin): The Ten Precepts and Religious Respect Words," *Journal of the International Association of Buddhist Studies,* vol. 13, no. 1 (1990), 19. There are Cambodian and Lao precept-keeping women too, but not much information is available about them at present.

37. Khaing, op. cit., pp. 79–82, 85–86; Melford E. Spiro, *Buddhism and Society, A Great Tradition and Its Burmese Vicissitudes* (New York: Harper & Row, 1970), p. 396.

38. Karma Lekshe Tsomo, *Sakyadhita,* 109–111; Kawanami, op. cit., pp. 20–22; Khaing, op. cit., pp. 83–85.

39. Kawanami, op. cit., pp. 19–21.

40. NIBWA, no. 15 (1988), pp. 15–20.

41. NIBWA, no. 31 (1992), pp. 5–6. The *Vinaya* accounts of the founding of the *bhikshuni sangha* conclude with the Buddha's prediction that Buddhism will not last more than a thousand years because women had been admitted into the *sangha.* This passage, too, is challenged by modern critics.

42. Hanna Havnevik, *Tibetan Buddhist Nuns. History, Cultural Norms and Social Reality* (Oslo: Norwegian University Press, 1989), p. 200.

43. Mahayana Buddhism in the form of Vajrayana or Tantric Buddhism is what is practiced in Tibet, and in the Himalayan countries Nepal, Sikkim, and Bhutan, which derived their religion from Tibet. Tantric Buddhism is the same as Mahayana doctrinally. But Tantric Buddhism stresses elaborate rituals and a vast array of esoteric meditative practices that are imparted directly and secretly by teacher to disciple.

44. Karma Lekshe Tsomo, "Tibetan Nuns and Nunneries," in *Feminine Ground: Essays on Women and Tibet,* ed. Janice D. Willis (Ithaca, N.Y.: Snow Lion Publications, 1989), pp. 118–134; Karma Lekshe Tsomo, *Sakyadhita,* pp. 150–151.

45. Havnevik, op. cit., p. 44. Because *ani* is the term most commonly used in published literature, I will use it in this chapter.

46. Havnevik, op. cit., pp. 149–155.

47. Havnevik, op. cit., pp. 47–52, 130–140.

48. Havnevik, op. cit., pp. 137–138, 173–178.

49. Havnevik, op. cit., pp. 161–162, 190–201. The American nun, Karma Lekshe Tsomo, is one of the most vocal of these Western women who have been trained in the Tibetan tradition. She has become a leading spokesperson for Buddhist women's issues in Asia and the West.

50. Havnevik, op. cit., pp. 151, 200–201. NIBWA, no. 9 (1986), pp. 9–12; no. 10 (1987), p. 7.

51. Kathryn Cissell, "The *Pi-ch-iu-ni chuang,* Biographies of Famous Chinese Nuns from pp. 317–516 c.e.," Ph.D. dissertation, University of Wisconsin, 1972, pp. 62–70.

52. E. W. Adikaram, *Early History of Buddhism in Ceylon* (Colombo: M. D. Gunasena and company, 1953), pp. 88–100.

53. Andre Bareau, *Les sectes bouddhiques du Petit Vehicule* (Saigon: E. F. E. O., 1955), pp. 181–200, 205–208. Both the Dharmaguptaka and the Theravada schools emerged out of the conservative groups that referred to themselves as "The Elders," meaning those who preserved the Buddha's teachings and intentions most faithfully. The Theravada became the "School of the Elders" that flourished in Sri Lanka; the Dharmaguptaka was a school that was active in northwest India and along the Central Asian trade routes that linked India and China.

54. Miriam Levering, "Women, the State, and Religion Today in the People's Republic of China," in *Today's Woman in World Religions,* ed. Arvind Sharma (Albany: State University of New York Press, 1994), p. 212.

55. C. K. Yang, *Religion in Chinese Society* (Berkeley: University of California Press, 1961), pp. 310–320, 332–334. NIBWA, no. 24 (1990), pp. 26–27.

56. Karma Lekshe Tsomo, *Sakyadhita*, pp. 119–123; Barbara Reed, "Women and Chinese Religion in Contemporary Taiwan," in *Today's Woman in World Religions*, ed. Arvind Sharma (Albany: State University of New York Press, 1994), p. 386, note 7; NIBWA, no. 24 (1990), p. 28. Figures on numbers of Buddhist clerics and laypeople, and numbers of temples, in Taiwan vary somewhat in the available sources. The Chinese Buddhist Association of Taiwan (quoted by Reed) estimates there were about 9,000 Buddhist clerics in 1989 and more than 4,000 temples.

57. NIBWA, no. 5 (1985), 20–22; no. 28 (1991), pp. 19–21; no. 35 (1993), pp. 16–17.

58. Venerable Master Hsing Yun, *How to Be a Fo Kuang Buddhist*, vol. 1 (Kaohsiung, Taiwan: Fo Kuang Publisher, 1987); *The Free China Journal*, October 1, 1991, p. 5.

59. Approbation of Fo Kuang Shan is not universal, however. The organization has some vocal critics, too. See NIBWA, no. 24 (1990), pp. 24–28.

60. Karma Lekshe Tsomo, ed., *Sakyadhita: Daughters of the Buddha* (Ithaca, N.Y.: Snow Lion Publications, 1988); NIBWA, no. 11 (1987), pp. 4–12.

61. NIBWA, nos. 29–30 (1991–92), pp. 3–28.

62. There are other extra-*Vinaya* communities of women and of men and women, in Buddhist Asia and in the West. See Bartholomeusz, op. cit., chaps. 7 and 9; Kabilsingh, *Thai Women in Buddhism*, pp. 55–67. But Sri Lanka's *dasa sil matavo* are one of the largest and most interesting of these groups in Asia.

63. Steven Collins, in his Introduction to the English translation of Mohan Wijayaratna, *Buddhist Monastic Life According to the Texts of the Theravada Tradition* (Cambridge: University Press, 1990), pp. xiv–sviii, points out that it is not possible to conclusively identify early versus later strata in the composition of the Theravada *Vinaya* on linguistic grounds, because all the Theravada canonical texts were first written down several centuries after the death of the Buddha. As they exist today, they represent an evolved text tradition. No doubt there were accretions to the rules before they were written down in the first century B.C.E., but it is impossible to prove that (for example) rule A is two generations older than rule B. The same applies to the other *Vinaya* books, most of which are extant only in their Chinese translations.

64. For example, see Walpola Rahula, *History of Buddhism in Ceylon* (colombo: M. D. Gunasena & Co., Ltd., 1966), p. 157, and Francois Bizot, *Les traditions de la pabbajja en Asie du Sud-Est* (Göttingen, Germany: Vandenhoeck and Ruprecht, 1988), passim.

65. Gustav Roth, *Bhikshuni-vinaya, Including Bhikshuni-prakirnaka and a Summary of the Bhikshu-prakirnaka of the Arya-mahasanghika-lokottaravadin* (Patna: K. P. Jayaswal Research Institute, 1970).

66. NIBWA, no. 12 (1987), p. 13.

67. Karma Lekshe Tsomo, *Sakyadhita*, p. 149.

68. Interview with Venerable Bhikshuni Il Jin Sunim, October 1993.

69. Havnevik, op. cit., pp. 159–160.

70. Interview with Venerable Bhikshuni I Fa, of Fo Kuang Shan, December 1993.

71. Ishii, op. cit., 14, pp. 49–50; Bartholomeusz, op. cit., pp. 148–149.

72. Letter of September 6, 1993, from Venerable Bhikshuni Man Ho.

Bibliography

Barnes, Nancy J. "Buddhism." In *Women in World Religions*. Arvind Sharma, ed. Albany: State University of New York Press, 1987.

———. "Women in Buddhism." In *Today's Woman in World Religions*. Arvind Sharma, ed. Albany: State University of New York Press, 1994.

Bartholomeusz, Tessa. "Women Under the Bo Tree." Ph.D. dissertation. University of Virginia, 1991.

Bechert, Heinz, and Gombrich, Richard, eds. *The World of Buddhism*. New York: Facts on File, 1984.

Bloss, Lowell W. "The Female Renunciants of Sri Lanka: the *Dasasilmattawa*." *Journal of the International Association of Buddhist Studies*. Vol. 10, no. 1, 7–32, 1987.

Gombrich, Richard. *Theravada Buddhism, A Social History from Ancient Benares to Modern Colombo*. London: Routledge and Kegan Paul, 1988.

Havnevik, Hanna. *Tibetan Buddhist Nuns. History, Cultural Norms and Social Reality*. Oslo: Norwegian University Press, 1989.

Horner, I. B. *Women Under Primitive Buddhism, Laywomen and Almswomen*. Delhi: Motilal Banarsidass, 1975. (Originally published London: Routledge and Kegan Paul, 1930.)

Ishii, Yoneo. *Sangha, State and Society: Thai Buddhism in History*. Honolulu: University of Hawaii Press, 1986.

Kabilsingh, Chatsumarn. *Thai Women in Buddhism*. Berkeley, Calif.: Parallax Press, 1991.

Karma Lekshe Tsomo, ed. *Sakyadhita: Daughters of the Buddha*. Ithaca, N.Y.: Snow Lion, 1988.

Kawanami, Hiroko. "The Religious Standing of Burmese Buddhist Nuns *(thilashin)*: the Ten Precepts and Religious Respect Words." *Journal of the International Association of Buddhist Studies*. Vol. 13, no. 1, 17–39, 1990.

Khaing, Mi Mi. *The World of Burmese Women.* London: Zed Books, 1984.

Willis, Janice D. ed. *Feminine Ground, Essays on Women and Tibet.* Ithaca, N.Y.: Snow Lion, 1989.

Yang, C. K. *Religion in Chinese Society.* Berkeley: University of California Press, 1961.

8

Buddhist Principles in the Tibetan Liberation Movement

José Ignacio Cabezón

> He who uses mankind badly, uses himself badly.
>
> Sextus the Pythagorean[1]

Tibet: An Overview

Tibet is a Buddhist country of 6 million inhabitants, occupying an area about the size of Western Europe, in the very heart of Asia. With China to the east and India to the west, it managed to serve as a buffer between these two great civilizations, interacting with both but maintaining its own cultural identity. Tibet had its own unique language, its own currency and postal system, and an independent government that integrated the religious and secular spheres *(chos srid gnyis 'brel)* under the leadership of the Dalai Lama. It developed distinctive traditions of painting, metalwork, and the performing arts and preserved a unique form of Mahayana Buddhism that was monastic, scholastic, and tantric in character.

In 1949 the Chinese invaded Tibet, an event that led to their slowly establishing considerable, and eventually complete, dominion over the country. For ten years the Tibetan government, posing little threat to Chinese colonial interests, was allowed to retain nominal power. Various attempts were made by the Dalai Lama and his representatives during this time to regain political control of their homeland. On May 23, 1951, under duress and threats of a full-scale invasion by the People's Liberation Army, a group of Tibetan delegates sent by the Dalai Lama as representatives of the Tibetan government, signed the Seventeen-Point Agreement that, while ceding control of Tibet's external affairs to China, guaranteed the country's *internal* autonomy.[2] Receiving little support from the outside world, the

Dalai Lama's government felt they had no choice but to accept the agreement already signed by the Tibetan delegates, despite the fact that the delegates had been prohibited from ever conferring with the central Tibetan government during the negotiation process. Because it promised some semblance of internal autonomy, the Tibetan government hoped that the agreement would allow them to keep Tibetan society, and especially their unique religious heritage, intact.

These hopes were unfounded, however, and relations between the Tibetan government and the Chinese continued to deteriorate. Finally, in 1959, after a series of events in which the Dalai Lama's safety was threatened, the people of Lhasa rose up against the Chinese. No match for the overwhelming might of Chinese forces, this culminated in the final military overthrow of one Tibetan government, and the Dalai Lama's flight to India. Together with almost 100,000 Tibetan refugees, the Dalai Lama continues to live in exile in India to this day.

Tremendous damage was done to the Tibetan culture, people, and land during and following the final Chinese takeover of the country in 1959: multitudes of Tibetans were executed, imprisoned, or forced to enter "re-education camps," monks and nuns were forced to enter lay life against their will, and a great deal of the country's cultural, religious, and artistic heritage was pillaged and sold. This was nothing compared to the losses that would be sustained later during the Cultural Revolution, however. By some estimates, all told, more than 1 million Tibetans have lost their lives at the hands of the Chinese, either directly through torture and execution or indirectly through mismanagement of Tibet's agricultural resources, that is, through policies that led to two 5-year periods of widespread famine and starvation in Tibet. In addition, more than 6,000 monasteries, temples, and historic structures have been destroyed.[3] As regards the natural environment, there has been systematic clearcutting of Tibetan forests, especially in eastern Tibet, and a great deal of Tibet's unique wildlife (the gazelle, wild ass, bar-headed geese, and brahmany duck) has been threatened, in some cases almost to the point of extinction.[4] Although the situation has improved somewhat since the end of the Cultural Revolution, Tibetans still lack the most basic human rights, such as freedom of speech and the right to peaceful protest. Just days before my own arrival in Lhasa, Tibet's capital, in the summer of 1991, for example, five Tibetans were arrested and imprisoned, and one killed, simply for engaging in peaceful protest outside Lhasa's Central Cathedral (Jo khang). Based on his interviews with former prisoners, John Avedon wrote that prison life in Tibet is:

> . . . characterized by unremittant labor, regular interrogation sessions in which the prisoner is beaten, ineffective medical care, borderline rations

of black tea and barley, and an ongoing death toll resulting from the harsh conditions. Prisoners sleep on the floor, are chained at night and only have bedding if the family members donate it.[5]

The systematic torture of prisoners has been documented in greater detail in a 1988 report by the Boston-based organization, Physicians for Human Rights, titled *The Suppression of a People: Accounts of Torture and Imprisonment in Tibet.*

To this day, the Chinese continue to practice a racist policy of covert cultural genocide—the systematic destruction of Tibetan cultural identity—that includes the massive population transfer of Han Chinese into Tibet (a policy whose end it is to make Tibetans a minority in their own homeland).[6] This, coupled with the repression of religious freedoms and the systematic destruction of traditional Tibetan learning, poses grave threats to the continued existence of Tibetan culture.

The Dalai Lama

The Dalai Lamas have been the spiritual and temporal leaders of the Tibetan people since the seventeenth century, when the fifth Dalai Lama consolidated political power and unified the country under his rule. Since that time the Dalai Lama has been considered by his followers to be the physical manifestation *(sprul pa)* of Avalokitesvara, the "buddha of compassion" and the mythical progenitor of the Tibetan people. Successive Dalai Lamas are considered the reincarnations of previous ones, and upon the death of a Dalai Lama a regent assumes power and takes on the responsibility of finding the new incarnation. The present Dalai Lama, Ngag dbang blo bzang bsTan 'dzin rgya mtsho (Ngawang lozang tenzing gyatso), is the fourteenth such incarnation *(sku phreng).*

The fourteenth Dalai Lama was born to humble peasant parents in 'A mdo (Amdo), one of the eastern provinces of Tibet, on July 6, 1935. He was recognized as the reincarnation of the thirteenth Dalai Lama and was enthroned in Lhasa on February 22, 1940. The regent continued to rule and the young Dalai Lama began his studies, which focused primarily on the religious texts of the monastic curriculum of the great monasteries *(gden sa).* Within a few years, however, a series of events, not the least of which was the Chinese invasion, brought great political instability to the country, and on November 17, 1950, the fourteenth Dalai Lama assumed full temporal power as head of state and government. Although he was responsible for the political affairs of the country from this time forward (at least to the extent possible, given the Chinese threat), he continued his religious studies, and in the year 1959, after sitting for public examinations during the annual Great Prayer Festival *(sMon lam chen mo)*, he was awarded the highest academic degree, that of *dge bshes lha ram pa* (geshe lharampa).

Within a matter of weeks, as we have seen, the Dalai Lama was forced to leave his homeland and to seek political asylum in India. For the past thirty years, based in the village of Dharamsala in the Himalayan foothills of north India, he has been the major force behind the Tibetan people's efforts at preserving their cultural identity in exile—setting up schools, monasteries, handicraft centers, and even an academy for the performing arts. He has been instrumental in the drafting of a Tibetan constitution, in reorganizing the Tibetan government in exile along representative and democratic lines, and in making major reforms in the monasteries. And, of course, he has been the indefatigable spokesman for Tibetan independence throughout the world.

The Dalai Lama has consistently eschewed violence as a means for achieving Tibetan independence, and on more than one occasion he has been instrumental in actually preventing violent retaliation against the Chinese, both in Tibet and abroad. Instead, he has sought repeatedly to engage in negotiations with the Chinese, and has put forward several proposals that could serve as the basis for such negotiations. The most famous of these is the Five Point Peace Plan that calls for:

1. Transformation of the whole of Tibet into a zone of peace;

2. Abandonment of China's population transfer policy that threatens the very existence of the Tibetans as a people;

3. Respect for the Tibetan people's fundamental human rights and democratic freedoms;

4. Restoration and protection of Tibet's natural environment and the abandonment of China's use of Tibet for the production of nuclear weapons and dumping of nuclear wastes.

5. Commencement of earnest negotiations on the future of Tibet and of relations between the Tibetan and Chinese peoples.[7]

On June 15, 1988, he made even greater public concessions to the Chinese in an address before the European Parliament at Strasbourg.[8] But these and other proposals have fallen on deaf ears, and there has been no positive response by the Chinese to the Dalai Lama's repeated call for dialogue.

In 1989 the Dalai Lama was awarded the Nobel Peace Prize in recognition of his unswerving commitment to the peaceful and nonviolent struggle for Tibetan independence. In his Nobel acceptance speech the Dalai Lama especially stressed the necessity of making of Tibet a zone of *ahimsa* or nonviolence through the demilitarization of the Tibetan plateau; of protecting its natural environment by ending the testing and stockpiling of nuclear weapons and by turning Tibet into "the world's largest natural park or biosphere"; and of maintaining it as a buffer zone between the two most populous states in the world, China and India.[9] Today, under the aegis of the International Campaign for Tibet, hundreds of chapters of the "Friends of Tibet" in every corner of the globe have joined the Dalai Lama in making the plight of the Tibetan people known throughout the world.

With this by way of background, I now move on to the main subject of this chapter, the social philosophy of the Dalai Lama. What are the principles guiding the Tibetan liberation movement? To what extent are they uniquely Buddhist, and to what extent universal? What are the doctrinal and scriptural foundations for these principles? How does a Buddhist social philosophy of liberation contrast with liberation theologies in Latin America?

Some Principles in the Tibetan Liberation Movement and Their Buddhist Heritage

What began as a response to a specific sociopolitical problem, the Tibetan response to the Chinese occupation of their homeland, has in recent years emerged as a systematic set of universal principles based on Buddhist teachings. Such a movement today might best be described as a Buddhist philosophy of social transformation. The tendency of the Tibetan liberation movement, and others like it, to become more universalized with time is discussed in more detail later. For now it must only be remembered that the universal principles characteristic of the movement today have their roots in a unique historical crisis: the Tibetans' loss of their homeland and their subsequent oppression at the hands of the Chinese. In what follows I shall be discussing some of the main points of the Dalai Lama's more developed and universal philosophy of social transformation, but I hope that in so doing the particular historical origins of these principles will not be lost. The Dalai Lama speaks of love for the enemy, and *for him* this means especially love for the Chinese. When he speaks of truth having the power to overcome evil, for him this means that, despite their small numbers and poor resources, the power of truth shall eventually prevail and Tibetans shall one day regain their independence.

Inner Transformation, Material Development, and the Rhetoric of Peace

It is one of the Dalai Lama's unique characteristics as a human being that he likes to tinker with things. In recent years this has led to a very

profound interest in the physical and natural sciences, an̲ᵤ   ₁ogy.
This has also brought him to meet on several occa͜ions wᵢₜ   ₙtists,
medical doctors, and psychologists; and has led to his repeated pᵣₐᵢ꜀ₑ of the
scientific and technological advances of the West.

This interaction with Western scientists has undoubtedly also influenced his belief that science and technology are not the inherent causes of
human alienation. If there exists human misery in technologically advanced
societies it is the fault of human beings, not of science. Hence, in the
industrialized West it is not scientific advancement that has brought alienation, but the fact that that level of material development has been achieved
at the expense of inner spiritual development.[10] It is in this context that he
frequently compares the Tibetan situation with that of the industrial West:

> Despite an often-stated desire to go beyond this materialistic emphasis,
> scientific and technological advancement seem to be the greatest pride of
> the Western world. This point of view stands in direct opposition to that of
> my own country, Tibet. We were technologically backward, but spiritually
> very rich.[11]

And it is inner, spiritual development that is perceived to be the true source
of peace. Hence, "things depend more on the mind than on matter. Matter
is important, we must have it, we must use it properly, but this century
must combine a good brain—intelligence—with a good heart."[12]

Science and technology, therefore, are not the enemy. Instead, the true
enemy lies within. "Many problems are created by our own mental defects;
we suffer due to an internal lack."[13] This means that the most fundamental
social problems that we face today are human-made and that their solution
involves personal transformation. This is not, of course, to denigrate social
action as an external practice, but it is to put it in its place. Without some
commitment to personal spiritual transformation, to the betterment of one's
mind, talk of peace is only so much rhetoric. "Everybody loves to talk about
calm and peace, whether in a family, a national or an international context,
but without *inner* peace, how can we make real peace?"[14] Therefore, true,
lasting peace is something that requires inner peace as a prerequisite. "The
only alternative is to achieve world peace through peace of mind."[15]

Is the inner transformation required to achieve a socially stable and
peaceful world sectarian in character? Is it necessarily Buddhist? The answer seems to be that it is not, that what is needed is a sense of brotherhood and sisterhood, compassion, and the genuine realization of the oneness
of all humankind,[16] which are principles espoused by all of the world's
religions. Nonetheless, there is a sense in which the Buddhist heritage of
Tibet is seen as making a particularly important contribution in this regard:

Traditionally, Tibetans are a peace-loving and non-violent people. Since Buddhism was introduced to Tibet over one thousand years ago, Tibetans have practiced non-violence with respect to all forms of life.[17]

The Interdependence of Contemporary Society

The fact that the Dalai Lama begins what is arguably his most important political proposal, "The Five Point Peace Plan," invoking the principle of interdependence, is indicative of its importance to his philosophy of social transformation:

The world is increasingly interdependent, so that lasting peace—national, regional and global—can only be achieved if we think in terms of broader interest rather than parochial need. . . . As the world grows smaller, we need each other more than in the past.[18]

Interdependence in this sense of the term is a modern phenomenon and is due, among other things, to improved communications. As a result of this, problems—social, economic, and political—can no longer be solved in isolation:

In ancient times problems were mostly local and therefore tackled at the local level. But now the situation is transformed and we have become very closely connected on the international level. One nation's problems can no longer be solved by itself completely.[19]

The principle of interdependence has its origins in classical Buddhist philosophy.[20] Especially as it is developed by Nagarjuna and his followers, it comes to be the positive analogue of emptiness, the final nature of all phenomena. This is undoubtedly the initial source for the Dalai Lama, but in applying it within the context of his philosophy of social transformation the concept takes on a new life. It takes on a historical tone, becoming a way of distinguishing modernity from "ancient times," and a dynamic, pragmatic principle for solving a variety of practical problems.

Discrimination and the Recognition of Equality

One of the most important principles in the Dalai Lama's social philosophy is that of the equality of all human beings. Philosophically, this has several loci in Buddhist doctrine. It is, of course, a corollary to the theory of buddha-nature *(tathagatagarbha)*—the fact that all beings are equal in their potential for perfection. It is also implicit within the discussion of the nature of mind, for according to classical Tibetan Buddhist psychology every individual's mind is of the nature of clarity and cognition, and at the most subtle level all beings, even buddhas, are equal in having as the substratum for all thought an extremely subtle mental state that, although usually hidden beneath grosser mental functions, does manifest itself in the case of ordinary beings at the time of death. It is this same subtlemost mind, present in every living being, that transforms into the enlightened state at the culmination of the process of mental purification. These two doctrines, the theory of buddha-nature and speculation concerning nature of the mind, give a metaphysical basis to the principle of the equality of all beings. Perhaps the most important *ethical* source for this idea comes from the *Bodhicaryavatara* of the Indian sage Santideva (8th century), a constant classical locus for much of the Dalai Lama's thought. A particular source of inspiration has been the eighth chapter, on meditation, where the specific form of *bodhicitta* meditation known as "the exchange of self with other" *(bdag gzhan nyams brjed)* is taught. It is in this context, and specifically as an antecedent to the actual exchange of self and other, that the equality of self and others is expounded. We are all equal in that we desire happiness and loathe suffering. As Santideva says:

> Hence, I should dispel the misery of others
> Because it is suffering, just like my own,
> And I should benefit others
> Because they are sentient, just like my body.
>
> When both myself and others
> Are similar in that we wish to be happy
> How are they different from me?
> Why do I strive for *my* happiness alone?
>
> And when both myself and others
> Are similar in that we do not wish to suffer,
> How are they different from me?
> Why do I protect myself alone?[21]

This equality of self and other has been taken as a theme, and expanded upon, in most of the Dalai Lama's writings. As with the principle of interdependence, it is the practical consequences of this idea that are stressed. Hence:

> We are the same human flesh. I want happiness; you also want happiness. From that mutual recognition we can build respect and mutual trust for each other. From that can come cooperation and harmony, and from that we can stop many problems.[22]

In many instances the principle of human equality is used to emphasize the superficiality of cultural differences and the unity of our basic humanity:

> During my travels abroad I have noticed many things which seem to differentiate West from East, and particularly from Tibet. It is easy enough to understand these superficial differences in terms of the varying cultural, historical and geographical backgrounds which shape each particular way of life and pattern of behavior, but I feel that the far more relevant point to be stressed is the unity of these varying cultures and peoples. That unity is basically the human quest for happiness. . . .[23]

It is interesting that this principle of human equality is also, in this system, the philosophical basis for human rights. Our wanting happiness and our desire to avoid suffering is philosophically fundamental in that it is self-evident and requires "no further justification."[24] Moreover,

> Based on that feeling we have the right to obtain happiness and the right to get rid of suffering. Further, just as I myself have this feeling and this right, so others equally have the same feeling and the same right.[25]

Just as equality can serve as the foundation for peace and for respecting human rights, discrimination (in a broad sense that includes not just prejudice but also the act of simply emphasizing differences) is considered the cause of strife and turmoil. Hence, sociocultural, ideological, religious, ethnic, and economic differences are considered both superficial and artificial.[26] At worst, emphasizing such differences can be the cause of discord:

> Philosophical teachings are not the end, not the aim, not what you serve. The aim is to help and benefit others, and philosophical teachings to support those ideas are valuable. If we go into the differences in philosophy and argue with and criticize each other, it is useless.[27] (Dalai Lama, 1984:47)

And in the secular realm:

> Also, in the world of politics such small discriminations create uncontrollable problems . . . sometimes from race, sometimes from ideology. The same is true for my own country, Tibet, due to certain attitudes of our great neighbor, the People's Republic of China, that appeared during the Cultural Revolution. In this manner human ways of thinking create problems in addition to the basic ones that we must face.[28]

Hence, ideology, religion, and culture are the constructs of human beings. As such they should serve us and bring us happiness. If instead they become sources of suffering, then we are creating unnecessary grief for ourselves, grief that, unlike natural catastrophes, is within our control.[29] Pragmatically, this suffering can be eliminated by stressing human equality rather than human differences.[30]

Love of One's Enemy and the Practice of Non-violence

In his monumental essay, *Civilization and its Discontents,* Freud states that if there is a "commandment" that he finds "even more incomprehensible and arouses still stronger opposition" in him than the commandment that one should love one's neighbor as oneself, it is the commandment, "Love thine enemies," and in the footnote he cites Heine's line that "One must, it is true, forgive one's enemies—but not before they have been hanged."[31] Freud's opposition notwithstanding, love of the enemy has been a pivotal way of expressing the principle of universal love (love for all humans or all beings) in many of the world's religions. It is of course an especially important ethical principle for those peoples who find themselves unjustly persecuted: the Hebrews at different periods in their history, the early Christians under Roman rule, and of course the Tibetans under Chinese domination.

Enemies, like human differences, are an undeniable fact of life. In the Dalai Lama's writings the existence of enemies is not denied, nor does he deny the fact that it is sometimes necessary to react aggressively to a situation:

> For example, if you are genuinely a humble and honest person and *act that way, some people may take advantage of you.* So in such a situation, it may be necessary to react. But we should react without bad feelings. Deep down, tolerance, compassion and patience must still be present. . . .[32]

External circumstances may demand different types of outward responses—some peaceful, some not. But regardless of the variety of possible external manifestations, one thing that must remain invariant is the internal positive motivation. Even when aggressive behavior is called for externally, the only proper internal motivation remains love and compassion. Indeed, it is love of the enemy that is perceived as being the true test of love:

> Love which is limited to near and dear ones is invariably alloyed with ignorance and attachment. The love being advocated here is the kind one can have even for another who has done one harm.[33]

In the Dalai Lama's analysis, based especially on the sixth chapter of the *Bodhicaryavatara* ("Patience"), gratitude becomes the correct response to the enemy:

> Only when someone criticizes and exposes our faults are we able to dis-
> cover our problems and confront them. Thus is our enemy our greatest
> friend. He provides us with the needed text of inner strength, tolerance
> and respect for others. Instead of feeling anger toward this person one
> should respect him and be grateful.[34]

Hence, enemies are to be valued in that they provide us with the opportunity to practice patience.

This attitude toward the enemy is not a mere theoretical principle.
In his recent autobiography, *Freedom in Exile,* the Dalai Lama applies
this to the case of the Chinese.[35] There he deplores the violence perpetrated against the Chinese by Tibetans in recent years, and although also
criticizing the Chinese human rights abuses against Tibetans, he emphasizes that these are the actions of a few and that in many cases the
Chinese populace has itself been deprived of fundamental human rights,
just as Tibetans have.[36]

A corollary to the Dalai Lama's views on universal love are his views
on the ultimate inefficacy of anger and violence as means to resolving
problems. Anger-motivated violence is at most a short-term answer to a
problem:

> Anger, jealousy, impatience and hatred are the real troublemakers; with
> them problems cannot be solved. Though one may have temporary suc-
> cess, ultimately one's hatred or anger will create further difficulties. With
> anger all actions are swift. When we face problems with compassion, sin-
> cerely and with good motivation, it may take longer, but ultimately the
> solution is better, for there is far less chance of creating a new problem.[37]

The doctrinal basis of this idea of nonviolence is to be found especially in
the *Vinaya* literature of Buddhism, the corpus of monastic discipline that
focuses on the avoidance of harm to others. For the Dalai Lama, a prime
exemplar of this principle is to be found in Mahatma Gandhi. In his autobiography, the Dalai Lama describes his visit to Rajghat, Gandhi's crema-
tion site, in the following words:

> It was a calm and beautiful spot and I felt very grateful to be there, the
> guest of a people who, like mine, had endured foreign domination; grate-
> ful also to be in the country that had adopted *Ahimsa*, the Mahatma's
> doctrine of non-violence. As I stood praying, I experienced simultaneously
> great sadness at not being able to meet Gandhi in person and great joy at
> the magnificent example of his life. To me he was—and is—the consum-
> mate politician, a man who put his belief in altruism above any personal
> considerations. I was convinced too that his devotion to the cause of non-
> violence was the only way to conduct politics.[38]

Universal Responsibility and Compassion

Perhaps the most important principles in the Dalai Lama's philosophy of social transformation are those of universal responsibility and compassion. Whereas love is traditionally defined as the wish to bestow happiness on others, compassion is considered the wish to rid others of their suffering. These, together with a third principle called "the superior thought" *(lhag bsam)*, taking upon oneself the burden or responsibility of liberating others,[39] are the three prior causes to the generation of *bodhicitta*, the "mind directed to enlightenment," which is the bodhisattva's wish to attain enlightenment for the sake of all sentient beings. It is in the context of the discussion of the doctrine of *bodhicitta* that we find the most extensive discussions of compassion in Tibetan Buddhism. This, then, is the doctrinal locus for the Dalai Lama's discussions of this subject. The reason why the concept of *bodhicitta* is not introduced as a universal principle within this philosophy of social transformation is clear. The notion of *bodhicitta* is one with clear Buddhist overtones. However, the Dalai Lama has consistently stressed the fact that the principles he is espousing are universal ones that should have applicability even in the secular sphere and "in this life."[40] For the Dalai Lama, making the message universal has meant in part divesting it of religious ideology, that is, making it as religiously neutral, and therefore as widely acceptable, as possible.

> Developing a kind heart does not involve any of the sentimental religiosity normally associated with it. It is not just for people who believe in religion; it is for everyone, irrespective of race, religion and political affiliation.[41]

This would of course exclude from the Dalai Lama's philosophy of social transformation notions with an overtly sectarian religious basis, such as *bodhicitta*, a notion that requires an understanding and acceptance of the specifically Buddhist conception of human perfection.

As we have mentioned, much of the Dalai Lama's discussion of the more general concepts of love, compassion, and universal responsibility are extracted from the discussion of *bodhicitta* and given a pragmatic, worldly flavor. It is a compassionate attitude, and especially *bodhicitta*, that is considered to be the perfect motivation *(kun slong)* for action in Mahayana Buddhism. In the Dalai Lama's thought the notion of proper motivation also plays an extremely important role. Ethically, it is the chief factor that determines whether an action is virtuous or not. When an action is motivated by compassion it becomes virtuous. To use a metaphor from the *Bodhicaryavatara*, like an elixir that can transform ordinary metal into gold, compassion has the capacity to transform worldly action into liberative action. Hence, even politics can become virtuous when properly motivated:

> Sometimes we look down on politics, criticizing it as dirty. However, if you look at it properly, politics in itself is not wrong. It is an instrument to serve human society. With good motivation—sincerity and honesty—politics becomes an instrument in the service of society. But when motivated by selfishness, with hatred, anger, or jealousy, it becomes dirty.[42]

The Power of Truth

There is an ancient pan-Indian tradition that ascribes power to truth. Truth has the power to protect the one who speaks it and to set injustice right. In the *Ramayana,* Sita proves her fidelity to her husband, Rama, thereby defending herself against the unjust charge of adultery by stating her position and throwing herself into a fire. Her emerging unscathed serves as proof of the truth of her position. The notion is also present in the Buddhist tradition,[43] and it finds an interesting expression in the context of the Tibetan liberation movement.

In 1960, the Dalai Lama wrote a short work called "Prayer Words Supplicating Truth, to Request the Compassion of the Three Supreme Jewels" *(mChog gsum thugs rje'i skul ba'i bden gsol smon tshig).* It is a work that invokes the power of the truth of the Buddha's doctrine to bring about the desired goal of universal happiness and Tibetan liberation. Now although it is primarily the truth of the Buddha's words that is invoked, there is also a sense in which the Dalai Lama's own words of prayer are considered words of truth. Hence, in the very first verse the Dalai Lama invokes the Buddhas of the past, present, and future and asks them to "please hear my anguished words of truth *(bden pa'i smre ngag)."*[44]

Truth, then, both as the reality of a given situation, that is, as the resolution sought by those who find themselves the object of oppression in a given situation, and as the words that express it, has the power to overcome evil, the oppression itself. The truth quite literally has the power to set free the oppressed. Hence,

> I believe that human determination and willpower are quite sufficient to challenge outside pressure and aggression. No matter how strong the evil force is, the flame of truth will not diminish. This is my belief.

Truth, in much of the Dalai Lama's writings, is frequently associated with the will of the people and pitted against the power and propaganda of government. Hence, when he states in his recent autobiography that "no matter what governments do, the human spirit will always prevail," he means in part that truth has a power mightier than institutional power and force. Applied to the Tibetan case this means that Tibetans under Chinese rule should never lose hope, for, in spite of their few numbers and relative military backwardness, the truth is with them, and it has a power greater than material might.

Is Social Transformation Idealistic?

It is not uncommon for proponents of social transformation, even those who do not proclaim utopian goals, to be accused of having idealistic visions. That this has in part been the response to the Dalai Lama's social philosophy is witnessed by the fact that he has found the need to defend himself against this charge. There is even at times in his writings the acknowledgment that his views on nonviolence may in fact *be* idealistic, at least for those who find themselves under the yoke of oppression.

> Yet, in truth, I realise that for most people such words are unrealistic. It is too much to ask. It is not right for me to expect Tibetans, who live their daily lives under such terrible hardships, to be able to love the Chinese. So, whilst I will never condone it, I accept that some violence is inevitable.[45]

For the most part, however, the Dalai Lama attempts to justify his social philosophy as plausible and practical. He concludes a recent talk, "Compassion in Global Politics," with the following words:

> ...no doubt you feel I am talking of an impractical dream. However, we human beings have a developed brain and limitless potential. Since even wild animals can gradually be trained with patience, the human mind can also gradually be trained, step by step. If you test these practices with patience, you can come to know this through your own experience.[46]

Therefore, the defense against the impracticality of such a vision comes in the form of reflection on human nature. If human beings were limited in their ability to change, so too would be society. Since they are not, since it is possible to change through training, the transformation of society is possible.

The idea of the limitless capacities of sentient beings has as one of its doctrinal sources the doctrine of buddha-nature, which, as we have mentioned earlier, is the claim that all beings with minds have the capacity to achieve perfection. More to the point as regards the doctrinal basis for the limitless capacity of sentient beings, perhaps, is Dharmakirti's defense of the possibility of buddahood in the *"Pramanasiddhi"* chapter of his *Pramanavarttika*. Be that as it may, in the present context, the claim is more modest and, although not philosophically neutral, inasmuch as it contains metaphysical presuppositions about the limitless possibilities available to human beings, it is at least doctrinally neutral in that it makes no specific reference as to the nature of that limitless state.

At the same time, the Dalai Lama acknowledges that the individual human transformation that is the basis for the transformation of society is difficult at best.[47] It is not something that can be achieved overnight. In fact, even though such a transformation is theoretically possible, there is no guarantee that it will actually take place:

> [A] troubled atmosphere is our current reality. It is very bad, but it is reality. People may feel that the opposite of this, the internal transformation about which I have been speaking is merely idealistic and not related to our situation here on earth. . . . Although to bring about inner change is difficult, it is absolutely worthwhile to try. This is my firm belief. What is important is that we try our best. Whether we succeed or not is a different question. Even if we could not achieve what we seek within this life, it is all right; at least we will have made the attempt to form a better human society on the basis of love—true love—and less selfishness.[48]

Buddhism and Liberation Theology

The Buddhist social philosophy that is emerging from the Tibetan liberation movement is one of a class of religiously based philosophies of social action in the world today. Although each of these movements address distinct, and even unique, problems and issues, it is illuminating to see how the Dalai Lama's philosophy contrasts with another such movement, Liberation Theology. Comparing the two, it seems to me, gives us greater insight into both.

It is one of the central features of Latin American Liberation Theology[49] that it views itself not simply as an addendum or complement to theology as it is currently done but as a critique of the entire theological enterprise. Hence, liberation theologians urge a shift from the traditional concern with the speculative and ahistorical to concern with giving "priority to historical critical thinking as such"[50] and from concern with orthodoxy as "right thinking" and "right speaking" to orthopraxis as "right doing."[51] Hence, for the liberation theologian the starting point of a religiously based philosophy of social action is not theory but practice. It is not ahistorical speculation, but action from within the ranks of the poor that leads to "the whole process of questioning the present social order . . . leading eventually to the abolition of the current oppressive culture."[52]

There is also a sense in which we might say that the Tibetan social philosophy of liberation is grounded in history, for surely it is a direct result of a historical crisis, the Chinese occupation of Tibet. But although it is born as a concrete response to oppression, it has, not unlike some strands of Liberation Theology itself, taken on a life of its own. It has become universalized, and the principles that it espouses are seen by its followers to have universal applicability. Hence, the message of the Buddhist social philosophy of liberation still developing among the Tibetans is no longer solely aimed at understanding and resolving the particular historical crisis in which the Tibetans find themselves but is instead aimed at a wider, even global, audience.[53]

This tendency for religiously based social philosophies to become universalized, to go beyond their particular historical crises to expound a more general message to humanity, is evident in the African-American freedom movement as well. In his most recent book, *Hope and History,* my colleague Vincent Harding writes:

> When we search deeply enough into the struggles for truth, justice and hope of any human community, moving with disciplined compassion and vision, we emerge from the exploration with lessons that were meant for us all. In other words, when approaching the movement from this perspective, what we realize is that the story of the African-American struggle for freedom, democracy and transformation is a great continuing human classic whose liberating lessons are available to all seekers and discoverers. . . .[54]

In other words, the lessons of the African-American freedom movement too are universal.

In both the Tibetan and the Latin American case it may be the oppressed that are the inspiration behind the emerging philosophies of liberation, but in both cases it is an intellectual elite that is the source of this new thinking. It is interesting, however, that the Buddhist social philosophy developing among the Tibetans is evolving not as a bottom-up phenomenon in which ecclesial structures and doctrines become the object of critique but as a top-down one in which the source of the new thinking is the religious hierarchy itself. This is in part due to the fact that the critique is not economic in nature. Whether or not the chief critique in the Latin America case is an economic one, it is certainly the case that such a discussion, and especially a discussion of the Church's role in legitimizing the economic exploitation of the poor, is high on the list of important topics for most Latin American liberation theologians. Such concerns are not absent in the Tibetan case, and indeed the Dalai Lama has himself, on a number of occasions, admitted that internal religious corruption was partly responsible for the eventual demise of the Tibetan government. This being said, it is clear that the most pressing problem, from the Tibetans' own perspective, is not internal corruption but the foreign domination of the Tibetan people by the Chinese. This is understandable. For a country under foreign domination, an economic critique of indigenous, precolonial, political, and ecclesiastical polity can only be considered a secondary task and one that might very well siphon energy away from the primary one of bringing an end to foreign domination. This explains in part why the Tibetan critique has been primarily directed externally by the hierarchy rather than internally toward the hierarchy.

What this has meant as well is that the Buddhist social philosophy emerging out of the Tibetan liberation movement is not envisioned as a radical rethinking of traditional Buddhist philosophy. Although suggesting a new reading of Buddhist texts, a new hermeneutical lens, it does not do so at the expense of the traditional understanding of Buddhist scripture. Instead, the tone in the Tibetan case is internally conciliatory rather than confrontative, it views itself more as a complement to traditional Buddhist philosophical speculation rather than as an undermining of it, and it stresses continuity with the tradition rather than rupture. The idea is not that orthopraxis must supplant orthodoxy but that it must supplement it. Traditional philosophical speculation and scriptural interpretation are not seen as obstacles to social action, the case with various liberation theologians.[55] Rather, as we have seen, they are perceived as providing the theoretical and spiritual *basis* for action. In the Tibetan case it is not that the traditional goals of Buddhism (e.g., *nirvana,* the universal emancipation of all beings, and so on) are discarded in favor of action in the world. Instead the two goals, worldly and supramundane, are seen as reinforcing each other, for virtuous action on behalf of the oppressed creates merit and aids in the task of mental purification, while the more traditional spiritual exercises, especially the practice of compassion and wisdom, are seen as providing the basis that ensures the moral goodness of an action and its efficacy.[56]

Among many Latin American liberation theologians there appears to be a rejection (or what might be the same, a radical redefinition) of tradition, especially of contemplative tradition and classical spiritual practice, in favor of immersing oneself into "the very midst of political activity, recognizing all its elements of conflict."[57] In the words of Vidales:

> Right from the start we must realize that human history, the one and only history that exists, is not only the circumstantial locale of salvation but also salvation itself—as yet unfinished but moving toward its final fulfillment.[58]

Such a rejection of traditional doctrine and spiritual practice in favor of worldly involvement is alien to the form of Buddhist social philosophy developing among Tibetans. Nonetheless, even in the Tibetan case there is recognition of the age-old tension "between personal soteriological goals and the concern for proper ordering of this-worldly life."[59] The resolution, in the Tibetan case, is achieved not from without, through the critique of tradition, but from within, through its exegesis, in such a way that both the personal soteriological element and the element of social action are preserved. Part of the Dalai Lama's task, then, is to draw out for a Buddhist audience the social implications of Buddhist philosophical theory. Here the Dalai Lama is functioning as a homiletician, encouraging Buddhists to action by making clear the practical and social dimensions of doctrine. For example, the Dalai Lama, when asked whether it was better to be in retreat or to be active in the world responded as follows:

> In general, if one can do both, it is best. I think this is the practical way to do it. For the greatest part of the year we have to live in society, we have to lead a good life . . . but for a few weeks, for two months or three months, to make retreat, to forget other types of worldly business and to concentrate solely on one's practice, I think this is the best way. If, however, someone has a special vocation for the hermetic life, if someone has this talent for living and practicing in isolation . . . then it may be worthwhile to . . . put all of one's energies toward spiritual practice. But this is the exception and quite rare. I think that among one million people there may be one or two with this type of talent or vocation.[60]

Hence, for the vast majority of humanity it is a balance between interior cultivation and external work in the social sphere that is considered the ideal life. No amount of social activism can supplant private spiritual practice. Indeed, social activism that is devoid of a proper spiritual/humanitarian foundation is questionable, to say the least. Also, for most people, no amount of meditation can take the place of involvement in the world. In the Tibetan Buddhist case, then, the soteriological, other-worldly element is neither abandoned nor redefined. The path of liberation is not reduced to social activism. At the same time, the practice of the soteriological dimension does not, except in rare cases, permit one to isolate oneself from the world. In the Tibetan case, the duality and tension between the two realms is resolved without being denied, and this results in a vision of the two realms as complementary.

Sociologically, Buddhism has traditionally conceived of the religious and secular worlds as interdependent but separate—the monastic community teaching and giving guidance to the laity, and the laity providing economic sustenance for monks and nuns. A Buddhist philosophy of social action, however, maintains that the religious and secular ideals should be united *within individuals* through a balance of their activities (each community taking on part of the work of the other), but this is a relatively novel development in the history of Indo-Tibetan Buddhism. The fact that such complementarity is to be achieved at the individual level, however, implies neither the sociological nor the soteriological equality of the two realms. Even for the contemporary Buddhist who follows the path that unites spiritual cultivation and social action, it is the exalted state of buddhahood, achieved through the practice of the doctrine and exemplified in the monastic community, that remains the object of greatest veneration and the highest state of human fulfillment, both for self and for other. Although responsible engagement in the world is part of the obligations of the contemporary Buddhist, such engagement alone is incapable of bringing about true and permanent human happiness, either for oneself or for the world.

It is worth noting that the social philosophy emerging out of the Tibetan liberation movement has not allied itself ideologically with any existing political worldview or form of economic analysis, as have many theologies of liberation in Latin America.[61] There are a variety of reasons for this, but perhaps the chief one is this: the Tibetan liberation movement is not a socioeconomic critique of Tibetan political institutions. Instead, as we have stated, its chief goal is the end of Chinese rule in Tibet. Ideological affiliation has little place in helping the Tibetans to achieve this end. Historically, neither the capitalist West nor the formerly Communist Eastern bloc has gone out of its way to support the Tibetan cause. This has led to a general skepticism on the part of the Tibetan intelligentsia concerning political ideology in general. Of course, in regard to the particular brand of Marxist-Leninist-Maoist thought espoused by the Chinese there is no skepticism on the part of the Tibetans, only abhorrence. This is hardly surprising, given what it has meant for them as a people.

Cultural, historical, and religious differences obviously account for the different ways that Liberation Theology and the Dalai Lama's philosophy have developed. The Dalai Lama's thought on its own undoubtedly emerges as a unique philosophy of social transformation; but the comparative dimension, it seems to me, gives us greater insight into the "hows" and "whys" of this uniqueness. In discussing the Buddhist principles behind the social philosophy emerging from the Tibetan liberation movement in the first portion of this chapter my goal has been to demonstrate the continuity of the Dalai Lama's thought with the Buddhist tradition. But there is novelty here as well, and even though that novelty does not manifest itself as a challenge to tradition, it does manifest itself as a reinterpretation of tradition that makes explicit the social implications of Buddhist doctrine. This new message is important not only for Tibetans and for those of us who support them in their struggle to regain their independence but also, it seems to me, for humankind as a whole.

Notes

1. Taken from Thomas Taylor's *Iamblichus' Life of Pythagorus,* and cited in Whitall N. Perry, *A Treasury of Traditional Wisdom* (San Francisco: Harper & Row, 1986), p. 600.

2. Marvin C. Goldstein, *A History of Modern Tibet: 1913–1951, The Demise of the Lamaist State* (Berkeley, Los Angeles, and London: University of California Press, 1989), p. 769.

3. *Tibet Briefing* (New York: The Office of Tibet, 1991), p. 1; John Avedon, *Tibet Today: Current Conditions and Prospects* (New York: The U. S. Tibet Committee, 1987).

4. John Avedon, "Inside Tibet," *Utne Reader* (April 1989), pp. 34–36.

5. Avedon (1987), p. 15.

6. Michael van Walt van Praag, *Population Transfer and the Survival of the Tibetan Identity* (New York: The U. S. Tibet Committee, 1986).

7. *Tibet Briefing,* pp. 10–11.

8. Given that the generous concessions of the Strasbourg Proposal, which included placing Tibet's foreign policy in the hands of the Chinese (*Tibet Briefing,* p. 15), received no positive Chinese response, the Strasbourg Proposal has since been withdrawn under pressure from Tibetans, both in Tibet and in exile, and is considered no longer binding. (*Tibet Briefing,* p. 17.)

9. Dalai Lama, "Nobel Lecture by the His Holiness Tenzing Gyatso, The Fourteenth Dalai Lama," in *News Tibet,* vol. 23, no. 2 (1989).

10. For an interesting discussion that parallels the Tibetan Buddhist one in some respects see Eric Fromm, *The Art of Loving* (New York and Evanston, Ill.: Harper & Row, 1962), pp. 27–28.

11. Dalai Lama, "The Principle of Universal Responsibility," pamphlet and material gathered from various talks given in Europe (New York: Potala Publications, n.d.), p. 6.

12. Dalai Lama (1984), p. 62.

13. Ibid., p. 11.

14. Ibid., p. 62.

15. José Cabezón, *H. H. The Dalai Lama, The Bodhgaya Interviews* (Ithaca, N.Y.: Snow Lion, 1988), p. 47.

16. Ibid.

17. Dalai Lama, "Five Point Peace Plan," pamphlet (1987), p. 2.

18. Ibid., p. 1.

19. Dalai Lama (n.d.), p. 2. See also Dalai Lama (1984), pp. 48, 58, 61, where the doctrine is worked out in more detail and illustrated with examples.

20. For an example of the Dalai Lama's discussion of the principle of interdependence in the context of Buddhist philosophical theory, see Dalai Lama, "A Brief Teaching by His Holiness the Fourteenth Dalai Lama," commentary on the *Eight Verse Mind Training* (Los Angeles: Thubten Dhargye Ling, 1979), p. 10.

21. *Bodhicaryavatara* (VII, 94–96); my translation here differs slightly from Stephen Batchelor's, upon which I base it. See Stephen Batchelor, *A Guide to the Bodhisattva's Way of Life by Shantideva* (Dharamsala: Library of Tibetan Works and Archives, 1979), pp. 113–114. For the Sanskrit and Tibetan of these verses, see the Bhattacarya edition (1960), pp. 60–61.

22. Dalai Lama (1984), p. 16.

23. Dalai Lama (n.d.), p. 1.

24. Dalai Lama (1984), p. 11. Compare this to the following passage from Plato's *Symposium.* " 'And what does he gain who possesses the good?' 'Happiness,' I replied; 'there is no difficulty in answering that.' 'Yes,' she said, 'the happy are made happy by the acquisition of good things. Nor is there any need to ask why a man desires happiness; the answer is already final.' " From B. Jowett, trans. *The Works of Plato* (New York: Tudor Publishing Company, n.d.), p. 334.

25. Dalai Lama (1984), p. 11.

26. Dalai Lama (n.d.), p. 2; (1984), pp. 11, 16.

27. Dalai Lama (1984), p. 47.

28. Ibid., p. 59.

29. The difference between the two types of suffering being discussed here has obvious parallels to the distinction between natural and moral evil in Western philosophical discussions of the problem of evil.

30. At the same time, there are many instances in which human diversity is celebrated in the Dalai Lama's writings; see (1984), p. 49, 60; (1988) pp. 38–39; (1985), pp. 4–5. A distinction needs to be made, therefore, between accepting and celebrating human differences, on the one hand, and using human differences as a basis for creating discord. The differences exist; it is, practically speaking, a question of what we do with them.

31. Sigmund Freud, *Civilization and Its Discontents,* James Strachey, trans. and ed. (New York: W. W. Norton, 1961), p. 57.

32. Cabezón (1988), p. 32

33. Dalai Lama (n. d.), p. 2.

34. Ibid., p. 5.

35. A more detailed discussion of other Buddhist principles (an understanding of karma, the ability to grow from living in adverse situations, etc.) that come into play in the Dalai Lama's own understanding of the present Tibetan situation are to be found in an interview with Daniel Goleman, "The Experience of Change" in *Parabola,* Spring (1990b), pp. 8–9.

36. Dalai Lama, *Freedom In Exile.* Autobiography (New York: Harper Collins, 1990a), p. 261.

37. Dalai Lama (1984), p. 62.

38. Dalai Lama (1990a), p. 116.

39. Dalai Lama, *Kindness, Clarity, and Insight,* J. Hopkins and E. Napper, eds. (Ithaca, N. Y.: Snow Lion, 1984), pp. 46–47, 60, 62.

40. Dalai Lama, "Emerging Consciousness for a New Humankind," in Michael von Bruck, ed. *Emerging Consciousness for a New Humankind* (Bangalore: Asian Trading corporation, 1985), p. 3.

41. Dalai Lama (n. d.), p. 3.

42. Dalai Lama (1984), p. 62.

43. For a discussion of this idea in the context of the long-life prayer *(zhabs brten)* literature of Tibetan Buddhism, where the truth of the Buddha's doctrine (especially interdependence), or of the three jewels, is invoked as a way of praying for the long life of the spiritual master, see my forthcoming article in *Tibetan Literature,* J. I. Cabezón and Roger Jackson, eds.

44. Dalai Lama, "A Prayer of Words of Truth and the Tibetan National Anthem," translated by the Translation Bureau of the Library of Tibetan Works and Archives (Dharamsala: Library of Tibetan Works and Archives, 1950), p. 1.

45. Dalai Lama (1990a), p. 261.

46. Dalai Lama (1984), p. 64.

47. Ibid., p. 87.

48. Ibid., pp. 15–16.

49. I am not unaware of the fact that there is great divergence of opinion in Liberation Theology in Latin America. For the purposes of this chapter, however, I

am allowing myself some pedagogical license and purposely simplifying points that might otherwise lead to major discussions of differences in these various movements. The focus of this chapter is not, after all, Latin American theological polemics but Buddhist social philosophy.

50. Raul Vidales, "Methodological Issues in Liberation Theology," in R. Gibellini, ed., and J. Drury, trans., *Frontiers of Theology in Latin America* (Maryknoll, N. Y.: Orbis Books, 1983), p. 36.

51. Ibid., p. 38.

52. Gustavo Gutiérrez, "Liberation Praxis and Christian Faith," in Gibellini and Drury (1983), p. 18.

53. This tendency in the direction of universality can also be attributed in part to the fact that underlying the Tibetan social philosophy under question are Buddhist principles, which are themselves viewed as having universal applicability.

54. Vincent Harding, *Hope and History: Why We Must Share the Story of the Movement* (Maryknoll, N. Y.: Orbis Books, 1990), p. 10.

55. Gutiérrez (1983), p. 10, for example, states that, "because of an upbringing that was ahistorical and focused on abstract principles, Christians were generally insensitive, if not actually hostile, to any scientific reasoning applied to the political realm." See also Joseph Comblin, "What Sort of Service Might Theology Render?" In Gibellini and Drury (1983), p. 62.

56. This is in marked contrast to the theory of the development of a Buddhist social ethnic that assumes the kammatic/nibbannic distinction, in which social action belongs in the kammatic, that is, "secular," realm, and is therefore related primarily to the goal of higher rebirth, as opposed to the nibbanic aspect of the religion whose goal is emancipation from all rebirth. In the Tibetan setting, and perhaps more generally in Mahayana Buddhism, the case can convincingly be made that such a distinction is unwarranted. Social action is as much the cause of *nirvana* as monastic discipline is; and vice versa, typically "nibbannic" practices such as wisdom and compassion are as relevant to properly acting within the world as is the concept of *karma*. One of the best treatments of the development of a Buddhist social ethic in a Theravada Buddhist society is to be found in Bardwell Smith, "Toward a Buddhist Anthropology: The Problem of the Secular," in *Journal of the American Academy of Religion*, vol. 36, no. 3 (1968), pp. 203–216.

57. Gutiérrez (1983), p. 16.

58. Vidales (1983), p. 40.

59. Frank Reynolds, "The Two Wheels of Dhamma: A Study of Early Buddhism," in Bardwell Smith, ed., *The Two Wheels of Dhamma: Essays on the Theravada Tradition in India and Ceylon* (Chambersberg, Penn.: AAR Studies in Religion, 1972), p. 62.

60. Cabezón (1988), p. 62.

61. The Dalai Lama has on several occasions in the past spoken out in favor of Marxism in its pure form, but this has been qualified in the following way in his recent autobiography, *Freedom in Exile:* ". . . The pursuit of Communism has been one of the greatest human experiments of all time, and I do not deny that I myself was very impressed with its ideology at first. The trouble was, as I soon discovered, that although Communism claims to serve 'the people' . . . 'the people' does not mean everyone, only those who hold views that are held by a minority to be 'the people's view' " (Dalai Lama, 1990a, p. 268).

That the Dalai Lama's political views are ultimately eclectic, and that he sees advantages and disadvantages in different political ideologies is evidenced by the following passage: ". . . inasmuch as I have any political allegiance, I suppose I am still half Marxist. I have no argument with Capitalism as long as it is practiced in a humanitarian fashion, but my religious beliefs dispose me far more towards Socialism and Internationalism. . . . Against this, I set the fact that those countries which pursue capitalist policies within a democratic framework are much freer than those which pursue the Communist ideal. . . . Having said that I remain half Marxist; if I were actually to vote in an election it would be for one of the Environmental parties" (Dalai Lama, 1990a, pp. 268–269).

References

Avedon, John. *Tibet Today: Current Conditions and Prospects.* New York: The U. S. Tibet Committee, 1987.

———. "Inside Tibet," *Utne Reader,* March-April 1989, pp. 33–41.

Batchelor, Stephen (trans.). *A Guide to the Bodhisattva's Way of Life by Shantideva.* Dharamsala: Library of Tibetan Works and Archives, 1979.

Cabezón, José I. *H. H. the Dalai Lama, The Bodhgaya Interviews.* Ithaca, N. Y.: Show Lion, 1988.

———. "Firm Feet and Long Lives: the *Zhabs brtan* Genre of Tibetan Literature." Forthcoming in *Tibetan Literature* coedited by José Cabezón and Roger Jackson. Ithaca, N. Y.: Snow Lion, forthcoming.

Comblin, Joseph. "What Sort of Service Might Theology Render?" in R. Gibellini (ed.) and J. Drury (trans.), *Frontiers of Theology in Latin America.* Maryknoll, N. Y.: Orbis Books, 1983.

Dalai Lama. "The Principle of Universal Responsibility," (pamphlet of material gathered from various talks given in Europe). New York: Potala Publications, n.d.

———. "A Prayer of Words of Truth and The Tibetan National Anthem." Translated by the Translation Bureau of the Library of Tibetan Works and Archives. Dharamsala: Library of Tibetan Works and Archives, 1975.

————. "A Brief Teaching by His Holiness the Fourteenth Dalai Lama," commentary on the *Eight Verse Mind Training.* Los Angeles: Thubten Dhargye Ling, 1979.

————. *Kindness, Clarity and Insight,* J. Hopkins and E. Napper (eds). Ithaca, N. Y.: Snow Lion, 1984.

————. "Emerging Consciousness for a New Humankind," in Michael von Bruck, ed., *Emerging Consciousness for a New Humankind.* Bangalore: Asian Trading Corporation, 1985, pp. 1–11.

————. "Five Point Peace Plan," pamphlet, 1987.

————. "Nobel Lecture By His Holiness Tenzing Gyatso, the Fourteenth Dalai Lama of Tibet," in *News Tibet* vol. 23, no. 2, 1989, pp. 4–6.

————. *Freedom in Exile* (Autobiography). New York: HarperCollins imprint of a Cornelia and Michael Bessie Book, 1990a.

————. "The Experience of Change," an interview with Daniel Goleman, *Parabola,* Spring 1990, pp. 5–10.

Freud, Sigmund. *Civilization and its Discontents.* Translated and edited by James Strachey. New York: W. W. Norton, 1961.

Fromm, Erich. *The Art of Loving.* New York and Evanston, Ill.: Harper & Row, 1962.

Goldstein, Melvyn C. *A History of Modern Tibet: 1913–1951, The Demise of the Lamaist State.* Berkeley, Los Angeles, and London: University of California Press, 1989.

Gutiérrez, Gustavo. "Liberation Praxis and Christian Faith," in R. Gibellini (ed.) and J. Drury (trans.), *Frontiers of Theology in Latin America.* Maryknoll, N. Y.: Orbis books, 1983.

Harding, Vincent. *Hope and History: Why We Must Share the Story of the Movement.* Maryknoll, N. Y.: Orbis Books, 1990.

Jackson, Roger. *Is Enlightenment Possible? Dharmakirti and rGyal tshab rje on Knowledge, Rebirth, No-Self and Liberation,* Ithaca, N. Y.: Snow Lion, forthcoming.

Jowett, B. *The Works of Plato.* New York: Tudor Publishing Company, n.d.

Perry, Whitall N. *A Treasury of Traditional Wisdom.* San Francisco: Harper & Row, 1986.

Reynolds, Frank. "The Two Wheels of Dhamma: A Study of Early Buddhism," in Bardwell L. Smith (ed.), *The Two Wheels of Dhamma; Essays on the Theravada Tradition in India and Ceylon.* Chambersburg, Penn.: AAR Studies in Religion, 1972, p. 3.

Smith, Bardwell. "Toward a Buddhist Anthropology: The Problem of the Secular," *Journal of the American Academy of Religion.* vol. 36, no. 3, 1968, pp. 203–216.

Tibet Briefing, New York: The Office of Tibet, 1991.

van Walt van Praag, Michael. *Population Transfer and the Survival of the Tibetan Identity*. New York: The U. S. Tibet Committee, 1986.

Vidales, Raul. "Methodological Issues in Liberation Theology," in R. Gibellini (ed.) and J. Drury (trans.), *Frontiers of Theology in Latin America*. Maryknoll, N. Y.: Orbis Books, 1983.

9

Thich Nhat Hanh
and the Unified Buddhist Church of Vietnam:
Nondualism in Action

Sallie B. King

History shows a paucity of ethically based social action in most of East Asian Buddhist history. In Vietnam, however, the massive suffering caused by the recent wars convinced many Vietnamese Buddhist monastics and laypersons that it was imperative for them to actively engage in the political and social struggles of their country. To determine the form this engagement should take required the forging of a new Buddhism. Arguably the most important theoretician of this Vietnamese movement was the monk Thich Nhat Hanh. In this chapter, I examine the way in which Nhat Hanh drew upon the resources of Buddhist nondualism (no good/no bad, no self/ no other) to meet the need for ethical social action by bringing experiential and theoretical nondualism directly to bear upon a socially active "Engaged Buddhism." I discuss Nhat Hanh's wartime actions together with those of the closely related Unified Buddhist Church of Vietnam and examine the theory behind those actions. Finally, I reflect upon the interface, in this Vietnamese engaged Buddhism, between theory and practice, between nondualism and social action.

Thich Nhat Hanh is a contemporary Vietnamese Zen master and poet. He was chair of the Vietnamese Buddhist peace delegation during the war and was nominated by Dr. Martin Luther King, Jr., for the Nobel Peace Prize. He is the author of over sixty books ranging from scholarship to poetry, from mindfulness training to engaged Buddhism. He currently lives in exile in France where he continues his writing, teaching and helping Vietnamese refugees. He is a leader of the international "engaged Buddhism" movement, which seeks to create and nurture vehicles for social action among Buddhists.

Nhat Hanh was born Nguyen Xuan Bao in 1926 in South Vietnam, the son of a petty government official.[1] At 17 he entered Tu Hieu monastery in Hue (central Vietnam) as a novice. His teacher was the Zen master Thich Chan That of the fortieth generation of the Lam Te (Lin-chi, Rinzai) Zen school and of the eighth generation of the Lieu Quan school, an indigenous Vietnamese branch of the Lam Te school. Vietnamese Buddhism has long embraced both Theravada and Mahayana (especially Pure Land and Zen) traditions, with Theravada most popular in the south and Mahayana in the north.[2] Nhat Hanh's studies included both traditions, with emphasis upon mindfulness, *gatha* (short verses) and *koan*.[3]

After a one-year novitiate, Nhat Hanh attended the Bao Quoc Institute and received full ordination in 1949. The name he took, Nhat Hanh, evokes the name of Van Hanh, an eminent monk of the tenth to eleventh centuries, who was proficient in the three teachings of Buddhism, Confucianism, and Taoism and who served effectively as adviser to the reigning Vietnamese kings. The name Van Hanh means "ten thousand actions," while Nhat Hanh means "one action"; Nhat Hanh declared that he, unlike his eminent predecessor, needed to concentrate on one thing.[4] The evocation of Van Hanh proved apt for Nhat Hanh, who also proved himself dedicated to broad learning both within and without the Buddhist tradition and who followed the politically engaged footsteps of his religious forebear.

Already in the course of his studies, Nhat Hanh stepped out of the well-trod path and asked staff members to change the curriculum "to include more emphasis on philosophy, literature, and foreign languages."[5] When this request was rejected, Nhat Hanh and four others left. He proceeded to establish himself in Saigon, supporting himself by writing novels and poetry while studying at Saigon University. When he graduated, placing first in four subjects, "the elders in Hue wrote asking him to come back and promised to institute a new policy allowing monks to follow studies outside the pagoda."[6] Although he returned vindicated, harmony with the elders was short-lived due to Nhat Hanh's radical ideas.

In 1950 Nhat Hanh and Thich Tri Huu founded Ung Quang Temple in Saigon; this later became An Quang Buddhist Institute, the foremost center of Buddhist Studies in South Vietnam and a center of activism in the Buddhist struggle movement. In 1956 Nhat Hanh founded a new monastic community, Phuong Boi, near Dalat. At this time he taught in a local high school[7] and was appointed Editor-in-Chief of the magazine *Vietnamese Buddhism* (Phat Giao Viet Nam), the official voice of the Association of All Buddhists in Vietnam (Tong Hoi Phat Giao Viet Nam). In this magazine he began to express in print the ideas of Engaged Buddhism.

In 1961 Nhat Hanh traveled for the first time to the United States, where he studied religion at Princeton and, in 1963, lectured on contemporary Buddhism at Columbia. He maintained contact with the more radical wing of the Buddhist church in Vietnam and at the appeal of one of its leaders, Tri Quang, returned to Vietnam in early 1964, after the fall of Diem. This was a time of tremendous creative activity for Nhat Hanh. Together with other radical Buddhist monks, he quickly began planning the establishment of Van Hanh University, a Buddhist university to fulfill his concept of Buddhist higher education, incorporating the kind of broad curriculum on which he had earlier insisted. He also founded the School of Youth for Social Service, one of the primary vehicles of Engaged Buddhism during the war in Vietnam. During this period, Nhat Hanh and others established a publishing house, which grew to be quite large and influential during the war. He edited the weekly journal *Sound of the Rising Tide,* the official publication of the Unified Buddhist Church, as well as another weekly. He kept up a steady stream of articles, books, and poems calling for peace and reconciliation. His publications were threatening to the governments of both North and South; both banned his collection of poetry *Prayers for the White Dove of Peace to Appear.*

The manner in which Van Hanh University was established is revealing.[8] An Quang pagoda monks agreed to set up a new university with Nhat Hanh's assurance that he would handle the financing. Friends, professors, writers, and others agreed to teach without pay since they were all employed elsewhere. He persuaded the abbots of some pagodas and a nunnery to loan rooms and furniture. Then groups of three went door to door with a letter signed by Nhat Hanh asking for contributions. "If you do kind things with a pure heart, I think you will get support. Money is not the most important thing." Nhat Hanh stresses the importance of relying on the people, not the rich but the poor, who are the source of its strength. "If you have too much, you don't rely on the support of the poor people. You might become arrogant or be cut off from your true resources."

In 1965 Nhat Hanh founded the Tiep Hien Order, the Order of Interbeing, a new branch of the Lam Te school, designed as a manifestation of engaged Buddhism. The order is composed of laypersons as well as monks and nuns. Its charter gives four principles as the foundation of the order: (a) nonattachment to views, "the most important teaching of Buddhism"; (b) direct practice-realization; (c) appropriateness—conformity to the "basic tenets of Buddhism" while engaging oneself to "truly help people"; although there are 84,000 Dharma doors, "even more doors should be opened"; and (d) skillful means.[9]

In 1966 Nhat Hanh made a speaking tour of nineteen countries, arranged by the Fellowship of Reconciliation.[10] In the United States, Nhat Hanh met members of the Senate and House, spoke with then Secretary of Defense Robert McNamara, spoke on nationwide television, and addressed a large meeting at Town Hall in New York. After a long talk with Martin Luther King, Jr., they held a joint press conference, in which King for the first time publicly repudiated the war, comparing the Vietnamese Buddhist peace movement with the American civil rights movement. Nhat Hanh also met with Thomas Merton; afterwards, Merton declared, "he and I see things exactly the same way."[11]

As the trip widened to international scope, Nhat Hanh spoke before the Canadian and the Swedish parliaments and before the British House of Commons. He spoke with the Queen of Holland, the Archbishop of Canterbury, and Dutch and French cardinals. His meeting with Pope Paul VI at the Vatican precipitated a papal mission to Saigon, the aim of which was to encourage Vietnamese Catholic involvement in the peace effort. (Vietnamese Catholics frequently tended to side with the United States and the Saigon government, while the Buddhists struggled against these.)

During this tour, Nhat Hanh publicized his influential "Five Point Proposal to End the War," proposed in Washington, D.C., on June 1, 1966. The proposal asked the United States to:

1. State clearly that it respects the right of Vietnamese to choose the kind of government they want.

2. Cease all bombing, North and South.

3. Declare a unilateral cease-fire.

4. Set a date for total withdrawal of all U.S. troops from Viet Nam (in terms of months) and begin the withdrawal immediately.

5. Help rebuild Viet Nam, all aid being completely free of ideological and political strings.[12]

This tour, and the questions from Western audiences it engendered, led Nhat Hanh to write *Vietnam: Lotus in a Sea of Fire,* which explained the Vietnamese Buddhist position to the West and in Vietnam became an underground best-seller, though banned by the government; the book was also published in eight translations in other countries.[13] The tour ended on a sorry note for Nhat Hanh personally. Colleagues in the Buddhist struggle movement advised him most strongly not to return. As a result of his speeches around the world, they were sure that upon his return to Vietnam he would either be imprisoned or assassinated (there had been an assassination attempt shortly before he left on his international tour).[14] The Buddhist leadership asked him instead to serve as an expatriate representative of the Buddhist movement. Thus began his life in exile, which continues to the present.

In 1968, at the request of the Unified Buddhist Church, Nhat Hanh established an office in Paris to further the work of the movement outside

Vietnam. In 1969 this office became the Vietnamese Buddhist Peace Delegation, which Nhat Hanh headed. To help support the group, Nhat Hanh taught Buddhist history at the Sorbonne; other members of the delegation tutored or worked in a Vietnamese restaurant.[15] They worked to publicize the Buddhist position and to influence the Paris Peace Talks, though they were formally barred from participating in them. They worked to "supply information on the situation in Vietnam, send out speakers, put visitors to Saigon in touch with Buddhist social workers, and seek financial help for orphans in Vietnam."[16]

When the Paris Peace Accords were signed, the delegation decided to stop criticism of either side and to devote themselves entirely to reconstruction and reconciliation work.[17] They themselves could not return to Vietnam, as the Saigon government would not respond to their request for visas; on one occasion "a plane was held at the Saigon airport for an hour because of a rumor that Thich Nhat Hanh was aboard."[18]

The Paris office was closed and Nhat Hanh began a retreat period of several years duration in rural France, where he meditated, gardened, and practiced mindfulness, seeking constructive engagement with his new circumstances. During this period he, and members of the group with him, largely curtailed their public visibility, though they worked actively to get information out of Vietnam and to help the boat people fleeing the war's aftermath. In 1976–1977 they organized an effort to pick up the boat people who were drowning in the Gulf of Siam; this effort was ultimately discontinued due to the hostility of the governments of Thailand and Singapore.

Nhat Hanh emerged from this period of relative retreat from public life with his energies devoted to the people both of Vietnam and the West. He and his associates continue to work on behalf of political prisoners in Vietnam and to ease the plight of the Vietnamese people, especially refugees and the very poor. Their base is a practice center in the south of France, Plum Village. Nhat Hanh contributes to the international engaged Buddhism movement with a steady stream of publications, public talks, and frequent workshops in many Western countries. On the day on which this paper was originally given, he conducted a walking meditation at the Vietnam Veterans Memorial in Washington, D.C.[19] This is an example of both his creativity and his ongoing efforts to heal the wounds which continue to be suffered on all sides of the war.

The Unified Buddhist Church of Vietnam: The Struggle Movement

Nhat Hanh's relationship with the political activism of the Unified Buddhist Church (U.B.C.) is a matter of some complexity. The Buddhist

Struggle Movement was not monolithic. Individual monks and nuns' views differed and factions did develop. A contemporary witness of these events, Don Luce, characterizes the Buddhist movement as composed of three main factions.[20] (1) The most visible, politically active group were the An Quang pagoda monks, among whom Thich Tri Quang, Thich Tam Chau, and Thich Thien Minh were the most prominent. This group was aligned with neither Saigon nor the National Liberation Front (NLF). This was the group that was able to stage massive street demonstrations at will, shoring up and bringing down governments. The headlines were theirs. As the war went on, they became progressively angrier and progressively more anti-Saigon and anti-United States, though certainly never pro-NLF. (2) Thich Nhat Hanh, the School of Youth for Social Service and some Van Hanh University people comprised the second group. These were very close in outlook to the first group but less angry and more thorough-going in their pacifism. While some of them certainly engaged in street demonstrations, Nhat Hanh was less inclined to do so, more averse to having anything to do with political machinations, and much more interested in pure, spiritually based pacifism motivated by love and compassion. (3) There was also a pro-NLF faction, though their story has not yet been told. In addition to these three, there were of course also monks and nuns who wanted nothing to do with politics or activism of any kind.

In the following pages I give a brief account of the actions of the U.B.C. during the 1963–1966 period. Nhat Hanh would not necessarily have agreed with all of the actions taken. Nevertheless, he was an important leader in the U.B.C., took actions as he saw appropriate that were in harmony with the overall aims of the U.B.C., and arguably made the most important theoretical contributions to the evolving U.B.C. program. By the same token, the Unified Buddhist Church of Vietnam was also the institution, which, more than any other, nurtured Thich Nhat Hanh as an engaged Buddhist. Thus the relationship between Nhat Hanh and the U.B.C. was mutually formative, though the two cannot be simply identified.

The political power of Vietnamese Buddhists first came to international attention in 1963 with the struggle against Diem. Ngo Dinh Diem, president of South Vietnam, was pro-Catholic and, of course, pro-United States. His strong Catholic identity and sympathies, reinforced by his brother, Ngo Dinh Nhu, and sister-in-law, Madame Nhu, in itself put him out of touch with the 80 percent of the Vietnamese who were at least nominally Buddhist. On May 8, 1963, Buddhists in Hue flew Buddhist flags as part of a celebration of Buddha's birthday.[21] Religious flags were technically illegal, but this had heretofore always been ignored and Vatican flags had only recently been flown for a ceremony honoring Diem's brother. On this occasion, Buddhist flags were torn down. That evening, a crowd gathered at a radio station when an expected Buddhist program failed to be aired.[22] Thich Tri Quang was inside, arguing with the head of the station and occasionally emerging to calm the crowd. The crowd continued to grow. Government officials arrived and ordered the crowd to disperse. Shortly thereafter, without warning, troops opened fire on the crowd. Eight people were killed, including seven children and one woman. Diem claimed that a Viet Cong hand grenade was responsible, despite a film showing government troops firing. When the American public watched these events on television, American support for the Diem government began to erode.

This event radicalized the Buddhist public of Vietnam and propelled more radical monks into positions of leadership in the Buddhist Church. On May 10, over ten thousand people participated in a protest demonstration in Hue. Buddhist monks demanded "legal equality with the Catholic Church, an end to arrests, greater freedom to practice their faith, and indemnification of the families of victims of the May 8 shootings."[23] Diem ignored these demands and jailed many activist monastics and students.

Note that it was originally government harassment and oppression of the Buddhist Church and its faithful that Buddhists organized to oppose. This kind of Buddhist activism, which struggles against the government expressly for the sake of religious freedom, has a historical precedent.[24] It is, of course, less common for this kind of struggle to escalate into one which can bring down governments and struggle with the greatest military power on the planet, as occurred during the war in Vietnam.

On June 11, the monk Thich Quang Duc burned himself to death in protest of these events. Photographs of the burning monk dominated the front pages of U.S. newspapers the next day, stunning the American public. Under U.S. pressure, Diem signed an agreement acceding to Buddhist demands but failed to change his actions. Tension continued to raise as increasing numbers of monks, nuns, and students protested with marches, strikes, and fasts. The pagodas were the center of many of these activities. Diem, under the influence of the Nhus, identified the Buddhist movement with activities of the Communist National Liberation Front and continued his policy of persecution and arrest. Further self-immolations by Buddhists occurred, which Madame Nhu mocked as "barbecues," as was widely reported in the American news media.[25]

The situation came to a head, from the Buddhist perspective, on the night of August 21, when Diem's forces raided Buddhist pagodas in Saigon, Hue, and other cities in South Vietnam. In the assault, monks were forcefully ousted, 1,420 of them arrested, several killed, about thirty injured and pagodas ransacked. From this point on, coup planning by top South Vietnamese generals became serious. In the United States, the Kennedy administration recognized the politically disastrous nature of Diem's actions in a country that was 80 percent Buddhist and worried about "the continued reliability of 'the predominantly Buddhist composition of the armed forces' if further Buddhist suicides or demonstrations were attempted."[26] Under the circumstances, the U.S. government gave encouragement to the coup planners.[27] Protests and arrests of protesters continued throughout September and October.

On October 8, Thich Nhat Hanh, who was at Columbia University at the time, presented documents on human rights violations in South Vietnam to the United Nations; the UN General Assembly authorized a fact finding mission. On October 27, in the midst of this mission, a Vietnamese monk immolated himself. Finally, on November 1, the coup occurred; the coup was bloodless except for the executions of Diem and his brother Nhu. Thich Nhat Hanh has said this about these events:

> Some said the coup was not entirely nonviolent, because, at the end, the army intervened. But even the soldiers did not open fire, although they assassinated Diem and his brother after the coup had taken place.
>
> There was much discussion, though I think it's very hard to draw conclusions. . . . And all the things that we did were done without any prescribed doctrine, from the circulation of mimeographed documents to the self-burning of the Buddhist monks and nuns. In particular, the self-immolations were not planned by any movement at all. They were the decision of individuals.
>
> There was no conscious ecumenical movement either. Christians and Buddhists, Catholics and Caodaists—they just struggled together. And we never said, 'Now we have done all we can do. Now you, the army, you have to do the last thing.' Members of the army worked side by side with nonarmy people.
>
> There were people who described it as a holy struggle, because the intention was so pure. The struggle in 1966, 1967, and on up to the present has never been as pure as it was in 1963. Because, when we speak of a third force, of replacing the government, of all those things, there is always an intention of seizing or at least sharing power. During the 1963 struggle nobody thought of toppling the Diem government in order to come to power. But after that, in 1964, 1965, and 1966, Buddhists, Catholics, Caodaists, thought of themselves, thought of their own power.
>
> I certainly don't mean to say that the more we carry the struggle forward, the more we fall spiritually or morally. But I think the motive of the struggle determines almost everything. You see that people are suffering and you are suffering, and you want to change. No desire, no ambition, is involved. So, you come together easily! I have never seen that kind of spirit again, after the 1963 coup. We have done a lot to try to bring it back, but we haven't been able to.
>
> . . . It was so beautiful.[28]

The new regime, headed by General Duong Van Minh, lost no time in establishing good relations with the Buddhists. His first day in office, Minh began freeing 75,000 political prisoners, including many Buddhist monks.

At this time, a four-day Buddhist congress was held that unified Theravada and Mahayana in Vietnam and resulted in the creation of the Unified Buddhist Church of Vietnam. In an opening speech, Thich Tam Chau, who would become one of the leading activists in the Church, enunciated the basic assumptions behind an engaged Buddhism:

> The experiences of recent months have shown us that social events can deeply influence the religious life, because Buddhists are at the same time the citizens of the country. . . . This organization does not aim to dominate, but to guide, educate, and aid disciples to fulfill their social duties. What are those social duties? They are the practice of Buddhist doctrine in daily life, the propagation of this doctrine to the people around them. In other words, the Buddhists have to participate in social and cultural activities.[29]

Again, we see the basic motivation to be the creation and protection of conditions to allow for the free and authentic practice of Buddhism. Here it is made explicit that since social and political conditions can "deeply influence the religious life" it is not only justified, it is a Buddhist's duty to be involved in influencing those social and political conditions in such a way as to permit freedom of religion.

Minh's short-lived administration was noted both for its good relations with the Buddhists and for its disinclination to pursue an aggressive military policy, preferring to look for a negotiated political settlement, possibly involving a "neutralist" government unaligned with any military bloc. "Neutralism" was very much in the air at the time. The United States was very unsympathetic to any talk of neutralism or negotiated political settlements, believing that this would result in defeat for perceived U.S. interests and victory for the North Vietnamese Communists. As the voice claiming to represent the majority of the people, the Buddhist movement became increasingly identified with "neutralism" (the refusal to side with North or South) and a negotiated political, as opposed to military, solution to end the war. Here was the basis for the subsequent chasm between the goals of the American government and those of the Vietnamese Buddhist movement. Through their opposition to the American prosecution of the war, the Buddhist movement also became popularly identified with Vietnamese nationalism, which was expressed in strong opposition to foreign, that is, American, domination.

The Minh regime was overthrown by a coup on January 30, 1964. Discontent among South Vietnamese generals and American mistrust of the Minh regime both played a role in the coup.[30] Minh's successor, Major General Nguyen Khanh, initially cooperated enthusiastically with American personnel and policy, but he was much more out of step with the wishes of the Vietnamese people, among whom antiwar and neutralist feelings were strong. This was a matter of great concern in Washington. President Johnson instructed Ambassador Lodge that the latter's mission was "precisely for the purpose of knocking down the idea of neutralization wherever it rears its ugly head and that on this point I think that nothing is more important than to stop neutralist talk wherever we can by whatever means we can."[31]

On August 16, Khanh promulgated a new constitution rearranging the government (the "Vungtau Charter"), giving himself sweeping new powers and sharply curtailing civil liberties.[32] Massive demonstrations led by Buddhist activists of the U.B.C. and enthusiastically joined by students followed almost immediately. On August 24, Khanh met with the top three leaders of the U.B.C.—Thich Tri Quang, Thich Tam Chau, and Thich Thien Minh— who demanded "that he abolish his new constitution, establish a civilian government, assure full freedom of religion and expression, and schedule free elections by November 1, 1965."[33] Khanh made concessions that did not fully meet these demands and demonstrations continued to mount.

U.S. General Westmoreland worried that the Buddhist spokesman, Thich Tri Quang, "had not repeat had not agreed to denounce the Communists" and observed that although the army continued to be "the key power factor, it is, at the moment, effectively neutralized . . ."[34] by the Buddhist-led popular movement. A contemporary CIA report reflected American lack of understanding of Buddhist motives, stating that Tri Quang "is capable of allying himself with the Communists at any time such an alliance strikes him as advantageous for his own political ambitions and religious objectives—two causes he almost certainly views as one." It describes him as "a fanatic nationalist, undoubtedly anxious to see the U.S. out of Vietnam at the earliest possible moment. . . . Consequently, some negotiated or neutralist solution which would expedite the U.S. departure must have considerable appeal in his eyes."[35] Such was the American understanding of the Buddhist desire for a negotiated peace, an end to the killing and freedom from foreign domination. The judgment of the final sentence, however, was essentially accurate, as was borne out by subsequent statements and actions of the U.B.C.

Kahin summarizes the situation well. Already at this time,

> the abiding problem for American officials was that the more broadly based and responsible to public opinion a Saigon government became, the less disposed it would be to continue with the fighting, and the greater the popular pressure it would be under to negotiate a neutralist political settlement incompatible with any continuing U.S. presence.[36]

In other words, any government acceptable to the United States, which wanted to pursue the war, would be unacceptable to the Vietnamese people, who wanted to stop the war, and vice versa. It was the Buddhist movement that voiced this popular dissatisfaction with American policy and actions.

This fundamental incompatibility of American and popular Vietnamese wishes that was already well established in 1964 only grew more pronounced. Thich Nhat Hanh's important 1967 work, *Vietnam: Lotus in a Sea of Fire*, refers to the same phenomenon, by then exacerbated by the expansion of the war.

> The business of war itself has been taken over almost completely by the American troops now, with the South Vietnamese army occupying a strictly subordinate role. . . . The more American troops sent to Vietnam, the more the anti-American campaign led by the NLF [National Liberation Front, communist forces in South Vietnam] becomes successful. Anger and hatred rise in the hearts of the peasants as they see their villages burned, their compatriots killed, their houses destroyed. Pictures showing NLF soldiers with arms tied, followed by American soldiers holding guns with bayonets, make people think of the Indochina war between the French and the Viet Minh and cause pain even to the anti-Communist Vietnamese. . . . The spirit of patriotism among the peasants is very high. They are not informed about world history or ideological struggles; what they see is a large force of white Westerners doing their best to kill their fellow countrymen, many of whom previously fought against the French. The peasants do not see the victims of the American military effort as dead Communists, but as dead patriots.[37]

From Nhat Hanh's perspective, it was quite impossible for America to win the war, since every short-term American "success"—killing Vietnamese Communists—alienated the Vietnamese masses and thus promised long-term defeat for America. He wrote, "I know it is a hard fact for Americans to face, but it is a fact that the more Vietnamese their troops succeed in killing, and the larger the force they introduce into Vietnam, the more surely they destroy the very thing that they are trying to build."[38]

Of course, opposition to the American war effort did not constitute the full Buddhist position, the uniqueness of which lay in its refusal to side with either the North or the South, with communism or capitalism. Nhat Hanh wrote:

> The majority of the peasants take little or no interest in the problems of communism or anti-communism. They are direct victims of the war, and consequently they welcome every effort in the direction of ending the war. . . . The more the war is escalated, the more they are its victims, since

both sides threaten their lives and property. Since early 1964 I have fre-
quented the remote villages of Vietnam. . . . Peasants in these villages hated
both sides. The Viet Cong ordered them to dig caves as shelters from the
possible bombing, while government troops warned them that if they dug
caves, the Viet Cong would use them for resistance against the government. They were warned that if they refused to dig the caves, they would
suffer the consequences from the Viet Cong, and they were warned by the
government that if they did dig the caves they would be beaten by the
government troops. We talked with some peasants . . . and when we had
established confidence between ourselves I asked them the question: 'Whom
would you follow: the government of South Vietnam or the National Liberation Front?' They replied: 'We do not follow either. We follow the one
who can end the war and guarantee that we can live.'[39]

The desire to put an end to the suffering of the powerless was the deepest
motivation of the Buddhist antiwar activists. Since both the NLF and the
American-backed Saigon government were propagating the war, the Buddhists sided with neither, but with their shared victims: the Vietnamese masses.

In January 1965, when the United States allocated funds to expand the
South Vietnamese armed forces from 560,000 to 660,000 men, with a con-
comitant increase in the draft, Buddhist and student opposition exploded.[40]
Huge demonstrations took place in Saigon, Dalat, Nhatrang, Hue, and Danang.
The demonstrators were anti-American as well as antiwar and attacked the
United States Information Service buildings in Saigon and Hue.

At this juncture, CIA analysis declared that the Buddhists were now
"strong enough to make unworkable any set of political arrangements their
leaders care to oppose."[41] Ambassador Taylor declared that the Buddhists
were "in a position of 'increased prestige and influence in [the] country,'
whereby they 'could create an atmosphere conducive to pressures for a
negotiated settlement.' "[42] In early 1965, South Vietnamese military weakness, political factionalism, and dramatic growth in the Buddhist movement combined to convince many American leaders that a neutralist
government in South Vietnam was immanent.[43] Khanh, souring on the U.S.
role in Vietnam, reached an agreement with Buddhist leaders to oust the
prime minister they fiercely opposed as too much under the control of
American influence. He also began a covert dialogue with the NLF. This was
too much for American officials and a number of South Vietnamese generals and Khanh was soon removed from power.

As the war expanded with more and more U.S. ground troops, large
numbers of civilians in South Vietnam were being killed in the effort to
eliminate Viet Cong. An American Congressional hawk admitted in early
1966 that "an average of two civilians were killed for every Viet Cong,
and . . . in some recent search-and-find missions against the VC the ratio

has been six civilians to one enemy soldier."[44] This resulted in huge numbers of refugees within South Vietnam and, as Nhat Hanh pointed out, the continued strengthening of antiwar sentiment, channeled by the Buddhists.

Reluctant to directly confront the United States and forbidden to speak of neutralism or negotiations, the Buddhist leadership focused antiwar sentiment on a demand for elections. The Saigon government felt forced by public opinion to promise elections but kept the promise vague and indefinite. The Buddhists continued to press this point. However, elections were strenuously opposed by the U.S. mission who believed that "if any elected assembly sits in Saigon, it will be on the phone negotiating with Hanoi within one week."[45]

In mid-March in Danang, Hue, and Saigon, mass rallies called for the military government to step down and allow free elections. Troops in northern South Vietnam (especially the Danang and Hue areas) were very sympathetic to these demands. Generals in that region refused to use military force against the movement as demanded by the Saigon regime. To buy time, the Saigon government made conciliatory promises to Buddhist leaders Thich Tri Quang and Thich Tam Chau that they soon broke. Demonstrations broke out again in Hue and in Saigon, the latter joined by leaders of the South Vietnamese Catholic community. The movement used explicitly anti-American language.

Things came to a head as the Saigon regime lost control of northern South Vietnam. "On April 2 [President] Johnson was advised that in Hue and Danang 'the police, civil servants, and large elements of the local 1st Division [troops] are in total sympathy with the [Buddhist-led] "struggle" group' and that 'anti-American themes have been increasing.' "[46] With American urging, planning, and assistance, the Saigon junta brought Saigon military forces headed by General Ky himself into Danang to crush the opposition, using a U.S. base as a staging ground. However, the local commander, General Nguyen Van Chuan, would not permit the Saigon forces to leave the base. Another general, headquartered in Hue, also declared for the Struggle Movement. Ky was forced to back down. Publicly, concessions were made to the Buddhists and Ky promised to withdraw his troops from Danang. Privately, Ky left his troops out of sight on the American base and organized a larger build-up. Ky promised elections for a constituent assembly to be held within three to five months, the resignation of the military government immediately after the elections and a political, rather than a military, solution in the area of the uprisings. "On the basis of these promises, which they understood [Ambassador] Lodge had concurred in," Tri Quang and other Buddhist leaders called off the demonstrations, with Tri Quang himself making a personal appeal in Hue.[47]

During a few weeks of calm, the Saigon government prepared their assault. In early May, Ky announced that the government would break most of the promises it had made to the Buddhists. On May 15 the military crackdown on Danang was begun. Using American arms, tanks, and bases, and moving at a time when local troops supportive of the Struggle Movement had been lured away, the junta crushed the opposition. Thousands of Buddhist families placed their sacred family altars in the streets to block the tanks' passage, to no avail. After two days "of bitter fighting . . . Ky's forces had captured the Struggle Movement's strongholds, including one pagoda compound described by [the *New York Times*'s Neil] Sheehan as looking like 'a charnel house.' The 700 local troops who backed the Struggle Movement surrendered, along with the monks, Buddhist boy scouts, students, and other civilians aligned with them."[48] On the heels of these events, Thich Nhat Hanh narrowly escaped an assassination attempt and left Vietnam on May 22, invited by the Fellowship of Reconciliation to represent the Buddhist cause before the American people. This became the international tour that ended in his exile.

In Vietnam, "Ky moved quickly against the Buddhists in Saigon, his troops using fixed bayonets and tear gas to drive some two thousand monks, nuns, and others into a pagoda compound, and arrested twenty leaders at the Buddhist Youth headquarters along with several labor leaders."[49] When "student supporters of the Struggle Movement in Hue . . . burned the U.S. consulate and USIS library there," Ky moved against Hue. "By June 19 his troops were in control of all Hue, and soon arrested Tri Quang and several hundred other Buddhist monks and university and high-school students."[50] Tri Quang was quickly released, but many other monks "were still in prison nine years later when the Saigon government fell."[51] Shortly thereafter, the crackdown on the Saigon Buddhist movement was completed. On June 25, Ambassador Henry Cabot Lodge "publicly praised Ky's regime for its stand in putting down the Struggle Movement, referring to this as 'a solid political victory.' "[52]

This was the end of the last major challenge the Buddhist movement posed to the South Vietnamese government and the United States. Although Buddhist struggle and protest continued with massive popular support and many successful peace campaigns, it never regained momentum sufficient to bring down a government or change the course of the war. The two main reasons for this were: first, the Thieu-Ky regime in Saigon stayed in step with American expectations and thus enjoyed firm political and military backing from the latter; and second, the Buddhist movement was fiercely suppressed by the Saigon government from the May 1966 crackdown until the end of the war. As an illustration, the U.B.C. obtained documents in 1968 showing that of 1,870 prisoners in Chi Hoa Prison, Saigon, 1,665 were listed on the daily census as "Buddhists," fifty as "Communists."[53]

Forms of Buddhist Engagement

As noted previously, the beginning of Buddhist engagement in Vietnam was the struggle to protect the practice of Buddhism. The goal of the movement steadily widened, however, to a struggle against political oppression and for peace. In the following we briefly consider some of the forms that the Struggle Movement took during the war. Nhat Hanh lists many such actions in *Love in Action,* of which I can mention only a few.[54] Note that the following were variously participated in by clergy and laity.

1. The works of "anti-war writers, composers, poets and artists"[55] were used to inspire and educate people on the popular level. Antiwar songs in particular spread quickly and were an effective vehicle for education, for promoting solidarity within the movement, and for holding attention on a given issue. A number of Nhat Hanh's poems were used in this way.

> A peace song based on a poem of Thich Nhat Hanh's was one of several widely used in every province of South Vietnam as teams travelled to explain and sing about "Do Not Shoot Your Brother":
>
> Our enemy has the name of hatred
> Our enemy has the name of inhumanity
> Our enemy has the name of anger
> Our enemy has the name of ideology
> Our enemy wears the mask of freedom
> Our enemy is dressed in lies
> Our enemy bears empty words
> Our enemy is the effort to divide us.
> Our enemy is not man.
> If we kill man, with whom shall we live?[56]

2. Fasting was engaged in by individuals and by large and small groups. "One fasts to pray, to purify one's heart and strengthen the will—or to arouse the latent awareness and compassion of the population."[57]

3. Family altars were placed in the street in the path of approaching tanks. In the context of traditional Vietnamese values, this was a drastic action. Placing the family altar before an approaching tank, one symbolically placed one's ancestors, the embodiment of the family, before the tank. In other words, one risked everything.

4. Some shaved their heads in protest against the government. In shaving one's head one took on the appearance of a Buddhist monk or nun, reminding government officials of Buddhist values and showing one's support of them. A foreign minister and a senator took this act in protest against government policies.

5. Noncooperation with the government was broadly adopted. Noncooperation included strikes, the return of government licenses, mass resignations of university professors and administrators, the boycott of classes by students, and the refusal to participate in the war. "All of these have been met with atrocious reprisals."[58]

6. The aid and protection of deserters and draft resisters was crucial. Buddhist activities formed an underground network to help hide those who refused to serve in the government army. Both deserters and those who hid them were imprisoned upon discovery. "In cases where a draft resister has been found hidden in a family's home, the entire family—including children—has been arrested."[59]

7. The most drastic act was self-immolation by Buddhist clergy and laypersons for the sake of awakening and educating the people.[60] This subject requires extra attention. Although this was a very powerful form of the Buddhist antiwar struggle, Nhat Hanh emphasized that it should not be conceived as violent. It was a manifestation of the individual's inability to bear the suffering of the people and a powerful attempt by the individual to reach the hearts of others. By demonstrating in this way the suffering of war, the self-immolator hoped that those who supported or perpetuated the war would likewise become unable to bear the pain of war and stop the actions that allowed it to continue.

Although these acts were associated with the U.B.C. and the Buddhist antiwar struggle, they were not sanctioned by these groups. Nhat Hanh writes, "Self-immolation usually occurs at a most unexpected moment and is not included in the program of action. No one has the courage to arrange for someone else's self-immolation. Whenever a person has declared his intention to burn himself the Buddhist Church has appealed to preclude the tragic act. But once such an important decision has come to a man, the authority of the Church is no longer important."[61] And again:

> We do not intend to say that self-immolation is good, or that it is bad. It is neither good nor bad. When you say something is good, you say that you *should* do that. But nobody can urge another to do such a thing. So such a discussion is not pursued in order to decide whether self-immolation is a good tactic in the nonviolent struggle or not. It is apart from all that. It is done to wake us up.[62]

Neither is the act a suicide. Nhat Hanh personally knew at least two of those who immolated themselves: Thich Quang Duc, a monk, and Nhat Chi Mai, a student. Nhat Hanh wrote, "It was because of life that they acted, not because of death."[63] Before her death, Nhat Chi Mai happily devoted herself to her parents for a month. Then she baked a cake and brought it to the Buddhist community, wearing a beautiful dress. "We had never seen her in that dress before, and many thought that she was going to marry and that was why she had deserted the community for one month. She brought a banana cake that she had made at home. She divided it up and gave it to every one of us. And how she laughed! Many suspected that she was going to get married. She was so joyful. And then two days later they heard the news."[64]

Nhat Chi Mai wrote Nhat Hanh "a simple letter": "Tomorrow I go to burn myself for peace; please don't worry, peace will come soon."[65] As she died, Chi Mai embodied reconciliation, kneeling in a position of worship before statutes of the Virgin Mary and the Bodhisattva of Compassion Quan Am (Kuan Yin, Kannon) that she had placed before her.

In addition to these struggle actions, the Buddhist movement led, organized, and inspired many kinds of action for relief, healing, and reconstruction, which should also be mentioned.[66]

1. Perhaps best known was the Buddhist role in evacuating villagers caught in the cross fire or lying before the approaching line of battle. In such cases, Buddhist monks and nuns dressed in their yellow robes and carrying the Buddhist flag for visibility would form a double column and walk the villagers out of immediate danger. As a rule, neither of the battling sides would fire on such Buddhist phalanxes, though without the yellow robes in evidence, they would surely have been targeted.

2. Sometimes monks helped establish cease-fire lines outside of villages by approaching both sides, at considerable risk, and convincing them to retreat to lines outside the villages.

3. Buddhist social workers worked to reconstruct villages destroyed in battle. This meant doing everything from rebuilding buildings, to mending the social fabric and healing psychological wounds. They sometimes had to return to rebuild the same village time and again.

4. Buddhist social workers worked actively on behalf of war orphans. Their programs were diverse. They built and operated familylike orphanages, sometimes staffed partially "with 'grandparents'—old people who had lost their families in the war." Based on the old tradition of relatives taking in a parentless child, they raised money with their "orphans-in-families" program to make it possible for desperately impoverished relatives to take in an orphan. Their "school-home" program provided a place for fatherless children, "half orphans," to go during the day and be cared for by social workers while the mother worked.[67]

5. Even during the war, Buddhist social workers were actively engaged in working to renew Vietnamese society, especially in the countryside. They worked to educate, to teach new agricultural methods, basic medicine, sanitation, and so on. This was conceived as a "rice-roots" effort in which "Buddhist social workers see themselves as catalysts for the common discussions where people themselves have to take a stand with regard to what should be done and how."[68]

Thich Nhat Hanh: Engaged Buddhist Ethics

When Diem fell, the activist Buddhists of Vietnam found themselves virtually overnight in a position of tremendous power and prominence. The eyes of the people of Vietnam, as well as of all the global parties to the conflict, were upon them. What should they do next? Completely unprepared, they needed to understand their role both in the light of their immediate situation and in the context of Buddhist values.

Events moved too fast, with crisis following crisis, and time was too short for anything like an adequate consideration of the issues. Yet the issues were there, were wrestled with, and continue to be wrestled with. Prominent among Buddhist activists publicly contemplating the principled foundation of Buddhist social activism was and is Thich Nhat Hanh. In his works written during the war and since, we see one creative attempt to come to Buddhist terms with the imperative posed by the "lotus in a sea of fire": Vietnam.

What kind of ethical principles are embodied in the engaged Buddhism of Thich Nhat Hanh? We can open this by examining one of his poems.

Please Call Me By My True Names

Do not say that I'll depart tomorrow
because even today I still arrive.

Look deeply: I arrive in every second
to be a bud on a spring branch,
to be a tiny bird, with wings still fragile,
    learning to sing in my new nest,
to be a caterpillar in the heart of flower,
to be a jewel hiding itself in a stone.

I still arrive, in order to laugh and to cry,
    in order to fear and to hope,
the rhythm of my heart is the birth and
    death of all that are alive.

I am the mayfly metamorphosing on the
    surface of the river,
and I am the bird which, when spring comes,
    arrives in time to eat the mayfly.

I am the frog swimming happily in the
    clear water of a pond,
and I am also the grass-snake who
    approaching in silence,
    feeds itself on the frog.

I am the child in Uganda, all skin and bones,
      my legs as thin as bamboo sticks,
and I am the arms merchant, selling deadly
      weapons to Uganda.

I am the 12-year-old girl, refugee
      on a small boat,
who throws herself into the ocean after
      being raped by a sea pirate,
and I am the pirate, my heart not yet capable
      of seeing and loving.

I am a member of the politburo, with
      plenty of power in my hands,
and I am the man who has to pay his
      "debt of blood" to my people,
dying slowly in a forced labor camp.

My joy is like spring, so warm it makes
      flowers bloom in all walks of life.
My pain is like a river of tears, so full it
      fills up the four oceans.

Please call me by my true names,
so I can hear all my cries and my laughs
      at once,
so I can see that my joy and pain are one.

Please call me by my true names,
      so I can wake up,
and so the door of my heart can be left open,
the door of compassion.[69]

This poem locates ordinary human morality in the same realm as animal and even plant behavior. He says "I" am a bud, a tiny bird, a caterpillar. This reflects traditional Buddhist ideas about the nature of human being: we humans are not a special class, different in our essential nature from other forms of life. We are beings who live many lives, and in the endless round of birth after birth, we are born sometimes in the form of human beings, sometimes in animal forms, sometimes as gods, sometimes as hell beings, sometimes in other mythological forms. Given this idea, it is natural to locate human behavior and even human morality in the same realm as that of other life forms.

How, then, do animals behave? The mayfly metamorphoses; the bird eats the mayfly. The frog swims happily, the grass-snake eats the frog. Is there good and evil here? Is there right and wrong? We certainly do not ordinarily think so. As the Taoists say, "The Tao is not humane"; in other words, Mother Nature does not operate by our standards of right and wrong; morality does not apply in the nonhuman world of nature.

Nhat Hanh goes on to create a parallel between the snake eating the frog and the arms merchant selling deadly weapons to Uganda, to the detriment of the starving Ugandan child. Again, he parallels these with the sea pirate who rapes a 12-year-old Vietnamese boat-girl, who in her anguish throws herself into the sea. Is there not right and wrong here? Are these not great evils being committed against innocent children? Any moral system would surely recognize the unequivocal wrong of such acts. How can Nhat Hanh suggest that the sea pirate and the arms merchant are in any way like the blameless bird or the snake?

In Nhat Hanh's view, the sea pirate and the arms merchant are indeed like the bird and the snake. All are driven in their actions by the same forces: hunger seeks satiation, fear seeks to avoid what is feared, revulsion seeks to avoid the repulsive, desire seeks to attain the desired, power seeks to exercise dominance. Human ideas of good and bad are meaningless in this context, as Nhat Hanh reveals by his repeated use of the word "I." I am the frog and I am the snake: if I were born a frog I would enjoy swimming in the pond; if I were born a snake, I would seek a frog for dinner. Likewise, Nhat Hanh says, "if I had been born in the village of the pirate and raised in the same conditions as he was, I am now the pirate."[70] It is important to recall that in the Buddhist view there is no soul or self that could be in its essence good or bad. While we live in samsara—the world of birth after birth after birth, the world of confusion and ignorant passions—we are conditioned beings. What I am is the product of my karma, my past actions in this life and previous lives. But if my karma causes me to be born in conditions of abject poverty, ignorance, and hopelessness, the person I become in this life will be the product of these conditions. So just as the snake behaves as it does on the basis of the conditions of its birth and its experiences in this life, so do human beings.

Two implications follow from this perspective. First, there is of course sorrow for the starving Ugandan child and the Vietnamese boat-girl; they also are the victims of the conditions of their birth. The first principle of Buddhism is suffering. The entire point of Buddhism from beginning to end is to eradicate suffering; this is the goal of each and every sincere Buddhist. So this is by no means a heartless view, despite the parallel drawn between the mayfly and frog on the one hand and the Ugandan and Vietnamese children on the other.

If the first principle of Buddhism is suffering, the second principle is the necessity of looking carefully at suffering, not turning one's face from it, seeing it clearly and understanding its roots. And part of seeing suffering clearly is feeling strongly that suffering; Nhat Hanh says I am the Ugandan child, I am the Vietnamese boat-girl. He not only feels sorry for them, he indicates that it is possible and necessary to feel complete empathy with the victims of hardship. Nhat Hanh says, "I feel the hunger, the misery, the despair that those children feel; the identical feelings that are in their hearts are in mine; there is no separation between us." This is surely the very opposite of heartlessness, and in fact suggests a degree of emotional commitment more intense than that usually expected in our Western ideas of pity.

Second, there is no judgment called for with respect to the sea pirate or the arms merchant, any more than there is for the snake and the bird. If you or I had been born under those conditions, you or I would be the sea pirate or arms merchant and as Nhat Hanh puts it, "I cannot condemn myself so easily." Furthermore, "If you take a gun and shoot the pirate," he says, "you shoot all of us," not only because that could and would be me if I were born under such circumstances but also "because all of us are to some extent responsible for this state of affairs."[71] This reflects Nhat Hanh's emphasis upon the interconnections that constitute conditioned origination, *pratitya-samutpada*. Everything that exists comes into being as a result of certain causes and conditions. These causes and conditions, in turn, are all interlocking and interdependent in an endlessly complex way. Therefore, in this view, everything that happens is related, albeit distantly for the most part, to everything else that happens. In that sense, I am, and each one of you is, partially responsible for the arms merchant's and the sea pirate's actions. In that sense, there is clearly no place for one person to sit in judgment upon another here.

Does it follow that morality is to be ignored altogether? By no means; we have already seen the morality implicit in Nhat Hanh's identification with both victim and victimizer. The end of his poem suggests the hoped-for state of morality. "Please call me by my true names" says Nhat Hanh. I am the joy and the sorrow; I am the killer and the killed. We cannot simply identify with the boat-girl and affirm her suffering while negating the sea pirate as "bad." Through identifying with both, we can overcome such a dualistic attitude toward the complexities of suffering. Through this identification with both good and bad, through meditative discovery of the impulses behind one's own "goodness" and "badness" one can finally put aside these categories and "wake up," opening one's heart to compassion.

We may take the compassion of which Nhat Hanh speaks as a reference to Buddha nature. Buddha nature is our "true self," our true identity, whose nature is constituted by wisdom and compassion. In Mahayana thought, Buddha nature is absolutely differentiated from ego personality. The latter lives in and is conditioned by the samsaric world of ethical judgment.

Buddha nature has no relation to that world, but is naturally and spontaneously compassionate, selfless, and altruistic. Thus there is a "goodness," called "compassion," beyond dualistic, judgmental good and evil.[72] This is the hoped-for moral condition.

In sum, this poem expresses an affirmation of a naturally compassionate Buddha nature as well as experiential identification with both victim and victimizer. In the context of an imperative to eliminate suffering, this produces Nhat Hanh's engaged Buddhism.

Regarding the means for making this vision a reality, all of Nhat Hanh's writings on socially engaged Buddhism emphasize the necessity of meditative and/or mindfulness practice. That this must be so follows directly from what was just stated. Both experiential identification with victim and victimizer and actualization of Buddha nature ordinarily are not attained without meditative practice. Both require self-knowledge beyond the level of ego personality as well as the ability to act in a way free of ego involvement. These are fruits of meditative practice. Consequently, an emphasis upon the necessity of meditative practice for the social activist is probably the most fundamental of Nhat Hanh's teachings. His work, *The Miracle of Mindfulness*, was written during the war years for the sake of students of the School of Youth for Social Service. Its message was the integration of meditation into their social work; its content was instruction in mindfulness practices that could be used in the context of wartime service to others. *Being Peace*, written for Western peace activists, has the same message: in order to make peace, one must "be peace"—that is, by practicing mindfulness in the midst of all one's activities.

From Theory to Action

What principles for action can we see in Nhat Hanh's thought—specifically, what principles for action in wartime? I perceive two core principles of action in Nhat Hanh's words and deeds. These also can be discerned, in my view, as the larger outlines of action of the Buddhist Struggle Movement as a whole.

1. The first principle of action is always to stop all killing and acute suffering as quickly as possible and to ameliorate suffering when stopping it is impossible. During the war, this meant first and foremost unswerving efforts to end U.S. bombing and to bring about a cease-fire. No other principles, allegiances, concern about subsequent consequences, or other considerations were allowed to compromise this most basic principle. On this principle, Nhat Hanh and the Buddhist Struggle Movement both were unbending.

As Nhat Hanh said, "I always put peace and human life above every-thing."[73] In one conversation, he made clear that peace in Vietnam was more important than the survival of Buddhism, and the survival of the Vietnamese people was more important than the survival of the Vietnamese nation.[74]

In Nhat Hanh's Buddhism, as I see it, there *are* some absolutes and these follow very much in the spirit of the Four Noble Truths. All of Bud-dhism is founded upon the First Noble Truth and its practical implication: there is suffering and it is a problem. All of Buddhism amounts to no more than the determined effort to eliminate suffering (truths Two, Three, and Four). This absolute withstands even the *Heart Sutra*'s emptying of the Four Noble Truths. Without recognition of the problematic nature of suf-fering and the determination to eliminate it, there is no Buddhism. Although Mahayanists empty the Noble truths, in practice the Four Vows of the Mahayana practitioner reinstate the absolute status of the imperative to eliminate suffering.

In fact, even the emptying of the Four Noble Truths can be seen as reinforcing this imperative, to the extent that emptying the Four Noble Truths guards against dogmatism and idolatry, agents of ignorance and suffering. Nhat Hanh makes this plain in his commentary on the first precept of the Tiep Hien Order, the "Order of Interbeing" that he founded during the war, which reads: "Do not be idolatrous about or bound to any doctrine, theory, or ideology, even Buddhist ones. All systems of thought are guiding means; they are not absolute truth." His commentary states, "In the name of ideologies and doctrines, people kill and are killed. . . . This precept includes the precept of not killing in its deepest sense."[75]

Arguably, certain forms of suffering, for example, mild humiliation, rejection, disappointment, loss, and so on may be a necessary part of a practitioner's path and may even be engendered by his or her teacher (Nhat Hanh himself burned down a monk's hut to deliver a lesson in imperma-nence). But such things are in a totally different category from the kinds of suffering endured by the peasants of Vietnam during the war (death, torture, dismemberment, persistent mortal terror, starvation, orphanhood), perpetrated upon them by strangers with no concern for their well-being. These are simply evils.

Perhaps the word "evil" here evokes the wrong connotations, a Chris-tian worldview of negative judgment upon evil. That kind of judgment does not play a role here. It is not that the Buddhist observes the suffering of the innocent from outside (from a God-like position of removal, or a scientific neutrality), makes a judgment that what she or he sees is wrong and then determines to take action. Rather, the scenario, as described by Nhat Hanh, is one in which the Buddhist identifies with those who are suffering in the sense that he or she experiences that suffering as his or her own and on that basis acts to remove the suffering. Nhat Hanh said during the war that being "on the spot," the suffering caused by bombing and oppression "hurts us too much. We have to react." In Cambodia also, he said, the bombing "hurt" so much that the monks went out to demonstrate.[76] Monks and nuns were pained by the suffering that they took as their own and acted out of that pain to try to remove the cause of pain. Nhat Hanh describes this in terms of the Buddhist elimination of the isolated ego, resulting in the end of an experiential sense of an absolute separation between self and other, and an ability to experience the "other" as in some sense "self." Here he discusses the relevance of this manner of experiencing for "social work":

> When reality is perceived in its nature of ultimate perfection, the practitioner has reached a level of wisdom called non-discrimination mind—a wondrous communion in which there is no longer any distinction made between subject and object. . . . I have a pile of orphan applications for sponsorship on my desk. I translate a few each day. Before I begin to translate a sheet, I look into the eyes of the child in the photograph, and look at the child's expression and features closely. I feel a deep link between myself and each child, which allows me to enter a special communion with them. . . . [This is] a kind of non-discrimination mind. I no longer see an "I" who translates the sheets to help each child, I no longer see a child who received love and help. The child and I are one: no one pities; no one asks for help; no one helps. There is no task, no social work to be done, no compassion, no special wisdom. These are moments of non-discrimination mind.[77]

There is also in this activist Buddhist response to suffering an echo of the Mencian "heart that can't bear" suffering. Nhat Hanh says of Thich Quang Duc and Nhat Chi Mai, two of the Vietnamese Buddhists who immolated themselves during the war and whom he knew well, "Both have left very lucid poetry and letters. When you read them, you sense their desire to live. But they could not bear the sufferings of others. They wanted to do something or to be something for others."[78]

The principle of absolute opposition to the suffering occasioned by war is articulated in the twelfth precept of the Tiep Hien Order. It states: "Do not kill. Do not let others kill. Find whatever means possible to protect life and to prevent war."[79]

2. The second principle of action that I perceive in Nhat Hanh and, to an extent, in the Struggle Movement, is nonseparation from all parties involved in conflict. This involves both a refusal to take sides with one party against another and a commitment to work toward reconciliation and healing. Certainly, no victory of any side or party against any other is envisioned. Success is the overcoming of distrust, antipathy, blame, and so on

and the creation of harmonious community in which the former enemies all participate. In practice for both Nhat Hanh and the Struggle Movement, this meant the Buddhist refusal to take side with either the North or the South, with the NLF or with the Saigon government, with the U.S. or with "Communism."

Action to bring about reconciliation is based upon sympathy for and identification with all parties engaged in a conflict and, in Nhat Hanh's case, reflects the nondualism and nonjudgmental quality of his ethics. These values are expressed in the following mindfulness exercise, which Nhat Hanh recommends to Buddhist social activists.

> [T]ake the situation of a country suffering war or any other situation of injustice. Try to see that every person involved in the conflict is a victim. . . . See that the situation is possible because of the clinging to ideologies and to an unjust world economic system which is upheld by every person through ignorance or through lack of resolve to change it. See that two sides in a conflict are not really opposing, but two aspects of the same reality. See that the most essential thing is life and that killing or oppressing one another will not solve anything. Remember the Sutra's words:
>
> > In the time of war
> > Raise in yourself the Mind of Compassion
> > Help living beings
> > Abandon the will to fight
> > Wherever there is furious battle
> > Use all your might
> > To keep both sides' strength equal
> > And then step into the conflict to reconcile.
> > *Vimalakirti Nirdesa*[80]

The practice of nonseparation from all parties engaged in a conflict is less straightforward than the practice of acting to end suffering. The element of complexity seems to lie in the practice of identification with both the oppressed and the oppressor. Nhat Hanh has said,

> . . . If nonviolence is a *stand,* then it would be an attack on violence. But the most visible form of violence is revolutionary and liberational violence. So if you stand for nonviolence, you automatically stand against actual revolution and liberation. Quite distressing! No! we are not against revolution and liberation. We are against the other side, the side of the institutions, the side of the oppressors. The violence of the system is much more destructive, much more harmful, although it is well-hidden and not so visible. We call it institutional violence. By calling ourselves nonviolent

we are against all violence, but we are first against the *institutional violence.*[81]

Contrast this with the poem, "Please Call Me By My True Names." There we saw Nhat Hanh say "I am" the frog and the snake, the Ugandan child and the arms merchant, oppressor and oppressed. Here, on the other hand, is language of siding with one side against another, standing with the oppressed against the oppressors. And while it is true that during the war the Buddhist Struggle Movement sided with neither North nor South (and the difficulty of this neutrality in time of war is not to be minimized), is it not the case that the Buddhist Church and Nhat Hanh as well sided with the Vietnamese people against the foreign perpetrators of the war, the United States? How are we to understand this? This is not an idle question; the question at stake is how it might be possible to reconcile Mahayana nondualism (here, unity with oppressed and oppressor) with concrete social action.

As I see it, it is entirely correct to say that the Buddhists sided with the Vietnamese people, but not entirely correct to say that they took sides against the United States. In the first place, siding with Vietnamese people meant adhering to principle #1, working to end suffering. Again, in this ethic, opposition to suffering is a noncompromisable absolute to which all other concerns are subordinate. Who was suffering the most during the war? The Vietnamese people. Hence the necessity of taking their side. Moreover, in this particular conflict, taking the side of the Vietnamese people already entailed siding with neither North nor South. We have already seen how the peasants were victimized by both powers. In that situation, as Nhat Hanh put it, "Peasants may give rice as tribute to the NLF, have a son in the government army—and demonstrate with the Buddhists"[82]

Second, what does it mean to "oppose the United States?" The Buddhist movement obviously never opposed the American soldiers fighting in Vietnam in the sense of perpetrating or advocating any harm to them. They saw Vietnamese and American soldiers alike as victims of more powerful forces that created a confluence of events in which these people were caused to kill and be killed. As Nhat Hanh put it earlier, "See that two sides in a conflict are not really opposing, but two aspects of the same reality." The single reality of which all were victims was a fearful world divided into American and Soviet camps. Seeing the American soldiers as victims in the same way that the Vietnamese soldiers were victims, they were not the target to be opposed. In opposing the United States, the Buddhists were opposing the underlying cause of the suffering of all involved, Vietnamese peasant and soldier as well as American soldier. During the war, Nhat Hanh in particular saw the underlying cause of suffering to be the policies emanating from Washington. It was this that he opposed. Others in the Struggle Movement leadership came progressively to share this view, especially after the crushing of the movement in Danang and Hue in 1966.

An incident that occurred during Nhat Hanh's wartime tour of the United States illustrates this. After Nhat Hanh addressed an audience in St. Louis, a man rose during the question period to scornfully ask Nhat Hanh why he was there, in the United States, if he cared so much for his people and their suffering. Nhat Hanh's reply was, "If you want the tree to grow, it won't help to water the leaves. You have to water the roots. Many of the roots of the war are here, in your country. To help the people who are to be bombed, to try to protect them from this suffering, I have to come here."[83] Note that the answer refers back to principle #1 and to the Four Noble Truths: to put an end to suffering is the motive and goal; to attain the goal one must determine the cause of suffering and remove that cause. It was the cause of suffering that Nhat Hanh and the Struggle Movement opposed.

It is important to recognize that in opposing American policies, the Buddhists were not in actual opposition to any living persons. Should we say that they were in opposition to the American president? I have heard Nhat Hanh speak of the extent to which our presidents are the product of forces outside of themselves and that their actions are largely controlled by their perception of the American public's views, political constraints, and the like. The same would apply to the small circle of men surrounding the president and filling his ear. Examining the situation, Nhat Hanh sees conditioned origination, nonseparation, or to use his own word, interbeing. As a consequence, an individual president or powerful policymaker cannot be singled out for personal blame. His actions are inextricably interconnected with a vast network of conditions, including the American public's views, the American political system, global economics, Cold War ideology, and so on. These interconnections make it impossible to target a particular individual for personal blame or scorn. They do not, however, freeze the Buddhist movement into inaction. The imperative to put an end to suffering impels them to act, while the web of interbeing prevents one-sided blaming.

> I believe with all my heart . . . that the monks who burned themselves did not aim at the death of the oppressors but only at a change in their policy. Their enemies are not man, they are intolerance, fanaticism, dictatorship, cupidity, hatred and discrimination which lie within the heart of man. . . . If we kill man, with whom shall we live?[84]

Note how much this resembles Gandhi's principle of opposing the deed, but not the doer. In both cases, social action is forwarded by opposing deeds that cause suffering while adhering strictly to nonviolence in an atmosphere ideally characterized by a freedom from personal animosity with an ultimate goal of reconciliation. This similarity is particularly striking, given the difference in underlying beliefs. Gandhi's principle is based upon reverence for the eternal Atman within each individual, Nhat Hanh's upon the very absence of such a thing, that is, the emptiness of self manifested in the web of interbeing.

Thus far we have considered the issue of taking sides with or against oppressor and oppressed on the large geographic scale of nations and regions and the large time scale of a war of many years duration. Now we must briefly consider the small scale in which questions arise of supporting or opposing particular individuals, their policies, and their actions on a day-by-day basis; here I refer to the actions of the U.B.C., rather than Nhat Hanh. We have seen the complexity and the urgency of such judgments in my summary of the influential role played by the Unified Buddhist Church during the war. Prime ministers and cabinet members rose and fell with the support of or withdrawal of support by the U.B.C. The Buddhist struggle movement made specific demands regarding such things as elections, constitutions, and the military draft. They mobilized tens of thousands of people to voice their demands in mass demonstrations. Here is clear siding for and against both policies and individuals. How shall we understand these actions in the context of the second core principle entailing the avoidance of siding with one party against another?

As I see it, the determination to proceed with such acts as demanding elections or calling for the removal of an official is based upon a process we have already identified. The Buddhist leadership decided to take a particular move when they judged that that move would help to attain the larger goal of removing the cause of suffering. The Buddhist leadership and the members of the movement as a whole met frequently, especially during crises, to analyze the situation and decide upon effective action.[85] Tactical and pragmatic considerations played a major role in these deliberations: Did they have sufficient popular backing to make this move? What were its chances of success? Was it too risky, given the likely response of the Americans or any of the powerful Vietnamese groups? Was the time right for this? Did they have the necessary resources? Did they have any allies for this move?

Whereas I have argued that considerations such as these were not allowed to compromise the core principle of working to end suffering, such tactical and pragmatic matters did and clearly *had to* influence decisions about particular moves under particular conditions. Given the absolute adherence to principle #1, the imperative to end the suffering, they could not risk failing in the larger aim of stopping the war for the sake of some lesser goal, such as demanding the ouster of a particular prime minister, which was conceived as leading to that larger goal. On the level of practical action in a prolonged struggle, means-ends considerations are inescapable; this requires the careful study of detailed information, brainstorming (conceiving of alternative possible actions), weighing alternative actions, judging which action will be most effective in the light of the countless interconnections of the web of interbeing, and deciding upon a course of action and implementing it.

Moreover, while the particular actions taken by the U.B.C. frequently did involve opposing powerful government individuals, in a sense, the Gandhian principle of opposing the action of the individual, but not the individual himself, was still in place. That is, clearly no individuals were opposed in the sense that any physical harm was done to them, and members of the Buddhist movement did struggle not to wish ill to any individuals personally. This was not always easy. After members of the movement were killed, students of the School of Youth for Social Service "declared that they couldn't hate those who killed their friends." Sister Phuong, Nhat Hanh's close associate, admits though, "For myself . . . I must confess that sometimes I find it very difficult not to hate."[86]

In sum, principle #1, the imperative to stop suffering, takes the engaged Buddhist out of a frozen position and demands action. Principle #2, nonseparation from all parties, requires that that action accord with Mahayana nondualism. However, principle #2, nonseparation from all parties, is less straightforward in practice and opens up difficult theoretical and practical issues.

I must reemphasize that Nhat Hanh himself did not engage in, or necessarily support, all the particular acts of the Buddhist Struggle Movement. I see three main reasons for this. First was temperament: as a human being he was and is more of a philosopher than the kind of activist who takes to the street. He did not, however, by any means negatively judge those who did take to the streets and in fact very much supported them. As we have seen, he composed some of the most effective slogans and songs used by those in the streets. He spoke of Thich Tri Quang as, "a man of action, and of courage and intelligence, whose life is good."[87]

Secondly, Nhat Hanh had an aversion to politics and political machination, to strategy and tactics. This comes out repeatedly in his writings. "Out of love and the willingness to act, strategies and tactics will be created naturally from the circumstances of the struggle. Thus, the problems of strategy and tactics are of secondary importance. They should be posed, but not at the beginning."[88] He hoped for a movement motivated by love and compassion; questions of political power muddied the waters. Of that most political of the activist monks, he wrote:

> *Only love and sacrifice can engender love and sacrifice.* This chain reac-
> tion is essential to the nonviolent struggle. Thich Tri Quang did not make
> strategy: he fasted 100 days. And everyone who passed by the Duy Tan
> clinic at that time had to hold his breath.[89]

Nhat Hanh's own contributions to the movement were of a nature that
attempted to keep the focus on bringing about peace, ending suffering,
recognizing that my enemy is not man, that I should not "shoot my brother."
He spent much of his time in the countryside, working for the peasants in
an atmosphere far less politicized than that of the urban centers. Thomas
Merton said of Nhat Hanh, "He represents the least 'political' of all the
movements in Viet Nam."[90]

    Finally, Nhat Hanh was as active as anyone during the war, but the acts
in which he engaged were different from those of most activist Buddhists.
Nhat Hanh was the single most prominent expatriate Vietnamese Buddhist
activist. He chose/was asked to fill this role partially because of his Western
expertise and partially because of his conviction that the roots of the war
were found in the United States. He saw himself as working on the root of
the problem in his talks with Western leaders and his missions to the
United Nations and to the Paris Peace Talks. He wrote:

> . . . Thich Tri Quang believes that we may attain peace indirectly by means
> of political maneuvering and through elections. . . . I doubt myself that
> much will be gained by indirect political maneuvering against the govern-
> ment and the Catholics, so long as the United States is determined to
> continue the war. Underlying the struggle with the government in Danang
> and other cities is the unstated question whether the war will go on; and
> this the United States will decide. . . . Only America can stop this war
> which is destroying not only our lives, but our culture and everything of
> human value in our country.[91]

This was written during the suppression of the Struggle Movement in Danang.
I believe history shows that while Tri Quang and his followers owned the
headlines, Nhat Hanh's judgment regarding what was needed to end the war
was finally correct. This by no means reduces the importance of the Struggle
Movement in the streets: this remains an example of the deepest courage in
attempting to invent Buddhist direct action literally under the gun.

Engaged Buddhism and Christian Liberation Theology

    A few comparative notes on Nhat Hanh's Buddhism and Christian
Liberation Theology will be instructive. One prominent similarity between

the two is the close ties of both with the poor. As we have seen, while seeking funds for the establishment of Van Hanh University, Nhat Hanh stressed the importance of relying upon many small contributions from the poor. In his view, the poor were "the strength" of the Buddhist movement and, moreover, could be relied upon. Again, during the war, while the more political Buddhist activists worked energetically in the cities with urban dwellers and especially with students, Nhat Hanh's group was particularly effective and had a natural closeness with the peasants, mostly living subsistence lives, in the countryside. The Buddhists' extensive rural network was based upon the social work of students from Nhat Hanh's School of Youth for Social Service, which involved living in peasant villages and knowing them and their needs on a first-hand, individual basis.

Second, as with the Catholic Church in Latin America, in Vietnam the Buddhist Church was really the only institution available to the people for work on a national basis outside the government (in fact, the government of Vietnam during the war years was a poor second to the Buddhist Church in this regard). Moreover, in both churches there is respect for traditional authority to encourage approval from the mature and tradition-minded population combined with the excitement of a new form of idealism to inspire the young and free-thinkers. Perhaps most important, there is an organization that actively demonstrates its helpfulness to the desperate.

An anecdote points to another similarity between the engaged Buddhism movement and Liberation Theology: justification of new principles in terms of reinterpreted traditional language. Nhat Hanh tells of a boy named An at the School of Youth for Social Service who worked with the villagers showing them a modern way to raise chickens. They assumed he was paid by the government for this work and when they found that he was not, they asked him why, in that case, he was working so hard. He replied: "Well, we are performing merits. . . . In times like this when people suffer so much, the Bodhisattvas don't stay in the temple; they are out here. That's why we are not winning merits in the temple; we are winning them here."[92] In other words, the traditional practice of earning merit by such actions as meditation, chanting, and the like was replaced in time of crisis by actions of service to the people that also won merit. Nhat Hanh comments, "It was a kind of popular theology. Nobody taught him to say that; it just came from his own heart and understanding. That created a kind of immediate understanding, and afterwards the peasants accepted our workers."[93] The peasants understood winning merits; they did not, initially understand activists monks. When the latter was explained in terms of the former, engaged Buddhism found acceptance.

One important point of contrast between the Unified Buddhist Church of Vietnam and Liberation Theology should be noted. "Uniquely, the Unified

Buddhist Church is not a prophetic minority group opposing both social injustice and the complicity of the churches. It is the country's [Vietnam's] principal religious body."[94]

Politics

The Christian and the Buddhist forms of engaged spirituality share a similar problem: divided opinions and a basic lack of clarity regarding the proper relationship between the church, its clergy, and the holding of political power. This is a difficult and controversial matter which deeply divided the Buddhist Church in Vietnam during the war. Let us open this up with the following words of Nhat Hanh taken from a conversation with Daniel Berrigan that took place during the war.

> Since the success of 1963, at least one million people have come and said, 'We need a Buddhist political party. If you are not organized politically, you cannot succeed.' Everyone has been saying that. There are politicians now who want the support of the Buddhist bloc. They call themselves Buddhist politicians and they compete with Christian politicians. The trust we had in each other in 1963 had disappeared.
>
> Then, after the signing of the Paris accords, we made another effort. We said, 'Now let us disassociate ourselves from any political party, including people who call themselves Buddhist politicians. We don't need a political party. Let's act as a religious community only, doing work of reconciliation and healing.' I was one of the members who strongly advocated that. . . .
>
> After we had adopted that attitude, we began to be attacked by politicians—Buddhist politicians as well—because of our determination to return to a purely religious stance. But we made the right decision. . . .
>
> We monks know that our strength is not as a political group; our strength is as a religious group. . . .
>
> The vocation of a priest is quite different from the vocation of a politician.[95]

As I see it, there is widespread agreement in both Christian and Buddhist circles that it is inappropriate and ultimately self-defeating for a priest or monk (or, potentially, a nun) to hold elected political office. Nhat Hanh cites as particularly problematic in this regard the inability of such a person to be free of either the appearance or the reality of self-interested action (i.e., acting on the basis of desire). "In Vietnam today, most people would not consider a monk as a serious monk if he ran for public office."[96]

This appears to be a sensible and clear principle, but even this is not so simple. The journalist Takashi Oka, in arguing for the necessity of a

Buddhist political party, pointed out that the Buddhist "lay leaders did recognize the political reality, but could do nothing without the bonzes [monks]—for the Buddhist masses still responded to their bonzes rather than to their lay leaders."[97] In other words, in the view of Buddhist lay leaders, it was not enough to say that a political movement should be led by the laity, since the people by and large would not respond to a lay movement but ultimately trusted only the monastics. In practice, of course, this was a catch-22 inasmuch as a monk running for office would no longer be considered a true monk. This, moreover, would be the rule in any traditional, un-Westernized Buddhist country.

Nhat Hanh advocated separating the Buddhist movement from public support of any political party or candidate, including Buddhists. This clearly is in line with his principle of nonalignment with any party against another. With the ultimate goal of reconciling all parties, Nhat Hanh and those associated with him were loath to set themselves up as yet another "side" interested in gaining power for itself and thus alienating it from all other parties. Nhat Hanh also argued against supporting a political entity because of his observation that when the Buddhist Church had supported "Buddhist politicians" they found that such politicians were only eager to use the Buddhist name for the support and votes that it produced, but then "deceived" the movement, failed to embody its principles and failed to join in the actions undertaken by the movement.[98] As a consequence, the image and integrity of the Buddhist movement itself was corrupted.

Yet we have seen during the war that support of and removal of support from individuals was an effective force regularly used by the Buddhist Struggle Movement. The "one million people" who wanted to see a Buddhist political party emerge sought a vehicle to channel the political expression of the principles embodied in the Buddhist Struggle Movement. Given the deep involvement in politics of the Buddhist Struggle Movement, and the claim of the latter to represent the wishes of the masses of South Vietnamese people, was this not a natural expectation?

Further difficulties are raised by Nhat Hanh's stated desire for the movement to return to a "purely religious stance," that is, to separate politics and religion. He remained unshaken in his enthusiasm for combining social work and religion but wanted to draw a line somewhere between social work and politics. It is unclear to me, however, how such a line could be drawn, especially during times of political crisis. For example, during the war in Vietnam, the engaged Buddhist's nonpolitical aim may have been to protect the people from suffering, but when it was the political system itself that was largely responsible for that suffering, it was impossible to avoid engagement in politics. Moreover, as Oka emphasized throughout his newsletters, after the fall of Diem the Buddhists *had* political power, whether they wanted it or not. The only real question was, how were they to respond to that reality in a responsible way?[99]

Does Nhat Hanh's position mean that an engaged Buddhist can only engage in political protest and opposition and that there is no constructive role that a Buddhist can play in politics, no contribution to the creation of a more just and humane political system? Perhaps such constructive work should be left to others, but in a case such as Vietnam's, when millions of people identified their vision with the Buddhists' (and this was by far the most popular view in the country, with which no politician or extant political party had any hope to compete) some way of identifying a political party with Buddhism was needed.[100] Should the line of prohibition be drawn between clergy and laity? Should a new category be found, something like the *anagarika* concept of Anagarika Dharmapala?[101] But even if one could name some such category of persons as eligible to participate in politics on the basis of Buddhist principles, or even if a purely lay Buddhist political party could be founded, would the imperfections and misjudgments that would inevitably emerge as these people engaged in active political life be received as an unacceptable corruption of the nonpolitical Buddhist life?

In Vietnam, all these questions remained moot. In fact, a Buddhist political party of sorts was founded in Vietnam, named the "Vietnamese Buddhist Force." The party was a lay-monastic amalgam. Thien Minh and a monk named Ho Giac were named chairman and vice-chairman, respectively, of the party; Tri Quang took no formal post, though he sat on the podium at the press conference while Thien Minh announced the existence of the new party. Prominent Buddhist laypersons served on the central committee. However, the party was never fully organized, much less put to the test, before it was suppressed. The theoretical questions in the background of a party such as this remain, however, and it is to be hoped that Buddhist activitists will contribute their further reflections on them.[102]

Conclusion

In the wake of all these questions, I will end on a positive note. Nhat Hanh's work breaks new ground for Buddhist thought and action. He has modernized Buddhism, making it "appropriate" to contemporary culture and conditions, while adhering to the "basic tenets" of Buddhism, which for him mean the Four Noble Truths, the vows of the *bodhisattva*, interbeing/ emptiness, and compassion. He has significantly contributed to the forging of a way to bring Buddhism out of monastic seclusion to engage with and serve all aspects of ordinary life. Beyond the Buddhist context, his nondualism in action has made a major contribution to international discussions and programs of spiritually based social action. Thus his ideas, forged in the particular context of wartime Vietnam, have been taken up by a global audience, and they address the major issues facing Buddhists today—modernization, lay-monk relations, social withdrawal versus social activism—as well as the major world issues of war and peace, spirituality and materialism, human community, and human well-being.

Of the Unified Buddhist Church and the Buddhist Struggle Movement it can only be said that theirs is one of the great examples of courage, altruism, and activist spirituality of all time. While they are in the company of Gandhi's *satyagraha* movement and Martin Luther King, Jr.'s, civil rights movement, they differ significantly in that theirs was not a movement led by a single, outstanding, charismatic leader. The Buddhists who participated in the Struggle Movement, who worked in the countryside to help peasants survive, who immolated themselves for peace—these people were moved, in fact, by the ideals of their Buddhist faith.

Nhat Hanh's own retrospective views on the Struggle Movement are characteristic:

> Despite the results—many years of war followed by years of oppression and human rights abuse—I cannot say that our struggle was a failure. The conditions for success in terms of a political victory were not present. But the success of a nonviolent struggle can be measured only in terms of the love and nonviolence attained, not whether a political victory was achieved. In our struggle in Vietnam, we did our best to remain true to our principles. We never lost sight that the essence of our struggle was love itself, and that was a real contribution to humanity.[103]

Epilogue

Nhat Hanh and the activist Buddhists in Vietnam were optimistic at the end of the war that they would quickly enter into a cooperative relationship with the new regime that would be of benefit to the entire country. After all, "the UBC had been responsible for a mass movement of opposition to the Saigon regimes and American intervention"[104] and had a well-established rice-roots network in place throughout the countryside ready to offer social service to the peasants. The Buddhists hoped and expected that they could offer their services to the new government to help repair the war damage and heal the psychological and social wounds of the people. To demonstrate good will, the U.B.C. organized 20,000 Buddhists to celebrate Ho Chi Minh's birthday.[105] Tragically, these hopes, and this potential source of healing, were quickly crushed.

> [R]eports quickly began reaching the UBC . . . of brutal treatment of Buddhist workers and clergy: orphanages confiscated, social service centers closed, pagodas seized or destroyed, religious statues smashed, the same

Buddhist flag that Diem had attempted to ban once again prohibited.

The School of Youth for Social Service, so many of whose staff and volunteers died in opposition to the war, was confiscated, its director imprisoned, his monk-assistant badly beaten.[106]

The help and healing that the Buddhists offered was utterly cast aside. Once again, Buddhist monks and nuns were detained, tortured, imprisoned, forbidden to leave their pagodas, forbidden to meet in large groups, forbidden to perform any but the most traditional Buddhist functions. The new regime's fear of the power—the political power—of the Buddhists was plainly evident. Once again, though they may not have wanted it and did not acknowledge it, the Buddhists were recognized by the government as possessing massive political power. The government was afraid of a group that could amass 20,000 people at will. They were afraid of a group that had a better network than they in the countryside. This group had to be suppressed and strictly controlled. Thus the government, spurning Buddhist assistance, proceeded on its own to utterly botch the reconstruction of the country, leading to further misery, especially in the forms of devastating poverty and hunger, on the part of the long-suffering Vietnamese people.

At this writing, the U.B.C. is still suppressed and strictly controlled. There are still prisoners of conscience, including Buddhists, in prison.[107] Others have died in jail. Virtually the entire leadership has had its movements restricted with house arrest or internal exile. As this goes to press in January 1995, the top two monks of the U.B.C., Thich Huyen Quang and Thich Quang Do, have just been arrested two days after Thich Huyen Quang began a hunger strike to protest the arrest of several other monks (the movements of both leaders had been restricted for years). This is a struggle that is still not over. Still, Vietnam, like many other Communist countries, is tolerating carefully measured liberalization outside of the political arena. Buddhists associated with Nhat Hanh, still hopeful despite everything, look forward to the day when they can return to the service of the Vietnamese people to work for reconciliation and healing.

Acknowledgment

I would like to thank several people and institutions who shared words and/or publications that substantially contributed to this paper: William Turley, Department of Political Science, Southern Illinois University at Carbondale; Patricia Hunt-Perry, Ramapo College, New Jersey; Steve Denny, Indochina Archives, University of California at Berkeley; the Fellowship of Reconciliation; Mobi Ho; Arnold Kotler, Parallax Press; Therese Fitzgerald,

Community of Mindful Living; Roger Rump, Asia Resource Center; Don Luce; and Sister Annabel Laity, Plum Village.

Notes

1. Marjorie Hope and James Young, *The Struggle for Humanity: Agents of Nonviolent Change in a Violent World,* Ch. 6 "The Third Way: Thich Nhat Hanh and Cao Ngoc Phuong." (Maryknoll, N.Y.: Orbis Books, 1977), p. 193; and "Biography of Thich Nhat Hanh" available from the Unified Buddhist Church at Plum Village, France. The following biography of Nhat Hanh relies primarily on the latter. Other sources are as cited.

2. Theravada and Mahayana formally united during the war, forming the Unified Buddhist Church of Vietnam.

3. Nhat Hanh's own teachings emphasize mindfulness and *gatha* practices, while his philosophy is a blend of Theravada and Mahayana.

4. Mobi Ho, conversation with the author, July 25, 1990.

5. Hope and Young, p. 193. This entire paragraph is summarized from Hope and Young.

6. Ibid., p. 194.

7. Ibid.

8. The following synopsis is taken from Thich Nhat Hanh's words in his conversation with Daniel Berrigan in Daniel Berrigan and Thich Nhat Hanh, *The Raft is Not the Shore: Conversations Toward a Buddhist/Christian Awareness* (Boston: Beacon Press, 1975), pp. 93–94.

9. Thich Nhat Hanh, *Interbeing: Commentaries on the Tiep Hien Precepts.* Edited, with an Introduction by Fred Eppsteiner. (Berkeley, Calif.: Parallax Press, 1987), pp. 17–18.

10. The following is taken from the "Biography of Thich Nhat Hanh" and from Hope and Young, pp. 195–196. The quoted material is from the latter.

11. Thomas Merton, "A Statement Concerning Thich Nhat Hanh," *Fellowship* 32 (7) (July 1966), p. 22.

12. Vietnamese Buddhist Peace Delegation, July 1, 1971, quoted by Bo Wirmark, *The Buddhists in Vietnam: An Alternative View of the War.* Introduction by Daniel Berrigan. Edited by Joseph Gerson. (Brussels, Belgium: War Resisters' International, 1975), p. 32.

13. Thich Nhat Hanh, *Vietnam: Lotus in a Sea of Fire,* with a Foreword by Thomas Merton and an Afterword by Alfred Hassler (New York: Hill and Wang, 1967).

14. "Biography of Thich Nhat Hanh."

15. This and the following are taken from Hope and Young, pp. 212–215.

16. Ibid.

17. Cao Ngoc Phuong, quoted in Ibid., p. 214.

18. Cao Ngoc Phuong in Ibid., p. 215.

19. Part of the 10th Annual Common Boundary Conference, "Compassionate Living," November 16–18, 1990, Crystal City, Virginia.

20. Don Luce, telephone conversation with the author, June 26, 1992.

21. In my account of the Buddhist Struggle Movement, I have relied most heavily upon the following. (1) George McT. Kahin, *Intervention: How America Became Involved in Vietnam* (New York: Alfred A. Knopf, 1986). Kahin's account is one of the few histories of the war to give substantial coverage of the role of the Buddhist movement in Vietnam from 1963 to 1966 and draws upon recently declassified U.S. government documents. (2) Takashi Oka, "Buddhism as a Political Force" I–VI. Institute of Current World Affairs, *Newsletter*, TO 24–27 and TO 34–35 (July 17, 1966, July 21, 1966, July 29, 1966, August 4, 1966, May 29, 1967, May 30, 1967). Oka, a Japanese-American, was one of very few Western journalists who took the Buddhist movement seriously and maintained ties with them; he knew Thich Tri Quang well. (3) I also rely heavily on both the account and the chronology given in James H. Forest, *The Unified Buddhist Church of Vietnam: Fifteen Years for Reconciliation* (International Fellowship of Reconciliation, published by Hof van Sonoy, the Netherlands, 1978).

22. This account is summarized from Oka, TO-25 (July 21, 1966), p. 5ff.

23. Kahin p. 149.

24. Jan Yun-hua discusses this point in his "Buddhist Self-Immolation in Medieval China" *History of Religions* 4 (1964–1965), pp. 243–269, esp. pp. 252–255.

25. See Oka, TO-25 (July 21, 1966) and Kahin, Ch. 6.

26. Kahin, p. 152.

27. Ibid., pp. 152–181.

28. Thich Nhat Hanh in Berrigan and Hanh, pp. 80–81.

29. Cited in Kahin, p. 184. Kahin found the speech in a cable from Mavin L. Manfull, Counsellor of Embassy for Political Affairs, American Embassy, Saigon to the Department of State, "Recent Buddhist Developments," March 26, 1964.

30. Ibid., pp. 198–202.

31. Ibid., p. 208. Kahin quotes a cablegram from Johnson to Lodge, March 20, 1964, published in the *Pentagon Papers as Published by "The New York Times,"* by

Neil Sheehan, Hedrick Smith, E. W. Kenworthy, and Fox Butterfield (Bantam Books, 1971), p. 285.

32. The following is summarized from Ibid., pp. 227–235.

33. Ibid., p. 228. And see Oka, TO-26 (July 29, 1966), p. 11.

34. Westmoreland quotation cited in Ibid., p. 228 taken from "Resume of Questions and Answers Telecon with General Westmoreland," August 25, 1964, p. 2; plus addendum.

35. CIA Memorandum, "Tri Quang and the Buddhist-Catholic Discord in South Vietnam," September 19, 1964, cited in Ibid., p. 234.

36. Ibid.,, p. 238.

37. Thich Nhat Hanh, Lotus, pp. 63–68.

38. Ibid., p. 68.

39. Ibid., pp. 64–65.

40. Kahin, p. 267f.

41. Ibid., taken from CIA, Memorandum for the national Intelligence Board, SNIE 53–65, "Short Term Prospects in South Vietnam," February 2, 1965.

42. Ibid., p. 271 cables from Taylor to State, January 29, and 31, 1965.

43. Ibid., p. 272.

44. Representative Clement Zablocki quoted in the New York Times March 17, 1966, and cited in Kahin, p. 403.

45. Quote attributed to a "most authoritative spokesman for U.S. policy in Saigon," believed in Kahin to be Ambassador Lodge, quoted by Emmet John Hughes in Newsweek, May 30, 1966, p. 23; cited by Kahin, p. 416.

46. Memorandum for the President from Dean Rusk, "Political Situation in South Vietnam," April 2, 1966, cited in Ibid., p. 421.

47. Ibid., p. 425. Also see Oka TO-34 (May 29, 1967) on the suppression of the Struggle Movement.

48. Ibid., p. 429. Sheehan quote from New York Times May 21, 22, 23, or 25, 1966.

49. Ibid., p. 430.

50. Ibid.

51. Ibid.

52. Lodge quote from the New York Times, June 25, 1966; cited in Ibid., p. 431.

53. Forest, p. 34.

54. Thich Nhat Hanh, *Love in Action: The Nonviolent Struggle for Peace in Vietnam* (Paris: Vietnamese Buddhist Peace Delegation, n.d.); cited in Wirmark, pp. 22–24. See also Thich Nhat Hanh, "Love in Action: The Nonviolent Struggle for Peace in Vietnam," *Fellowship* 36 (1) (January, 1970), pp. 23–25.

55. Thich Nhat Hanh, "Love in Action," p. 25.

56. Forest, p. 12.

57. Ibid.

58. Wirmark, p. 23.

59. Ibid., p. 24.

60. It is less well known that some Americans did the same. See Daniel Berrigan's comments in Berrigan and Hanh, pp. 59 and 62.

61. Thich Nhat Hanh, *Love in Action,* pp. 11–12; cited in Wirmark, p. 23.

62. Berrigan and Hanh, p. 62.

63. Ibid., p. 61.

64. Ibid., p. 63.

65. Ibid., p. 43.

66. This list is composed from information found in Wirmark, Hope and Young and *The Mindfulness Bell* (newsletter produced by friends and students of Thich Nhat Hanh, c/o Parallax Press), as well as conversation with Mobi Ho.

67. Cao Ngoc Phuong in Hope and Young, pp. 215–216.

68. Wirmark, p. 24.

69. Thich Nhat Hanh, *Being Peace,* edited by Arnold Kotler (Berkeley, Calif.: Parallax Press, 1987), pp. 63–64.

70. Ibid., p. 62.

71. Ibid.

72. Winston King makes a similar distinction in "Motivated Goodness and Unmotivated Perfection in Buddhist Ethics," *Anglican Theological Review* 71 (2), pp. 143–152.

73. Berrigan and Hanh, p. 20.

74. Ibid.

75. Thich Nhat Hanh, *Being Peace,* p. 89.

76. Berrigan and Hanh, p. 99.

77. Thich Nhat Hanh, *The Miracle of Mindfulness: A Manual on Meditation,* Revised Edition, Translated and with a Preface by Mobi Ho, Afterword by James Forest (Boston: Beacon Press, 1975, 1987), p. 57.

78. Berrigan and Hanh, p. 60.

79. Thich Nhat Hanh, *Being Peace,* p. 98; also see Thich Nhat Hanh, *Interbeing,* pp. 54–55.

80. Nhat Hanh, *Miracle,* p. 95.

81. Vietnamese Buddhist Peace Delegation, December 1, 1973, p. 7, cited in Wirmark, p. 19.

82. Hope and Young, p. 211.

83. Thich Nhat Hanh, *Miracle,* p. 103.

84. Thich Nhat Hanh quoted in "Visit from a Buddhist Monk," *Fellowship: The Magazine of the Fellowship of Reconciliation* 32 (7) July 1966, p. 3.

85. Mobi Ho, conversation with the author.

86. Hope and Young, p. 213.

87. Thich Nhat Hanh, "A Buddhist Poet in Vietnam," *New York Review of Books* June 9, 1966, pp. 4–5.

88. Thich Nhat Hanh, "Love in Action," p. 24.

89. Ibid.

90. Merton, p. 22.

91. Ibid.

92. Berrigan and Hanh, p. 43.

93. Ibid.

94. Forest, p. 17

95. Thich Nhat Hanh in Berrigan and Hanh, pp. 82–83.

96. Nhat Hanh in Ibid., p. 84.

97. Oka, TO-27, August 4, 1966, p. 8.

98. Nhat Hanh in Berrigan and Hanh, p. 83 and 85.

99. See, for example, TO-25, July 21, 1966, pp. 11–13.

100. "Two million South Vietnamese were the active corps—the monks, nuns and lay people whose lives centered on their commitment as Buddhists, many of them the shock troops of the resistance to Diem." Forest, p. 6.

101. An *anagarika* is in the world but not of it, keeps his hair but wears a white robe, obeys the ten *sila* of the monk, but takes as his task social and political service work. See Gananath Obeyesekere, "Religious Symbolism and Political Change in Ceylon," in Bardwell L. Smith, ed., *The Two Wheels of Dhamma: Essays on the Theravada Tradition in India and Ceylon,* AAR Studies in Religion Number Three (Chambersburg, Penn.: American Academy of Religion, 1972), pp. 68–73.

102. See Oka, TO-22, July 4, 1966, pp. 9–11 on this ephemeral party.

103. Thich Nhat Hanh, *Love in Action: Writings on Nonviolent Social Change* (Berkeley, Calif.: Parallax Press, 1993), p. 47.

104. Forest, p. 13.

105. Ibid.

106. Ibid.

107. See the annual reports on Vietnam by Amnesty International.

Bibliography

Berrigan, Daniel, and Nhat Hanh, Thich. *The Raft Is Not the Shore: Conversations toward a Buddhist-Christian Awareness.* Boston: Beacon Press, 1975.

Forest, James H. *The Unified Buddhist Church of Vietnam: Fifteen Years for Reconciliation.* Hof van Stony, Netherlands: International Fellowship of Reconciliation, 1978.

Hassler, Alfred. *Saigon, U.S.A.* Introduction by Senator George McGovern. New York: Rich W. Baron, 1970.

Hope, Marjorie, and Young, James. *The Struggle for Humanity: Agents of Nonviolent Change in a Violent World.* Chapter 6, "The Third Way: Thich Nhat Hanh and Cao Ngocc Phuong," pp. 185–221. Maryknoll, N.Y.: Orbis Books, 1977.

Kahin, George McT. *Intervention: How America Became Involved in Vietnam.* New York: Alfred A. Knopf, 1986.

Luce, Don, and Sommer, John. *Viet Nam: The Unheard Voices.* Chapter 6, "Defending the Interests of the Believers." Foreword by Edward M. Kennedy. Ithaca, N.Y.: Cornell University Press, 1969.

Nhat Hanh, Thich. "A Buddhist Poet in Vietnam," *New York Review of Books* June 9, 1966, pp. 4–5.

———. *The Miracle of Mindfulness: A Manual on Meditation,* Rev. ed. Preface and translation by Mobi Ho. Afterword by James Forest. Boston: Beacon Press, 1975, 1981.

————. *Interbeing: Commentaries on the Tiep Hien Precepts.* Edited by Fred Eppsteiner. Berkeley, Calif.: Parallax Press, 1987.

————. "Love in Action: The Nonviolent Struggle for Peace in Vietnam." *Fellowship: The Magazine of the Fellowship of Reconciliation* 36 (1) (January 1970): 23–25.

————. *Vietnam: Lotus in a Sea of Fire.* Foreword by Thomas Merton. Afterword by Alfred Hassler. New York: Hill and Wang, 1967.

Oka, Takashi. "Buddhism as a Political Force," I–VI. Institute of Current World Affairs, *Newsletter,* TO 24–27, TO 34–35; July 17, 1966; July 21, 1966; July 29, 1966; August 4, 1966; May 29, 1967; May 30, 1967.

Wirmark, Bo. *The Buddhists in Vietnam: An Alternative View of the War.* Introduction by Daniel Berrigan. Edited by Joseph Gerson. Brussels, Belgium: War Resisters' International, 1974.

10

The Soka Gakkai: Buddhism and the Creation of a Harmonious and Peaceful Society

Daniel A. Metraux

The Soka Gakkai is a unique phenomenon in modern Japanese history. No other modern Japanese religious organization has succeeded in creating such a widespread social and political movement on the foundation of Buddhist ideas. The Soka Gakkai movement is actively involved in a wide range of areas including education, peace activism, environmental concerns, the promotion of traditional and modern arts, international diplomacy, and domestic politics. Because the Soka Gakkai "represents the most significant blend of religious ideals and sociopolitical action in present-day Japan,"[1] it has attracted widespread attention both in Japan and abroad.

In some respects the Soka Gakkai has been very successful. In 1992 it claimed a membership of over 8 million households in Japan and 1.26 million members in nearly 120 countries.[2] It sponsors an influential political party, the Komeito, an educational system that includes two high schools and a large university, two art museums and other cultural institutions, several publishing companies and mass circulation newspapers, and various other Japanese national and international cultural organizations. It has also acquired large amounts of money and property.

However, the Soka Gakkai's success coupled with what was once a very rigid fundamentalistic and evangelical stance have made the Soka Gakkai one of the most controversial movements in postwar Japan. Other Buddhist groups have accused the Soka Gakkai of perverting basic Buddhist doctrines, while rival political parties denounce the Soka Gakkai as a false religious movement whose leaders use the votes and donations of its members to advance their wealth and political power. The Japanese media has continually accused Gakkai leaders of corruption.

The Soka Gakkai began as a strictly religious movement to propagate the doctrines of Nichiren Shoshu, which, until the 1940s, was one of the smaller of the many Nichiren sects in Japan. Its fervent proselytization campaigns in the 1950s and 1960s won many new members among lower middle-class groups, as well as widespread criticism. The Soka Gakkai broadened its range of activities in the 1960s and 1970s and today is as much a political and social movement as it is religious. During the 1980s and early 1990s Gakkai leaders and the membership as a whole began "to ascend the sociological escalator to positions of greater power and respectability."[3] The result has been a mellowing process leading to greater compromises with the status quo and greater acceptance by establishment circles.

The Soka Gakkai and Nichiren

The Soka Gakkai has inherited both the fighting spirit and the determination of its patron, Nichiren (1222–1282), who founded the only major native school of Japanese Buddhism. Nichiren lived during the Kamakura era (1185–1333), one of the most turbulent periods of Japanese history, during which the country was beset by domestic strife, two full-scale invasions by Mongol armies, and a series of natural disasters including earthquakes and mighty storms. Many Japanese believed that they were living in the age of *mappo* (the period of degeneration of the Dharma) when people turned away from the saving truths of Buddhist scripture and turned to evil and violent ways.[4] Nichiren, who subscribed to these ideas, devoted his life to a search for the resolution of these problems.

The worldview of the Soka Gakkai today is based on an eschatological view of *mappo*. It asserts that twentieth-century man with all of his wars, pollution, and suffering still lives in *mappo*. Gakkai leaders assert that they have inherited Nichiren's mantle and that their charge is to propagate his teachings throughout the world in order to lead man into a peaceful and righteous period. In other words, although evil prevails in the world today, the Soka Gakkai can guide man to a brighter "promised land" here on earth.

Nichiren was profoundly affected by the idea of *mappo*. After studying at the Tendai center on Mount Hiei near Kyoto and elsewhere, he developed the idea that Japan was on the verge of total collapse. He predicted that Japan would suffer major natural disasters, social chaos, and foreign invasions. Nichiren proclaimed that Japan was suffering such agonies because of the propagation of false Buddhist teachings. He concluded that the ultimate religious truth lay only in the *Lotus Sutra*,[5] which he believed to be the last and greatest teaching of the Buddha Shakyamuni. In this work the

Buddha reveals that all people have the potential for Buddhahood. Nichiren believed that when the priest Dengyo-Daishi founded the Tendai (Chinese: T'ien-t'ai) sect in Japan in 806, its doctrines were based on the Lotus Sutra. Nichiren charged that the followers of Tendai over the next four centuries had corrupted the sect by adding some new teachings and practices that were very different from Dengyo's doctrines.[6] Nichiren declared that the suffering of Kamakura–era Japan was due to the lack of attention to the Lotus Sutra. He insisted that salvation for mankind and for Japan could only be achieved through absolute faith in the Lotus Sutra. One could demonstrate one's faith and achieve salvation merely by uttering the title (daimoku) of the Lotus, Namu-myo-ho Renge-kyo ("Praise to the Wonderful Dharma of the Lotus Sutra").[7]

The teachings developed by Nichiren are based on four key points. First, the Lotus Sutra is the highest and only valid scripture for the age of mappo. It is the only vehicle that can bring salvation and, moreover, one need only show complete faith in its creed to be saved. Second, Nichiren believes in an eternal, omnipresent, and omnipotent Buddha. Third, this Buddha is immanent in every aspect of reality. All humans can attain salvation because they possess Buddha nature. Fourth, the means by which one can attain salvation is the path consisting of the "Three Great Secret Laws" (San Dai Hiho): (a) the gohonzon, or object of worship, a mandala or symbolic representation of the eternal Buddha inscribed by Nichiren himself; (b) the daimoku, the recitation of which is supposed to bring divine blessings on the believer; (c) the kaidan, or national sanctuary, which was to be built once the country's salvation had occurred.[8]

Nichiren introduced several new elements into Japanese Buddhism. One was a sense of intolerance. He insisted that his was the only religion that could save humankind during mappo and that all other faiths would lead humankind to damnation. He advocated a highly aggressive form of proselytism called shakubuku ("to break and flatten"), which, though harsh, he believed to be the only way to overcome the depravity of the age. Nichiren was also very politically oriented. He claimed that the nation would crumble unless the government led the people to the True Buddhism. Failure of the government to make this move, he said, would bring natural disasters and social calamity.[9]

These traditions are important for understanding the modern Soka Gakkai. Its exclusivism is based on Nichiren's assertion that the Lotus is the sole source of man's salvation. Its missionary zeal stems from Nichiren's idea that it is the responsibility of the devotee to convert others. Another key point is that spiritual benefit (kudoku) and material benefits (riyaku) are correlated. This concern for material welfare has become a very important component of the Soka Gakkai's belief system.

The Soka Gakkai, like Nichiren Shoshu, teaches that Nichiren was the physical incarnation of the highest spiritual principle, even superceding Shakyamuni. Further, it teaches that Nichiren's *Gohonzon* (mandala), on which is drawn the title of the *Lotus Sutra*, embodies the teachings of the true Buddha and contains the power to bring happiness to those who worship before it. According to the Soka Gakkai:

> Nichiren Daishonin[10] embodied his enlightenment—the fusion of reality and wisdom—in the form of the Gohonzon, the object of worship. The Gohonzon itself is the entity of the fusion of reality and wisdom. . . . With faith in the Gohonzon, one can realize the Buddha-nature inherent in one's own life. Thus faith equals wisdom. Again, our Buddha-nature is reality and our faith in the Gohonzon corresponds to wisdom. This fusion of reality and wisdom takes place within our own lives. Hence Nichiren Daishonin says in his Gosho, "Never seek this Gohonzon outside yourself. The Gohonzon exists only within the mortal flesh of us ordinary people who embrace the Lotus Sutra and chant Nam-myoho-renge-kyo.[11]
>
> The True Law which the Daishonin revealed is the object of worship of Nam-myoho-renge-kyo. Any person who believes in this object of worship and chants Nam-myoho-renge-kyo to it can expiate all negative karma and attain Buddhahood.[12]

According to the Soka Gakkai, Nichiren envisioned the establishment of a peaceful and harmonious world once mankind returned to the efficacy of the *Lotus*. He felt that people could become truly happy and that a nation could prosper only when everybody accepted the sacred teachings of the Lotus Sutra. He predicted that when the people of Japan accepted the *Lotus*, the age of *mappo* would end and Japan would enter a new period of peace and harmony.

Nichiren accepts the Tendai concept of the Ten Worlds (*jukai*), according to which there are at least ten states of mind always present in the personality of every human. Everybody is dominated by one of these ten psychological states, which range from pure rage (Hell) to shear joy (Buddhahood). Man need not await death to achieve salvation.[13] The cause of humankind's sad state is bad karma. The key to a better life is changing one's karma. A perfectly clean or pure karma allows one to become a Buddha—a kind and loving person whose wisdom and devotion to others makes him a superior human. The tragedy of *mappo*, according to Nichiren, was that the world was dominated by too many people with hellish natures.

The goal of Nichiren's Buddhism, therefore, is to move as many people as possible from the misery of a hellish mind/bad karma to the joyful state of Buddhahood. Nichiren believed in the Lotus' power to save humanity and consequently strongly felt that during the age of *mappo*, the *Lotus*

Sutra must be spread to save humanity. He concluded that the *Lotus* was expounded for the sake of all people living at the beginning of *mappo*.

Nichiren's ideas concerning the ideal state for society are clearly expounded in his 1260 tract, *Rissho Ankoku Ron* (RAR; "Establishment of the Legitimate Teaching for the Protection of the Country"). He begins with a graphic portrait of the ugly state of affairs in Japan during his life:

> In recent years, there are unusual disturbances in the heavens, strange occurrences on earth, famine and pestilence, all affecting every corner of the empire and spreading throughout the land. Oxen and horses lie dead in the streets, the bones of the stricken crowd the highways. Over half the population has already been carried off by death, and in every family someone grieves.[14]

Nichiren diagnosed the cause of Japan's turmoil in the Kamakura period to be the fact that people had spurned the *Lotus Sutra*. The result is that "the benevolent deities and sages abandon the nation and leave their accustomed places. As a result, demons and followers of heretical doctrines create disaster and inflict calamity upon the populace."[15] However, the country may achieve "prosperity through the Buddhist Law. . . . One must first of all pray for the safety of the nation and then work to establish the Buddhist Law."[16]

The Soka Gakkai agrees with Nichiren, asserting that people who have achieved enlightenment have undergone a "Human Revolution" (*ningen kakumei*) and that their responsibility is the propagation (*kosen rufu*) of the faith to other people. Moreover, their social and political view of the modern world is based on the ideas expounded in RAR. Like Nichiren, Toda Josei, who reorganized and built the Gakkai after World War II, exclaimed that the disasters that befell Japan during and after World War II came as a result of the government's decision to ignore the words of Nichiren and to propagate Shinto. Toda thus saw himself as the modern disciple of Nichiren who was charged with the propagation of his Buddhism and the salvation of the world after the disaster of World War II.

The Nichiren School splintered into several sects following their patron's death in 1282. One of these sects, Nichiren Shoshu, teaches that Nichiren appointed one of his disciples, Nikko Shonin (1246–1333), as his designated successor. This sect was founded in the late thirteenth century when Nikko built its head temple, Taiseki-ji, near Mount Fuji. The major difference between Nichiren Shoshu and other Nichiren sects is Nichiren Shoshu's assertion that Nichiren is the true Buddha of the age of *mappo*, while other Nichiren sects believe that Shakyamuni is the true Buddha. Nichiren Shoshu claims that Shakyamuni was a precursor, a kind of John the Baptist, who brought Buddhist teachings to mankind, while Nichiren himself was born in the age of *mappo* to save mankind in its hour of greatest need.

The Origins of the Soka Gakkai

The Soka Gakkai dates its origins to 1930 when two educators, Makiguchi Tsunesaburo (1871–1944) and a younger disciple, Toda Josei (1900–1958) formed an organization, the Soka Kyoiku Gakkai (SKG; Value-Creation Education Society). The goal of the SKG was to study, discuss, and publicize the educational theories of Makiguchi. Makiguchi, an educational philosopher and writer, had devoted his entire career to teaching, educational administration, and the development of a philosophy of education. The philosophy was based on the premise that the goal of human life is the attainment of happiness and that man can only become happy if he becomes a value-creator. Value consists of three related ingredients: Goodness, Beauty, and Benefit or Gain. A happy person is defined as one who maximizes his potential in his chosen sphere of life and who helps others maximize theirs.

Makiguchi felt that the goal of education must be to help train the student to think independently and creatively. He denounced the educational system of 1930s Japan as being too rigid. Rote memorization of facts, noted Makiguchi, stifled a child's creativity and natural curiosity. He wanted teachers to give students more personal attention, to encourage independent learning activities, and to have schools teach the children more about their community. His ideas appeared in his book *Soka Kyoiku Gaku Taikei* ("A System of Value Creation Education"; 1930–1934).

The Soka Kyoiku Gakkai began as a journal and discussion group to publicize Makiguchi's ideas. But Makiguchi had also converted to Nichiren Shoshu in 1928, and when his educational ideas received little public response or attention, he turned increasingly to religion. By the late 1930s he became convinced that human happiness could best be achieved through the religious doctrines of Nichiren. He then refocused the SKG's activities to the proselytization of his view of Nichiren Buddhism. By the end of the 1930s the membership became diversified and included people from various walks of life, including students and housewives, as well as educators.[17]

The SKG was nearly totally destroyed due to the hostile treatment it received from the government during World War II. The wartime Japanese government, determined to have totalitarian control over all areas of thought and association, tried to force Nichiren Shoshu to unite with the other Nichiren sects. In 1943 both Toda and Makiguchi were imprisoned for their refusal to participate in Shinto worship. Makiguchi died in prison in 1944.

The Soka Gakkai that grew up under the aegis of Toda Josei after World War II had a very different focus from the old SKG and grew for entirely different reasons. It is said that Toda devoted much of his time in prison during World War II to reading the *Lotus Sutra* and chanting it continuously. While in prison, he suddenly became aware of the fact that he had been anointed as the person who was to spread the teachings of Nichiren to bring true happiness to the people of Japan and the rest of the world who had endured so much suffering due to the war. Toda considered himself to be Nichiren's personal delegate who bore the "awesome responsibility" of ending the "misery of mankind."[18] Accordingly, he organized the Gakkai as the vehicle to achieve this end.

Toda changed the name of the SKG to the Soka Gakkai (Value Creation Society) to reflect a change of emphasis from education to religion. The Soka Gakkai grew rapidly as an independent lay religious teaching and evangelistic organization. It promised happiness, meaning in life, and the comfort of close group membership to the restless, rootless, searching, and deeply frustrated people of postwar Japan. Toda was a tireless speaker, counselor, evangelist, and organizer who by 1950 had attracted a core of followers, many of them quite young, who worked as hard as he did. The result was tremendous growth; Toda vowed in 1951 to attain a membership of 750,000 households in seven years. In 1957 it was announced that the goal had been reached.

During the Soka Gakkai's period of astounding growth in the 1950s and 1960s, young Gakkai zealots, claiming that every religion other than Nichiren Shoshu is an evil religion, attacked temples of other Buddhist sects, headquarters of other new religions, and even Christian churches. The extreme measures of these activists won the Gakkai a very bad reputation in the press. Toda made matters worse in 1954 by noting, "We must consider all religions our enemies and we must destroy them."[19]

On the other hand, there was a very tender side to Toda and other Gakkai leaders. His own familiarity with the postwar suffering of the Japanese, his genuine ability to counsel the many miserable people who came to his door, and his hard work and organizational abilities guaranteed the success of his group. When he died in 1958, Toda had become a nationally known figure whose funeral was attended by many of Japan's ruling elite.

Ikeda Daisaku (1928–   ), Toda's disciple and chosen successor, continues to lead the Soka Gakkai today. Ikeda formally relinquished the presidency and day-to-day administration of the Soka Gakkai in the late 1970s,[20] but he remains as the movement's spiritual leader, teacher, and major spokesman. Ikeda is a widely known figure in Japanese society and is recognized abroad as a major Japanese figure.

Ikeda is the spiritual architect who took the firm foundation developed by Toda and built the Soka Gakkai into a strong national and international movement. Under his direction the Soka Gakkai has grown into a huge, stable, and mature organization that wields tremendous influence throughout Japanese society. Ikeda is also responsible for making the Soka Gakkai into a truly international movement with strong bases in the United States and Europe and chapters in over a hundred countries. Ikeda was the driving force behind the growth of the Soka Gakkai's school system. He organized the Komeito, which remains today as the second-largest opposition political party in Japan.[21] Ikeda is the author of an astounding number of books and articles. When he is not writing, Ikeda travels across Japan and to foreign countries speaking to Soka Gakkai chapters and providing religious guidance to members. Ikeda also makes what the Gakkai calls "pilgrimages for peace," which consist, first, of proposals for disarmament and the lessening of tension between nations and, second, meetings with major world figures. He is deeply revered by Gakkai members as a religious leader and teacher and as a symbol of the Soka Gakkai. The Soka Gakkai apparently envisions Ikeda as an international spiritual leader like Gandhi. The Gakkai on occasion publishes articles praising the work of Gandhi and then compares the work of Ikeda to that of Gandhi. Ikeda is called a "crusader for world peace" and a "hope for suffering humanity."

Although Ikeda is revered by Soka Gakkai members, he has received considerable criticism by the vernacular press and opponents of the Soka Gakkai. He has been accused of power-seeking and some journalists have tried to link him with a number of scandals, but none of these charges has been actually proven. One Liberal-Democratic Party (LDP) member of the House of Representatives charges that Ikeda is a major political powerbroker and much more of a political leader than a religious figure.[22] Despite this criticism, however, Ikeda remains as the respected leader of the Soka Gakkai.

Soka Gakkai Membership

The Soka Gakkai is a predominantly urban-based religious movement with a membership of between 8 and 10 million believers. It grew from a tiny band of followers at Toda's presidential inauguration in 1951 to a following of 750,000 at his death in 1958. Membership swelled throughout the 1960s and 1970s and reached the 8 million–level in the 1980s. It appears that membership stabilized at this level in the early 1990s.

The Soka Gakkai achieved its massive size not only through the power and appeal of its practice and teaching but also through thorough organization, passionate proselytization by members, and the image that the Soka Gakkai projected a very modern and streamlined version of Buddhism that was offered to the citizenry of a Buddhist nation in which the traditional forms of Buddhism and Shinto had been discredited by the disaster of World War II. Another reason for the Soka Gakkai's rise is its organizational strength. The Gakkai is carefully organized into prefectural, city, district, and block groups. Its real sociological strength lies in the tightness of its neighborhood groups where members pay a great deal of attention to the needs of fellow believers. One finds evidence of continual contact and mutual help. The Soka Gakkai's leaders in Tokyo cannot cater to the needs of the average member in Fukuoka, but a carefully chosen chain of leaders and the loving concern of another local believer can. Gakkai members always say that they belong to a caring and compassionate movement. Disgruntled members exist in every organization, but they are outnumbered by contented members. The existence of an intensely loyal and dedicated membership is the key to the Gakkai's long-term success.

Another key factor in the Soka Gakkai's success is that members act as support groups for each other. When a member is experiencing some form of distress, she or he quickly receives the sympathetic help of a neighboring Gakkai member or leader. Members at local meetings are strongly urged to articulate problems in their lives, and it is common for other members in attendance to lend them advice and support.

Membership in the Soka Gakkai is not an all-encompassing activity. Unlike some religious cults that demand huge monetary dues, along with the total time and dedication of their membership, isolating them from the mainstream of society, the Soka Gakkai, like other traditional Mahayana Buddhist sects in Japan, seeks to improve the life of the member in society. The member carries on a very normal life at home and at work where she or he mingles freely and inconspicuously with other members of society. The Gakkai, however, expects the faithful member to devote some of his or her time to movement-related activities, including *gongyo* or daily prayer, attendance at the various meetings (*zadankai*) that are usually held on a monthly basis, and proselytization (*shakubuku*). Members are strongly encouraged to purchase and read a wide variety of organizational publications including its daily newspaper, the *Seikyo Shimbun*. Many members take written examinations that are supposed to improve their understanding of Buddhism.

James White, in his study of the Soka Gakkai in the late 1960s, discovered that the Soka Gakkai was an urban and predominantly lower-middle class movement with a predominance of laborers, self-employed small businessmen, and housewives.[23] In the early 1990s, however, one gets the impression that while housewives and blue-collar workers may still form an important element, the occupational and financial levels and achievements are now much higher than they were in the 1960s. This partly reflects a strong national trend that has made the average Japanese far better educated and materially and occupationally more successful in the 1990s than he was a generation earlier. But today the Soka Gakkai, with its own excellent school system and its political, social, and economic successes, attracts many well-educated and articulate leaders and members. In general the Soka Gakkai membership profile would generally conform to the residents of most urban areas in Japan. There is a smaller but significant rural following as well.

People join the Soka Gakkai for a variety of reasons. Many younger followers become members because they were brought up in families that had at least one other member. Others find membership attractive because of the contentment and satisfaction of friends or colleagues who are members. One young male recruit in 1992 stated that "I joined the Soka Gakkai because many of my friends who are members seemed much happier than my friends who are not members."[24]

Other members list some form of physical or psychological suffering as a reason. The common tale is of a person who is ill or suffering from depression due to financial or occupational hardships who is approached by a Gakkai member who pledges that membership will bring relief and a new sense of happiness to the sufferer. Members often say that membership has significantly changed their lives for the better—they feel much happier, have a new sense of confidence, are much more successful in their jobs or careers, and enjoy a new set of friends and supporters.

Members often speak of a "Soka Gakkai spirit," referring enthusiastically to the ways that this Buddhism has changed their lives. Robert Eppsteiner, an American member, provides a good example of this spirit:

> In the 1960s, issues of human rights, equality, and the debate on the Vietnam war were constantly on the 'front pages' of my mind as well as those of my fellow students. As I studied Buddhism and participated in Soka Gakkai activities as a lay person, I started to build bridges where ordinary citizens could start to climb out and over many of their problems of daily living. I learned to respect individuals for who they were, not for who I wanted them to be. I started to develop an inner awareness of personal responsibility that to be human was not only to share the joys, but the sufferings of another human being. When I studied about the successive presidents of the Soka Gakkai, I could feel that their deep inner conviction and determination to serve humanity flowed from the currents of Buddhism. There was no greater joy for me than to see another person overcome his or her suffering and become a citizen committed to serve society. I became hopeful that I could personally effect positive change in society and that the Soka Gakkai as an organization was contributing value, based on Buddhism, to human society.[25]

Buddhism and Society

Cultural activities (defined as the activities that people perform in their everyday lives, ranging from ordinary human relationships to education, politics, and the arts) form an important part of the Soka Gakkai movement. The Soka Gakkai is unique among the new religions in Japan in the depth and scope of its sociocultural activism. Gakkai activities range from education and culture to politics and publishing. The Gakkai never enters a new field in a temporary or token manner. It always commits its considerable resources and skilled leaders to each new enterprise and invests in careful long-term development. The emphasis is on quality and durability. An example is Soka University near Tokyo, which opened in 1971 as a very small institution but which has grown steadily in size and quality ever since. The result of this careful planning and development is that Soka has become one of the better universities in Japan. Similarly, the Komeito is now an established and powerful political party, Soka Gakkai–sponsored cultural events attract world-famous artists, and its newspaper, the *Seikyo Shimbun*, is the third-most-read daily paper in Japan.

The Soka Gakkai is involved in a wide variety of cultural activities. It believes that international exchange in the fields of arts and letters is an important way to bring different cultures together and to promote international understanding. The Min-On Concert Association, which was founded by the Soka Gakkai in 1963, has sponsored exchanges with many nations throughout the world in opera; ballet; choral singing; orchestral, chamber, and popular music; and popular and folk dancing. It has brought major orchestras and world-famous artists to Japan. The Tokyo Fuji Art Museum in Hachioji regularly displays paintings and other works of art from around the world. The Institute of Oriental Philosophy coordinates and sponsors research on Buddhism in close coordination with scholars of religion outside of the Soka Gakkai.

With respect to society, the professed goal of the Soka Gakkai is not to radically alter major social institutions but to improve and cleanse them so as to rid humanity of the "three great poisons—greed, anger and folly." Its leaders state that a world following the "true" teachings of Nichiren would bear a strong physical resemblance to its predecessor, but the worldview and attitudes of its citizens would be far more humane, generous, and peaceful than before. Such social evils as warfare and environmental pollution would recede, and concerned Buddhists in every walk of life would work diligently to redress the economic and social imbalances of society.

The Soka Gakkai believes that religion must serve as the basis of any morally just society. As they see it, the primary social role of religion is to remove the basic causes of human discontent and to lead humankind to true happiness, harmony, and prosperity in life. Religion is essential for the philosophical, social, and political betterment of society as a whole, and it must enter into every phase of society, including politics, in order that change may occur for the better. Ikeda Daisaku, for example, criticizes the greed and corruption in Japanese politics, on the basis of his belief that Japan's politicians are unprincipled men who pursue power and wealth for themselves while ignoring the welfare of the Japanese people. He suggests that Japan would be much better led by principled leaders whose thinking and actions are based on Buddhist ideals of justice and respect for the dignity of human life.[26]

This combination of religion and social activism is based on the concept of *Obutsu Myogo*, the "fusion of Buddhist beliefs with every phase of social behavior, the veritable reconstruction of society on a comprehensive base of religious values and norms."[27] According to Ikeda:

> The purpose of the Soka Gakkai lies in the attainment of *Kosen rufu*, propagation of True Buddhism throughout the country, and further to the entire world. From a cultural viewpoint, *Kosen rufu* means the construction of a highly civilized nation. Religion should be the base of all cultural activities. In a sense, the Soka Gakkai aims at an unprecedented flowering of culture, a Third Civilization.[28]

Although the professed goal of the Soka Gakkai is the conversion of the rest of humanity to its beliefs, its leaders realize that their movement will remain comparatively small within their own lifetimes. A more tangible social and cultural goal of the Soka Gakkai is to act as an exemplary model of social behavior for nonmembers to emulate. Thus, the Komeito, even if it remained a minority force in the Diet, could strengthen democratic values in Japan by exposing corruption and by showing larger parties how to better respond to the needs of the people. Soka Gakkai schools, though few in number, could lead the way to the general improvement of the quality of Japanese education if educators saw the superiority of Soka-based education.

The Soka Gakkai regards itself as a teacher whose lessons can help others improve their lives. The Soka Gakkai's peace movement, for example, is in fact a peace education program based on books and exhibitions that is meant to remind the Japanese of the horrors of war. Gakkai leaders believe that if younger people knew the misery of modern warfare, they would work actively for the promotion of peace.

The Soka Gakkai also believes that even limited social activism can bring greater rewards for society as a whole. Large donations of money collected from the public and given to the United Nations can help refugees in certain countries. Exchanges of Japanese students from Soka Gakkai schools with children in Russia and China can foster better ties between Japan and the outside world, as can Ikeda's visits with world leaders. Consequently, the Soka Gakkai calls for a fundamental fusion of religious idealism and practical social action programs.

The Soka Gakkai Peace Movement

The professed goal of the Soka Gakkai is the realization of genuine world peace. It seeks a global environment in which each nation would live in harmony with its neighbors, problems such as global pollution would be brought under control, and individuals would be able to maximize their fullest potentials without inflicting harm on others. The Soka Gakkai has defined peace as a harmonious way of life where war would disappear as a method of solving disputes and a person would be free to work not only for the betterment of his or her own life but of the lives of other people as well.

The Soka Gakkai peace movement is based on the belief that its reading of the thinking of Nichiren provides the key to the achievement of genuine happiness. Man possesses within him both the potential for good and bad (Ten Worlds). People who devote themselves to the Buddhism of Nichiren will eventually get a purer karma which will allow them to become happier and more caring people. If everybody's karma changed for the better, mankind would experience true peace and happiness. Ultimately the universal application of Nichiren Buddhism is the best guarantor of peace.

Realistically speaking, however, the Soka Gakkai realizes that Nichiren Buddhism will not spread worldwide overnight. The Gakkai, however, stresses that there are other practical steps whose adoption could improve prospects for a more peaceful world and a safer environment. A key teaching of Buddhism is the truth of social interdependence, the idea that all living beings share the world together and that the act of one will have an effect on all others. The Soka Gakkai's peace movement is a set of activities that will encourage mankind to better understand its interdependence and to adopt measures that will foster the development of a safer world. Gakkai programs include extensive measures to promote peace education, communication between different societies, and an awareness of the dimensions of the environmental problems facing man.

The Soka Gakkai has a long documented record of antiwar activities. The Japanese government imprisoned Gakkai leaders in 1943 because of their criticism of its war effort. Toda Josei reconstructed the Soka Gakkai after World War II with the belief that Nichiren Shoshu Buddhism could lead to the creation of a new society devoid of militarism where people could live in peace and harmony. In 1957 Toda published his "Atomic and Hydrogen Bomb Ban Proclamation" in which he "condemned nuclear weapons as an absolute evil that threatens the people's right of existence and called on youth to launch a movement to disseminate the truth that anyone who resorts to the use of nuclear weapons is a diabolical fiend. This belief constitutes the basis of Soka Gakkai's peace movement."[29]

The philosophy behind the Soka Gakkai's peace activities today were summarized in a 1991 editorial in its newspaper, the *Seikyo Shimbun*:

> Dr. Johan Galtung, a prominent peace advocate, once spoke about the relationship between peace and karma, or the Buddhist theory which explains how potential energies residing in the inner realm of life manifest themselves as various results in the future. He said that in contrast to the thinking that peace can be preserved if the bad person apologizes for his deed, Buddhist teaching maintains that it is irrelevant to find fault or to blame since all people have a common karma. He said that war cannot be eliminated if the perpetrator apologizes. He observed that human karma itself is the problem.

> The same is true of nuclear weapons. The problem cannot be solved by getting rid of them physically, although their elimination is a condition for a solution. The know-how of producing nuclear weapons remains with us forever. The essential solution to the nuclear threat lies in unceasingly combatting the 'diabolical nature' of man which threatens the right of the very existence of mankind. A way must be found to transform human karma.

> In a letter to his disciples, Nichiren Daishonin states: 'Life itself is the most precious of all treasures. Even the treasures of the entire universe cannot equal the value of a single human life.'

> At a time when confrontation between ideologies is coming to an end and when the nature of state sovereignty is being questioned, the Buddhist philosophy implicit in President Toda's declaration against atomic and hydrogen bombs undoubtedly will take on added significance.[30]

Peace education is the heart of the Soka Gakkai's antiwar movement. The Gakkai insists that if people had a better idea of the hellish nature of war and the suffering it brings to mankind, they would be less prone to engage in violent activities. The result is a stream of publications, exhibitions, and films recounting the absolute horror of war.

History textbooks used in Japanese high schools do not give an in-depth analysis of Japan's involvement in World War II. Students are told that Japanese suffered greatly because of the war but are not told about the horrors Japanese forces inflicted on the Chinese and other Asians. The Japanese invasion of China was called an "advance"; the Japanese navy did not attack Pearl Harbor, but rather "engaged" the United States. In 1986 the education minister commented that the Rape of Nanking was no worse than atrocities committed by other nations. In 1988 another cabinet member called the Marco Polo Bridge Incident of 1937 an "accident."[31] The result is that Japanese born in the postwar era know little about World War II.

The Soka Gakkai shares the concern of some Japanese educators that if Japan's future leaders do not understand the full impact that the war had on Japan, they might adopt policies that might lead to a repeat of the war. One result is a significant effort by the Soka Gakkai to inform younger Japanese of what happened during World War II. Since the 1970s the Soka Gakkai's Youth and Women's Divisions have engaged in the publication of a lengthy series of books including the eighty-volume set, *Sensoo o Shiranai Sedai E* ("To the Generations Who Do Not Know War")[32] and a twenty-volume set, *Heiwa no Negai o Komete* ("With Hopes for Peace").[33] Gakkai members recorded the war experiences of hundreds of Japanese who fought in or lived through World War II and published these accounts in this series. The result is a very graphic portrait of the horrors of World War II that is generally unavailable in Japanese history texts. The goal of these publications is to "promote antiwar sentiments by keeping alive the memories of the horrors and cruelty of war and passing them on to posterity, in as much as the generation of people who do not have first-hand knowledge of war is increasing."[34]

A related campaign is a series of exhibitions depicting the ugliness and horror of war. Since the 1970s the Soka Gakkai has put on a series of shows detailing in photographs and charts the terrible impact that war, nuclear war in particular, can have on humankind. One exhibit, "War and Peace," was shown in Hiroshima in 1991. It was cosponsored by the International Bureau for Humanitarian Issues and International Physicians for the Prevention of Nuclear War and had the support of the United Nations Department for Disarmament Affairs. The exhibit previously had been shown at the United Nations (1989), Boston (1990), Geneva (1990), Moscow (1991), and Oslo (1991).

This exhibition emphasizes the themes of peace, human rights, and environmental protection and is divided into two main sections, "The 20th Century: A History of Conflict" and "The 21st Century: The Challenge for Humanity." The first section takes up the period from World War I through World War II, nuclear weapons and the arms race. The second section deals with humanitarian and environmental issues, such as hunger and poverty, refugees and displaced persons, apartheid and racism, global warming, ozone depletion, acid rain, radioactive pollution, toxic wastes, deforestation, desertification, and extinction of species.[35]

The Soka Gakkai is an active supporter of the United Nations. It is an NGO (Non-Government Organization) representative at the UN and participates in many official UN activities. The Soka Gakkai works particularly closely with the United Nations High Commissioner for Refugees (UNHCR). Gakkai officials have inspected refugee camps in Asia and Africa and have raised considerable sums of money that have been donated directly to the UNHCR for refugee relief. Some of this money was used for the construction of an electric power generating plant in 1990 for Palestinian refugees in the West Bank area of the Jordan River.[36]

Working as an NGO of the UN Economic and Social Council, Soka Gakkai International (SGI), the international arm of the Gakkai, has carried out environmental consciousness-raising activities around the world.[37] In 1992 these included a major conference on the environment convened in London by SGI, the Commonwealth Human Ecology association, and UNESCO. Some one hundred delegates including major experts on the environment discussed a wide-range of problems, such as pollution and the destruction of rain forests. SGI participated at the UN Conference on Environment and Development (UNCED) with an exhibition, "Toward the Century of Life: The Environment and Development." The exhibition concentrated on two themes: the global environmental crisis and development and protection of the great Amazon. Several SGI members in Brazil are actively involved with such organizations as the National Research Institute for Amazonia and the Brazilian Enterprise for Research on Agriculture and Cattle, which are playing a frontline role in the battle to save the region's fragile environment.

Another important element of the Soka Gakkai's peace movement is the intercultural exchange of people and ideas. The Soka Gakkai contends that international understanding can only come about if people from different countries get to know each other directly through face-to-face contacts. For several decades the Soka Gakkai has sent teams of its members to visit a large number of countries including the former Soviet Union and China. The Gakkai has invited a large number of foreign groups, especially students, to visit Japan. In 1990 and 1991, for example, eight pupils from the Beijing First Experimental Primary School and twelve pupils from the No. 1234 elementary and secondary school in Moscow visited Soka Primary Schools in Tokyo and Osaka while a 201-member Soka Gakkai youth cultural delegation made a one-week visit to China.

Soka Gakkai leaders, Ikeda Daisaku in particular, have developed dialogues and strong relationships with a variety of international political and cultural leaders. During one month (April 1992) Ikeda held lengthy discussions with violinist Yehudi Menuhin, Chinese Communist Party General Secretary Jiang Zemin, Czechoslovakian President Vaclav Havel, and former

Soviet President Mikhail Gorbachev. The point of these dialogues and relationships with world leaders, which have been going on for over two decades, is to increase understanding and communication between Japan and other nations and cultures. It is well known that the Soka Gakkai played an important role as a mediator between China and Japan prior to the establishment of diplomatic relations between the two countries in 1972.

The Soka Gakkai seeks to encourage the peace theme among its members in an ongoing series of meetings and cultural festivals in Japan and in countries with SGI chapters. The idea of the Peace Culture Festival series is to have many people from different regions and countries participating together with the hope that they will gain a greater appreciation for each other by working together.

Soka Gakkai leaders contend that its university, Soka University, encourages peace with its strong international curriculum and its exchange programs for students and scholars from North America, Europe, Asia, and Africa. The Soka Gakkai opened the Pacific Basin Research Center at Soka University's California campus in 1991 to study economic and political forces shaping the region and U.S.-Japan relations. In the fall of 1993, SGI President Daisaku Ikeda founded the Boston Research Center for the 21st Century as a focal point for the SGI's peace studies and to promote dialogue among scholars and activists on issues relating to peace, human rights, environmental protection, education, and culture.

Education

The Soka Gakkai was founded by a teacher as a movement dedicated to educational reform. Thus, it is no surprise that the Soka Gakkai has developed its own educational system. The Gakkai's school system is actually quite small in comparison to the size of the membership. It consists of a handful of kindergarten, elementary, junior high, and senior high schools; and Soka Women's Junior College and Soka University on a single campus near Tokyo. Soka University has overseas campuses near Los Angeles and Paris.

Soka University, founded in 1971, is the crown jewel of the Soka Gakkai educational system. In 1991 the large campus at Hachioji had an enrollment of 6,453 students; 277 faculty; six undergraduate faculties; graduate courses in economics, law, and letters; a series of correspondence courses; and an Institute of the Japanese Language for foreign students. There are six attached research institutes including the Institute for the Comparative Study of Cultures, the Institute for Peace Studies, and the Center for African Studies. Soka Women's Junior College is also located on the university campus.

Although it was founded in 1972, Soka University has already become one of the better universities in Japan. It does not have the prestige of Tokyo or Keio Universities, but the Soka Gakkai has spent vast sums to build a large modern campus with ultramodern facilities and to hire an excellent faculty with sound scholarly and teaching credentials.[38] It has an excellent reputation among Japanese educators and ranks with the best Japanese universities in placing students in good career positions.[39] An Adult Degree Program (correspondence division) fills the needs of some fourteen thousand students ranging in age from their early twenties to eighty. Many of these students are seeking certification in education. During the summer vacation the university holds special classes and programs for the correspondence students.

Soka University differs from most Japanese universities because it has a broad international focus,[40] a low student-faculty ratio with ready student access to faculty, and many small seminar classes. A nationwide poll of college seniors in 1992 ranked Soka University third in overall student satisfaction.[41] Speaking personally, I found the students I taught at Soka to be alert, curious, and very bright. They seem to be much more idealistic than students I met at other universities and to have a much better understanding of international affairs.

Soka Gakkai schools offer a standardized nonsectarian curriculum that conforms to Japanese law and traditions. Teachers at these schools often point out that what makes their institutions stand out from others in Japan is an enriched education that comes from having smaller classes, close ties between faculty and students, and a stress on the need for the students to learn how to think for themselves.

Virtually all of the students and over half the faculty are members of the Soka Gakkai, and there are many Gakkai-related activities on campus. Nevertheless, although Soka is a thoroughly Buddhist university, its classes are remarkably free of religious discussions and dogma. Indeed, it is surprising how many students are ignorant about the history of the Gakkai. Many of the students I interviewed at Soka University in 1992 were not terribly concerned with religious matters and attended Soka because they felt that they could get a good career preparation there.

The Soka Gakkai and Politics

The Soka Gakkai's participation in politics is not an anomaly in Japanese history. The fact that the Soka Gakkai is actively engaged in politics stems largely from a tradition in Japanese society that strongly links religion and other aspects of society. Americans have a long tradition of the separation of church and state, but such an idea does not exist in Japan. On the contrary, Japan has a long tradition that links politics and religion together under the divine authority of the emperor.

The pre–World War II imperial state system in Japan was "a kind of patriarchical absolutism based on the absolute divinity of the Emperor from whom all legitimate authority emanated."[42] State Shinto was fostered a century ago by the government and nationalistic Shinto theologians as a source by which to legitimize the newly built government and to unite the people under its authority. The government encouraged the spread of Shinto rituals and observances and ordered all citizens to adopt them, thus utilizing the Shinto ceremonial events to enhance nationalism. "State Shinto was a sort of new national religion introduced by the government after the Meiji period, but the government itself regarded it not as a religion, but as the Japanese national ideology which dominated other general religions."[43]

The New Religions that grew in the prewar era (such as Omotokyo) all had a strong concern with politics and with national political issues. Nakano orders prewar New Religious organizations into three groups in terms of their response to the government's policy of sponsoring National Shintoism.[44] The first consists of groups like Omotokyo, which criticized the government for its tampering with the authentic and original spirit of Shinto and called for a reconstruction of society based on a true unity of Shinto and the Imperial Way. Omotokyo was later suppressed by the government. A second group of New Religions, such as Tenrikyo and Reiyukai, supported the government's ideology of the emperor system and the national polity and were thus permitted some degree of spiritual independence in exchange for their support of the government. A third group denied the ideology of the emperor system and national polity. One of the leading organizations in this category was the Soka Kyoiku Gakkai (SKG), the forerunner of today's Soka Gakkai.

Makiguchi Tsunesaburo, the founder of the SKG, strongly opposed the measures incorporated in the Religious Organizations Law of 1939, which sought to impose government control over religions by forcing the amalgamation of denominations. The SKG leadership also refused to worship and enshrine replicas of the sacred tablets of Ise Grand Shrine, saying that this was contrary to its religious teachings. As a result, Makiguchi, his chief disciple, Toda Josei, and other SKG leaders were imprisoned in 1943 and the organization was dissolved. Makiguchi died in prison in 1944 and Toda, who reorganized the Soka Gakkai after World War II, was not released until July 1945.

The threefold political division of New Religions reemerged after World War II when all laws suppressing religious activity were abolished. The most radically conservative group was Seicho-no-I. It sought to abolish the liberal reforms of the Allied Occupation, which it said were alien to Japanese cultural traditions. It wanted to reconstruct the state in accordance with the traditional ideals of the Japanese nation including the rewriting of the Japanese constitution and the creation of a new educational system that was not dominated by left-wing teachers. A second grouping of New Religions including Rissho Koseikai, PL Kyodan, and Sekai Kyuseikai formed the Union of New Religious Organizations of Japan (UNROJ). The UNROJ has successfully run a number of candidates in House of Councillors and has cooperated closely with the ruling conservative Liberal Democratic Party (LDP). The third grouping consists of the Soka Gakkai, which created its own opposition party, the Komeito, in 1964.[45]

The Soka Gakkai's interest in politics is part of the Nichiren tradition of political activism in Japanese history. Nichiren himself remonstrated against the government's support of other sects of Buddhism, blaming the catastrophes afflicting Japan at the time on the government's neglect of the true laws and saving powers of the *Lotus Sutra*. The Soka Gakkai apparently has inherited much of his ardor, courage, and determination. Like Nichiren, the Soka Gakkai is like the angry gadfly that makes fervent disciples and angry enemies. Just as Nichiren tried to use the government to make certain religious changes for what he felt was the benefit of the nation, the Soka Gakkai today professes that it is using politics as a vehicle for bringing about meaningful change.

The Soka Gakkai itself has never shied away from political involvement. The essence of the Soka Gakkai's venture into politics stems from its interpretation of the worldview of Nichiren. The Gakkai regards itself as the preparer of a new civilization, a civilization where peace, freedom, and harmony will flourish. It supports the notion that a person and his environment are one. For this reason, it repudiates the notion that religion should be involved in spiritual things or in happiness only in another world after death. But in order to achieve happiness here and now, bold action to produce an environment more conducive to the flourishing of human society is necessary.

After the war, Toda Josei was well aware of the fact that both political power and action were necessary if Japan was to move away from its militaristic past. If a degree of political power could give the Soka Gakkai a public forum to express its views and an opportunity to influence legislation in its favor, then political action was an appropriate step for the Soka Gakkai to take.

Toda and other early Gakkai leaders also remembered their persecution at the hands of the government during World War II. Unrestricted political power gave government authorities complete control over the lives of most Japanese. Becoming a part of the power structure by sending representatives to local, regional, and national assemblies would mean that the Soka Gakkai would have some say over the making and implementation of government decisions and could perhaps prevent future persecution by the authorities. The democracy that came to Japan after the war provided each citizen an equal right in determining who his leaders would be. Toda quickly realized that the rapidly expanding membership base of the Soka Gakkai could be effectively utilized to provide the Gakkai with the political power that it sought.

The Soka Gakkai's Political Views

The Soka Gakkai justifies its political action on the basis of its concept of *Obutsu myogo*, the belief that one cannot separate religion from society. Religion must serve as the foundation for other activities, and it is the duty of the Soka Gakkai as a religious group to send envoys into all spheres of life.

The Soka Gakkai does not propose to alter the institutions of government, but it does call for the fusion of political ideas with a religious spirit of benevolence derived from Buddhism. This fusion can provide government with a strong ideological foundation, inspire politicians to work harder for the welfare of the people, and encourage the public to play a more active role in politics. The Gakkai further contends that national and social problems will be remedied when the spiritual unity of the nation is attained.

The Soka Gakkai has introduced two concepts, Human Socialism (*Ningen shakaishugi*) and Buddhist Democracy (*Buppo minshushugi*) that together are said to represent the ideals of the fusion of practical politics and religious principles (*Obutsu myogo*), the philosophy society must adopt for the creation of a truly democratic society.

Human socialism is the Soka Gakkai's program for the economic reconstruction of society. The goal is to merge the best aspects of capitalism and socialism (or Marxism) and to blend them with the humanistic philosophy of Nichiren Buddhism. Capitalism is good in that it provides man with the freedom to gain the best from life, but inevitably there are people who are impoverished by capitalism's "excessively bitter competition."[46] Socialism is praised for its emphasis on social equality, but is criticized for rigid governmental controls and failure to emphasize the unique wishes of each individual member of society.

The Soka Gakkai's practical solution to the imbalances of socialism and capitalism is the creation of a democratic welfare state in which a socially responsible government would provide people with good, inexpensive health care; a more progressive education; and a cleaner environment.

Government would help the needy with improved social services and hous-ing.[47] The state, however, would not be overbearing. People would enjoy complete freedom (Buddhist Democracy) and there would be a free and open social and economic environment. Government would remove the causes of social inequality, but people would be free to build their own lives. Since Buddhism promotes such ideals as the respect for human dignity, peace, and life, people would treat each other in a far more humane manner than in a non-Buddhist state.

The Evolution of a Unique Party

The Komeito is a type of political party without parallel in Japanese history. European political history is full of denominational political parties with a strong Christian base, but the Komeito is the first successful religion-based party in Japan. As a religious party with its base in the Soka Gakkai, the Komeito is difficult to classify in terms of the classical conservative-progressive division of Japanese politics. Komeito voters do not support the party for ideological reasons; rather, their support is based on the fact that they are Soka Gakkai members and since the party is still an unofficial arm of the Soka Gakkai, it is part of their religious duty to work hard for the Komeito during election campaigns and to vote for its candidates on elec-tion day.

The Soka Gakkai became actively involved in politics in the early 1950s when it successfully ran a number of candidates as independents for local offices in Tokyo, Osaka, and other parts of Japan. This success led to the successful election of Gakkai-supported candidates in Upper House elec-tions in the late 1950s and early 1960s. The Soka Gakkai formed the Komeito in 1964.

Prospects for the Komeito looked good from the start. There were already 6½ million families belonging to the Soka Gakkai, approximately 10 percent of Japan's total population. The fact that the membership was con-centrated heavily in Tokyo, Osaka, Fukuoka, and other urban areas, and that Japan has a multimember constituency system,[48] gave the Komeito a special advantage. These optimistic projections were borne out in 1967 and 1969 when the Komeito won twenty-five and forty-seven seats, respectively.

The problem for the Komeito is that it is unable to move much beyond its Soka Gakkai base. Soka Gakkai membership has remained at a fairly constant 8 to 10 percent of the Japanese population since the late 1960s. At the same time Komeito vote totals have remained in the mid-five-million range throughout the 1970s and 1980s. In Upper House elections the Komeito vote jumps up to the mid-six-million range in the proportional representation races because voters in every district have a chance to vote for Komeito candidates while isolated voters in districts with few Soka Gakkai voters are denied the chance to support the Komeito because it does not run candidates in those constituencies. Because of this strong unvarying base, the Komeito does well in elections with low voter turnouts and poorly in those with large turnouts. Thus, the Komeito's percentage of the total vote in the proportional representation race for the Upper House jumped from 10.9 percent in 1989 to 14.3 percent in 1992 although the total popular vote only went up by a bit more than 300,000 votes.[49]

It is clear that the Komeito would not win any elections without the Soka Gakkai religious base. Endo Otohiko, a Komeito member of the House of Representatives from Tokyo, estimates that at least half his votes come from Soka Gakkai voters and that the average Komeito candidate depends on Soka Gakkai for two thirds or more of his or her votes.[50] There are, of course, marginal non–Soka Gakkai voters who will vote for occasional Komeito candidates. For example, the Komeito put up a very attractive candidate, Hamayotsu Toshiko, in the 1992 Upper House election. Hamayotsu is one of the leading women attorneys in Japan. A number of independent voters I interviewed after the election said that they voted for her not because she was a Komeito candidate, but, rather, because they did not want to support the LDP and could not get themselves to vote for the socialists or communists.

Soka Gakkai–Komeito Relationship

Although the Komeito has managed to distance itself from the Soka Gakkai in terms of its day-to-day activities since their official separation in 1970, it proudly admits that it is a religious and Buddhist party whose goal is to promote the religious ideals of its creator in the secular world of politics. Ishida, chairman of the Komeito, stated in 1992 that "I do not deny that our party is a religious one. Our political philosophy of humanism is rooted in our religion."[51] Endo Otohiko confirms that the Komeito is a Buddhist party rooted in such ideals as pacifism and human welfare.[52]

The fact that the Komeito is a religious party is clearly indicated in surveys conducted in the early 1980s concerning the religious values and practices of its members. These surveys established that only 9 percent of LDP supporters, 5 percent of Japan Socialist Party supporters, and no supporters of the Communist party indicated that they engage in religious activities, while 46 percent of Komeito supporters responded that they do. When asked if they believe in a religion, positive responses range from 9 percent for the Communists to 29 percent for LDP supporters, while the figure for Komeito supporters was 83 percent.[53]

The Soka Gakkai and the Komeito gained a unique position of power in 1989 when the Liberal Democratic Party suffered a humiliating defeat in that year's Upper House elections. For the first time since its creation in 1955, the LDP lost its majority and had to rely on the votes of sympathetic opposition parties to get its legislation passed. The Komeito, which had been moving closer to the LDP during the 1980s, seized the opportunity to become an informal coalition partner of the LDP.

The Komeito sought to keep its own identity and independence by becoming a "friendly member" of the opposition. According to Endo Otohiko, a Komeito Diet member of the lower house:

> The Komeito does not automatically oppose or support any measure brought before the Diet by the government. Our party stands for peace, welfare, and the dignity of human life. If any bill meets these criteria, we will back it. If not, we will offer suggestions to amend the bill to bring it closer to what we stand for. . . . Our hope in future elections is that the LDP will do well enough to get a near majority so that it will have to rely on our support and influence, but not too well or too badly which would mean that we would have less influence.[54]

Since the Komeito is a member party of the Diet and participates in the day-to-day life of Japanese politics, it must vote on many measures. It has followed a more conservative line since its unofficial marriage with the LDP. Some Soka Gakkai members were outraged when the Komeito voted in favor of the 1992 Peace Keeping Operations (PKO) Bill that authorized the sending of Japanese troops to support UN peace-keeping projects, while others have criticized the party's decision in the 1980s to support the military alliance with the United States. The Komeito answers these criticisms by noting that in the difficult world of politics, compromise is necessary and if the Komeito is to have any impact, it must cooperate with other parties. The Komeito insists, for example, that it forced many restrictions into the PKO bill before it gave the LDP the votes it needed to pass it.

Soka Gakkai International (SGI)

The Soka Gakkai's base and the vast majority of its members are in Japan, but it regards itself as an international movement and asserts that the "Buddhism of Nichiren Daishonin" is applicable to all of mankind. Gakkai leaders stress that its Buddhism is a world religion with the power to bring peace and happiness everywhere.

The Soka Gakkai's approach is international. Virtually every branch of the Soka Gakkai stresses internationalism, and Gakkai publications are full of information about other countries. Gakkai leaders stress that the Japanese must move away from the chauvanism that was so predominant in Japan before 1945 and that the key to world peace is respect for and appreciation of other cultures. They insist that Japan must share its vast wealth and experience with other impoverished parts of the world. They back up these statements with large donations to the United Nations and exchanges of members with people from other countries. This international approach is especially evident at Soka University.

In the early 1960s the Gakkai launched a drive to build foreign branches in the United States and Europe. Later the drive was extended to all other parts of the world. In 1992 SGI reports that there were about 1.26 million believers in about 120 branches worldwide. Venezuela is typical of a country that started out with a tiny Soka Gakkai chapter. The first chapter was founded in 1973 with twenty charter members, but since then "the organization has grown and now encompasses members of all ages from all walks of life. In particular, the youth division has become so active that it is now organizing an annual summer training course."[55]

The foreign branches of the Soka Gakkai are at least technically independent of the headquarters in Japan and many are incorporated in their host countries. The Soka Gakkai coordinates its international activities through two offices centered in Tokyo: SGI and the Nichiren Shoshu International Center. Ikeda Daisaku holds the title of SGI president, which, in actuality, means that he is a moral leader who provides all believers with guidance. The foreign chapters have their own domestic leadership groups.

The SGI organization in the United States (SGI-USA) was established in 1960; its current general director is Fred Zaitsu. Its headquarters is in Santa Monica, California, but there are chapters all over the country. At first most of the members were of Japanese origin, but by the 1980s most members were native whites or blacks.

Sandy McIntosh, a journalist, professor, and former member of SGI-USA, makes the following observations concerning the Gakkai in the United States:

> Is Soka Gakkai/Nichiren Shoshu the true American Buddhism? To an observer, the practices of Soka Gakkai seem tailor-made for the American fast-food, instant wish-fulfillment culture. You can chant for money, for a better job, for love, for any of the 108 human desires symbolized by the 108 prayer beads that Nichiren Shoshu members hold when they chant. An observer would note that Soka Gakkai practitioners spend far more time in discussion meetings and other group activities than they do in disciplined contemplation or consultation with Buddhist teachers. Because its emphasis falls on action rather than view, Soka Gakkai appeals to a broad range of Americans with varying educational backgrounds, even as

it may alienate those who enjoy meditative Buddhist traditions. Without looking further, an observer might reasonably conclude that Soka Gakkai represents only a simplified version—or even a cynical perversion—of Buddhism created for American consumption. . . . The appeal [of materialism] attracts many Americans living in the inner cities who are desperate for a way to improve their lives. For these people who know little material prosperity, the more conventional Buddhist view—that enlightenment is encouraged by abandoning all attachment to material things—is virtually senseless.[56]

McIntosh raises a point that many non-Japanese Buddhists use to criticize the Soka Gakkai—their emphasis on materialism and material benefits and gain in this lifetime. They correctly point out that these Gakkai doctrines contradict traditional Buddhist ideals that identify material gain with the evil effects of desire. They forget that there is a strong tradition in Japanese Mahayana Buddhism on benefits one can secure in the secular world. Japanese religion and society is very "this-world" oriented, and there is little thought of what occurs after death. The orientation of Japanese Buddhism is based on the relief of suffering in this world.

The Dispute Between the Soka Gakkai and the Nichiren Shoshu Priesthood

In 1990 a vicious verbal war broke out between the Soka Gakkai and the leaders of the Nichiren Shoshu priesthood at Taiseki-ji. The dispute climaxed in November 1991, when the head priest, Nikken Abe, excommunicated the Soka Gakkai and its foreign chapters and ordered the Gakkai to disband itself. The Soka Gakkai refused to comply and in turn demanded the ouster of the head priest.

Although the Soka Gakkai and Nichiren Shoshu are legally two distinct organizations with their own leaders, the two groups worked together in general harmony through 1990. However, the priesthood claims that the Soka Gakkai is a subsidiary organization working on behalf of Nichiren Shoshu, but the Soka Gakkai has always regarded itself as a truly independent organization that has its own direct spiritual mandate from Nichiren. The result has been occasional tension between the two groups since World War II.[57]

The key questions concerning the Soka Gakkai and Taiseki-ji involve spiritual leadership and responsibility, the correct role of the clergy and laity, and the organizational problem of a small provincial priestly order suddenly growing into a mammouth national and international community of believers. The issues are very complex, but the priesthood claims that it is the sole custodian of religious authority and dogma. The Soka Gakkai leadership argues that the sacred writings of Nichiren, not the priesthood, represent the ultimate source of authority and that any individual with deep faith in Nichiren's teachings can gain enlightenment without the assistance of a priest. The Soka Gakkai supports the idea that because all people have equal access to enlightenment, in effect, all people are priests.

The Taiseki-ji priesthood charged that the Soka Gakkai, in forgetting its status as a lay group, had both attacked and subverted the authority of the head temple. It is apparent that the head temple felt that the Soka Gakkai had become too powerful and that it was eroding both the authority of the head priest and the functions of the general priesthood. In effect, it feared that Ikeda and his aides had seized the prerogatives and authority of the church and were becoming the de facto leaders of Nichiren Shoshu, thus rendering the priesthood irrelevant. Soka Gakkai members were charged with wrongly seeking religious instruction and leadership from Ikeda rather than Taiseki-ji.[58] A key point of contention appears to be the way that the faithful can attain enlightenment. The priesthood claims that its intervention on behalf of the believer is necessary. The Soka Gakkai insists that enlightenment can only come through the direct actions of the believer. True devotion expressed through prayer and chanting before a Gohonzon, a loving and respectful attitude toward other people, and sincere attempts at proselytization of the faith are all that are required. Because all people, clergy and laity, have equal opportunity for Buddhahood, priests and laymen are equal. Soka Gakkai president Akiya Einosuke insists that the goal of his movement is to "return Buddhism to the people." A believer does not attain enlightenment through the priesthood, but through direct prayer and faith in the Gohonzon, which as the embodiment of Nichiren's enlightenment constitutes the object of worship. Akiya insists that the Soka Gakkai is much like Luther in that it is restoring Buddhism to its essence.[59]

Although it may take many years for the current dispute to be resolved in one manner or another, the Gakkai will continue to thrive. The key to its success is its ability to translate traditional Buddhist concepts for a modern audience. Lay movements that directly address the needs of the common man often find a responsive cord in a nation whose people, according to a United Nations poll in the 1980s, were among the unhappiest on earth. At the same time, the Taiseki-ji priesthood has extensive wealth and could well survive a prolonged cloistered existence, but it is doubtful that it will attract many lay supporters.

One important and immediate result is the Soka Gakkai's denunciation of Nichiren Shoshu as a corrupt sect that has totally perverted the teachings of Nichiren. By 1992 the Soka Gakkai had dropped all mention of Nichiren Shoshu from its literature and had declared that it alone represented the true line of (Nichiren) Buddhism. In effect, the Soka Gakkai has established itself as an independent sect of Nichiren Buddhism.

The Soka Gakkai and Exclusivism

Buddhism's success as a religion and philosophy stems from its relatively easy adaptation to other, native traditions in the areas it colonized. It has been possible for Buddhists to maintain their indigenous beliefs for certain worldly, religious, or civil purposes while simultaneously holding Buddhist views about their own psychological nature and the ultimate ends of human action. "Buddhism, in other words, has had little of the imperiousness that has characterized missionary religions such as Christianity and Islam. It is quintessentially tolerant, cosmopolitan, and portable . . ."[60]

Nichiren Buddhism, however, is uncharacteristicly exclusivistic in terms of faith and doctrine. Nichiren declared that the nation will only prosper when the True Buddhism is revered. Nichiren envisioned the creation of a great Buddhaland in Japan, but this could only be achieved through devotion to the *Lotus Sutra*. It is ironic that the Nichiren School, which is based on the *Lotus Sutra* that "teaches universal salvation, developed into the most exclusivistic religious, social, and political society in Japan."[61]

Most of Japan's new religious groups are nonexclusive. They proclaim the superiority of their own beliefs, but state that they see value in other religions. Even Nichiren-based movements such as Rissho Koseikai have cooperated with other religious movements in a variety of areas. The Soka Gakkai, however, much like Nichiren himself, refuses to have anything to do with other religious organizations.

The Soka Gakkai has always remained true to the Nichiren tradition in terms of the orthodoxy of its faith, but since the 1970s it has developed a far more cooperative attitude in its strictly secular and social programs. The Gakkai makes an important distinction between its purely religious and its secular activities. Nonmembers are often restricted from Soka Gakkai religious events, but are openly welcomed at cultural activities. In the same way, Gakkai members are very much involved with nonmembers in their everyday lives. Today few Gakkai members "wear their religion on their arm."

The Soka Gakkai today remains exclusivistic in terms of the orthodoxy of its faith. There is no compromise possible in its belief structure and ultimately the "salvation of the world can only come through the Buddhism of Nichiren Daishonin."[62] On the other hand, the Soka Gakkai is less exclusivistic in terms of social programs. It often cooperates with other people, organizations, and nations in its peace, education, and music programs. Gakkai scholars and politicians participate in a wide range of international conferences and the Gakkai itself sponsors international conferences in which nonmember scholars participate. Ikeda and other Gakkai officials have developed strong relationships with many non–Soka Gakkai leaders across the world. Nonmember students and research scholars such as myself are greeted warmly at Soka University. The Soka Gakkai actively engages in debates and forums with nonmembers.

This degree of openness and sense of cooperation has come over the years as the Soka Gakkai has developed and matured as a movement. There was a time in the 1950s, when it was still young and small as an organization, when many of its leaders and members were more militant and exclusivistic, but this has changed considerably since the early 1970s. Today the Soka Gakkai projects a far more mellow, relaxed tone that reflects the self-confidence and stability of the movement today. In recent years the Soka Gakkai has not grown as fast as it did in the past, but neither has it declined.

The dichotomy between Soka Gakkai's religious and social activities creates a paradox. The Gakkai claims that it is a champion of world peace, and its support for refugees, the United Nations, and the environment have created tentative links with the outside world. However, its dogmatic orthodoxy places limits on its credibility and ability to influence Japanese society. Even the most sincere Gakkai advocate of world peace will not be taken too seriously by a highly skeptical Japanese public that regards the Gakkai peace movemenmt as a form of self-serving religious propaganda.

The Impact of the Soka Gakkai

Scholars and critics of the Soka Gakkai have often questioned the impact that the movement has had on Japan; what are its long-term contributions to society? One must be careful not to exaggerate the influence of the Soka Gakkai in Japanese society as a whole. Despite fervent activities by the Gakkai to win public attention and respect, most Japanese are very ignorant of the movement. They all have heard of Ikeda and are aware that mass media on occasion has linked the Gakkai to certain scandals, but they know little more.

The main reason for this situation is that few Soka Gakkai-generated activities are ever covered in the national media. Soka Gakkai leaders complain that the national news media has an "allergy" when it comes to covering their movement. A senior television news editor/journalist confirms these suspicions: "When Ikeda met with President Gorbachev or the prime minister of China, we did not cover the event because the meeting had no effect on Japan's national destiny. But we will cover a minor statement by a Komeito leader because his actions can have some impact on Japanese politics."[63]

The result is that outside of politics, the impact of the Soka Gakkai has been negligible. The Gakkai's strong adherence to its own doctrines and worldview is both the source of its strength and its weakness. Its anchor is its big following and strong leadership, but its exclusivism makes it a suspect organization to most Japanese, who distrust its motives. This distrust dooms most Soka Gakkai attempts to influence Japanese society and minimizes its influence on the national scene. Despite the high quality of many of its institutions and programs, public disdain will always leave the Gakkai on the periphery of Japanese life.

The Gakkai is more notable for its profound impact on its own membership. It greatly influences 6 to 7 percent of the population, which can be very important in such areas as politics. If the LDP splits into two or more political parties, the vote and support of the Komeito will become very important to Japan's political elite. In less than fifty years, the Gakkai has built a mass movement that has brought Buddhism back into the lives of millions of families that previously had had little interest in or commitment to Buddhism. Buddhism for most Japanese even today is a fossilized and largely irrelevant religion that people turn to only at times of funerals or when they pay a high fee to visit an ancient temple in Kyoto. In the eyes of its millions of members, however, the Soka Gakkai has recovered Buddhism's inner spirit. Of course, there are other Buddhist reform and lay movements in Japan, like Rissho Koseikai, that have revived Buddhism as a popular religion of the common person. The Soka Gakkai, however, has emerged as one of the most important of these reform movements in terms of membership and overall impact on society.

The Soka Gakkai is psychologically like a nation within a nation. If one defines a nation as a group of people who share common values and beliefs that distinguish them from their neighbors, a self-identity, and support a common set of leaders, then the Soka Gakkai is very distinct from the rest of Japanese society. Members are very devoted and loyal to their leaders, religion, and organizational ideology.

The Soka Gakkai is still a critically important movement because it drastically affects the lives of 8 million Japanese in the early 1990s. It has restored strong religious values to one of the few genuinely religious segments of Japan's increasingly secular society. The Gakkai strongly influences their voting patterns, their education, and their thinking on a broad range of issues including peace and the environment. The organizational strength of the Soka Gakkai and the devotion of its members will make the Gakkai an important force in Japan for years to come.

Epilogue

The Soka Gakkaoi's political party, Komeito, won fifty-one seats in the July 1993 election—up from the previous forty-five seats. These fifty-one seats became a vital building block in the 259-seat Hosokawa coalition government. Four Komeito leaders, all Gakkai members, serve in the Hosokawa cabinet (as of this writing) and three others hold key subcabinet positions. In effect, the Soka Gakkai has become a vital part of the Japanese government and political establishment.

Notes

1. T. P. Kasulis, "Religion and Politics: Cultural Background of the Soka Gakkai," in Charles Wei-hsun Fu and Gerald E. Spiegler, ed., *Movements and Issues in World Religions: A Sourcebook and Analysis of Developments Since 1945* (New York: Greenwood Press, 1991), p. 304.

2. *Soka Gakkai News*, September, 1992, p. 2.

3. Winston Davis, "Fundamentalism in Japan: Religious and Political" in Martin E. Marty and R. Scott Appleby, eds. *Fundamentalisms Observed* (Chicago: University of Chicago Press, 1991), p. 804.

4. *Mappo* or Latter Day of the Dharma is the "last of the three periods following Shakyamuni Buddha's death when Buddhism falls into confusion and Shakyamuni's teachings lose the power to lead people to enlightenment. . . . The *Daishitsu Sutra* predicts that this . . . will be an 'age of conflict,' when monks will disregard the precepts and feud constantly among themselves, heretical views will prevail, and Shakyamuni's Buddhism will perish."

The first two eras are *shobo* (true law), which began immediately after the Buddha's death and lasted 1000 years, and *zobo* (imitative law), which lasted during the second millenium following the Buddha's death. During *shobo* it was said that the world was a contented and peaceful place. The peace was maintained during *zobo*, but the world became an ugly chaotic realm during *mappo*. Asian Buddhist tradition holds that Shakyamuni died in 949 B.C. Calculating from this date, Japanese Buddhist scholars in the Kamakura period believed that *mappo* had begun in l052. They attributed the chaos of the Kamakura period to this concept. Nichiren Shoshu International Center, *A Dictionary of Buddhist Terms and Concepts* (Tokyo: NSIC, 1983), p. 244.

5. The *Lotus* (*Saddharma-pundarika*) *Sutra*, known as *Myoho-renge-kyo* in Japanese, was first translated into Chinese by Dharmaraksa in the Western Tsin dynasty (265–316), and was again translated by Kumarajiva in 407.

6. H. Paul Varley, *Japanese Culture* (Honolulu: University of Hawaii Press, 1984), p. 92.

7. According to the Soka Gakkai, the Daimoku is the "ultimate Law or true entity of life permeating all phenomena in the universe . . . the eternal and unchanging truth. . . . Nichiren Daishonin teaches that the Mystic Law encompasses all laws and teachings within itself, and that the benefit of chanting . . . includes the benefit of conducting all virtuous practices." *A Dictionary of Buddhist Terms and Concepts*, op. cit., p. 284.

8. James W. White, *The Soka Gakkai and Mass Society* (Stanford, Calif.: Stanford University Press, 1970), p. 33.

9. White, pp. 33–34.

10. "Daishonin" is the honorific title that the sect, Nichiren Shoshu, gives to Nichiren to denote his sacred status.

11. *Soka Gakkai News*, March 1991, p. 21.

12. Nichiren Shoshu International Center, *Buddhism and the Nichiren Shoshu Tradition* (Tokyo: NSIC, 1986), p. 157.

13. Japanese Buddhism, all of it Mahayana, is a Buddhism centered on benefits in the secular world. Its orientation is the relief of suffering in this world.

14. Quoted from RAR. Philip B. Yampolsky, *Selected Writings of Nichiren* (New York: Columbia University Press, 1990), p. 13.

15. Ibid., p. 19.

16. Ibid., pp. 30–31.

17. Dayle M. Bethel, *Makiguchi: The Value Creator* (Tokyo: Weatherhill, 1973), p. 97.

18. Ikeda Daisaku, *The Human Revolution*, vol. 2 (Tokyo: Weatherhill, 1974), p. 146.

19. Quoted in Kiyoaki Murata, *Japan's New Buddhism* (Tokyo: Weatherhill, 1969), p. 100.

20. The current president of the Soka Gakkai is Akiya Einosuke. He is in charge of the day-to-day management of the movement.

21. The Komeito and the Soka Gakkai became independent entities in 1970.

22. Interview with Mihara Asahiko, June 24, 1992.

23. White, pp. 61–80.

24. Interview with Tanaka Hideaki, July 4, 1992.

25. Robert Eppsteiner, "Forever on the Side of the People," in *Soka Gakkai News*, 227, June 1992, p. 23.

26. Interview with Ikeda, November 2, 1992.

27. White, p . 36.

28. Quoted in Edward Norbeck, *Religion and Society in Modern Japan: Continuity and Change* (Houston: Tourmaline Press, 1970), p. 179. The concept of a "Third Civilization" refers to a proposed fusion of the best ideas of capitalism and socialism. The society envisioned by the Soka Gakkai would enhance individualism and freedom of choice along with a cooperative spirit.

29. *Soka Gakkai News*, October 1991, p. 2.

30. *Seikyo Shimbun*, September 7, 1991.

31. Carol Gluck, "The Idea of Showa," in Carol Gluck and Stephen R. Graubard, eds., *Showa: The Japan of Hirohito* (New York: W. W. Norton & Co., 1992), p. 14.

32. The Youth Division of the Soka Gakkai published two English volumes presenting an abbreviated version of this series. See The Youth Division of Soka Gakkai, *Cries for Peace: Experiences of Japanese Victims of World War II* (Tokyo: The Japan Times, 1978) and *Peace is Our Duty: Accounts of What War Can Do to Man* (Tokyo: The Japan Times, 1982).

33. An English edition containing forty selected translations from the first twelve volumes was published in 1986 by Kodansha International (Tokyo, New York, San Francisco). It is titled *Women Against War*.

34. *Soka Gakkai News*, July 1991, p. 18.

35. *Soka Gakkai News*, August–September 1991.

36. *Soka Gakkai News*, February 1992, pp. 2–3.

According to the Soka Gakkai: "Since its initial fund-raising campaign for Indochinese refugees in 1973, major relief campaigns have been conducted by the Soka Gakkai. Donations to refugees in Africa and Asia to date (1992) total about Yen960 million (about U.S. $5 million). The funds raised have been allocated to relief projects geared to providing medical care, food supplies, education, and other services administered by the UNHCR and related agencies. SGI fact-finding missions have been sent to observe conditions in many countries and volunteers have been sent to Cambodia and Somalia." *SGI*. Soka Gakkai International Publication, 1992.

37. SGI is recognized as an NGO with consultative status in the UN Economic and Social Council. The Soka Gakkai is also recognized as a GO with the UN Department of Public Information and the UN High Commissioner for Refugees; the SGI is recognized as an international NGO with UNESCO.

38. Approximately half the faculty belongs to the Soka Gakkai, but virtually every student is a Gakkai member. Many younger faculty members are Soka graduates

who have received graduate training elsewhere. Many older faculty members are retirees from other prestigious universities such as Waseda and Tokyo universities who are invited to teach at Soka for a few additional years.

39. For example, in 1992 Soka University was among the top three Japanese universities in terms of students who passed the foreign service, bar, and CPA exams.

40. There are exchange programs with nearly forty universities abroad, many foreigners on the faculty, many exchange students from China and elsewhere, and a curriculum that strongly emphasizes international studies. A considerable number of Soka students study abroad each year—most often in China, Russia, and other parts of Southeast Asia. A growing number come to the United States.

41. International Christian University ranked first and Keio University came in second. Soka students were particularly impressed with the chance to get to know their teachers well, be in smaller classes, receive individual attention, and experience the emphasis on international studies and exchanges.

42. Nakano Tsuyoshi, "New Religions and Politics in Post-war Japan," in *Sociologica*, v.14.12, 1990.3, p. 3.

43. Ibid., p. 5.

44. Ibid., pp. 6–8. The rest of the paragraph is summarized from Nakano.

45. Nakano, pp. 8–9.

46. Ikeda Daisaku, *Seiji to Shukyo* [Politics and Religion] (Tokyo: Ushio Shinsho, 1969), p. 220.

47. Ohara Teruhisa, *Soka Gakkai no Shucho: Seimei e no Funade* [The Declaration of the Soka Gakkai: Mission Towards a Century of Life] (Tokyo: Daisanbunmeisha, 1975), p. 57.

48. Each election district in Japan has 3–5 representatives in the Diet, but each voter can only cast one ballot. This system is advantageous to smaller parties who can often elect their candidates with only a small percentage of the vote.

49. *Yomiuri Shimbun*, July 30, 1992.

50. Interview with Endo Otohiko in Tokyo, July 9, 1992.

51. *Asahi Shimbun Japan Access*, July 6, 1992, p. 1.

52. Endo interview, *op. cit.*

53. Gerald Curtis, *The Japanese Way of Politics* (New York: Columbia University Press, 1988), p. 226.

54. Endo interview.

55. "Venezuela: Paving the Way for a New Century," in *SGI Quarterly*, Summer 1992, p. 26.

56. Sandy McIntosh, "An Insider's View of Nichiren Shoshu," in *Tricycle* II.2 (Winter 1992), p. 22.

57. Today the Soka Gakkai claims that Nichiren Shoshu priesthood betrayed Nichiren and the Nichiren tradition when in 1943 it agreed to comply with government requests to merge the sect with other Nichiren sects and to allow Shinto prayer to be placed at Taiseki-ji. Soka Gakkai leaders like Makiguchi and Toda strongly objected to this compromise, stating that one must not stain the purity of Nichiren Buddhism. The Japanese government jailed Makiguchi and Toda when they refused to cooperate with the government and to stop their criticisms. Makiguchi died in jail in 1944. Today the Soka Gakkai points to this incident as an example of its ideological purity and of the priesthood's "betrayal" of Nichiren Buddhism. See the *Seikyo Shimbun*, April 2, 1992, p. 1.

58. Nikken Abe, "Soka Gakkai Kaiin ni Tsugu " [A Proclamation to Soka Gakkai Members] in *Bungei Shunju*, 2.92, pp. 386–398.

59. Interview with Akiya Einosuke, June 19, 1992.

60. Michael Carrithers, *The Buddha* (New York: Oxford University Press, 1983), p. 80.

61. Kitagawa, p. 120.

62. Interview with Yamaguchi Hiromu, Soka Gakkai International, June 30, 1992.

63. Interview in Tokyo, August 1992. The journalist requested anonimity.

Selected Bibliography in English

Bethel, Dayle. *Makiguchi: The Value Creator*. Tokyo: Weatherhill, 1973.

Carrithers, Michael. *The Buddha*. New York: Oxford University Press, 1983.

Davis, Winston. "Fundamentalism in Japan: Religious and Political," in Martin E. Marty and R. Scott Appleby, eds., *Fundamentalisms Observed*. Chicago: University of Chicago Press, 1991.

Ellwood, Robert S. *The Eagle and the Rising Sun: Americans and the New Religions of Japan*. Philadelphia: Westminster Press, 1974.

Ikeda Daisaku. *Human Revolution*, vols. 1–5. Tokyo and New York: Weatherhill, 1972–1986.

———., *A Lasting Peace*. Tokyo: Weatherhill, 1981.

———. and Arnold Toynbee, *Choose Life: A Dialogue*. Oxford: Oxford University Press, 1989.

Kasulis, T. P. "Religion and Politics: Cultural Background of Soka Gakkai" in Charles Wii-hsun Fu and Gerhard E. Spiegler, eds., *Movements and Issues in World Religions: A Sourcebook and Analysis of Developments Since 1945*. New York: Greenwood Press, 1991.

Kitagawa, Joseph. *Religion in Japanese Society*. New York: Columbia University Press, 1966.

McFarland, H. Neil. *The Rush Hour of the Gods*. New York: Harper & Row, 1967.

McIntosh, Sandy. "As American as Apple Pie? An Insider's View of Nichiren Shoshu" in *Tricycle: The Buddhist Review*, Winter 1992.

Metraux, Daniel. *The History and Theology of the Soka Gakkai*. Lewiston, New York: Edwin Mellen, 1988.

————, "The Split between the Soka Gakkai and Nichiren Shoshu" in *The Journal of Japanese Religious Studies*, December 1992.

Murata, Kiyoaki. *Japan's New Buddhism*. Tokyo: Weatherhill, 1969.

Nakano Tsuyoshi, Tamaru Noriyoshi, and Ikado Fujio, "Discussion: The Traditional and the Contemporary in Religion," in *The Journal of Oriental Studies*, vol. 4, 1992.

Nichiren Shoshu International Center, *Buddhism and the Nichiren Shoshu Tradition*. Tokyo: Nichiren Shoshu International Center, 1986.

Norbeck, Edward. *Religion and Society in Modern Japan: Continuity and Change*. Houston: Tourmaline Press, 1970.

SGI Quarterly. Issues since 1984.

Soka Gakkai News. Issues since 1975.

White, James. *The Soka Gakkai and Mass Society*. Stanford, Calif.: Stanford University Press, 1970.

11

Conclusion: Buddhist Social Activism

Sallie B. King

Colonialism, foreign invasion, war, Westernization, oppression, social injustice, poverty, discrimination—these are the contexts out of which contemporary Buddhist social activism was born. Each of the cases examined in this volume is unique; each developed independently in response to circumstances not found elsewhere. Yet among the individuals and movements represented in this book, similar themes repeatedly arise. This is perhaps not surprising, given that all emerge from a shared Buddhist heritage and all confront both the ills and the assets of modernity.

This concluding essay has two objectives: (1) to bring together and organize by theme the disparate material covered in the preceding chapters, providing thereby a synthetic account of Buddhist liberation movements in Asia as a whole and allowing us to determine what kind of patterns, if any, emerge in this movement; and (2) to reflect upon and offer occasional tentative assessments of engaged Buddhism as a whole.

Reformism

It may be useful to begin this discussion with a consideration of the conceptual framework suggested by Robert N. Bellah in his essay "Religion and Progress in Modern Asia."[1] Bellah suggests that as traditional societies are confronted by the demands of modernity, they often choose between reformist and neotraditionalist alternatives. "Reformist" movements advocate substantial change, often expressed, according to Bellah, in terms of "a return to the early teachers and text, a rejection of most of the intervening tradition, [and] an interpretation of the pristine teaching . . . as advocating social reform and national regeneration.[2] Moreover, such movements

401

necessarily entail an "intense self-criticism of tradition."[3] Neotraditionalism, on the other hand, is "an ideology designed to keep change to a minimum and defend the *status quo* as far as possible."[4] It uses "modern ideas and methods to defend traditional cultural values, which are held to be superior to those of any other tradition."[5]

It seems fair to say that all of our figures are reformers, though this judgment must be immediately qualified by noting that several of them also exhibit traditional or neotraditional features to one degree or another. One of the factors determining the degree to which the movements considered in this volume match the characteristics of "reformism" suggested by Bellah is the degree to which their fundamental concern is societal change. Sarvodaya, Ambedkar, TBMSG, and Sulak are particularly concerned to change the societies in which they live. With this major objective established as their first priority and *raison d'être,* each constructs a new form of Buddhism to help bring about the desired social change. These figures and movements fit the "reformist" profile as conceived by Bellah most closely.

Other individuals and the movements they lead prominently possess some features of reformism but upon closer consideration muddy the distinction between reformism and traditionalism or neotraditionalism. The nuns and quasi-nuns are highly interesting in this regard. They are entirely focused upon the reform of Buddhist institutions and certainly in this sense, they are reformist. However, from another perspective those whose objective is the reestablishment of the nuns order might well be conceived as very traditional insofar they simply look for the restoration that they conceive as integral to the Buddhism established by Sakyamuni, the replacement of something perhaps inadvertently lost over time; they therefore ardently defend what they see as the traditional form and values of Sakyamuni's Buddhism. Nor do these Buddhist women address larger societal concerns. On the other hand, those *dasa sil matavo* of Sri Lanka who do not care to see the nuns' order revived but prefer to create a new path for Buddhist women are more reformist than their aforementioned sisters, and indeed serve by their very existence as challenges to Buddhist tradition of potentially fundamental significance. What we see here are degrees of reformism and kinds of reformism.

Buddhadasa represents another variant of reformism. Reversing the priorities of figures like Ambedkar and movements like Sarvodaya, he was clearly most interested in a reformed Buddhism and only secondarily in a reformed society, though, philosophically, he regarded the two as inseparable. His interest in reforming Buddhism, though, was much broader than that of the nuns and quasi-nuns insofar as it ranged far beyond institutional reform to a fundamental and profound rethinking of basic beliefs, values, and practices.

Thich Nhat Hanh and the Dalai Lama fall in another category. Both find themselves in societies already undergoing traumatic, forced change provoked by the invasion of external forces. Change is not in question here, it is a reality. Their primary concern is to articulate a proactive Buddhist response to this challenge. Secondarily, each is also deeply interested in and expansive in his vision of the reform of Buddhism and of society, and, in this sense, both are classic exemplars of reform.

Our figures and movements also differ in terms of the degree to which they engage in "intense self-criticism of tradition." Indeed, for the most part, "criticism" is far too strong a word for what most of our reformers do. They do tend to return to the original texts (Pali *suttas*) and/or core principles (Four Noble Truths, selflessness, interdependence, compassion) and move directly from these to their own teachings. But they tend to see themselves more as reinterpreters of tradition than as its critics, stressing continuity with the basic principles of Buddhism as they see them. Especially in the instance of the Dalai Lama, who literally embodies the continuity of tradition, is this the case. For the people of Tibet he must be, literally, the very incarnation of tradition, his modern perspective and many enacted reforms notwithstanding. Indeed, in the Dalai Lama, reform and tradition, continuity and change, are one.

Similarly, Soka Gakkai is a movement deeply imbued with both reformist and neotraditional elements. Soka Gakkai's forebear, Nichiren, was himself a classic reformer, insofar as he understood himself to be returning to Buddhist roots in the *Lotus Sutra,* was intensely critical of intervening tradition, claimed that the *Lotus* mandated social activism of the kind he pursued, and in fact constructed a new Buddhism radically different from its predecessors in response to the demands of his time. Nichiren's inheritors, the Soka Gakkai, continue along the path proclaimed by Nichiren—but does their practice of firmly maintaining a venerable reform path make them neotraditional? While they are intensely socially active, this is in their case very much understood to be a continuation of what was begun by Nichiren. In this respect they seem to be a classic instance of "an ideology designed to keep change to a minimum and defend the *status quo* as far as possible," especially with respect to maintaining their own version of Buddhism. They are also well known for holding that their "traditional cultural values" are "superior to those of any other tradition." Yet they remain deeply concerned with the reform of society and expend vast amounts of time, money, and energy to this end. Thus, in Soka Gakkai also, reform and tradition are inseparable.

I call all of our figures and movements reformist, not in a sense that excludes neotraditionalism but in a sense that may be understood to include some of what Bellah identifies as neotraditional features. These figures and movements are all reformist in the sense that they are all deeply committed to the reform of something, although that something varies from case to case and differs in the degree to which it constitutes a challenge to Buddhist tradition itself. We will return to this point again.

Justification of a New Buddhism

Looking at these contemporary movements in a historical context, Chris Queen argues that there is no precedent for the kind of Buddhist social activism we now see throughout Buddhist Asia.[6] These movements represent something new, engendered by modern historical conditions. This being the case, it is no surprise that we find throughout our subjects conscious attempts to formulate a Buddhist justification for social action. These justifications vary widely in the extent to which they speak in traditional language, but in all cases they remain distinctively Buddhist.

Of all our movements, the social activism of Soka Gakkai is most clearly rooted in its own (Nichirenite) tradition. That Nichirenite tradition, however, sees itself as discontinuous with its own past. Thus members and leaders of Soka Gakkai can point to the social and political activism of Nichiren as their self-justification; they see themselves as amply continuing what he began. Nichiren himself, however, had to justify his radically new version of Buddhism by developing a rhetoric of *mappo;* for Nichiren, the crisis of the period of degeneracy not only justified but demanded the radical break with the tradition that he led. Soka Gakkai maintains this rhetoric, claiming, according to Metraux, that "twentieth-century man with all of his wars, pollution, and suffering still lives in *mappo.*" Hence the outlook, beliefs, and practices instituted by Nichiren are still viable, in this view, for the world today.

Most of our figures, of course, trace their roots to the Buddha. With varying emphases, many of them assert that they find in his words the social teaching that they espouse anew. Buddhadasa, for example, stressed that he always strove to live and work entirely within the boundaries set by the Buddha and, indeed, called himself the "Servant of the Buddha." He saw himself as simply carrying on the work of the Buddha, frequently quoting the latter's saying, "I teach only *dukkha* and the utter quenching of *dukkha.*" His social teachings emerged naturally within this purview. For him, "world peace is the Buddha's purpose."

This kind of justification of the new in the light of the old, of reference to the Buddha and to the Pali *suttas* to justify today's teachings, is typical of Buddhist reformism and of many of our figures. This pattern is particularly striking in Buddhadasa's case, who blazed a path for himself that followed precisely this route. As a student he felt himself to be adrift and lacking in the basic principles he needed until he abandoned the traditional monastic education, which stressed the commentaries, and set out alone to read the Pali *suttas* and *vinaya,* wherein he found the guidance upon which his lifework was built.

Also in other cases this "return to the source" is found. Sarvodaya often justifies itself by reference to the Pali *suttas,* emphasizing, naturally enough, those *suttas* in which the Buddha gave social and economic teachings, but also reinterpreting the Four Noble Truths, the Eightfold Path, and the Four Divine Abodes. Sulak Sivaraksa finds his foundations in the Four Noble Truths, the Five Precepts, and the Four Divine Abodes, appealing frequently to the Pali texts, but interpreting them in light of the pressing concerns of today. Similarly, those supporting the effort to reinstate branches of the *bhikshuni* order are engaged today in careful study of the ancient *Vinaya* to find a justification for and a proper manner of pressing forward.

On the same principle, our non-Theravadin figures add basic Mahayana and Tantric sources to these Pali text sources, the Dalai Lama referring to Santideva's *Bodhicaryavatara,* Nhat Hanh to the *Vimalakirti Nirdesa,* and Soka Gakkai to the words of Nichiren. These are all forms of returning to the source.

In addition to texts, our subjects also cite well-established Buddhist principles to justify and explain the underlying motivation of the social actions that they espouse. In fact, they refer to some of the most fundamental Buddhist principles for this purpose. The nuns and quasi-nuns are most paradigmatic in this respect: their motivation is simply the desire to follow the way of the Buddha and to make that way available to other women— surely, in a Buddhist context, the most inarguable of all possible motivations for action. On a level only slightly less fundamental, the leaders of Soka Gakkai explain their activism as motivated by a responsibility to propagate the faith (most popular Mahayana *sutras* stress this concern) and compassion for their members and for the world.

The Dalai Lama speaks consistently throughout the world of love and compassion as the only proper motivation for social action, emphasizing in this context the principle of the interchangeability of self and other. In Buddhadasa's case, it is very clear that his social teachings grew naturally out of his teachings about *dukkha* and egoism; they were an extension and an expression of these more fundamental principles. Along similar lines, Sulak emphasizes that selflessness must be expressed in the nonexploitation of oneself and others, and from this principle a host of social teachings naturally emerge. The Unified Buddhist Church of Vietnam emphasizes motivation in compassion expressed in action to relieve the suffering of others. Thich Nhat Hanh also emphasizes compassion and love, emphasizing, in particular, the nonduality of self and other as the foundation of one's actions on behalf of another. Thus love, compassion, and selflessness emerge again and again as the basic motivators of virtually all of our social activists.

Here we begin to see that Asian Buddhist activists understand the foundations of their efforts to be found not only in literary sources (preeminently the words of the Buddha) but also in practice and experience. Literary sources and philosophical principles can and do provide a rationale, a Buddhist justification for Buddhist social activism, but the actual motivation of social activism tends to be repeatedly described, as we have seen, in terms of love, compassion, and selflessness. These experiential conditions are to be cultivated with Buddhist practice, as all of our figures emphasize. While each teacher and movement has distinctive practices, the most prominently encountered ones are the Five Precepts, the Eightfold Path, the Four Divine Abodes, and mindfulness in daily life. Some examples: Soka Gakkai appeals to its own roots and stresses the ability of chanting to transform a person and develop compassion. Nhat Hanh wrote *The Miracle of Mindfulness* as "A Manual on Meditation for the Use of Young Activists," to quote its original subtitle. For him, mindfulness is the *sine qua non*, the essential foundation that makes Buddhist social engagement possible. For many followers of Ambedkar's movement and of TBMSG, preparation for conversion and then instruction in the basics of Buddhism is a prerequisite, to be followed by the application of those teachings to their own particular life circumstances to effect a kind of self-liberation from the trap in which their society has ensnared them. As in most of our movements, the Ambedkarites are taught mindfulness practices and the cultivation of loving-kindness (one of the Four Divine Abodes).

The Buddhist principle of interdependence is probably the most powerful conceptual tool used by the social activists to understand, express, and justify their perspective. The way in which this principle is used, of course, varies, ranging from observations upon the most obvious kinds of interdependence to the most subtle.

Soka Gakkai applies the principle of interdependence by emphasizing that all living beings share the world and therefore the acts of each of us affect all the others. Their program to nurture peace is fundamentally an educational program built upon this premise, designed to foster understanding of global interdependence, promote communication and sympathy between different societies, and address the environmental crisis that requires action by all. The Dalai Lama also emphasizes global interdependence, pointing out that the increasingly interdependent nature of the world mandates international approaches to the resolution of political, ecological, and other problems. Don Swearer contends that, in a different way, Sulak's activist style is based upon his Buddhist awareness of interdependence. Aware that multiple dimensions compose any issue, he multiplies his activist programs; aware that multiple constituencies are concerned in everything, he reaches out, creates networks and dialogues with anyone who is willing. Interdependence also emerges in everything from his interpretation of the Four Divine Abodes to environmental awareness.

Some of the most profound and far-reaching applications of the principle of interdependence can be found in the teachings of Buddhadasa and Thich Nhat Hanh. Interdependence is fundamental for each, and its implications are spelled out in countless ways.

For Buddhadasa, understanding interdependence "leads to clearly seeing that there is no real self," which, in turn, as Santikaro puts it, "allows us to set aside distinctions between self and other, between personal and social." The consequence is Buddhadasa's "Dhammic Socialism," an expression of his understanding that interdependence is all–pervasive, the inescapable law of nature ("the interdependence of nature makes nature inherently socialistic"). Thus Buddhadasa defines Dhammic Socialism as "the correctness necessary for living together in groups which nature has dictated" and contrasts this with individualism and with liberal democracy, both of which are based upon selfishness. For Buddhadasa, "Everyone is indebted to society and is bound by the social contract from the moment one was born from one's mother's womb, or even from the time one was in the womb." Hence, to live Dhammicly, or correctly, is to recognize our social nature, put aside selfishness, and create a society that can be peaceful because its members recognize the good of the whole as more important than the good of the individual.

Turning to Nhat Hanh, we see again that his social principles are outgrowths of the perspective that sees interdependence as the fundamental rule of life. In assessing moral issues, interdependence shows us that we cannot isolate ourselves from the harmful or criminal act of "another," we cannot pretend the criminal or the pirate is bad and I am good, "because all of us are to some extent responsible for this state of affairs." At the same time we cannot separate ourselves from the victim or the sufferer; throughout the war, the basic motivation of the Buddhist activists was that they felt the pain of the Vietnamese people as their own and consequently they had to act the relieve their own pain. For Nhat Hanh, then, interdependence means nonseparation from both the cause and the suffering of pain. Thus, mindful awareness of interdependence creates, on the one hand, an imperative to act to relieve the suffering of anyone who suffers and, on the other hand, the necessity to resolve conflict without acting "against" the welfare of anyone, including those who have caused others pain.

These examples illustrate an important point: the activists in this volume do not conceptualize, justify, and express their social activism in terms of minor themes found occasionally in insignificant places in the vast expanse of Buddhist heritage and tradition. On the contrary, they draw on the most basic points enunciated by the Buddha and emphasized ever since: compassion, interdependence, selflessness.

In my view, the dispute regarding the extent to which the Buddha himself was interested in social teachings is focused upon a relatively insignificant matter. He clearly had some social teachings, though we can debate the relative weight he gave them. However, Buddhadasa and Nhat Hanh seem to me to amply confirm the reformers' more important contention, namely, that the basic teachings of Buddhism can profitably be read with the *intention* of determining their implications for social ethics, and for social and political theory. The social teachings of Nhat Hanh and Buddhadasa develop completely naturally from their religious teachings, and the latter emphasize very traditional, central Buddhist principles, especially selflessness and interdependence. Thus their teachings are new and yet unquestionably Buddhist, natural extensions that are at the same time new applications.

Of course, not all Buddhists are content with the rereadings and interpretations some engaged Buddhists have made. For some, the distance between the word of the Buddha and the understanding of today's reformers is too great. The best example of one subjected to this criticism is Ambedkar, whose *The Buddha and His Dhamma* was judged by a reviewer in *Maha Bodhi* to be "enough to shock a real Buddhist." In the same vein, Sarvodaya is often criticized as distorting the Buddha's message with a too this-worldly message. Ariyaratne goes on the offensive when this criticism is made, charging in return that, to quote Bond, "it is this interpretation of Buddhism as a world-denying system that is in error. He [Ariyaratne] contends that this viewpoint began during the colonial period when the Western powers wanted to subvert the culture and marginalize the monks." Certainly, when one examines the history of Buddhism in Sri Lanka before, during, and after colonialism, one quickly sees that his argument has merit.[7]

A Question of Balance

Many engaged Buddhists make a point of insisting that the Buddha himself gave social teachings that have been overlooked in recent years. "The Buddha has a Social Message," says Ambedkar, "He answers all these questions. But they have been buried by modern authors." To speak of social issues in a Buddhist context is, for many of our subjects, to return to Buddhism its original wholeness. Thus Sarvodaya's Ariyaratne says that an interpretation limiting Buddhism to spiritual teachings erroneously ends up "confining Buddha's teachings only to the other world." This is obviously a mistake, he says, because there are many teachings about social issues preserved in the Pali *suttas*. Thus to bring out those social teachings today restores a lost balance to the teachings.

Materialism and Spirituality

The movements in our volume whose mission is to work with the poor (Ambedkar, TBMSG, and Sarvodaya in particular; Soka Gakkai to an extent) have taken as their purpose to secure the liberation of the poor from suffering in all its ramifications—material, psychological, social, cultural, and spiritual. They view these forms of suffering as interrelated and thus construct programs that target suffering in its many dimensions simultaneously. In this, they see themselves following in the footsteps of the Buddha. TBMSG, for example, refers to the *Dhammapada*'s saying that "hunger is the greatest of afflictions" and "health the greatest of possessions" and cites the Buddha's putting off a Dharma talk until a hungry man was fed.

Especially in the cases of Ambedkar, TBMSG, and Sarvodaya, service to the poor is the starting point, the *raison d'être*. Consequently, a Buddhism that overlooks or marginalizes the material and other specific needs of the poor will not be developed under their aegis. Ambedkar emphasizes that "the Buddha never cared to enter into a discussion which was not profitable for man's welfare." If one's concern is human welfare and if one's community is the very poor, it is then inevitable that programs designed to meet the multiple urgent needs of the poor will emerge. The Buddhism that Ambedkar brought into being was fully this-worldly, addressing the here-and-now needs of the Untouchables, and redefining liberation as the curing of the material and social suffering of the poor. According to Queen, Ambedkar

> knew that the traditional presentation of the Four Truths—which blame the victims for their own suffering—would be offensive and unacceptable to people whose sufferings were caused by others' cruelty and a heartless social system. . . . He knew that the voluntary poverty and contemplative pursuits of the traditional Bhikkhu could not offer a viable ideal for people locked in structural poverty.

Consequently, in Queen's view, Ambedkar read Buddhist texts through a hermeneutic lens that asked, in effect, what can an Untouchable find of value herein?

Soka Gakkai, though addressing and appealing to a community far less needy than the ex-Untouchables, has attracted its greatest numbers from the lower socioeconomic echelons of the societies in which it is found. One observer, reflecting upon Soka Gakkai's appeal in the United States, remarks in a vein quite similar to Ambedkar's,

> The appeal [of Soka Gakkai's materialism] attracts many Americans living
> in the inner cities who are desperate for a way to improve their lives. For
> these people who know little material prosperity, the more conventional
> Buddhist view—that enlightenment is encouraged by abandoning all
> attachment to material things—is virtually senseless.

There is no doubt that India's ex-Untouchables would share this sentiment.

Ambedkar emphasizes a kind of hierarchy of needs according to which
it is clear that human spiritual needs cannot be seriously attended to until
material needs are adequately satisfied. This notion, of course, is not unknown in traditional Buddhism. At the same time, he saw the two as interconnected. Speaking to political activists, he said, "The battle is in the
fullest sense spiritual. There is nothing material or social in it. For ours is
a battle, not for wealth or for power. It is a battle for freedom. It is a battle
for the reclamation of human personality."

Buddhadasa sounds a surprisingly similar note, emphasizing the fundamental unity of the material, physical, and social within the all-embracing
"spiritual." As a great scholar of Buddhism he speaks with authority, saying,
"Buddhism is neither materialism or mentalism, but is the correctness
between the two, or both of them in the right proportions. The religion
which can be taken as the best social science must not be a slave of materialism nor crazy about mental things."

Many engaged Buddhists see themselves as restoring balance to a Buddhist tradition that has been over-spiritualized by giving attention to the
material component of life, its sustenance, its nurturance, and its protection.
In my view, insofar as the Buddha emphatically did not teach a soul theory
but, on the contrary, taught that human beings are psychophysical organic
wholes, the reformers have impeccable Buddhist grounds for so believing.
Similarly, there are cultural and social components of the soulless "heap of
heaps" which is a person. The elimination of suffering throughout all components of human life-experience is the goal of the figures and movements
in this volume. As Buddhadasa put it, the social and the spiritual are two
interpenetrating aspects of the one reality (Dhamma); "Don't separate them,
otherwise world peace is not possible." Sarvodaya makes this particularly
clear with its program of nurturance of human life in society, believing that
the best support of spiritual development is the nurturance of all wholesome
influences on the person—material, psychological, social, and cultural.

In my view, it is natural that people working with the poor will emphasize material development. It is also inherent in the Buddhist Middle
Path that the poor be helped to have enough of the material support of life
to free them sufficiently of material worry that they will be capable of
attending to spiritual matters. Sakyamuni did not attain enlightenment

while he was starving, but after he ate. Thus an implicit notion of a hierarchy of needs—eat first, meditate second—is part of the discovery of the Middle Path. Moreover, when Buddhadasa says, "Buddhism is neither materialism nor mentalism, but is the correctness between the two or is both of them in the right proportions," I believe he is articulating a principle that all of our figures and movements would endorse. For example, those working on behalf of the quasi-nuns—the *mae ji* of Thailand, the *ani* of Tibet—explicitly emphasize the necessity of improving their economic and educational status in order to make it possible for them to pursue a serious spiritual path. While not all are equally concerned about the practicing conditions of Buddhist women, no one seriously disputes this vital and direct connection between the material and the spiritual.

It is true that not all of our activists are as concerned about the material realm as are Ambedkar, TBMSG, and Sarvodaya. However, not all of them are directly addressing communities as poor as those served by these movements. All of our activists do fashion versions of Buddhism that speak to or are appropriate to the particular needs of the particular community with which they are most concerned. The key phrases in the quotation from Buddhadasa are "the correctness between the two" and "the right proportions." Simply put, in keeping with the Middle Path, Buddhist principles mandate that the poor need more attention given to the material dimension of life than do those who have enough; those who have more than enough need their attention turned to that fact. Thus Nhat Hanh, for example, during the war years helped create a Buddhism appropriate to war conditions, one focused on preserving life and ameliorating the most intense forms of suffering. Since the war, his community has, among other things, organized an effort to feed the poorest of the poor in Vietnam. When speaking in recent years to Western audiences, however, he admonishes us to be mindful of the thievery implicit in rich nations' relations with poor nations (Sulak echoes this view) and to be mindful of the mental, spiritual, and physical poisons embedded in much of what we "consume" in our food, TV, films, and so on. Clearly, ample use is made by our subjects of *upaya*, skillful means, whether or not the term is used: the Buddhism must fit the community and their most urgent needs.

This Middle Path view leaves many of our activists quite ambivalent, in some cases quite antipathetic, toward capitalism. Buddhadasa articulates most incisively the selfishness inherent in capitalism, its reinforcement of our proclivity to think in terms of "I" and "mine," and its tendency to turn interdependent relationships into competitive or antagonistic ones. He turns his back on it entirely. For him, as for many another Buddhists, Buddhist understanding of the interdependence of all things necessitates a socialist ordering of our communal life.

Those among our figures who are seriously engaged with the development of their countries also are quite antipathetic toward capitalism. Following Ruskin's principle, "There is no wealth but life," Sarvodaya is highly critical of the exclusively materialistic, capitalist model of development in which, as Bond puts it, "the material aspects pertaining to social, economic and political development are balanced by the immaterial aspects having to do with spiritual, moral and cultural development." This is an excellent demonstration of Buddhadasa's principle of "the correctness between the two" and "the right proportions." Similarly, Sulak is a highly vocal critic of the capitalist model of development being pursued by his nation, advocating instead a model similar in its broad outline to that pursued by Sarvodaya, a model designed to enhance the lives of ordinary people (rather than the elite few) in economic, cultural, social, political dimensions and to preserve the environment and natural resources.

Soka Gakkai, headquartered in the most highly developed and richest nation of Asia, faces a scenario quite different from those encountered by Sulak and Sarvodaya. In Japan, it is not a matter of models or strategies for development, but of forging a Buddhist social and political presence in a highly capitalistic nation. Soka Gakkai, and its political wing, Komeito, make no pretense of attempting to alter the basic structure of the Japanese economy and society. Rather, they attempt to nudge the status quo in a direction harmonious with Buddhist principles. The rhetoric they use is quite in line with what we have seen earlier. Advocating "Human Socialism" and "Buddhist Democracy," they believe in merging the best features of capitalism (freedom), socialism (equality), and Buddhism (humanism) in a benevolent, democratic welfare state. The specific goods that they emphasize—health care, education, environmental protection, help for the needy, freedom, and equality—seem to be a Japanese, upscale version of the goods emphasized by Sarvodaya and Sulak, though it is important to note that the criticism of capitalism that we find voiced so clearly in our other figures is considerably muted in Soka Gakkai. If, as Metraux claims, Soka Gakkai's membership is indeed climbing the economic ladder, Soka Gakkai faces a significant fork in the road. Either its drive to enhance the material prosperity of its membership will be cut back, which would be in keeping with the broader principle of balance between the material and the spiritual; or it will continue with its materialistic emphasis at a time when, from the Middle Path point of view, a more spiritual emphasis is called for. The Soka Gakkai is currently undergoing significant change; time will tell how it responds to the challenge of its own success.

The Dalai Lama may have the most ambivalence of all our figures regarding the relative value of capitalist and socialist approaches to organizing society. Affirming plainly that his religious beliefs dispose him well toward socialism, he balances this against the trauma caused him and his country by a socialist country and acknowledges that countries pursuing "capitalist policies within a democratic framework are much freer." He clearly is torn between the ideological promise of socialism with its disastrous praxis and the ideological antipathy called up by capitalism conjoined with its comparatively benign praxis with respect, at least, to his own country. In the end, he washes his hands of them both, declaring his final sympathies to be in harmony with the "Environmental parties." This final position is, it seems to me, quite of a piece with the perspectives endorsed by Sulak and Sarvodaya. The embracing of greed inherent in capitalism and consumerism is an obstacle that our subjects simply cannot overlook. Neither can the exploitation of people or planet be tolerated. On the other hand, none of our figures are friends of poverty; they all endorse a principle of well-being held in a context of moderation and sharing." Thus a kind of "Green," environmentally friendly, people-friendly politics and economics emerges rather consistently among our subjects.

Balancing Spirituality and Social Activism

Just as engaged Buddhists strive for a balance between materialism and spirituality in their social action programs they also espouse a balance between spiritual pursuits and social activism itself. As a rule, the former is seen as the foundation of which the latter is the natural result. As Sulak puts it, ". . . people need to know how to *apply* the Four Noble Truths and the Noble Eightfold path today, and how these *methods* can inspire people in the creation of a desirable society in the near future." Swearer describes Sulak's view as a "practical spirituality" and characterizes it as one in which "spiritual development and dedication to the pursuit of a more humane world necessarily go hand in hand."

A very clear illustration of this principle can be found in Nhat Hanh, whose work, *The Miracle of Mindfulness* was precisely instruction in mindfulness practice for the students of the School of Youth for Social Service who were engaged with serving the need of peasants during wartime. It directly applies Buddhist practice to social engagement. Regarding the connection between the two, Nhat Hanh often points out that the first necessity in a crisis is to remain calm and mindful.

Looking at the matter from a comparatively traditional perspective, the Dalai Lama sees worldly goals (e.g., regaining the homeland) and supramundane, traditional Buddhist goals (*nirvana*) as mutually reinforcing, for, as Cabezón puts it, virtuous action on behalf of the oppressed creates merit and aids in the task of mental purification, while the more traditional spiritual exercises, especially the practice of compassion and wisdom, are seen as providing the basis that insures the moral goodness of an action, and its efficacy.

Significantly, Cabezón points out, this conception of the relationship between worldly and supramundane goals

> is in marked contrast to the theory . . . that assumes the kammatic/nibannic distinction, in which social action belongs in the kammatic, i.e., 'secular,' realm, and is therefore related primarily to the goal of higher rebirth, as opposed to the nibbanic aspect of the religion whose goal is emancipation from all rebirth.

This again can be taken as the rule for virtually all the subjects of this volume: the polarity between kammatic and nibbanic goals does not hold; the two realms are seen, even in purely Theravada cases such as Sarvodaya, as interpenetrating, or as two aspects of a single reality. Although not all our subjects by any means conceive of their goals in such traditional terms as either "higher rebirth" or "*nirvana*," it remains the case that they see work on behalf of the oppressed, the poor, or the suffering as both expression of, and training ground for, enlightenment. This is certainly a linchpin in the fundamental conception of engaged Buddhism.

George Bond discusses Sarvodaya with some very useful "betwixt and between" language (to use Swearer's helpful phrase) that applies in spirit to our other movements as well. He describes Sarvodaya as "an interpretation of Buddhism with a this-worldly focus and a form of social and economic development with a spiritual base." In the Sarvodayan view, development needs to be reinterpreted by Buddhism, but Buddhism also needs to be reinterpreted in the context of Sri Lanka's contemporary development needs. The path that a Sarvodaya volunteer embraces also is articulated in this "betwixt and between" language, insofar as it is described as one of "selfless service," "worldly asceticism," and "mundane awakening."

This language is a fine expression of the kind of balance that our subjects envision. Of course, the balance is not always one between two equal parts. Of our subjects, probably Ambedkar is the one who most stresses the political and social dimensions of the path and makes the least of the spiritual—but the spiritual dimension is still essential in his view as well. On the other side of the spectrum, probably the Dalai Lama and Buddhadasa give relatively the greatest emphasis to the spiritual dimension—but again, the social is essential for both of them also.

When we come to the subject of the goals of these paths we find greater variety among our subjects, a spectrum of views running from very traditional understandings of the goal as spiritual, to radical reinterpretations of the goal in social terms.

Buddhadasa's stance on this matter is at once utterly traditional and utterly new. He says, ". . . social goods and acting for the benefit of society are prerequisites of traveling beyond to *nibbana*." Again, as paraphrased by Santikaro, he says,

> The Buddhist goal of quenching or ending *dukkha* is not to be falsely spiritualized into an other worldly end, for the genuinely spiritual does not denigrate or reject the body. *Nibbana* can only be found right here in the middle of *samsara*, the whirlpool of birth and death. So when we talk about ending *dukkha*, we mean both personal and social problems.

Ultimately, social and spiritual peace are deeply interconnected for Buddhadasa insofar as neither can be found without getting to the root of the problem at the level of human desires. Buddhadasa always gave primacy to absolute peace, *nibbana*, but came to believe and articulated with increasing clarity and strength over the years that social peace is to be reached by the same path; hence his saying, "world peace is the Buddha's purpose." Thus the traditional goal is reconceived only slightly, leaving behind transmundane language but retaining language of enlightenment and freedom from desire. With the transmundane gone, it becomes possible, even inevitable, to articulate a concept of *nirvana* that incorporates world peace while retaining much of the traditional meaning of personal peace and awakening.

In Sarvodaya, we encounter language indicating a more extensive reinterpretation of the goal as traditionally conceived. Sarvodaya begins in much the same position as Buddhadasa. Ariyaratne says, "To change society we must purify ourselves, and the purification process we need is brought about by working in society." In this view, the social and spiritual goals are interdependent. Like Buddhadasa, Sarvodaya has no interest in a purely supramundane *nirvana*. However, unlike him, Sarvodaya's main emphasis is upon, in Bond's phrase, a "mundane awakening" in which the First Noble Truth, *dukkha*, is reinterpreted as "there is a decadent village"; the Second Noble Truth, the origin of *dukkha*, is reinterpreted as the causes of the village's decadence; and the Third Noble Truth, cessation or *nirvana*, is understood as hope that the village's suffering can be eliminated. While Ariyaratne acknowledges that this is not the equivalent of the Buddha's teaching, he defends this approach as one that can be meaningful to villagers in their present condition and one that has the potential to improve their spiritual condition sufficiently that they may go on to follow the path in the direction of the more traditional goal. In this way, though most of their activities seem to be of a social nature, spiritual goals remain the most important for Sarvodaya and the traditional goal continues to be respected, but certainly the rhetoric and action of Sarvodaya focuses upon the very new concept of "mundane awakening."

Turning to Ambedkar, we reach the furthest end of the spectrum, with reinterpretation of the goal going beyond reform to the radical level of change. Ambedkar goes further than the rest in negating tradition and, as we have seen, rejects the traditional version of the Four Noble Truths as blaming the victim. In particular, he rejects the traditional Buddhist emphasis on suffering as internally caused, replacing this with an emphasis on eliminating the external causes of the Untouchables' suffering: social, political, and economic. In Queen's summary, "Suffering is not chiefly the product of mental attachments . . . but the result of social exploitation and poverty." Ambedkar rejects also the traditional understanding of enlightenment and reinterprets it, in Queen's words, "as the amelioration of material conditions and social relationships in this life." In Queen's estimation all this is a radical rereading, but not a radical break from, the Buddhist tradition. He justifies this judgment by noting that all the central teachings are still there, though with markedly altered emphases. Significantly, the Five Precepts, always the most important components of the teachings for the laity, are emphasized, along with other teachings that would nurture in the follower a more proactive, take–charge–of–your–destiny approach to life. Queen argues that when seen in the company of the drastic transformations that Buddhism has undergone in the past, Ambedkar's reading cannot be considered to have gone too far; indeed the transformation he engendered may be considered comparable to those occasions when the Path veered off in the direction of early Mahayana, Tantra, and Ch'an. There is no question, though, that on our social-spiritual spectrum, Ambedkar is the farthest out on the social side, with spirituality almost, but not entirely, out of the picture.

It is noteworthy that the inheritor of the Ambedkar legacy that places the most emphasis on the spiritual training of its members, TBMSG, is also, according to Sponberg, probably the most successful in attaining social goals of the various Ambedkarite groups that have developed. This is especially significant insofar as TBMSG's respiritualizing of Ambedkar's vision brings the latter more closely into line with the other reformist movements discussed in this volume; while Ambedkar is the farthest out on the social end of the social-spiritual spectrum, TBMSG is comparable to Sarvodaya, which is somewhere near the middle of the group. Interestingly, the leaders of TBMSG find that they must carefully convince their followers that they are not betraying the political heritage bequeathed to them by the greatly revered Ambedkar, by "overly spiritualizing" his heavily social teaching. Thus while the leadership endorses a balanced spiritual-social program, their followers are not all necessarily content with that balance.

A Word on Behalf of Happiness

It may surprise some readers to discover that a number of our subjects and their followers speak, as Buddhists, of happiness. Thus a Soka Gakkai member stated, "I joined the Soka Gakkai because many of my friends who are members seemed much happier than my friends who are not members." Metraux goes on to observe, "Members often say that membership has significantly changed their lives for the better—they feel much happier, have a new sense of confidence, are much more successful in their jobs or careers, and enjoy a new set of friends and supporters." What is this talk of happiness?

It is to be hoped that the reader is not one of those who still believe that Buddhism is "pessimistic," but there may be many who find it somehow inappropriate to speak of Buddhism as a source of happiness. Is this not an impermissible softening of the harsh depths of Buddhist insight? To this, Nhat Hanh replies, "To suffer is not enough."

> Life is filled with suffering, but it is also filled with many wonders, like the blue sky, the sunshine, the eyes of a baby. To suffer is not enough. We must also be in touch with the wonders of life. They are within us and all around us, everywhere, any time. . . .
>
> Meditation is to be aware of what is going on—in our bodies, in our feelings, in our minds, and in the world. Each day 40,000 children die of hunger. . . . Yet the sunrise is beautiful, and the rose that bloomed this morning along the wall is a miracle. Life is both dreadful and wonderful. To practice meditation is to be in touch with both aspects. Please do not think we must be solemn in order to meditate. In fact, to meditate well, we have to smile a lot.[8]

Before jumping to conclusions about the superficiality of this view (vis-à-vis traditional Buddhism), the reader should recall that these words were written by a man who lived through the war in Vietnam in a state of mindful awareness, who saw countless friends and colleagues die in that struggle, who cherished hopes and acted tirelessly to bring about an early and peaceful conclusion to that conflict only to have those hopes mercilessly crushed, and who lives today in long-term exile from the country and people he dearly loves. This is a man who knows suffering! So why all this talk of happiness and smiling?

I think it is important to be aware that despite their many substantial differences, Nhat Hanh and the Soka Gakkai have one very significant point in common: they both think that happiness—the ordinary, garden-variety happiness of humankind—is important; indeed, they think it is the point of Buddhism and of Buddhist practice.

Buddhism has always been about the elimination of *duhkha*. Of course, when the Buddha spoke of *duhkha,* he was not speaking of simple unhappiness. Two related features of the worldview of our subjects have intervened since the time of the Buddha to allow for the reinterpretation of Buddhism in such a way that the goal of eliminating *duhkha* can be understood as at least partially equivalent to the nurturing of happiness. These two features are the this-worldly perspective of our subjects and their focus upon the laity.

The focus upon the laity is obvious. Most of these movements are conceived entirely as movements to improve the welfare of the people: Ambedkar's movement, TBMSG, Soka Gakkai, Sarvodaya, the Buddhist Struggle Movement in Vietnam, Sulak's various organizations, all are movements whose purpose was or is to protect or help people and to improve human society. The Tibetan liberation movement basically falls into this category as well, though it has the added complication of national sovereignty issues. Out of all our subjects, only Buddhadasa seems to have as his first priority the teaching of a correct Buddhism rather than the this-worldly welfare of the people *per se* (though the latter is clearly within the purview of his major concerns); and only the nuns' movement is more concerned with monastics than with the laity.

Having one's primary concern as the well-being of people does not inevitably mean that one will fashion a this-worldly Buddhism. However, when the bombs are falling, when the neighboring country's troops invade, when poverty or social injustice becomes extreme, then concern with the welfare of the people inevitably becomes translated into a this-worldly Buddhism. In particular, when, in the modern world, *duhkha* becomes injustice that can be redressed, lives that can be protected, illness that can be prevented, when tangible remedies that are the fruits of modernity are available, then a Buddhism concerned with the people's well-being becomes this-worldly.

In times of crisis, dramatic things have been done by many of our subjects and their followers in the name of the Buddha. In ordinary times, a kind of daily–life focus emerges, an attempt to make Buddhism appropriate to the mundane lives of ordinary people. This praxis matches Nhat Hanh's prescriptive words: though there are 84,000 Dharma doors, "even more doors should be opened." One good example of this is TBMSG, whose instruction to Buddhist ex-Untouchables, according to Sponberg, entails "seeking to find ways in the Dhamma to deal with specific social issues such as domestic violence and alcohol abuse as well as the broader problems of poverty, lack of self-esteem and confidence, and the difficulties encountered in taking advantage of educational and employment opportunities now guaranteed by law," along with the construction of residential communities "meant to be workshops for the development of spiritual friendship and community," schools, hostels, medical clinics, libraries, sports and cultural programs, and right livelihood cooperatives.

Soka Gakkai, similarly, has a daily–life focus, the core of which is the local neighborhood group, which acts as an immediate support for each member. As Metraux explains,

> When a member is experiencing some form of distress, she or he quickly receives the sympathetic help of a neighboring Gakkai member or leader. Members at local meetings are strongly urged to articulate problems in their lives and it is common for other members in attendance to lend them advice and support. . . . Gakkai members always say that they belong to a caring and compassionate movement.

Moreover, members believe that the benefits of their Buddhist practice will become manifest in the success and harmony of their family lives, jobs, schoolwork, and so on. Happiness in these dimensions is targeted and expected. Sarvodaya is much the same. With its emphasis upon a holistic approach to the well-being of Sri Lankan villagers, it nurtures joy in community, culture, and nature, along with economic sufficiency and inner peace.

Before leaving the subject of happiness, I should point out that the Dalai Lama also speaks in these terms: "All of us want happiness. In cities, on farms, even in remote villages, everyone is quite busy. What is the purpose? Everyone is trying to create happiness. To do so is right. However, it is very important to follow a correct method in seeking happiness. . . ."[9] We should also recall that happiness is likewise regarded as a *desideratum* in the early Buddhist discourses, where happiness is frequently mentioned as a characteristic of Buddhist practitioners. The *Dhammapada* devotes an entire chapter to happiness, which begins,

197. Let us live happily then, not hating those who hate us!
among men who hate us let us dwell free from hatred!

198. Let us live happily then, free from ailments among the ailing!
among men who are ailing let us dwell free from ailments!

199. Let us live happily then, free from greed among the greedy!
among men who are greedy let us dwell free from greed!

200. Let us live happily then, though we call nothing our own!
We shall be like the bright gods, feeding on happiness![10]

And, as is frequently cited, the Buddha advised his followers to cultivate the following thoughts: "May all beings be happy and secure; may their minds be contented."[11] Therefore, the notion that Buddhist practice should engender happiness is not a new one, though the analysis of what is needed for happiness certainly is.

Buddhism and Politics

The subject of the relationship between Buddhism and politics is an area in which we see widespread difference in both views and practice among our subjects; perhaps most interesting, the practice itself proves very difficult for many of our subjects.

On one extreme of our spectrum of views on the place of politics in activist Buddhism is the wholehearted endorsement of party politics by the Soka Gakkai, expressed in the founding of the Komeito, originally part of Soka Gakkai and now formally separated, though still having the closest of associations. Similarly, the most politically activist wing of the Unified Buddhist Church of Vietnam also founded a Buddhist political party, though the party did not survive long enough to take any substantive form. One notch down from this extreme is Ambedkar, who belongs in this category in spirit. Although the Republican Party Ambedkar founded was not expressly Buddhist, his role as a national statesman placed his engaged Buddhism in the context of mainstream politics. Perhaps the Dalai Lama also belongs in this category, inasmuch as he is himself a global political figure, though he does not engage in partisan politics and, indeed, is in no position to do so. For all these figures, political activism has been the rule; its practice has occasioned ideological trouble only for the Vietnamese Buddhists (a subject to which we shall return).

On the other end of this particular spectrum, several of our figures have nothing, or almost nothing, to do with politics, specifically, the nuns and quasi-nuns, Buddhadasa, and TBMSG. Buddhadasa, relatively more withdrawn from the world than the other monks in this volume, was still very seriously engaged with issues of political ideology and made some courageous statements in challenging the antisocialist ideological climate prevalent in Thailand. TBMSG, for its part, has consistently tried to work outside of partisan politics but, perhaps ironically given the larger Buddhist body of opinion, has been repeatedly castigated by other, more politically activist Ambedkarite movements for this practice.

Our other figures are embroiled in politics to one degree or another without engaging in party politics and with varying degrees of acceptance or aversion to politics. Sulak, while not a politician, is a political gadfly who repeatedly challenges the political status quo in terms explicit enough to earn himself imprisonment on charges of *lèse-majesté* and self-imposed exile to avoid the same. Sarvodaya, for its part, has consistently sought political neutrality, though it has not always been successful in this attempt. While it has often worked cooperatively with the government, recently the crisis afflicting the country has pushed Sarvodaya into a position openly critical of the government. Even before Ariyaratne began to voice this criticism, the government was sufficiently threatened by his popularity that they made strong moves to control and mute his influence. Under the circumstances in which Sri Lankans find themselves, many urge Ariyaratne to run for political office. He, however, consistently declines, citing his desire to remain apolitical and neutral. Here is a case in which an individual, because of his success in leading a movement of spiritually based social activism, has attained such prominence that he has spontaneously taken on the aura of a powerful political figure despite his own disinterest in such a role.

King
Malkalx

A more complex case is that of the Buddhists in Vietnam, who had political power sufficient to make or break one government after another but were extremely reluctant to admit that they held this power and were even more reluctant to put it to use in a frankly acknowledged way, though they were by no means averse to using it to attain the ends to which they were committed. Similar is Aung San Suu Kyi of Burma (Myanmar), who, though not represented in this volume, is another exemplar of a politically/socially engaged Buddhism. She protests throughout her speeches that she is involved in national affairs because of the crisis facing her country, because, as the daughter of a popular national leader, she can serve as a unifying focus for the people's yearning for democracy—but that she herself has no interest in political parties and power politics.[12] Yet the political power she held was a sufficient threat to the Burmese government that she was placed under house arrest for five years following her party's decisive victory at the polls.

In both the Burmese and the Vietnamese cases, then, we see a profound ambivalence about politics: a deep aversion to political machinations and, especially, the self-serving, self-aggrandizing nature of politics, coupled with an equally deep urge to serve the people by helping them to gain the political ends they seek. Clearly there are vital questions embedded in these situations that the Buddhist social activist movement urgently needs to resolve. Can Buddhism serve the needs of the people without engaging in politics in those cases in which politics are a major source of suffering for the people? And if Buddhists were to engage in politics, what sort of politics would it be? Should monks and nuns always remain outside politics? Is there a way to engage in political work while avoiding the polarizing and destructive nature of partisan politics? It is not the Buddhist way, traditionally, to denounce the other and elevate oneself. In a crisis, engaged Buddhists

Sallie B. King

are willing to act in this way, but they are rarely willing to settle into this pattern for the long run. They seem to want to invent a new kind of politics that would not involve this kind of thing, a politics that would be purely a service to the people. The Dalai Lama says,

> Sometimes we look down on politics, criticizing it as dirty. However, if you look at it properly, politics in itself is not wrong. It is an instrument to serve human society. With good motivation—sincerity and honesty—politics becomes an instrument in the service of society. But when motivated by selfishness, with hatred, anger, or jealousy, it becomes dirty.

Outside of times of crisis, such a politics, not surprisingly, has eluded Buddhists.

Buddhist Identity and Buddhist Self-Negation

A tremendously interesting tension exists within our group, often within a single thinker, in the dynamic interplay between Buddhist identity and Buddhist self-negation. My use of these terms requires some elaboration. On the one hand, Buddhism is, like many other religions, a highly institutionalized religion with a long history and a deeply symbiotic relationship with the cultures in which it is found. As such, Buddhism is a cultural artifact with a rich and highly particular form. This cultural Buddhism, or Buddhism as a phenomenon in the world, is greatly important to a number of our figures and their movements as the foundation of an identity, an identifier that is able to define an individual, a people, or a nation and to distinguish them from others.

On the other hand, there is in Buddhism a deep strain of self-negation, a theme that declares that Buddhism, as a cultural artifact, is a means and not an end, a way to something else, a finger pointing at the moon, a less-than-ultimate that makes available the ultimate. This is nicely expressed in the Parable of the Raft, which tells us quite bluntly that what we want is the other shore; the Raft (Dharma and, by extension, Buddhism itself) should be gratefully used and properly cared for, but it should not be confused with the ultimate end. All this is reemphasized for Mahayana followers by the teachings of emptiness and skillful means: Buddhism is a form, and as such is empty of any ultimacy; to be sure, it is a highly skillful form, but nonetheless a form. This strain of self-negation in Buddhist thought results, in some of our figures, in a strong insistence upon the nonultimacy of Buddhism, the nonviability of taking Buddhism as something final, the rejection of taking Buddhism as the end of our seeking rather than the vehicle of our seeking.

From this position several of our figures venture on to a position of religious inclusivism. For if Buddhism is a nonultimate vehicle making available what we seek, other forms, specifically other world religions, may also be such vehicles for what we seek, if they are sufficiently skillful. Several of the figures in the present group have taken this step and have explicitly embraced such a Buddhist inclusivism. Thus while they strongly affirm that Buddhism is a viable vehicle to Truth or Dhamma, they also readily acknowledge that other religions may be so as well. If this is so, then what really counts is Truth, not Buddhism per se. This attitude is the opposite of that held by those for whom Buddhism is important as an identity; for these, not any religion will do; it must be Buddhism and only Buddhism.

Both of these tendencies may be traced back to the origins of Buddhism. As we have seen, the Buddhist tendency to negate itself can be traced to the teachings of the Buddha, paradigmatically in the Parable of the Raft; and Buddhism as a cultural artifact goes back inevitably to the teachings of the Dharma, the founding of the Sangha, and the establishment of the Vinaya. Thus in the roots of Buddhism's establishment, in the teaching of the Dharma, lies a dialectical relationship between Buddhism's continual reestablishment and its occasional self-negation or disestablishment. But herein lies a problem: for what can survive with a recurrent urge in its core to negate itself?

The Buddhist propensity to de-absolutize itself has great appeal for those sickened by the spectacle of religious intolerance. But as the sociologist Robert Bellah points out, there is a problematic side to the Buddhist attitude just described, which may degenerate into what he labels "overtolerance." "An overtolerant religion is one that fails to communicate its message to important groups in the society and passively assents in their adherence to heterogeneous and often less developed orientations." While he identifies Hinduism as the most egregious offender in this respect, Buddhism is also singled out for special attention.

> Buddhism, through passive acceptance of pre-existing religious orientations, frequently found itself overwhelmed by them in time. The extreme case, perhaps, is Japan, where Buddhist universalism and individualism were almost entirely swallowed in a recrudescence of magical, collectivistic religious orientations of archaic type and semi-archaic Confucianism.[13]

I would argue that the extreme Buddhist case is India, where Buddhism was born and subsequently virtually disappeared, until the recent revival; but Bellah's point is well taken and most pertinent to the present subject.

Buddhism, a religion with self-negating and inclusivistic tendencies to the point of "overtolerance," has found itself struggling simply to survive in many parts of Asia. Major human-caused disasters of one form or another—colonialism, communist intolerance, war, genocide, foreign invasion—have been the rule, rather than the exception, for Buddhist countries in Asia in the modern period. Where it has not been a question of the people surviving—most drastically, in Cambodia—it has often been a question of Buddhism surviving—most drastically, in China and Tibet. But even short of these extremes, the fate of Buddhism has been closely tied to questions of identity and sometimes nationhood in much of Asia—resistance to social bigotry, resistance to colonialism, resistance to Westernization, and resistance to communism have been the daily fare of Asian Buddhists for decades. How, then, do our subjects handle the tension between the general Buddhist tendency toward self-negation and the present vital role of Buddhism as a particularizing identity, an identity that separates Buddhism as a culture from what it is not and thereby protects itself and the people to whom that identity is crucial?

First, some of our subjects are less interested in Buddhist self-negation and inclusivism than others. Soka Gakkai, notorious in the recent past for its exclusivism and utter intolerance of not only other religions, but other Buddhists as well, stands out among our subjects in this regard. As Metraux notes, however, Soka Gakkai's rhetoric and praxis of exclusivism have been considerably toned down in recent years. In fact, in 1993 Daisaku Ikeda founded the "Boston Research Center for the 21st Century" in order to foster interreligious and intercultural dialogue.[14] This opening is too new at present to assess.

Ambedkar's movement and the TBMSG are probably next in our group in giving the least weight to Buddhist self-negation, but theirs is an entirely different case from Soka Gakkai. In the first place, Buddhist tolerance plays an important role in each. One of the criteria by which Ambedkar selected Buddhism was its tolerance; Islam was rejected for its intolerance, which Ambedkar found repugnant and not conducive to morality and rationality. TBMSG, for its part, draws heavily on the pan-Buddhist teachings of Sangharakshita, which, while not inclusive of non-Buddhist religions, are obviously deeply ecumenical and thus work against any tendency toward dogmatic exclusivism. This said, however, it should be emphasized that neither ecumenicism nor inclusivism is a significant concern for either Ambedkar or TBMSG in their work with the ex-Untouchable community. Their concern, especially Ambedkar's, is precisely with identity, a Buddhist identity that changes the former Untouchable into a new being on a social, a psychological, and perhaps even an ontological level—an identity that transforms him or her from a being with negative value to a being whose value is the equal of anyone's. The whole point of these movements is Buddhist identity, an identity that functions precisely to separate the former

Untouchables from the Hindu world and its values, an identity that denies the claims which that world makes on the ex-Untouchables. The act of conversion—claiming this identity—is the crucial break from the Hindu world and the first act in the progressive realization of Buddhist identity. It is no surprise, then, that with this purpose, Buddhist self-negation makes no appearance in these movements; it would serve no purpose, and, as Ambedkar points out, Buddhism is always practical.

On the other side of this continuum are two figures, Buddhadasa and Nhat Hanh, who stress the self-negating qualities of Buddhism and make little of Buddhism as a form of particularizing identity. Nhat Hanh's Tiep Hien Order, for example, gives as its very first foundational principle, "non-attachment to views," which Nhat Hanh calls "the most important teaching of Buddhism." The first precept of this order reads, "Do not be idolatrous about or bound to any doctrine, theory, or ideology, even Buddhist ones. All systems of thought are guiding means; they are not absolute truth." His commentary states, "In the name of ideologies and doctrines, people kill and are killed." In the midst of a devastating war of both historical and ideological origin, Nhat Hanh is keenly aware that ideology kills. This experience strongly reinforces for him the importance of Buddhism's self-negating tendencies. Moreover, although he is vitally concerned with the lot of a particular Buddhist people, since ideology is part of the problem, he does not see Buddhist identity as in any way part of the answer he seeks, even though the answer he espouses is entirely inspired by his Buddhist perspective. He makes it clear that for him peace and the protection of human life are more important than anything and states explicitly that if it came down to a contest between them, these are more important than the survival of Buddhism.

Buddhadasa also endorses Buddhist self-negation as one of the cornerstones of his thought and ultimately takes the next step to explicit inclusivism. The motivating force behind his embracing of Buddhist self-negation is a kind of Buddhist pragmatism in which all that matters is *dukkha* and the overcoming of *dukkha*. As Santikaro notes, if asked whether something is "correct," Buddhadasa asks in return, "Does it quench *dukkha*?" with the obvious implication that whatever quenches *dukkha* is "correct." Again, Buddhadasa does not simply equate the Dhamma with the Buddha's teachings. As Santikaro puts it, for Buddhadasa, "Dhamma is the Truth, Reality, Law, or to whatever the teachings point.... Dhamma is Nature." Buddhadasa raised his "first major controversy" with this issue, declaring in a lecture that "the Buddha, Dhamma, and Sangha of most Buddhists were obstacles obstructing their way to *nibbana*. Because of their egoistic attachments to the Buddha, Dhamma, and Sangha, they did not have the true Buddha, Dhamma, and Sangha which alone can liberate us from *dukkha."* This is Buddhist self-negation *par excellence,* echoing Nhat Hanh's concerns about attachment to concepts and ideology, explicitly including the Buddhist variety.

This active embracing of Buddhist self-negation has borne fruit for both Nhat Hanh and Buddhadasa in long-standing interest and participation in Buddhist-Christian dialogue, Nhat Hanh mostly for religious reasons (though there were important political aspects to these discussions during the war), Buddhadasa initially out of suspicion of Christian missionaries in Thailand and subsequently out of purely religious interest. Buddhadasa has gone so far as to declare, as Santikaro puts it, that "all religions are the same in one central respect—eliminating selfishness." Here we find ourselves in explicitly inclusivist territory. On the basis of this shared concern he believed all religions share a common enemy in materialism and should work together for the well-being of humanity.

I have discussed those figures who make major use of Buddhism as an identity and those strongly committed to Buddhist self-negation; I shall now look at two figures who are simultaneously strongly committed to Buddhism in both respects: Sulak and the Dalai Lama.

Sulak is a great lover of traditional Thai culture and greatly concerned to support and protect it. Of course, Buddhism is a major and inseparable constituent of that culture. Sulak's concern is to protect that culture from the eroding influence of modernization and the encroachment of Western ways. As Swearer puts it, in the modern period,

> competing secular institutions, the dramatic social and cultural changes accompanying the building of an increasingly industrialized market economy, and the rapid erosion of a village-based subsistence way of life have undermined the integrity and future viability of the Thai Buddhist tradition.

In particular, "Sulak sees two complementary challenges to Siamese identity: an erosion of traditional cultural, religious and social values, and a wholesale appropriation of a Western lifestyle." This deep and rapid change has prompted what Sulak sees as an identity crisis, a crisis to which he has responded with many initiatives designed to promote and ensure the continuity of what he sees as the best in Thai Buddhist culture. Thus he approves of a figure like King Mongkut, whom he characterizes as one whose

> strength was not only his understanding of the West . . . but going back to the root of Siameseness which he claimed to be in accordance with the original teaching of the Buddha. . . . Mongkut altered Siamese 'outer identity,' e.g., learning English and Western technology, but preserved the essential core which was rooted in Buddhism.

In this way Thai Buddhist identity is for Sulak crucial to the resistance of Westernization, consumerism, and secularization and to the preservation of correct, that is, Buddhist, values in Thai society.

At the same time, Sulak is very aware of the oppressive use made of cultural Buddhism by Thai ruling powers. For this and other reasons, he has made a very clear statement endorsing Buddhist self-negation. Sulak distinguishes between small "b" buddhism and capital "B" Buddhism. The latter is "acculturated Buddhism, conventional ritualistic Buddhism, the *pro forma* Buddhism of civil religion, a Buddhism identified with Thai chauvinism and militaristic, aggressive values." Small "b" buddhism he understands to be "the essential core of all the great world religions"; following Buddhadasa, he identifies this with selflessness. Sulak's judgment of cultural Buddhism, then, ranges from disinterest ("You don't have to profess . . . [a particular] faith, you don't have to worship the Buddha, you don't have to join in any ceremonies") to outright disapprobation of that Buddhism that supports state oppression and militarism. Clearly, his heart is with small "b" buddhism, the Buddhism of self-negation and inclusivism. Yet, at the same time, he is deeply interested in and furthers the cause of cultural Buddhism insofar as it has the potential to carry into modern times the values of traditional Thai Buddhist culture currently struggling to survive under the onslaught of foreign, modern influences.

Before we consider a possible reconciliation of this apparent contradiction, let us take a look at the second figure who works wholeheartedly with both Buddhism as an identity and self-negating inclusivist Buddhism, the Dalai Lama. The Dalai Lama, of course, supports Tibetan efforts to maintain their cultural and religious identity; indeed, he embodies a good deal of that identity in his person. Under the circumstances, the effort to preserve Tibetan culture (which largely means religious culture), together with the effort to regain the homeland, must be first among his concerns. In this sense, the support, protection, and continuity of Tibetan Buddhist identity is the foremost daily working concern for him and his followers.

At the same time, and perhaps surprisingly for someone with his particular responsibilities (who also, perhaps surprisingly, calls himself an Internationalist), the Dalai Lama speaks consistently and eloquently from the Buddhist inclusivist perspective. Positively, the Dalai Lama, like Buddhadasa, sees core principles shared by all the world's religions, specifically, for him, "a sense of brotherhood and sisterhood, compassion, and the genuine realization of the oneness of all humankind." Indeed, what is really important to him—love, kindness, and compassion—is found not only in all religions but in secular culture as well. It is important to him to exclude no one from the call to the healing of humankind's woes; since the cause of suffering is everywhere, its cure must be everywhere.

On the critical side, as Cabezón summarizes it, the Dalai Lama believes that "ideological, religious, ethnic, and economic differences are . . . both superficial and artificial [and that] . . . emphasizing such differences can be the cause of discord." Indeed, the Dalai Lama expresses a rationale much like Nhat Hanh's:

> . . . in the world of politics such small discriminations create uncontrollable problems . . . sometimes from race, sometimes from ideology. The same is true for my own country, Tibet, due to certain attitudes of our great neighbor, the Peoples Republic of China, that appeared during the Cultural Revolution.

In short, Nhat Hanh and the Dalai Lama are both of countries that have faced disaster partially for ideological reasons. Hence they both have learned very well the serious danger embedded in ideology and have been concerned ever since to articulate a Buddhism that not only would not be party to the destructive potential of ideology but that at best could be a tool to fight against the destructive power of such ideology. This ability of Buddhism to be both a unique and powerful tool to be used for the undermining of dogmatic attachment to ideology and also potentially an ideology to which one could be dogmatically attached underlies the issue currently under consideration and accounts for the complexities and variability we see among the subjects of this volume with respect to this issue.

Cabezón, I think, sheds considerable light on this subject when he summarizes the Dalai Lama's view, saying,

> ideology, religion and culture are the constructs of human beings. As such they should serve us and bring us happiness. If instead they become sources of suffering, then we are creating unnecessary grief for ourselves, grief which . . . is within our control.

This brings to light again the pragmatic strain in Buddhism and, I think, helps us to make sense of the variability we have seen among our subjects on this issue. Soka Gakkai remains outside the following consensus that I believe, however, represents the rest of our subjects.

As we have seen, in our activists' view, happiness is good, suffering and unhappiness are bad; Buddhism should promote the former and help eliminate the latter. In their various ways, all our figures (except Soka Gakkai) are using the Buddhist identity/self-negation polarity to do just this with respect to the particular community each is addressing. Where Buddhist identity is an important component of the long-term happiness of a people, our movements support it. This is the case for Ambedkar and TBMSG first and foremost and for Sulak and the Dalai Lama also in crucial ways. Buddhism does make it clear that "ideology, religion and culture are the constructs of human beings." But this is a two-edged sword: a human construct where useful, where conducive to human happiness, should be used—cultural Buddhism itself is nothing more or less than this. But where such a construct causes pain, its nonultimate status can always be called into view. Thus where ideology has been a particular source of suffering, as for Nhat Hanh and the Dalai Lama, Buddhist self-negation is particularly clearly espoused. Also among the greatest intellectuals and scholars of our group—Buddhadasa, the Dalai Lama, and Nhat Hanh—the Buddhist tendency toward self-negation is picked up and developed. Perhaps most interesting of all, those who see both points and/or who have use for both points, espouse both. Within the context of Buddhist views, and in contrast to what might seem logical, this is not a trade-off situation. Given that cultural Buddhism is an artificial construct to be used or not as conditions warrant, it is very possible for a figure such as the Dalai Lama or Sulak to see some circumstances under which it is useful or necessary to take a particular form of Buddhist identity with the utmost seriousness, while at another time, in another context, Buddhist self-negation may be embraced as the most useful or appropriate.

One more movement, Sarvodaya, remains to be discussed in this context. I have saved this one for separate and final consideration because it is unique in its embodiment of the point of greatest tension between Buddhist identity and Buddhist inclusivism. On the one hand, this is a thoroughly and deeply Buddhist movement, the rhetoric of which, the vision and goals of which, and the greatest part of the labor of which are all Buddhist. Its very Buddhistness is one of the keys to its success in overwhelmingly Buddhist Sri Lanka and within the context of the larger Buddhist revival in that region. On the other hand, Sarvodaya has always recognized the limiting factors in religious particularism and has always struggled against them. Not everyone in Sri Lanka is Buddhist; but the Sarvodaya people believe they have a method and a program that is useful to the entire country and all its people. Of course, this tension has become acute and deadly serious with the escalation of violence between the ethnic Tamils and Sinhalese. In this respect, it is a very good thing indeed that Sarvodaya has, since its beginnings, downplayed the particularizing nature of its Buddhist foundations and consciously developed an inclusivist rhetoric and praxis, declaring, like Buddhadasa, Sulak, and the Dalai Lama, that all religions share a common spiritual core. Thus Sarvodaya declares itself founded upon this core as a nonsectarian entity, despite the fact that it is deeply Buddhist and, again, despite the fact that its Buddhistness is one of the keys to its success. Yet also its inclusivism is a key to its success; surely without the foundation of inclusivism it had established over many years, it would have been of far less use in the current tragic struggle between Tamils and Sinhalese. Sarvodaya does seek, as Bond says, "to build an inclusive society and an integrated nation" and it has made vast contributions to this end; yet it has this vision and is able to act successfully upon it, ironically, because of its Buddhistness, a Buddhistness that simultaneously is able to embrace both the history and identity of a people and the inclusivism always latent in Buddhism. In my view, Sarvodaya brings into sharpest focus the paradoxical nature of Buddhist identity/inclusivism.

Love and the Prophetic Voice

All of our figures want to change the world in some respect. As Buddhists articulate so clearly, change is usually a natural, evolutionary process; it is always inevitable. However, in some cases in the human social world, especially when vested interests, prejudice, or habit are involved, to bring about change requires a significant effort to displace the status quo. What a Buddhist way of displacing the status quo might be is one of the major issues of this volume.

The two basic modalities for changing a resistant status quo pursued by our subjects may be called "love" and the "prophetic voice," respectively. The prophetic voice maintains a separation between self and other and does not hesitate to denounce what it sees as error and those whose actions are in error. Those who use this approach take up an oppositional stance with respect to an opponent or entity that they wish to see displaced and take it as a goal to remove that opponent or entity from its position. In contrast, there are others who fundamentally and on principle recognize no enemy, who are averse to taking up an oppositional stance and who prefer to effect change in a manner that creates no enemies. This last example is described by some of its proponents as a way of love and compassion and is an expression of a view that sees no real separation between self and other.

Among our figures, Ambedkar, Sulak, and Soka Gakkai best exemplify the power of the prophetic voice. The Soka Gakkai's forebear, Nichiren, of course, is possibly the most outstanding exemplar of the prophetic voice in the entire Buddhist tradition.[15] His fiery denunciations of both the religious and the political status quo of his time and his dogged insistence upon their total displacement earned him the hatred of the powerful and the love of common people. The early leadership of Soka Gakkai closely followed this pattern, opposing the Japanese state's control of institutionalized religion at a time when most religions took the easy path of least resistance to the state's demands. Subsequently, Soka Gakkai earned notoriety by its excessively aggressive proselytization techniques that included denunciation of every other religious path. While that aggression has been sharply curtailed in recent years, the Soka Gakkai continues to avidly embrace the stance of the religious/social prophet. Moreover, Soka Gakkai's political wing, Komeito, takes as its ostensible goal the elimination of corruption in government, a natural expression of this tradition's prophetic heritage (though Komeito itself has not been immune from corruption scandals). Today Soka Gakkai is very interested in education and communication programs promoting world peace. In the past its strong stance within the prophetic perspective has made it difficult for other institutions, as well as individuals, to communicate, let alone cooperate, with it. It will be interesting to see whether this pattern changes with their new dialogical initiatives.

Ambedkar's is another strongly prophetic voice. With the cause of the Untouchables ranking first and foremost in his life, I think it is fair to say that Ambedkar was more than anything else a fighter for his people and only secondarily all the other things he was in life—government official, political activist, and religious leader. The invective that he heaped upon the caste system, orthodox Hinduism, and the governments that refused to challenge them is comparable to Nichiren's. Each sees moral and religious destitution utterly ruining his world and seeks only the most potent means to displace that fundamental corruption. After a lifetime of attacks upon Hinduism, Ambedkar finally decided to step outside of the Hindu world. This deceptively simple act was for him the deepest kind of attack, an act that utterly nullified not only the moral claims of the Hindu world but even its very existence; it was an attempt to render that world nothing for himself and, in time, for those who followed him. Insofar as a prophetic act affirms the self (and one's position) and negates the other (and the other's position), then Ambedkar's conversion was a prophetic act par excellence.

Sulak is another thoroughly prophetic figure, one who has denounced his government at great personal risk and has even carried on a long-running series of *ad hominem* attacks on an individual he opposes. At the same time, he has been highly critical of institutionalized Buddhism in Thailand and its subservience to the state. Of course, Sulak has conceived a very substantial revisioning of both Buddhism and Thailand, which he constantly advocates and refines. But it is clear that he feels that the oppressiveness and corruption of the government, the ruinous direction in which he believes it is leading the country, and the Buddhist Church's acquiescence in all this are obstacles that must be removed in order for a changed society to develop.

While Sulak is a student of Buddhadasa, the latter has taken an approach to change in Thailand, especially in Thai Buddhism, which contrasts with Sulak's. During his student years, Buddhadasa became deeply dissatisfied with institutional Buddhism as it existed in Thailand in those days and with the course of study to which that institution limited him. His dissatisfaction with that curriculum forced him to leave tradition behind and to chart a course of study for himself. But as Santikaro notes, "in making this move, he went beyond the official and politically controlled religious institution without breaking with it. There were no harsh words, judgments, or condemnations. . . ." He proceeded simply to speak and write from his own perspective, gradually winning a larger and larger audience, with more and more converts to his radically innovative views. In this manner, he eschewed the prophetic stance while still moving toward change. Similarly, at a time when to speak of socialism was virtually forbidden by the government, he did not attack the government for its oppressiveness, he simply began speaking of socialism—notably, not the government's caricatured version of socialism but a Buddhist socialism as he envisioned it. Thus, Buddhadasa strove to bring about change by using his greatest resource, his intellectual creativity, refusing the constraint of any power that tried to prevent him from following its lead, and articulating what he found along the way. In this manner he has not taken up a prophetic, that is, oppositional stance, but has produced change by simply charting his own course, which happens to be sharply distinct from the status quo, and progressively winning more and more followers. It is not accidental that this approach is in harmony with his Buddhist principles, in particular, his emphasis upon interconnection.

Like Buddhadasa, Thich Nhat Hanh and the Dalai Lama have avoided taking up an oppositional stance, but they have done so much more deliberately and under much more difficult conditions. During the war, Buddhists in Vietnam united in calling their approach the "Third Way," that is, a way not on the side of the North and opposing the South, again not on the side of the South and opposing the North, but a Third Way on the side of all the people and on the side of peace, opposing no side. This was a very conscious expression of the Buddhist perception of interconnectedness, a principle that could not be more poignant than in the context of a country divided in two, with brother literally fighting brother. They tried to articulate a position of love for all parties to the conflict, of well-wishing to all. Beyond this level of agreement, however, Buddhists divided between those, notably Nhat Hanh, who maintained a remarkably consistent practice of nonseparation from all parties to the conflict, and others, notably the more politicized leadership of the Unified Buddhist Church, who took active steps to bring about the displacement of particular leaders whom they opposed. Interestingly, Nhat Hanh approved of the movement that brought down the Diem government, but this seems to have been possible for him largely because it was a spontaneous movement "without any prescribed doctrine," with "pure intention," without any thought of "toppling the Diem government in order to come to power"; it was a spontaneous outburst of suffering and the desire to change: "No desire, no ambition, is involved." Once the Buddhists saw that they could gain power, the political situation became oppositional, a situation of our interest versus theirs. This was a stance unacceptable to Nhat Hanh, who continued to articulate a philosophy of nonseparation from all parties involved. This stance of nonseparation from all is expressive of the awareness of interconnectedness but, for Nhat Hanh, is also the only stance in harmony with "pure intention"—desirelessness. Thus Nhat Hanh is a thoroughgoing exemplar of the attempt to effect change through love, while the Unified Buddhist Church represents an uneasy amalgam of this stance with the oppositional stance.

The Dalai Lama also is an utterly striking exemplar of the modality of love. The head of a country invaded by an overwhelming foreign power, a power that took over control of the country, displacing its leadership and causing its people incalculable suffering, culminating in an effort to displace the culture itself, the Dalai Lama still avoids taking an oppositional stance against the Chinese. That is to say, if you compare the Dalai Lama to Soka Gakkai, Ambedkar, or even Sulak, you find not a word of invective; instead, you find language of love and gratitude. "Thus is our enemy our greatest friend. He provides us with the needed test of inner strength, tolerance and respect for others. Instead of feeling anger toward this person one should respect him and be grateful." He maintains patiently that the only proper motivation for him in his struggle with the Chinese, whom he calls "our great neighbor," is love and compassion. "The love being advocated here is the kind one can have even for another who has done one harm." Of course, this love for his neighbor by no means translates into condoning their actions or making light of the plight of the Tibetan people for whom he has unique responsibility. It refers, rather, to an awareness of one's own interconnectedness with them, one's ultimate nonseparation from them, which directly implies one's concern for their well-being. In other words, from the perspective of interconnection, the terms "self" and "other" break down and an oppositional stance becomes impossible. Therefore, in this case, he actively seeks a solution that furthers the well-being of both Chinese and Tibetans.

At the same time, the Dalai Lama also contends that such a solution is ultimately the only viable solution. Acting from an oppositional stance, in the extreme case acting from anger and hatred, will in his view only create new problems. Love and compassion are superior modalities with which to approach those with whom we are in conflict because it works better in the long run. "When we face problems with compassion, sincerely and with good motivation, it may take longer, but ultimately the solution is better. . . ." He no doubt has in mind teachings like those of the *Dhammapada*, which states, "For hatred is not appeased by hatred; hatred is appeased by love; this is the eternal law."[16]

A Word on Nonviolence

All of our figures, whether they embody the modality of love or of the prophetic voice, espouse nonviolence in major, substantive ways. A large portion of Soka Gakkai's social program is dedicated to the effort to bring about stable, long-lasting world peace and, in particular, to ensure that the nuclear threat is never again made real.[17] Sarvodaya actively struggles to end the violence between Tamils and Sinhalese in Sri Lanka and to bring about deep reconciliation. Nhat Hanh and the Buddhists in Vietnam struggled nonviolently to bring peace to a country devastated by war. Sulak opposes the militarism of the Thai state. The Dalai Lama advocates the "transformation of the whole of Tibet into a zone of peace." Buddhadasa articulated a holistic vision in which "the Buddha's goal is world peace" and in which social and global peace are expressions of individual realizations of personal peace while a peaceful world helps reinforce individual efforts to gain personal peace. Ambedkar and TBMSG nonviolently struggle to stop the social, psychological, and physical violence of Hinduism against the Untouchables and to bring about conditions and train the Untouchables in such a way that they will cease to engage in acts of violence against themselves. In addition, Soka Gakkai, Sarvodaya, Buddhadasa, Sulak, and the Dalai Lama all speak strongly for and create programs to help nurture nonviolence toward the planet. Thus nonviolence is universal among our figures.

It should also be remembered that Buddhist activists have earned a disproportionate share of Nobel Peace Prize awards in recent years: the Dalai Lama in 1989 and Aung San Suu Kyi in 1991. In addition, Thich Nhat Hanh was nominated for the prize by Martin Luther King, Jr. Given that Buddhists constitute only about 6 percent of the world's population, engaged Buddhists constitute a disproportionately large share of the world's peace leadership.

Conclusion

I do not usually like to hazard predictions, but in the present case it seems to me obvious that socially engaged Buddhism is both too broad and too deep, that is, it is too widespread and too well-rooted in fundamental, long-standing Buddhist principles for it to go away, to vanish into obscurity with little trace. This movement represents one major wing of the confrontation of Buddhism with modernity, and the forces of modernity are inexorable. In my judgment, the Buddhist response to modernity as exemplified in this volume has been remarkably successful in the following sense. As reformers, engaged Buddhists have articulated deeply insightful restatements of basic Buddhist principles that confront and challenge modern conditions. Many of these movements have attracted some of the brightest, and certainly the most idealistic and most forward-looking members of their populations. It is true that the Buddhist response to modernity also includes reactionary Buddhist conservativism. However, whereas in many parts of the world—the United States and the Middle East most strikingly—fundamentalist, reactionary responses to modernity clearly are on the rise at the expense of both mainstream and liberal outlooks, in the Buddhist world, reformist and prophetic Buddhism is maintaining its own alongside dynamic conservative groups. While progressive and conservative groups seem equally strong in some countries, such as Thailand, in many Buddhist countries—Vietnam, Burma, Tibet, India—the reformist view is clearly the far more significant one.

Engaged Buddhism need make no apologies for its status in Asia; it is a major influence on the social and political, as well as the religious world. While it is impossible to predict exactly what form this movement will take as it continues to evolve—a number of its exemplars will no doubt fade in importance in time, while the future influence of the conservative Buddhist responses to modernity is unpredictable—it is undeniable that the face of Buddhism in Asia has changed and will continue to change as Asia continues to confront modernity. Buddhist liberation movements, collectively, constitute a major turning point in the development of Buddhism and will continue to play a role of substantial importance in the evolution of Buddhism into the foreseeable future.

Notes

1. Robert N. Bellah, "Epilogue: Religion and Progress in Modern Asia," in Robert N. Bellah, ed., *Religion and Progress in Modern Asia* (New York: Free Press; London: Collier-Macmillan, 1965), pp. 168–229.

2. Ibid., p. 210.

3. Ibid., p. 213

4. Ibid.

5. Ibid., p. 201.

6. References, including quotations, to statements found elsewhere in this volume will not be provided with endnotes. Any references to materials found outside this volume will of course be properly referenced.

7. See George D. Bond, *The Buddhist Revival in Sri Lanka: Religious Tradition, Reinterpretation and Response.* Columbia: University of South Carolina Press, 1988.

8. Thich Nhat Hanh, *Being Peace.* Edited by Arnold Kotler. (Berkeley, Calif.: Parallax Press, 1987), pp. 34.

9. Tenzin Gyatso, the XIVth Dalai Lama, "Hope for the Future." In Fred Eppsteiner, ed. *The Path of Compassion: Writings on Socially Engaged Buddhism,* rev. 2nd ed. Berkeley, Calif.: Parallax Press, 1988, p. 4.

10. F. Max Muller, trans., *The Dhammapada: A Collection of Verses.* Delhi: Motilal Banarsidass, 1881, 1965, 1968, p. 53.

11. *Metta-sutta.* Cited in Walpola Rahula, *What the Buddha Taught,* rev. ed. Foreword by Paul Demieville. New York: Grove Press, 1974, p. 97.

12. Aung San Suu Kyi, *Freedom from Fear and Other Writings.* Foreword by Vaclav Havel. Edited with an Introduction by Michael Aris. New York: Penguin, 1991.

13. Bellah, pp. 191–192.

14. "The Center has three objectives: (1) to further the development of open, continuous dialogue among people of all points of view as means of creating peaceful relations and preventing violent confrontation; (2) to participate in the global movement among concerned citizens, scientists, and other intellectual leaders to evolve a broad consensus in favor of life-affirming human values; and (3) to develop a philosophical and practical basis for creating harmony among different peoples, cultures, and religions." Quoted from "About the Center," introductory matter in a pamphlet by Daisaku Ikeda, "Mahayana Buddhism and Twenty-First Century Civilization," a lecture given September 24, 1993, at Harvard University and published by the Boston Research Center for the 21st Century, 396 Harvard Street, Cambridge, Mass.

15. See Masaharu Anesaki, *Nichiren the Buddhist Prophet.* Cambridge, Mass.: Harvard University Press, 1916.

16. *Dhammapada,* p. 5.

17. Depending upon one's definition of violence, one might want to argue that Soka Gakkai has committed acts of violence with its extreme religious intolerance. Certainly its intolerance has made its peace work less viable. It is to be hoped that this sort of thing is in its past.

Contributors

Nancy J. Barnes received her Ph.D. in Sanskrit and Indian studies from the University of Toronto and is currently Visiting Professor at the University of Hartford and at Trinity College in Hartford, Connecticut. She is the author of a dozen articles and chapters including, "Changing the Female Body: Wise Women and the Bodhisattva Career in Some *Maharatnakuta Sutras*," (*J. of the International Association of Buddhist Studies*), "Women in Buddhism," in *Women in World Religions* (SUNY Press), and "Buddhist Women," in *Today's Woman in World Religions* (SUNY Press).

George D. Bond is Professor and Chair of the Department of Religion at Northwestern University. He is the author of *The Word of the Buddha: The Tipitaka and its Interpretation in Theravada Buddhism* (M.D. Gunasena, Colombo), *The Buddhist Revival in Sri Lanka: Religious Tradition, Reinterpretation and Response* (University of South Carolina Press), and, jointly with Richard Kieckhefer, *Sainthood: Its Manifestations in World Religions* (University of California Press).

José Ignacio Cabezón is Assistant Professor of the Philosophy of Religion, Iliff School of Theology. A graduate of the Buddhist Studies program of the University of Wisconsin, he is the author of *A Dose of Emptiness: An Annotated Translation of mKhas Grub rje's sTong thun chen mo* (SUNY Press) and the editor of *Buddhism, Sexuality and Gender* (SUNY Press) and *H.H. The Dalai Lama, The Bodhgaya Interviews: 1980–85* (Snow Lion).

Sallie B. King is Professor and Head of the Department of Philosophy and Religion at James Madison University. She is the author of *Buddha Nature* (SUNY Press) and *Journey in Search of the Way: The Spiritual Autobiography of Satomi Myodo* (SUNY Press), as well as "Buddhist Spirituality and Social Activism in the Twentieth Century" in *Buddhist Spirituality: Chinese, Tibetan, Japanese, Korean*, volume 9 in the Crossroad *World Spirituality* series.

Daniel A. Metraux is Chair and Associate Professor of Asian Studies at Mary Baldwin College. In 1992 he served as Visiting Scholar and Professor at Soka University in Tokyo and from 1975 to 1977 he was a Mombusho Fellow at Tokyo University. He is the author of *Taiwan's Economic and Political Growth in the late Twentieth Century, The Japanese Economy and the American Businessman,* and *The History and Theology of the Soka Gakkai,* all published by Edwin Mellen Press.

Christopher S. Queen is Dean of Students for Continuing Education and Lecturer on Religion in the Faculty of Arts and Sciences, Harvard University. He began his Buddhist studies under Donald Swearer at Oberlin College and completed his graduate studies in the philosophy and phenomenology of religion at Union Theological Seminary and Boston University. He has written on engaged Buddhism for *Dr. Ambedkar, Buddhism, and Social Change* (Delhi) and *Tricycle: The Buddhist Review.*

Santikaro Bhikkhu is Acting Abbot, Suan Atammayatarama in Thailand. Born and raised in Chicago, he first went to Thailand in 1980, where he was ordained as a *bhikkhu* in 1985. Since that time he worked closely with Ajarn Buddhadasa until his death, translating for him both orally and in writing, and assisting with retreats. At Suan Atammayatarama he trains monks, novices, and lay practitioners.

Alan Sponberg taught Buddhist studies at Princeton and Stanford universities for eleven years before moving to the University of Montana where he is Professor of Asian Religion and Philosophy. His research interests focus on cross-cultural transformations of Buddhism, both historical and contemporary, and his publications include *Maitreya, the Future Buddha* (Cambridge University Press).

Donald K. Swearer is the Charles and Harriet Cox McDowell Professor of Religion at Swarthmore College and was the Numata Visting Professor of Buddhist Studies at the University of Hawaii in 1993. He has written widely on Asian and comparative religions, especially Buddhism in Thailand. His recent publications include *Me and Mine: Selected Essays of Bhikkhu Buddhadasa* (SUNY Press), *Buddhism and Society in Southeast Asia,* rev. ed. (SUNY Press), *Opening the Eyes of the Buddha: Buddha Image Consecration in Northern Thailand* (forthcoming.)

Index

Ambedkar, Dr. Bhimrao Ramji: *The Buddha and His Dhamma*, 26, 55–63; as charismatic leader, 6–7; and Christianity, 52–53; childhood of, 21; on compassion, 57; conversion of, 12, 50–54, 113n. 6; enshrinement of, 77–78; on equality, 47, 51; on Four Noble Truths, 56–58, 62, 416; and Gandhism, 50, 63; hermeneutical principles of, 58–63; as inspiration of TBMSG, 75, 77–79, 103, 105–107, 109; life of, 48–55; on liberation, 46, 416; and meditation, 118n. 53; and monasticism, 90–92; as "premodern," "modern" and "postmodern," 45–46, 65–66; as prophetic voice, 431; and Sangharakshita, 81–84; as statesman, 27; on suffering, 56–59, 61–62; on taking Refuge, 92; on women, 109; Western influence on, 23, 26–27, 64

anagarika, 93, 354

ani, 272–275

antiwar activities: of Buddhist Struggle Movement, 326–334; of Soka Gakkai, 377–379. *See also* nonviolence; peace activism

Ariyaratne, A. T.: as charismatic leader, 137, 139, 141; founding of Sarvodaya, 134–135; and Gandhi, 122–123, 125; view of monasticism, 125. *See also* Sarvodaya Shramadana

asceticism, this-worldly: in Anagarika Dharmapala, 123; in Sarvodaya, 128

Asian Cultural Forum on Development, 201–202

Aung San Suu Kyi: and Nobel Peace Prize, 2; on politics, 421; Sulak on, 219–220

awakening, reconceptualization of: in Sarvodaya, 9–10, 129–130, 134, 415–416.

See also enlightenment, reconceptualization of

Ayya Khema, Venerable, 266, 278

Bandaranaike, S.W.R.D., 29

Bellah, Robert N., 223–224; 401–402, 423

Berger, Peter, 45

Berrigan, Daniel, 352

Bhagavad Gita, 128

Bharati, Agehananda, 31

bhikshuni sangha: Buddhadasa's influence on, 180; in China, 275–276; eight important rules of, 261, 282–284; International Conference on Buddhist Nuns, 278; and Fo Kuang Shan, 276–278, 287; founding of, 260–262; history of 259; institutional control issues, 280; and laity, 284–285; ordination rules for, 261–262; prospects for, 285–287; in Sri Lanka, 262–263; in Taiwan, 276–278, 287; and *Vinaya*, 260, 262. *See also* women

bhikshuni sangha, establishment of: in Thailand, 269–271; in Tibetan Buddhism, 274–275

bhikshuni sangha, restoration of: issues surrounding, 278–285; in Sri Lanka, 265–267, *Vinaya* rules and, 281–282

Bodhicaryavatara, 304–305

bodhicitta, 306

Brahmins, 73

Buddha nature: Dalai Lama on, 301–302, 308; in Nichiren and Soka Gakkai, 367, 368; in Thich Nhat Hanh, 341–342

Buddha, social teachings of the: Ambedkar on, 60; Buddhadasa on, 164–165; relative importance of, 408–409; Sarvodaya on, 125, 126, 137; TBMSG on, 97